Bald Eagles in Alaska

Bald Eagles
in Alaska

Bruce A. Wright and Phil Schempf, eds.

A co-publication of the:
Bald Eagle Research Institute
American Bald Eagle Foundation
Hancock Wildlife Foundation

hancock
house

ISBN 978-0-88839-695-2 (print)
ISBN 978-0-88839-696-9 (electronic—PDF)

Cataloging in Publication Data

Bald eagles in Alaska / Bruce A. Wright and Phil Schempf, eds.

Includes bibliographical references and index.
Issued also in electronic format.
ISBN 978-0-88839-695-2

1. Bald eagle—Alaska. I. Wright, Bruce A., 1952- II. Schempf, Philip F.

QL696.F32B355 2010   598.9'4309798   C2010-900268-7

Printed in the USA

Front cover photograph by David Predeger
Back cover photograph by David Hancock

A co-publication of the:
Bald Eagle Research Institute
American Bald Eagle Foundation
Hancock Wildlife Foundation

Published and distributed simultaneously in Canada and the United States by

hancock house

HANCOCK HOUSE PUBLISHERS LTD.
19313 Zero Avenue, Surrey, B.C. Canada V3Z 9R9

(604) 538-1114 Fax (604) 538-2262

HANCOCK HOUSE PUBLISHERS
#104-4550 Birch Bay-Lynden Rd, Blaine, WA U.S.A 98230

(800) 938-1114 Fax (800) 983-2262

Website: **www.hancockhouse.com**
Email: **sales@hancockhouse.com**

Contents

Foreword

Marshall Lind

Chancellor, University of Alaska, Southeast, Juneau, Alaska

As one who never tires of the presence of Bald Eagles in our Alaskan environment, it is a particular pleasure for me to introduce this unique book. I feel confident you will share my enthusiasm as you read through *Bald Eagles in Alaska*. The book is unique because almost all of the authors are long time Alaskans who know Bald Eagles, not as an endangered species, but as an integral part of the avifauna of the 49th state. Chapters in this text present a range of topics on culture, conservation and management as well as sound scientific data. Various papers cover the Alaska habitat from the northern rainforest to the treeless Aleutian Islands. Diverse human attitudes are presented from the Tlingit Indians to the bounty hunters; from the modern conservationists of Haines to the ambitious people of New York who are trying to replace their diminished eagle population with Bald Eagle stock from Alaska. In short, *Bald Eagles in Alaska* offers the best portrait that has ever been assembled in the status and ecology of Bald Eagles in Alaska.

Photo: Governor Hammond (left) and Chancellor Lind (right) enjoy a good laugh at a Bald Eagle Research Institute meeting in Juneau, Alaska. Photo by Scott Foster.

You can read from cover to cover or browse here and there from chapter to chapter. In either case, you will have a rewarding experience whether you are a casual reader, a biology student or a raptor scientist. As a bonus, you will get a bit of a sense of the enthusiastic reverence Alaskans (and some neighbors from Canada and other states) feel for their land and its resources. The genesis of this fine volume was at a Juneau conference in November, 1990, hosted by the American Bald Eagle Research Institute of the University of Alaska, Southeast (UAS). The objective was to produce a reader to complement the correspondence study course in Bald Eagles offered by the biology department at UAS and to produce a compendium of the most current information on Bald Eagles of Alaska and Yukon for use by the scientific community and enjoyment of the general public. My thanks to all the splendid authors who present their work here and my warmest regards to all the Bald Eagle enthusiasts who read this book.

Preface

Bruce A. Wright[1,2] James G. King[3] and
G. Vernon Byrd[4]

[1]Aleutian Pribilof Islands Association, [2]Conservation Science Institute, [3]U.S. Fish and Wildlife Service, retired, [4]Alaska Maritime NWR, 95 Sterling Hwy, Homer, AK 99603

In November 1990 the University of Alaska, Southeast (UAS) and the Bald Eagle Research Institute hosted a symposium on Bald Eagles in Juneau, Alaska. The original intent was to provide a reader for the UAS correspondence study course, Bald Eagles in Alaska's Coastal Rain Forest, but there was also a plan to publish the proceedings.

For various reasons, the work was not published in a timely fashion. After the passage of so many years, we almost abandoned this project because only "hard copies" of original contributions were available. Nevertheless, our "ad hoc" team decided that the information contained in these papers is important enough to justify the time and energy required to produce this book. We could not have done it without the significant contribution of Sharon Baur at Alaska Maritime National Wildlife Refuge, who methodically scanned every page, photograph and graphic from the only extant complete set of manuscripts.

Clearly, additional information has been learned about eagles in Alaska since these papers were written in 1990, but we have not asked all authors to update their contributions from the original symposium. Indeed some of the authors are now deceased. We did include some recent, invited contributions to make the volume a more complete picture of Alaska's Bald Eagles at the end of the 20th century. All papers have been peer reviewed.

We believe this book is still the best compilation of information about Bald Eagles in Alaska and therefore will be useful to scientists, resource managers, students and the public. Therefore we are pleased to offer this compilation to major libraries in Alaska and via the internet.

The volume should be cited as:
Wright, B. A. and P. F. Schempf, eds. 2008. Bald Eagles in Alaska. Bald Eagle Research Institute, University of Alaska Southeast, 11120 Glacier Hwy., Juneau, Alaska 99801

Citations for individual papers would be for example:
Isleib, M. E. "Pete." 2008. Avian Resources of Southeast Alaska: A Brief Review and Their Importance to Eagles. Pages 68-71. In: Wright, B. A. and P. F. Schempf, eds. Bald Eagles in Alaska.

Introduction

Bruce A. Wright and Phil Schempf

National Oceanic and Atmospheric Administration, Juneau, U.S. Fish and Wildlife
Service, Juneau, AK

*None of God's creatures more inspires patriotic pride, communion with the natural
world and majesty than does the eagle. May their tribe increase, along with the
ennoblement their presence brings to humankind.*
Jay S. Hammond (1922-2006)

What is it about Bald Eagles (*Haliaeetus leucocephalus*) that catches the eye of people?
Is it simply their size or striking appearance? Is it the power they display or the majesty they symbolize (King 1998)? Ever since man first entered the kingdom of the Bald Eagle more than 10,000 years ago, eagles have attracted the attention of humans. Bald Eagles continue to command our respect, challenge our understanding of the natural world and allow our hearts to soar as if lifted by their strong wings.

The editors, Bruce Wright (left) and Phil Schempf (right) admire a male Bald Eagle.
Photo by Scott Foster.

*Editor's note: Bruce Wright's new affiliations are Aleutian Pribilof Islands Association
and the Conservation Science Institute.*

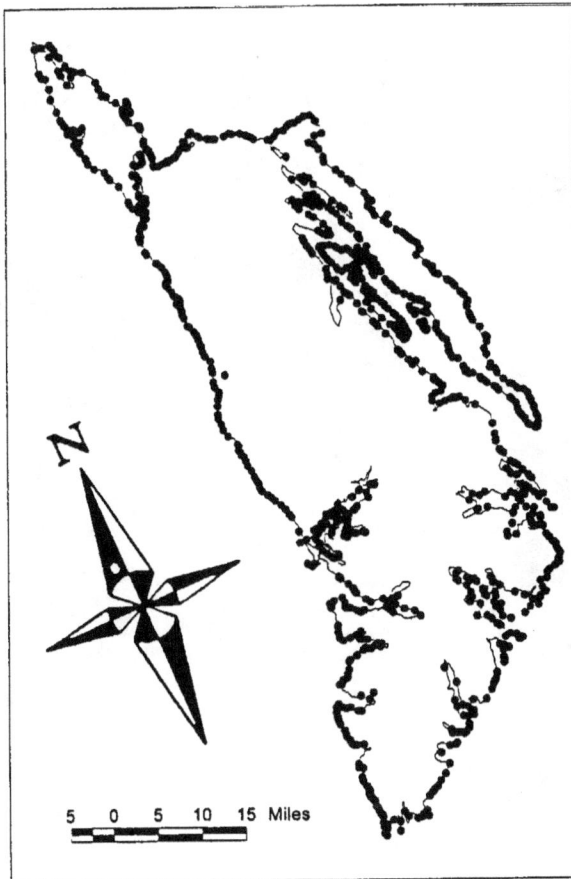

Figure 1. Bald Eagle nests outline the shores of Admiralty Island, a center of abundance for nesting Bald Eagles. USFWS unpublished data.

To many, the sight of a Bald Eagle in the wild adds a spiritual dimension to an outdoor adventure. When a visitor to Alaska stops to watch an eagle glide by or pass high overhead, one can picture that same person, months later, pausing in their busy life in a busy city, staring out a window into the smog and they again see the Bald Eagle, feel the Bald Eagle, know the Bald Eagle is the keeper of their wilderness spirit. People need to know that eagles fly free, wolves howl in the moonlight, Sandhill Cranes cover the Earth with their majestic yet forlorn calls as they migrate to their wilderness nesting grounds. These symbols hold our spirituality and allow people to understand we still belong to the wilderness.

In 1990, the University of Alaska Southeast hosted a two day symposium to discuss our understanding and share our enthusiasm for the Bald Eagles of Alaska. Appropriately, we met in Southeast Alaska, "the center of the universe for Bald Eagles" said Mike Jacobson, biologist for U.S. Fish and Wildlife Service. There may be more than 100,000 Bald Eagles across the continent from nesting areas in Florida and northern Mexico to their northern extent in the boreal forests of Canada and Alaska. The comparatively small area encompassed in Southeast Alaska is home to roughly one-fifth of the world's Bald Eagle population. The densest known breeding population occurs on Admiralty Island with nearly 1,029 catalogued nests along 860 shoreline miles (Figure 1). It's no wonder the symposium took place in the Bald Eagle's stronghold.

Scientific books tend to reduce their subject to a recitation of technical observations and statistical results. This book brings together writings from scientists and others in a diversity of disciplines, who provide key information on the ecology and management of Bald Eagles and who approach them with different perspectives. Within these pages are the facts and figures of Bald Eagle ecology (Boeker 2008, Cain 2008, Hansen et al. 2008, Suring 2008 and Thomas 2008) and current management issues (Canterbury 2008, Fraser and Anthony 2008, Reiser and Ward 2008, Johnson 2008, Menaker 2008, Samson 2008) to topics as disparate as the meaning of the eagle to the Tlingit people who lived with them for thousands of years (Marks 2008).

Bald Eagle nest on cliff. Note the two eaglets and the bright orange lichen along side the nest. This is a species of lichen usually associated with cliff nests. Photo by Cary Anderson.

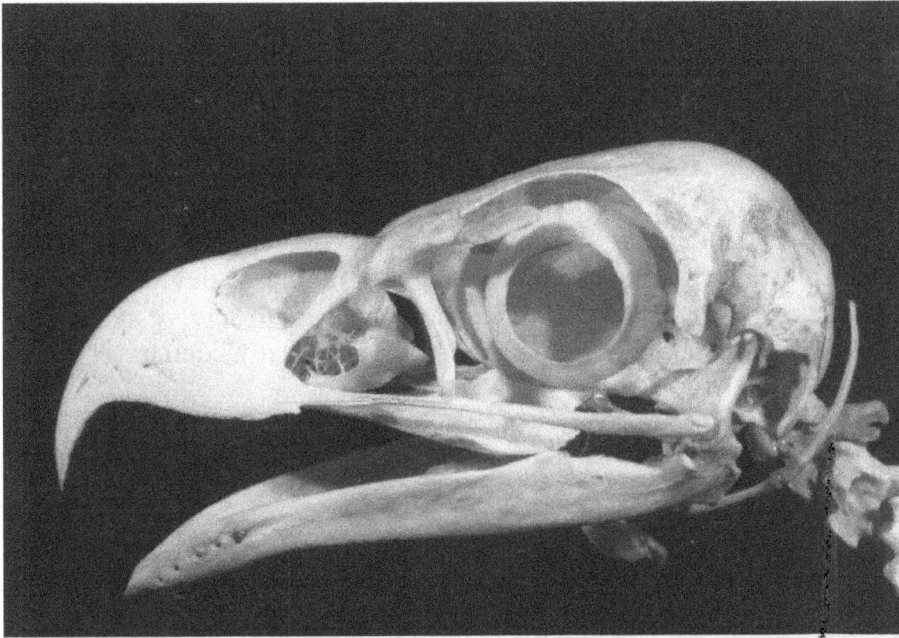

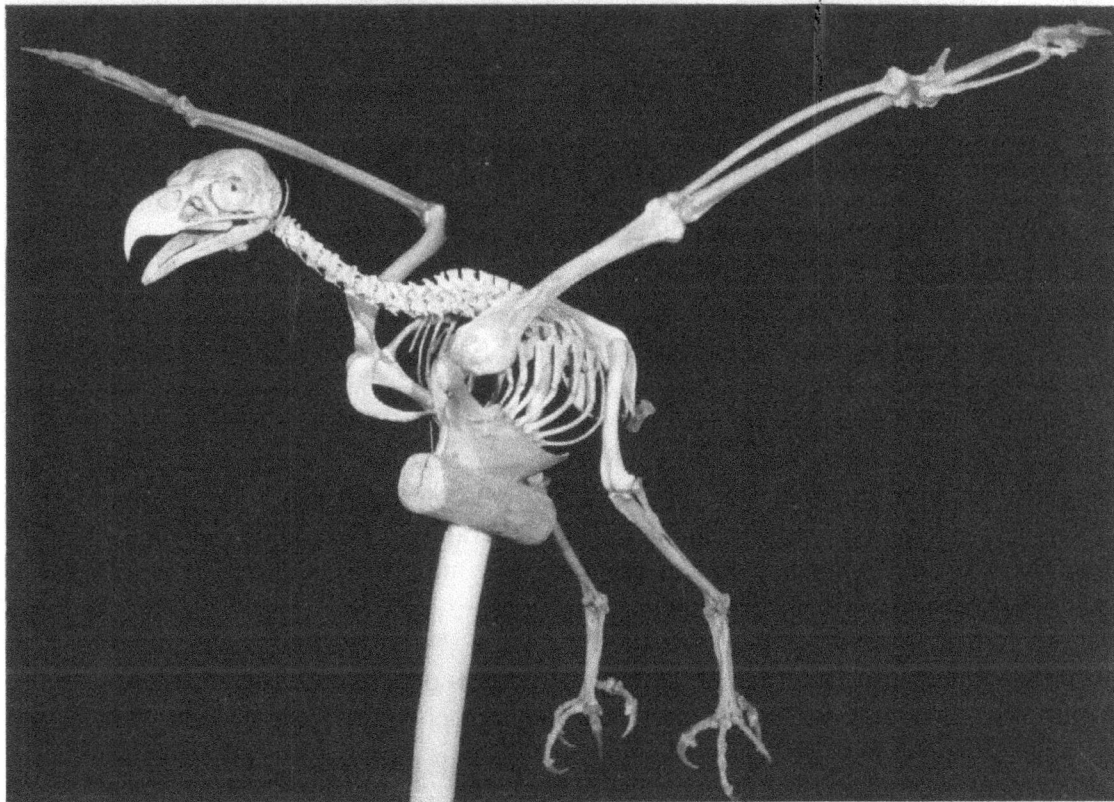

Bald Eagle skeleton assembled by Barbara Morgan and John Maniscalco, University of Alaska Southeast. Photos by Rita O'Clair.

Some of the papers reflect on the movements of eagles from nesting areas to wintering areas perhaps hundreds of miles away. These migrations are possible due to the Bald Eagle's strong flight, feasible by adaptations shared with most other birds: strong lightweight hollow bones (Figure 2), a lightweight beak instead of heavy teeth, keen eyesight and, of course, feathers. Central to the success of birds of prey is their keen eyesight. The eyes of an average 10 to 14 pound Bald Eagle are larger than that of a full grown person. The eye is held into place by bony plates called the sclerotic ring (Figure 2) and they are protected by a nictitating membrane (Figure 3). Bald Eagles have many other adaptations, including a variety of behaviors, that allow them to survive in a wide variety of habitats, varying from human communities to the remotest wilderness.

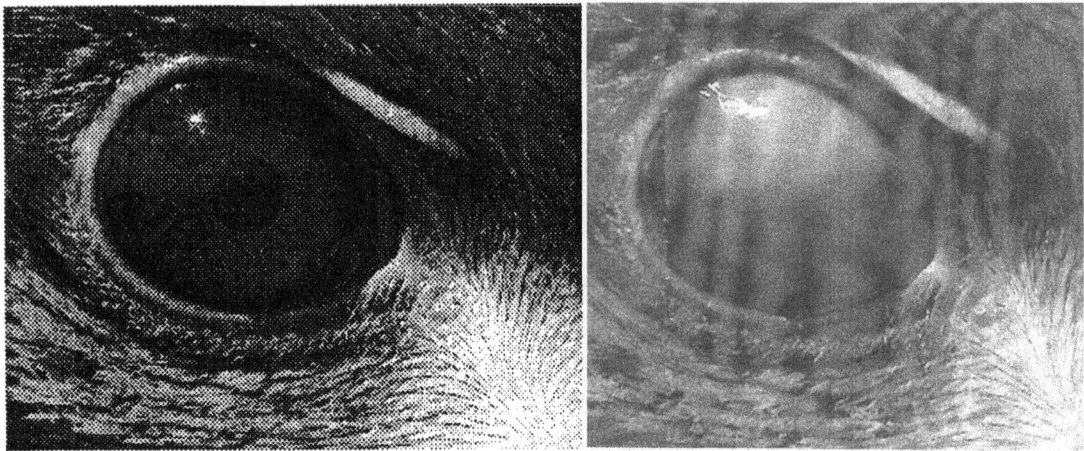

These photographs are close-ups of a Bald Eagles eye, one photo shows the nictitating membrane and the other does not. Photos by Daniel Zatz.

Bald Eagles in Alaska presents a great deal of technical information on Bald Eagle biology summarizing years of research and study. Notably, this is the first compendium discussing the status of eagles throughout Alaska (Bailey et al. 2008, Bernatowicz et al. 2008, Byrd and Williams 2008, Dewhurst 2008, Jacobson 2008b, Ritchie and Ambrose 2008, Wright 2008 and Zwiefelhofer 2008). Much of the data that are presented has been very difficult to collect because of the Bald Eagle's protected status in this region of vast wilderness. Alaska represents a unique natural laboratory for the study of abundant Bald Eagle populations living under essentially pristine conditions, controlled by conditions that have seen little influence by man.

Although much of the information presented in this book was collected in Alaska, its utility extends far beyond the borders of the state (Fluehler 2008, Titus and Fuller 2008). Managers in other parts of the eagle's range can benefit from the lessons we've learned. This is demonstrated by the translocation of eagles from Alaska to supplement populations where their numbers were severely reduced (Jacobson 2008a, Nye 2008). We cannot only share information about eagles, but actually share eagles as well. Although Bald Eagles have been extensively studied in many places, we are still ignorant of basic life history facts (Gende 2008).

Much of the research on Bald Eagles concentrates on their spring and summer nesting period. Over-winter survival plays a critical role in the Bald Eagle population's health. Bald Eagles' energy needs are accentuated during the late fall and winter when salmon are scarce. During this period some Bald Eagles take to stealing ducks from hunters, some find food in garbage dumps and others switch prey to whatever is available, often large gulls and waterfowl.

One fall a plastic duck decoy washed up on the beach. Its lead anchor was missing, but otherwise the plastic hen mallard was unscathed. A rock was tied to the anchor string and it was placed in several feet of water. For weeks not much happened. The decoy didn't even attract another ducks, as the plastic hen mallard weathered the fall storms. Later that winter the decoy went missing, but it was thought the ice or a log had carried it off. On a nice sunny, although cold, February day an adult Bald Eagle was cruising the beach. As it passed where the decoy once floated the eagle made a quick maneuver, side-slipped, dove and with extended talons, scraped the water creating a flash of spray then regained its elevation and continued down the beach. What had the eagle attacked as no prey was obvious? Perhaps a small fish had caught its eye. The next week a juvenile Bald Eagle struck the water twice in the same place before continuing on. Upon investigation it was discovered that just below the surface was the plastic mallard, only now it was scraped, torn and punctured with multiple holes. The eagles could see the nearly sunken decoy from their lofty search for food and, as food became more scarce in winter, the attacks ensued.

During late winter and early spring Bald Eagles must contend with scarce food resources, but lower temperatures and inclement weather increase energy demands and the days are short, decreasing important hunting time. During the summer and fall Bald Eagles use and depend upon their `wait and see' strategy to efficiently obtain food. But during the winter their hunting strategies may shift to more active searching and their prey switches from mostly fish to over 50% ducks and geese (Isleib 2008). During this lean period their white heads may help cue other eagles that food has been found, come and get it.
The white head and tail of adult Bald Eagles also functions to denote an eagle's status and is used to communicate to other eagles. Adults maintaining a nesting territory only need to position themselves in a prominent location such as a tree top to signal to other eagles this place is taken. They often add a screaming call to accent their determination to exclude other eagles, but sometimes more aggressive behavior is necessary. The intensities of these displays often change throughout the nesting season. The all white Bald Eagle seen in northern Southeast Alaska (Figure 4) in the early 1980s consummated as a super releaser of this territorial behavior. The subtleties of these and other Bald Eagle behaviors are another chapter of eagle biology needing further investigations.

In addition to this book, the University of Alaska Southeast has developed a series of distance delivery wildlife courses, the most popular of which is the Bald Eagle course, Bald Eagles of Alaska's Coastal Rain Forest. This book was to become part of the course curriculum. Also, the University of Alaska Southeast, American Bald Eagle Foundation and Bald Eagle (Jay Hammond) Research Institute, in cooperation with the National Wildlife Federation and the U.S. Fish and Wildlife Service have produced a compre-hensive Bald Eagle bibliography which has already attracted researchers world-wide

(Nelson-Wright 2008). The author of *Alaska's Magnificent Eagles* (Anderson 1997) used the bibliography and several raptor researchers continue to depend on this unique resource. The bibliography is updated with the most current Bald Eagle literature.

The 1990 symposium, this book and updating of the Bald Eagle bibliography are activities made possible by the American Bald Eagle Foundation and Bald Eagle (Jay Hammond) Research Institute. The American Bald Eagle Foundation was established in 1982, soon after establishment of the Alaska Chilkat Bald Eagle Preserve. The Foundation is headquartered in Haines, Alaska, close to the Bald Eagle Preserve. In 1989, the Foundation established the Bald Eagle (Jay Hammond) Research Institute which is headquartered in Juneau, Alaska. The Institute's principle objectives are to promote research, education and rehabilitation programs designed to enhance the survival and preservation of the Bald Eagle.

In the years since the symposium, work on eagles has continued in Alaska and other parts of its range. The effects of the *Exxon Valdez* oil spill have faded and eagle numbers in the Prince William Sound region have rebounded and continue to expand (Bowman, et al. 1995). Eagle numbers in Southeast Alaska appear to have stabilized. The recently signed land management plan for the Tongass National Forest establishes a beach buffer that will protect thousands of miles of prime nesting and foraging habitat. In the contiguous United States, where there are approximately 4,500 nesting pairs, the Bald Eagle was down-listed in 1995 from endangered to threatened.

However, development and industrialism are not allies to Bald Eagles, other wildlife or wilderness (Lee 1993) and climate change will certainly have an effect on Bald Eagles. In the past the damage has been dramatic. One of the most abundant bird species on the planet, Passenger Pigeons, are now extinct. What appeared to be an endless resource is forever gone. Countless other examples exist today in which exploitation rates are not supported by good scientific knowledge. For example, Harlequin Ducks and some other sea ducks have a low reproductive rate, but they are managed as if they reproduced like mallards. Sea duck populations are declining and in some regions are in danger of extinction, requiring restrictive management measures. "Management by extinction" need not be a standard technique for controlling resource exploitation if our society is willing to require conservative use and knowledge-based resource management. If sound science and not resource experimentation, was the standard for resource management, the list of threatened and endangered species would not be so extensive. With extinctions and subsequent loss of biodiversity, ecosystems change, possibly without a chance to ever recover (Kricher 1997). The editors hope *Bald Eagles in Alaska* will serve as a springboard for continuing work on Alaska's Bald Eagles to meet the needs of land managers and educators. Perhaps more importantly, we hope this book shares the enthusiasm we feel for this conspicuous resident of our lands.

This all-white Bald Eagle was seen for several weeks in Juneau, Alaska. Photos by Bruce Wright.

The last chapter of this book looks to the future, how eagles benefit people in the state today and what our information needs will be for tomorrow. In the early days of Alaska, eagles were viewed as vermin and a competitor for resources of importance to people (Cegelska 2008, DeArmond 2008). As such, eagles were often shot on sight. Today people recognize that eagles are a resource in their own right and can be of local economic significance (Shuler 2008).

A final note on the future of the Bald Eagle: How can we insure their prosperity? What does it take to maintain healthy eagle populations and the continued prosperity of people? Bald Eagles were once on the brink of extinction in the contiguous United States and their dwindling population was an indicator of their pending demise and quite possibly the demise of humankind. Indicators of an unhealthy environment were recognized and DDT was banned, eagle protection laws were passed and enforced, habitat was protected and Bald Eagles now appear to be thriving. In a sense, humankind is repaying the Bald Eagle for alerting us to the dangers of misusing chlorinated hydrocarbons (Sindermann 1996) and wrecking havoc on the environment. This is, after all, what an indicator species is supposed to do. Look around and what are the indicator species telling us now? Killer whales in the Gulf of Alaska have alarmingly high loads of DDT, DDE and PCBs. Sea otters and Bald Eagles from the Aleutian Archipelago have high levels of organochlorines (Estes, et al. 1997); some salmon populations are declining in Washington, Oregon and California; there are increasing numbers of species' extinctions; the list is almost endless. Watch for what happens in the future, for the indicators of effects from global warming (Gore 1992), global climate change, increased habitat destruction, pollution and increased human population.

Our way out of this quagmire of self-destruction is knowledge, education and conservation. Knowledge of what is wrong, knowledge of what humankind can accomplish as the dominant species and education for the decision makers who must put aside their self-interests and do what is right to make the world a better place. Conservation might be obtained by establishing reserves for fish, wildlife and habitats, some of which would be off-limits to human disturbance thus allowing natural evolution. Conservation means giving back to the Bald Eagle and their kin what they have given to humankind, a source of spirituality only found in wilderness.

Acknowledgements

We would like to acknowledge the efforts of the following people for their help with planning and coordination of the symposium and with the preparation of this book; Sharon Baur, Vern Byrd, Amy Carroll, Dan Egolf, Kathleen Everest, Marge Hermans, Barbara Hyde, Jim King, Marshall Lind, Charlotte Olerud, Lee Paavola, Dennis Russell, Jeff Williams and Brie Drummond.

Literature Cited

Anderson, C. 1997. Alaska's Magnificent Eagles. Alaska Geographic: Vol. 24, No. 4.

Bailey, T. N., E. E. Bangs, W. W. Larned, A. J. Loranger, M. F. Portner, T. V. Schumacher and E. A. Jozwiak. 2008. Nesting and wintering Bald Eagle population parameters on and adjacent to the Kenai National Wildlife Refuge, Alaska, 1979-1990. In: Wright, B. A. and P. F. Schempf, eds. Bald Eagles in Alaska.

Bernatowicz, J. A., P. F. Schempf and T. D. Bowman. 2008. Bald Eagle productivity in Southcentral Alaska in 1989 and 1990 after the *Exxon Valdez* oil spill. In: Wright, B. A. and P. F. Schempf, eds. Bald Eagles in Alaska.

Boeker, E. L. 2008. Eagles on the Chilkat: Winter ecology. In: Wright, B. A. and P. F. Schempf, eds. Bald Eagles in Alaska.

Bowman, T. D., P. F. Schempf and J. A. Bernatowicz. 1995. Bald Eagle survival and population dynamics after the *Exxon Valdez* oil spill. Wild. Manage. 59(2):317-324.

Byrd, V. G. and J. C. Williams. 2008. Distribution and status of Bald Eagles in the Aleutian Islands. In: Wright, B. A. and P. F. Schempf, eds. Bald Eagles in Alaska.

Cain, S. L. 2008. Time budgets and behavior of nesting Bald Eagles. In: Wright, B. A. and P. F. Schempf, eds. Bald Eagles in Alaska.

Canterbury, J. 2008. Bald Eagle reaction to construction on Back Island, Alaska. In: Wright, B. A. and P. F. Schempf, eds. Bald Eagles in Alaska.

Cegelske, J. A. 2008. Law enforcement and the Bald Eagle Protection Act. In: Wright, B. A. and P. F. Schempf, eds. Bald Eagles in Alaska.

DeArmond, R. N. 2008. Shoot the damned things! Alaska's war against the American Bald Eagle. In: Wright, B. A. and P. F. Schempf, eds. Bald Eagles in Alaska.

Dewhurst, D. A. 2008. History and status of Bald Eagle population and productivity studies on the Alaska Peninsula, Alaska. In: Wright, B. A. and P. F. Schempf, eds. Bald Eagles in Alaska.

Estes, J. A., C. E. Bacon, W. M. Jarman, R. J. Norstrom, R.G Anthony and A. K. Miles. 1997. Organochlorines in sea otters and Bald Eagles from the Aleutian Archipelago. Marine Pollution Bulletin,

Vol. 34, 6: 486-490.

Fluehler, H. C. 2008. American Bald Eagles at home in the world. In: Wright, B. A. and P. F. Schempf, eds. Bald Eagles in Alaska.

Fraser, J. D. and R. G. Anthony. 2008. Human disturbance and Bald Eagles. In: Wright, B. A. and P. F. Schempf, eds. Bald Eagles in Alaska.

Gende, S. M. 2008. Perspectives on the breeding biology of Bald Eagles in Southeast Alaska. In: Wright, B. A. and P. F. Schempf, eds. Bald Eagles in Alaska.

Gore, A. 1992. Earth in the balance, ecology and the human spirit. Houghton Mifflin Co., New York.

Hansen, A., E. L. Boeker and J. I. Hodges. 2008. The population ecology of Bald Eagles along the Pacific Northwest coast. In: Wright, B. A. and P. F. Schempf, eds. Bald Eagles in Alaska.

Isleib, M. E. "Pete". 2008. Avian resources of Southeast Alaska: A brief review and their importance to eagles. In: Wright, B. A. and P. F. Schempf, eds. Bald Eagles in Alaska.

Jacobson, M. J. 2008a. Removal of Alaskan Bald Eagles for translocation to states. In: Wright, B. A. and P. F. Schempf, eds. Bald Eagles in Alaska.

Jacobson, M. J. 2008b. The status of the Bald Eagle in Southeast Alaska. In: Wright, B. A. and P. F. Schempf, eds. Bald Eagles in Alaska.

Johnson, N. P. 2008. Nesting Bald Eagles in urban areas of Southeast Alaska. In: Wright, B. A. and P. F. Schempf, eds. Bald Eagles in Alaska.

Kricher, J. 1997. A neotropical companion. Princeton University Press.

Lee, K. N. 1993. Compass and gyroscope: integrating science and politics for the environment. Island Press, Washington, D.C.

Marks, P. 2008. Bald Eagles and their meaning to the Tlingit people of Southeast Alaska. In: Wright, B. A. and P F. Schempf, eds. Bald Eagles in Alaska.

Menaker, R. R. 2008. The Alaska Chilkat Bald Eagle Preserve: How it all began. In: Wright, B. A. and P. F. Schempf, eds. Bald Eagles in Alaska.

Nelson-Wright, A. 2008. The Bald Eagle bibliography. In Wright, B. A. and P. F. Schempf, eds. Bald Eagles in Alaska.

Nye, P. E. 2008. A review of the natural history of a reestablished population of breeding Bald Eagles in New York. In: Wright, B. A. and P. F. Schempf, eds. Bald Eagles in Alaska.

Reiser, M. H. and J. P. Ward, Jr. 2008. Habitat structure of Bald Eagle nest sites and management zones near Juneau, Alaska. In: Wright, B. A. and P. F. Schempf, eds. Bald Eagles in Alaska.

Ritchie, R. J. and R. E. Ambrose. 2008. Distribution, abundance and status of Bald Eagles in Interior Alaska. In: Wright, B. A,. and P. F. Schempf, eds. Bald Eagles in Alaska.

Samson, F. B. 2008. Cooperative management of the Bald Eagle in south coastal Alaska. In: Wright, B. A. and P. F. Schempf, eds. Bald Eagles in Alaska.

Shuler, J. 2008. Bald Eagles and the tourist industry in Alaska. In: Wright, B. A. and P. F. Schempf, eds. Bald Eagles in Alaska.

Sindermann, C. J. 1996. Ocean pollution on living resources and humans. CRC Press, New York.

Suring, L. H. 2008. Habitat relationships of Bald Eagles in Alaska. In: Wright, B. A. and P. F. Schempf, eds. Bald Eagles in Alaska.

Thomas, N. J. 2008. Causes of mortality in Alaskan Bald Eagles. In: Wright, B. A. and P. F. Schempf, eds. Bald Eagles in Alaska.

Titus, K. and M. R. Fuller. 2008. Bald Eagle banding in Alaska. In: Wright, B. A. and P. F. Schempf, eds. Bald Eagles in Alaska.

Wright, J. M. 2008. Bald Eagles in Western Alaska. In: Wright, B. A. and P. F. Schempf, eds. Bald Eagles in Alaska.

Zwiefelhofer, D. C. 2008. History and status of Bald Eagle nesting and productivity on the Kodiak Island Archipelago, Alaska. In: Wright, B. A. and P. F. Schempf, eds. Bald Eagles in Alaska.

The Southeast Alaska Environment

Bald Eagles and Their Meaning to the Tlingit People of Southeast Alaska.

Paul Marks

Sealaska Corporation, Juneau, AK

The Eagle and the Raven are important as representatives of the two moieties in Tlingit culture. The Eagle is a prominent figure in stories handed down by elders to instruct their children and grandchildren and Eagle parts were used for various purposes in traditional Tlingit society.

I appreciate the invitation to share a little of what I have learned from our elders. This is what I would say in Tlingit: It is Tlingit Tundataani, which means "the way we think as Tlingit people" or "human thinking."

Our grandparents would always instruct us in the things that we were to learn-the stories that we were to begin to understand and learn from the time that we were children and even before then. Our grandparents or our parents would begin speaking to the children while they were still in the womb. We believed that our children would listen. We felt that at that time the child was beginning to record in his memory what was being said to him.

The stories that we have today were told by our grandparents as instruction. These stories existed way before you and I were even thought of. All we knew, through the Raven stories, was how the Raven taught us how to get our food and taught the Tlingit people how to live.

One of my grandparents, Woosh Kiyadagweich was his Tlingit name, was from Sheetkaa, Sitka in English. He and another grandfather of mine, from DeiShu, Haines, would get together and tell the stories back and forth to one another of the old ways. It was at a time when our people began to recognize that there would be one day that our land would be flooded over with non-Natives. So they began to instruct a young man, his name in Tlingit: Donawaak. Some of you may know him. His English name is Austin Hammond. He received an honorary doctor's degree of humanities from the University of Alaska Southeast in 1989.

He's the one who told me some of the stories from his grandparents. He was told, "You're going to be the one that's going to pass these stories on because there's going to come a time that you're going to need these stories. There are going to be people coming in that will flood our land and you're going to need to learn or know these stories."

At that time we did not know our Heavenly Father as we know him now. We only knew the Raven stories. Raven had three titles. Yell Dleit, the first title, means in translation "the White Raven." The second title, Yell Tlein, meant "the Bigger Raven." The third, Yell Yaadi, meant "the Child of the Raven." These three were one. He was white at the beginning and then he turned black when he stole the water and put all the lakes and the different waterways that we have today in Southeast Alaska.

Yeil Yaadi, the story that I'm going to share with you, comes from Austin Hammond.

Our grandfathers would say: "Woosh Kiyadi gweitch" as their time on this earth was coming to an end: Grandson, be of good courage. Be of good courage. Tell these stories to your children and to your grandchildren. Let them know and whoever will listen, tell them these stories. My dear grandchildren, I want you to know, I want you to hear my voice, that it is my desire now that you will think of this story I am about to tell. Through this story, my hope is that you will think about your lives.

The Story of the Raven and His Brother-in-Law

As the Raven began his journey he headed out to sea and as he paddled out to sea he saw what he called his brother-in-law. From there he began to talk with his brother-in-law. The Raven called out, Is that you, brother-in-law? Aax Kaani is how he called in Tlingit. Aax Kaani. Waa eigwe. My brother-in-law, is that you?

This seemed to be a planned meeting as they came together and talked. And Raven, being inquisitive, asked him, How long ago were you born, Aax Kaani? How long ago were you born?

And his brother-in-law told him: Before primitive tools were made.
And the Raven replied, I guess you are just a young boy or a young child yet. Then he added, I was born before the crust of the earth was formed.

The lesson of this story, as our parents and grandparents would instruct us, is that always an argument starts with little troubles. Also, let me point out, that since I am a Raven, as I was telling this story, an Eagle would know that I am calling him brother-in-law because we have two moieties, the Eagle and the Raven.

His brother-in-law told the Raven, well, I guess you were born before me.
Then he put his hat on. It was the Fog Hat. Soon the fog was so thick Raven couldn't see anything. But it brought a new insight to the Raven. Before the fog he didn't think what he was saying to his brother-in-law. He was just trying to out-talk him. He spoke impulsively.

So the Raven called out to his brother-in-law, changing his mind: Aax Kaani. Aax Kaani. I guess you were born before I was. But his brother-in-law did not pay any attention to him. And out there on the ocean it was very calm. One could hear not a thing. The fog was so thick Raven couldn't even see the bottom of his canoe.

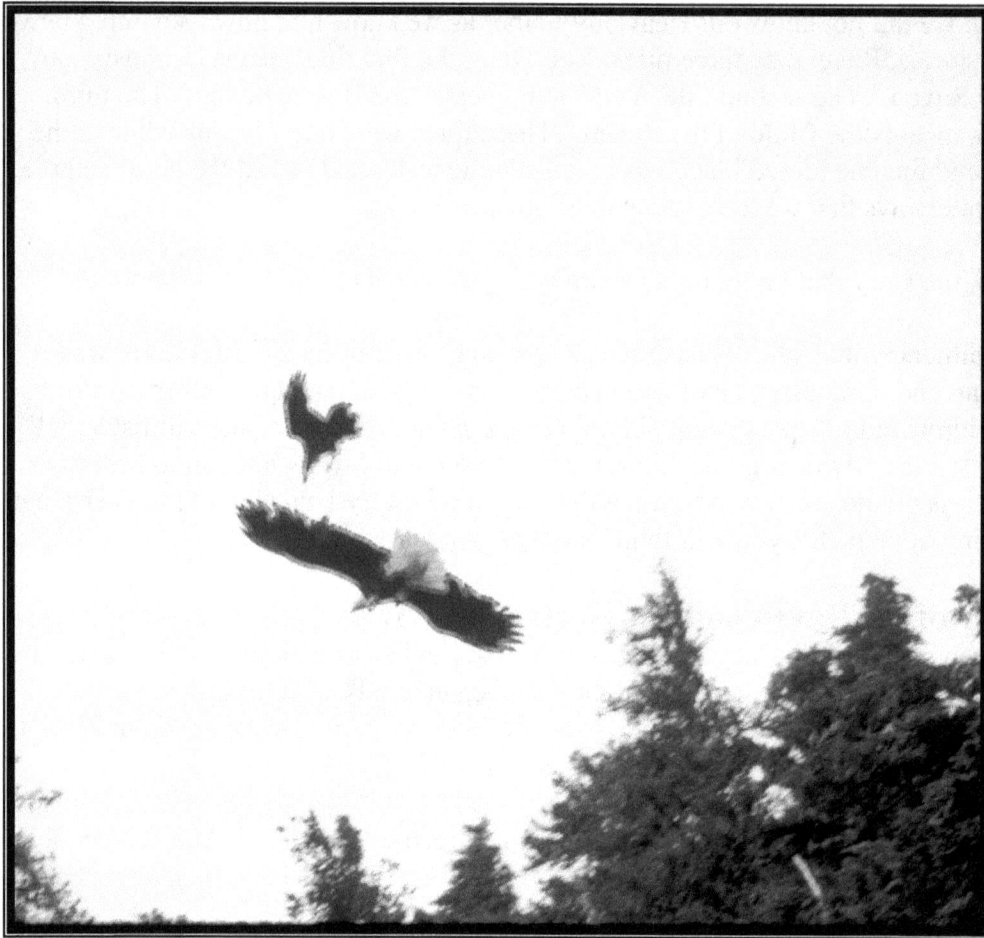

An eagle and a raven. Photo by Bob Armstrong.

After awhile Raven called to his brother-in-law again. Aax Kaani. Aax Kaani. I guess you were born way before me, the tone of his voice starting to change. He was getting frightened. It felt as if the boat was shaking with him. He didn't know what was going to happen and feared the boat might tip over.

This is how we are sometimes when we say something wrong. We get frightened just as the Raven was frightened.

Raven called to his brother-in-law the third time, now with softness in his voice: Aax Kaani. Aax Kaani. I guess you were born way before me.

Raven's voice turned to crying as he called out and suddenly the Raven grabbed the side of his canoe as his brother-in-law shook the canoe with him in it.

What are you saying? his brother-in-law asked as he began to take his Fog Hat off.
I guess you were born before me-way before I was born, Raven said, wiping the tears from his eyes.

This is how it is in our lives when we say the wrong thing. We think of our mistakes after they are made. This is why it is as it was with Raven and his brother-in-law. From that point on they worked together building this world. They would not do anything without the other.

Importance of the Eagle in Tlingit Culture

As mentioned earlier, the Eagle is part of the Tlingit social structure. There are two moieties, the Eagle and the Raven. They are both equal. In Tlingit society we are all equal and this is how we balance out things.

We also used parts of the eagle's body, as I learned from asking our elders. There is not much information about this, but I will continue to ask for more information. I was told that the eagle's wing was used for sweeping out the tribal houses. And the tail of the eagle was used for dancing regalia: Dancers would put them in their hands and move them back and forth. Sometimes the beak was used for a spoon.

I was also told that the parents would tie the wings to the children's wrists, to the boys' wrists. I suppose they were tied in such a fashion that it would be very difficult for the child to move, it wouldn't be as natural. There would be a little tug on his arms when he was moving his arms. It was believed that this would give him arm strength while he was growing up.

The Shaman [Fee-Kee]

One story tells of a powerful shaman called Fee-Kee, who was Ixt', a helper of the people. The shaman often journeyed into the wilderness and up into the mountains to seek out hardship to give himself strength. One time the shaman went up on top of a mountain in the Haines area. While there he saw an eagle flying high above him. As he looked at the eagle he began chanting. He had a drum with him and he drummed four times and upon the fourth drum it is told it sounded like a rifle shot and the eagle came down from where he was at .. dead. And this is one of the reasons how our shaman took the spirit of the eagle away from him for his own possession. And in Tlingit terms that's Atoow and that was property that was owned by that particular shaman or that clan that he belonged to.

His name was Fee-Kee. He was known to be very powerful.
He was also known to eat the eagle and he would let the eagle go rancid and they said that it tasted like fish, because basically that's one of the eagle's main diets. I've asked two people about that and both brothers, elders, once said that we as people used to eat it and they said it was pretty good meat. It may not sound tasty but I guess when we thought of chickens we probably felt the same way.

The Eagle As Gift-Giver

But there is another story of a man or a family in Klawock. I understand that today there are people who bring wounded or injured eagles back to health. A family in Klawock did the same thing for an eagle. And as he gained strength they let the eagle go. And the eagle caught a king salmon and he dragged it to shore where the family was, in front of the family's house and left it there and he flew up into the woods and sat in a tree watching. The family throughout the day didn't pay attention to the king salmon and the eagle became very angry and flew down to the king salmon and tore the king salmon up and devoured it. And so we are told the story as to when in need the eagle will help you or bring food to you as he tried to pay back his gift. And the respect that we are paying to the eagle today: that gift will be paid back to us.

Other Significance of the Eagle

We also have a river we call Ch'aak-Heeni. That's just a little ways from Klukwan area. And the original name, Ch'aak being our Tlingit term for eagle and it's spelled Ch'aak in Tlingit. The original name was Gie, I believe. And that's what the river was called Gie y nee, Eagle River, which is a small river across from Klukwan.

We also had houses, Ch'aak it, Eagle House.

In closing as I mentioned earlier that we as a people have two moieties, the Eagle and the Raven and they are both equal. Our father comes from Chookanheeni, Grass River. He was from the Xoot Hit, the Brown Bear House and he was an Eagle, from the Eagle moiety.

The Bald Eagle in American Culture

James G. King

U.S. Fish and Wildlife Service (retired), Juneau, AK

The emotions and symbolism Americans associate with the United States national symbol are traced through the history of our nation and world cultures. These associations have proven of real benefit to Bald Eagles and other species struggling for survival in a changing modern world.

United States citizens are surrounded by millions of Bald Eagle images. We find them as statues, as adornments on buildings, over doors, atop flag poles, on post office trucks, on stamps, on flags, on church lecterns, in art markets, on athletic trophies and on dollars and quarters in our pockets. No other bird or beast enjoys such prominence in our culture. Why?

The artistic record of man's interest in eagles goes back at least as far as ancient Mediterranean civilizations and cave dwellers in what is now Europe. In Greek mythology, Zeus had an attendant eagle that bore his lightning bolts in its talons. Ancient Roman legions were known by the eagle standards they carried. In early Christian art the eagle was associated with St. John the Evangelist, symbolizing divine vision and spiritual flight. Spiritual flight was demonstrated through the eagle's ability to get nearer God by soaring beyond human vision into the heavens above.

The eagle has often been a symbol of military power and triumph. It was used to adorn body armor and shields from the time of Charlemagne (about 800 A.D.) and in this heraldic form it became somewhat stylized and slimmed, with its wings and legs spread. The slender eagle was given a second head on emblems of Austria, Germany and Russia, symbolizing their power and influence to both the east and west of their borders. Napoleon Bonaparte decorated his palaces with eagle motifs and used them on his military insignia (Coumbe 1966). And so the eagle evolved in the Old World as a symbol of physical and spiritual power.

European symbolic eagles do not seem to represent a particular species. Sometimes, in fact, they are shown with a crest, which none of the European eagles have. And, of course, they were not Bald Eagles.

During these same times, however, the Bald Eagle had taken a similar place in the culture and ceremonies of North American Indians from the Atlantic to the Pacific. People worldwide are familiar with the classic Indian eagle feather headdress.

At the time of the American Revolution, official documents were generally authenticated by "sealing" them with a drop of hot wax on which an engraved impression was stamped. Right after signing of the Declaration of Independence on July 4, 1776, the Continental Congress appointed Thomas Jefferson, John Adams and Benjamin Franklin to a committee charged with developing such a seal for the new nation. Various designs were

Adult Bald Eagle, our national symbol. Photo by Bob Armstrong.

proposed based on European heraldry and a six-year debate erupted. As we are reminded by the press every Thanksgiving Day, Ben Franklin thought the turkey a better symbol than the eagle, which he called a bird of "bad moral character" (Evans 1966), perhaps contributing to the delay.

On June 20, 1782, Congress finally adopted a design by William Barton modified by Charles Thompson (Evans 1966). This seal included an eagle purported to be an "American Eagle." It was a peculiar bird, skinny like some of its symbolic cousins and with a crest. It was splayed out in an unnatural "spread eagle" position, its middle hidden by a large medieval shield with 13 vertical bars. The lightning bolts of Zeus had evolved into 13 arrows, representing the 13 colonies, held in the left talons. In the right talons was an olive branch, perhaps suggesting the spirituality of St. John or perhaps a symbol of peace. Near its head was a cluster of stars.

Peculiar or not, this bird became the symbol of our country. The symbolic eagle was improved in 1841 with removal of the crest and addition of a white head. It was modified again in 1902 to put a little meat on its bones. The shield, stars and arrows remain as you see them today on any dollar bill. Superstitions about the number 13, so frequently indicated on the great seal, do not seem to have detracted from the popularity of the dollar.

As time went by, our eagle cast off some of its earlier connotations and came to be considered primarily a symbol of American freedom. As such, the Bald Eagle has found a prominent place on postage stamps, coins, state seals, insignia, trophies and decorations of all sorts. In Alaska the Russian two-headed eagle can still be found on the cannons at the Castle Hill State Historic Park in Sitka and on various memorabilia in museums. Recently, when queried about the two-headed bird, however, Russian ornithologist A. A. Kistchinski told me, "I think it is extinct."

Eagle/Raven Logo of the Sealaska Corporation.
The American Eagle carries on and is dignified in place names across the country. In Alaska, there are no less than 91 bluffs, bays, creeks, harbors, islands, mountains, points and other features bearing the eagle moniker (Orth 1967).

The living eagle has not enjoyed comparable popularity. For much of our history eagles tended to be lumped with the so-called "chicken hawks." They were often shot on sight by farmers, fishermen and "varmint" hunters in a misguided effort to protect domestic and more favored wild animals.

As people prospered and the nation's population increased-and as improvements were made in varmint hunting equipment-eagle numbers declined. In the West sheep farmers, who accused eagles of taking their lambs, learned to use poisons, traps and eventually aircraft in their vendetta (Green 1985). In Alaska, the Territorial Legislature maintained a bounty on eagles from 1917 to 1953 in response to fears by some fox farmers and salmon fishermen (DeArmond 2008).

Concern for declines in birds of many species began to develop about the turn of the century, leading to the 1916 Convention with Great Britain for Protection of Migratory Birds in the United States and Canada (Ossa 1973). The Migratory Bird Convention Act of 1918 excepted raptors. Eagles remained fair game until passage of the Bald Eagle Protection Act of 1940 and even that legislation excepted eagles in Alaska until it was amended in 1959.

The Bald Eagle Protection Act was amended again in 1962 to protect Golden Eagles and to prevent any further losses to varmint hunters who could not distinguish golden from immature Bald Eagles. Other raptors were brought under protection by amendments to the Migratory Bird Treaty between the United States and Mexico in 1972 (Green 1985). But all was not right, much to the consternation of ornithologists and conservationists, who had led the campaign to stop eagle shooting. Bald Eagles responded by going into a sharp decline. Studies showed that the pesticide DDT, widely used since 1947, was disrupting reproduction in Bald Eagles and a number of other raptors by causing the birds to lay eggs with abnormally thin, fragile shells that broke under the weight of their incubating mothers. In the face of widespread national concern, the Environmental Protection Agency banned the use of DDT in 1972 (Green 1985).

By this time the Bald Eagle was an important figure in the debate over what to do about endangered species. Congress passed three Endangered Species Acts-in 1966, 1969 and 1973-each of increasing strength and effectiveness (Bean 1977).

Protection and restoration of Bald Eagles began in earnest under provisions of the Endangered Species Act of 1973. Research into eagle mortality soon disclosed a new problem, however: eagles were dying in significant numbers from lead poisoning, a result of preying on waterfowl wounded by hunters.

Figures 1-3: The symbolic eagle dominates the Great Seal of the United States and is featured in the insignia of a number of American Government and private agencies. The first seal is from 1782, the second seal is from 1841 and the third seal is from 1902.

Lead had long been recognized as a poison to waterfowl and efforts to develop and require a nontoxic shot go back at least to the 1960s. But resistance to the use of steel shot proved very strong in spite of the knowledge that 2 or 3 percent of all ducks in America were thought to die from ingesting spent lead shot (Bellrose 1964). In some places, where exhaustive study showed severe problems, steel shot was required by state action, but the struggle to ban lead shot nationwide moved very slowly.

In 1985 the National Wildlife Federation, because of the loss of eagles, filed suit under the Endangered Species Act to end the use of lead shot in the U.S. The federal judge ruled favorably and directed that use of lead shot for hunting waterfowl must end by 1991 (Gerrard and Bortolotti 1988).

In many respects, the Bald Eagle remains a symbol of individual liberty, not only to American citizens but to less free people everywhere and to a continuing stream of immigrants who fulfill their dreams by coming to this country. In addition, the Bald Eagle in America is evolving into something of a standard bearer for conservation and environmental protection. Other species, too, have benefited from public concern about eagles. Had there not been strong popular concern for the security of our national symbol, the protection of Golden Eagles and other raptors, the banning of DDT, the passing of effective endangered species legislation and the banning of lead shot might have taken much longer. Less well documented is the probability that human health has benefited from phasing out the environmental poisons that so nearly exterminated the eagles.

Mark Stalmaster (1987) suggested a growing sentiment when he wrote, "If the Bald Eagle returns, it will be more than a wildlife achievement: it will symbolize the growing concern and appreciation for life on earth." And the Bald Eagle is returning.

Our country has evolved enormously since 13 tiny, rural states adopted the Bald Eagle as symbol of their strength and freedom. This nation now leads the world in developing technology and solving associated environmental problems. Still carrying the image of strength and freedom, the Bald Eagle has assumed a new mantle as symbol of the power of free people to solve environmental problems.

Literature Cited

Bean, M. J. 1977. The evolution of national wildlife law. Council on Environ. Quality, U.S. Gov. Printing Off., Washington, D.C. 485pp.

Bellrose, F. C. 1964. Spent shot and lead poisoning. Pages 479-485. In: Waterfowl tomorrow. U.S. Geological. Inter., Fish Wild. Serv., Gov. Printing Off., Washington, D.C. 770pp.

Coumbe, C. W. 1966. Eagle in art and symbolism. Encyclopedia Americana 9:474.

DeArmond, D. A. 2008. Shoot the damned things! Alaska's war against the American Bald Eagle. In: Wright B. A. and P. F. Schempf, eds. Bald Eagles in Alaska.

Evans, T. 1966. The Nation's symbol. Pages 105-113. In: Steferud, A. and A. Nelson, eds. Birds in our lives. U.S. Geological. Inter. Fish Wild. Serv., Gov. Printing Off., Washington, D.C. 561pp.

Gerrard, J. M. and G. R. Bortolotti. 1988. The Bald Eagle-haunts and habitats of a wilderness monarch. Smithsonian Inst. Press, Washington, D.C. 178pp.

Green, N. 1985. The Bald Eagle. Pages 509-531. In: The Audubon wildlife report. Natl. Audubon Soc., New York, NY. 671pp.

Orth, D. J. 1967. Dictionary of Alaska place names. U.S. Geol. Surv. Prof. paper 567, U.S. Gov. Printing Off., Washington, D.C. 1084pp.

Ossa, H. 1973. They saved our birds. Hippocrene Books, New York. 227pp.

Stalmaster, M. V. 1987. The Bald Eagle. Universe Books, New York. 227pp.

Geology of Southeast Alaska: With Special Emphasis on the Last 30,000 Years

Cathy L. Connor

University of Alaska, Juneau, AK

The unique habitats of Southeastern Alaska are the end result of its geologic history. Southeast Alaska is a geologically complex region. Known as the Alexander Archipelago and named after Tsar Alexander of Russia, this land now covered by a temperate rainforest has had a long and dynamic geologic history.

Some of this region's bedrock formed within 15° latitude of the equator and later moved via sea-floor spreading and ocean plate movement to its present location beginning about 200 million years ago. The journey included joining with other geologic terranes or unique packages of rocks and their ultimate collision with the North American continent. Southeast Alaska began to take shape as the ocean crust conveyor belt moved fragments of volcanic island arcs, old coral atolls, deep sea sedimentary rocks and even pieces of continents across the northeastern Pacific and caused their accretion onto ancient North America.

Within the past 30,000 years, the Alexander Archipelago was scoured and polished by late Pleistocene ice and subsequently flooded as a warming climate caused glaciers and ice caps to melt, resulting in a worldwide sea level rise. This unique geologic history has given Southeast Alaska the steep-sided mountains and deep fjords that make the region so distinctive today.

Southeast Alaska and its Terranes

Three very different terrenes now lay side-by-side in Southeast Alaska. In Middle Triassic time about 220 million years ago, the Wrangellia, Alexander and Stikine terranes were somewhere offshore.

The Stikine terrain is made up of andesite, basalt and rhyolitic volcanic flow rocks and sedimentary rocks of late Paleozoic age that are interbedded with marine sandstone and limestone. This group of rocks probably began as a volcanic island chain much like Indonesia today. The Stikine terrain docked with North America by the early Jurassic about 200 million years ago, attaching itself onto what is now interior British Columbia. The Alexander terrane includes lower and middle Paleozoic deep ocean trench deposits, volcanic rocks, shallow water limestone and late Paleozoic limestone, chert and volcanic rocks. The limestones and marbles found today in the Heceta-Tuxekan Islands west of Prince of Wales Island and in Glacier Bay were formed as part of the early Alexander Terrane.

To the west, rocks of Wrangellia record a volcanic island arc capped by shallow-water marine shale. Limestones interbedded with the shale are Permian (240-280 million years) in age and contain distinctive marine fossils. Following the reef environment, a thick unit of volcanic basalt records a rifting of the ocean floor that began beneath sea level but was so thick that it surfaced eventually producing 100,00 to 200,00 cubic kilometers of basalt (Jones et al. 1982). The volcanism ended by about 200 million years ago and was followed by carbonate deposition similar to that presently occurring in the Persian Gulf. The copper deposits of the Wrangell Mountains ultimately came to reside in these shallow water carbonates.

The Wrangellia and Alexander terranes joined together off the North American coast by Middle Jurassic time and before they accreted onto North America, rocks of the Gravina Belt were deposited upon this superterrane. Rocks in Auke Bay, Douglas Island, eastern Admiralty, Kupreanof Island and Gravina Island opposite Ketchikan are all part of the Gravina belt.

Early Cretaceous folding and faulting in Wrangellia/Alexander terrane rocks record the initial collision of that superterrane with North America. Deformation of the rocks caused regional metamorphism and generated large volumes of granite rock intruding this newly forming coastal mountain region. Metamorphic and intrusive igneous rocks crop out in the Juneau area and extend eastward under the Juneau Icefield (Ford and Brew 1977).

The beginning of the Tertiary Period records the arrival of the Chugach terrane outboard of Wrangellia around 65 million years ago. About 25 million years ago the Yakutat block was sliced off the continental margin southeast of Chatham Strait and moved 330 miles northwest along the Queen Charlotte-Fairweather transform fault system. This coastal crash, much like India against Asia, is uplifting the St. Elias Mountains in the Yakutat area.

North of the St. Elias Mountains, right lateral movement along the Denali Fault beginning as early as Cretaceous time, has deformed Miocene and Oligocene cobbles in conglomerate rocks and offset sandstones 180 miles. Branches of the Denali Fault extend into the Chilkat Valley and have deformed Tertiary rocks there.

Alaska's Glacial History; Evidence From the Gulf of Alaska

The Gulf of Alaska region has been glaciated since late Miocene time (Molnia 1986). Evidence from the Yakataga Formation northwest of Icy Bay had shown that sediments about six million years old were deposited by glaciers into a marine environment. Drill hole information for Middleton Island (Plafker 1971) reveals that 1000 km off the coast there are at least 1,150 m of the Yakataga Formation glacial deposits.

Pleistocene Glaciation in the Alexander Archipelago

Between Icy Bay and the Queen Charlotte Islands, the extent and timing of ice advances over the past two million years or Pleistocene epoch is not well known. The ubiquitous U-shaped valleys and numerous rounded passes provide evidence for a long history of intensive glaciation that spared only the mountains of central Baranof Island and a few scattered summits above 1,000 m on Chichagof, Admiralty and Prince of Wales Islands. Local island ice caps and valley glaciers were later invaded by ice from the Coastal Mountains and interior British Columbia that spilled over the archipelago. An ice sheet 1,000 m thick sculpted this landscape.

In the Juneau area, radiocarbon dated peats yielded ages greater than 39,000 years ago (Miller 1973a). These peats are covered by glacial marine deposits and record a pause in the latest Pleistocene phase of glaciation. Fossil pollen recovered from this interstitial peat records a flora dominated by shrubs and ferns with rare trees. The peat beds suggest that glaciers had receded out of the inner fjord zone of Southeast Alaska sometime prior to 39,000 years ago (Mann 1986).

Capps (1931) was the first to propose that large outlet glaciers of the past 25,000 years ended along the outer continental shelf of Southeast Alaska in deep submarine valleys beyond the large fjord entrances. Acoustical studies of sediments on the continental shelf between Cross Sound and Prince William Sound have helped to map some of these sea valleys and delineate glacial deposits. Unfortunately, these techniques do not provide age control. It is, therefore, not possible to say whether the entire continental shelf was glaciated during the last Pleistocene glacial advance beginning about 25,000 years ago. Mann (1986) believes that during the last Pleistocene, glacial maximum outlet glaciers 20-50 km wide flowed out of the Alexander Archipelago at Dixon Entrance, Sumner Strait, Chatham Strait and Icy Strait with surfaces as high as 600 m above present sea level. Deglaciation was probably rapid with much catastrophic calving.

Raised Marine Deposits Record Deglaciation

As glaciers melted and sea level began to rise, the landscape was still depressed by the weight of the newly departed ice. The glacier-carved valleys, once flooded with seawater, form steep-sided fjords with poor foraging for eagles. However, the head of these valleys have wonderful outwash plains with superlative eagle foraging space.

In Juneau, beach gravels were deposited at an elevation as high as 230 m above sea level just before 13,000 years ago (Miller 1973a). Along the south coast of the Chilkat Peninsula, raised beaches and bedrock terraces record three episodes of crustal depression associated with ice loading in nearby Glacier Bay beginning about 13,350 years ago (Ackerman et al. 1979). Twelve thousand year old marine shells occur at 70 m on Northeast Chichagof (Mann 1986). Glacial marine material exists at 213 m on Admiralty Island (Miller 1973b) and at 150 m on the mainland east of Prince of Wales Island (McConnell 1913). Near Petersburg, marine shells dated to about 12,400 years occur at an elevation of about 62 m (Ives et al. 1967). Marine terraces were found by Berg (1973) at 60 m near Ketchikan and Sainsbury (1961) found shells and glacial-marine deposits up to 61 m on Prince of Wales Island. These altitudes of marine limits result in part from ice loading and they provide a rough indication of ice thickness.

Bald Eagles and the Pleistocene

Somewhere in southeast Asia before about 25 million years ago, the group of birds known as kites provided the ancestors for the sea eagle (Stalmaster 1987). From this Asian ancestor, the Bald Eagle emerged, but no fossil evidence of this evolution is found until about 1 million years ago when eagle bones appear in the Rancholabrean faunas of California's tar deposits (Howard 1932).

Meanwhile the steelhead trout (*Oncorhynchus mykiss*), formerly (*Salmo gairdneri*) had moved northward into the North Pacific from North America. These fish provided the ancestral pool for five species of Pacific salmon which are thought to have evolved during the Pleistocene (McPhail and Lindsey 1970, Neave 1958). Isolated groups of salmon survived in fresh water streams on the Bering land bridge during maximum glacial advances and in the Columbia River basin in Washington.

Bald Eagles may have invaded Alaska prior to 1,000,000 years ago, following Asian shorelines around the Pacific rim to feed on the newly evolving taste sensation, salmon and then continued down the coast to become entombed in the La Brea tar pits of southern California.

Bald Eagles feeding on spawned-out chum salmon. Photo by Bob Armstrong.

Ice retreated from Southeast Alaska beginning about 16,000 years ago in the Queen Charlotte Islands (Clague et al. 1982) and by 12,000 years ago in the inner fjord areas to the north, setting the scene for the arrival of the "People of the Tides" (Tlingit) by way of the Nass and Skeena River canyons from the interior. The numerous members of the Tlingit Eagle Clan can attest to the presence of the Bald Eagle in Southeast Alaska upon the arrival of their ancestors, the first Southeast Alaskans.

Editor's note: To this day northern Southeast Alaska is rising either as a result of rebound of the land now that the glaciers have retreated (isostatic rebound) or due to mountain building and uplift. The Glacier Bay area is rising at about 3cm per year.

Literature Cited

Ackerman, R. E., T. D. Hamilton and R. Stuckenruth. 1979. Early culture complexes on the northern northwest coast. Canadian Journal of Archeology 3:195-209.

Berg, H. C. 1973. Geology of Gravina Island, Alaska. U.S. Geological Survey Bulletin 1373. 41 pp.

Capps, S. R. 1931. Glaciation in Alaska. U.S. Geological Survey Professional Paper 1700A, pp. 1-8.

Clague, J. J., J. R. Harper, R. J. Hebda and D. E. Howes. 1982. Late Quaternary sea levels and crustal movements, coastal British Columbia. Canadian Journal of Earth Sciences 19:597-618.

Ford, A. B. and D. A. Brew. 1977. Preliminary geologic and metamorphic-isograd map of northern parts of the Juneau a1 and a-2 quadrangles, Alaska. U.S. Geological Survey Miscellaneous Field Studies, Map MF-847.

Howard, H. 1932. Eagles and eagle-like vultures of the Pleistocene of Rancho LaBrea: Carnegie Institution of Washington D.C. Publ. 429. 82 pp.

Ives, P. C., G. Levin, C. L. Oman and R. Meyer. 1967. U.S. Geological Survey radiocarbon dates IX. Radiocarbon 9:505-529.

Jones, D. L., A. Cox, P. Coney and M. Beck. 1982. The growth of western North America. Scientific America 247(5):70-84.

Mann, D. H. 1986. Wisconsin and Holocene glaciation of Southeast, Alaska. Glaciation in Alaska, Hamilton et al., eds. Alaska Geological Society. pp. 237-265.

McConnell, R. G. 1913. Portions of Portland Canal and Skeena mining divisions, Skeena District, British Columbia. Canadian Geological Survey Memoir 32. 101 pp.

McPhail, J. D. and C. C. Lindsey. 1970. Freshwater fishes of northwestern Canada and Alaska. Fisheries Research Board of Canada Bulletin 173. 381 pp.

Miller, R. D. 1973a. Gastineau Channel formation, a composite glaciomarine deposit near Juneau, Alaska. U.S. Geological Survey Bulletin 1394. pp. C1-C20.

Miller, R. D. 1973b. Two diamictons in a landslide scarp on Admiralty Island, Alaska and the tectonic insignificance of an intervening peat bed. U.S. Geological Survey Journal of Research. 1:309-314.

Molnia, B. F. 1986. Glacial history of the northeastern Gulf of Alaska-A synthesis. Glaciation in Alaska, Hamilton et al., eds. The Geological Society of Alaska. pp. 219-236.

Neave, F. 1958. The origin and speciation of "*Oncorhynchus*" (SALMON). Transactions of the Royal Society of Canada Vol., LII, Series III, Section 5. pp. 25-39.

Plafker, G. 1971. Pacific margin Tertiary basin. In: Cram, I.H., ed. Future petroleum provinces of North America. American Association of Petroleum Geologists Mermoir. 15:120-135.

Sainsbury, C. L. 1961. Geology off part of the Craig C-2 quadrangle and adjoining areas, Prince of Wales Island, southeastern Alaska. U.S. Geological Survey Bulletin 10058-H. pp. 299-362.

Stalmaster, M. V. 1987. The Bald Eagle. Universe Books, New York. 227 pp.

Ecological Characteristics of Temperate Rain Forests: Some Implications for Management of Bald Eagle Habitat

Paul B. Alaback

University of Montana, Missoula, MT

Some of the world's densest populations of eagles thrive in the temperate rainforest regions of Alaska and adjacent British Columbia. Although many human-caused factors may be attributed towards population declines in other regions, in the North Pacific the unique climate and the rainforests that have developed still play a key role in defining why these habitats are so productive for eagles. In order to set the stage in understanding how eagles interact with these forests we need to first establish how unique these forests really are, define what a temperate rainforest is and how it functions.

Temperate rainforests are of great scientific interest and have been the focus of intense public debate on both conservation and management throughout their geographic range. They include some of the longest-lived and massive tree species as well as the largest remaining virgin landscapes outside of the tropics (Franklin and Waring 1980, Alaback 1989a, 1990a). Temperate rainforests function in a uniquely wet and cold climate which has direct implications to many ecological processes and to their conservation. They occur at high latitudes where their sensitivity to and history of rapid climatic change make them ideal subjects for monitoring global climatic change. Many critical scientific questions relating to landscape level processes may be best studied in temperate rainforests since their fauna and landscapes are more intact than in most other ecosystem types. Important decisions on conservation and management options for these pristine ecosystems will also require that we understand in much greater detail how temperate rainforests respond to both logging and climatic perturbations and how they differ from other forest types.

In this paper the composition, structure and function of the temperate rainforests of Alaska and adjacent British Columbia is described and a review of scientific literature relating to their ecology is provided. In addition, implications of this research to management of eagle habitat is discussed in the context of current practices and under new concepts collectively called by the USDA Forest Service "New perspectives in

36

Forestry."

A Definition for Temperate Rainforest

The term temperate rainforest is not new to ecology, but has been applied to a range of vegetative types throughout the world (Kuppen 1918, Kuchler 1949, Franklin and Dyrness 1973, De Laubenfels 1975, Webb 1978, Alaback and Juday 1989). One of the most distinctive features of rainforest climate is cool summers and wet weather year around. An ecological consequence of this unique climate is frequent disturbance by wind and the lack of fire as an important factor in forest dynamics. In the southern hemisphere, lightning caused fires appear to be rare events (Wardie et al. 1983). Throughout the northern hemisphere fire plays a key role, either as an infrequent catastrophic event in humid regions, or as a chronic event in drier climates. Only in the coastal rainforest is fire of minor importance (Harris and Farr 1974).

Rainforests are difficult to distinguish floristically or physiognomically from related forest types (Webb 1968, 1978, Cockayne 1971, De Laubenfels 1975). The upper canopy is often composed of a large number of species with few in a position of dominance and trees form clumped patterns reflecting gap-phase disturbance regimes. Epiphytes are often associated with rainforests, but they also frequent timberline and arctic environments with a high frequency of fog.

As a whole, temperate rainforest ecosystems are quite distinct from those of the tropics. Obviously tropical rainforests are among the most species rich ecosystems on earth and are a dramatic contrast with the relatively species impoverished temperate rainforests. But many other important differences occur as well. Temperate zone forests have proportionately fewer species in the upper canopy. Canopy trees tend to have smaller, more coriaceous, or even needle shaped leaves in the temperate rainforest formation, although conifers can occur in some lowland tropical rainforests (New Guinea, Queensland, Fiji, Borneo, Malaya). Temperate rainforests have proportionately fewer lianas when compared with the tropics (De Laubenfels 1975, Webb 1978). Dense mats of mosses and liverworts often carpet the forest floor and the upper canopy.

For purposes of discussion, the temperate rainforest climatic zone is defined with the following four factors:
1) greater than 1400 mm annual precipitation, 10% or more occurring during the summer months,
2) cool frequently overcast summers, July (or austral January) isotherm < 16 ° C,
3) fire infrequent and not an important evolutionary factor and
4) dormant season caused by low temperatures, may be accompanied by transient snow.

Temperate rainforests are relatively rare world-wide since most large land masses have continental climates which produce rain-shadows or extremes in temperature that prevent the development of rainforest (Figure 1). Most rainforest regions are bathed in ocean-born winds which bring moderate temperature and continuous rain. The principle rainforest zones are along the northern Pacific coast of North America, from a narrow band along the Olympic Peninsula in Washington State (46° N), to a broad band reaching the coastal cordillera in British Columbia and southeastern Alaska (61° N); and along a similar latitudinal range and physiographic pattern in southern Chile from approximately Valdivia in the coast and Conguillio in the Andes (38° S) south to western Tierra del Fuego (55° S). In North America "seasonal rainforests" extend from Vancouver Island, British Columbia south to the redwood region. Annual rainfall often approaches or even exceeds that in the temperate rainforest region, but is usually concentrated in winter, with extended droughts during the summer (Waring and Franklin 1979). Because of these summer droughts, fire is much more common and destructive in seasonal rainforests and plays a key role in their ecology relative to temperate rainforests. All other temperate rainforest zones are in isolated patches in mid-montane regions or in smaller islands, with the possible exception of western South Island, New Zealand. Temperate rainforests cover approximately 23 million hectares, or about 5% of that covered by tropical rainforests.

Climate

The key characteristic that distinguishes major forest formations and that of the temperate rainforest zone itself is the duration and intensity of cool summer rain. Although summer rains occur in other temperate forest types, they are usually associated with intense storms of short duration and do not lead to a cool climate. In temperate rainforests, long periods of fog, drizzle and light rain are common. This may be why the cloud forests of the tropics share so much in common both climatically and biologically with temperate rainforests. Within the temperate rainforest zone, duration and intensity of summer rains are closely associated with forest structure and composition.

Moving northward along the northern Pacific coastline there is a steady decline in growing season temperatures which is closely related to species richness and tree productivity (Farr and Harris 1979). In the southern hemisphere, climates tend to be more maritime so that cool climates begin at much lower latitudes than in North America. The rainforest of North America begins at nearly 10° higher latitude than it does in South America. In Chile, tidewater glaciers begin at only 45° S, or nearly 12° lower in latitude than tidewater glaciers in Alaska. Winter photosynthesis can play a significant role in carbon uptake in cool northern climates especially towards the south (Waring and Franklin 1979).

As in the tropics, the limit of the rainforest zone is mostly a function of precipitation rather than temperature (De Laubenfels 1975). Forest extends to the highest latitudes where heavy rainfall persists (e.g. contrast the climate of Punta Delgata, Chile and Adak Island, Alaska). Wind may also play a role in restricting forest growth as in the case of the Aleutian Islands in Alaska where planted *Picea* seedlings only survive in sheltered micro-sites (Alden and Bruce 1989), or in the exposed moorlands of the southern Chilean coast (Holdgate 1961, Young 1972).

Historical fluctuations in climate also have played a major role in shaping the modern day forests of coastal Alaska. Relatively small changes in global climate often result in major glacial advances or recessions in coastal Alaska. Extensive repeated glaciation, as recently as 200 years ago has constrained species diversity and species distributions by isolating populations, removing habitat, or by eliminating migration corridors.

This Sitka spruce tree, known locally as the Akutan forest, struggles to survive in the windy Aleutian Islands. Photo by Bruce Wright.

Contemporary forest communities have existed in Prince William Sound and western Alaska for less than 3,000 years. The spruce/hemlock forest has only developed over the last 5,000-8,000 years. The excellent pollen record of this region suggests continual and rapid change in tree species composition since the last major glaciation (Heusser 1960), some of which has been recorded in changes in the cultures of indigenous peoples in the region.

Soils

Soils play a key role in determining ecosystem structure, composition and function in the rainforest zone. In many cases, the effects of the excessively wet cool climate are primarily expressed to plants through soils. High rainfall and low temperatures usually translate into a faster rate of plant litter accumulation than of litter decomposition resulting in thick organic layers in the soil. Although large quantities of nutrients may exist in soils, the availability of these nutrients is usually low and is closely related to plant species abundance (Bormann and Sidle 1990, Klinka et al. 1990). Roots cannot extract nutrients efficiently under anaerobic conditions, likewise nutrients are often difficult to utilize when they are imbedded in large insoluble compounds. Both conditions are prevalent in temperate rainforest soils. As a consequence, many plant species are dependent on mycorrhizal species of fungi and microbes to help extract and uptake nutrients from soils or from complex organic compounds in soils. On the most poorly drained sites, plants must adapt a stress toleration strategy including slow growth rates and more efficient nutrient retention. Perpetually wet or flooded soils are also difficult for plants to colonize and establish, further restricting plant growth.

Subtle differences in soils fertility can translate into significant differences in tree growth rates or in vegetation composition and structure in coastal rainforests (Gagnon and Bradfield 1987, Alaback and Juday 1989, Martin 1989). All five major types of forest in coastal Alaska can be distinguished on the basis of soils characteristics – primarily by water drainage classes. The best drained sites occur on the loose, poorly developed gravelly or loamy alluvial soils in riparian floodplain sites. Sitka spruce, red alder, devil's club and salmonberry are common species in this zone. The best drained upland sites are dominated by western hemlock, blueberry and shield ferns. Somewhat poorly drained sites usually have a mixture of hemlock and either or both (yellow cedar and western red cedar). Poorly drained sites are usually dominated by mountain hemlock in mixture with shore pine. The only major plant community type in coastal Alaska which cannot be distinguished on the basis of soils is the high elevation mountain hemlock type-which primarily occurs in areas with a persistent snow pack, well drained soils and a short growing season either at high latitudes (e.g. Prince William Sound) or at high elevations.

A key consequence of the unique climate of temperate rainforests to soils is the rapid rate of soils morphogenesis. High rates of runoff result in rapid leaching and podzol formation (Holdgate 1961, Bowers 1987, Alexander 1988). Heavy accumulations of organic matter and nutrient immobilization lead to the development of a hardpan layer, impeding water drainage (Ugolini and Mann 1979). Without chronic disturbance, soils in Southeast Alaska are hypothesized to develop into waterlogged acidic, peat-like soils which can only support stunted bog-like forest plants. The causes of bog formation and the determinants of the ecotone between bog and forest have been long debated in both hemispheres (Holdgate 1961, Neiland 1971, Hennon 1986). A leading hypothesis is that the balance between bog and forest may reflect changes in regional climates (Winkler 1988). In both of the principal rainforest regions cupressid (cypress) tree species have rapidly diminished their former geographic range or are experiencing disease and decline (*Fitzroya cupressoides*, *Chamaecyparis nootkatensis*). For *Chamaecyparis*, it appears that the forest-bog ecotone is a key factor (Hennon 1986). Another cupressid, *Pilgerodendron uvdera*, although uncommon, plays a similar ecological role in Chile.

Forest Structure and Composition
The conifer forests of the Pacific coast of North America are unique in many ways, but their most outstanding characteristic is in "evergreenness," structure and age. Most other temperate rainforest types have an upper canopy of 30-45 m in height (e.g. Wardie et al. 1983). In North America, Sitka spruce can attain heights of 70-80 m as far north as Southeast Alaska. The great stature of these forests gives a complex structure relative to

Figure 1. World distribution of temperate rainforests. Ellipses indicate principal regions with temperate rainforests. This figure represents potential maximum historical distribution and does not take account of current land-use practices. Adapted from Alaback 1986.

Temperate Rainforests

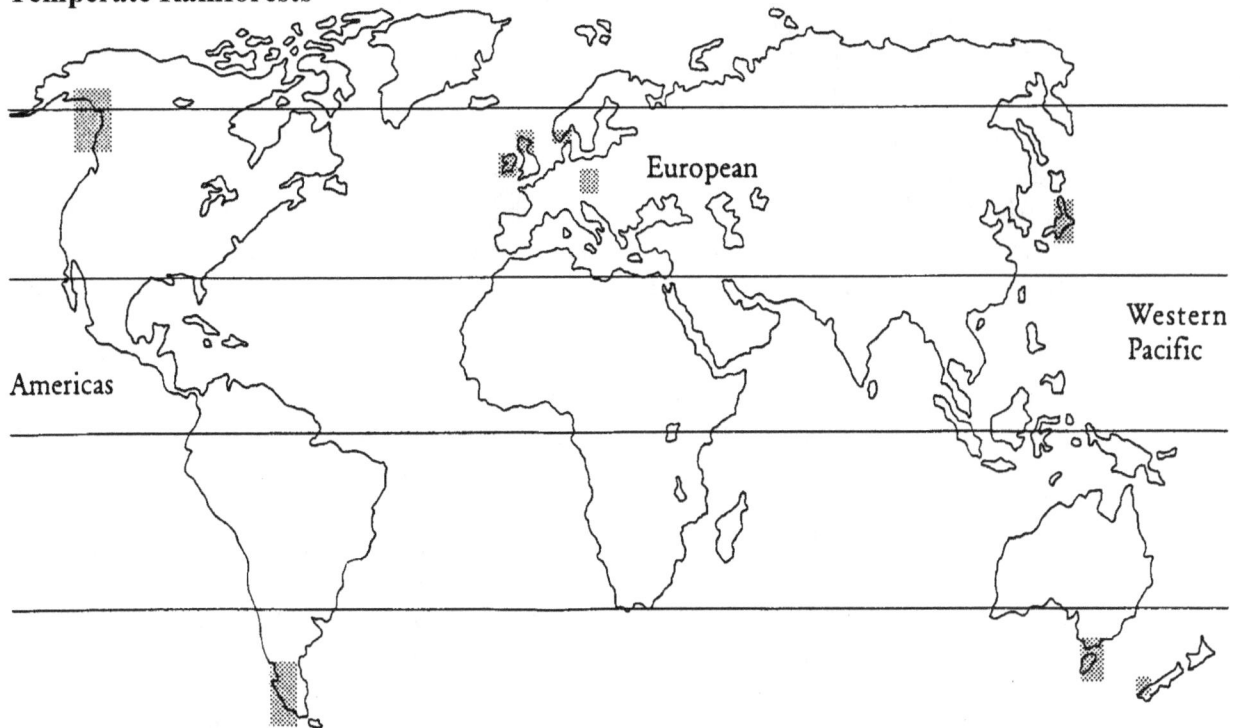

many other forest types. Only the mixed *Araucaria-Nothofagus* forests of New Guinea compare in stature and structure (Enright 1982). The conifer forests of the Pacific slope are also quite unique in their domination over hardwood or deciduous species. Most other parts of the world with similar climates have either a mixture of conifer and hardwood species or a domination of hardwood species with occasional conifers (Waring and Franklin 1979, Ash 1982, Wardie et al. 1983). It appears that this domination of conifers is due to historical causes, principally the development of a summer drought period in the Pacific Northwest and subsequent colonization of the rainforest region by trees from this southerly region (Waring and Franklin 1979).

Within the riparian zone, typically a mixture of western hemlock and western red cedar forms a main canopy layer approximately 30-45 m high with occasional patriarch Sitka spruce trees emerging 30-40 m above the canopy. These dominant spruce may be unshaded throughout their lives, resulting in long periods of maximal growth rates and rapid establishment in the upper canopy. Oftentimes these trees will be as little as 200 years old, or occasionally as much as 750-800 years old (Alaback unpubl., Waring and Franklin 1979). Dominant trees are typically 70-300 cm in diameter. It is not clear whether these Sitka spruce forests typically establish simultaneously, following a major catastrophic disturbance, or can continually establish following localized small-scale disturbances. Occasionally, on larger flood plains, cathedral forests of pure Sitka spruce may develop attaining as much as 800 mt biomass/ha. Productivity of individual trees is high, but because of low density, overall ecosystem productivity is usually not significantly greater than on well drained upland sites.

Western hemlock occupies the majority of productive forested land in the Pacific rainforest zone. Its great tolerance of shade and preference for organic seedbeds leads to a complex multilayered structure. Typical canopy heights are 35-50 m. Tree diameters typically range from 50-150 cm. Small canopy disturbances can result in the release of slow growing saplings which then can grow fast enough to eventually make it into the upper canopy. The complex history of small-scale disturbances is thought to be closely related to maintenance of species diversity and habitat patchiness (Armesto and Figueroa 1987, Alaback 1990b). A lush understory of herbs, short and tall woody shrubs and trees provides for an optimal condition for many herbivorous mammals (Hanley et al. 1989). Hemlock forests typically accumulate 200-600 mt biomass/ha (Alaback 1989a, Bormann and Sidle 1990).

Thin bark and poor vigor often combine to make hemlock highly susceptible to heart rot and root decay. This internal rot then predisposes dominant trees to stem breakage or root throw. Decay of hemlock logs can appear to be quite rapid, since the standing tree may have had extensive and advanced internal decay before dying and falling down. A full-sized tree, 50-70 cm in diameter, may be reduced to a shallow hump on the forest floor 50 years following falling to the ground (Graham and Cromack 1982). Western hemlock snags and logs are therefore not as useful habitat as other species which have higher persistence following death (Alaback unpubl., Noble and Harrington 1981).

Mixed forests of hemlock and cedar have among the oldest trees in Southeast Alaska, but are generally less productive than pure hemlock or spruce forest types. Canopy heights can reach 45 m but more typically fall in the range of 24-35 m (DeMeo 1989). The canopy is usually more open so that a more vigorous woody shrub understory can develop. Yellow cedar and red cedar can both exceed 1000 years of age in this forest type. Red cedar occurs primarily in the southern portion of Southeast Alaska and at lower elevations within this region. Preliminary data from both British Columbia and Alaska suggests red cedar is abruptly restricted in its geographic distribution by temperature, perhaps by ice and snow breakage of its fragile terminal leader. Often the transition between a high dominance of western red cedar and its complete disappearance can occur within a 100 m difference in elevation or less. Because of their high resistance to decay, snags are often abundant and long-lived in this forest type (Hennon and Loopstra 1991). Cedar snags are of relatively low value for cavity nesting animals however (Noble and Harrington 1981). Wood hardness and the toxicity of secondary compounds within these snags may be important in restricting their use by animals.

The most diverse but least productive type of coastal rainforest occurs on poorly drained sites throughout coastal Alaska and adjacent British Columbia. In Southeast Alaska this forest is often called the mixed conifer type because no single species appears to dominate this forest type consistently (Martin 1989). Common dominant species include mountain hemlock, shore pine, western red cedar and yellow cedar types (Banner et al.

1990). In British Columbia these ecosystems are called mostly mountain hemlock or western red cedar. Stand height is typically 20-35 meters. Forests are relatively open grown and usually include a wide representation of forest forb, herb, shrub and tree species as well as many wetland or bog species (Ver Hoer et al. 1988, Martin 1989). Small hummocks formed by old windthrow mounds or by geological anomalies often have a distinctly taller and more productive vegetation than surrounding areas. Low nutrient availability and high water tables often lead to severe stunting of tree growth, as in shore pines less than 30cm in diameter which can attain 300-500 years of age.

In the most poleward sites a distinctly open and depauperate forest develops. In Alaska this subarctic rainforest is best represented in Prince William Sound with a mixture of *Picea sitchensis*, *Tsuga heterophylla* and *T. mertensiana* (Cooper 1942, Eck 1984, Alaback and Juday 1989, Borchers et al. 1989). Growing sites are poor and mature canopies of 20-35m are common (Young 1972, Farr and Harris 1979). Thickets of *Rubus spectabilis* and other tall woody shrubs are less common than in the spruce rainforest type. The understory is dominated by ericaceous woody shrubs and carpets of bryophytes and ferns on the forest floor. The landscape in both hemispheres is a dynamic fine-grained mosaic of bog or moorland, ice fields and rainforest. These are among the least well known rainforest types.

Bald Eagles on a sunny Southeast Alaska beach with a lush old-growth forest in the background. Photo by Mike Jacobson, USFWS.

Productivity

Abundant rainfall and moderate temperatures year around combine to make the temperate rainforest zone one of the most productive in the temperate zone. Western hemlock produces a phenomenal load of leaf biomass and leaf area compared to most other species (Gholz 1982). As a consequence it can grow under dense shade and can outgrow many other species. One of the most ecologically important effects, though, is its efficiency at capturing solar radiation. The dense shade created by hemlock stands, combined with low solar altitudes and one of the worlds most cloudy climates, results in poor growth of understory shrubs, herbs and trees. Because of this, gaps in the canopy caused by geologic or soils anomalies or by canopy disturbance play a key role in maintaining the productivity and diversity of understory plants (Alaback 1982, Tappeiner and Alaback 1989). These understory plants are of key importance to many bird and mammal species for fruits, foliage, insects and cover (e.g. Willson et al. 1982). They also represent the major component of plant species diversity in these forests.

Key constraints to productivity include soils, climate, biogeography and possibly genetics. As discussed above, poor nutrient availability and fluctuating water tables can pose severe constraints to plant colonization and growth. Soils disturbance can improve nutrient availability by mixing organic and mineral fractions, improving water drainage, increasing soil temperatures and thereby should increase rate of decomposition and nutrient release (Bowers 1987, McClellan et al. 1990).

Climate restricts growth within this region by low growing season temperatures, short growing seasons and frost. Height growth of Sitka spruce is closely related to accumulated temperature (growing degree days) throughout the region (Farr and Harris 1979). Variability in snow fall or snow persistence during the spring can also have a large effect on primary productivity. Over a four-year period, timing of flowering and beginning of above ground shoot growth for early blueberry varied by a month or more in the Juneau area (Alaback, unpubl.). The complex interplay of ice fields, cold air drainages and the movement of air around the complex of fjords and straights, often result in wide variation in plant productivity and phenology.

Because of the relatively recent colonization of Southeast Alaska following the Pleistocene glaciations, there may also be a genetic constraint on primary productivity. Yellow cedar, for example, is distributed more commonly in the outer coast and other regions without recent glaciation more commonly than on the mainland. Poor reproductive success has greatly limited its distribution, even to the point of losing the species in some sites after logging. Planted seedlings by contrast, appear to grow perfectly well in areas in which no yellow cedar trees now occur. Western hemlock and Sitka spruce may also benefit from other seed sources because of the insufficient time for them to become adapted to the continuously changing climate of coastal Alaska.

Forest Dynamics
Catastrophic disturbance
Temperate rainforests are extremely dynamic systems with disturbances occurring at several spatial and temporal scales. In the Valdivian and Olympic rainforest zones, catastrophic disturbance appears to be an important component of stand structure, whether caused by fire, landslides, or volcanism (Franklin and Waring 1980). At higher latitudes and along exposed coastlines, continual disturbance by wind may become a

more important factor (Armesto and Figueroa 1987, Harris 1989, Taylor 1990). Forest stand structure is often an integration of both scales of disturbance due to the longevity of dominant trees. *Picea* and *Tsuga* are at least moderately shade tolerant and can regenerate effectively under partial forest canopies, although forests with a high component of *Picea* are normally subject to large scale catastrophic disturbances. In the Valdivian Andes *Nothofagus* species, by contrast appear to require catastrophic disturbance for regeneration. The mixed forest of myrtles, laurels and podocarps appears the most ecologically analogous to the *Tsuga* forests of North America (Armesto and Figueroa 1987).

The first work on plant succession in the temperate rainforest zone focused on succession following deglaciation (Cooper 1937, Crocker and Major 1955, Reiners et al. 1971). A simple chronosequence was used to characterize this succession from bryophytes (e.g. *Rhacomitrium* spp.), to a shrub stage (*Salix* spp.), to a *Picea sitchensis* forest, finally to a climax *Tsuga heterophylla* forest. This primary succession can proceed remarkably quickly, with a dense mature *Picea* forest established on land scraped bare by glaciers only two centuries ago.

In North America, *Alnus sinuata* is widely recognized for playing an important role in soils nutrition following deglaciation by fixing atmospheric nitrogen (Crocker and Major 1955). Following establishment of *Alnus* forests, *Picea* seedlings grow slowly in the understory, eventually overtopping the short-lived *Alnus*. The initially nitrogen-rich soils then allow for rapid growth of *Picea* and the establishment of a pure *Picea* forest within two centuries of deglaciation (Cooper 1937). Bormann and Sidle (1990) established that across this chronosequence a dramatic change in soils structure and fertility also occurs. Although the succession is rapid, low nutrient availability develops in the mature Sitka spruce forests and has probably been a key factor in predisposing these forests to insect attack and decline which will, in turn, accelerate a change towards climax forest species such as western hemlock. In Chile, *Gunnera chilensis* appears to play a similar role to *Alnus*, although few field studies have been conducted to verify how important its nitrogen fixation is to soils development and plant succession following glacial retreat (Veblen et al. 1989).

Recent work on post glacial succession has emphasized plant life history strategies and competitive relationships to examine if succession truly follows the facilitation model of Connell and Slatyer (1977) or simply relay floristics (Egler 1954). Preliminary results of some of this work suggests that post glacial succession is a far more complex and multi-faceted process than first believed. For example, in Glacier Bay the original work was done only on the eastern arm of the Bay where glacial retreat occurred rapidly (e.g. Cooper 1937). In the western arm where calcareous parent materials predominate, a wide range of plant successional trajectories develop following deglaciation. The speed of deglaciation and physical processes associated with it such as scour, fill, the texture of outwash materials and other soil changes, lead to divergent successional pathways. It also appears that late sere species occur at the earliest stages of the succession, imposing some constraints on the facilitation model.

Few studies have been conducted on succession following landslides or mudflows in the northern temperate zone (Miles and Swanson 1986, Smith and Commandeur 1986, Dale 1989). Chronosequences are difficult to establish because of the individualistic nature of each disturbance event and the wide range of soil conditions which may result from different kinds of disturbances or within different terrains contained in a single landslide area. The succession resembles post glacial succession in its dominance by nitrogen fixing species such as *Lupinus* and *Alnus* and early establishment of *Picea*. Similarly in Chile the nitrogen fixer *Gunnera chilensis* is an early colonizing species, along with the climax species, *Nothofagus dombeyi*. Much of the climax old-growth *Nothofagus* and Fitzroya is presumed to originate from landslide or mudflow events. Yet little information is available on the timing and nature of primary succession either following deglaciation or slope failures in the region.

Secondary succession also proceeds, rapidly following non-catastrophic disturbance in the northern temperate rainforest zone. Following windthrow or logging, most of the pre-disturbance propagules survive intact allowing growth release of tree seedlings and layering or resprouting of shrubs and herbs. The most characteristic aspect of the succession is an extended period of species impoverished, understory vegetation following the establishment of a dense overstory canopy layer. Less than 1% of the understory biomass of old-growth forests are maintained in these younger forests for 100 years or more (Alaback 1982, 1984). As stands mature, shade tolerant shrubs and tree seedlings invade the understory, often leading to a dense secondary canopy layer. Only after the principle overstory stratum senesces, to follow a pattern of gap-phase dynamics does the full structural diversity of shrubs, herbs and tree seedlings develop (Alaback 1990b). Many herbaceous species (e.g. *Cornus canadensis, Rubus pedatus, R. lasiococcus, Oxalis oregona*) which are important sources of highly nutritious forage are most abundant in chronically disturbed old-growth or in the oldest age class of seral dominants (500-1000 years old) (Alaback 1982, 1989b, Spies and Franklin 1988).

Windthrow and gap-phase dynamics
Only recently has research on the ecology of northern rainforests begun to examine how the natural pattern of localized disturbance by windthrow affects plant community processes and forest structure. Windthrow disturbance is widespread throughout coastal Alaska and appears to be a vital factor in maintaining the diversity, productivity and the structural complexity of temperate rainforests (Harris and Farr 1974, Armesto and Figueroa 1987, Alaback 1989a, Harris 1989). Two basic forms of windthrow disturbance occur: a) catastrophic windthrow and b) localized windthrow.

Catastrophic windthrow is highly variable in space and time, but tends to be more common at higher elevations on steep slopes with thin soils which are fully exposed to southeasterly storms off the ocean. Greater than 80% of the standing trees usually are knocked over during this kind of storm and damage usually extends over many hectares of forest land. A key question is how large and extensive catastrophic windthrow patches are and how frequently they impact different landscapes. Indirect evidence from tree age distributions in a few locations around Southeast Alaska suggests, for example, that many forests regenerated after a widespread disturbance approximately 200 years ago.

Extensive areas on western Prince of Wales Island and western Admiralty Island have forest dominants approximately 200 years old.

Localized windthrow, or gap phase dynamics, is hypothesized as being of central importance to the maintenance of structure and diversity of old-growth forests in coastal rainforests. Studies in both British Columbia and Alaska have shown a high frequency of localized disturbance with clear implications to regeneration and establishment of tree seedlings (Lertzman 1989, Hocker 1990). In the subalpine zone of British Columbia, gaps are created at any given place every 600-700 years. In the low elevation spruce-hemlock forests in Southeast Alaska, sub-dominant trees were affected by gaps every 32 years, or an average of seven times in the life of dominant trees. While the subalpine sites were disturbed less frequently than in the tropics, sea level forests were being disturbed much more frequently than most temperate forests and at about the same frequency as in tropical rainforests.

Windthrow creates a hole in the canopy and disturbs the soil, creating habitat for either the colonization of new plants, or the increased growth of established plants. Windthrow imparts a large degree of heterogeneity to a forest since windthrow can occur at different times of the year, with varying levels of seed availability of different species and can cause varying levels of soils or canopy disturbance. All of these factors will affect which species will respond most effectively to the disturbance and what the composition and structure of the forest will be in the future. Repeated disturbances of different intensities at a site will also allow the co-occurrence of several different kinds of species and have different effects than any single disturbance.

When windthrow results in root throw and the creation of mounds and pits on the forest floor, it sets off a whole series of ecological processes important both for the maintenance of site productivity and biological diversity. The mounds are first colonized by a series of moss and liverwort species, then are colonized by several herb, shrub and tree species (den Ouden 1988). In general, the effects of gap creation are much greater when the gap involves root throw than if it only involves stem breakage or canopy disturbance (Clebsch and Busing 1989, Nakashizuka 1989).

The present composition and structure of rainforests directly reflects their history of disturbance and regeneration, sometimes spanning centuries. Sitka spruce, for example, requires more light and disturbance than hemlock if it is to establish under a forest canopy. Dense forests with a large component of spruce, therefore, reflect a response to catastrophic disturbance and cannot be perpetuated without subsequent disturbances of similar magnitude. Along the Oregon coast, for example, Taylor (1990) discovered that Sitka spruce could not be maintained in small canopy gaps (<0.25 ha) and required gaps at least 800-1000 m² in size to maintain present composition. At higher elevations or in alluvial or shoreline ecosystems, spruce regenerates readily under the forest canopy with or without disturbance since there is sufficient light under the canopy. At low elevation upland forests, the dense canopy that develops requires disturbance for species like Sitka spruce to regenerate and maintain itself. Pure stands of hemlock, by contrast, can be readily perpetuated by small scale gap disturbances (Christy and Mack 1984). By looking at forest composition and structure, it is therefore, possible to gain some insight into long-term patterns of forest disturbance and ultimately patterns of climatic change (Lertzman 1989).

Management Implications

Eagles have a well known preference for large dominant trees or snags for nesting and roosting and for riparian habitat (Hodges and Robards 1982). Trees commonly used by eagles often exceed 30 m height and 110 cm in diameter. In typical upland old-growth forests, these trees would range 400-500 years old, but in open beach fringe habitats trees of this size could be as little as 200-300 years old (Alaback and Juday 1989, W. Farr, pers. comm.). Forest management for optimal eagle habitat would then require at a minimum, maintaining a forest structure that includes a significant number of trees with these characteristics and maintaining the integrity of the riparian zone.

Conventional, even-aged management, in which large areas are clear cut and grown for approximately 100 years until cut again, is unlikely to produce trees of sufficient size for eagles at any time during the rotation (Taylor 1934). Planting and thinning can be used to increase growth rates, but it would still be unlikely that trees of the mean size of eagle nesting trees could be produced in less than the period of a 100 year timber rotation (W. Farr, Juneau Forest Sciences Lab., pers. comm.). Management of eagle habitat for average sized nesting trees would then most likely require at a minimum an extended rotation, generally in the range of 150-250 years. An additional problem would be to make the trees sufficiently wind firm (through early thinnings for example) to have an adequate probability for persistence. Silvicultural strategies ideally should also ensure the maintenance of sufficient abundance, size and broad representation of snag and log decay classes in habitat management areas (Cline et al. 1980, Franklin 1989). A spatial or landscape scale planning analysis would also be required to ensure that at any point in time a sufficient number of trees with adequate size for eagle nesting would be available.

Alternatively less commonly used, uneven-aged, or "new forestry" techniques could be used to manage eagle habitat areas (Franklin 1989). In principle, trees could be harvested frequently, but not more than 30-50% at a time, thus emulating small-scale windthrow disturbance. A key problem would be providing sufficient light and soils disturbance to maintain an adequate equilibrium of spruce, hemlock and other species. Rather than evenly distributing harvest across a stand, for example, it may be more effective to harvest trees in small patches, similar in size to that required by spruce naturally for regeneration in gaps (ca. 1000 m²). As in even-aged management, careful attention would also have to be paid to windthrow. As patches are created in the forest, trees on the edge of the gap are usually windthrow prone. The more dense the forest the more likely that trees surrounding the gap will be wind thrown. A similar strategy could also be applied to the riparian zone in which it is necessary to maintain an intact forest canopy continuously over time.

Many questions remain regarding the dynamics of native rainforests and how principles learned from these studies could be applied to forests managed for timber as well as for eagles. Because shoreline habitats and riparian habitats are among the most wind exposed and frequently disturbed habitats along the coast, they will likely be more difficult to manage than protected upland habitats.

Studies of rainforest dynamics need to be directed to model the frequency and scale of disturbance that is required to maintain the forest structure needed for eagles. To successfully manage forests for these specific characteristics will likely require a high level biological and technological knowledge, which does not exist for most rainforest types. Considerable modeling, experimentation and detailed trials will be required before a high degree of confidence can be attained in predicting the ultimate long-term effects of these manipulations on ecosystem structure and function.

Literature Cited

Alaback, P. B. 1982. Dynamics of understory biomass in Sitka spruce-western hemlock forests of Southeast Alaska. Ecol. 63:1932-1948.

Alaback, P. B. 1984. Secondary succession following logging in the Sitka spruce-western hemlock forests of Southeast Alaska: Implications for wildlife management. U.S. Geological. Agric., For. Serv., Gen. Tech. Rep. PNW-173. Portland, Oreg. 26pp.

Alaback, P. B. 1989a. Endless battles, verdant survivors. Nat. History August 45-48.

Alaback, P. B. 1989b. Logging of temperate rainforests and the greenhouse effect--some ecological factors to consider. Pages 195-202. In: E. B. Alexander, ed. Proc. Watershed '89. March 21-23,1989, Juneau, Alas., U.S. Geological. Agric, For. Serv., Reg. 10, Juneau, Alas.

Alaback, P. B. 1990a. Alerce: The South American giant. The World and I. October 316-321.

Alaback, P. B. 1990b. Dynamics of old-growth temperate rainforests in Southeast Alaska. In:: A. M. Milner and J. D. Wood, eds. Proc. 2nd Glacier Bay Sci. Symp., Sept. 19-22, 1988, Gustavus, Alas. Natl. Park Serv., Alaska Reg., Anchorage, Alas.

Alaback, P. B. and G. P. Juday. 1989. Structure and composition of low elevation old-growth forests in research natural areas of Southeast Alaska. Nat. Areas J. 9:27-39.

Alden, J. and D. Bruce. 1989. Growth of historical Sitka spruce plantations at Unalaska Bay, Alaska. U.S. Dept. Agric., For. Serv., Portland, Oreg., Gen. Tech. Rep. PNW-GTR-236. 18pp.

Alexander, E. B. 1988. Rates of soil formation: implications for soil-loss tolerance. Soil Sci. 145:37-45.

Armesto, J. J. and J. Figueroa. 1987. Stand structure and dynamics of rainforests in the Chiloe Archipelago. J. Biogeogr. 14:367-376.

Ash, J. 1982. The *Nothofagus* Blume Fagaceae of New Guinea. Pages 355-380. In: J. L. Gressitt, ed. Monogr. Biol. Vol 42. W. Junk, The Hague.

Banner, A., R. N. Green, A. Inselberg, K. Klinka, D. S. McLennan, D. V. Meidinger, F. C. Nuszdorfer and J. Pojar. 1990. Site classification for coastal British Columbia. Minist. For., Victoria, B.C.

Borchers, S. L., J. Wattenbarger and R. Ament. 1989. Forest plant associations of Montague Island, Chugach National Forest: preliminary results. Pages 29-46. In: E. B. Alexander, ed. Watershed '89. March 21-23,1989, Juneau, Alaska, U.S. Geological. Agric, For. Serv., Reg. 10, Juneau, Alas.

Bormann, B. T. and R. C. Sidle. 1990. Changes in productivity and distribution of nutrients in a chronosequence at Glacier Bay National Park, Alaska. J. Ecol. 78:561-578.

Bowers, F. 1987. Effects of windthrow on soil properties and spatial variability in Southeast Alaska. Ph.D. Diss., Univ. Wash., Seattle. 200pp.

Christy, E. J. and R. N. Mack. 1984. Variation in demography of juvenile *Tsuga heterophylla* across the substratum mosaic. J. Ecol. 72:75-91.

Clebsch, E. C. and R. T. Busing. 1989. Secondary succession, gap dynamics and community structure in a southern Appalachian cove forest. Ecol. 70:728-735.

Cline, S. P., A. B. Berg and H. M. Wight. 1980. Snag characteristics and dynamics in Douglas-fir forests, western Oregon. J. Wildl. Manage. 44:773-786.

Cockayne, L. 1971. The subtropic and subantarctic rainforests of New Zealand. Pages 109-136. In: S. R. Eyre, ed. World Vegetation Types. Columbia Univ. Press, New York.

Connell, J. H. and R. O. Slatyer. 1977. Mechanisms of succession in natural communities and their role in community stability and organization. Am. Nat. 111:1119-1144.

Cooper, W. S. 1937. The recent ecological history of Glacier Bay: An initial report upon a long term study. Ecol. 4:355-65.

Cooper, W. S. 1942. Vegetation of the Prince William Sound region, Alaska; with a brief excursion into post-Pleistocene climatic history. Ecol. Monogr. 12:1-22.

Crocker, R. L. and J. Major. 1955. Soil development in relation to vegetation and surface age at Glacier Bay, Alaska. J. Ecol. 43:427-448.

Dale, V. H. 1989. Wind dispersed seeds and plant recovery on the Mount St. Helens debris avalanche. Can. J. Bot. 67:1434-1441.

De Laubenfels, D. J. 1975. Mapping the world's vegetation. Syracuse Geogr Ser. 4., Syracuse Press, Syracuse, N.Y.

DeMeo, T. 1989. Preliminary forest plant association guide, Ketchikan area, Tongass National Forest. U.S. Dept. Agric., For. Serv., Ketchikan, Alaska. 164pp.

den Ouden, J. 1988. Some investigations on forest mosses in Southeast Alaska. M.S. Thesis. Landbouwuniversiteit, Wageningen, The Netherlands. 40pp.

Eck, K. C. 1984. Forest characteristics and associated deer habitat values, Prince William Sound islands. Pages 235-246. In: W. R. Meehan, T. R. Merrell and T. A. Hanley, eds. Fish and wildlife relationships in old-growth forests. Proc. Symp., Juneau, Alaska, 12-15 April 1982. Am. Inst. Fish. Res. Biol. and U.S. Dept. Agric., For. Serv., Pacific Northwest Res. Stn., Portland, Oreg.

Egler, F. E. 1954. Vegetation science concepts: Initial floristic composition a factor in old field vegetation development. Vegetation 4:412-417.

Enright, N. J. 1982. The Araucaria forests of New Guinea. Pages 381-399. In: J. L. Gressitt, ed. Monogr. Biol. Vol 42. W. Junk, The Hague.

Farr, W. A. and A. S. Harris. 1979. Site index of Sitka spruce along the Pacific coast related to latitude and temperatures. For. Sci. 25:145-153.

Franklin, J. F. 1989. Toward a new forestry. Am. For. November/December 37-44.

Franklin, J. F. and C. T. Dyrness. 1973. The natural vegetation of Washington and Oregon. U.S. Dept. Agric., For. Serv., Pac. Northwest For. Range Exp. Stn., Portland, Oreg., Gen. Tech. Rep. PNW-8. 417pp. illus.

Franklin, J. F. and R. H. Waring. 1980. Distinctive features of the Northwestern coniferous forest: development, structure, function. Pages 59-89. In: R. H. Waring, ed. Forests: fresh perspectives from ecosystems analysis Proc. 40th Ann. Biol. Colloq., Oregon State Univ. Press. Corvallis.

Gagnon, D. and G. E. Bradfield. 1987. Gradient analysis of west central Vancouver Island forests. Can. J. Bot. 65:822-833.

Gholz, H. L. 1982. Environmental limits on aboveground net primary production, leaf area and biomass in vegetation zones of the Pacific Northwest. Ecol. 63:469-481.

Graham, R. L. and K. Cromack, Jr. 1982. Mass, nutrient content and decay rate of dead boles in rain forests of Olympic National Park. Can. J. For. Res. 12:511-521.

Hanley, T. A., C. T. Robbins and D. E. Spalinger. 1989. Forest habitats and the nutritional ecology of Sitka black-tailed deer: a research synthesis with implications for forest management. U.S. Dept. Agric., For. Serv., Pac. Northwest For. Range Exp. Stn., Portland, Oreg., Gen. Tech. Rep. PNW-230.

Harris, A. S. 1989. Wind in the forests of Southeast Alaska and guides for reducing damage. U.S. Dept. Agric., For Serv., Pac. Northwest For. Range Exp. Stn., Portland, Oreg., Gen. Tech. Rep. PNW-244: 63pp.

Harris, A. S. and W. A. Farr. 1974. The forest ecosystem of Southeast Alaska. Forest ecology and timber management. U.S. Dept. Agric., For. Serv., Pac. Northwest For. Range Exp. Stn., Portland, Oreg., Gen. Tech. Rep. PNW-25. 109pp.

Hennon, P. E. 1986. Pathological and ecological aspects of decline and mortality of *Chamaecyparis nootkatensis* in Southeast Alaska. Ph.D. Diss., Oregon State Univ., Corvallis. 279pp.

Hennon, P. E. and E. M. Loopstra. 1991. Persistence of western hemlock and western red cedar trees 38 years after girdling at Cat Island in Southeast Alaska. U.S. Dept. Agric., For. Serv., Pac. Northwest For. Range Exp. Stn., Portland, Oreg., Res. Note (5pp).

Heusser, C. J. 1960. Late-Pleistocene environments of North Pacific North America. Am. Geogr Soc. Spec. Publ. No. 35: 308pp.

Hocker, K. M. 1990. Influence of canopy gaps on forest dynamics in Southeast Alaskan hemlock spruce forests. Senior Thesis, Harvard Univ., Dept. Biology. Cambridge, Mass. 43pp.

Hodges, J. I., Jr. and F. C. Robards. 1982. Observations of 3,850 Bald Eagle nests in Southeast Alaska. Pages 37-54. In: W. N. Ladd and P F. Schempf, eds. Proc. of a symposium and workshop on raptor management and biology in Alaska and Western Canada, 17-20 February 1981, Anchorage, Alas. U.S. Dept. Inter., Fish Wildl. Serv., Anchorage, Alas. 335pp.

Holdgate, M. W. 1961. Vegetation and soils in the south Chilean islands. J. Ecol. 49:559-580.

Klinka, K., Q. Wang and R. E. Carter 1990. Relationships among humus forms, forest floor nutrient properties and understory vegetation. For. Sci. 36:564-581.

Kuppen, W. 1918. Klassifickation der klimate nach temperature niederschlag and jahreslauf. Petermann"s Mitteilungen 64:193-203.

Kuchler, A. W. 1949. A geographical system of vegetation. Geogr. Rev. 37:233-240.

Lertzman, K. 1989. Gap-phase community dynamics in a sub-alpine old growth forest. Ph.D. Diss., Univ. British Columbia, Vancouver.

Martin, J. R. 1989. Vegetation and environment in old growth forests of northern southeast, Alaska: a plant association classification. M.S. Thesis, Arizona State Univ., Tempe. 221 pp.

McClellan, M., B. T. Bormann and K. Cromack, Jr. 1990. Cellulose decomposition in Southeast Alaskan forests: effects of pit and mound microrelief and burial depth. Can. J. For. Res. 20:1242-1246

Miles, D. W. R. and F. J. Swanson. 1986. Vegetation composition on recent landslides in the Cascade Mountains of western Oregon. Can. J. For. Res. 16:739-744.

Nakashizuka, T. 1989. Role of uprooting in composition and dynamics of an old-growth forest in Japan. Ecol. 70:1273-1278.

Neiland, B. J. 1971. The forest bog complex of Southeast Alaska. Vegetation 26:3-62.

Noble, R. E. and P. Harrington. 1981. Snag characteristics in old growth forests on Prince of Wales Island, Alaska. U.S. Dept. Agric., For. Serv., Alas. Reg. Rep. 125. Juneau, Alas. 88pp.

Reiners, W. A., I. A. Worley and D. B. Lawrence. 1971. Plant diversity in a chronosequence at Glacier Bay, Alaska. Ecol. 52:55-59.

Smith, R. B. and P. R. Commandeur. 1986. Soils, vegetation and forest growth on landslides and surrounding logged and old-growth areas on the Queen Charlotte Islands. British Columbia Minist. For., Victoria, Land Manage. Rep. No. 41: 95 pp.

Spies, T. A. and J. F. Franklin. 1988. Old growth and forest dynamics in the Douglas fir region of western Oregon and Washington. Nat. Areas J. 8:190-201.

Tappeiner, J. C. and P. B. Alaback. 1989. Early establishment and vegetative growth of understory species in the western hemlock - Sitka spruce forests of Southeast Alaska. Can. J. For. Res. 67:318-326.

Taylor, A. H. 1990. Disturbance and persistence of Sitka spruce *Picea sitchensis* bog. Carr. In: coastal forests of the Pacific Northwest, North America. J. Biogeogr. 17:47-58.

Taylor, R. F. 1934. The yield of second growth western hemlock-Sitka spruce stands in southeastern Alaska. U.S. Dept. Agric. Tech. Bull. 412. 30pp.

Ugolini, F. C. and D. H. Mann. 1979. Biopedological origin of peatlands in Southeast Alaska. Nature 281:366-368.

Veblen, T. T., D. H. Ashton, S. Rubulis, D. C. Lorenz and M. Cortes. 1989. *Nothofagus* stand development on in-transit moraines, Casa Pangue Glacier, Chile. Arctic and Alpine Res. 21:144-155.

Ver Hoer, J. M., B. J. Neiland and D. C. Glenn-Lewin. 1988. Vegetation gradient analysis of two sites in Southeast Alaska. Northwest Sci. 62:171-180.

Wardie, P., M. J. A. Buffin and J. Dugdale. 1983. Temperate broad-leaved evergreen forests of New Zealand. Pages 33-72. In: J. D. Ovington, ed. Temperate broad-leaved evergreen forests. Ecosystems of the World 10. Elsevier, New York.

Waring, R. H. and J. F. Franklin. 1979. Evergreen coniferous forests of the Pacific Northwest. Sci. 204:1380-1386.

Webb, L. J. 1968. Environmental relationships of the structural types of Australian rain forest vegetation. Ecol. 49:296-311.

Webb, L. J. 1978. A general classification of Australian rainforests. Aust. Plants 76:349-363.

Willson, M. F., E. A. Porter and R. S. Condit. 1982. Avian frugivore activity in relation to forest light gaps. Caribbean J. Sci. 18:1-4.

Winkler, M. 1988. Effect of climate on development of two Sphagnum bogs in south-central Wisconsin. Ecol. 69:1032-1043.

Young, S. B. 1972. Subantarctic rain forest of Magellanic Chile: distribution, composition and age and growth rate studies of common forest trees. Ant. Res. Ser. 20:307-372.

The Importance of Fish to Bald Eagles in Southeast Alaska: A Review

Robert H. Armstrong

Alaska Department of Fish and Game; University of Alaska Southeast, Juneau, AK

Fish are the most important prey for Bald Eagles in Southeast Alaska, yet not enough is known about which species are most important to eagles, how and where eagles obtain them and how secure various fish populations are. This study explores those questions and proposes a number of studies that should be conducted to acquire adequate data for making management decisions.

Throughout their range Bald Eagles feed on fish more than any other group of organisms. After reviewing 2,000 references on Bald Eagles, Lincer et al. (1979) concluded that "without a doubt" fish are the primary prey and often represent 80-90% of their diet. Similar statements were made by Stalmaster (1987) and Gerrard and Bortolotti (1988) in their reviews of the life history and biology of the Bald Eagle in North America.

Fish are also the most important item in the diet of Bald Eagles in Southeast Alaska. In a review of literature on Southeast Alaska's Bald Eagles Sidle et al. (1986) concluded that fish are the eagles' dietary mainstay. In an analysis of nearly 500 eagle stomachs collected in Southeast Alaska, Imler and Kalmbach (1955) found that fish averaged 66% of their year-round diet. An even higher percentage of fish (78%) were included among prey brought to nests by adult eagles in the area (Ofelt 1975).

Which species of fish are being eaten by eagles in Southeast Alaska? Which species are most important and how do eagles obtain them? How large are these fish populations now and what can we predict about future populations? Only a couple of dietary studies have been conducted on Bald Eagles in Southeast Alaska. Are these adequate or should more studies be conducted? These questions will be discussed in this paper.

Importance of Fish to Eagles in Southeast Alaska

Bald Eagles feed on a variety of fish species in Southeast Alaska. Usually these feedings occur when fish concentrate in shallow water to spawn. The following species are probably most important to Southeast Alaska's Bald Eagles.

Salmon

All species of salmon are of particular importance to Bald Eagles because salmon enter fresh water to spawn, often in large numbers and then die and wash up along stream and river bars and banks, lake and ocean shores and tidal flats. Compared to most other fish available to eagles, salmon are large. One carcass may satiate several eagles. The importance of salmon and their use by Bald Eagles is well documented. Several studies, in fact, correlate the abundance of Bald Eagles with the abundance of spawned-out salmon (Servheen 1975, Fitzner and Hansen 1979, Hansen et al. 1984).

The largest concentration of eagles feeding on spawned-out salmon occurs in the Chilkat River near Haines, Alaska. More than 3,000 eagles may feed at one time on the carcasses of chum salmon that spawn in spring-fed stretches of the river. Bald Eagles travel to this river from all over Southeast Alaska and some scientists believe the entire region's carrying capacity for eagles may depend on these salmon (Hansen et al. 1984). The large size of chum salmon (4.5-6.0 kg) and their habit of spawning late (September to November) in several Southeast Alaska rivers, including the Chilkat, make this species especially important to Bald Eagles (Morrow 1980).

Pink salmon may be particularly important to nesting Bald Eagles in Southeast Alaska. Pinks are the most numerous salmon and spawn in more than 2,000 streams throughout the region. They utilize all sizes of streams, even the intertidal portions of streams that have blocks to migrating fish at tidewater. Probably any coastal fish stream within a nesting eagle's territory will contain spawning pink salmon. Most pink salmon spawn at a time when the eaglets are large (July-August) and pink salmon are small enough (1-3 kg) to be carried to the nest (Morrow 1980). Pink salmon may also be particularly important to fledged eagles, as their carcasses would be widely available in mid to late August, when most Southeast Alaska's Bald Eagles fledge (Sidle et al. 1986).

Coho salmon, although not nearly as numerous as pink salmon, are also known to spawn in more than 2,000 streams throughout the region. Coho are one of the latest spawners in Southeast Alaska; many spawn in November and December (Morrow 1980). They spawn when water and air temperatures are dropping and often just before and during ice formation on streams, rivers and lakes. Also, coho spawn when other fish scavengers are either leaving the region (as in the case of gulls) or denning (as in the case of bears). Coho carcasses decompose slowly in the colder water and many become trapped in ice. These carcasses are thus available to eagles in late fall, often during mid-winter and even during spring thaws in some systems. I have observed coho salmon entering the Mendenhall River system near Juneau to spawn in late December. Bald Eagles can often be seen in this area throughout the winter feeding on coho salmon carcasses.

Sockeye salmon in Southeast Alaska usually spawn in systems associated with lakes (Morrow 1980). They choose lake systems because most young sockeye rear for 1 or 2 years in a lake before migrating to sea (Margolis et al. 1966). In Southeast Alaska, 189 lakes are accessible to sockeye salmon (Reed 1971). Although sockeye are restricted to relatively few systems as compared to pink and coho salmon, they are no doubt important to local populations of Bald Eagles. For example, Bald Eagles feed on sockeye salmon in the shallow channels of the Chilkat River delta while the fish are enroute to Chilkat Lake near Haines (Hansen et al. 1984).

Chinook salmon spawn in only 33 streams and rivers in Southeast Alaska and most of these streams are used by fewer than 1,000 spawners. Most chinook spawning in our three highest producing rivers (the Stikine, the Taku and the Alsek rivers) do so within tributaries in Canada; nevertheless the chinook are no doubt important to local populations of Bald Eagles. Since chinook are the largest of the Pacific salmon, with many weighing between 12 to 18 kg (Morrow 1980), one carcass would satiate several eagles.

The Alaska Department of Fish and Game closely monitors commercial and sport catch and escapement of salmon in Southeast Alaska and most runs are strong. Recent commercial catches of all salmon species in Southeast Alaska have been among the highest on record. The 1989 Southeast Alaska salmon catch was approximately 65.8 million fish and this ranked second only to the 1941 salmon harvest (Geiger and Savikko 1990).

Dolly Varden
Dolly Varden char are the most widely distributed fish in Southeast Alaska. They can be found in all types of fresh and salt water capable of supporting fish (Armstrong and Morrow 1980). The anadromous form of charr is probably the most available as prey for Bald Eagles. These charr concentrate in lakes and larger rivers for the winter (Armstrong 1974), where they may exceed 100,000 in a single lake or river (Armstrong 1965). In April and May I have seen lake outlets completely full of migrating Dolly Varden.

Dolly Varden may be more important in the diet of Bald Eagles than the literature indicates. Eagles were always present during the spring out-migrations of charr at Lake Eva on Baranof Island. Dolly Varden overwinter in the Chilkat River near Haines Baade (1955) and Hansen (1987) mentioned that the breeding eagles of the Chilkat Valley fed upon them.

Successful management of anadromous Dolly Varden is difficult because they move from one freshwater system to another and because each system contains mixed stocks. Over-harvest has apparently occurred in the Juneau area where the sport catch rate dropped considerably over a 10 year period (Armstrong 1979). I have outlined management strategies for the maintenance of Dolly Varden populations in Southeast Alaska (Armstrong 1974).

Pacific Herring
In spring, Pacific herring move inshore in large numbers to spawn in bays and estuaries (Eschmeyer and Herald 1983). They usually lay their eggs on beach rocks, eel grass, kelp, rockweed and pilings at depths between high tide and 36 feet (Hart 1973). In Southeast Alaska, thousands to perhaps millions of herring spawn on a single beach (Alaska Dept. Fish & Game 1978). The peak of spawning is in mid-March (Ibid.) but may occur anytime from February through June (Hart 1973). Bald Eagles, particularly non-breeders, concentrate to feed on spawning herring (Hodges et al. 1979). Up to 300 eagles have been observed feeding on Pacific herring at Klawock in Southeast Alaska (Bailey 1927).

The Alaska Department of Fish and Game conducts detailed stock assessments of Pacific herring and the stocks are strong and well managed. The allowable harvests range from 10 to 20% of these estimates only when they fall above an established threshold level. Otherwise the fishery is closed. The strength of Southeast herring stocks currently is reflected in the 1989 harvest, which was the highest since 1964 (Funk and Savikko 1990).

Eulachon

Eulachon concentrate to spawn in the mainland rivers of Southeast Alaska from March through May (Hart 1973). Most spawn over coarse sand and pea-sized gravel (Morrow 1980) in the lower parts of glacier fed rivers. Since they spawn in relatively shallow water and die after spawning (Eschmeyer and Herald 1983), the eulachon would be accessible to feeding eagles.

An important location where Bald Eagles feed on eulachon is in the Stikine River near Wrangell. During April from 500 to 1,500 eagles gather there to feed on spawning eulachon (Hughes 1982b). On April 13, 1990, 1,073 eagles were concentrated where the eulachon spawn in the Stikine River (Walsh 1990a). This concentration is considered to be the second highest number of feeding eagles in Southeast Alaska and this food supply may be critical to the survival of the area's eagles (Hughes 1982b). Bald Eagles also feed on eulachon in the Chilkat River near Haines (Hansen 1987) and I have observed numerous eagles feeding on them in the mouth of Mendenhall River near Juneau.

Eulachon are harvested commercially in Washington and Oregon, where more than 454,000 kg per year are taken (Morrow 1980). In Southeast Alaska they are harvested only by subsistence fishermen. In 1987, approximately 20,000 pounds of eulachon were taken by subsistence fishermen in Southeast Alaska (Bosworth 1990). More than half of this harvest came from the Chilkat and Chilkoot rivers (Betts 1990).

Pacific Sand Lance

As a source of food for marine birds and mammals, the Pacific sand lance is one of the most important fish in our marine waters (Sealy 1975, Beacham 1986, Armstrong and O'Clair 1987). Sand lance are particularly vulnerable to predators and are flushed easily from the sand when disturbed (Hobson 1986). When not buried they occur in large schools near the water surface in both inshore and offshore marine waters (Eschmeyer and Herald 1983).

Sand lance may be important in the diet of Southeast Alaska eagles. On numerous occasions I have counted between 20 and 80 Bald Eagles feeding on Pacific sand lance during minus tides on the Mendenhall Wetlands near Juneau. On a minus tide the sand lance's burial grounds are often exposed.

Bald Eagles at the mouth of the Mendenhall River feeding on sand lance. Photo by Bob Armstrong

I have observed Bald Eagles walking over these areas. This seems to panic the sand lance, which squirt out of the sand, making them easy prey for the eagles. Concentrations of Bald Eagles near the edge of sandy tidal flats, especially at minus tides, may be feeding on Pacific sand lance.

Other Fish Species
Many other species of fish concentrate to spawn in areas that would make them available to Bald Eagles of Southeast Alaska; however, I could find little or no information on their use by eagles.

Cutthroat and steelhead trout would be available to Bald Eagles when the fish spawn in the spring (Jones 1977a, b). The anadromous cutthroat trout may be available to eagles during their migrations to sea in May and June and again when they return in September and October (Armstrong 1971).

Capelin are vital food for almost all vertebrate creatures of the marine ecosystem of coastal northeast Canada (Thurston 1988). I believe they are also important forage fish for Bald Eagles and other fish eaters in Southeast Alaska because they spawn in large schools where eagles could get to them and they die after spawning. They move inshore between April and October to spawn on fine gravel or sandy beaches (Eschmeyer and Herald 1983). Capelin have been observed trapped in intertidal ponds on the Mendenhall Wetlands during May and again in July (Bishop et al. 1987). Other smelt, including surf smelt, rainbow smelt, night smelt and longfin smelt, occur in Southeast Alaska and have spawning characteristics that could make them vulnerable to predation by Bald Eagles (Eschmeyer and Herald 1983).

Starry flounders and Pacific staghorn sculpins frequent shallow intertidal sloughs and ponds, sometimes in considerable numbers (Bishop et al. 1987). Sculpins and flatfish have been observed among prey items brought to eaglets in Southeast Alaska (Ofelt 1975) and in eagle stomachs (Imler and Kalmbach 1955). The use of benthic fish, such as flounders and sculpins, has also been documented elsewhere for the Bald Eagle (Cash et al. 1985, Haywood and Ohmart 1986, MacDonald and Austin-Smith 1989). Walleye pollock, other cod species and rockfish also occur in the diet of Bald Eagles in Southeast Alaska (Imler and Kalmbach 1955).

Special Considerations During Nesting

Bald Eagles typically nest near the best foraging areas (MacDonald and Austin-Smith 1989). In Southeast Alaska, Hodges and Robards (1982) found that nests were located in areas where the eagles could most easily obtain fish, such as near the waterfront along exposed coasts and on prominent points and islets.

Availability of fish not only influences the number of eagles breeding in an area but also increases the survival of their offspring. In general, birds that are solitary nesters adjust their breeding density to correspond with available food (Newton 1976). In the Chilkat River Valley, the availability of fish influenced breeding rates, egg laying dates and offspring survival of nesting eagles and caused eagle productivity to fluctuate greatly between years (Hansen et al. 1984).

Nesting eagles are very territorial and defend their territories against other eagles from at least mid-March through August (King et al. 1972). During this time they may seldom forage for fish beyond their territory, which may only be 1-2 km (Stalmaster 1987). The adults typically perch near their nesting sites and wait for fish to appear (Stalmaster 1987, Gerrard and Bortolotti 1988).

Since food abundance in spring strongly influences where, when or if eagles lay eggs (Hansen et al. 1986), fish species available at this time are especially important to the eagles. In Southeast Alaska, the first salmon are not available until July. Pacific herring, eulachon and a few other species concentrate to spawn in spring, but these spawning concentrations are widely scattered and would be available to only a relatively small percentage of the region's nesting eagles. On the other hand, non-breeding eagles, which do not have territories, can search widely for these spring spawning concentrations and probably benefit most from them (Hodges et al. 1987).

Most nesting Bald Eagles are probably dependent on the occasional fish swimming near the surface of the water and the dead and dying fish that float or wash up on the beach within their territory. Most fish species sink to the bottom when they die and probably get scavenged before bacterial action can refloat them.

Whether or not a fish floats after being killed probably depends on the presence or absence of a gas bladder and the type of gas bladder that it has. Some fish have a gas bladder that opens into the esophagus (physostomous condition) while others have a gas bladder that lacks a duct to the esophagus (physoclistous condition). When physostomous fish are handled, as when they are caught and released by fishermen, the gas bladder may collapse and the fish will sink. But when physoclistous fish are brought to the surface their gas bladder expands, hence they usually float after being released.

Of the fish commonly caught by fishermen, only members of the cod family such as walleye pollock and rockfish have a physoclistous condition and float after being killed. Also, walleye pollock are known to float or swim about at the water's surface when they are sick or injured. Most other fish such as salmon, trout, flounders and sculpins, are physostomous and sink after being killed.

Walleye pollock, then, may be easily captured by nesting eagles. In addition, they may be one of the most abundant marine fish in Alaska. They make up 73% of the total harvest of groundfish (Kruse 1988). In the 1960s they were the fish that I most frequently caught while trolling for salmon. Also, I would see them in large numbers swimming about Juneau area boat docks. Pollock have even been observed entering stream mouths during the advancement of tide waters (Armstrong and Winslow 1968).

Walleye pollock are utilized by nesting eagles in Southeast Alaska. Pollock and cod were present in about one-third of the 325 eagle stomachs with fish examined by Imler and Kalmbach (1955). They were the most frequently consumed fish during May and June before salmon spawning began and during a critical time for nesting eagles.

Walleye pollock were abundant in the northern half of Southeast Alaska in the early 1970s, but they essentially had disappeared by 1982 or 1983 (Bracken 1990). This disappearance may have been related to an apparent epizootic that caused an unusual die-off of walleye pollock within the major inside passages and inlets of northern Southeast Alaska during April 1977 (Kingsbury 1977). This noted die-off of pollock may have caused the increasingly higher proportion of adult eagles that failed to breed between 1970 and 1979 (Hansen and Hodges 1985), or the significant drop in the total number of offspring in nests observed between 1972 and 1986 (Hansen 1987). The evidence may indicate a relationship and the importance of walleye pollock and other cod to nesting eagles in Southeast Alaska should be investigated.

How Bald Eagles Obtain Fish in Southeast Alaska
Bald Eagles obtain fish in a variety of ways. In general, non-nesting eagles search for fish; nesting eagles wait for fish to come near their nesting site (Hansen et al. 1984).

According to Stalmaster (1987), Bald Eagles acquire food by stealing prey from others, scavenging on carrion and hunting and killing (Hansen et al. 2008).

Eagles find fish not only by searching themselves but also by following other eagles and other birds to dead fish and concentrations of fish (McClelland et al. 1982, Harmata 1984). Bald Eagles often prefer to acquire fish by stealing from other eagles and other species rather than acquiring it on their own (Stalmaster and Gessaman 1984). On several occasions, I have seen eagles follow river otters and steal their catch. They also steal food from sea otters (White et al. 1971), Ospreys (Hughes 1982a), mergansers and gulls (Stalmaster 1987).

Bald Eagles also take advantage of fish captured, injured, or driven to the surface of the water by other fish predators. They will feed on fish killed by bears and wolves (Gard 1971, Hansen et al. 1984), injured by whales and sea lions (Hyde 1990) and driven to the surface by loons (Dixon 1909), seals (Ofelt 1975) and salmon (Beebe 1974).

Human activities also may provide fish for Bald Eagles. Commercial, sport and subsistence fishermen often catch and release unwanted fish. Many of the released fish are crippled or dead and eagles feed upon them (Beebe 1974, Dunstan and Harper 1975, Hansen et al. 1984, Dennis 1990). Eagles also take advantage of fish and their parts that are discarded by fish hatcheries in Southeast Alaska (Walsh 1990b).

Among all of the different ways that Bald Eagles obtain fish, two in particular are probably more important. (1) The number of salmon carcasses that bears scoop out of rivers and streams seems quite significant. When food is abundant, particularly late in the summer, bears foraging spawned out salmon carcasses tend to eat only the fat-rich brains and eggs, leaving the rest of the carcasses on river bars and banks. The remaining larger portions of the carcasses can then be eaten by Bald Eagles. Many spawned out salmon carcasses originally settle into deep pools. Were it not for the bears they would be difficult or impossible for eagles to obtain.

The widespread commercial, sport and subsistence fisheries in Southeast Alaska must provide an abundance of unwanted fish carcasses for eagles. A high correlation was found between eagle breeding success and the amount of fish caught and discarded by commercial fishermen in central Saskatchewan (Whitefield and Gerrard 1985). In Southeast Alaska most fishing occurs during the eagles' nesting period, from May through August and dead fish from fishing may be crucially important in regulating eagle populations.

Concerns for the Future
Although most fish stocks utilized by Bald Eagles in Southeast Alaska are healthy, I am concerned about their future. The demand for human use of fish in Alaska has increased substantially in recent years. Commercial, subsistence and sport harvests have increased about three-fold since 1976 (Kruse 1988). There is also a trend toward more utilization of other fish species. If commercial utilization of capelin, eulachon and Pacific sand lance were allowed in Southeast Alaska the effects on Bald Eagles could be considerable.

Many other human activities can negatively affect fish. Logging, mining, power developments, urbanization and pollution have all had profound negative impacts on fish populations throughout the nation. The mining industry is rapidly expanding in Southeast Alaska. Release of toxic materials, both accidentally and deliberately, has been commonplace with the mining industry elsewhere (Laycock 1989). Fish assimilate toxic chemicals from their environment and pass them up the food chain to Bald Eagles (Stalmaster 1987).

While contributing significantly to our knowledge of the fish species utilized by Bald Eagles studies need to be supplemented with others if we are to understand the relative importance of different species of fish. Ofelt's direct observations (1975) of the food brought to eaglets at three nests covered only the period between June 30 and August 10 and 38% of the fish could not be identified. Imler and Kalmbach (1955) examined the stomach contents of about 500 eagles killed in Alaska under the bounty program. While their study gave a clearer picture of the year-round utilization of fish by eagles, the examination of stomach contents may be biased toward mammals, birds and larger-boned fish. Small-boned fish such as Pacific herring, Pacific sand lance, eulachon, capelin and other smelt were found only in small numbers in their study. But fine-boned fish are more easily digested by eagles and their remains are more difficult to find because of their small size (Dunstan and Harper 1975).

Other methods may also not yield accurate results. For example, studies of the food habits of White-tailed Eagles in Greenland by Danish ornithologists have revealed several problems associated with examining prey fragments and pellets found near nesting sites (Kampp and Wale 1979, Wille 1979). The Danes assessed prey most accurately when they used automatic cameras to photograph each food item carried to the nest by the White-tailed Eagle adults.

There are several major gaps in our knowledge of the relationship between fish and eagles in Southeast Alaska. Some of these gaps may be critical to future management of Bald Eagles, especially as we develop our land and as we increase our utilization of fish resources. Although any further information on fish as food for eagles will help us to better understand these relationships, we need certain types of data more than others. I believe we should give priority to four kinds of studies:

1. Determine the distribution of nesting Bald Eagles in relation to the fish resources and related activities in Southeast Alaska. We need an overall survey that would plot on a single map: eagle nest locations, salmon streams, herring spawning areas, Dolly Varden wintering areas, tidal flats, locations of commercial, subsistence and sport fisheries and other fish resource information. This information could be gathered from the area management biologists of the Alaska Department of Fish Game Divisions of Commercial, Subsistence and Sport Fisheries. Such a study could help reveal whether prey availability affects the pattern of nest distribution. It could then be used to plan more detailed studies as the need for them is indicated.

2. Determine the species of fish utilized by nesting Bald Eagles prior to the availability of

salmon carcasses. Spring and early summer is important to nesting success. The success of this type of study may require direct observations of nesting eagles. Observations from a boat to determine where and when nesting eagles fish and which fish species they catch could be compared with fish depicted in photographs of the eagles bringing prey to their nests.

3. Determine the importance of fish discarded by commercial, subsistence and sport fishermen to Bald Eagles in Southeast Alaska. At the Northern Regions Conference in Anchorage (1990) a proposal was made that fishermen be required to keep and utilize all fish caught rather than throw unwanted fish overboard. If implemented, what effect would this proposal have on nesting Bald Eagles? Perhaps this type of information could be gathered by observers stationed within or near selected fisheries in the region.

4. Determine the year-round utilization of Pacific sand lance by Bald Eagles. Sand lance burial grounds are often exposed or nearly exposed during minus tides. An ideal study site is a burial ground associated with the Mendenhall Wetlands near Juneau, where numerous eagles feed on sand lance at low tide. This study could be done with a spotting scope without disturbing the eagles and other aspects of food gathering by eagles over tidal areas could also be determined. The utilization of flounder, sculpins and eulachon by eagles could be documented here as well.

Acknowledgements

I thank Rita O'Clair and Bruce Wright of the University of Alaska Southeast for their helpful comments on the manuscript.

Literature Cited

Alaska Department of Fish and Game. 1978. Alaska's Fisheries Atlas. State of Alaska Department of Fish and Game. V. 1.

Armstrong, R. H. 1965. Some migratory habits of the anadromous Dolly Varden *Salvelinus malma* (Walbaum) in Southeastern Alaska. Alaska Department Fish and Game Research Report 3:36pp.

Armstrong, R. H. 1971. Age, food and migration of sea-run cutthroat trout *Salmo clarki*, at Eva Lake, Southeastern Alaska. Trans. Amer. Fish. Soc. 100: 302-302.

Armstrong, R. H. 1974. Migration of anadromous Dolly Varden *Salvelinus malma* in Southeastern Alaska. J. Fish. Res. Board Can. 31:435-444.

Armstrong, R. H. 1979. Where have all the dollies gone? Alaska Fish and Game Trails. pp. 18-19. March/April.

Armstrong, R. H. and J. E. Morrow. 1980. The Dolly Varden charr *Salvelinus malma*. In: CHARRS Salmonid Fishes of the Genus Salvelinus. Perspectives in Vertebrate Science. Vol. 1, pp. 99-140.

Armstrong, R. H. and R. O'Clair. 1987. Sand lance key food link. Nature Southeast. Southeastern Log. July pp. 1-4.

Armstrong, R. H. and P. C. Winslow. 1968. An incident of walleye pollock feeding on salmon young. Trans. Am. Fish. Soc. 97(2):202-203.

Baade, R. T. 1955. Dolly Varden trout investigation in the Chilkat River. Alaska Game Fish Invest. Fed. Aid in Fish Restoration. Q. Prog. Rep. (Proj. F-1-R-4) 4:39-41.

Bailey, A. M. 1927. Notes on the birds of Southeastern Alaska. Auk 44:184-205.

Beacham, T. D. 1986. Type quantity and size of food of Pacific salmon *Oncorhynchus*, in the Strait of Juan de Fuca, British Columbia, Canada. U.S. National Marine Fisheries Service Fish Bulletin. 84(1):77-90.

Beebe, F. L. 1974. Field studies of the Falconiformes (vultures, eagles, hawks and falcons) of British Columbia. Occasional Papers of the British Columbia Provincial Museum No. 17: 163 pp.

Betts, M. 1990. Chilkat and Chilkoot Rivers subsistence eulachon harvest May 1990: Interim Report Division of Subsistence, Alaska Department of Fish and Game. June, 1990. 18pp.

Bishop, D., R. Armstrong and R. Carstensen. 1987. Environmental analysis of lower Jordan Creek and nearby wetlands in regard to planned airport taxiway extension. A report prepared by Environaid, Juneau, Alaska. 69pp.

Bosworth, R. 1990. Alaska Department of Fish and Game. Personal communication.

Bracken, B. 1990. Region I Groundfish Project Leader. Personal communication.

Cash, K. J., P. J. Austin-Smith, D. Banks, D. Harris and P. C. Smith. 1985. Food remains from Bald Eagle nests on Cape Breton Island, Nova Scotia. Wildl. Manage. 49:223-235.

Dennis, E. 1990. Commercial fisherman. Personal communication.

Dixon, J. S. 1909. A life history of the northern Bald Eagle. Condor 11:187-193.

Dunstan, T. C. and J. F. Harper. 1975. Food habits of Bald Eagles in north-central Minnesota. J. Wildl. Manage. 39(1):140-143.

Eschmeyer, W. N. and E. S. Herald. 1983. A field guide to Pacific coast fishes of North America. Houghton Mifflin Co., Boston. 336pp.

Fitzner, R. E. and W. C. Hanson. 1979. A congregation of wintering Bald Eagles. Condor 81:311-313.

Funk, F. and H. Savikko. 1990. Preliminary forecasts of catch and stock abundance for 1990. Alaska herring fisheries. Alaska Department of Fish and Game. Regional Information Report No. 5J90-02.

Gard, R. 1971. Brown bear predation on sockeye salmon at Karluk Lake, Alaska. J. Wildl. Manage. 35(2):193-204.

Gerrard, J. M. and G. R. Bortolotti. 1988. The Bald Eagle haunts and habitats of a wilderness monarch. Smithsonian Institution Press, Washington and London. 178pp.

Geiger, H. J. and H. Savikko. 1990. Preliminary forecasts and projections for 1990. Alaska salmon fisheries. Alaska Department of Fish and Game. Regional Information Report No. 5J90-03.

Hansen, A. J. 1987. Regulation of Bald Eagle reproductive rates in Southeast Alaska. Ecology 68(5):1387-1392.

Hansen, A. J. and J. I. Hodges, Jr. 1985. High rates of nonbreeding adult eagles found in Southeast Alaska. J. Wildl. Manage. 49:454-458.

Hansen, A. J., E.L. Boeker, J. I. Hodges and D. R. Cline. 1984. Bald Eagles of the Chilkat Valley, Alaska:

ecology, behavior and management. Final Report of the Chilkat River Cooperative Bald Eagle Study. National Audubon Society and U.S. Fish and Wildlife Service. 27pp.

Hansen, A., E. L Boeker and J. Hodges. 2008. The population ecology of Bald Eagles along the Pacific Northwest coast. In: Wright, B. A. and P. F. Schempf, eds. Bald Eagles in Alaska.

Hansen, A. J., M. I. Dyer, H. H. Shugart and E. L. Boeker. 1986. Behavioral ecology of Bald Eagles along the Pacific Northwest coast: A landscape perspective. Oak Ridge National Laboratory, Environmental Sci. Div. Pub. No. 2548. Oak Ridge, Tennessee. 166pp.

Harmata, A. R. 1984. Bald Eagles of San Luis Valley, Colorado: Their winter ecology and spring migration. Ph.D. Thesis, Montana State University, Bozeman.

Hart, J. L. 1973. Pacific fish of Canada. Fisheries Research Board of Canada. Bulletin 180. 740pp.

Haywood, D. H. and R. D. Ohmart. 1986. Utilization of benthic feeding fish by inland breeding Bald Eagles. Condor 88:35-42.

Hobson, E. S. 1986. Predation on the Pacific sand lance *Ammodytes hexapterus* (Pisces: Ammondytidae) during the transition between day and night in Southeastern Alaska. Copeia: 1:223-226.

Hodges, J. I. and F. C. Robards. 1982. Observations of 3,850 Bald Eagle nests in Southeast Alaska. Pages 37-66. In: W. N. Ladd and P F. Schempf, eds. Proc. of a symposium and workshop on raptor management and biology in Alaska and Western Canada, 17-20 February 1981, Anchorage, Alas. U.S. Dept. Inter., Fish Wildl. Serv., Anchorage, Alas. 335pp.

Hodges, J. E., E. L. Boeker and A. J. Hansen. 1987. Movements of radio-tagged Bald Eagles, *Haliaeetus leucocephalus*, in and from Southeast Alaska, Can. Field Nat. 101:136-140.

Hodges, J. I., J. G. King and F. C. Robards. 1979. Resurvey of the Bald Eagle breeding population of Southeast Alaska. Wildl. Manage. 43:219-221.

Hughes, J. 1982a. The Osprey in Southeast Alaska. Pages 197-204. In: W. N. Ladd and P F. Schempf, eds. Proc. of a symposium and workshop on raptor management and biology in Alaska and Western Canada, 17-20 February 1981, Anchorage, Alas. U.S. Dept. Inter., Fish Wildl. Serv., Anchorage, Alas. 335pp.

Hughes, J. 1982b. Spring concentration of Bald Eagles along the Stikine River estuary. Page 82. In: W. N. Ladd and P F. Schempf, eds. Proc. of a symposium and workshop on raptor management and biology in Alaska and Western Canada, 17-20 February 1981, Anchorage, Alas. U.S. Dept. Inter., Fish Wildl. Serv., Anchorage, Alas. 335pp.

Hyde, J. 1990. Alaska Department of Fish and Game, Personal Communication.

Imler, R. H. and E. R. Kalmbach. 1955. The Bald Eagle and its economic status. U.S. Fish and Wildlife Service Circular 30.

Jones, D. E. 1977a. Life history of sea-run cutthroat trout. Alaska Department of Fish and Game. Federal Aid in Fish Restoration. Completion Report. Study AFS-42. 18:78-105.

Jones, D. E. 1977b. Life history of steelhead trout. Alaska Department of Fish and Game. Fed. Aid in Fish Restoration. Completion Report. Study AFS-42. 18: 52-77.

Kampp, K. and F. Wille. 1979. Fodevaner hos den Gronlandske Havorn *Haliaeetus albicilla* groenlandicus Brehm. (Food habits of the Greenland White-tailed Eagle) Dansk Ornitologisk Forenings Tidsskrift, 73:157-64. (In Danish with English summary).

King, J. G., F. C. Robards and C. J. Lensink. 1972. Census of the Bald Eagle breeding population in Southeast Alaska. J. Wildl. Manage. 36:1292-1295.

Kingsbury, A. P. 1977. Mortality of walleye pollock *Theregra chalcogramma* in Southeastern Alaska during 1977. Alaska Department of Fish and Game. Division of Commercial Fisheries. Juneau, Alas.

Kruse, G. H. 1988. An overview of Alaska's Fisheries: Catch and economic importance of the resources, participants in the fisheries, revenues generated and expenditures on management. Alaska Department of Fish and Game. Fishery Research Bulletin 88-01. 72pp.

Laycock, G. 1989. Going for the gold. Audubon, July. pp. 70-81.

Lincer, J. L., W. S. Clark and M. N. LeFranc, Jr. 1979. Working bibliography on the Bald Eagle. Nat. Wildl. Fed. Tech. Ser. No.2.

MacDonald, P. R. N. and P. J. Austin-Smith. 1989. Bald Eagle, *Haliaeetus leucocephalus*, nest distribution on Cape Breton Island, Nova Scotia. Canadian Field-Naturalist. 103(2):293-296.

Margolis, L., F. C. Cleaver, Y. Fukuda and H. Godfrey. 1966. Salmon of the north Pacific Ocean. Part IV. Sockeye salmon in offshore waters. Bull. Int. N. Pac. Fish. Comm. 20:1-70.

McClelland, B. R., L. S. Young, D. S. Shea, P. T. McClelland, H. L. Allen and E. B. Spettigue. 1982. The Bald Eagle concentration in Glacier National Park, Montana: Origin, growth and variation in numbers. Living Bird 19:133-155.

Morrow, J. E. 1980. The freshwater fishes of Alaska. Alaska Northwest Pub. Co., Anchorage, Alas. 248pp.

Newton, I. 1976. Population limitation in diurnal raptors. Can. Field Nat. 90(3):274-300.

Ofelt, C. H. 1975. Food habits of nesting Bald Eagles in Southeast Alaska. Condor. 77(3):337-338.

Reed, R. D. 1971. Lakes in Southeastern Alaska which are accessible to anadromous fish. Alaska Department of Fish and Game, Sport Fish Division, Administrative Report. 16pp.

Sealy, S. G. 1975. Feeding ecology of the Ancient and Marbled Murrelets near Langara Island, British Columbia, Canada. Can. Zool. 53(4):418-433.

Servheen, C. W. 1975. Ecology of the wintering Bald Eagles on the Skagit River, Washington, M.S. Thesis, Univ. Wash, Seattle.

Sidle, W. B., L. H. Suring and J. I. Hodges, Jr. 1986. The Bald Eagle in Southeast Alaska. Wildlife and Fisheries Habitat Management Notes. U.S. Forest Service, Juneau, Alaska. 29pp.

Stalmaster, M. V. 1987. The Bald Eagle. Universe Books, New York. 227pp.

Stalmaster, M. V. and J. A. Gessaman. 1984. Ecological energetics and foraging behavior of overwintering Bald Eagles. Ecological Monographs 54:407-428.

Thurston, H. 1988. The little fish that feeds the North Atlantic. Audubon. January. pp. 52-71.

Walsh, P. 1990a. Mitkof Island bird observation. The Raven 14(9):4.

Walsh, P. 1990b. U.S. Forest Service, Petersburg, Personal Communication.

White, C. M., W. B. Emison and F. S. L. Williamson. 1971. Dynamics of raptor populations on Amchitka Island, Alaska. BioScience 21(12):623-627.

Whitefield, D. W. A. and J. M. Gerrard. 1985. Correlation of Bald Eagle density with commercial fish catch. Pages 191-193. In: J. M. Gerrard and T. N. Ingram, eds. 1985. The Bald Eagle in Canada, White Horse Plains Publishers, Headingley, Manitoba.

Wille, F. 1979. Den gronlandske Havorns *Haliaeetus albicilla* groenlandicus Brehm. fodevalg-methde og forelobige resultater. (Choice of food of the Greenland White-tailed Eagle-method and preliminary results) Dansk Ornithologisk Forenings Tidsskrift, 72:165-70.

Avian Resources of Southeast Alaska: A Brief Review and Their Importance to Eagles

M. E. "Pete" Isleib

1938-1993, Juneau, AK

The wealth and diversity of Southeast Alaska's avian populations are important to the area's Bald Eagles. Geographic position, maritime climate and diverse and rich marine environments all affect the abundance and diversity of the avian resources of Southeast Alaska.

Six major geographic regions have been recognized and defined for Alaska relative to bird distribution (Kessel and Gibson 1978). Southeastern Alaska, including its contiguous offshore waters south of Cape Fairweather, is the farthest east and smallest of these biogeographic regions. The region's southerly position and proximity to birds of continental climates and its position on the Pacific coastal migration corridor contribute to its avian diversity.

Relatively little has been published on the distribution and abundance of birds in the region. Historically, data prior to the end of the nineteenth century are extremely limited. During the late nineteenth century and the first half of this century, Southeast Alaska for the most part was bypassed by ornithological investigators seeking more discovery-oriented results from arctic and subarctic Alaska. However, two major natural history investigations, the Harriman Expedition in 1899 (Keeler 1910) and the Alexander Expeditions of 1907 (Grinnell 1909) and 1909 (Swarth 1911) visited numerous localities in Southeast Alaska and provided the first abundance of material and information on the birds of the region.

Subsequently and prior to statehood in 1959, several individuals added appreciably to our knowledge of the region's avifauna, including Alfred M. Bailey (1927), George G. Cantwell (1897), Joseph S. Dixon (1907), Ira N. Gabrielson (1944), Joseph Grinnell (1898, 1909), Stanley G. Jewett (1942), Harry S. Swarth (1911, 1922), J. Dan Webster (1941, 1950), George Willett (1914, 1915, 1921, 1928) and Ralph B. Williams. Brief summaries of the work of these people, as well as specific data and syntheses, are included in Gabrielson and Lincoln (1959).

Since statehood, governmental agencies have conducted several studies of the region's waterfowl, raptors and seabirds. Some threatened species such as Bald Eagles and Trumpeter Swans have received special attention.

Of late, most recent agency studies have taken a more ecological or ethological approach. Comprehensive information on the status, distribution, abundance and breeding biology of all birds in the region has been gathered and compiled principally by Brina Kessel and Daniel D. Gibson at the University of Alaska Museum and by volunteers.

Volunteers working with programs of the National Audubon Society annually conduct breeding bird censuses in June at a few sites in the region. They also conduct Christmas Bird Counts at eight of the region's population centers and contribute observations to Alaska's seasonal columns in the Audubon Society's field journal American Birds. During the past 25 years, American Birds has contained much of the new information and information about trends regarding birds in Southeast Alaska.

Bald Eagle searching for food from spruce tree perch. Photo by Jack Hodges, USFWS.

Many states have completed or are compiling breeding bird atlases. These are comprehensive censuses and surveys of all breeding bird populations within their geographic borders. Mostly because of Alaska's vastness, Alaskans will probably lack this depth of information for the foreseeable future. For Southeast Alaska such information is available on some colony nesting seabirds and Bald Eagles. Brina Kessel and Daniel D. Gibson, however, are preparing a new comprehensive publication on Alaska's birds. The authors have been amassing a tremendous volume of material on the birds in the various biogeographic regions of Alaska for more than 30 years.

Of the 430 species of birds that have occurred in Alaska, more than 300 have been recorded in Southeast Alaska-more species than have been reported in any other biographic region of Alaska. (Gibson, pers. comm.). Several species are represented by hundreds of thousands, even millions, of individuals, while about 70 species have been "vagrants" beyond the periphery of their annual range. Many species reach their distributional limits within the region and some occur in very small numbers or only in restricted habitats or locations. Approximately 130 species breed in the region, about 120 species occur during winter, 210 during spring, 160 during summer and 215 during fall. Of the birds recorded in Southeast Alaska, approximately 50% are marine or water-dependent species and they constitute more than 80% of the total avian biomass utilizing the region during any season of the year. Waterfowl, shorebirds and seabirds each represent millions of individuals.

The diversity and quantity of birds in the region is important to water-dependent predators and scavengers such as *Haliaeetus* eagles, that depend on avian resources for much of their diet. The Bald Eagle, nearly ubiquitous in the region, represents a biomass of more than 100 tons and it captures and consumes even the largest of other birds. An investigation of the stomach contents of nearly 400 Southeast Alaska Bald Eagles conducted during the bounty years revealed that birds, principally waterfowl, constituted a large percentage of eagle diet during the colder months of October through April (Imler and Kalmbach 1955). During November more than 50% of the volume was ducks and geese and on an annual basis birds represented nearly 20% of the eagle's diet.

At seabird colonies on Forrester Island National Wildlife Refuge, another investigation of eagle pellets revealed birds were the most frequently found prey in summer and contributed the greatest volume to the diet (DeGange and Nelson 1978). Food habit studies elsewhere in Alaska and in the Pacific Northwest have reported that the proportion of birds in the diet of Bald Eagles may vary from nearly 20% to 86% by volume, depending on general area and time of year (Imler and Kalmbach 1955).

I leave you with a final note on the avian resources of Southeast Alaska: A healthy and productive environment for Bald Eagles depends on a similar environment for all birds.

Literature Cited

Bailey, A. M. 1927. Notes on the birds of Southeastern Alaska. Auk 44:1-23, 184-205, 351-367.

Cantwell, G. C. 1897. Notes from Alaska. Nidologist 4:59.

DeGange, A.R. and J. W. Nelson. 1978. Additional studies of seabirds in the Forrester Island National Wildlife Refuge, 31 May-17 June 1977. Unpubl. rep., U.S. Fish Wildl. Serv, Anchorage, Alas. 29pp.

Dixon, J. S. 1907. Some experiences of a collector in Alaska. Condor 9(5):128-287.

Gabrielson, I. N. 1944. Some Alaskan notes. Auk 61:105-130; 270-287.

Gabrielson, I. N. and F. C. Lincoln. 1959. The birds of Alaska. The Stackpole Co., Harrisburg, Pa. 922pp.

Grinnell, J. 1898. Summer birds of Sitka, Alaska. Auk 15(2):122.

Grinnel, J. 1909. Birds and mammals of the 1907 Alexander expedition to Southeastern Alaska. Univ. Calif. Publ. Zool. 5:171-264.

Imler R. H. and E. R. Kalmbach. 1955. The Bald Eagle and its economic status. U.S. Geological. Int., Fish Wildl. Serv. Circular 30. 51 pp.

Jewett, S. C. 1942. Bird notes from Southeastern Alaska. Murrelet 23: 67-75.

Keeler, C. 1910. Days among Alaskan birds. Harriman Alaska Expedition, Vol. II, pp. 205-234.

Kessel, B. and D. D. Gibson. 1978. Status and distribution of Alaska birds. Studies in Avian Biol. No. 1, Cooper Ornithol. Soc., 100pp.

Swarth, H. S. 1911. Birds and mammals of the 1909 Alexander Alaska expedition. Univ. Calif. Publ. Zool. 7:9-172.

Swarth, H. S. 1922. Birds and mammals of the Stikine River region of northern British Columbia and Southeastern Alaska. Univ. Calif. Publ. Zool. 24(2):125-314.

Webster, J. D. 1941. Notes on the birds of Sitka and vicinity, Southeastern Alaska. Condor 43:120-121.

Webster, J. D. 1950. Attitudinal zonation of birds in Southeastern Alaska. Murrelet 31(2):23-26.

Willett, G. 1914. Birds of Sitka and vicinity, Southeastern Alaska. Condor 16(2):71-91.

Willett, G. 1915. Summer birds of Forrester Island, Alaska. Auk 32(3):32.

Willett, G. 1921. Bird notes from Southeastern Alaska. Condor 23(5):156-159.

Willett, G. 1928. Notes on some birds of Southeastern Alaska. Auk 45:445-449.

Bald Eagle Biology

Time Budgets and Behavior of Nesting Bald Eagles

Steven L. Cain

U.S. Fish and Wildlife Service, Juneau, AK; National Park Service, Moose, WY

As "multiple use " of public lands increases, the potential for humans to disturb Bald Eagles increases. Detailed information about Bald Eagle behavior is needed as a basis for managing eagles and their nest sites where potential for human disturbance exists. This study used time-lapse photography to document Bald Eagle incubating, brooding, prey deliveries and feeding at several sites on Admiralty Island in Southeast Alaska. It provides a number of insights into male/female role differentiation, how roles and behavior change over time and environmental factors such as how weather and time of day affected sex roles and activities of Bald Eagles nesting and rearing young. Based on results of the study, recommendations are given for protecting nesting Bald Eagles from human disturbance.

Abstract

Time budgets for adult Bald Eagle (*Haliaeetus leucocephalus*) activities at nests were documented from mid-incubation to fledging at one nest and from hatching into the post-fledging period at two nests. Time-lapse cameras recorded instantaneous samples of activity at 90 second intervals. Both sexes incubated eggs and brooded young. Eggs were incubated for 95% of daylight hours, with the female and male contributing 53% and 42% respectively. Total brooding time averaged 79% of each day 1-10 days after hatching and declined to 6% of each day 41-50 days after hatching. Both sexes delivered prey and the frequency of prey deliveries did not vary with the age or number of young in the nest. Females fed young 81-91% of the time and the number of feedings increased with the number of young in the nest. Weather variables had significant impact on nearly all nesting activities. Incubating and brooding rates increased with wind velocity and decreased with daily high temperature. Brooding rates also increased with daily precipitation and decreased with sunniness. Females tended to incubate and brood more and males less during periods of cold, wet, windy and cloudy weather. Prey delivery rates decreased with precipitation and feedings decreased with daily high temperature. Comparisons with other raptor species indicate that Bald Eagles share nesting duties between the sexes more than many birds of prey. Recommendations for minimizing human disturbance during the nesting cycle and the possible role of reversed sexual dimorphism in determining sex role differentiation are discussed.

Acknowledgements

This study was funded by the U.S. Fish and Wildlife Service, the University of Montana and the National Rifle Association. Jack Hodges, Dirk Derksen and Phil Schempf were instrumental in making this study a reality. Andy Anderson, Dave Irons, Bruce Conant and Jim King provided logistical and technical support. Margi Shamonski, Becky Landingham, Mark Watowa, Karen Bollinger, Robin Hunter and Mike Jacobson all provided critical field support at various times during the study. Riley McClelland generously offered guidance and several beneficial discussions throughout the study. Riley McClelland, Phil Schempf, Dave Buehler and an anonymous reviewer improved the manuscript by providing helpful comments on earlier drafts.

Introduction

Few studies have documented detailed observations of nesting Bald Eagles. Herrick (1924a, 1924b, 1932, 1933) provided in-depth accounts of Bald Eagle nesting activities, but most of his observations included little quantified data. Sprunt et al. (1973) considered Herrick's work a monumental contribution but added that many gaps existed. Broley (1947, 1952) briefly described nesting behavior and Gerrard et al. (1979) reported on time budgets and nesting behavior of captive breeding eagles.

Detailed and quantified accounts of the nesting activities of other raptors include studies of captive and wild Golden Eagles (*Aquila chrysaetos*) in Montana (Ellis 1979, Craighead 1980), Peregrine Falcons (*Falco peregrinus*) in Alaska (Enderson et al. 1972), Osprey (*Pandion haliaetus*) in California, Nova Scotia and Washington (Levenson 1979, Jamieson et al. 1982, Stinson et al. 1988) and Gyrfalcons (*Falco rusticolus*) in Greenland Jenkins 1978), one written by Charles Broley and the other by his wife Myrtle Broley.

As Bald Eagles repopulate historic habitat in the lower 48 states and urban centers expand into Bald Eagle habitat in Canada and Alaska, the protection of nesting Bald Eagles will become even more difficult. Beyond the legal protection of adequate nesting habitat lies the challenge of protecting the birds that occupy it. Protection implies that the birds be able to live year-round and reproduce undisturbed by human activities. However, the vast majority of Bald Eagle habitat in North America today exists on government-owned land. These lands often are subject to various degrees of multiple use (e.g. recreation, logging, grazing and mining) that compete for the same resources eagles require. Consequently, the agencies administering these lands knowingly and regularly compromise the protection of Bald Eagle nesting efforts to accommodate other uses. Thus, there is an important need for detailed accounts of nesting time budgets to develop criteria for managing nest sites where the potential for human disturbance exists. I report on the time budgets of nesting Bald Eagles from mid-incubation to fledging at one nest and from hatching into the post-fledging period at two nests. My objectives were to document incubating, brooding and feeding at the nests with specific emphasis on sex role differentiation, temporal changes and the effects of several environmental parameters on these activities.

Study Area and Methods

The study was conducted on the northern tip of Admiralty Island, approximately 32 km west of Juneau, in Southeast Alaska. The island's 1,400 km of pristine coastline support approximately one Bald Eagle nest for every 1.6 km; 30-40% of these nests are productive each year (Hodges 1982, Robards and King 1998). The climate is maritime with an average annual precipitation of 230 cm and average temperatures in January and

July of -1°C and 15°C respectively. Extreme temperatures during the study season (April-August 1984) were -2° C on 25 April and 26°C on 6 July. Other than researcher visits, eagles in the study area were undisturbed by human activities.

Instantaneous samples (Altmann 1974) of nesting activities were recorded at 90 s intervals with remote, time-lapse camera units. Each camera unit consisted of a Minolta XL-601 super-8 movie camera, an intervalometer, a photocell and a battery pack housed in a 50 caliber ammunition box. The intervalometer and photocell circuits were similar to those described by Diem et al. (1977). Occupied nests were located during the incubation period by boat and helicopter. Monitored nests were selected based on nest tree and adjacent tree characteristics that enabled timelapse monitoring. Efforts to habituate eagles to my presence were made by decreasing the distance to the nest sites during successive visits over a period of several days, finally culminating with placement of the camera within the nest territory. Cameras were mounted in adjacent trees, 10-30 m from the nest, until nestlings were approximately 25 days old, to allow the adults to become familiar with the system from a distance. Cameras were then moved into nest trees and mounted 3-4 m above the nest platform.

Monitored nest sites each differed in nest tree structure, nest orientation in relation to the tree bole and exposure to the elements. The "Horse" nest tree was a dominant Sitka spruce (*Picea sitchensis*) approximately 20 m from the shoreline and 35 m high. The nest bowl was south of the tree's trunk, about 10 m from the top of the tree, with a substantial canopy above. The "Sand" nest tree was a small, deformed Sitka spruce approximately 15 m from the shoreline and 15 m high. Although small, this tree was sheltered by other trees only to the west. The nest bowl was 3 m from the top and north of the tree trunk, with no canopy above. The "Barlow" nest tree was a sub-dominant western hemlock (*Tsuga heterophylla*) approximately 60 m from the shoreline and 20 m high. The nest bowl was 4 m from the top and northwest of the trunk, with a substantial canopy above. This tree was protected by taller trees on all sides except for a narrow flight corridor to the north.

To differentiate between the sexes, one eagle at each monitored site was captured (Cain and Hodges 1989) and marked. Following procedures recommended by Ellis and Ellis (1975), marking consisted of bleaching a small patch of primary coverts on the carpel joint of each folded wing. This proved to be an easily applied, effective, non-permanent method of marking. Throughout the nesting season marked birds were easily identified from any angle, from both direct and film observations and dyed feathers appeared to remain undamaged. Measurements from each bird (Bortolotti 1984a) and comparison of relative size during field observations were used to determine the sex of marked birds. A total of 298 days were monitored at three different nests (Table 1). The "Barlow" nest, was monitored from mid-incubation (15 days before hatching) to fledging. The "Horse" and "Sand" nests, were monitored from hatching well into the post-fledging period. Fourteen monitoring days were lost due to investigator error or equipment malfunction. Prey deliveries were recorded at all nests from 30 days after hatching into the post-fledging period. Prior to this period, when cameras were mounted in adjacent trees, prey deliveries could not always be confirmed. Feedings were recorded at all nests from hatching to fledging and were classified as either eaglet feedings, when adults fed eaglets, or adult feedings, when adults fed at the nest. Eaglet feedings consisted of feeding bouts where the eaglet was in feeding position: head and neck erect, close to and facing the feeding adult. Feeding bouts that occurred without an eaglet in feeding position were recorded as adult feedings. Bouts of eaglets feeding themselves were not included in these analyses. Since it is likely that adults occasionally fed during eaglet feeding bouts, the number and duration of eaglet feedings were probably over estimated and those for adult feedings at the nest underestimated.

Films were viewed with a time-lapse analyzing projector. As the films were observed, data were entered into a computer using customized programs that maximized efficiency. The date and time of day were recorded on the beginning and end of each roll of film. Relative dates and times were then assigned to each frame analyzed. Activity states were assumed to last for 90 s for each frame on which they were observed. Non-parametric correlations of time budgets with weather variables were performed with Spearman's coefficient of rank correlation, yielding Spearman's coefficient r_s. Tests for differences between means were accomplished with the T-test and the MannWhitney U test (Sokal and Rohlf 1981). Weather data were taken from the National Oceanic and Atmospheric Administration weather station at the Juneau International Airport, approximately 13 km from the center of the study area.

Nests were monitored only with time-lapse cameras, consequently there were no control nests monitored to assess possible investigator-induced disturbance associated with the presence of the cameras (Bortolotti et al. 1985). However, this was investigated by comparing results of this study with similar studies of undisturbed Bald Eagle nests. Patterns of nest attentiveness in this study were essentially identical to those documented in other studies (Bortolotti et al. 1985). Furthermore, when behavior patterns on nest visit days, when trees were climbed, were compared with other days, significant differences (p < 0.05) were found for only three of over 70 nest visit days. Each of these three occurred at the Barlow nest during incubation and the differences observed were due to extended nest absence periods by the adults before and immediately after the researchers climbed an adjacent tree. These days were not included in incubation time budget analyses. No behavioral differences (p > 0.05) were found between nest visit and non-visit days at any of the nests after eggs had hatched. These comparisons indicate that the results of this study were not significantly biased by investigator-induced disturbance.

Results and Discussion
Incubation
The daily incubation routine (n = 12 days) was characterized by alternating male and female incubation bouts throughout the period. Total incubation time averaged 95% (range 89-100%, SE = 1.1) of each day with the female incubating 53% (range 30-74%, SE = 3.6) of the time and the male 42% (range 22-68%, SE = 3.8) (Figure 1). The number of incubation bouts/day averaged 4.5 (range 3-10, SE = 0.55) for the female and 3.1 (range 2-5, SE = 0.29) for the male. Incubation bout duration averaged 144 (range 82-261, SE = 7.2) minutes for the female and 164 (range 76-273, SE = 10.1) minutes for the male.

Few other Bald Eagle time budget data exist for comparison. Herrick (1933) described similar routines for incubating Bald Eagles but did not quantify his observations. Based on 55.5 hours of mid-incubation observation on a pair of captive Bald Eagles, Gerrard et al. (1979) reported a total incubation time of 98% (71% by the female) and shorter incubation bout durations (84 compared to 155 minutes). These discrepancies probably can be attributed to differences in environment as well as differences between individual nesting pairs. With little time devoted to seeking food, captive birds may initiate nest exchanges more often. The tendency of the male eagle at the Barlow nest to contribute more time to nearly all nesting activities than males at the other two nests I monitored probably accounted for some of the greater male participation in incubation. Similar variation in the sexual division of incubation duties among nesting pairs has been documented in other raptors (Enderson et al. 1972, Levenson 1979, Craighead 1980, Clevenger 1987, Stinson et al. 1988).

o Total ■ Female □ Male

Percent
Daylight
Hours

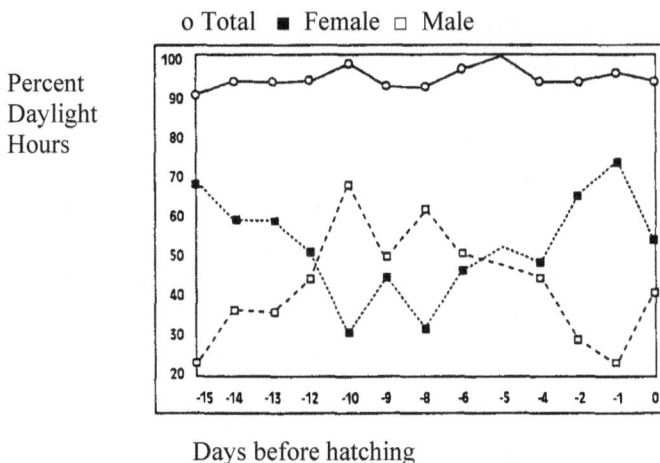

Days before hatching

Figure 1. Percent of daylight hours eggs were incubated by male and female Bald Eagles (film changes occurred on days -11, -7 and -3).

The incubation rate was relatively constant throughout the day, with a slight decrease during mid-day, probably as a result of warmer mid-day temperatures (Figure 2). Sharp increases in female incubation at approximately 0500 and 1100 hrs. probably occurred after feedings. Female incubation increased dramatically during the afternoon and evening hours to nearly 100% by nightfall. This suggests that the female exclusively incubated throughout the night, being relieved by the male early in the morning. On several occasions I observed eagles flying in the early morning hours in almost complete darkness. Thus, the timelapse cameras did not always record the first nest exchange of the day.

Vocalizations just prior to nest exchanges, observed on the films and directly, were common. Usually the incubating bird initiated the exchange by calling to its mate and then, after several vocal exchanges, the birds switched positions on the nest. Periods when both birds were at the nest usually occurred during nest exchanges, but these were brief and accounted for less than 1% (range 0-1.5%, SE = 0.08) of each day. Captive Bald

Figure 2. Average hourly incubating rates for Bald Eagles at the Barlow nest.

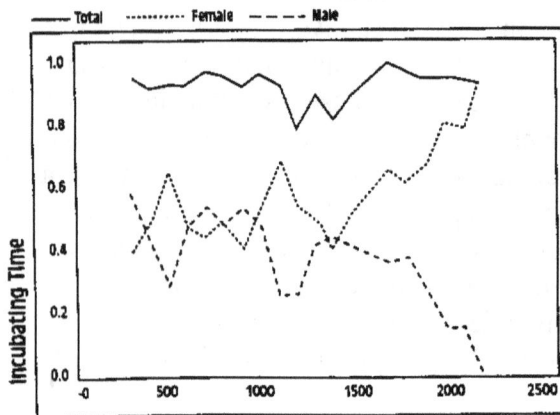

Eagles, in contrast, spent an average of 3.7% of the day on the nest together (Gerrard et al. 1979). Birds were absent from the nest bowl an average of <4% each day, with absence periods averaging 11.2 minutes duration. Field observations indicated that at least one of the adults was perched within 50 m and in clear view of the nest during most absence periods.

Other behavioral events recorded during incubation included postures suggesting egg turning (eagle bent over with its beak contacting the egg) and nest raking. Because these events can be of short duration, the time-lapse sampling probably underestimated their frequency. Egg turning, important to prevent egg membranes from sticking together (Newton 1979), occurred an average of 4.2 (range 0-11) times daily; male and female rates were approximately equal. Gerrard et al. (1979) reported an egg turning rate of once per hour during continuous, mid-incubation observations, but, since egg turning is believed to be more important during the early stages of incubation (Newton 1979), egg turning rates may decline as the embryo develops. Although egg turning is generally accomplished with the adult's beak, in one case film records showed the male eagle erect and looking at the egg with his foot in definite contact with it, possibly attempting to turn it in this manner. Nest raking, when incubating birds picked at moss and dry grass in the nest, often using it to maintain and re-shape the nest cup, was common. This has been observed in raptors elsewhere (Enderson et al. 1972, Jenkins 1978, Ellis 1979, Gerrard et al. 1979, Craighead 1980, Bortolotti et al. 1985) and seems to be common in birds of prey. In this study it seemed to isolate the nest cup from cold drafts and insulate the eggs, as suggested by Ellis (1979).

No prey deliveries or feedings occurred at the nest during incubation until four days prior to hatching, when the female delivered at least 2 prey items and fed in the nest on 4 occasions. The male fed at the nest once during this period.

Incubation patterns were modified in response to changing environmental conditions. Total incubation time by day increased with increases in daily average wind velocity (r_s = 0.556, $p = 0.024$) and decreased with increases in maximum daily temperature (r_s = -0.499, $p = 0.04$). Responses to precipitation and percentage of the day that was sunny were also evident, but these were not statistically significant. Changes in weather also seemed to influence how incubation duties were shared by the sexes. Although not statistically significant, correlations indicated that the proportion of female incubation increased on cold, wet and windy days whereas male incubation increased on warm, dry and calm days. Similarly, Gerrard et al. (1979) found that eagles left eggs exposed

Incubating Bald Eagle. Photo by Mike Jacobsen, USFWS.

for significantly longer periods during relatively high temperatures and low wind velocities; Jamieson et al. (1982) reported significantly less incubation by male Ospreys during periods of rain.

Egg Hatching

Hatching dates spanned a period of 20 days among the 3 nests (Table 1) and were similar to hatching dates known for adjacent areas of Southeast Alaska (Hodges 1982, M. Jacobson, pers. comm.). Hatching of both eggs was documented at the Barlow nest where the camera position afforded the best view, although some details, such as small, fine cracks in the eggs, could not be seen. From the time when eggs were last seen completely intact until the egg was completely hatched, 6.7 hrs elapsed for the first egg and 2.5 hours elapsed for the second egg. While brooding the day after the first egg hatched, the female removed the egg shell fragments from underneath her and placed them outside of the nest cup.

Brooding

The primary brooding period lasted for 50 days at all three nests. Combining the three nests, brooding time averaged over 80% of each day during the first five days after hatching and tapered off gradually to approximately 6% 41-50 days after hatching (Figure 3). Total brooding time fell to less than 3% of the day 51-60 days after hatching and to less than 1% 61-70 days after hatching. No brooding was observed after eaglets were 71 days old. The most rapid decline in total brooding time, between 11 and 20 days after hatching (Figure 3), coincided with development of the eaglets' second (grey) down stage and their ability to thermoregulate (Bortolotti 1984b). Ellis (1979) also reported a 50 day brooding period for Golden Eagles and a similar brooding curve, with the most rapid descent occurring five days after completion of the second down stage.

Table 1. Nest chronology, productivity and monitoring dates for the three Bald Eagle nests studied.

	Sand	Barlow	Horse
Eggs laid	2	2	3
Eggs Hatched	2	2	3
Hatching Dates	21 May,* 23 May 2	3 June, 5 June	17 May, 19 May, 23 May **
Young Fledged	2	1	1
Fledging Date(S)	10 Aug., 15 Aug.	24 Aug.	11 Aug.
Age at Fledging (days)	80, 84	82	86
Camera Installed	23 May	18 May	16 May
Camera Removed	26 Aug.	26 Aug.	24 Aug.
Camera Days lost***	53-56	17-20	73-78
Total Monitoring Time (days)	96	101	101

*estimated hatching date
**date third eaglet first observed in the nest
***nest chronology days where the day of hatching = 0

Figure 3. Average percent of daylight hours eaglets were brooded by male and female Bald Eagles at three nests.

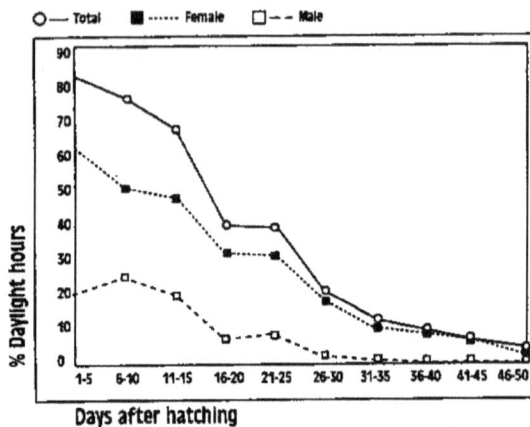

Figure 4. Average nest attendance in percent of daylight hours at three Bald Eagle nests.

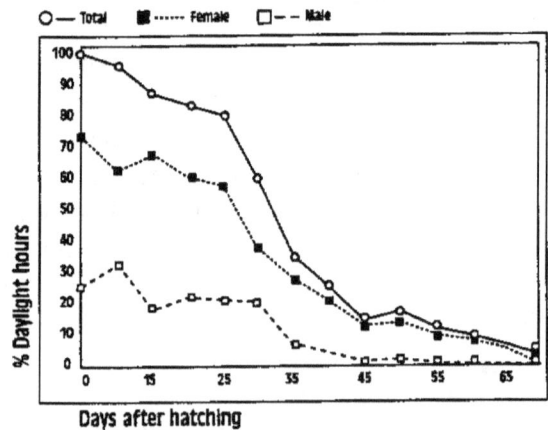

The primary brooding period consisted of an average of 29% male brooding and 71% female brooding. This represents a considerably greater contribution to brooding by the male than found in other raptors. For example, average female brooding proportions were nearly 100% for Golden Eagles (Ellis 1979), 99% for Peregrine Falcons (Enderson et al. 1972), 95-100% for Ospreys (Levenson 1979, Jamieson et al. 1982) and 87% for Gyrfalcons (Jenkins 1978). Greater participation of the male Bald Eagle in brooding corresponds to greater participation of the female in other nesting activities, particularly procuring food. While males brooded, females spent much of the time foraging for themselves and the eaglets.

Adults brooded much of the time they were at the nest, but they also engaged in other activities (Figure 3 and 4). The proportion of non-brooding nest presence, usually spent standing, feeding, or preening, increased gradually throughout the brooding period, from approximately 15% 1-5 days after hatching to over 70% 46-50 days after hatching.

During the first half of the brooding period, when eaglets were most dependent on adults for protection from the elements, the daily brooding pattern was characterized by a gradual decrease in total brooding time per hour from sunrise until mid-day, followed by a sharp increase into the night (Figure 5). Total brooding time was significantly greater from first light until 0900 hrs and from 2000 hrs until dark, when compared to the period 0900-2000 hrs ($p < 0.001$). The proportion of total brooding accomplished by the female was also significantly greater during the morning (first light to 0900 hrs, $p < 0.05$) and evening (2000 hrs to dark, $p < 0.001$) hours. The male's contribution to total brooding, while still proportionately less than the female's, was greatest during the first hour of daylight. As observed during incubation, the females' contribution rose rapidly during the late afternoon and evening, suggesting that she was the primary brooder during the night.

Figure 5. Average hourly brooding rates of Bald Eagles at three nests, during the period 1-25 days after hatching.

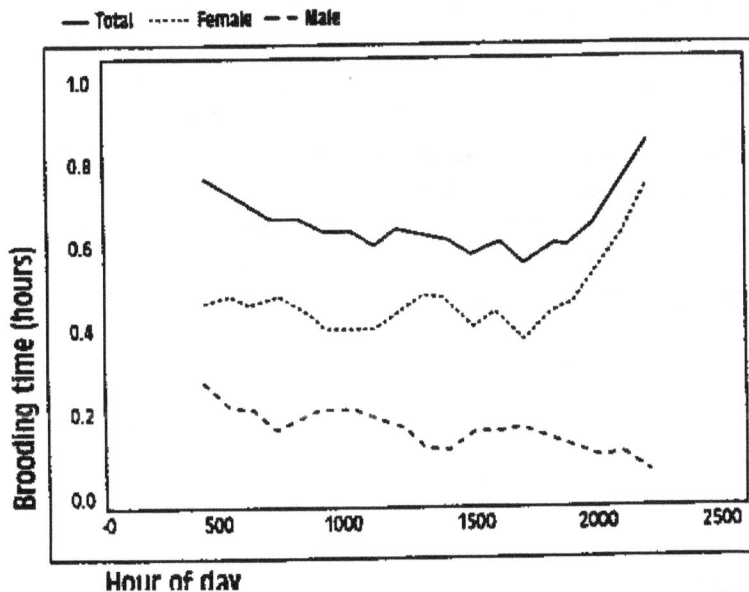

Significant variations in brooding patterns among nests were evident, especially during the first 30 days after hatching (Table 2). Total brooding time at the Horse nest was significantly greater than total brooding time at the Sand nest 11-20 days after hatching ($p < 0.001$) and significantly greater than total brooding time at the Sand and Barlow nests 21-30 days after hatching ($p < 0.01$). Male and female proportions of the total brooding time were significantly different among all nests ($p < 0.05$) throughout the brooding period. Males brooded an average of 16% of the total brooding time at the Sand nest, 280/o at the Horse nest and 42% at the Barlow nest.

Eaglets in nest. Photo by Jack Hodges, USFWS

Three eaglets died shortly after hatching at two of the nests studied. At the Barlow nest, the second eaglet hatched two days after the first. A day after hatching it was erect and being fed by the adults, but apparently died later in the day and the female removed its body from the nest cup while brooding. The day after it died, the male removed the carcass from the nest when departing from a brooding session. Eight days after the first of three eggs hatched at the Horse nest, the two older eaglets were much larger than the youngest. The youngest eaglet died during an intense 3-day spring storm when little food was brought to the nest. Another died between two and five days after the storm. The survival rate for nestlings and productivity for nests in this study were similar to those reported for Southeast Alaska (Hodges 1982, Robards and King 2008). There was no indication that monitoring activities were related to any of the mortalities documented.

Table 2. Ten day Interval averages for brooding time In percent of daylight hours at 3 Bald Eagle nests.

Days after Hatching		Sand			Barlow			Horse			Mean		
		%	Range	SD	%	Range	SD	%	Range	SD	%	Range	SD
1-10	Male	15	(1-31)	10.2	33	(17-63)	9.8	23	(12-32)	6.7	23	(1-50)	11.4
	Female	69	(50-86)	14.8	41	(16-50)	12.3	58	(38-74)	12.8	56	(17-86)	17.5
	Total	84	(74-95)	6.1	73	(51-85)	9.8	80	(66-91)	8.7	79	(51-95)	9.3
11-20	Male	3	(0-9)	4.2	27	(7-58)	20.3	11	(<1-28)	10.1	14	(0-58)	16.9
	Female	36	(9-60)	15.4	29	(10-50)	11.0	66	(42-89)	14.8	41	(9-89)	20.3
	Total	39	(19-65)	15.5	56	(17-85)	25.7	78	(67-93)	8.5	55	(17-93)	24.0
21-30	Male	<1	(0-6)	1.9	2	(0-13)	4.4	14	(0-39)	14.5	6	(0-39)	10.5
	Female	25	(0-55)	21.1	12	(0-39)	11.6	43	(10-70)	18.9	26	(0-71)	21.4
	Total	25	(0-60)	22.1	14	(<1-52)	14.7	57	(18-76)	16.8	36	(0-76)	25.4
31-40	Male	0			<1	(0-2)	0.6	3	(0-19)	6.2	1	(0-19)	3.7
	Female	14	(0-50)	14.5	7	(0-39)	12.0	11	(2-27)	7.9	11	(0-50)	11.7
	Total	14	(0-50)	14.5	7	(0-39)	12.2	14	(2-35)	11.0	1	(0-50)	12.6
41-5	Male	<1	(0-2)	0.6	0			0			<1	(0-2)	0.3
	Female	5	(0-28)	9.2	7	(0-34)	10.3	6	(0-21)	5.9	6	(0-34)	8.5
	Total	5	(0-28)	9.4	7	(0-34)	10.3	6	(0-21)	5.9	6	(0-34)	8.5

Effects of Weather on Brooding

Bald Eagles in this study modified brooding patterns in response to several environmental variables. Total daily brooding time 1-25 days after hatching decreased with increases in daily high temperature at all nests (Barlow $r_s = -0.584$, $p = 0.001$; Horse $r_s = -0.312$, $p = 0.08$; Sand $r_s = -0.765$, $p < 0.001$). Total brooding time also increased with increases in the average wind velocity at the more exposed nests (Horse, $r_s = 0.464$, $p = 0.01$; Sand, $r_s = 0.639$, $p < 0.001$). At the Sand nest, by far the most exposed to the elements, brooding time increased with increases in daily precipitation ($r_s = 0.549$, $p = 0.002$) and decreased with increases in percent of the day that was sunny ($r_s = -0.483$, $p = 0.007$). Similar relationships with percent sunshine and precipitation at Horse and percent sunshine at Barlow were also evident but were not statistically significant. The modification of brooding patterns in response to inclement weather has been observed in other species of raptors. Brooding time was correlated with wind chill values at Golden Eagle nests (Ellis 1979) and with mean daily temperatures at Peregrine Falcon nests (Enderson et al. 1972). Jenkins (1978) noted that brooding was influenced by weather extremes in general at Gyrfalcon nests.

The relative distribution of correlations between brooding and weather among nests suggests that relative nest exposure to the elements may have a considerable influence on the amount of time adults spend protecting their eggs and young. At the Sand nest, where the nest bowl was completely exposed to sun, rain and prevailing winds, each of these variables significantly affected parental investment in brooding. In contrast, at the Barlow nest, where an overhead canopy protected the nest from rain and sun and surrounding trees provided an effective shield from prevailing winds, only daily high temperature affected brooding time. The Horse nest, protected from the sun and rain by a substantial overhead canopy but with direct exposure to prevailing winds, was affected only by the wind and daily high temperature. Protected nest sites may incur disadvantages, however. For example, at the less protected Sand and Horse nests, the nest bowls served as effective hunting and lookout sites, where adults scanned for prey and potential predators while tending their young. Adults tending young at the Barlow nest could not perform these activities simultaneously, which may have placed additional demands on the non-tending adult and made foraging less efficient in general.

Weather variables also caused shifts in the division of brooding duties between the female and male, with a significant premium placed on female brooding during wet, cold, windy and cloudy conditions. Similar to the pattern observed for incubation, the proportion of female brooding decreased with increases in daily high temperature at all nests (Barlow, $r_s = -0.356$, $p = 0.04$; Horse, $r_s = -0.664$, $p < 0.001$; Sand, $r_s = -0.713$, $p < 0.001$). At the two most exposed nests, female brooding proportions also increased with increasing wind velocities (Horse, $r_s = 0.759$, $p < 0.001$; Sand, $r_s = 0.606$, $p = 0.001$) and increasing daily precipitation (Horse, $r_s = 0.461$, $p = 0.015$; Sand, $r_s = 0.507$, $p = 0.005$) and decreased with increasing sunshine (Horse, $r_s = -0.686$, $p < 0.001$; Sand, $r_s = -0.500$, $p = 0.005$).

Female/male brooding shifts in response to changing environmental conditions were best exhibited at the Horse nest, where significant reversed responses were observed for all four weather variables (Figure 6). Because of the Horse nest's relative location, its microclimate was probably more closely approximated by the weather in Juneau (where weather data were collected) than were microclimates at the other two sites, which could have accounted for the more clearly defined relationships documented there. Monitoring weather at the actual nest sites could document microclimatic fluctuations that went unrecorded in this study and provide further evidence of the patterns I observed.

Sexual Dimorphism
I suggest that the weather-induced female/male shifts in incubating and brooding observed during this study are directly related to sexual dimorphism in Bald Eagles. Bald Eagle females are larger and heavier than males (Snyder and Wiley 1976). In addition, female brood patches are approximately three times larger than male brood patches (Cain, pers. obs.). The female's larger body size, resulting in a reduced surface area to mass ratio and greater fasting tolerance and larger brood patch enable her to transfer heat to eggs and young more effectively and for longer durations. Because of this, a premium has evolved for female attendance of eggs and nestlings during periods of inclement weather. This was well illustrated during a very intense, 3-day spring storm when the Horse nest female did virtually 100% of the incubating and brooding for the entire duration of the storm.

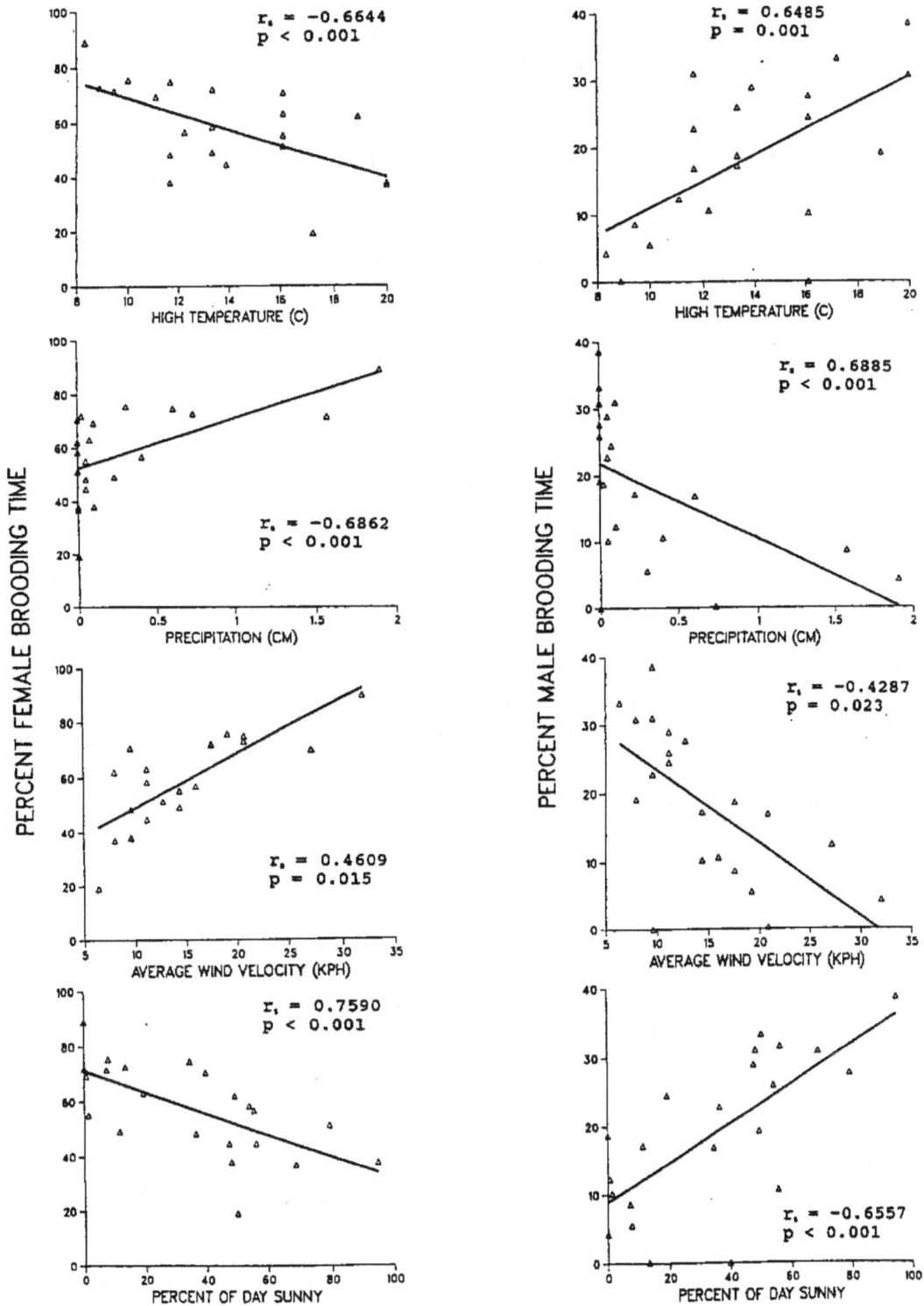

Figure 6. Female–male Bald Eagle brooding shifts in response to changing environmental conditions during brooding at the Horse nest.

Others have proposed similar explanations for reversed sexual dimorphism in raptors (Cade 1982, Snyder and Wiley 1976), but most of the 14 (at least) hypotheses put forth on the subject revolve around niche partitioning for reducing intraspecific competition for food and the importance of female dominance in maintaining pair bonds (see review in Mueller and Meyer 1985). Mueller and Meyer (1985) argued that the roles of the sexes in incubating and brooding were not important in the evolution of reversed sexual dimorphism because degree of dimorphism in raptors is not correlated with these traits. However, their analysis considered only the division of total incubation and brooding time between the sexes and did not address the driving factors (e.g. weather) responsible for the daily distribution of such divisions. Granted, this would have been difficult because such documentation, for the most part, does not exist. This current lack of information among raptors likewise precludes further support for the importance of sex role differentiation in the evolution of reversed sexual dimorphism. Results of this study do indicate, however, that sexual dimorphism plays an important role in the adult eagles' ability to protect their eggs and young during periods of inclement weather, regardless of whether these factors were a cause for or simply an effect of the evolution of reversed sexual dimorphism.

Sexual dimorphism in adults and different demands for protecting young among the three nests studied may be partly responsible for differences observed in the proportion of female and male brooding at each nest. Because egg hatching was later in the season at Barlow, the average high temperature during the brooding period was greater at this nest than at either of the other nests (p < 0.05). This nest was also the most protected from the elements. Together these factors would have favored more brooding by the male and less by the female and may partially account for the highest proportion (42%) of male brooding observed. Conversely, hatching dates and mean temperature during the brooding period were similar at the Sand and Horse nests, but the Sand nest was more exposed and contained two eaglets, which would have favored more brooding by the female and less by the male. Accordingly, the proportion of male brooding (16%) at this nest was the lowest observed.

Prey Deliveries
The number of prey deliveries per day and the proportion of deliveries by each sex varied substantially, both within and among nests (Table 3) and did not increase with the number of young in the nest or as the eaglets matured. More prey items per day were brought to the Horse nest than to either the Sand (p = 0.06) or Barlow (p < 0.05) nests, even though the Sand nest contained 2 young. The number of deliveries fluctuated greatly from day to day and showed no consistent trends throughout the nesting season. Stinson (1978) reported similar results for Osprey and found that neither age or number of unfledged young affected the rate of fish delivery at nests. Herrick (1924a) reported comparable prey delivery rates of 2.5 and 4.0 per day at 2 Bald Eagle nests and Wallin (1982) reported a mean rate of 0.24 deliveries/hr at 3 nests. However, comparing prey delivery rates may not be meaningful without accompanying estimates of prey biomass, especially where prey habitat varies among nests as it did in this study. High prey delivery rates could simply be a result of adults securing consistently smaller prey. The Sand and Barlow nests were adjacent to very similar, primarily deep water foraging

areas. In contrast, the Horse nest, where prey delivery rates were highest, was adjacent to a large tidal flat that may have contained an abundance of smaller prey species unavailable to the birds at the other two nests.

Daily precipitation was the only weather variable that influenced prey deliveries. Although correlations were weak, the Sand and Barlow nests showed decreases in the number of prey deliveries per day as daily precipitation increased (Sand, r_s = -0.217, p = 0.06; Barlow, r_s = -0.269, p = 0.04), possibly as a result of poor visibility. Grubb (1977) found that cloud cover and disturbed water surfaces both decreased capture success of Ospreys, but Stinson et al. (1988) found no correlations between Osprey prey delivery rates and weather variables, including precipitation.

Participation of each sex in delivering prey seemed to parallel participation in brooding. The male delivered more items than the female at the Barlow nest only, where male participation in brooding was also greatest. Female deliveries were two and three times more numerous than male deliveries at the Sand and Horse nests respectively.

Table 3. Average number of prey deliveries per day at 3 Bald Eagle nests during the period 30-80 days after hatching.

	Sand (range)	SE	Barlow (range)	SE	Horse (range)	SE
Prey deliveries per day	2.7(0-8)	0.26	2.3(0-6)	0.25	3.6(0-11)	0.35
Male deliveries	21 (0-100)	3.7	40(0-100)	8.7	15 (0-100)	3.6
Female deliveries	48(0-100)	6.3	26(0-100)	5.2	46(0-100)	5.6
Unknown deliveries	31 (0-100)	4.3	34(0-100)	5.5	39(0-100)	8.2

Comparable prey delivery ratios for male and female Bald Eagles were observed by Herrick (1924b), where females delivered twice as many items as the male and by Ofelt (1975), where deliveries were approximately equal between the sexes. The number of prey items delivered by unknown adults (i.e. when the delivering adult was not recorded on film) was similar at all nests and increased as the eaglets became self-sufficient feeders.

Prey deliveries occurred throughout the day, but the highest rates were observed between 0700 and 1100 hrs. An increase in prey deliveries by females was largely responsible for the peak during these hours. Prey delivery rates for males, although low during the very early morning, were somewhat consistent throughout the day (Figure 7).

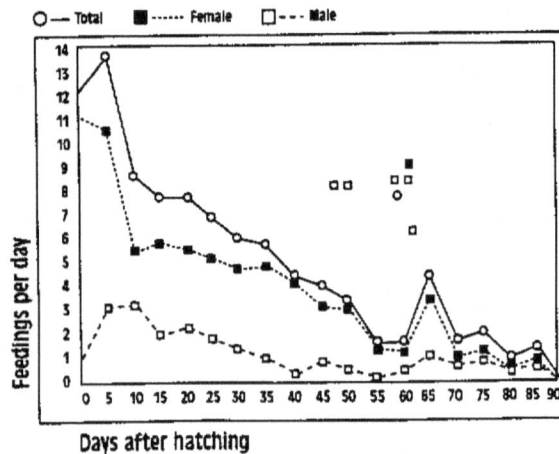

Figure 7. Hourly prey delivery rates at three Bald Eagle nests during the period 30-80 days after hatching.

Feedings

Eaglet feeding rates at one-eaglet nests were similar and averaged 8.6/day 1-10 days after hatching, declining gradually to 1.9/day 71-80 days after hatching. Male participation declined from 22% of all feedings 1-10 days after hatching to no feedings 7180 days after hatching (Figure 8). Female-male ratios for eaglet feedings were similar at the Sand and Barlow nests but greater at the Horse nest ($p < 0.01$).

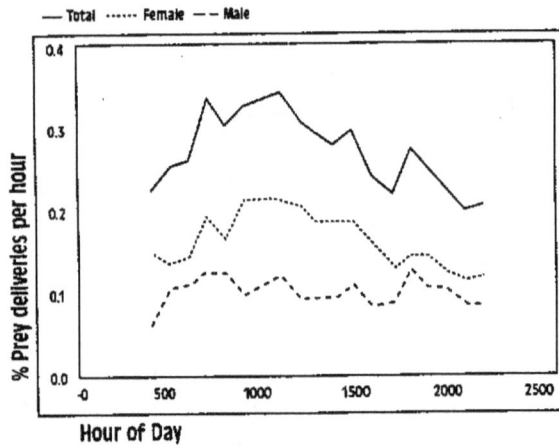

Figure 8. Average number of eaglet feedings (adults feeding eaglets) per day at two Bald Eagle nests containing one eaglet each.

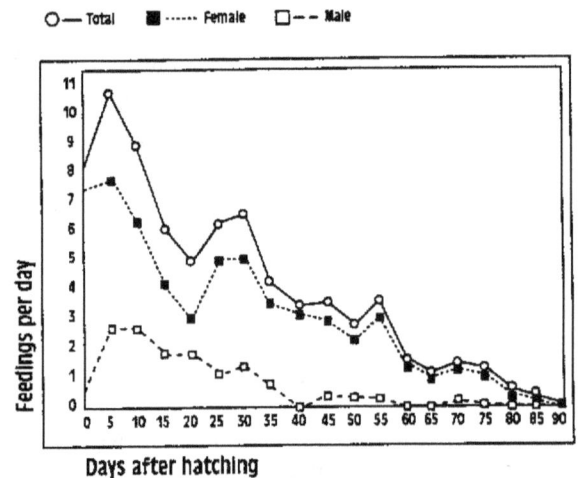

Figure 9. Average number of eaglet feedings (adults feeding eaglets) per day at a Bald Eagle nest containing two eaglets.

Eaglet feedings at the Sand nest, which contained two eaglets, occurred more frequently than at the other two nests ($p < 0.05$) (Table 4). Eaglet feedings averaged 12.0 per day 1-10 days after hatching and declined to 2.8 per day 71-80 days after hatching. The male fed eaglets 30% of the time 1-10 days after hatching and 16% 71 to 80 days after hatching at the 2-eaglet nest (Figure 9). Although eaglet feeding bout duration was similar for females at all nests, male bout duration was significantly longer at the two eaglet nest (Horse, $p < 0.001$; Barlow, $p < 0.05$). Thus, adults at the 2-eaglet nest dealt with the greater feeding demand by feeding more often and, in the male's case, feeding for longer durations. Enderson et al. (1972) found similar correlations between the number of feedings per day and the number of young in Peregrine Falcon nests. Eaglet feedings at all nests occurred throughout the day but occurred more often during two relatively distinct periods, from 0500-1000 hrs and from 1400-1900 hrs (Figure 10).

Table 4. Average number, percent male and female and bout duration for eaglet feedings (adults feeding eaglets) at 3 Bald Eagle nests.

	SAND (range)	SE	BARLOW (range)	SE	HORSE (range)	SE
Feedings per day	5.9(0-17)	0.48	4.7(1-19)	0.43	4.3(1-15)	0.38
% Male feedings	19(0-57)	2.1	19(0-67)	1.5	9 (0.50)	1.5
Female feedings	81(43-100)	2.1	81(33-100)	1.7	91 (50-100)	1.7
Male feeding duration (min)	5.8(0-38)	0.80	3.3(0-33)	0.57	2.9(0-23)	0.57
Female feeding duration (min)	7.9(0-21)	0.55	6.9(0-23)	0.50	7.5(0-22)	0.50

The number of eaglet feedings per day, characterized by a rapid increase during the first five or six days after hatching followed by a gradual decline through the nestling period, was very similar to feeding patterns observed in Golden Eagles (Ellis 1979). However, Bald Eagles in this study were atypical among other raptors in regard to observed levels of male participation in feeding young (Table 4). Male Golden Eagles, Ospreys, Peregrine Falcons and Gyrfalcons all play an insignificant role in feeding their young; the female feeds nearly 100% of the time (Enderson et al. 1972, Ellis 1979, Jenkins 1978, Levenson 1979, Jamieson et al. 1982).

Figure 10. Hourly eaglet feeding rates (adults feeding eaglets) for Bald Eagles at three nests.

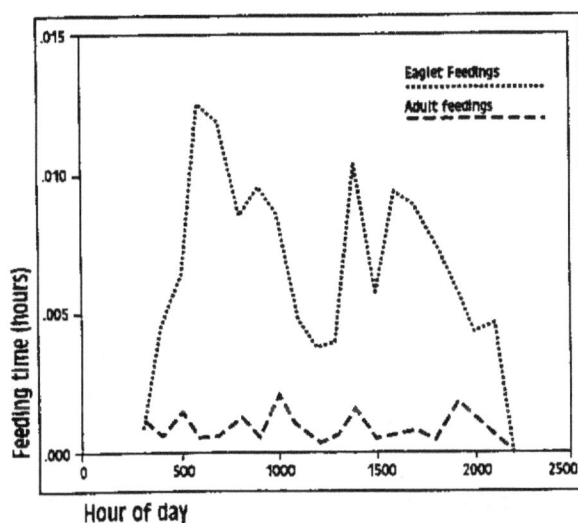

Daily high and low temperatures were the only weather variables that affected eaglet feeding rates, but correlations were weak. Eaglet feedings per day decreased with increasing high temperatures ($r_s = -0.2641$, $p < 0.001$) and increased with decreasing low temperatures ($r_s = -0.466$, $p < 0.001$). Eaglet feeding bout durations also increased as daily low temperature decreased (female, $r_s = -0.268$, $p < 0.001$; male, $r_s = -0.201$, $p = 0.001$). These responses were probably stimulated by different levels of eaglet food begging as they responded to fluctuating energy demands.

Adult feedings at the nest usually occurred immediately after an eaglet feeding bout, when the eaglet became satiated. Occasionally, an adult would arrive at the nest with a prey item and feed while the eaglet, apparently not hungry, remained in a non-feeding position. Adult feeding rates were similar at all three nests, but varied with the stage of the nesting cycle. Female and male rates were approximately equal during the primary brooding period. Females fed at the nest an average of 0.44 (range 0-5, SE = 0.073) times/ day and males 0.42 (range 0-6, SE = 0.078) times/day. Feeding bout duration averaged 4.0 (range 1.5-23.5) minutes for females and 3.0 (range 1.5-13.5) minutes for males. After the brooding period, daily feeding rates for females increased to 0.58 (range 05, SE = 0.083) whereas rates for males declined to 0.11 (range 0-2, SE = 0.031). Bout lengths for both sexes remained similar after the brooding period. Adults fed at the nest throughout the day with no apparent preference for any particular time (Figure 10).

Management Implications

With a basic knowledge of Bald Eagle nesting activities and some of the factors that drive them, informed decisions on how best to protect the species from potentially disturbing human activities can be made. Although the magnitude varies, disturbance can be defined as any human activity that results in a deviation from Bald Eagle behavioral patterns that would normally occur under conditions not disturbed by humans. Ideally, nesting behavior patterns would be observed in all potentially disturbing situations to ensure protection of the nesting effort. However, the time that is required to monitor individual nest sites and identify any but the most gross deviations from the norm, such as nest abandonment, is not available to most wildlife managers. Therefore, the establishment of conservative general guidelines, combined with providing specific recommendations when necessary, may be the best protective strategy.

General guidelines for protecting Bald Eagle nests from disturbance on public land typically revolve around establishing buffer zones within which human activities are prohibited or restricted. These zones are usually expressed as a radius around the nest, but ideally they also contain other high use areas such as favored perch trees and foraging areas. Such general guidelines, if adhered to, may be effective and their use should be encouraged. Fraser (1985) pointed out that buffer zones can create problems for land managers; examples of eagles tolerating disturbance within the zone are often cited. However, nest sites occupied by eagles habituated to increasing levels of disturbance over several years may not be reoccupied after the death of one or both of the occupants. Such nest sites may be lost over time. Thus, long-range concern requires the establishment of general, conservative guidelines and enforcing buffer zones at all nesting territories.

In day-to-day land management, general guidelines are often temporarily subverted for special needs, including research activities, variously justified by the administering agencies. In these cases, specific recommendations are necessary to ensure that activities do not create potentially harmful effects. Specific recommendations can also help safeguard active nest sites on private land, where land use cannot be controlled. Results of this study can be used to base several specific recommendations for regulating human activities inside normally restricted buffer zones. These recommendations assume that the potential for disturbance and the consequences of it are highest when nest attendance and levels of associated activities (e.g. brooding) are also high. But since weather was a significant factor in determining behavioral patterns in this study, some of these recommendations, especially numbers two and three, may only apply in areas of northern latitude with similar climatic regimes.

1. During the incubation period and for the first 15 days after hatching, no human activities should occur in the vicinity of the nest. With the possible exception of the early courtship and territory establishment phase of the nesting cycle, Bald Eagles are most prone to disturbance during the incubation period and while young are less than two weeks old (Bortolotti et al. 1985, Cain 1985). Because of the constant level of nest attendance required during incubation and early brooding, any human activity that results in even a slight deviation from normal behaviors could put the eggs or young at risk to mortality due to predation or excessive cooling. In addition, adults startled while incubating or brooding small young can damage eggs or young as they abruptly leave the nest (Yates and McClelland 1989). Behavioral patterns of the adults are also easily disturbed during this period, especially during incubation and nest abandonments may occur as a result of any intrusion (Cain 1985). Researcher visits to the nest may be especially risky during this period and are not recommended. However, Bortolotti et al. (1985) provided evidence that visits of 15 min. or less may not be detrimental, indicating that duration of dis-turbance is important. What is considered the "vicinity" of the nest will vary depending on physiography, presence of natural screening and the type of disturbance involved, but a 0.5 km radius around the nest should be considered an absolute minimum disturbance-free buffer zone (Fraser 1985). In many cases, buffer zones should be larger than this.

Eaglet in nest. Photo by Mike Jacobson, USFWS.

2. From 16 to 35 days after hatching, human activities should not occur in the vicinity of the nest. However, if circumstances require isolated and justified exceptions (e.g. researcher visits) to this guideline, activities should take place during mid to late afternoon only, be of short duration and not take place during periods of inclement weather. During this period nest attendance and brooding diminish rapidly and young are least likely to require brooding during the mid to late afternoon and during periods of fair weather (see effects of weather on brooding discussion). By this time, parental behaviors

are well established and the risk of nest abandonment has diminished considerably. Hourly brooding rates are still high in the morning and evening throughout this period, thus early or late activities are not advised. Because nest attendance and feeding rates are still relatively high, duration of any allowed activities should be very short (perhaps 10-30 minutes).

3. From 36 days after hatching to fledging, human activities should not occur in the vicinity of the nest. However, if circumstances require isolated and justified exceptions (e.g. researcher visits) to this guideline, activities should occur only during mid-day, should not exceed two hours duration and should not occur during periods of inclement weather. By 35 days after hatching, daily brooding curves have flattened out, exhibiting little or no increases during the early or late hours of the day. But since prey deliveries and eaglet feedings peaked during the morning hours and eaglet feedings peaked again during the afternoon, activities should be restricted to mid-morning (1000 hrs) through early afternoon (1400 hrs). Since brooding was recorded until eaglets were 70 days old, activities should not occur during periods of inclement weather, when late brooding was most likely to occur.

Under 2 and 3 above, justified exceptions do not include any activities that could occur at other times of year (i.e. outside of the nesting cycle). These recommendations are based on nesting chronology; therefore, it is imperative that chronology is known for nests in question. If the precise chronology is not known, recommendations for a specific period should extend to the end of the known range of the same chronology for that geographic region or population.

It should be reemphasized that these recommendations are not intended to replace recommended or established buffer zones that prohibit human activities near eagle nests throughout the nesting cycle. Neither are they intended for recurring, daily activities, which may result in detrimental levels of disturbance, even if they are applied as above.

Rather, they are intended to help minimize disturbance from isolated, sporadic, human activities that cannot be avoided. Based on this study, these recommendations are conservative. However, since each nesting pair reacts differently to disturbance (Grier 1969, Bortolotti et al. 1985, Cain 1985), even conservative approaches may not adequately safeguard some active nests. Whenever possible, nesting behavior and activity time budgets should be monitored during potentially disturbing situations and remedial measures taken if any deviations from natural behavior patterns arise.

Literature Cited

Altmann, J. 1974. Observational study of behavior: sampling methods. Behav. 49:227-265.

Bortolotti, G. R. 1984a. Sexual size dimorphism and age-related size variation in Bald Eagles. J. Wildl. Manage. 48:72-81.

Bortolotti, G. R. 1984b. Physical development of nestling Bald Eagles with emphasis on timing of growth events. Wilson Bull. 96:524-542.

Bortolotti, G. R., J. M. Gerrard, P. N. Gerrard and D. W. A. Whitfield. 1985. Minimizing investigator-induced disturbance to nesting Bald Eagles. Pages 85-103. In: J. M. Gerrard and T M. Ingram, eds. The Bald Eagle in Canada, Proceedings of Bald Eagle Days. Winnipeg, Manit., Can.

Broley, M. J. 1947. Migration and nesting of Florida Bald Eagles. Wilson Bull. 59:3-20.

Broley, C. L. 1952. Eagle man. Pelligrini & Cudahy, N.Y. 210pp.

Cade, T. J. 1982. The falcons of the world. Cornell Univ. Press, Ithaca, N.Y. 192pp.

Cain, S. L. 1985. Nesting activity time budgets of Bald Eagles in Southeast Alaska. M.S. Thesis, Univ. Montana, Missoula. 47pp.

Cain, S. L. and J. I. Hodges. 1989. A floating fish snare for capturing Bald Eagles. J. Raptor Res. 23:10-13.

Clevenger, A. D. 1987. Atypical incubation rates at a New Mexico Peregrine Falcon eyrie. J. Raptor Res. 21:33-35.

Craighead, D. J. 1980. Sex differences in nest construction, incubation and parental behavior in captive American Golden Eagles (*Aquila chrysaetos*). M.S. Thesis, Univ. Montana, Missoula. 64pp.

Diem, K. L., L. A. Ward and J. C. Cupal. 1977. Cameras as remote sensors of animal activities. Int. Congr. Game Biol. 11:503-509.

Ellis, D. H. and C. H. Ellis. 1975. Color marking Golden Eagles with human hair dyes. J. Wildl. Manage. 39:445-447.

Ellis, D. H. 1979. Development of behavior in the Golden Eagle. Wildl. Mono. 70:1-94.

Enderson, J. H., S. A. Temple and L. G. Swartz. 1972. Time-lapse photographic records of nesting Peregrine Falcons. Living Bird 11:113-128.

Fraser, J. D. 1985. The impact of human activities on Bald Eagle populations-a review. Pages 68-84. In: J. M. Gerrard and T. M. Ingram, eds. The Bald Eagle in Canada, Proceedings of Bald Eagle Days, Winnipeg, Manit., Can.

Gerrard, P. N., S. N. Wiemeyer and J. M. Gerrard. 1979. Some observations on the behavior of captive Bald Eagles before and during incubation. Raptor Res. 13:57-64.

Grier, J. W. 1969. Bald Eagle behavior and productivity responses to climbing to nests. J. Wildl. Manage. 33:961-966.

Grubb, T. G. 1977. Weather-dependent foraging in Ospreys. Auk 94:146-149.

Herrick, F. H. 1924a. An eagle observatory. Auk 41:89-105.

Herrick, F. H. 1924b. The daily life of the American eagle: late phase. Auk 41:389-422.

Herrick, F. H. 1932. The daily life of the American eagle: early phase. Auk 49:307-323.

Herrick, F. H. 1933. Daily life of the American eagle: early phase. (concluded). Auk 50:35-53.

Hodges, J. I. 1982. Bald Eagle nesting studies in Seymour Canal, Southeast Alaska. Condor 84:125-127.

Jamieson, I., N. Seymour and R. P Bancroft. 1982. Time and activity budgets of Ospreys nesting in northeastern Nova Scotia. Condor 84:439-441.

Jenkins, M. A. 1978. Gyrfalcon nesting behavior from hatching to fledging. Auk 95:122-127.

Levenson, H. 1979. Time and activity budgets of Ospreys nesting in northern California. Condor 81:364-369.

Mueller, H. C. and K. Meyer. 1985. The evolution of reversed sexual dimorphism in size-a comparative analysis of the Falconiformes of the Western Palearctic. Current Ornithol. 2:65-101.

Newton, I. 1979. Population ecology of raptors. Buteo Books, Vermillion, S.D. 399pp.

Ofelt, C. H. 1975. Food habits of nesting Bald Eagles in Southeast Alaska. Condor 77:337-338.

Robards, F. C. and J. G. King. 2008. Nesting and productivity of Bald Eagles in Southeast Alaska, 1966. In: Wright, B.A. and P. F. Schempf, eds. Bald Eagles in Alaska.

Sokal, R. R. and F. J. Rohlf. 1981. Biometry. W. H. Freeman and Co., San Francisco, Calif. 859pp.

Snyder, N. F. R. and J. W. Wiley. 1976. Sexual size dimorphism in hawks and owls of North America. Ornithol. Monogr. 20:196.

Sprunt, A., W. B. Robertson, Jr., S. Postupalsky, R. J. Hensel, C. E. Knoder and F. H. Ligas. 1973. Comparative productivity of six Bald Eagle populations. Trans. North Am. Wildl. Nat. Resour. Conf. 38:96-106.

Stinson, C. H. 1978. The influence of environmental conditions on aspects of the time budgets of breeding Ospreys. Oecologia 36:127-139.

Stinson, C. H., J. Lauthner and R. T. Ray. 1988. Breeding behavior of Ospreys in northwestern Washington. Murrelet 69:24-27.

Wallin, D. O. 1982. The influence of environmental conditions on the breeding behavior of the Bald Eagle (*Haliaeetus leucocephalus*). M.S. Thesis, College of William and Mary, Williamsburg, Virg. 64pp.

Yates, R. E. and B. R. McClelland. 1989. Unusual leg injury in a nestling Bald Eagle. J. Raptor Res. 23:14-16.

Perspectives on the Breeding Biology of Bald Eagles in Southeast Alaska

Scott M. Gende

U.S. Forest Service, Forestry Sciences Lab., Juneau, AK

Southeast Alaska (hereafter Southeast) has one of the highest densities of breeding Bald Eagles in North America (Gende et al. 1997). With relatively pristine habitat, low levels of disturbance and minimal contaminant influence, Southeast is a prime area to study factors that naturally regulate population levels, reproduction and general ecology of Bald Eagles. My several years of field research with hundreds of hours of observation of Bald Eagles have led to some perspectives on the breeding biology of eagles in Southeast. I will discuss some of these observations in context of other research that has been done on the life history of Bald Eagles and suggest potential topics for future research.

Three distinct stages of reproduction for eagles in Southeast will be discussed: pre-laying, incubation and nestling. The post-fledging period is also an extremely important period as fledglings exhibit the highest rates of mortality during the first year out of the nest (e.g., McCollough 1986, Hodges et al. 1987). Although I have observed adults feeding fledglings for 3 weeks after they leave the nest, I have little insight concerning the post-fledging ecology and thus will not discuss this period (1). (The numbers in the text such as (1) refer to text found in the section entitled Potential Research Questions). All related research questions are listed by number at the end of the manuscript.

Pre-laying

The pre-laying stage of reproduction is the time when nesting activities resume in the spring (e.g., courtship, talon-locking, nest building) to the time just before females lay their first egg. The pre-laying period cannot be defined as the time breeding pairs arrive on the territories, because the population of adult eagles in Southeast is thought to be non-migratory (Sidle et al. 1986). Some sub-adults will migrate south during the winter but many adults stay and, in fact, exhibit fidelity to their nest sites throughout the winter (Hodges et al. 1987, Kralovec 1994). This does not mean territorial adults will not stray from the territory. On the contrary, eagles are often on the move in the winter, traveling between food patches (e.g., to the winter chum run in the Chilkat River) for up to 10 d at a time (Kralovec 1994). Throughout the winter, pairs will return to the nest territory for brief periods to re-establish their claim. For eagles to be non-migratory, there must be sufficient food during the winter. Sporadic trapping efforts have provided some evidence that food levels in Southeast are sufficient during the winter. For example, in January 1995, Phil Schempf and I trapped an adult female that weighed nearly 7.4 kg, much heavier than normal mass estimates of eagles.

95

In early spring, breeding activity resumes and eagles spend more time in their territories. I have seen activities such as talon-locking, nest building and copulation in early March, although the majority of the breeding population doesn't exhibit this behavior until late March or early April. Before egg laying, territoriality does not seem to be rigorously enforced. Adults are still floating between food patches and an intruding adult on a pair's nesting territory is often ignored.

Nest-building or maintenance is a major activity for eagles before egg laying. Nests are built up by adding sticks or nest lining (moss or grass). Although nest maintenance is carried out throughout the summer, most of the re-building occurs in the spring. Pairs building a completely new nest often dedicate much of their springtime activities to carrying nesting material and working on the new nest. Rates of nest loss (due to windthrow) has been estimated to be about 6% annually (Hodges 1982). Thus, most of the nest-building activities observed in the spring are for maintenance or building up of old nests.

Bald Eagle nest with commanding view of Southeast Alaska waters. Photo by Scott Gende.

The density of nest structures is very high along saltwater shores in Southeast, as territorial pairs often have more than one nest in their territory. I know of one nesting pair that has five nest structures in their territory. This is a far cry from some populations elsewhere in the country, where a lower density of eagles allow for a larger territory (and thus more nests) to be defended. In Wisconsin, for example, some nesting pairs have as many as 12 nest structures in their territory (K. Warnke, Minnesota Coop. Fish and Wildl. Research Unit, Univ. Minnesota, pers. comm.). In Southeast, it is very difficult to determine territorial borders and ascribe nest structures to particular pairs because of the high density of adults and nest structures and the convoluted shoreline. However, from long-term productivity surveys, nest use (but not fate) was found to be related to nest success the previous year, nests that failed were less likely to be used the following year (Gende et al. 1997) (2). Without marked birds, it is difficult to tell if nesting pairs switched nests or are nonbreeding in a given year. Using different nests from year to year seems to be the rule, although some nests are used consistently. I know of several nesting pairs that have used (and successfully fledged young) from the same nest for seven straight years (3).

By mid-April, copulation is seen more often for pairs in Southeast. Copulation is thought to precede egg laying by 3-6d (Wiemeyer 1981). The eggs of Bald Eagles are small relative to the size of the adult, averaging approximately 130 g (Hensel and Troyer 1964). In fact, the ratio of egg weight to female body weight for Bald Eagles is one of the smallest of any bird (approximately 3% of female's body weight; Stalmaster 1987), suggesting it is relatively inexpensive energetically for eagles to produce eggs (4). By comparison, the Pine Siskin, a small passerine that nests in Southeast Alaska, lays eggs that weigh approximately 11% of the female's body weight. With an average clutch size of 4 eggs, female Pine Siskins would lay almost half of her body weight during 4 days of laying-quite an investment compared to the Bald Eagle.

Not all adult eagles establish territories every year. Estimates of the frequency of non-breeding adults in Southeast have been as high as 38% (Hansen and Hodges 1985), although other estimates are closer to 25% (P. Schempf pers. comm.). Of those adults that exhibit some form of territorial behavior, not all lay eggs every year. I have observed territorial pairs repair nests, copulate and even sit down into the nest bowl for short stints as if laying, yet fail to lay eggs (5). There is some evidence that habitat manipulation is one factor that may affect the density of pairs that lay eggs. The density of active nests decreased significantly as the proximity to clear cuts increased on Chichagof and Catherine islands in Chatham Strait (Gende et al. 1998).

Incubation Stage
In the last week of April or the first week in May, most nesting females can be seen sitting down in nests in incubation posture, signifying that laying has occurred or is about to occur. Although the majority of nesting pairs lay during these two weeks, the range of laying dates include mid-April to early June. This contrasts with nesting populations further north (e.g., the Gulkana River basin in Southcentral Alaska) where the breeding season is more compact and the range of laying dates is shorter (Steidl and Anthony 1995). During the several days before laying, females will often spend some time sitting in and tending to the nest bowl. During a two-year study in Southeast, the average clutch size for eagles in Southeast was 1.94 eggs, with 81% of nests containing a clutch of two eggs, 13% containing a clutch of 1 egg and 6% containing a clutch of 3 eggs (Gende and Willson 1997) (6). These clutch size frequencies are similar to those in nesting

populations elsewhere in the country (Stalmaster 1987).

Eggs are usually laid several days apart, although inter-egg intervals can be up to a week (Wiemeyer 1981). Eagles begin incubating eggs immediately after laying. Although males and females share incubation duties (Cain 1985), I have observed females doing most of the incubation immediately after laying.

Once females complete their clutch, the eggs must be incubated almost 24 hours a day. The embryos in eggs left unattended for more than a few minutes in Southeast will probably die of exposure, or possibly predation by corvids. Reflecting this constraint, eagles seldom leave an active nest during incubation. While one adult sits tediously on the nest, the other adult perches nearby. The non-incubating adult forages and, once a fish is caught, will fly back to a tree and eat it completely. On only two occasions have I observed an incubating adult come off the eggs to try to capture a fish. In both instances, the nest was eventually abandoned before the eggs hatched, suggesting that the incubating birds may have been food stressed. Duration of incubation bouts depends on the weather. Eggs are incubated for much longer periods during windy, rainy days, usually by the female (Cain 1985). When the incubating bird wants to switch duties with the foraging bird, it often calls to its mate and stands up on the rim of the nest before flying off. Or the foraging bird will fly onto the rim of the nest before the two switch incubation duties. For successful incubation, therefore, nesting pairs must have good timing and communication.

Once chicks hatch, almost all prey caught by either adult is taken directly to the nest. During supplemental feeding experiments, adults (mostly males) would, on occasion, eat part of the fish before bringing it to the nest, although in most instances adults took fish directly to the nest. During one climb to a nest with newly hatched young, I found over 18 uneaten adult herring and several partially eaten walleye pollock. The nest eventually fledged both young. Second, the change in behavior of an incubating eagle is another good indication of when hatching occurs. There are few activities in nature more boring to observe than an incubating eagle. On average, eagles in Southeast will stand and turn the eggs every 75 minutes or so, longer if the weather is cold or wet. During or after hatching, however, eagles will stand and examine the contents of the nest much more frequently, about every half hour just after hatching.

Nestlings develop for 10-12 weeks before fledging, which occurs, on average, in mid-August. From the time they hatch to just before fledging, eaglets will gain up to 6 kg (Bortolotti 1986). As eaglets get older, adults spend less time at the nest. Often, when chicks are 6 weeks old or older, adults will catch a fish and simply drop it in the nest, rather than stay in the nest and feed the chicks. Nesting birds will take only food small enough to carry immediately to a safe place to eat, avoiding any major confrontations with pirating eagles that would require the incubating adult to leave the nest (10).

The average Southeast Alaska Bald Eagle clutch size is slightly less than two eggs. Photo by Scott Gende.

Nestling stage

Hatching occurs after approximately 35 days of incubation. There are several behavior clues that indicate eggs have hatched. First, when an eagle is observed bringing prey to the nest, hatching has occurred or is about to occur. In captive breeding trials, eaglets have been heard vocalizing at least 12 hours before pipping (Wiemeyer 1981). With hatching occurring 24-48 hours after the onset of pipping (Wiemeyer 1981), adults probably have some clue as to when to start bringing food 36-60 hours before eaglets hatch. This caching behavior is thought to serve as a buffer for periods of food shortage once the eaglets hatch or as a means of reducing sibling competition (Gerrard and Bortolotti 1988).

With more beaks to feed, the nestling stage of reproduction would appear to be the critical period in terms of food availability. However, this does not appear to be the case for eagles in Southeast Alaska. Until pink salmon become available in late June, eagles seem to be able to supplement their diet with a wide variety of fish. I have often observed 4 or 5 species of fish (including walleye pollock, starry flounders, herring, sand lance and rockfish) cached in the nest at one time in early June (11). Once pink salmon begin milling in near-shore water by late June or early July, they are utilized extensively by eagles (Imler and Kalmbach 1955, Ofelt 1975, Cain 1985). From fish remains in nests and from foraging observations, I think that eagles use pink salmon almost exclusively from the time they arrive in the shallows until after eaglets have fledged. Without pink salmon present, the nestling period would almost surely be more taxing in terms of food availability for adults and likely to be more limiting to nestling survival (12).

Bald Eagles cache food in their nest as seen in this photo. Also, note the size difference of these siblings. Photo by Scott Gende.

Another possible reason eagles are not food limited during the nestling stage is that adults are less constrained to the nest once eggs hatch. Adults will spend less time at the nest as chicks develop (Cain 1985), thereby leaving more time to forage (Watson et al. 1991).

They are also not required to be in the nest around the clock. With no natural predators of large eaglets, adults are free to travel for longer stints to food patches, leaving nestlings to fend for themselves.

Conclusions

Although some work has been completed on certain aspects of the reproductive biology of eagles, more work is needed. Studying eagle biology not only lends insight into factors that control nesting success, but also figures prominently in the ecosystem as a whole. Eagles serve as a strong tie between the aquatic and terrestrial habitats and low productivity from eagles may serve as an indicator of problems in the aquatic and terrestrial environment. Understanding the viability of the population of eagles in Southeast hinges on continual understanding of the factors that influence each stage of reproduction. Furthermore, understanding factors that regulate reproduction is needed as conflicts continue to arise over development and extraction of resources utilized by humans and nesting eagles (Gende et al. 1998). Thus, prudent long-term management depends on an understanding of Bald Eagle nesting biology (Willson et al. 1997).

Potential Research Questions:

(1) (The numbered Potential Research Questions relate to the numbers in the preceding text.) Information on the post-fledging ecology of eagles, e.g., movements, diet and general ecology is sorely needed for eagles in Southeast. One interesting aspect would be the relationship between spawning salmon and young-of-year (YOY) eagles. How much YOY eagles rely on spawning salmon and changes in the weight of YOY eagles with and without access to spawning salmon are obvious questions. In addition, documenting movements of eaglets once they fledge and following these birds for 4 or 5 years would provide information on plumage characteristics of known-age eaglets in a high density population. Sub-adult eagles in Southeast, who seem to be tolerated by territorial pairs much more than other adults, may delay adult plumage to enhance survival and food acquisition in a population that may already saturate the habitat (Hansen 1987).

(2) It would be interesting to monitor whether nesting pairs attempt to breed each year and which nests are used.

(3) A tremendous amount could be learned about the breeding dynamics of eagles in Southeast Alaska by marking a large number of individuals. Monitoring individually marked birds would aid in understanding the number of nest structures in each territory, the extent of nest fidelity between years and rates of turnover for nesting pairs (pair-bond duration). For the latter, I get the impression from watching behavior of pairs that have failed in consecutive nesting attempts that mating for life is not always the rule in Southeast, especially for pairs associated with nests that consistently fail.

(4) Although eggs may be energetically inexpensive to produce, clutch formation may be limited by nutrients, such as calcium. Identification of the proximate factors that limit clutch size would aid in understanding which prey items are essential before laying.

(5) An important research question is to identify factors that control the density of nesting

pairs that lay eggs every year. There is much variation in the number of nests that are active every year vs. the number that are successful. How does the variation compare and what factors affect each? What determines whether or not eggs are laid?

(6) Determining clutch size for many nests is difficult because nest climbs disturb incubating eagles. Climbs made during our research averaged only 25 minutes (from the time we approached the nest from a boat to the time we motored away). Nevertheless, more data are needed on the annual variation of clutch size, the factors that determine the number of eggs laid and fledging success in different circumstances (for example, nests that fledge 1 young on average have a much different interpretation if the clutch size was 2 vs. 1, a difference of 50% in fledging success).

(7) It would be interesting to compare certain aspects of behavior of pairs that successfully breed vs. those that fail in a given year, including the frequency of switching during incubation, nest attentiveness (how long eggs are exposed), length of pair bond and foraging success of pairs during incubation. These clues may provide a clearer picture as to why most nests fail during incubation.

(8) More research is needed on the physiological costs of incubation for eagles once the clutch is completed. How much does basal metabolic rate increase as a result of heating and reheating eggs? This, in conjunction with foraging success and weight changes during incubation (See #6), may provide insight as to the threshold at which eagles may abandon the current nesting attempt.

(9) It would be interesting to see the daily weight fluctuation of eagles during incubation. Monitoring weight changes year round would also provide insight to physiological stress experienced by eagles during the different seasons.

(10) Despite evidence that food is limiting during incubation, it is curious that nesting pairs will not take supplemental food during this period. A series of supplemental feeding experiments using different prey sizes could resolve whether or not prey size is a limiting factor.

(11) The wide diversity of prey available to nesting eagles may be a reason that breeding dynamics, including the density of active nests and nesting success, are higher, on average, along saltwater shores vs. freshwater shores (e.g., the Chilkat River Valley). Studying the natural history of prey species taken by nesting eagles in both habitats would aid in understanding not only eagle biology but productivity of coastal vs freshwater habitats.

Researcher Scott Gende, preparing to measure a captured adult Bald Eagle. Note that Scott keeps control of the sharp talons and is wary of the sharp hooked beak. Photo by Phil Schempf, USFWS.

(12) Comparing diet, growth rates and post-fledging survivorship of nesting pairs that do and do not have access to pink salmon (e.g., up a river that has barrier falls, or nests associated with an early run of pinks) would aid in understanding the importance of pink salmon to nesting eagles.

Literature Cited

Bortolotti, G. R. 1986. Evolution of growth rates in eagles: sibling competition vs energy considerations. Ecology 67:182-194

Cain, S. M. 1985. Nesting activity time budgets of Bald Eagles in Southeast Alaska. MS Thesis, University of Montana, Missoula, Montana. 46pp.

Gende, S. M., M. F. Willson and M. Jacobson. 1997 Reproductive success of Bald Eagles (*Haliaeetus leucocephalus*) and its association with habitat/landscape features and weather in Southeast Alaska. Can. J. Zool. 75:1595-1604.

Gende, S. M., M. F. Willson, B. H. Marston, M. Jacobson and W. P. Smith. 1998. Bald Eagle nesting density and success in relation to distance from clearcut logging in Southeast Alaska. Biol. Conserv. 83:121-126.

Gende, S. M. and M. F. Willson. 1997. Supplemental feeding experiments of nesting Bald Eagles in southeastern Alaska. J. Field Ornithol. 68: 590-601.

Gerrard, J. M. and G. R. Bortolotti. 1988. The Bald Eagle; haunts and habits of a wilderness monarch. Smithsonian Institution Press, Washington, D.C.

Hansen, A. J. 1987. Regulation of Bald Eagle reproductive rates in Southeast Alaska. Ecology 68:1387-1392.

Hansen, A. J. and J. I. Hodges. 1985. High rates of nonbreeding adult Bald Eagles in Southeastern Alaska. J. Wildl. Manage. 49:454-458.

Hensel, R. J. and W. A. Troyer. 1964. Nesting studies of the Bald Eagle in Alaska. Condor 66:282-286.

Hodges, J. I. 1982. Evaluation of the 100-meter protective zone for Bald Eagle nests in Southeast Alaska. U.S. Dept. Interior, Fish and Wildlife Service, Raptor Management Studies, unpublished report. Juneau, Alas. 11 pp.

Hodges, J. I., E. L Boeker and A. J. Hansen. 1987. Movements of radio-tagged Bald Eagles, *Haliaeetus leucocephalus*, in and from Southeastern Alaska. Can. Field-Nat. 10:136-140.

Imler, R. H. and E. R. Kalmbach. 1955. The Bald Eagle and its economic status. U.S. Dept. of the Interior, Fish and Wildlife Service, Circular No. 30.

Kralovec, M. L. 1994. Bald Eagle movements in and from Glacier Bay National Park and Preserve. Final Report. Glacier Bay National Park, Gustavus, Alas. 67pp.

McCollough, M. A. 1986. The post-fledging ecology and population dynamics of Bald Eagles in Maine. Ph.D. Dissertation. University of Maine, Orono, Maine. 46pp.

Monaghan, P. and R. G. Nager. 1997. Why don't birds lay more eggs? TREE 12:270-274.

Ofelt, C. H. 1975. Food habits of nesting Bald Eagles in Southeast Alaska. Condor 77:337-338.

Sidle, W. B., L. H. Suring and J. I. Hodges. 1986. The Bald Eagle in Southeast Alaska. Wildlife and Fisheries Habitat Management Notes. U.S. Forest Service. R10-MB-9. 29pp.

Stalmaster, M. V. 1987. The Bald Eagle. Universe Books, New York.

Steidl, R. J. and R. G. Anthony. 1995. Recreation and Bald Eagle ecology on the Gulkana National Wild River, Alaska. Unpublished Final Report to the Bureau of Land Management, Alaska. 71 pp.

Swenson, J. E., K. L. Alt and R. L. Eng. 1986. Ecology of Bald Eagles in the greater Yellowstone ecosystem. Wildl. Monogr. 95:146.

Watson, J. W., M. G. Garrett and R. G. Anthony. 1991. Foraging ecology of Bald Eagles in the Columbia

River estuary. J. Wildl. Manage. 55:492-499.

Wiemeyer, S. N. 1981. Captive propagation of Bald Eagles at Patuxent Wildlife Research Center and introductions in the wild, 1976-1980. Rapt. Res. 15:68-82.

Willson, M. F., S. M. Gende and B. H. Marston. 1997. Wildlife habitat models and land management plans: lessons from the Bald Eagle (*Haliaeetus leucocephalus*) in Tongass National Forest. Nat. Areas. J. 17:26-29.

Habitat Relationships of Bald Eagles in Alaska

Lowell H. Suring

U.S. Forest Service, Anchorage, AK

Studies of Bald Eagles in Alaska show that they consistently select areas with specific landscape features for nesting, perching, roosting and foraging. They also choose different landscape features, or habitat, for different activities. This paper describes the kinds of habitat Bald Eagles use in Southeast Alaska, Kodiak Island, the Kenai Peninsula, the Alaska Peninsula, the Aleutian Islands and Interior Alaska.

Bald Eagle nests, which may measure up to 1.8 m (6 ft) in diameter and 1.2 m (4 ft) tall, are placed in large dominant or co-dominant trees or on prominent land forms. Nest sites are usually close to water where Bald Eagles can forage for fish and other prey. When Bald Eagles are not at their nest site or moving about, they usually find a place to perch. Perches are usually located along the coast or along rivers and streams where food is available.

Roosts are areas where Bald Eagles spend the night. Roosts are usually located in protected areas that minimize the effects of adverse weather. Foraging sites are selected by Bald Eagles to maximize availability and accessibility of food items.

These habitat relationships have been extensively studied throughout the range of Bald Eagles (e.g., Gerrard et al. 1975, Servheen 1975, McEwan and Hirth 1979, Steenhof et al. 1980, Andrew and Mosher 1982, Anthony et al. 1982, Mathisen 1983, Grubb 1988, Anthony and Isaacs 1989, Johnsgard 1990). In this paper I review the information available on the use of habitats by Bald Eagles throughout Alaska.

Nesting Habitat
Southeast Alaska
A clear description of nest sites selected by Bald Eagles in Southeast Alaska has emerged from the extensive surveys conducted by the U.S. Fish and Wildlife Service. The typical nest site in this area is associated with old-growth forests near salt water (Hodges and Robards 1982). Nearly all (98%) of the nest trees were within 183 m (600 ft) of the shoreline (Figure 1). The mean distance of the nest tree to salt water was 37 m (121 ft) (Table 1).

Most (94%) of 3,850 nests examined by Hodges and Robards (1982) were found in live trees. Sitka spruce provided sites for 78% of 3,850 nests (Table 2). Although 20% of the nests were located in western hemlock, this species is usually not preferred because its branches are shorter than those of Sitka spruce. Hemlock do not live as long as spruce and their terminal branches are much finer (Grubb 1976). Western red cedar is found throughout southern Southeast Alaska, but it is rarely used for nesting by Bald Eagles because of its fine branching structure. Corr (1974) reported a very similar distribution in the species of nest trees near Petersburg, Alaska (Table 2).

Bald Eagle nests have usually been found near the top of large, old trees (Table 1). Nest trees averaged 30-36 m (98-118 ft) tall and had an average diameter of 1.1 m (3.6 ft). Trees of this size are usually at least 400-500 years old (Corr 1974, Hodges and Robards 1982). Height of nest trees was shown to have a significant, positive relationship to the percentage of active nests (Hodges and Robards 1982, Hansen 1987). Perhaps Bald Eagles with nests in trees that extend above the surrounding canopy are better able to locate prey.

Figure 1. Frequency distribution of distances of nests to water for Bald Eagle nests In Southeast Alaska (from Hodges and Robards 1982).

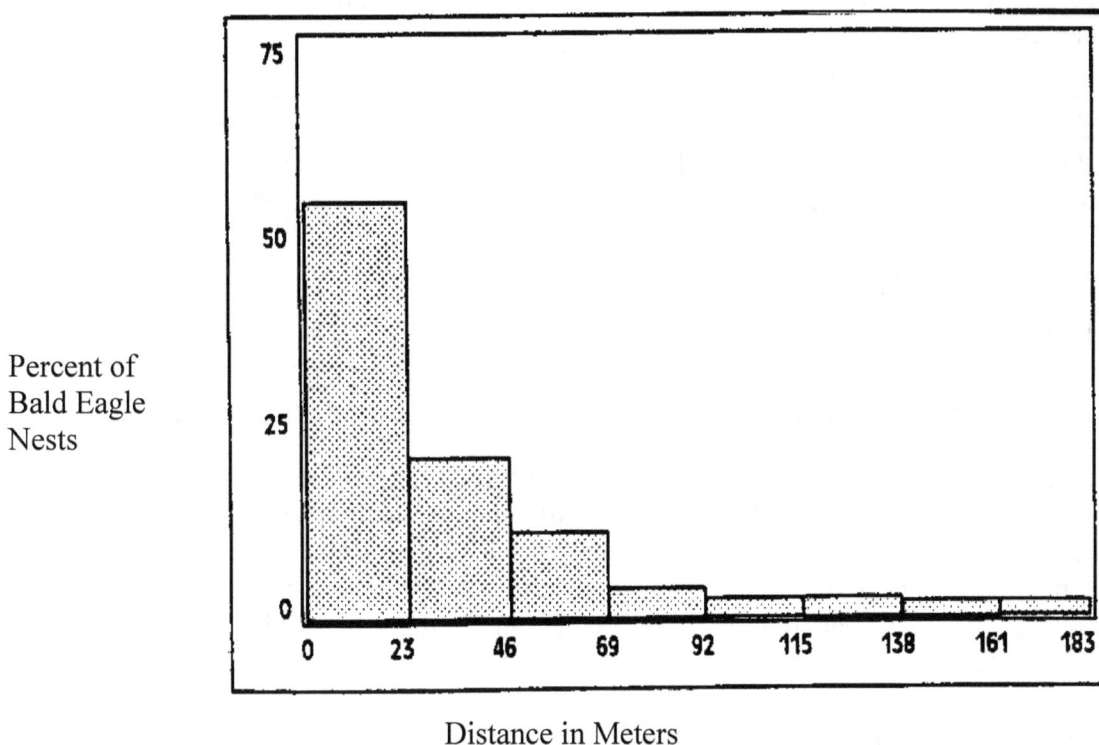

Percent of Bald Eagle Nests

Distance in Meters

The major mainland river systems in Southeast Alaska also support approximately 200 Bald Eagle nests (Hodges 1979). The flood plains of these rivers support stands of large, mature black cottonwood trees that serve as nest sites (Hodges 1979, Hughes 1980, Hansen et al. 1986). Black cottonwood also provided the majority of nest trees along rivers in the Yakutat area (Patten 1981) (Table 2).

Kodiak Island/Kenai Peninsula
Although the preference Bald Eagles have for placing their nests on prominent locations does not change throughout Southcentral Alaska, the actual sites of nests vary. Trees are preferred nest sites and are used whenever available. Black cottonwood is the preferred

species on Kodiak Island and the Kenai Peninsula (Table 1) (Chrest 1964, Troyer and Hensel 1965, Bangs et al. 1982a). However, on Kodiak Island, where trees grow only in riparian areas, 20-30% of nests were found on rocky cliffs or at the bases of alder trees on rock cliffs along the coast. All nests were near water and areas without trees or cliffs did not have nests (Table 1).

Alaska Peninsula/Aleutian Islands

Although the Alaska Peninsula and the Aleutian Islands are nearly treeless, approximately 17% of the breeding Bald Eagles in Alaska occur there (Sidle et al. 1986). Bald Eagles breed on every major island in the Aleutian chain except the Near Island group (Early 1982). Hehnke (1973) reported locating 43 Bald Eagle nests from Unimak Island north to Bear Lake on the Alaska Peninsula. All of the nests were on rocky pinnacles or cliffs.

Table 1. Characteristics of locations of Bald Eagle nests in Alaska

Location	Mean Distance	Height of Nest Tree	Height of Nest	Source
Southeast Alaska	37 m	30 m	25 m	Hodges & Robards (1982)
Southeast Alaska	33 m	36 m	30 m	Corr (1974)
Chilkat Valley	75 m	30 m	23 m	Hansen et al. (1986)
Prince William		24 m		Anthony et al. (1982)
Kodiak Island	73 m	22 m	16 m	Chrest (1964)
Kenai Peninsula	0.2 km	13 m	8-10 m	Bangs et al. (1982)
Alaska Peninsula	20 m			Hehnke (1973)
Amchitka Island			12 m	Sherrod et al. (1976)
Tanana River			18 m	Ritchie (1982)

On Amchitka Island, Bald Eagles selected one of five types of sites on which to build nests: 1) sea stacks or pinnacles sticking out of the ocean, which had been formed by the erosion of small peninsulas; 2) ridges, which are small peninsulas still connected to the mainland; 3) connected sea stacks, which are partially eroded ridges; 4) islets, which are similar to sea stacks but are broader and flatter; and 5) the sides of hills adjacent to saltwater (Sherrod et al. 1976, Byrd and Williams 2008).

Pinnacles or similar sites were preferred Bald Eagle nesting sites (Murie 1959, Sherrod et al. 1976). Pinnacles and sea stacks are most similar to trees in that they are the dominant structure on the landscape and they provide protection from potential nest predators. Hillsides and cliffs close to good foraging areas may have functioned as nest sites as well as pinnacles did prior to the introduction of mammalian predators on these islands. The introduction of arctic fox for fur farming in the early 1900s and the introduction of dogs, cats and Norway rats during World War II may have influenced selection of nest sites by Bald Eagles (Kenyon 1961, Sherrod et al. 1976). The elimination of foxes, dogs and cats from Amchitka Island may have allowed Bald Eagles to reestablish nests on hillsides adjacent to intertidal beaches where they forage for fish, shorebirds and waterfowl.

Interior Alaska

Although the Bald Eagle is generally considered to be uncommon to rare throughout interior Alaska, it is known to breed throughout the area (Gabrielson and Lincoln 1959, Armstrong 1980). Several major river systems, such as the Tanana River and the Yukon River, support well-established populations of Bald Eagles (Metcalf 1976, Ritchie 1982). Less dense populations of Bald Eagles nest in association with the numerous lakes, ponds and wetlands throughout the area (Spindler et al. 1981).

Bald Eagles prefer to nest in trees that are close to water (e.g., within 600 m on the Tanana River) and that are the dominant member of the stand (Ritchie 1982). Stands of balsam poplar and spruce are common adjacent to rivers in interior Alaska and balsam poplar is favored as a nest site (Table 2). Spruce, primarily white spruce, is also used often and occasionally nests are located in quaking aspen trees.

Perching Habitat

Perches are integral features of habitat for Bald Eagles because the birds spend significant portions of time perching. Non-breeding adults and wintering Bald Eagles may spend up to 90% of daylight hours perching (Gerrard and Whitfield 1980, Stalmaster 1981). Often Bald Eagles hunt from perches, waiting there for prey to pass by (Stalmaster 1987). Once food is secured, the birds often return to the perch to consume their prey. Perching requires less energy than flight and exposure to the sun warms the birds. Both factors reduce metabolic demands (Hayes and Gessaman 1980, Stalmaster 1981).

Perches also serve important functions for breeding adults. Perches may be used as sites to attract mates and to advertise territory occupation (Fraser 1981, Mahaffy 1981). They may also provide locations from which nests may be protected from other predatory birds (Sidle et al. 1986).

Bald Eagles usually select tall trees with large lateral branches near the top for perching (Stalmaster et al. 1985). In winter they choose such trees that are close to water and associated food sources. More than 80% of wintering Bald Eagles on the Skagit River in Washington were observed to perch within 25 m of water (Figure 2) (Hunt et al. 1980 as cited in Stalmaster et al. 1985). Nesting Bald Eagles choose perch sites close to their nests. Bald Eagles prefer dominant or co-dominant trees in small groups, or single trees near water, over large uniform stands of trees (Stalmaster and Newman 1979). Snags also provide preferred perching sites for Bald Eagles (Stalmaster and Newman 1979, Hansen and Bartelme 1980).

Table 2. Nest Sites of Bald Eagles in Alaska

Location	Number of Nests Observed	Nest Site	Percent	Source
Southeast Alaska	3829	Sitka spruce	(78)	Hodges and Robards (1982)
		Western hemlock	(20)	
		Cedar Cottonwood	(2) (t)	
Southeast Alaska	128	Sitka spruce	(77)	Corr (1974)
		Western hemlock	(14)	
		Cedar	(2)	
		Dead Tree	(7)	
Chilkat Valley	59	Sitka spruce	(12)	Hansen et al. (1986)
		Cottonwood	(88)	
Yakutat	32	Sitka spruce	(6)	Patten (1981)
		Cottonwood	(84)	
		Other tree	(6)	
		Rocky knob	(3)	
Kodiak Island		Cottonwood	(66)	Chrest (1964)
		Cliff	(34)	
Kodiak Island	326	Cottonwood Cliff	(81)	Troyer and Hensel (1965)
		Rocky	(13)	
		Alder	(6)	
Kodiak Island	12	Cottonwood	(100)	Trudgeon (1980)
Kenai Peninsula	36	Cottonwood	(77)	Bangs et al. (1982)
		Aspen	(19)	
		White spruce	(3)	
Amchitka Island	251	Sea stack	(38)	Sherrod et al. (1976)
		Ridge	(24)	
		Connected stack	(20)	
		Islets	(8)	
		Hillsides	(10)	
Tanana River	48	Balsam poplar	(69)	Ritchie (1982)
		White spruce	(29)	
		Aspen	(2)	
Interior Alaska	23	Balsam poplar	(78)	Roseneau and Bente (1979)
		Spruce	(22)	

Roosting Habitat

Roosting sites are generally those areas where wintering Bald Eagles spend the night; however, roosts may also be used throughout the day during severe weather (Stalmaster et al. 1985). Roosting sites are selected for characteristics that reduce exposure of the birds to wind, precipitation and low temperatures. The presence of protective land forms and stands of conifer trees appears to be more important than distance to foraging areas. Roosts in Oregon have been reported up to 20 km from food sources (Keister and Anthony 1983). Large, old-growth trees located on slopes or in protected valleys are preferred roosting sites (Steenhof 1978, Hansen et al. 1980, Keister 1981, Anthony et al. 1982). Bald Eagles often choose coniferous forests over deciduous forests for roosting even though the birds may have to travel greater distances from the conifers to obtain food (Stalmaster and Gessman 1984). The energy saved by roosting in the greater protection of the conifer trees more than compensates for the extra energy expended in travel (Stalmaster and Gessman 1984).

Figure 2. Frequency distribution of distances of perches to water for Bald Eagles In Washington State (from Stalmaster et al. 1985)

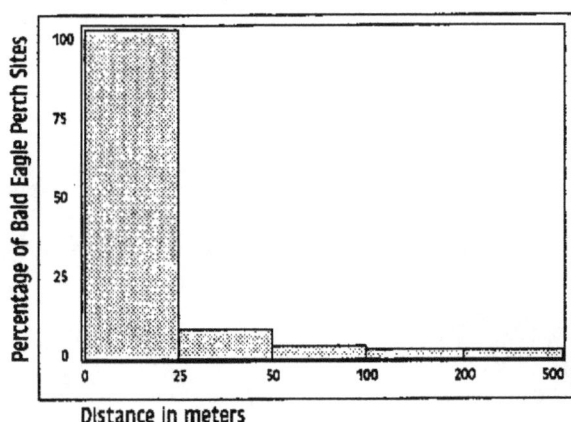

Very little published information is available describing the roosting habits of Bald Eagles during winter in Alaska. Black cottonwood and conifer trees were used for night roosting in the Chilkat Valley in northern Southeast Alaska (Hansen et al. 1986). Bald Eagles in this area roosted mainly in black cottonwoods until late fall. From late fall through winter the birds roosted in stands of western hemlock and Sitka spruce that were protected from prevailing winds by topographic features such as ridges and mountains.

Even less is known of roosting behavior of Bald Eagles during spring and summer. Bald Eagles concentrating in response to food sources in spring and early summer have been reported for the Copper River Delta (Bucaria 1979, Michelson et al. 1980), Yakutat Forelands (Peterson et al. 1981) and the mouth of the Stikine River (Hughes 1980). However, roosting areas used in association with these seasonal concentrations have not been identified. At the mouth of the Stikine River the Bald Eagles apparently do not use specific roosting areas but are dispersed throughout the forested hillsides close to the feeding area (Hughes 1980).

Foraging Habitat

Populations of various raptors may be limited by the availability of food (Newton 1979). Several studies have suggested that this phenomenon applies to Bald Eagles (Sherrod et al. 1976, Stalmaster 1981, Hansen 1987). Availability of food appears to be extremely important in the relationship of Bald Eagles to their habitat. Although Bald Eagles are opportunistic feeders, they are strongly associated with aquatic environments for foraging. Studies in Canada have shown that as the distance to aquatic foraging habitat increased the percentage of nests with young decreased (Gerrard et al. 1975).

The large foraging areas provided by inland seas and broad channels are preferred by Bald Eagles in Southeast Alaska. Approximately 55% of nests examined occurred adjacent to such areas (Hodges and Robards 1982). Nearly 30% of observed nests were associated with salt water bays and 11% were found on narrow salt water channels. Heads of bays and brackish lagoons were avoided (Robards and King 2008). Most nest sites in Southeast Alaska were associated with intertidal margins of less than 45 m (Robards and Hodges 1976). Fewer nest sites than expected were located adjacent to broad expanses of mud flats (Corr 1974). The increased distance over extensive mud flats to foraging sites may be a disadvantage to nesting Bald Eagles.

Bald Eagle sitting in its nest atop a western hemlock tree overlooking the ocean. Photo by Scott Gende.

The location of Bald Eagle nests found in the Yakutat area and on the Kenai Peninsula suggested that the birds preferred sites near clear, slow moving, relatively shallow streams that support spring and fall spawning fish (Patten 1981, Bangs et al. 1982). Streams and rivers that are free from ice throughout the winter or early in the spring are preferred foraging sites (Ritchie 1982, Gerrard and Bortolotti 1988). Reduced visibility of fish in silty or turbid rivers reduces the success of hunting efforts by Bald Eagles (Grubb 1977). Hunting conditions for Bald Eagles tend to be more variable in glacier-fed rivers than in salt water because of turbidity and fluctuation of river level associated with glacier melt (Hansen 1987).

Summary

A pattern for a general description of Bald Eagle habitat in Alaska may be extracted from this review. Nest sites are located on a dominant structure near good foraging sites. If the nest is placed in a tree, the tree is generally live, is dominant or co-dominant in the stand and has large branches. Large snags that serve as perches are close to the nest tree. If the nest is not in a tree it is located on a cliff or rock structure such as a sea pinnacle that provides protection from predators and disturbance.

Perch sites for immature and non-nesting adult Bald Eagles are usually large, tall trees with large lateral branches and close to foraging sites. Single trees or trees in small groups are preferred. Snags are preferred but live trees are readily used.

Roosting sites for wintering Bald Eagles are located in areas protected from prevailing winds by topographic features. Although Bald Eagles use deciduous trees for roosting, they prefer conifers during severe weather. Large trees with open horizontal branches are preferred within the roosting site.

Bald Eagle nests are built close to foraging areas where prey are available. These foraging areas include large salt water channels and clear, shallow streams that are ice free.

Literature Cited

Andrew, J. M. and J. A. Mosher. 1982. Bald Eagle nest site selection and nesting habitat in Maryland. J. Wildl. Manage. 46:382-390.

Anthony, R. G., R. L. Knight, G. T. Allen, B. R. McClelland and J. I. Hodges. 1982. Habitat use by nesting and roosting Bald Eagles in the Pacific Northwest. Trans. North Am. Nat. Resour. Conf. 47:332-342.

Anthony, R. G. and F. B. Isaacs. 1989. Characteristics of Bald Eagle nest sites in Oregon. J. Wildl. Manage. 53:148-159.

Armstrong, R. H. 1980. Guide to the birds of Alaska. Alaska Northwest Publ. Co., Edmonds, Wash. 332pp.

Bangs, E. E., T. N. Bailey and V. D. Bems. 1982. Ecology of nesting Bald Eagles on the Kenai National Wildlife Refuge, Alaska. Pages 47-54. In: W. N. Ladd and P F. Schempf, eds. Proc. of a symposium and workshop on raptor management and biology in Alaska and Western Canada, 17-20 February 1981, Anchorage, Alas. U.S. Dept. Inter., Fish Wildl. Serv., Anchorage, Alas. 335pp.

Bucaria, G. P. 1979. Copper River Delta area wildlife resource review. U.S. Dep. Agric., For. Serv., unpublished rep. Chugach Nati. For., Anchorage, Alas. 114pp.

Byrd, V. G. and J. C. Williams 2008. Distribution and status of Bald Eagles in the Aleutian Islands. In: Wright, B.A. and PF. Schempf (eds). Bald Eagles in Alaska.

Chrest, H. 1964. Nesting of the Bald Eagle in the Karluk Lake drainage on Kodiak Island, Alaska. M.S. Thesis, Colorado State Univ., Fort Collins. 73pp.

Corr, P. O. 1974. Bald Eagle (*Haliaeetus leucocephalus* alaskanus) nesting related to forestry in Southeastern Alaska. M.S. Thesis, Univ. Alaska, Fairbanks. 144pp.

Early, T. J. 1982. Abundance and distribution of breeding raptors in the Aleutian Islands, Alaska. Pages 99-111. In: W. N. Ladd and P F. Schempf, eds. Proc. of a symposium and workshop on raptor management and biology in Alaska and Western Canada, 17-20 February 1981, Anchorage, Alas. U.S. Dept. Inter., Fish Wildl. Serv., Anchorage, Alas. 335pp.

Fraser, J. D. 1981. The breeding biology and status of the Bald Eagle on the Chippewa National Forest. Ph.D. Thesis, Univ. Minnesota, St. Paul. 235pp.

Gabrielson, I. N. and F. C. Lincoln. 1959. The birds of Alaska. The Stackpole Co., Harrisburg, Pa. 922pp.

Gerrard, J. M., P. Gerrard, W. J. Maher and D. W. A. Whitfield. 1975. Factors influencing nest site selection of Bald Eagles in northern Saskatchewan and Manitoba. Blue Jay 33:169-176.

Gerrard, J. M. and D. W. A. Whitfield. 1980. Behavior in a nonbreeding Bald Eagle. Can. Field-Nat. 94:391-397.

Gerrard, J. M. and G. R. Bortolotti. 1988. The Bald Eagle, haunts and habits of a wilderness monarch. Smithsonian Inst. Press, Wash. D.C. 177pp.

Grubb, T. G. 1976. A survey and analysis of Bald Eagle nesting in western Washington. M.S. Thesis, Univ. Washington, Seattle. 87pp.

Grubb, T. G. 1988. Pattern recognition-a simple model for evaluating wildlife habitat. U.S. Dep. Agric., For. Ser. Res. Note RM487. 5pp.

Grubb, T. R. 1977. Why Ospreys hover. Wilson Bull. 89:149-150.

Hansen, A. J. 1987. Regulation of Bald Eagle reproductive rates in Southeast Alaska. Ecology 68:1387-1392.

Hansen, A. J. and J. W. Bartelme. 1980. Winter ecology and management of Bald Eagles on the Skokomish River, Washington. Pages 133-144. In: R. L. Knight, G. T Allen, M. V Stalmaster and C. W. Servheen, eds. Proc. of the Washington Bald Eagle symposium. The Nature Conservancy, Seattle, Wash.

Hansen, A. J., M. V. Stalmaster and J. R. Newman. 1980. Habitat characteristics, function and destruction of Bald Eagle communal roosts in western Washington. Pages 221-229. In: R. L. Knight, G. T. Allen, M. V. Stalmaster and C. W. Servheen, eds. Proc. of the Washington Bald Eagle symposium. The Nature Conservancy, Seattle, Wash.

Hansen, A. J., M. I. Dyer, H. H. Shugart and E. L. Boeker. 1986. Behavioral ecology of Bald Eagles along the Pacific Northwest coast: a landscape perspective. Oak Ridge Natl. Lab., Environ. Sci. Div. Publ. 2548. Oak Ridge, Tenn. 166pp.

Haves, S. R. and J. A. Gessaman. 1980. The combined effects of air temperature, wind and radiation on the resting metabolism of avian raptors. J. Thermal Biol. 5:119-125.

Hehnke, M. F. 1973. Nesting ecology and feeding behavior of Bald Eagles on the Alaska Peninsula. M.S. Thesis. California State Univ., Humboldt. 56pp.

Hodges, J. I., Jr. 1979. Southeast Alaska mainland river Bald Eagle nest survey. U.S. Fish and Wildl. Serv., unpublished rep. Juneau, Alas.

Hodges, J. I. and F. C. Robards. 1982. Observations of 3,850 Bald Eagle nests in Southeast Alaska. Pages 37-54. In: W. N. Ladd and P F. Schempf, eds. Proc. of a symposium and workshop on raptor management and biology in Alaska and Western Canada, 17-20 February 1981, Anchorage, Alas. U.S. Dept. Inter., Fish Wildl. Serv., Anchorage, Alas. 335pp.

Hughes, J. H. 1980. Bald Eagles on the Stikine River, Alaska. U.S. Dep. Agric., For. Serv., unpublished rep. Petersburg, Alas.

Hunt, W. G., B. S. Johnson, J. B. Bulger and C. G. Thelander. 1980. Impacts of a proposed Copper Creek Dam on Bald Eagles. BioSystems Analysis, unpublished rep. San Francisco, Calif. 143pp.

Johnsgard, P. A. 1990. Hawks, eagles and falcons of North America. Smithsonian Inst. Press, Wash., D.C. 403pp.

Keister, G. P., Jr. 1981. Characteristics of winter roosts and populations of Bald Eagles in the Klamath Basin. M.S. Thesis, Oregon State Univ., Corvallis. 82pp.

Keister, G. P. and R. G. Anthony. 1983. Characteristics of Bald Eagle communal roosts in the Klamath Basin, Oregon and California. J. Wildl. Manage. 47:1072-1079.

Kenyon, K. W. 1961. Birds of Amchitka Island, Alaska. Auk 78:304326.

Mahaffy, M. S. 1981. Territorial behavior of the Bald Eagle on the Chippewa National Forest. M.S. Thesis, Univ. Minnesota, St. Paul. 92pp.

Mathisen, J. E. 1983. Nest site selection by Bald Eagles on the Chippewa National Forest. Pages 95-100. In: D. M. Bird, ed. Biology and management of Bald Eagles and Ospreys. Harpell Press, Ste. Anne de Bellevue, Quebec.

McEwan, L. C. and D. H. Hirth. 1979. Southern Bald Eagle productivity and nest site selection. J. Wildl. Manage. 43:585594.

Metcalf, L. 1976. Ornithological investigations in the Yukon-Charley area. Pages 237-261. In: S. Young, ed. The environment of the Yukon-Charley rivers area, Alaska. Cent. North. Stud., Contrib. from the Cent. North. Stud. 9.

Mickleson, P. G., J. S. Hawkings, D. R. Herter and S. M. Murphy. 1980. Habitat use by birds and other wildlife on the eastern Copper River Delta, Alaska. Alas. Coop. Wildl. Res. Unit, unpublished rep., Univ. Alaska, Fairbanks. 158pp.

Murie, O. J. 1959. Fauna of the Aleutian Islands and the Alaska Peninsula. U.S. Fish and Wildl. Serv., North Am. Fauna 61. 406 pp.

Newton, I. 1979. Population ecology of raptors. Buteo Books, Vermillion, S.D. 399pp.

Patten, S. M., Jr. 1981. Seasonal use of coastal habitat from Yakutat Bay to Cape Fairweather by migratory seabirds, shorebirds and waterfowl. N.O.A.A. Environ. Assessment Program, unpublished rep., Juneau, Alas. 138pp.

Peterson, M. R., J. C. Greilich and N. M. Harrison. 1981. Spring and fall migration and habitat use by water birds in the Yakutat Forelands, Alaska-1980. U.S. Fish and Wildl. Serv., unpublished rep., Anchorage, Alas. 106pp.

Ritchie, R. J. 1982. Investigations of Bald Eagles, Tanana River, Alaska, 1977-80. Pages 55-67. In: W. L.

Ladd and P. F. Schempf, eds. Raptor management and biology in Alaska and western Canada. U.S. Fish and Wildl. Serv., FWS/AK/PROC-82. Anchorage, Alas.

Robards, F. C. and J. G. King. 2008. Nesting and productivity of Bald Eagles. Southeast Alaska-1966. In: Wright, B.A. and P.F. Schempf, eds. Bald Eagles in Alaska.

Robards, F. C. and J. I. Hodges, Jr. 1976. Observations from 2,760 Bald Eagle nests in Southeast Alaska. Progress report 1969-1976. U.S. Fish and Wildl. Serv., unpublished rep., Juneau. Alas. 27pp.

Roseneau, D. and P. Bente. 1979. A raptor survey of the proposed Northwest Alaska Pipeline Company gas pipeline route: the U.S.-Canada Border to Prudhoe Bay, Alaska. Unpubl. rep., LGL Ecol. Res. Assoc. Inc., Fairbanks, Alas. 82pp.

Servheen, C. W. 1975. Ecology of the wintering Bald Eagles on the Skagit River, Washington. M.S. Thesis, Univ. Washington, Seattle. 96pp.

Sherrod, S.K., C. M. White and F. S. L. Williamson. 1976. Biology of the Bald Eagle on Amchitka Island, Alaska. Living Bird 15:143-182.

Sidle, W. B., L. H. Suring and J. I. Hodges, Jr. 1986. The Bald Eagle in Southeast Alaska. U.S. Dep. Agric., For. Serv., Wildl. and Fish. Habitat Manage. Note 11. Juneau, Alas. 29pp.

Spindler, M. A., S. M. Murphy and B. Kessel. 1981. Ground censuses of waterbird populations in the upper Tanana Valley, Alaska. Pages 133-148. In: F L. Miller and A. Gunn, eds. Symposium on census and inventory methods for population and habitats. Proc. Northwest Sec. Wildl. Soc., Univ. Idaho, For. Wildl. and Range Exp. Stn. Contrib. 217. Moscow.

Stalmaster, M. V. 1981. Ecological energetics and foraging behavior of wintering Bald Eagles. Ph.D. Thesis, Utah State Univ., Logan. 157pp.

Stalmaster, M. V. 1987. The Bald Eagle. Universe Books, New York. 227pp.

Stalmaster, M. V. and J. R. Newman. 1979. Perch-site preferences of wintering Bald Eagles in northwest Washington. J. Wildl. Manage. 43:221-224.

Stalmaster, M. V. and J. A. Gessaman. 1984. Ecological energetics and foraging behavior of overwintering Bald Eagles. Ecol. Monogr. 54:407-428.

Stalmaster, M. V., R. L. Knight, B. L. Holder and R. J. Anderson. 1985. Bald Eagles. Pages 269-290. In: E. R. Brown, tech. ed. Management of wildlife and fish habitats in forests of western Oregon and Washington. Part 1-Chapter narratives. U.S. Dep. Agric., For. Serv., Pac. Northwest Reg. Publ. R6-F&WL192-1985. Portland, Oreg.

Steenhof, K. 1978. Management of wintering Bald Eagles. U.S. Fish and Wildl. Serv., Biol. Serv. Program, FWS/OBS-78/79. Wash., D.C. 59pp.

Steenhof, K., S. S. Berlinger and L. H. Fredrickson. 1980. Habitat use by wintering Bald Eagles in South Dakota. J. Wildl. Manage. 44:798-805.

Troyer, W. A. and R. J. Hensel. 1965. Nesting and productivity of Bald Eagles on the Kodiak National Wildlife Refuge, Alaska. Auk 82:636-638.

Trudgeon, D. E. 1980. Environmental studies of the proposed Terror Lake hydroelectric project, Kodiak Island, Alaska. Raptor studies and intergravel water temperature studies. Univ. Alaska, Arctic Environ. Inf. and Data Cent., unpublished rep. Anchorage, Alas. 57pp.

The Population Ecology of Bald Eagles Along the Pacific Northwest Coast

Andrew Hansen, Ervin L. Boeker and
John I. Hodges

National Audubon Society, U.S. Fish and Wildlife Service, Juneau, AK

Snow crystals sparkle in cold moonlight. The frozen stillness is interrupted only by the splashing of a restless salmon in an ice-rimmed pool. The beam of a flashlight illuminates the fish. "The last one. That brings the count to 8032." Our fish survey completed, we hurry off the snow-covered gravel bar as the dull glow of dawn creeps into the southeastern sky.

Once on shore, we look back over the expanse of braided streams. Two brown bears, faintly visible in the dim light, leave their nightly fishing and fade into the forest. A scream pierces the silence and a Bald Eagle lights in the tree above us. Soon a scattering of eagles is visible on the gravel bars. More and more dark silhouettes descend from the sky in a cacophony of cries.

The strengthening light reveals a spectacular sight: Bald Eagles are everywhere. They blanket the gravel bars, heavily weigh the branches of streamside trees and crowd into the salmon-filled pools. Eagles atop fish carcasses throw back their heads in ritualistic display while others make bold aerial assaults on the feeders. The chaotic scene of thousands of Bald Eagles in a feeding frenzy is accented by an equal number of gulls, magpies and ravens scurrying for fish scraps left by eagles.

We are witnessing a typical winter morning on the Chilkat River in Southeast Alaska (Figure 1). Here, along a 5 km stretch of river, occurs perhaps the greatest gathering of eagles in the world. Each autumn more than 3000 Bald Eagles crowd into a place that the Tlingit Indians call the "Council Grounds" of the eagles.

Studying the birds for the National Audubon Society, we eventually learned that they come to the Council Grounds for food. An unusual hydrological condition results in large volumes of groundwater flowing up through the bed of the Chilkat River. In fall and winter, when most of the river is ice covered, the springs in the Council Grounds maintain a temperature favorable to the maturation of salmon eggs. The upwelling water also clears the spawning gravel of fine silts and enhances aeration of the eggs. This prime

Figure 1. Map of the Northwest coast of North America.

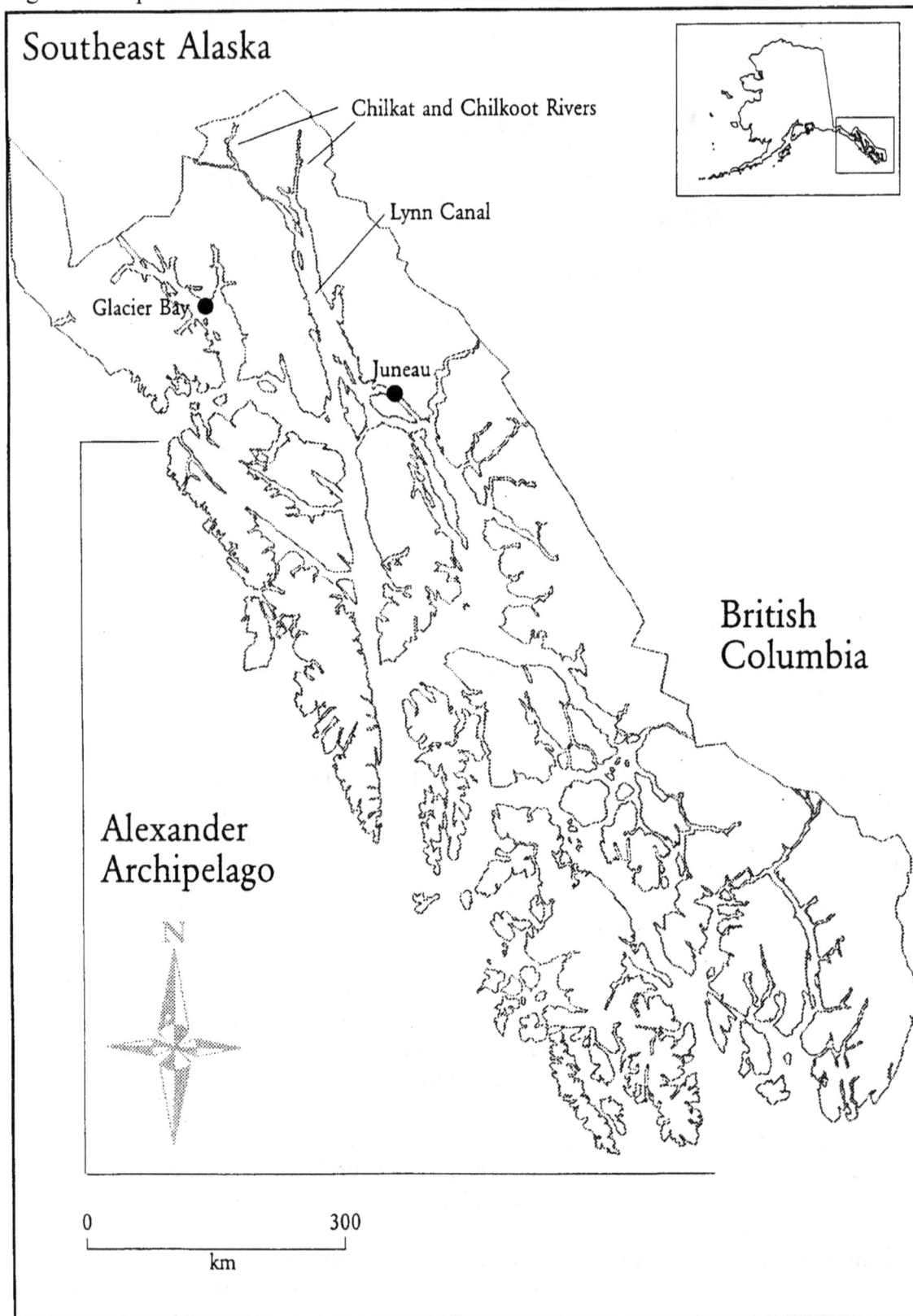

Southeast Alaska

Chilkat and Chilkoot Rivers

Lynn Canal

Glacier Bay

Juneau

British
Columbia

Alexander
Archipelago

N

0   300
       km

spawning habitat attracts the largest run of chum salmon in Southeast Alaska. As many as half a million fish leave the ocean and swim up the Chilkat River each autumn to spawn and die in the Council Grounds.

The spawned-out carcasses of these fish comprise a rich food supply for several types of birds and mammals, including gulls, waterfowl, ravens, magpies, coyotes, wolves, brown bear and, of course, Bald Eagles. The great store of carrion is typically depleted by mid-winter; most animals then disperse to find food elsewhere. Hundreds of eagles remain in the Chilkat Valley, however, some nesting in the valley's 90 breeding territories.

Although no other aggregation of Bald Eagles compares in size to that in Chilkat Valley, the species is remarkably abundant along the entire Pacific northwest coast from Washington State to the Aleutian Islands. The southern half of this region along coastal British Columbia and Southeast Alaska supports an estimated 20,000 eagles (Hodges et al. 1984). Bald Eagle nests line the convoluted shoreline at an average density of about one nest every 2 km (Hansen and Hodges 1985). People visiting the region by boat are often surprised to find that the eagle is one of the most common birds they encounter. The relatively pristine northwest coast with its primeval forests and abundant fishes appears to be ideal habitat for the Bald Eagle.

The significance of the Northwest Coast population is put into perspective when compared with populations in the 48 conterminous United States. There, the eagle is sufficiently uncommon that most Americans have probably never seen their national symbol in the wild. Historical records suggest that present eagle abundance in the 48 contiguous states is only a fraction of what it was prior to European settlement. Early explorers described massive aggregations of Bald Eagles on both the east and west coasts of the continent (Dawson and Bowles 1909). European colonization, however, brought extensive changes to the North American landscape. Large portions of the Atlantic Coast states were already deforested by 1840 (Cronan 1983). Stocks of Atlantic salmon were severely depleted through overfishing by the mid-1800s (Netboy 1974). To the west, catches of Pacific salmon in the Sacramento and Columbia rivers began to diminish by the 1890s (Smith 1979).

Such reductions in the prey and habitats of the Bald Eagle may have precipitated its decline. Elliott Coues noted in 1883 that Bald Eagles, though still common in New England, were less abundant than in earlier times. Just 43 years later, Edward Forbush (1927) declared that breeding eagles had been extirpated from southern New England. The eagle's abatement was further hastened after the 1940s by the widespread use of toxic chemicals such as DDT. Alexander Sprunt IV (1969) has summarized several early studies and reported that the breeding population in a portion of Florida dropped from 72 pairs in 1946 to 43 pairs in 1957 and then to 35 pairs in 1964. New Jersey had 35 pairs in 1937 and only two in 1965. Breeding losses continued through the 1960s. Fortunately, after a ban on the use of DDT in 1972, Bald Eagle productivity stabilized in some regions and began to improve in others (Grier 1982).

Bald Eagles along the Chilkat River, Alaska. Photo by Scott Gende.

Eagle populations have been so depauperate in the United States in recent years that biologists have had difficulty learning very much about the factors that regulate Bald Eagle populations, the adaptive significance of many morphological and behavioral traits and the effects of any environmental change on eagle ecology (Stalmaster 1987, Gerrard and Bortolotti 1988).

The large and stable population of the Pacific northwest coast offers a unique opportunity to address these questions. To that end, the U.S. Fish and Wildlife Service (USFWS) has performed extensive surveys of Bald Eagle reproduction in Southeast Alaska since 1966 (Hodges et al. 1979, Hodges et al. 1984, Hansen and Hodges 1985, Robards and King 2008). More recently, the National Audubon Society conducted an intensive study of Bald Eagles in the Chilkat Valley in cooperation with the USFWS (Hansen et al. 1984). This paper highlights what was learned via these studies about the factors that limit Bald Eagles in natural environments, their adaptations for survival and reproduction and the population attributes resulting from these adaptations. We also examine the implications of these findings for eagle conservation along the Pacific coast and elsewhere in North America.

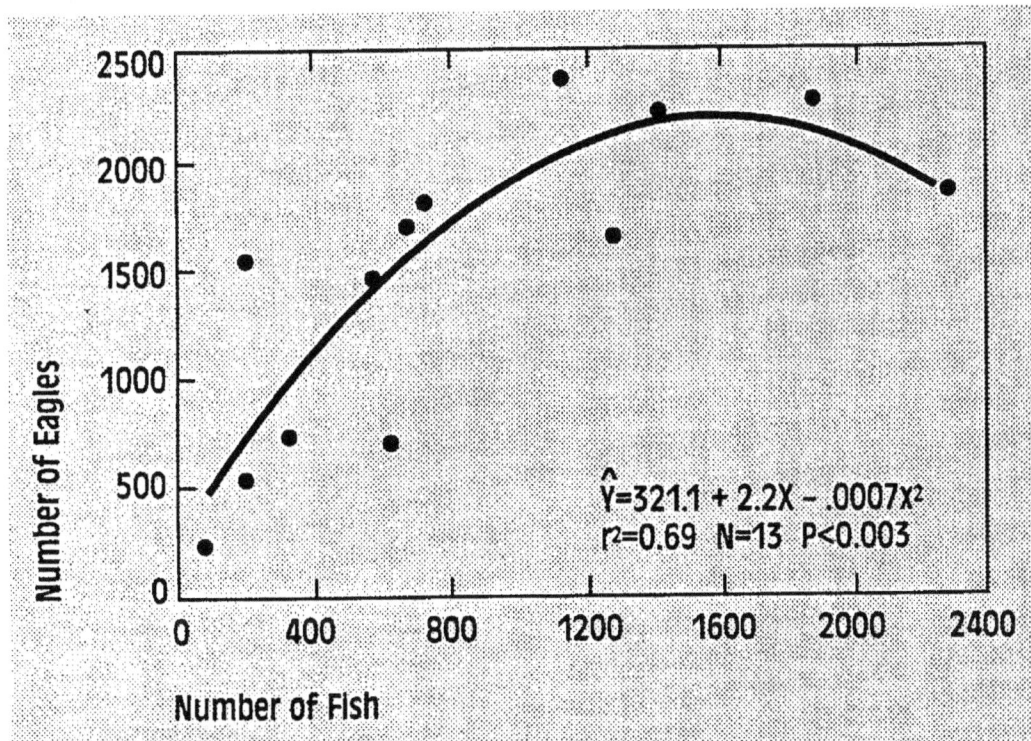

Figure 2. Relationships between food availability and eagle numbers in the Council Grounds, Chilkat River, Alaska. From Hansen et al. 1986.

The Northwest Coast Environment

The Pacific northwest coast is a stunning landscape where the glaciated Coast Mountains abut the Pacific Ocean. The region's elevated topography and cool, maritime climate maintain vast ice fields which for millennia cut deep U-shaped valleys and fiords and left countless coastal islands. An expansive coniferous rainforest dominates the lowlands and the coastal waters are among the most productive in the world.

Extensive upwellings bring nutrient-rich deep water to the ocean surface. Productivity is further enhanced by mineral sediments flowing from glacier-fed rivers. These nutrients are harvested by plankton and eventually move up the food chain to support a diverse fish community including Pacific herring, the eulachon, cod, flatfishes and five species of Pacific salmon. All of these fish provide food for Bald Eagles (Armstrong 2008).

The northwest coast is remarkably dynamic. A hierarchy of natural disturbance regimes generates cycles of landscape dynamics at various temporal and spatial scales (Hansen et al. 1986). Each of these disturbance cycles has a unique influence on the eagle. For example, one very large-scale perturbation is the fluctuation in global climate that results in ice ages about every 100,000 years. Continental glaciers overrode the northwest coast repeatedly during the Pleistocene. The ice forced salmon to spawn south of the glaciers and scoured the land of vegetation. When the glaciers retreated, they left newly carved valleys that eventually were colonized by expanding salmon populations. These successive range restrictions are thought to have resulted in the divergence of Pacific salmon into the five species of today (Neave 1985).

Thus, long-term glacial cycles controlled the vegetation of the northwest coast and influenced the distribution and evolution of Pacific salmon. In turn, the abundance and range of the Bald Eagle undoubtedly waxed and waned with its food supply and habitats. It is likely that these events led to evolution of the traits we see in Bald Eagles today.

Importance of Food to Bald Eagle Survival

The agents that regulate survival in Bald Eagles are little known. For carcasses recovered in the Lower 48 states, gunshot wounds and collision with power lines are determined to be the leading causes of death (Evans 1982) and most researchers assume that these are primary factors limiting survival. Ecologists Mark Stalmaster (1981) and Steve Sherrod and colleagues (1976) suggest, however, that survival of eagles in Washington state and the Aleutian Islands is limited primarily by starvation.

Our studies in the Chilkat Valley support this hypothesis. In fact, we found that food is the web that interconnects virtually every aspect of Bald Eagle ecology. For example, eagle abundance in the Council Grounds correlated directly with the number of salmon available to the birds (Hansen et al. 1984. Figure 2).

Furthermore, eagles were concentrated in the valley where food was abundant but scarce elsewhere. Eagle population size was not, however, related to ambient temperature, ice coverage of the river, snow depth, or cloud cover.

The eagles' migratory movements also show their affinity for food patches. We placed small radio transmitters on 31 birds and then located them monthly from an airplane (Hodges et al. 1987). When winter food supply was depleted in the Council Grounds, the radio-tagged birds all rode the cold winds southward.

The adults remained in Southeast Alaska. Some of the adults joined feeding aggregations while others dispersed along the shoreline, presumably to obtain breeding territories. In contrast, the subadults, not constrained by breeding, moved much father south-up to 1,600 km away-and wintered along the coasts of British Columbia and Washington where salmon were still spawning. When food levels improved in Southeast Alaska in summer, some of the subadults returned north.

The ways eagles use habitat is further evidence of the ecological importance of food stress. The birds perch and roost in forests to minimize energy expended in thermoregulation. (See discussion in following section on Other Survival Strategies.) Along the northwest coast, then, periods of overwhelming food abundance are offset by times of great scarcity. It is during those bottlenecks when food is sparse that eagle survival is limited primarily by starvation.

Importance of Food to Bald Eagle Reproduction

We learned that food also regulates many phases of reproduction in eagles of the northwest coast. Early investigators attributed the great losses in eagle productivity in eastern North America during the 1950s and 1960s to human disturbance, loss of habitat and shooting (Sprunt 1969). Subsequent studies strongly implicated chemical contaminants. James Grier (1982) of North Dakota State University found an inverse relationship between DDE (a metabolite of DDT) in eagle eggs and the number of young produced per breeding area. As DDE levels decreased after the ban on DDT, eagle productivity increased.

In the pristine haunts of the northwest coast, where use of pesticides and human development have been less acute, we expected eagle reproduction to be consistently high. We were wrong. More than half of the adults in the region failed to breed in 3 of 4 years of study in the 1970s (Hansen and Hodges 1985). Such a preponderance of non-breeding adults was particularly surprising because of the seemingly endless number of suitable nesting trees along the coast.

Even more alarming, however, was the pattern of eagle productivity in Seymour Canal on Admiralty Island, an area considered the richest eagle breeding habitat in North America. The average number of offspring produced there has fallen almost by half since 1978 (Hansen 1987). Also puzzling was the wide variability in nest success in the Chilkat Valley: 5 eaglets were fledged in 1980 compared to 38 in 1982 (Hansen et al. 1986). What factors regulate breeding in what is thought to be prime Bald Eagle habitat? Has natural disturbance produced long-term population cycles that include periodic breeding depressions? Or has human disturbance artificially reduced breeding?

In hopes of resolving the query, we tested hypotheses on chemical contaminants, habitat quality and food limitations (Hansen 1987). Data provided by Stanley Wiemeyer of the USFWS Patuxent Wildlife Research Center indicated that Bald Eagles in Southeast Alaska generally harbor no abnormal levels of toxins or heavy metals. Thus we rejected chemical contaminants as a factor limiting reproduction.

We found also that habitat quality was not strongly related to eagle productivity (Hansen 1987). The characteristics of nest sites that fledged young were not different from those of unsuccessful nest sites.

Our third hypothesis involved the importance of food abundance to reproduction. A combination of fortuitous natural events and planned field experiments provided strong evidence that food availability does indeed regulate many phases of reproduction in eagles. In 2 of the 4 years we worked in the Chilkat Valley, the carcasses of salmon that spawned in autumn, froze in the river ice and were preserved through winter. When the ice melted in spring, the fish were once again available to eagles.

We found that when these large food patches were present in spring, the density of breeding eagles was greater in the Council Grounds than along other river sections where food was scarce. But, in years when the rich food supply did not develop, breeding density was similar throughout the valley. We also found that eagles that nested near the food patches laid eggs earlier in spring than those more distant from food. (In many species of birds, individuals that lay earliest in the year fledge the most young.)

Later in the season, after food became scarce everywhere, we performed an experiment whereby food was regularly provided to some breeding pairs and not to others. The survival rates of offspring where food was supplemented were considerably greater than in other nests (Table 1). In experimental nests, 4 of 12 offspring survived while only 2 of 48 survived in the control nests.

Table 1. Effect of supplemental feeding of breeding Bald Eagles in the Chilkat Valley, Alaska on nest success and offspring survival between May 7 and June 7 1983. From Hansen 1987.

	Nest Status				Offspring Survival			
	Successful		Unsuccessful		Survived		Died	
Treatments	No.	%	No.	%	No.	%	No.	%
Food Provided	3	43	4	57	4	33	8	67
Control	2	8	27	93	2	4	46	96

We concluded from these breeding studies that: (1) food abundance in spring strongly influences if and when northwest coast eagles lay eggs, (2) habitat quality is important when eagles select a breeding area, partially because habitat aids in foraging and (3) feeding conditions during incubation and rearing regulate offspring survival.

These findings are useful for interpreting the seemingly odd reproductive patterns described earlier. First, the disparity in the number of chicks fledged among years in the Chilkat Valley was probably related to differences in foraging conditions. The glacier-fed Chilkat River is notoriously unstable in flow rate and turbidity so that foraging conditions vary greatly. Presumably, fledging rates were higher in years when feeding conditions were good.

The declining productivity in Seymour Canal in recent years was probably also food related. Food shortages there may have been caused by natural fish cycles, weather fluctuations, or overfishing by humans (Armstrong 2008).

Lastly, the surpluses of nonbreeding adult eagles throughout Southeast Alaska may have resulted because only a portion of the potential breeding sites in the region offer food supplies sufficient for females to attain breeding condition. When those sites are saturated, the remaining adults are forced to forego breeding that year. Because food supplies fluctuate, the number of suitable breeding sites and breeding rates changes between years. Thus, in contrast to findings in the Lower 48 states, our work shows that along the northwest coast both eagle survival and reproduction are limited by food shortages.

Pirating and Displays in Foraging

Bald Eagles have evolved elaborate feeding behavior to stave off starvation (Hansen 1986, Stalmaster 1987). For example, they obtain food both by hunting and by stealing from Ospreys, gulls and even other eagles. Naturalists have long noted this proclivity for pirating food. In fact, Benjamin Franklin thought the practice so cowardly that he campaigned against the eagle's placement on the seal of the new United States. More recently, Mark Stalmaster (1987) determined that stealing from conspecifics is very common even when food is abundant. He watched eagles stumble over fish carcasses as they moved to steal food from others.

Another intriguing feature of eagle foraging behavior is how quickly feeding eagles lose ownership of food items. Even the most aggressive pirates, after winning food, are themselves soon displaced. This situation is unusual among animals. Resource defenders typically enjoy a substantial advantage over challengers.

A third interesting characteristic of foraging eagles is their high rate of displaying. Both feeders and challengers perform ritualized postures and calls and we questioned the function of these behaviors.

In order to make sense of the eagles' elaborate foraging behavior we turned to evolutionary game theory (Maynard-Smith 1982). Classical game theory was developed to analyze human economic behavior. The theory has now been adapted to evolutionary problems where the currency is not money but Darwinian fitness. Game theory considers the costs and benefits of the resource procurement strategies open to organisms and identifies "unbeatable" strategies that may become fixed in a population over evolutionary time. These are called evolutionary stable strategies, or ESS. ESS theory has been applied to a variety of problems in ecology involving sex ratios, parental investment in offspring and plant growth, but it has probably been most useful for understanding animal contests.

Is the Bald Eagles' proclivity for pirating food even when food levels are high a maladaptive behavior? Game theory predicts that the frequencies of hunting and stealing will be balanced such that the payoffs of each strategy are equal. Our data support the predictions of game theory (Hansen 1986).

We closely observed eagles at feeding grounds, recording both their behavior and the number of bites of fish they consumed. We found that the benefits of hunting and stealing in terms of feeding rate were nearly identical (Figure 3). The risks of injury were also about the same for each strategy. Thus, contrary to the claims of Ben Franklin, pirating by eagles is neither cowardly nor suboptimal. The birds appear to employ evolutionary stable strategies, where they hunt and steal at frequencies that maximize food intake and minimize injury.

We also learned that individuals are not equally successful at winning contests. Larger eagles usually defeated smaller ones. Hungry eagles often won over those that were replete and birds descending from the air had a positional advantage over those on the ground. Furthermore, the eagles displayed the ability to assess their own size and hunger level relative to that of others. Individuals most often attacked others that were smaller and more satiated than themselves. In other words, attackers selected the opponents least likely to fight back.

These findings make clear why successful pirates were themselves soon displaced. Food holders simply had the odds against them. First, attackers held a more favorable position. Second, as feeders ate more, their likelihood of winning a contest decreased. And, third, pirates assessed the relative size and hunger level of opponents and chose to displace those most likely to yield. So, when the feeder lost a contest, it could gain the advantage of attacking and was likely to win the next contest. This unusual situation where resource defenders are at a disadvantage to challengers led to the chaotic scene at the feeding grounds, where hundreds of eagles continually supplanted one another at salmon carcasses. Interestingly, this type of infinite regress was predicted by game theorists a decade ago.

Finally, we gained insights into the function of ritualistic displays. Hungry eagles apparently capitalize on the assessment capabilities of others. They dissuade opponents from fighting by advertising that they are hungry and likely to win the contest. As a result, disputes over food are usually settled without escalated fighting. We observed talon-to-body contact in only 10 of 541 interactions. In none of the cases did the victim appear to be hurt.

Other Survival Strategies

High rates of pirating, elaborate displays and assessment behavior are but some of the strategies eagles use to obtain sufficient food in an environment where food supplies range from abundant to almost nonexistent. A boom-bust economy of this type was probably prevalent over much of North America in pre-settlement times and was perhaps a major force in shaping the evolution of Bald Eagles. How have the birds responded, then, to the selective pressures imposed by periodic food shortages?

Bald Eagles have adapted strategies that enhance food intake, reduce energy output and reduce injury (Hansen et al. 1986). One adaptation for maximizing food intake is an opportunistic diet. Although Bald Eagles are primarily fish eaters, they will consume virtually any vertebrate or crustacean they can safely catch or that they find dead. This "broad palate" has allowed the birds to adjust to novel food sources such as city dumps and fish kills at hydroelectric stations.

Bald Eagles locate ephemeral food patches through broad-scale movements. Our telemetry studies revealed that individuals may forage over an area exceeding 100,000 km² during the course of a year. Subadults, not constrained by the demands of breeding, are free to forage over much greater areas than are adults and natural selection appears to have favored a unique morphology for the subadult life history phase. Young birds have longer wing and tail feathers than adults, which gives them a greater wing area to body weight ratio (light wing loading) and facilitates the soaring flight necessary for broad-scale movements. In other words, subadults are built for distance rather than speed. The relatively heavy wing loading of adults, on the other hand, probably aids in the agile flight required for defending nests. (Incidentally, longer feathers make young birds look larger than adults, but adults and subadults actually weigh about the same.)

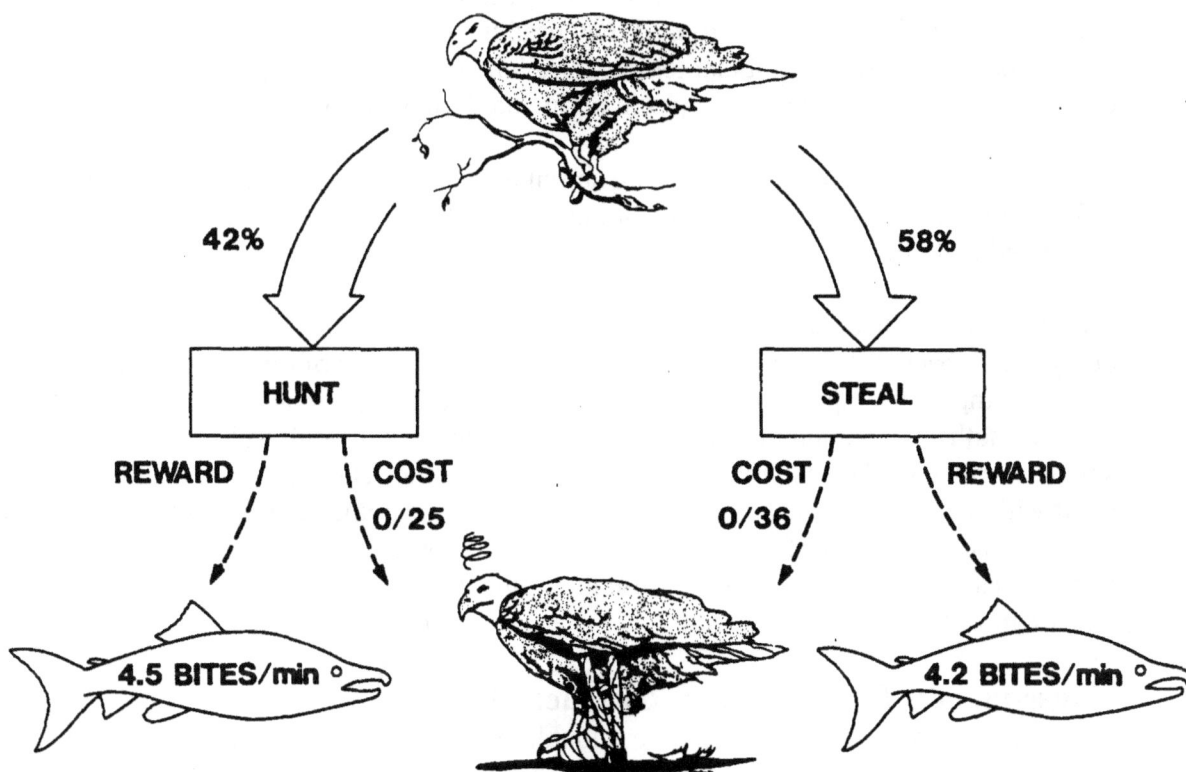

Figure 3. The frequencies of hunting and stealing and respective payoffs in feeding rate (bites/unit search and consumption time) and costs in incidence of injury for 14 eagles monitored over full feeding periods. From Hansen 1986.

Once Bald Eagles find a good place to forage, they locate food by searching for prey and for other eagles that appear to be near food. An eagle on the ground is more conspicuous than a prey item and thus a hungry eagle can increase its chances of finding food by cueing on both. The maximum distance at which an eagle can see a perched conspecific is unknown, but McClelland and his coworkers (1982) at Montana State University have estimated that an eagle can detect a soaring conspecific at a distance of more than 23 km. After eagles locate food, they often select those prey items that are most profitable. Stalmaster (1981) found that birds prefer salmon carcasses that have the tough skin already torn - these can be consumed more rapidly. They also avoid frozen and thus inedible carcasses by taking those that are in water.

Breeding Bald Eagles sometimes store food in their nests, perhaps for days. This apparent stockpiling may be a hedge against times when hunting is temporarily poor. Eagles reduce the threat of starvation not only by maximizing consumption but also by conserving energy. Stalmaster (1981) found in Washington that ambient temperature, wind speed, long-wave radiation and rainfall all were most stressful to eagles on gravel bars, intermediately stressful to eagles perched in streamside deciduous trees and least stressful to eagles in conifers. Further, he calculated that eagles saved 6% of their daily energy budget by roosting in conifers rather than in deciduous trees.

In the Chilkat Valley, eagles maximized time spent in protected habitats when the weather was harsh. At feeding grounds they used the gravel bars less and streamside cottonwood trees more as ambient temperature fell. They also sought refuge in the thick conifer forests on the mountain slopes at night and during storms.

Eagles also conserve energy by avoiding activities that are not essential. Stalmaster (1981) found that wintering eagles spent only about 1% of each day in flight and he concluded that idleness is an important strategy for winter survival.

Injury also jeopardizes eagle survival, so birds minimize risks by feeding on carrion that doesn't fight back as live prey does and by judging the abilities of other eagles so as to avoid getting into scrapes where they may be hurt. The dark plumage of subadult eagles may be another adaptation that serves to thwart attackers. A feeding subadult clothed in splotchy brown feathers is probably less visible to pirating fellow eagles than a feeding adult with brilliant white head and tail feathers. A cryptic plumage also may allow subadults better access to foraging in the territories of breeding adults, either because they are less likely to be seen, or because their plumage signals that they cannot breed and are not a threat to the owners.

Consequences for Population Characteristics

Thus far we have discussed the resources that limit eagles and the birds' resulting adaptations for reproduction and survival. Let's now use this information to interpret some of the characteristics of eagle populations.

Because of their mobility and their broad diet, Bald Eagles are distributed over much of North America. On the Pacific Northwest Coast, nesting eagles regularly space themselves along shorelines because of territorial behavior. But in times of food scarcity, nonbreeders congregate in the few places where food is abundant, such as in the Chilkat Valley. An important consequence of eagles being drawn together at such food patches is sociality.

To an individual eagle, neighboring conspecifics are features of the environment that may be an aid or a hindrance in obtaining food. When an individual bird can follow others to food, it benefits from sociality. However, a cost of group living is the possibility of having prey pirated by other eagles.

Pirating behavior has important ramifications at the population level. Pirates usually try to steal from small or young eagles because small, inexperienced birds are easy victims. When food is scarce these "low status" birds often do not get enough to eat and must either move elsewhere or starve. Thus, pirating is an internal regulating mechanism that influences survival rates and, in turn, population size. This mechanism results in at least some birds obtaining enough food to survive stress periods.

E.L. Boeker conducting Bald Eagle studies on the Chilkat River. Photo by Phil Schempf, USFWS.

Aggressive behavior related to breeding also helps regulate eagle populations along the Northwest Coast. Territorial eagle populations claim a disproportionately large share of the suitable habitat. Although many eagles can survive in the region by making distant flights to ephemeral food patches, the only birds that can breed are those that can find and defend territories that offer a predictable food supply for a full six months. Such habitat is limited in the region, so a surplus of nonbreeders is probably typical. The size of the surplus probably varies from year to year as feeding conditions change.

Dorsal view of juvenile Bald Eagle fitted with radio transmitter on the Chilkat River. Photo by Andy Hansen.

The important implication here is that Bald Eagle breeding rates and nesting success may fluctuate drastically in natural systems. Thus, the reduced productivity in Seymour Canal since 1978 and low breeding rates throughout Southeast Alaska may be part of a natural population cycle (Figure 4). Another possibility is that human activities have reduced fish stocks in the area and thereby decreased suitable breeding habitat for eagles. If the latter is the case, surpluses of nonbreeders may be harbingers of serious population declines. The permanent presence of nonbreeders may also have evolutionary implications. Bald Eagles do not acquire adult plumage until they are four to six years of age. This prolonged subadult period may be an adaptation to strong competition for nest sites. Young eagles, being poor competitors for suitable nest sites, may maximize the number of offspring they produce over a lifetime by avoiding the risks of breeding too early. Delayed maturation also enhances survival because young birds unburdened by the traits necessary for reproduction, are free to have the cryptic plumage and lighter wing loading that improve their ability to find and defend food.

Implications for Conservation and Land Management

This look at the Bald Eagle in the fairly pristine habitats of the Pacific Northwest Coast has answered some of the questions about the birds' behavior and population dynamics. It is evident that the fabric of Bald Eagle ecology and evolution was woven by an ever-changing environment. A hierarchy of natural disturbances ranging from local storms to continental glaciers drove the dynamics of the two resources on which birds depend-food and habitat. Eagles responded to the changing resource patterns by evolving various adaptations to enhance survival and reproduction. These adaptations define the characteristics we see today in the Northwest Coast population.

With an awareness of the intricate relationship between environment and eagle ecology, it is easier to understand why populations in parts of North America have nearly collapsed in historic times. Disturbances imposed upon the landscape by European settlers were catastrophic compared to anything the eagles had experienced previously. Much of the continent was denuded of old-growth forests and anadromous fishes in only a few hundred years. These changes occurred too rapidly for eagles to adapt and consequently their numbers plummeted. The introduction of toxic chemicals into their environment further exacerbated the situation and the birds became nearly extinct in parts of their range.

Fortunately, in the 1970s the United States government unleashed a massive campaign to save its national symbol. Laws were promulgated to protect the eagle nationwide and to maintain critical habitats in the Lower 48 states. A total ban was placed on DDT. Many states funded programs to reintroduce the eagle into its former haunts.

Figure 4. Theoretical tong-term population cycles in Bald Eagles. (a) The number of breeders (solid line) increases until suitable habitat is saturated. Continued recruitment results in formation of a floating population (dashed line) which competes with breeders for food causing a reduction in breeding habitat. The reduced productivity leads to a drop in the number of floaters, food available to breeders increases and the cycle begins anew. (b) In time an equilibrium may be reached where breeding and floating populations remain stable. It is unlikely, however, that the carrying capacity of the breeding habitat remains constant as shown in (a) and (b). The abundance of suitable breeding habitat probable fluctuates between years to the populations of breeders and floaters do not reach equilibrium. From Hansen et al. 1986.

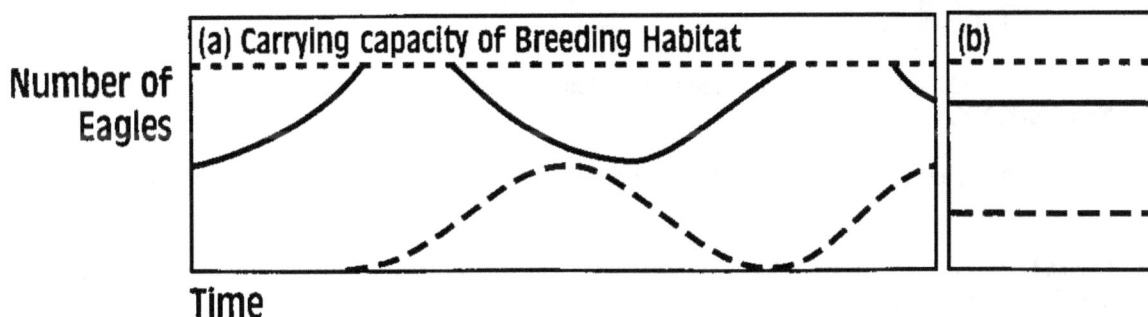

This conservation effort has yielded rewards. Eagle populations have stabilized in some places and are slowly increasing in others. But more can be done. The environment needs to be cleansed of deadly poisons such as PCBs, lead and mercury. The foods and habitats of eagles in the 48 contiguous states must be maintained where they still exist and reestablished where they have been destroyed. Human disturbance at eagle nests and wintering areas should be controlled.

Conservation efforts should be no less stringent along the Northwest Coast. The large eagle population there is as vulnerable to human-caused disturbances as were populations in eastern North America 300 years ago. Currently, the forest haunts of eagles are being destroyed by logging at an alarming rate in British Columbia and Southeast Alaska. Prudent management dictates that a coastal fringe of timber be maintained there. Furthermore, additional research is needed to determine if the poor productivity of eagles in Southeast Alaska is a result of overfishing by people.

Indeed, the Chilkat Valley itself is serving as a testing ground for new management techniques. The view from the banks of the Council Grounds reveals that the Chilkat Valley is now at an interface between a pristine past and a present of increasing resource development. Whether these landscape changes will allow the perpetuation of the Chilkat eagles or encourage their demise is dependent upon a bold experiment. In response to the urging of conservationists nationwide in 1980, the state of Alaska established a 25,000 hectare sanctuary for eagles. Lands surrounding the Alaska Chilkat Bald Eagle Preserve were at the same time open to logging and mining.

The outcome of this experiment may have considerable significance beyond the Chilkat Valley; eagles throughout the region may suffer if their great winter food supply in the Council Grounds is degraded. However, the talents and sincerity of the people managing the eagle preserve and surrounding state forest, along with the concern expressed by people nationwide, give cause for optimism about the fate of Bald Eagle populations on the Pacific Northwest Coast and throughout the United States.

Literature Cited

Armstrong, R. H. 2008. The importance of fish to Bald Eagles in Southeast Alaska: A review. In: Wright, B. A. and P. F. Schempf, eds. Bald Eagles in Alaska.

Cronan, W. 1983. Changes in the land. Indians, colonists and the ecology of New England. Hill and Wang, New York, NY.

Dawson, W. L. and J. H. Bowles. 1909. The birds of Washington, Vol. 2. Occidental Publ. Co., Seattle, Wash.

Evans, D. L. 1982. Status report on 12 raptors. U.S. Dept. Int., Fish Wildl. Serv., Spec. Sci. Rep. Wildl. Vol. 238. 66pp.

Forbush, E. H. 1927. Birds of Massachusetts. Norwood Press, Norwood, Mass.

Gerrard, J. M. and G. R. Bortolotti. 1988. The Bald Eagle-haunts and habitats of a wilderness monarch. Smithsonian Inst. Press, Washington, D.C. 178pp.

Grier, G. W. 1982. Ban of DDT and subsequent recovery of reproduction in Bald Eagles. Science 218:1232-1234.

Hansen, A. J. 1986. Fighting behavior in Bald Eagles: a test of game theory. Ecology 67 (3):787-797.

Hansen, A. J. 1987. Regulation of Bald Eagle reproduction rates in Southeast Alaska. Ecology 68 (5):1387-1392.

Hansen, A. J., E. L. Boeker, J. I. Hodges and D. R. Cline. 1984. Bald Eagles in the Chilkat Valley, Alaska: ecology, behavior and management. Final Rep., Chilkat River Coop. Bald Eagle Study. Nat. Audubon Soc., Anchorage, AK. 27pp.

Hansen, A. J., M. I. Dyer, H. H. Shugart and E. L. Boeker. 1986. Behavioral ecology of Bald Eagles along the Pacific Northwest coast: a landscape perspective. Oak Ridge National Laboratory, Environmental Sci. Div. Pub. No. 2548. Oak Ridge TN. 166pp.

Hansen, A. J. and J. I. Hodges, Jr. 1985. High rates of nonbreeding adult bald eagles in Southeastern Alaska. J. Wildl. Manage. 49:454-458.

Hodges, J. I., Jr., J. G. King and F. C. Robards. 1979. Resurvey of Bald Eagle breeding population of Southeast Alaska. J. Wildl. Manage. 43:219-221.

Hodges, J. I., Jr., J. G. King and R. Davies. 1984. Bald Eagle breeding population survey of coastal British Columbia. J. Wildl. Manage. 48(3):993-998.

Hodges, J. I., Jr., E. L. Boeker and A. J. Hansen. 1987. Movements of radio-tagged Bald Eagles, *Haliaeetus leucocephalus*, in and from Southeast Alaska. Can. Field. Nat. 101:136-140.

Maynard-Smith, J. 1982. Evolution and theory of games. Cambridge Univ. Press, New York, NY.

McClelland, B. R., L. S. Young, D. S. Shea, P. T McClelland, H. L. Allen and E. B. Spettigue. 1982. The Bald Eagle concentration in Glacier National Park, Montana: Origin, growth and variation in numbers. Living Bird 19:133-135.

Neave, F. 1985. The origin and speciation of *Oncorhynchus*. Trans. Royal Soc. Can. Ser. 3, 52 (5):25-40.

Netboy, A. 1974. The salmon: their fight for survival. Houghton Mifflin Co., Boston, MA.

Robards, F. C. and J. G. King. 2008. Nesting and productivity of Bald Eagles in Southeast Alaska - 1966. In: Wright, B. A. and P. F. Schempf, eds. Bald Eagles in Alaska.

Sherrod, S. K., C. M. White and F. S. L. Williamson. 1976. Biology of the Bald Eagle on Amchitka Island, Alaska. Living Bird 15:143-182.

Smith, C. L. 1979. Salmon fisheries of the Columbia. Oregon State Univ. Press, Corvallis, OR.

Sprunt, A., IV. 1969. Population trends of the Bald Eagle in North America. Pages 347-351. In: Hickey, J. J., ed. Peregrine Falcon populations: their biology and decline. Univ. Wisconsin Press. Madison, WI.

Stalmaster, M. V. 1981. Ecological energetics and foraging behavior of wintering Bald Eagles. Ph.D. Thesis, Utah State Univ., Logan, UT. 157pp.

Stalmaster, M. V. 1987. The Bald Eagle. Universe Books. New York, NY. 227pp.

Eagles on the Chilkat: Winter Ecology

Erwin L. Boeker

National Audubon Society, U.S. Fish and Wildlife Service (retired), Denver, CO

During fall and early winter, when food for Bald Eagles is limited in most parts of Southeast Alaska, thousands of eagles congregate in Alaska's Chilkat Valley just north of Haines. There, upwellings of warm water in the river and a late run of chum salmon provide abundant and accessible food. From 1979 to 1983, the National Audubon Society and the U.S. Fish and Wildlife Service conducted cooperative research that affirmed the importance of this world-class eagle habitat.

The Bald Eagle (*Haliaeetus leucocephalus*), the United States national symbol, inhabits the North American continent from the Gulf of Mexico to the Arctic. Although highly mobile and opportunistic in its feeding habits, it is usually found near seacoasts, inland lakes and rivers in association with fish.

In the contiguous 48 states, the largest breeding populations of Bald Eagles occur around the Great Lakes, in Florida, along the Atlantic coast, especially Chesapeake Bay and along the Pacific Northwest Coast. As a result of human encroachment, including the harvest of old-growth forests along coasts and rivers and the introduction of chemical toxins and other pollutants into the environment, populations in these regions steadily declined from 1940 to 1980. By 1978 numbers were so low the Federal Government classified all Bald Eagles in the contiguous 48 states as either endangered or threatened. Fortunately, with the banning of DDT in 1972 this trend has been reversed and presently populations are increasing in the lower 48 states.

With 30,000 miles of tidal shoreline on hundreds of islands and inland waterways still in relatively pristine condition, it is not surprising that Southeast Alaska and coastal British Columbia contain the largest breeding and wintering populations of Bald Eagles remaining in North America. To better understand the habits and needs of Bald Eagles in winter, an ecological study was conducted in the Chilkat Valley of Southeast Alaska during the winters of 1979-1983. This paper briefly summarizes the results of the study. In Alaska, although congregations of several hundred Bald Eagles normally occur on Kodiak Island, the Copper River Delta, Berners Bay near Juneau, the Stikine and Taku rivers and other salmon spawning areas in winter, none surpasses numbers of eagles found in the Chilkat Valley. This valley, located at the northern reaches of the inland waterway, 80 miles northwest of Juneau, is the winter home of the largest concentration of Bald Eagles in North America.

Thousands of eagles choose to winter in the Chilkat Valley simply because this area contains all their basic requirements for survival. As in all winter habitats, the abundance and availability of food is most important. In this regard the Chilkat Valley is unique, as it supports the largest and latest chum salmon (*Oncorhynchus keta*) run in Southeast Alaska. In addition, since portions of the Chilkat River remain ice-free due to unusual upwellings of warmer water, the eagles are assured an abundant and dependable food source throughout much of the critical winter period.

Other important components of winter eagle habitat, such as proper dispersion of perch and roost sites and shelter from strong winds and storms, are well provided by physical features of the Chilkat Valley. The valley is bordered by mountains ranging to 6,000 feet in elevation. Steep slopes are covered by Sitka spruce (*Picea sitchensis*), western hemlock (*Tsuga heterophylla*) and mountain hemlock (*T. mertensiana*). The valley floor is dominated by the Chilkat River which is joined on its path to the sea by the Klehini, Tsirku and Takhin rivers. The Chilkat River originates in Canada as a glacier-fed stream some 50 miles north of Haines, Alaska. It broadens to a wide flood plain with braided channels, extensive gravel bars and islands covered with dense stands of black cottonwoods (*Populus trichocarpa*) in the vicinity of Klukwan, a Chilkat Indian village 23 miles north of Haines. Here the cottonwoods are well-distributed near feeding areas along the river and they provide eagles with optimum roost sites and perches for hunting and resting in the fall and early winter. Later in the winter, during periods of cold weather, many eagles abandon the cottonwood roosts for more protected conifer sites on the slopes of the valley.

The climate of the Chilkat Valley is largely maritime. Moist air uplifted by the coastal mountains produces typically cool summers, moderate winters and considerable precipitation well distributed throughout the year. Barometric instability between the warm, moist air mass and cold, dry interior high pressure systems causes wide variations in temperature and wind conditions in winter. For example, temperature differences of 10°F are common between the mouth of the Chilkat River and points 20 miles upstream. On occasion, when winds are blowing in excess of 60 mph at the mouth of the river, it is calm upstream. Thus, the Chilkat River eagles are not subjected to much of the harsh winter weather experienced by other wintering eagle populations in Southeast Alaska. Beginning in September and continuing through late autumn, thousands of Bald Eagles move into the Chilkat Valley from surrounding areas. Population peaks, as determined by combined aerial and ground counts during the course of our study, varied from 3,100 to 3,700 birds. Early in the season eagles are found widely distributed throughout the valley. By late October, as ice begins to form and fish become less abundant in tributary streams, the birds begin to concentrate along a 5-mile stretch of the Chilkat Valley below the village of Klukwan. This area, where on occasion more than 2,000 eagles can be viewed from one spot, is known as the Council Grounds and includes the mouth of the Tsirku River, which is the source of the Chilkat Valley's unusual warm water upwellings.

Although much of the surface water in the "Council Grounds" remains ice free during the winter, there are times when shelf ice builds from the edges of open channels to a point where salmon carcasses are either frozen in the ice or are in water so deep they cannot be reached by the eagles. When this happens, usually in late December or January, the birds are forced to leave the valley and search for a new food source.

Tracking data for 31 eagles, marked with radio transmitters in the Chilkat Valley during the course of the study, revealed that upon leaving the valley the birds initially move into the northern half of Southeast Alaska. Adults tended to remain in this area; immatures spread out southward. Half of the marked immatures ended up in British Columbia and Washington state, which attests to their remarkable mobility.

Bald Eagle along the Chilkat River, Alaska. Photo by E. L. Boeker.

The total number of individual eagles that annually use the Chilkat Valley is unknown. However, some radio marked eagles moved out of and back into the area several times before their final departure. These data suggest some degree of population turnover during the winter and may indicate that the valley actually supports considerably more eagles than recorded on daily and weekly counts.

There can be little doubt that the Chilkat Valley contributes much to the overall well being of Alaska Bald Eagles. The timing and size of the fall chum salmon run is especially important for first-year eagles because it provides an easily accessible and abundant food supply at a time when these birds are learning to survive on their own. Frequently, in areas where food is more limited, post fledging mortality due to starvation is common because young birds simply do not have sufficient time to develop the hunting skills needed to survive. The food in the Chilkat Valley also greatly benefits breeding eagles because here, as opposed to other winter areas where food is not as abundant, the birds are not required to expend vast amounts of energy to maintain body condition. As a result, they are in prime physical condition at the onset of the breeding season.

To assure permanent protection for this special and unique habitat, legislation establishing the 49,000 acre Alaska Chilkat Bald Eagle Preserve was signed into law in 1982. This action was certainly an important first step in assuring a more secure future for Alaska Bald Eagles, but much more needs to be done. Threatening landscape changes are occurring at a rapid pace in Alaska with the steadily increasing demand for fish, timber and minerals. Also, industrial accidents such as the 1989 *Exxon Valdez* oil spill in Prince William Sound demonstrate that even Alaska Bald Eagles are living in a rapidly changing and perilous world.

For a detailed account of the Chilkat Bald Eagle study see: Hansen, A. J., E. L. Boeker, J. I. Hodges and D. R. Cline. 1984. Bald Eagles of the Chilkat Valley, Alaska: ecology, behavior and management. Natl. Audubon Soc., Anchorage, Alas. 27 pp.

Causes of Mortality in Alaskan Bald Eagles

Nancy J. Thomas

U.S. Fish and Wildlife Service, Madison, WI

The U.S. Fish and Wildlife Service has been documenting the causes of death in Bald Eagles (*Haliaeetus leucocephalus*) from all parts of the United States including Alaska for more than 25 years. The process involves conducting a complete postmortem examination called a necropsy. A necropsy provides a more accurate assessment of the cause of death than would reliance on external appearances or field circumstances alone.

Problems with environmental contaminants and dwindling populations often focus attention on the causes of Bald Eagle deaths in the Lower 48 states. In contrast, understanding the causes of Alaskan Bald Eagle deaths is of particular interest because of the unique population status of eagles in Alaska: They are a stable population, not listed by the Federal Government as threatened or endangered and they're in a relatively contaminant-free environment. The following report summarizes the necropsy findings from 344 Alaskan Bald Eagles.

Methods

From 1975 through February 1989, 344 Alaskan Bald Eagles collected in the wild were submitted to the National Wildlife Health Research Center, Madison, Wisconsin for necropsy (Figure 1). All birds were collected prior to the *Exxon Valdez* oil spill. Necropsy results from 27 eagles collected prior to 1975 were published previously (Coon et al. 1970, Mulhern et al. 1970, Prouty et al. 1977). Any Alaskan Bald Eagle found dead in the wild during the study period was accepted for necropsy; however, it is unlikely that every dead Bald Eagle found was submitted. Bald Eagles found sick or injured and treated for a short period prior to death were also included. Each bird was assigned to one of seven collection locations representing census areas (Figure 2). Carcasses were generally frozen and submitted within weeks or months of collection. Eleven different pathologists performed the examinations over the 15 year period of this study.

The necropsy entailed a methodical and complete examination of all external structures, all internal organs and the selection of appropriate tissue samples for laboratory tests as indicated by examination findings or history (Whiteman and Bickford 1989). Available laboratory tests included bacterial, fungal or viral isolations; parasite collection and identification; histopathology (microscopic examination of tissues); and chemical analysis for selected poisons or environmental contaminants. At the conclusion of all laboratory tests, the results of the necropsy and supportive tests were considered together to reach a knowledgeable conclusion regarding the cause of death. We determined the primary cause of the bird's death to be the initial factor responsible for its demise, not a complication of an original problem. A gunshot wound that resulted in a fatal infection, for example, would be listed as a gunshot mortality.

Bonferroni simultaneous confidence intervals were used to identify differences in the proportionate causes of death between the sexes or age groups (Kirk 1982). The chi-square test was used to compare body condition indices or the proportionate causes of death at different collection locations (Daniel 1978).

Number of Bald Eagles

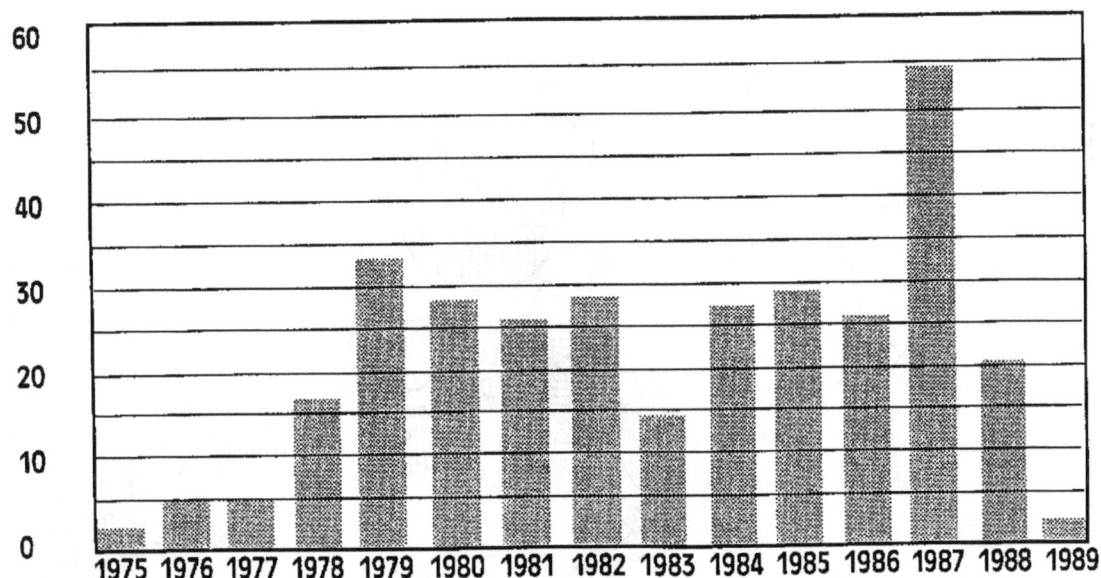

Figure 1. Collection date (year) of 322 Alaskan Bald Eagles, 1975–1989. (Twenty-two eagles with no collection date record are omitted).

Results and Discussion
Certainly every Alaskan Bald Eagle that died during the 15 years of the study is not present in the data set; this fact must be considered in interpreting the results. Public use of an area and public interest can affect the likelihood of a carcass being found and submitted. The mortality factor itself may influence collection probability; for example, an eagle that dies immediately after being struck by a vehicle is more likely to be found than a sick debilitated bird that can hide in remote habitat. However, the data set does identify Bald Eagle mortality factors and documents the minimum number of occurrences.

The causes of mortality by sex and age class for 344 Alaskan Bald Eagles are presented in Table 1. Fifty-six percent of the eagles submitted were males. Sixty-one percent had primarily white head and tail plumage (non-juvenile plumage). There were no significant differences in the causes of death of males versus females (P>0.1) or adults versus non-adults (P>0.1), so all groups were combined (Figure 3). The causes of death and their proportions were similar to those reviewed by Schmeling and Locke (1982) in reporting the results from examinations of 87 dead eagles early in the study. Statistical comparisons of the causes of death were made among only five collection locations and among the four most frequent diagnoses because only small numbers of birds fell into the other categories (Table 2). The proportion of electrocution, emaciation and gunshot diagnoses varied significantly (P<0.01) among the collection sites.

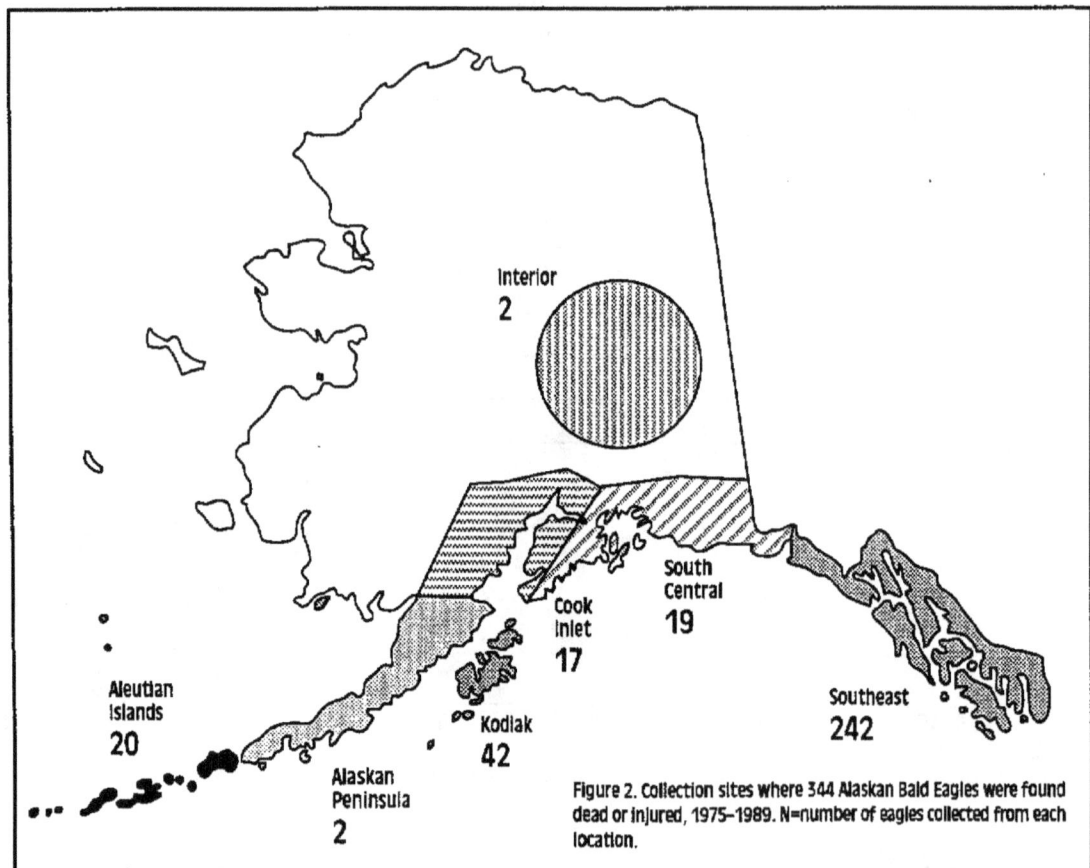

Figure 2. Collection sites where 344 Alaskan Bald Eagles were found dead or injured, 1975–1989. N=number of eagles collected from each location.

The four most frequent diagnoses of trauma, electrocution, emaciation and gunshot accounted for the deaths of 70% of the eagles submitted. Trauma was the single most frequent diagnosis (24.7%). Trauma was diagnosed at similar rates (P=0.47) in all five collection sites. Eagles that died from traumatic injuries most often showed the effects of blunt or impact trauma, such as fractured bones or internal hemorrhage. The exact cause of the injuries usually could not be identified by the wounds but the case histories often suggested these birds were hit by vehicles or collided with power lines or power poles. Trauma diagnoses also included birds with injuries that suggested aggressive encounters with other raptors, probably other eagles. Wounds in these cases consisted of relatively shallow punctures that were often associated with extensive muscle tearing or shredding, hemorrhage and sometimes fractures or bone perforations. These injuries were distinctly different from the deeply penetrating tracts of gunshot wounds. Aggression wounds had a somewhat characteristic anatomic distribution that could include the upper shoulders, back of the neck, legs below the knees, head and face and pectoral region.

Table 1. Causes of mortality in 344 Alaskan Bald Eagles, 1975-1989.

Cause of Death	Frequency		Sex*				Age*			
			Male		Female		Adult		Juvenile	
	No.	Percent	No.	Percent	No.	Percent	No.	Percent	No.	Percent
Trauma	85	24.7	44	24.7	36	25.9	57	5	27	20.5
Electrocution	60	17.5	33	18.5	26	18.7	32	15.5	28	21.2
Emaciation	53	15.4	33	18.5	18	13.0	31	15.1	21	15.9
Gunshot	44	12.8	20	11.3	17	12.2	30	14.6	14	10.6
Poisoning	25	7.3	11	6.2	14	10.1	14	6.8	11	8.3
Infectious Disease	13	3.8	5	2.8	6	4.3	5	2.4	7	5.3
Trapping	7	2.0	5	2.8	1	0.7	5	2.4	2	1.5
Other	57	16.5	25	15.2	21	15.0	32	15.5	22	16.7
Total	344	100.0	178	100.0	139	100.0	206	100.0	132	100.0

*Individuals In which sex/age were not recorded are omitted. There were no significant (P>0.1) differences in the causes of death of males versus females or adults verses juveniles.
+Percent of eagles per sex or age group.

Table 2. Causes of mortality in 340 Alaskan Bald Eagles from five collection sites, 1975-1989.

Cause of death					Frequency					
	Southeast		Kodiak		Aleutians		South Central		Cook Inlet	
	No.	Percent	No.	Percent	No.	Percent	No.	Percent	No.	Percent+
Trauma+	57	23.5	12	28.5	5	25.0*	7	36.8	2	11.8
Electrocution+	43	17.8	3	7.1	12	60.0*	0	0.0	2	11.8
Emaciation+	48	19.8	2	4.8	1	5.0	1	5.3	0	0.0
Gunshot+	23	9.5	13	30.9	0	0.0	1	5.3	7	41.2
Poisoning	15	6.2	2	4.8	1	5.0	7	36.8	0	0.0
Infectious	11	4.5	2	4.8	0	0.0*	0	0.0	0	0.0
Trapping	6	2.5	1	2.4	0	0	0	0	0	0.09
Other	39	16.2	7	16.7	1	5.0	3	15.8	6	35.2
Total	242	100.0	42	100.0	20	100.0*	19	100.0	17	100.0%

*Four eagles collected from the Alaska Peninsula and Interior Alaska are omitted because of the small sample size at these sites.
+Collection sites were compared by the chi-square test. Emaciation, electrocution and gunshot varied significantly (P<0.01) among the collection sites; trauma did not vary significantly.

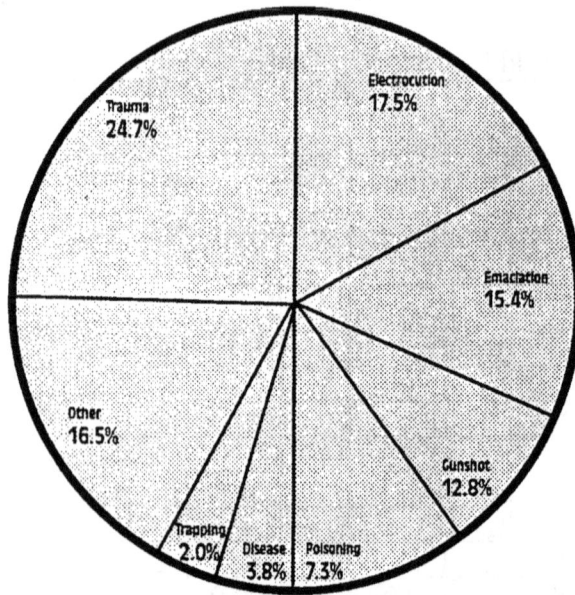

Figure 3. Proportionate causes of mortality in 344 Alaskan Bald Eagles, 1975-1989.

Electrocution was the second most frequent diagnosis (17.5%) among Alaskan eagles. The key to identifying this cause of death was the recognition of burns which could be as subtle as a small perforation in feathers or minute blisters on the feet. Electrocuted eagles were collected at the highest rate (60.0%) in the Aleutian Islands. However, electrocution also caused the death of a substantial number of eagles in Southeast Alaska and occurred in other locations as well.

Raptor electrocution is a manageable problem that can be virtually eliminated by power line or pole modifications and standards for new power line installations (Olendorff et al. 1981). The problem of Bald Eagle electrocution at the military base on Adak Island has been well documented and successfully addressed (see Byrd and Williams 2008).

Emaciation was found in 15.4% of the eagle carcasses examined. This diagnosis was reserved for cases in which there was no apparent physical explanation for the bird's debilitated condition. Birds diagnosed as emaciated had no evidence of crippling injuries that might have caused starvation. No toxicity was found despite the fact that most were tested for a variety of toxic compounds that can lead to emaciation. (Toxicological tests were not available for all emaciated eagles but 87% of the emaciated eagle carcasses were tested for lead; 51% for various organochlorine compounds such as "DDT", dieldrin, endrin and related compounds; and 23% for toxic levels of heavy metals other than lead.)

Eagle deaths that were attributed to emaciation occurred seasonally (Figure 4). The majority (83%) of the emaciated eagles were found dead from February through July. Emaciation was a consistent diagnosis, found in each of the 11 years from 1978 through 1988. Emaciation from unknown causes was diagnosed at a higher rate (19.8%) in Bald Eagles from Southeast Alaska than in eagles from other locations (0-5.3%).

No single explanation for the cause of emaciation in Alaskan Bald Eagles emerged from the data. A number of problems can be manifested as emaciation. Any individual bird could have had a metabolic or neurological problem that interfered with its nor mal food-gathering functions without leaving anatomic clues visible at necropsy. Some birds could have been affected by toxicity from one or more unrecognized compounds. In Southeast Alaska there is potential environmental contamination from organic compounds such as polychlorinated biphenyl compounds (PCBs) associated with pulp mills or with heavy metals such as mercury, which is found in mine tailings or natural deposits. A third possibility is that these birds had an inadequate or inaccessible food supply. The seasonal occurrence of emaciation sub gests that inclement weather could be a contributing factor.

This Bald Eagle was obviously this young person's prize and probably was shot to collect the bounty. Photo courtesy of Alaska State Library.

Gunshot mortalities were diagnosed in 12.8% of the eagles submitted. Birds in this category had crippling or fatal injuries characteristic of gunshot wounds. Many of the diagnoses were confirmed by the identification of metal fragments or shot pellets in the wound tissue or by radiograph. The proportion of gunshot mortalities was highest in eagles submitted from Kodiak Island (30.9%) and from Cook Inlet (41.2%). All of the gunshot mortalities from Cook Inlet were collected on the Kenai Peninsula. The gunshot birds from these two locations were collected during every month of the year except July and August.

The remainder (30%) of the submitted eagles had diagnoses divided among poisoning, infectious diseases, trapping, or miscellaneous categories that were combined as "other." Poisoning caused the deaths of 7.3% of the Bald Eagles examined. The majority of these poisoned birds (16 of 25) died from lead poisoning. Generally the source for Bald Eagle lead poisoning is assumed to be lead shot ingested with the tissues of prey, particularly waterfowl (Pattee and Hennes 1983). The stomachs of lead poisoned eagles are usually empty so there is no specific clue to the source of the lead, but occasionally the birds' stomachs contain lead shot or lead fragments. The 16 lead poisoned Alaskan Bald Eagles all had empty stomachs, but there was some circumstantial evidence suggesting lead shot caused the poisonings. In documenting over 200 Bald Eagle lead poisonings throughout the United States, we found that these cases peak following fall hunting season and occur only from October through June. Alaskan Bald Eagle lead poisonings occurred only from December through June (Figure 5). The majority (13 of 16) of the lead poisoned birds were collected in Southeast Alaska where Bald Eagles prey heavily on waterfowl from October through April (Imler and Kalmbach 1955). Alternatively there has been concern that environmental contamination from lead ore in Southeast Alaska presents a toxic hazard to wildlife. Since there is evidence that bioaccumulation of lead through tissues does not cause raptor lead poisoning (Pattee and Hennes 1983, Custer et al. 1984), it is generally assumed that eagles must ingest the highly concentrated metal itself to become poisoned. What is not clear is how spilled lead ore could become directly accessible to eagles.

Several Bald Eagle poisonings were caused by compounds other than lead. Two eagles died from strychnine poisoning in the Ketchikan area during summer 1979, but we have no further details on the circumstances surrounding this incident. On Kodiak Island in 1987, two Bald Eagles died and two were reported sick with barbiturate poisoning. These birds had been scavenging on the carcass of a horse that had been euthanized with pentobarbital. Five other Bald Eagles died from barbiturate poisoning during one episode on Spike Island in southcentral Alaska. Thirty-eight percent of the 344 eagles examined were screened for organochlorine compounds but none were found to have died from organochlorine poisoning (Kaiser et al. 1980, Reichel et al. 1984, Patuxent Wildlife Research Center, unpubl. data).

Infectious diseases caused the deaths of 3.8% of the Alaskan Bald Eagles examined. The single most common disease identified was avian pox, found in six eagles collected in Southeast Alaska and on Kodiak Island. Pox infection in Alaskan eagles was reported previously (Schmeling and Docherty 1982). Avian pox is a viral disease which can cause massive eruption of proliferative skin nodules, particularly in non-feathered skin. The nodules can impair vision and hearing and lead to severe debilitation or secondary bacterial infections. As in many other viral diseases, pox is more common in young immunologically naive birds, so this disease poses a particularly serious threat to translocation projects. The early lesion of avian pox may be only an unapparent small blister. If unrecognized, the disease may spread rapidly by contact among all birds in a hacking tower. If infected birds are released, pox may spread to other wild free-flying eagles in the area. Even if the infected birds are not released, the disease may be spread to wild birds via mechanical transmission by insects (Karstad 1971).

Number of Emaciated Bald Eagles

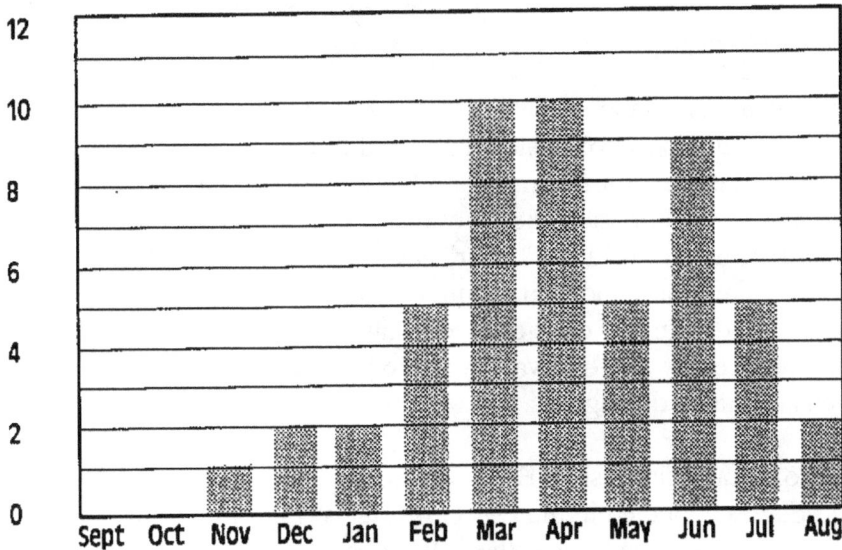

Figure 4. Collection date (month) of 51 emaciated Alaskan Bald Eagles (two emaciated eagles with no collection date record are omitted).

Number of Lead Poisoned Bald Eagles

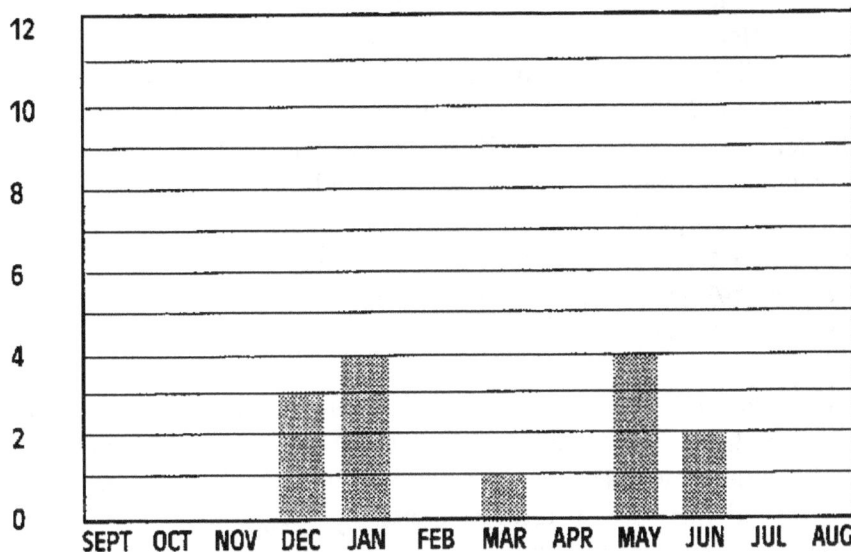

Figure 5. Collection date (month) of 14 lead poisoned Alaskan Bald Eagles. Two lead poisoned eagles with no collection date record are omitted.

Additional infectious diseases diagnosed in the Alaskan Bald Eagles examined included fungal and bacterial infections. Three eagles died from aspergillosis, a respiratory infection named after the causative agents, fungi of the genus *Aspergillus*. This disease is most common in eagles held in close confinement; however, only one of these three birds had any history of captivity for rehabilitation. Three eagles died from bacterial infections that were either generalized or confined to a joint. The bacterium identified in two of these birds was *Staphylococcus aureus*, a bacterium that may gain entry through skin wounds and tends to localize in the joints of young birds. One eagle had both a bacterial joint infection and avian pox.

Accidental trapping in leghold traps caused the deaths of 2.0% of the Bald Eagles submitted. Trapped eagles had constrictive or lacerating trap injuries to toes or legs. Some birds had additional physical complications from capture such as abrasions, bruising, evidence of drowning or emaciation.

The last diagnostic category, a miscellaneous category called "other," included 16.5% of the Alaskan Bald Eagles submitted. Approximately one-third of these carcasses were too decomposed to allow a meaningful examination. In another one-third no cause of death could be identified; and, in fact, the common causes of death were ruled out in these birds. The remaining one-third of eagles in the "other" category had complicated diagnoses in which the causes of their conditions could be one of several factors or several factors combined. Included in this category were eagles that died with visceral gout, the final condition produced by any of a variety of toxic, infectious or even nutritional factors that cause kidney damage.

The proportionate causes of death for Alaskan Bald Eagles were compared with similar data for 1919 other Bald Eagles collected in the Lower 48 states (Figures 3 and 6). Both data sets were similar. In both cases trauma was the most frequent diagnosis and trauma along with electrocution and gunshot comprised three of the four most frequent mortality factors. There were, however, two notable differences in the data sets. Emaciation was diagnosed in Alaskan Bald Eagles at almost three times the rate for eagles in the Lower 48 states. To examine this difference a little further, we also compared the adequacy of fat and muscle deposits described at necropsy in Alaskan Bald Eagles versus that in eagles from the Lower 48 states. We confined the comparison to the mortality factors that were not expected to be debilitating. Although 72% of the Alaskan Bald Eagles dying from trauma, electrocution and gunshot injuries were in normal body condition, a significantly ($P<0.002$) greater proportion (82%) of the eagles dying from the same factors in the Lower 48 states were in normal body condition. This finding suggests that the general state of nutrition of Alaskan Bald Eagles may be relatively poor in comparison to eagles in the Lower 48.

In the second notable difference, poisoning was diagnosed at more than twice the rate in Bald Eagles in the Lower 48 states than it was in eagles from Alaska. Approximately one-half of the poisonings in the Lower 48 states were caused by lead and the majority of the remainder were due to pesticides. The historic problems with organochlorine compounds such as DDT were represented in the earlier period of the data set, however, recent poisonings in the Lower 48 states were often due to the organophosphorus or carbonated pesticides, the pesticides that replaced "DDT." Although the compounds used in later years break down relatively rapidly in the environment, birds including Bald Eagles are exquisitely sensitive to many of them. These new pesticides are the documented cause of more than 100 Bald Eagle deaths, usually subsequent to the eagles' feeding on carrion or bait in secondary poisoning episodes. Fortunately it appears that Alaska has been spared this problem to date, due to the sparsity of agricultural pesticide use.

Documentation of the causes of Alaskan Bald Eagle "sea" deaths over the past 15 years has provided an extensive database for future reference and has identified several problems pertinent to the management of this species. Losses of eagles due to electrocution have been greatly reduced in the Aleutian Islands by developing raptor-safe power line and power pole configurations. Similar management techniques could be successful in other areas. Because avian pox poses a threat to the success of translocation projects, particular caution must be applied to screening or quarantining eagles donated to such programs. Cases with law enforcement implications such as gunshot or trapping mortalities are probably underrepresented in this study since the carcasses of birds killed by these means may be purposely hidden. The numbers in this data set could indicate just the tip of the iceberg.

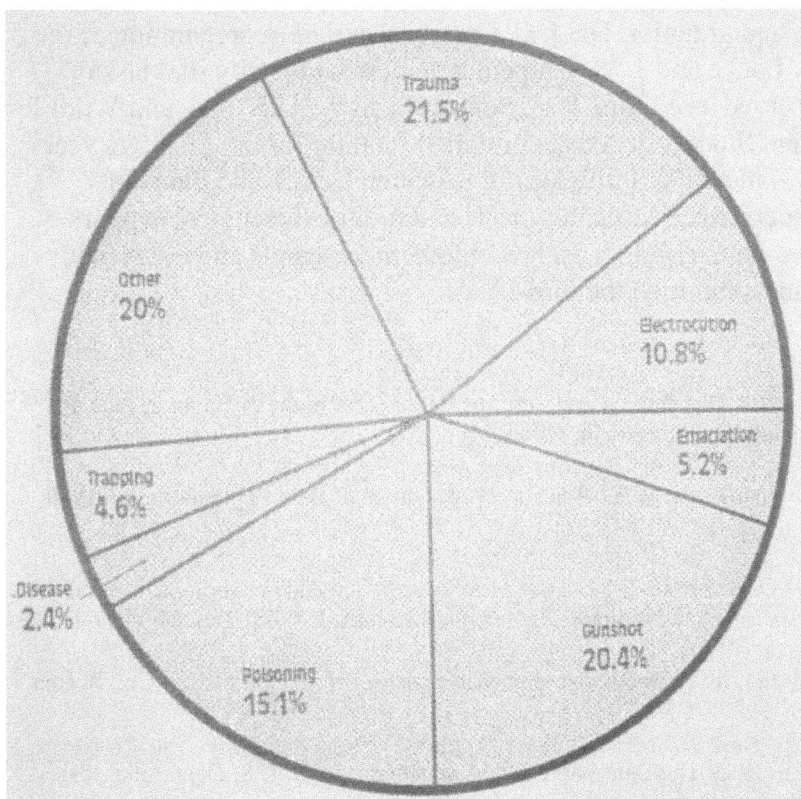

Figure 6. Proportionate causes of mortality in Bald Eagles collected in the contiguous United States, 1975-1988. N=1919.

These data also raise a number of interesting questions. What is the source of the lead that poisons Alaskan Bald Eagles? There are similarities to lead poisoning patterns in the remainder of the United States, but, alternatively, unique environmental sources may exist in Alaska. Why does emaciation appear to be particularly common in Bald Eagles of Southeast Alaska? As some other papers in this volume suggest, nutrition, toxins or other factors may be affecting the body condition or reducing the survival of Alaskan Bald Eagles. These and other questions will be answered only by future investigations.

Acknowledgements

Diagnostic work depends on the coordinated efforts of many people. I wish to acknowledge the efforts of the other pathologists who examined these eagles: Drs. L. N. Locke, S. K. Schmeling, L. Sileo, R. K. Stroud, L. Siegfried, S. Kerr, S. Hurley, P. Gullett, T. J. Roffe and K. Woods. Dr. M. D. Samuel provided statistical consultation. D. Johnson prepared the data and graphics. Dr. J. C. Franson assisted in preparation of the manuscript and Drs. L. N. Locke and J. W. Carpenter and the University of Alaska Southeast Editorial Staff served as editors. P. F. Schempf and the U.S. Fish and Wildlife Service Raptor Management Studies in Alaska provided funding for the final two years of the project. Staff at the National Wildlife Health Research Center and Patuxent Wildlife Research Center performed laboratory tests and provided technical support. Finally this study depended on the biologists, law enforcement agents and other field personnel who collected and submitted the birds.

Literature Cited

Byrd, V. G. and J.C. Williams. 2008. Distribution and status of Bald Eagles in the Aleutian Islands. In: Wright, B.A. and P.F. Schempf, eds. Bald Eagles in Alaska.

Coon, N. C., L. N. Locke, E. Cromartie and W. L. Reichel. 1970. Causes of Bald Eagle mortality, 1960-1965. J. Wildl. Dis. 6:72-76.

Custer, T. W., J. C. Franson and O. H. Pattee. 1984. Tissue lead distribution and hematologic effects in American Kestrels (*Falco sparverius L.)* fed biologically incorporated lead. J. Wildl. Dis. 20(1):39-43.

Daniel, W. W. 1978. Pages 174-184. In: Applied nonparametric statistics. Houghton Mifflin Co., Boston, Mass.

Imler, R. H. and E. R. Kalmbach. 1955. The Bald Eagle and its economic status. U.S. Dept. Inter, Fish Wildl. Serv. Circular 30. Washington, D.C. 51 pp.

Kaiser, T. E., W. L. Reichel, L. N. Locke, E. Cromartie, A. J. Krynitsky, T. G. Lamont, B. M. Mulhern, R. M. Prouty, C. J. Stafford and D. M. Swineford. 1980. Organochlorine pesticide, PCB and PBB residues and necropsy data for Bald Eagles from 29 states-1975-77. Pestic. Monit. J. 13:145-149.

Karstad, L. 1971. Pox. Pages 34-41. In: J. W. Davis, R. C. Anderson, L. Karstad and D. O. Trainer, eds. Infectious and parasitic diseases of wild birds. Iowa State Univ. Press., Ames.

Kirk, R. E. 1982. Pages 106-109. In: Experimental Design: Procedures for the behavioral sciences, Second ed. Brooks/Cole Publ. Co., Monterey, Calif.

Mulhern, B. M., W. L. Reichel, L. N. Locke, T. G. Lamont, A. Belisle, E. Cromartie, G. E. Bagley and R. M. Prouty. 1970. Organochlorine residues and autopsy data from Bald Eagles, 1966-68. Pestic. Monit. J. 4(3):141-144.

Olendorff, R. R., A. D. Miller and R. N. Lehman. 1981. Suggested practices for raptor protection on power lines-The state of the art in 1981. Raptor Res. Found., Inc., Raptor Res. Rep. No. 4., St. Paul, Minn. 111 pp.

Pattee, O. H. and S. K. Hennes. 1983. Bald Eagles and waterfowl: the lead shot connection. Trans. North Am. Wildl. Nat. Resour. Conf. 48:230-237.

Prouty, R. M., W. L. Reichel, L. N. Locke, A. A. Belisle, E. Cromartie, T. E. Kaiser, T. G. Lamont, B. M. Mulhern and D. M. Swineford. 1977. Residues of organochlorine pesticides and polychlorinated biphenyls and autopsy data for Bald Eagles, 1973-74. Pestic. Monit. J. 11:134-137.

Reichel, W. L., S. K. Schmeling, E. Cromartie, T. E. Kaiser, A. J. Krynitsky, T. G. Lamont, B. M. Mulhern, R. M. Prouty, C. J. Stafford and D. M. Swineford. 1984. Pesticide, PCB and lead residues and necropsy data for Bald Eagles from 32 states1978-81. Environ. Monit. and Assessment 4:395-403.

Schmeling, S. K. and D. Docherty. 1982. Fatal avian pox in Bald Eagles from Alaska. Pages 255-262. In: W. N. Ladd and P F. Schempf, eds. Proc. of a symposium and workshop on raptor management and biology in Alaska and Western Canada, 17-20 February 1981, Anchorage, Alas. U.S. Dept. Inter., Fish Wildl. Serv., Anchorage, Alas. 335pp.

Schmeling, S. K. and L. N. Locke. 1982. Causes of mortality in 87 Alaskan eagles. Page 253. In: W. N. Ladd and P F. Schempf, eds. Proc. of a symposium and workshop on raptor management and biology in Alaska and Western Canada, 17-20 February 1981, Anchorage, Alas. U.S. Dept. Inter., Fish Wildl. Serv., Anchorage, Alas. 335pp.

Whiteman, C. E. and A. A. Bickford. 1989. Pages 241-242. In: Avian Disease Manual, Third ed. Am. Assoc. Avian Pathol., Kennett Square, Penn.

Population History and
Status

The Status of the Bald Eagle in Southeast Alaska

Michael J. Jacobson

U.S. Fish and Wildlife Service, Juneau, AK

Within the twentieth century the Bald Eagle (*Haliaeetus leucocephalus*) population in Alaska has undergone considerable change (Imler and Kalmbach 1955, Robards and King 1966, Hodges et al. 1979, Jacobson 1989). A lengthy period of outright persecution toward Bald Eagles occurred in Alaska between 1917 and 1952 when a bounty was placed on them. Records from the Alaska Territorial Treasurer show that a minimum of 128,273 Bald Eagles were killed and presented for bounty, with more than 100,000 coming from Southeast Alaska (Robards and King 2008).

No doubt many fishermen and fur farmers routinely shot eagles, whether turned in for bounty or not. It is also likely that a large number of eagles were killed or injured and never retrieved (Imler and Kalmbach 1955). Even though the last bounty was paid in 1952 and the territorial eagle bounty was finally repealed in 1953, many eagles continued to be killed. Human attitudes that eagles were an undesirable predator were slow to change.

Figure 1. Estimated number of adult Bald Eagles in Southeast Alaska.

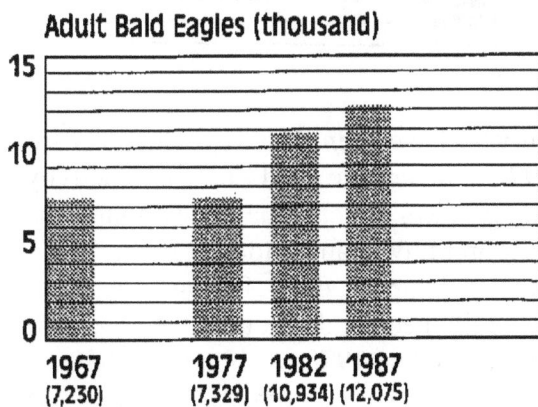

Adult Bald Eagles (thousand)

1967 (7,230)   1977 (7,329)   1982 (10,934)   1987 (12,075)

Figure 2. Peak counts of Bald Eagles in the Chilkat River Valley, Southeast Alaska, during fall 1984–1990.

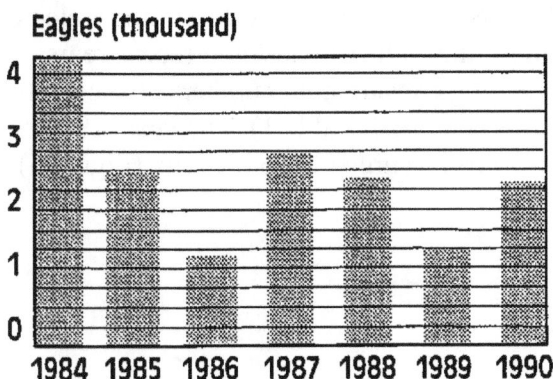

Eagles (thousand)

1984 1985 1986 1987 1988 1989 1990

Thus the number of eagles in Alaska was certainly reduced, but to what extent is unknown. Imler (1941) recorded the number of Bald Eagles seen during the summer of 1941 in various parts of Southeast Alaska and his findings show eagle density at about half of more recent years (Hansen and Hodges 1985).

Current Status

The most recent census of the adult population of Bald Eagles in Southeast Alaska was conducted in 1987 (Jacobson 1989, See editor's note.) This aerial survey was based an a sample of random plots originally devised by King et al. (1972). The same plots have been surveyed over a span of twenty years: 1967, 1977, 1982 and 1987. During this period, the Bald Eagle population of Southeast Alaska has shown a significant increase, from an estimated 7,230 ± 896 adults in 1967 to 12,075 ± 2,438 in 1987 at 95% confidence level (Figure 1). The population has recovered from the bounty period, stabilized and increased. Further, assuming that immature birds comprise 20% to 30% of the population, the total number of Bald Eagles in Southeast Alaska is estimated at 14,000 to 16,000. This represents about half of Alaska's Bald Eagles (J. Hodges unpubl. data, Schempf 1989), perhaps 35% of all Bald Eagles in the United States and about 20% of the total population (i.e., world population) in North America (Gerrard 1983, Stalmaster 1987, Johnsgard 1990).

The largest gathering of Bald Eagles - in fact the largest gathering of any eagle species in the world - occurs during the fall (October - December) in Southeast Alaska's Chilkat River drainage at the head of Lynn Canal. Peak counts from aerial surveys conducted in the valley during 1984-1990 have fluctuated from 1,124 to 3,988 birds, with an average of 2,277 (Figure 2).

Figure 3. Number of Bald Eagle eggs and chicks in nests in Seymour Canal, Southeast Alaska, during 1972-1990.

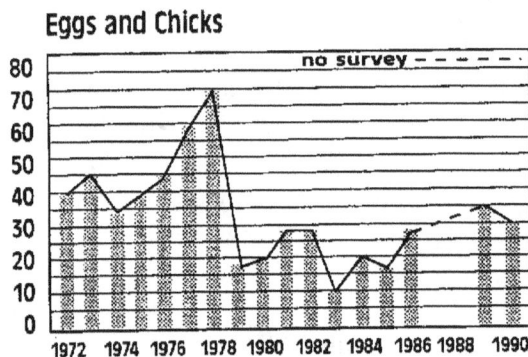

Figure 5. The number of Bald Eagle young produced from surveyed areas of Southeast Alaska.

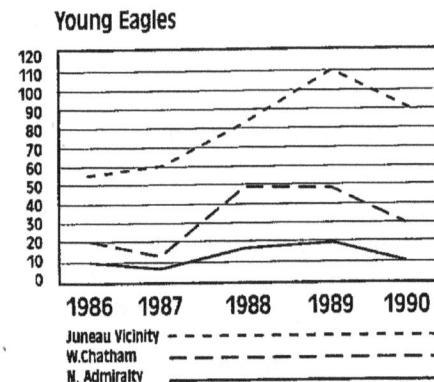

Figure 4. Map of Southeast Alaska showing areas surveyed for Bald Eagle productivity, and the Chilkat River region.

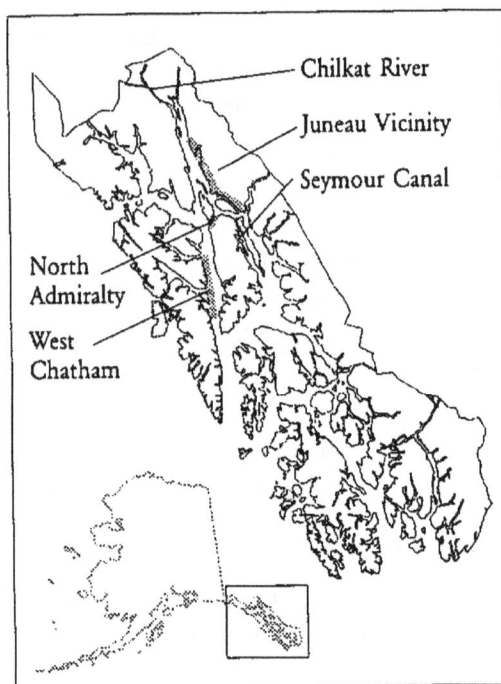

Surveys have been flown by helicopter since 1972 to determine Bald Eagle productivity along 87 km of coastline in Seymour Canal on Admiralty Island (Hodges 1982, Jacobson unpubl. data). Productivity has generally been high, though there was a period in the late 1970s and into the 1980s where it dropped (Figure 3). This decrease may be related to changes in the amount of food available (Hansen and Hodges 1985, Hansen 1987). Reproduction surveys have been consistently conducted in other selected areas of Southeast Alaska in recent years, showing considerable numbers of successful nests (Figure 4, Table 1). The years 1988-1990 had a surge of productivity (Figure 5).

Little is known about the survival rates of Bald Eagles in Southeast Alaska and survival may actually be the most important factor in Bald Eagle population maintenance and growth. Relatively small changes in survival rates may have a significant affect on Bald Eagle populations (Grier 1980). Since the population has increased in recent times, it can be assumed that survival rates for Southeast Alaska's Bald Eagles have been favorable.

Table 1. Bald Eagle productivity in Southeast Alaska.

Area Surveyed	Years Surveyed	Shoreline km (miles)	Average no. of active	Average no. of successful	Average no. of young produced	Young/ active nest	Young/ successful nest
Juneau vicinity	1986-90	219(136)	79.8	52.0	80.4	1.05	1.53
West Chatham	1986-90	84(52)	34.8	21.6	32.6	0.90	1.46
North	1986-90	59(36)	17.6	10.0	13.6	0.77	1.36
Seymour Canal	1972-90*	87(54)		22.4	33.1		1.41

* Not surveyed in 1987-88.

Discussion

I believe the population increase documented since the first comprehensive survey of 1967 is due to the following basic factors:

Elimination of the bounty (eagles are now protected by law, particularly the Bald Eagle Protection Act (16 U.S.C. 668-668d).

Most fish populations (the primary food of Bald Eagles) in Southeast Alaska have remained strong. Peoples' attitudes have changed. There has been increased public concern for the welfare of Bald Eagles. Alaskans no longer view eagles as undesirable predators. In turn, many eagles have become more tolerant of people. Eagles are seen living adjacent to most communities of Southeast Alaska. They have nested successfully among subdivisions, near roads and airports and other areas of human activity (Jacobson unpubl. data).

Problems

The situation is not so pleasant for Southeast Alaska's Bald Eagles as it may appear however. There has been steady growth and expansion of the human population; mining is undergoing a surge of growth; air traffic has multiplied; and there are many hatchery reared salmon which can compete with wild stocks, a situation which may ultimately prove detrimental to eagles. Also, an unknown number of eagles continue to be shot each year; they are frequently electrocuted; they are accidentally trapped; they have collisions with power lines and moving vehicles; and they suffer from contaminants such as lead. Moreover, eagles face the continuing threat of habitat loss. Suitable habitat for Bald Eagles is being altered and even eliminated, with the main problem being the elimination of waterfront areas which eagles have used since time immemorial. Large areas of public lands have been transferred to private ownership and there has been a tremendous increase in logging and road construction.

Bald Eagle nest tree left in a clear cut on Peratrovich Island, Southeast Alaska. Without the other trees creating a natural windbreak this eagle nest tree is susceptible to windthrow Photo by Mike Jacobson, USFWS.

Since 1969, the US. Fish and Wildlife Service vessel M/V Surfbird has provided support for Bald Eagle nest surveys and associated studies in Southeast Alaska. Photo by Mike Jacobson.

Furthermore, Alaska continues to have the least restrictive of all Bald Eagle habitat protection measures in the United States. The Bald Eagle Protection Act helps to protect the birds, their eggs, nests and nest trees, but it does not specifically protect surrounding habitat. Maintaining Bald Eagle habitat is essential to provide for the long term maintenance of the population.

In conclusion, the Bald Eagle population of Southeast Alaska has responded favorably to decreased persecution and is at its highest recorded level, but the coming years will have to increasingly focus on the need for protection of their habitat if the population is to remain in abundance.

Editor's Note: Aerial surveys to estimate the size of Southeast Alaska's adult Bald Eagle population were conducted in 1992 and again in 1997. The estimated number of adult eagles in 1992 was (13,341 +7-2,348 at 95% confidence level. The 1997 estimate was 12,026 (+ or - 3,108). The U.S. Forest Service's Tongass Land Management Plan Revision now restricts most timber harvest within 1,000 feet of the beach, the same area where the majority of Bald Eagles are found on the forest.

Literature Cited

Gerrard, J. M. 1983. A review of the current status of Bald Eagles in North America. Pages 5-21. In: D. M. Bird, ed. Biology and management of Bald Eagles and Ospreys. Harpell Press, Ste. Anne de Bellevue, Quebec. 325pp.

Crier, J. W. 1980. Modeling approaches to Bald Eagle population dynamics. Wildl. Soc. Bull. 8:316-322.

Hansen, A. J. and J. I. Hodges. 1985. High rates of non-breeding adult Bald Eagles in Southeastern Alaska. J. Wildl. Manage. 49(2):454-458.

Hansen, A. J. 1987. Regulation of Bald Eagle reproductive rates in Southeast Alaska. Ecol. 68(5):1387-1392.

Hodges, J. I., J. G. King and F. C. Robards. 1979. Resurvey of the Bald Eagle breeding population in Southeast Alaska. J. Wildl. Manage. 43(1):219-221.

Hodges, J. I. 1982. Bald Eagle nesting studies in Seymour Canal, Southeast Alaska. Condor 84:125-127.

Imler, R. H. 1941. Alaska Bald Eagle studies. U.S. Fish Wildl. Serv., Denver, Colo. 17pp.

Imler, R. H. and E. R. Kalmbach. 1955. The Bald Eagle and its economic status. U.S. Fish Wildl. Serv. Circ. 30. 51 pp.

Jacobson, M. J. 1989. A survey of the adult Bald Eagle population in Southeast Alaska. Unpubl. rep., U.S. Fish Wildl. Serv., Juneau, Alas. 6pp.

Johnsgard, P. A. 1990. Hawks, eagles and falcons of North America. Smithsonian Inst. Press, Washington, D.C. 403pp.

King, J. G., F. C. Robards and C. J. Lensink. 1972. Census of the Bald Eagle breeding population in Southeast Alaska. J. Wildl. Manage. 36(4):1292-1295.

Robards, F. C. and J. G. King. 2008. Nesting and productivity of Bald Eagles in Southeast Alaska. 1966. In: Wright, B.A. and P.F. Schempf, eds. Bald Eagles in Alaska.

Schempf, P. F. 1989. Raptors in Alaska. Pages 144-154. In: B. G. Pendleton, ed. Proc. West. Raptor Manage. Symp. and Workshop. Natl. Wildl. Fed. Sci. and Tech. Ser. No. 12, 317pp.

Stalmaster, M. V. 1987. The Bald Eagle. Universe Books, New York, N.Y. 227pp.

Nesting and Productivity of Bald Eagles in Southeast Alaska-1966

Fred C. Robards and James G. King

U.S. Fish and Wildlife Service, Juneau, AK

Southeast Alaska supports a dense population of Bald Eagles (*Haliaeetus leucocephalus*). At the time of this writing, there is little information on the past or present status of these birds. Bounty hunting, logging and reduction in salmon stocks may have altered the population level from pristine times. Future development of the area may cause changes in the population. Thus, in 1966, a study was set up to determine the present breeding population and productivity of Bald Eagles on Admiralty Island.

Southeast Alaska consists of steep, glacier ridden, fjord cut, mainland coast fringed with innumerable offshore mountain islands, islets and rocks. Most of the lower elevations of this land are covered with climax rain forest of Sitka spruce (*Picea sitchensis*) and western hemlock (*Tsuga heterophylla*). Several large river valleys have extensive growths of cottonwood (*Populus trichocarpa*), a successional species. The climate is mild and moist with annual precipitation averaging about 99 inches but varying locally due to the effects of the high mountains. The average January temperature is 30 degrees F and the July average is 59 degrees F. Thousands of streams and rivers provide spawning habitat for millions of salmon and other fish. The area contains an estimated 13,000 miles of salt water shoreline.

Admiralty Island lies in the northern portion of Southeast Alaska, is about 100 miles long and up to 30 miles wide. Its mountains rise to an elevation of 4,000 feet. The island is separated from the mainland by 4 to 16 miles of salt water and separated from the Pacific Ocean by another range of islands. The spruce and hemlock forest overhangs the entire beach line and less than 10% has been logged. The Admiralty Island study area contains 6.5% of the total coastline of Southeast Alaska.

The Chilkat Valley lies 66 miles north of Admiralty Island on the mainland and contains extensive growths of cottonwood. The Chilkat River system provides spawning habitat for numerous salmon runs.

Although Southeast Alaska has not been badly marred by the hand of man, it is not an untouched ecosystem. Between 1785 and 1910 sea otters were exterminated from Southeast Alaska. Salmon fishing began about 1878 and after about 1942 salmon stocks began a decline and were reduced from former abundance. A small amount of logging was done in connection with the mining, fur and salmon industries. Since 1940 the logging industry has been steadily increasing.

Table 1. Bald Eagle bounty data 1917 to 1952.

Period	Appropriation	Bounty Per Eagle	Eagles Bountied	Funds Expended
1917-1918	$7,500	$.50	5,229	$ 2,614.50
1919-1920	5,000	.50	4,239	2,119.50
1921-1922	2,500	.50	4,528	2,263.50
1923-1914	18,000	1.00	20,497	20,497.00
1925-1926	20,000	1.00	7,312	7,312.00
1927-1928	12,500	1.00	27,843	27,843.00
1929-1930	10,000	1.00	8,196	8,196.00
1931-1932	8,000	1.00	4,999	4,999.00
1933-1934	10,500	1.00	7,490	7,490.00
1935-1936	12,000	1.00	3,009	3,009.00
1937-1938	15,000	1.00	12,793	12,793.00
1939-1940	10,000	1.00	7,970	7,970.00
1941-1942	none	1.00	1,872	1,872.00
1943-1944	none	-	-	
1945-1946	1,528*	1.00	1,528	1,528.00
1947-1948	no bounty	-	-	
1949-1950	15,000**	2.00	6,450	12,900.00
1951-1952	17,000	2.00	4,318	9,363.00
1953	no bounty***			
Totals	$164,528		128,273	$133,042.50

*Bounty Act of 1917 repealed. $1,528.00 appropriated to pay 1941-1941 claims
**Bounty Act of 1949 enacted. Bounty raised to $2.00 per eagle.
*** Bounty Act of 1949 repealed.

The Territorial Legislature established a $.50 bounty on eagles in 1917 in hopes of protecting salmon. In 1923 the bounty was increased to $1.00. After 1941 the Legislature failed to appropriate bounty money and the system was discarded in 1946. A new Bounty Act was passed in 1949 paying $2.00 per eagle and remained in effect until nullified by Federal protection in 1952.

Most of the records dealing with the eagle bounty system have been destroyed thus it is no longer possible to know how many eagles were killed in any given year. The annual reports of the Alaska territorial treasurer do show how many eagles were bountied for each two year legislative period. These records show 128,273 eagles were killed and presented for bounty from 1917 to 1952. Bald Eagle data for the treasurer's reports are included in Table 1.

Of course, not all eagles bountied were taken from Southeast Alaska. Some of the treasurer's reports do break down the number of bounties by judicial Division indicating that about 80% of those bountied were from Southeast Alaska. Table 2 summarizes eagle bounties paid by area.

In recent years pesticides have been used in a few isolated areas of Southeast Alaska, but we can assume this region is largely free from this menace.

Table 2. Bald Eagles Bountied in Judicial Divisions.

Period of Record	Southeast 1st Judicial Division	Northwest 2nd Judicial Division	South/Southwest 3rd Judicial Division	Interior 4th Judicial Division
1917-18	3,958	0	1,270	1
1921-22	2,023	0	240	1
1923-24	11,475	2	3,195	0
1925-26	7,008	1	299	3
1939-40	5,551	3	2,408	8
1941-42	1,110	0	762	0
Totals	31,125	6	8,174	13

Objectives:

The overall objectives of this study were to determine the status and productivity of Bald Eagles on relatively undisturbed areas in Southeast Alaska.

We intended to develop survey methods that could be used in other parts of Alaska and also that could be repeated from time to time to determine any change in status or productivity at some time in the future.

Methods:

Admiralty Island was selected as the primary study area as it represents a large relatively undisturbed block of Bald Eagle habitat. The shoreline was measured on one inch to the mile U.S.G.S. maps and divided into 86 plots of ten miles each. Islets immediately adjacent to the main island were included in the measurement. Ten plots were picked at random for intensive study. Observations were made from a four place Cessna 180 float plane, from a three place helicopter, from a 50 foot motor vessel and from a skiff with an outboard motor.

Most of the nests were located with the airplane using two or three observers. Repeated passes, sometimes as many as ten, would be made along the study area. All nests located were marked on one inch to the mile maps and other data were recorded (Table 3). The initial survey was made at a time when the snow had fallen from the branches of the trees but remained piled in nests. Subsequent searches were made after the presence of eagles in or near nests helped attract the observers' attention. A search was also made from the deck of the vessel and from the skiff. A few additional nests were located by this means. The searchers would continue surveys until repeated effort produced no new results. Nests were frequently difficult to see and obviously some nests must have been missed in spite of our best efforts.

The airplane was of no use in counting eggs or young, but the helicopter proved most effective. Eagles could be flushed from the nests successfully and they usually got well out of the way although returned to the nest almost immediately when the helicopter moved away. Two eagles showed some hostility toward the helicopter but the pilot maintained a position above any nearby birds where he could frustrate an intended attack with the blast of the prop wash.

Observations from the water, in spite of the opportunity to use binoculars, proved largely ineffective for locating nests. All observations in this report were made by the authors and Keith Banning and Karl Alstead of the Bureau of Sport Fisheries and Wildlife in Juneau.

Results:
Nest Location
Nests within the study area were all located in trees. A single ground nest, an active nest, was located on a treeless grass covered islet four miles offshore from Admiralty Island. This nest type is limited in this area, but is more common in treeless areas of western Alaska.

On Admiralty Island the entire beach fringe is covered with spruce-hemlock forests. Probably due to their larger, more suitable limb structure, 90% of the nests are located in spruce trees. Nest trees may be either alive or dead, but are always of the larger size in the area. Nests may be located at the extreme top of a tree where something has broken the tip above a whorl of branches. Nests may also be located in crotches or on clusters of branches below the top of the tree but always in the top third of the tree. Nests below the top of the growing tree are obviously the most difficult to see.

In the Chilkat Valley most nests are located in crotches of large cottonwood trees which fringe the channels of the river. These nests are easy to see before the leaves come out in the spring.

Most of the nests are located in trees near the water's edge, but some may be behind the beach fringe and up to 200 yards from the water. All nests are located in such a way that there is a clear flight path to a near point on the beach or river with no obstructions the bird would have to fly up over.

Table 3. Eagle data card.

Eagle Data Card - Bald or Golden

Observer's Name:
Address:
Transportation Used:
Date:
Geographic Location of Nest:
Usable Landmark to Relocate Nest:

Nesting Site
Merchantable Timber:
Tree Species:
Shrub Species:
Cliff or Other Location, Describe:
Height From Ground:
Height From See Level:

Nest Activity
No Activity:
Adults in Locality:
Active Nest Building:
Incubating Eggs:
Brooding Young:
Eggs in Neat, Number:
Young in Nest, Number:
Date of Hatch:
Date Young Fledged:
Mortality Observed:
Cause of Mortality:

Complete a data card for each observation of change
in nest status. Use reverse side for supplemental data
or to add notes on above.

Prevailing weather, soil type and other factors affect the overall height of tree growth and in some areas the timber is markedly stunted. Bald Eagles nest in the stunted timber at about the same rate as in the full growth stands, but always in the larger trees of the stand.

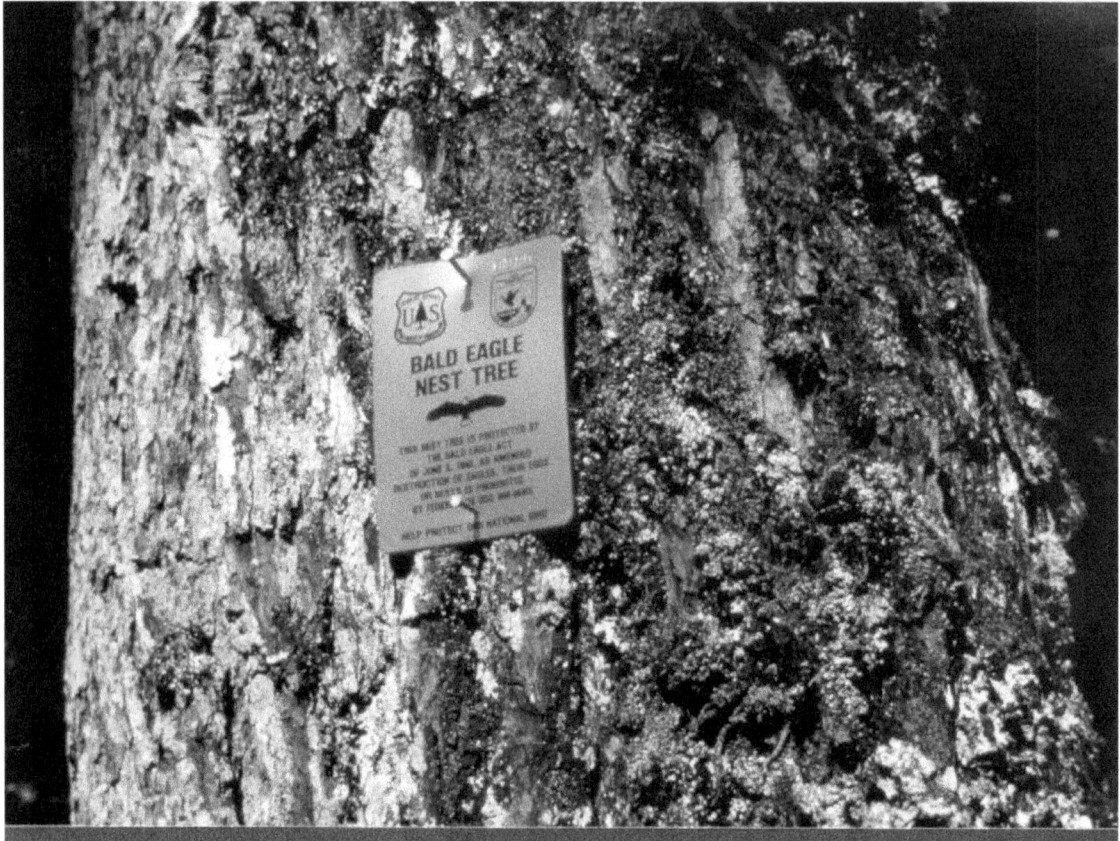

Bald Eagle nest tree sign used to mark nest trees under the cooperative agreement between the U.S. Fish and Wildlife Service and the U.S. Forest Service. Photo by USFWS.

Nest location on the Admiralty Island study area shows some selectivity toward certain types of beach frontage. The greatest density was found in areas fronting a wide expanse of open water. Second preference appeared to be small islands. Small confined bays seem to be less attractive and bays that are ice covered into the nesting season are not used at all (Table 4). Beach types were classified by one-half mile divisions for the entire study area. We found that the ten primary study plots were quite representative of the entire area. Beaches exposed to an open expanse of salt water may provide the best source of food.

Nests were fairly uniformly distributed (Table 4) except in the iced-in bays, in the several small patches of second growth timber where suitable trees were not available and in a few small areas adjacent to settlements where human harassment may be a factor. Exposure to the sun, locations of salmon streams and prevailing winds do not seem to influence nest site selection.

162

Nest Construction

Nest material can be drift picked from beaches or branches collected from dead trees and bushes. The nest platform is composed of sticks of all sizes up to four feet in length and two inches in diameter. The nest is lined with grass, twigs, seaweed and other debris. Many of the nests appear to have been in use for many years. Some nests, evidently not recently used, support a heavy growth of moss and grass.

Nest Density

The ten mile plot size proved large enough to contain a relatively representative amount of beach front types as described in the preceding section. Table 5 shows the density of nests per plot to be remarkably uniform. The Admiralty Island, Douglas Island and Auke Bay plots contain ten miles of beach. The Chilkat River plots contain ten miles of river frontage each.

Table 4. Relation of active nests to beach front type on Admiralty Island.

Total Indicated Type	Habitat Study Plot Active Nests Mileage	Study Plot by Type Mile	Nest Incidence by Type	Total Mile	Active Nests for Admiralty Is.
Open Coast	23	31.0	0.74	287	212
Protected Coast	6	15.5	0.39	80	31
Ice Free Bay	11	24.5	0.45	289	130
Iced-In Bay	0	6.5	0	85	0
Islands & Islets	13	22.5	0.58	119	69
Total	53	100.0	0.54	860	442

The function of the large number of inactive nests could not be determine from a one year study, but only a few a them had been abandoned long enough to support a dense growth of grass and other vegetation. The direct distance between nests on the plots was measured with calipers on the map. Table 6 shows the distance between active nests, between inactive nests and between all nests regardless of activity on the Admiralty Island and Chilkat River plots. It appears that these eagles do not nest closer than 700 yards to each other and this suggests a territory size.

Table 5. Comparison, nesting density, Admiralty Island, Douglas Island, Auke Bay and Chilkat River areas.

Study Area	Plot Number	Total Nests	Active Nests	Average Active Nests Per Mile	Percent of Total Active Nests
Admiralty Is.	7	14	5	0.5	
	19	13	7	0.7	
	21	10	5	0.5	
	24	14	5	0.5	
	27	11	5	0.5	
	36	14	5	0.5	
	45	14	6	0.6	
	53	16	6	0.6	
	54	11	4	0.4	
	82	16	5	0.5	
Totals		133	53	0.5	40%
Douglas Is.	1A	8	5	.5	
	2A	8	4	.4	
Auke Bay	3A	12	7	.7	
Totals		28	16	.5	57%
Chilkat River	1	7	5	.5	
	2	12	6	.6	
	3	9	4	.4	
	4	6	3	.3	
	5	6	2	.2	
	6	12	4	.4	
Totals		52	24	.4	46%
Total for all Plots 217		93	0.5	43%	

Nesting Period

During most of the year eagles are not observed using nest platforms for perching. Early in April eagles are seen perched in nests indicating the rehabilitation of nests has begun. The helicopter was used to check 72 nests on and adjacent to the Admiralty Island study area. During 1966, all birds with eggs were incubating on or before May 9, all eggs had hatched by June 7 and all young were well feathered and nearly ready to fly by July 7. A variation in size of nestlings was observed on June 7, indicating hatching dates may vary as much as two weeks.

Editors' Note: More recent studies have identified the inactive nests as old nests or nests not otherwise used by the eagles maintaining the territory. These nests may be used in subsequent years.

Table 6. Distance between nests in miles in SE Alaska.

Admiralty Island			
Number of Nests	43.00	68.00	119.00
Average Distance	1.12	.85	.55
Closest Nests	.40	.10	.10
Farthest Nests	4.00	2.50	4.00
Chilkat Valley			
Number of Nests	18.00	24.00	48.00
Average Distance	1.18	1.15	.76
Closest Nests	.60	.50	.20
Farthest Nests	2.00	2.60	1.70

Productivity

Table 7 summarizes data for the 72 nests checked by helicopter. The clutch size was from 1 to 3 eggs with an average of 1.96 eggs per nest. An 82% hatching success and a 72% survival rate to fledgling was determined.

Table 7. Productivity and survival rate of 72 SE Alaska nests.

No. In Nest	Eggs 5/9/66	Downy Young 6/7/66	Preflight Nestlings 7/7/66
0	0 nests	4 nests	9 nests
1	6 nests	20 nests	24 nests
2	63 nests	48 nests	39 nests
3	3 nests	0 nests	0 nests
Total	141 eggs	116 downy young	2 feathered nestlings

Survival rate in 72 SE Alaska nests

	Egg Survey 5/9/66	Downy Young Survey 6/7/66	Preflight Nestlings 7/7/66
Number	141 eggs	116 eaglets	102 eaglets
Average	1.96 per nest	1.61 per nest	1.42 per nest
Survival	100%	82%	72%

The 1966 production data from the 72 nests checked by helicopter was combined with data on active nests from the ten Admiralty Island study plots. This indicates that the entire study area may have produced 648 ±69 fledgling eaglets (Table 8).

Table 8. Indicated bald eagle production on Admiralty Island.

	Eggs (May)	Downy Young (June)	Pre-flight Nestlings (July)	
Minimum Nests	408	800	657	579
Maximum Nests	504	988	811	716
Average	894 ±94	734 ±77	648 ±69	

Conclusions

The objectives of the study were met. The researchers involved with this study did not expect eagles nests to be so numerous or to have such an even distribution. Of particular interest is the indication that the marine environment is the primary source for food for nestling Bald Eagles and the association to salt water appears to effect nestling densities more than any other factor. Only the very largest of the salmon streams, such as the Chilkat River, produce enough food to effect nesting distribution.

This Bald Eagle is watching for salmon along the Chilkat River.
Photo by Bob Armstrong.

The study method used proved to be satisfactory and might be appropriate for use in other areas. For instance, with this strip plot census technique, it would be possible to sample all of Southeast Alaska and develop statistically reliable figures for not only eagle production, but for habitat types, iced-in bays, etc. Money and time are the only limiting factors.

Editors' Note: This paper has been cited numerous times since 1966 yet it remained in the gray literature and difficult to obtain. It describes the earliest work for assessing Bald Eagle nesting and productivity in Southeast Alaska using methodology that continues to be the basis for collecting these data today. For these reasons the editors decided to include this important historical work in Bald Eagles of Alaska.

Bald Eagle Productivity in Southcentral Alaska in 1989 and 1990 after the *Exxon Valdez* Oil Spill

Jeffrey A. Bernatowicz, Philip F. Schempf and Timothy D. Bowman

U.S. Fish and Wildlife Service, Juneau, AK

On 24 March 1989, the oil tanker *Exxon Valdez* ran aground spilling more than 40 million liters of crude oil into Prince William Sound, Alaska. The oil moved southwest, fouling approximately 2,500 km of shoreline from Prince William Sound to the Alaska Peninsula (Table 1 and Figure 1). In the cleanup effort during the following two springs and summers, thousands of workers and a variety of equipment scoured the oiled shoreline. An estimated 8,000 Bald Eagles (*Haliaeetus leucocephalus*) inhabit the spill area and their nesting season coincided with the arrival of oil and cleanup crews. Bald Eagles in coastal areas are highly dependent on the nearshore ecosystem for nesting (Hodges and Robards 1982, J. I. Hodges, Jr., S. L. Cain. and P. F. Schempf, U.S. Fish and Wildlife Service, unpublished data) and foraging (Imler and Kalmbach 1955, Garrett et al. 1993). Their opportunistic feeding strategy and willingness to enter the water make them susceptible to oiling (Todd et al. 1982).

There is no documentation on the effects of crude oil on Bald Eagle reproductive success; however, crude and refined oil have been found to cause significant embryo mortality in other avian species (Hartung 1965, Szaro 1977, Albers 1978, Albers and Szaro 1978, Szaro et al. 1978, Coon et al. 1979, King and Lefever 1979, Szaro 1979, Albers 1980, Szaro et al. 1980). Fresh and weathered crude oil in amounts greater than or equal to 5 µL applied to eggs significantly reduced hatching success of gulls and ducks, the only species tested. The long-term survival of avian nestlings ingesting oil is uncertain (Szaro 1977, Flemming et al. 1982, Pattee and Franson 1982, Leighton 1986), but oiled down and feathers lose insulation value and birds suffer from hypothermia (Szaro 1977).

Oiled Bald Eagle at the Valdez Sorting Station, summer of 1989. Photo by USFWS.

Figure 1. Areas in south-central Alaska affected by the *Exxon Valdez* oil spill of March 24, 1989. Shaded areas represent the range of the moving oil slick. Dated lines represent the time of arrival of the oil slick at the indicated location.

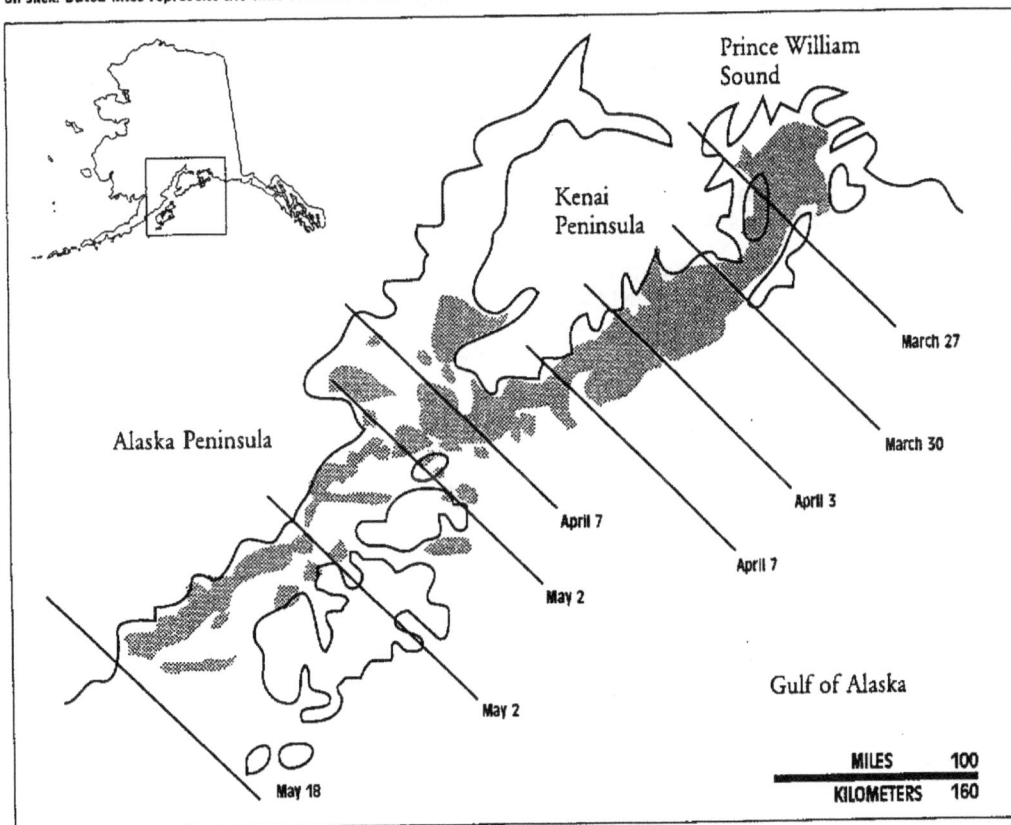

Reproductive success of Bald Eagles is evaluated using two surveys. An occupancy survey is conducted to count the number of breeding pairs in the population (occupied nests) and identify the number of pairs that laid eggs (active nests). Occupancy surveys should be timed after all eggs have been laid and before any nesting failures have occurred (Postupalsky 1974, Fraser et al. 1983). In most cases, this will be a compromise, because failures probably begin before the last eggs are laid. A second survey, the productivity survey, is conducted to identify failed nests and to count older young that are likely to fledge. The productivity survey needs to be timed late enough so few additional nestling mortalities will occur but before any chicks leave the nest. Failure to time the surveys correctly will bias estimates of reproductive success (Steenhof and Kochert 1982, Fraser et al. 1983).

Table 1. Cumulative maximum oiled shorelines in southcentral Alaska, by region, after the oil spill.

Regions [a]	Heavy oiling [b]	Medium oiling [c]	Light oiling [d]	Very light oiling [e]	Total oiling	No oiling
PWS						
km	169.1	125.3	218.3	215.3	728.0	1,278.2
%	8.4	6.2	10.9	10.7	36.3	63.7
Kenai						
km	36.1	51.6	111.6	136.7	336.0	1,514.0
%	1.9	2.8	6.0	7.4	18.2	81.8
Kodiak						
km	10.7	53.9	108.2	724.6	897.4	1,516.0
%	0.4	2.2	4.5	30.0	37.2	62.8
Katmai/APBNWR						
km	9.5	35.2	192.9	292.1	529.7	913.0
%	0.6	2.8	13.4	20.2	36.7	63.3

[a] PWS = Prince William Sound; Kenai = Kenai Peninsula; Kodiak = Kodiak Archipelago; Katmai/APBNWR = Katmai National Monument and Alaska Peninsula–Becharof National Wildlife Refuge.
[b] A band of surface and/or subsurface oil greater than 6 m wide or more than 50% coverage of the intertidal zone.
[c] An oil band of 3 6 m wide or 10–50% coverage of intertidal zone.
[d] An oil band less than 3 m wide or 10% coverage of intertidal zone.
[d] An oil band less than 1 m wide or beach having less than 1% coverage.
[e] Percent of all surveyed shoreline.

The standard measure of Bald Eagle reproductive success is young per occupied nest. Estimates should be based on all occupied nests, including those in which no eggs were laid (i.e., nonbreeding pairs) (Postupalsky 1974, Steenhof 1987). Determining the actual number of occupied nests is difficult because not all adults are visible (Bowman et al. 1993) or in the vicinity of the nest (Whitfield et al. 1974, Fraser et al. 1983). This determination also assumes the ability to delineate individual territories. There is potential to grossly underestimate the number of occupied territories, especially in areas with high Bald Eagle densities (Hansen and Hodges 1985).

Figure 2. Subregions surveyed for productivity of Bald Eagles *Haliaeetus leucocephalus* in southcentral Alaska, 1989 and 1990, after the *Exxon Valdez* oil spill.

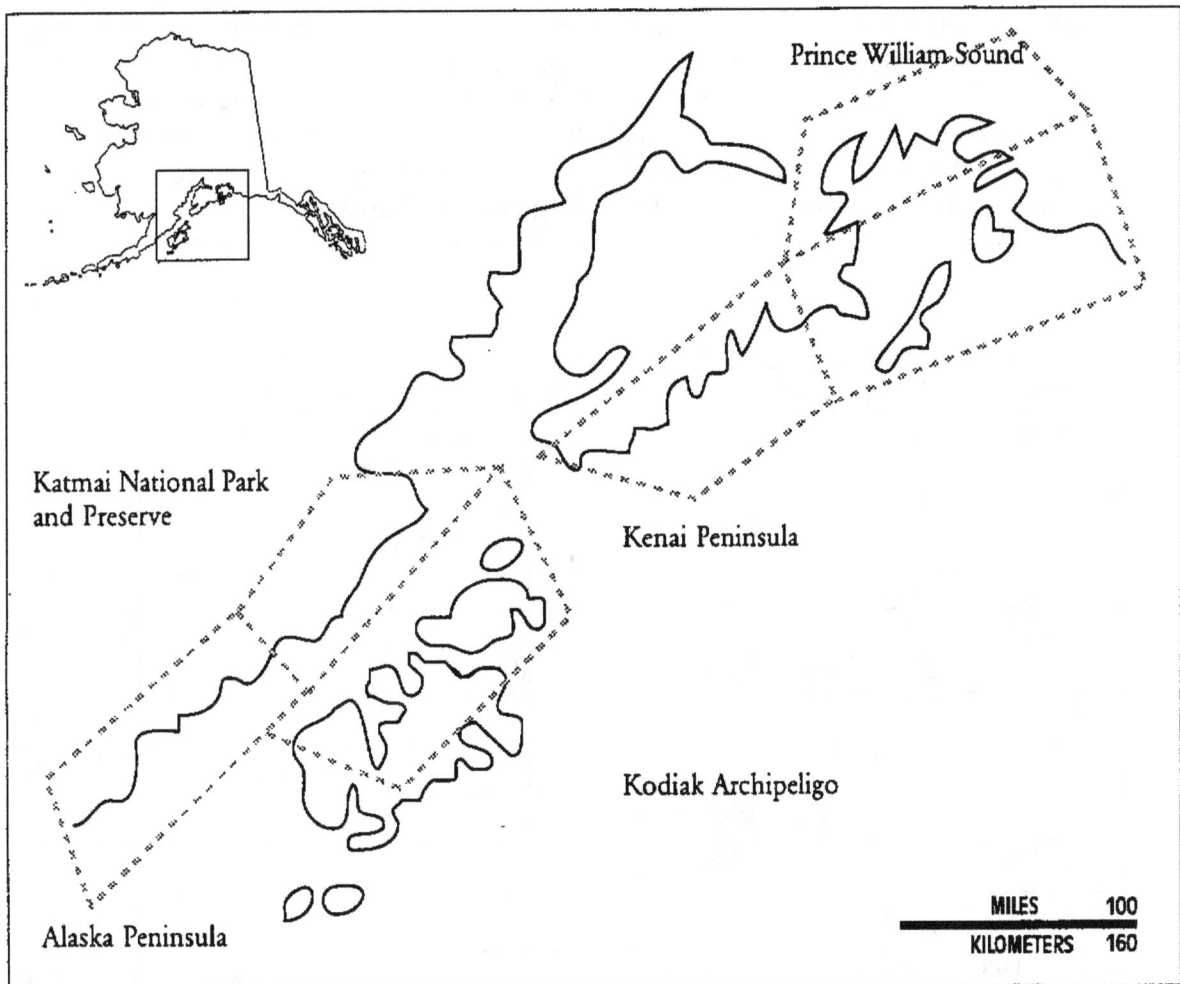

Figure 2. Subregions surveyed for productivity of Bald Eagles *Haliaeetus leucocephalus* in southcentral Alaska, 1989 and 1990, after the *Exxon Valdez* oil spill.

Bowman et al. (1993) analyzed Bald Eagle productivity in relation to shoreline oiling in Prince William Sound and D. Zwiefelhofer (USFWS, unpublished data) compared Bald Eagle productivity in 1989 to historical data in survey plots affected by oiling. The objectives of our study were to gather, collate and reanalyze all available data on Bald Eagle productivity in the entire region affected by the *Exxon Valdez* oil spill during 1989 and 1990 to determine if the spill influenced reproductive success. This study was part of an assessment of potential damage caused by the spill to identify reparation and restoration needs.

Methods
Study Area
The study area encompassed all shorelines influenced by the oil spill which included: Prince William Sound (PWS), the southeastern coast of the Kenai Peninsula (Kenai), the Kodiak Archipelago (Kodiak) and the southern coast of the Alaska Peninsula within the Katmai National Park and Preserve (Katmai) and Alaska Peninsula-Becharof National

Wildlife Refuge (APBNWR) (Figure 2). Bald Eagles in Prince William Sound and Kenai nest primarily in western hemlock (*Tsuga heterophylla*) and Sitka spruce (*Picea sitchensis*). In Kodiak, black cottonwood (*Populus trichocarpa*) is the predominant nest tree and approximately 18% of the active nests are on cliffs or sea stacks. The majority of nests within Katmai are ground nests, although alders (*Alnus crispa*) are occasionally used. All Bald Eagles within APBNWR nest on the ground. Ground nests are often built of driftwood, debris and kelp but quickly become overgrown when they are inactive. The climate in the coastal areas is relatively mild, with an average range of 7 to 25 C in summer and -5 to 1 C in winter. Only a few sheltered, brackish bays freeze in winter. Precipitation ranges from 120 cm on the Alaska Peninsula to more than 500 cm in some areas of Prince William Sound.

Table 2. Dates and methods for nesting success and production surveys of Bald Eagles in Southcentral Alaska, 1989 and 1990, after the *Exxon Valdez* oil spill.

Occupancy survey			Occupied nests found after June 1 (%)	Productivity survey	
Regions	Dates	Methods		Dates	Method
PWS 1989	18 Apr-5 May	Wing	0	15 Jul-8 Aug	Helicopter
	20-27 May	Helicopter	0		
1990 (1)	10-19 Apr	Helicopter	0	21-25 Jul	Helicopter
	13-19 May	Helicopter	0	12-14 Aug	Helicopter (2)
	11-20 Jun	Helicopter	0		
Kenai 1989	Jun	Boat	ND (3)	27 Jul-8 Aug	Helicopter
1990	19 May-7 Jun	Helicopter	30	4-5 Aug	Helicopter
Kodiak 1989	10 May-7 Jun	Helicopter	36	28 Jul-S Aug	Helicopter
1990	7 May-3 Jun	Helicopter	1	28 Jul-5 Aug	Helicopter
Katmai 1989	11 Jun	Helicopter	ND (3)	26 Jun-I5 Aug	Boats (3)
1990	26-27 May	Helicopter	0	24-25 Jul	Helicopter
APBNWR 1989	10 May-3 Jun	Helicopter	78	4-5 Jul	Helicopter
	19-20 Jun	Helicopter	0	2-25 Jul	Wing (2)
	9-31 May	Helicopter	0	26-28 Jul	Helicopter
	19-21 Jun	Helicopter	0		

(1) In addition to surveys listed, approximately 50% of the area was surveyed once every 10 d.
(2) Resurvey of nests with young that were not near fledging on previous survey.
(3)Surveys were conducted, but locations of individual nests were not recorded or data were lost.

Survey Methods

Crews from the USFWS and National Park Service conducted the surveys. In 1989, nesting surveys were often conducted opportunistically while performing other duties related to the spill. Therefore, survey timing, area and methods were not standardized. In 1990, at least two surveys were conducted to assess Bald Eagle productivity. An occupancy survey was conducted during the incubation period (May to early June) and a productivity survey was conducted after eggs had hatched but before young had fledged (July to early August). Survey methods and timing are given for each area in Table 2.

Prince William Sound

Initial nest occupancy data were collected opportunistically during Bald Eagle population surveys in 1989. The population surveys followed methods presented by Hodges et al. (1984) and included all island shorelines and 23 random plots (16,828 ha) along the mainland shoreline. The locations of active nests were recorded as they were seen, but the primary effort was to count adults. The second occupancy survey was flown using mapped nest locations from the population survey and a study in the early 1980s of nest locations within Prince William Sound (USFWS, Juneau, Alaska, unpublished data). The second occupancy survey focused on finding occupied nests within the immediate spill area. Subsequent nest surveys were flown ad hoc throughout the remainder of the summer. The main purposes of the flights were to coordinate oil spill cleanup activities, collect addled eggs and prey remains and attach a band and radio transmitter to nestlings. Some flights were made specifically to collect productivity information, but there was no systematic survey schedule or area because of the availability of personnel and aircraft focused on the spill zone in western Prince William Sound.

In 1990, all shorelines directly affected by the spill were included in the survey area. Because of the low productivity observed in 1989, we also surveyed shorelines in eastern Prince William Sound that were not directly within the spill's path to determine the extent of damage. Approximately 80% of the nesting habitat in the sound was surveyed in 1990.

Kenai Peninsula

No occupancy survey was flown in 1989. Limited nesting information was collected at random in June by personnel working on the oil spill cleanup. Productivity surveys in 1989 covered approximately 90% of the outer coast of the Kenai Peninsula (Figure 2) and concentrated on Kenai Fjords National Park. In 1990, single occupancy and productivity surveys were conducted along the same coast surveyed in 1989.

Kodiak Archipelago

Approximated 60% of the Kodiak Archipelago shoreline (Figure 2) was surveyed once for occupancy and productivity in both 1989 and 1990. Active nests were not distinguished from those occupied by nonbreeding pairs in 1989. Surveys concentrated on the areas within the path of the oil spill (N, NW and NE parts of the archipelago).

Katmai National Park and Preserve

The survey area included the entire Katmai National Park and Preserve coastline on the south side of the Alaska Peninsula (Figure 2). In 1989, occupancy surveys were conducted by helicopter in June, but the data were lost. Productivity information in 1989 was collected by boat throughout the summer as time permitted, but data were recorded only in field notes, without using a data sheet, resulting in inconsistent records. In 1990, single occupancy and productivity surveys were conducted.

Alaska Peninsula-Becharof National Wildlife Refuge
Surveys were conducted along the south side of the Alaska Peninsula within the APBNWR in 1989 and 1990. Only active nests were noted on the occupancy surveys in 1989.

Oiling Data
We examined reports issued by the Alaska Department of Environmental Conservation (ADEC). Alaska Department of Natural Resources, USFWS, U.S. Coast Guard and Piatt et al. (1990) to determine the timing and extent of oil contamination. There were major differences in degree and extent of oiling between reports. We used a summary of extent and degree of oiling provided by ADEC (W. Lane, ADEC, unpublished data) because it was the most recent and presumed to be the most accurate. Also, the data provided by ADEC pertained to areas that matched our nest survey areas to a large extent.

Data Analysis
We were responsible for collecting data in Prince William Sound. In other regions, all reports, data summaries and available raw data came from other sources and were reviewed by us for this report.

Whenever possible, field investigators were interviewed. We mapped and assigned a number to each individual nest. Dates and nest status were assigned to each nest for individual observations. When discrepancies existed in the raw data, summaries and reports for a nest, it was omitted from the data set. In 1989, only data summaries containing the final fate for each nest were available for the Kenai Peninsula and Katmai National Monument.

We used terminology and calculated measures of reproductive success based on definitions adapted from Postupalsky (1974) and Fraser et al. (1983) (Table 3 and Figure 3). Survey area, methodology and timing were not consistent between areas and years. To reduce the potential biases, we used subsets of data for comparison between years. Within the spill zone (western Prince William Sound), we compared nests that were found on occupancy surveys before 1 June and on productivity surveys, in both 1989 and 1990. In eastern Prince William Sound, the 1989 sample was too small for meaningful comparison between years; thus, we included all nests with complete survey data from 1990. On Kenai, we were unable to determine which or how often areas were surveyed; therefore, we used only nests that were found in both 1989 and 1990 in the subset. Survey methods were similar between 1989 and 1990 in APBNWR, but the area was more extensive in 1990. There were also potential mapping errors in 1989. For comparison between years, we used only nests in the area surveyed in both years. Reported observations for individual nests were either not mapped or did not match available field notes for Katmai in 1989. Total young produced and number of occupied nests were the only data available for Katmai in 1989. No subsets were needed for Kodiak as methods and observer experience were similar between years. We do not think it is appropriate to compare survey results between years and among subregions using statistical techniques because of the biases involved in the way the data were collected.

Pre-spill estimates of Bald Eagle productivity and nesting success were lacking for most of the regions studied. We reviewed the literature and unpublished data of Alaska Bald Eagle nesting studies for comparative data. Most historical studies provide sampling data only for the actively nesting eagles. When nonbreeding birds were surveyed, there was little difference in productivity estimates based on occupied versus active nests. Therefore, we only included active nests in estimates of productivity and nest success in the comparative data.

Bald Eagle nest locations were either not recorded, vague or of questionable accuracy in many regions in 1989. The accuracy of the oiling data was also questionable. Furthermore, Bowman et al. (1993) found that even non-oiled beaches within the spill zone had high rates of nest failure. Therefore, we only considered productivity in the context of oiling data on a regional basis rather than by nest site (Bowman et al. 1993) or sample plot (Zwiefelhofer, unpublished data).

Table 3. Definitions of terms used in calculations of nest success and productivity for Bald Eagles (after Postupalsky 1974 and Fraser et al. 1983) as used in this study.

Term	Definition
Occupied nest	An adult in incubating posture or two adults actively defending, near or at nest. Includes nesting (active) nonbreeding eagle pairs.
Active nest	A nest with an adult in incubation posture or with aerie or chicks.
Nonbreeding pair	A territorial pair of eagles that do not produce eggs during the survey year. Defined on a survey as two adult eagles obviously associated with a nest (generally within 300 m).
Total young produced [a]	Number of young produced to an advanced stage of development (fully feathered).
Young per occupied nest [b]	Total number of young produced divided by total number of occupied nests.
Young per active nest [b]	Total number of young produced divided by total number of active nests.
Percent successful [b]	Number of nests in which at least one young was raised to an advanced stage of development divided by total number of active or occupied nests.

[a] Calculated using all nests found in survey area.

[b] Calculated using only nests found on both the occupant survey and productivity survey.

The oil remained in a smooth liquid form as it traveled NE to SW through Prince William Sound, reaching the Gulf of Alaska at the end of March (Figure 1). Approximately 36% of the Prince William Sound shoreline in the spill path was coated with more than 14% receiving heavy or moderate oiling (Table 1). More than 7.6 million liters of oil (17% of original spill) escaped the sound and traveled the length of the Kenai Peninsula in 2 weeks, reaching the Barren Islands by 11 April (Figure 1). Less than 5% of the area surveyed along the Kenai Peninsula received heavy or moderate oil (Table 1). The oil became weathered, emulsified into "mousse," and broke up into patches before reaching Kodiak Island and the Alaska Peninsula by the end of April

(Figure 1). Total percent of shorelines oiled on Kodiak Island and on the Alaska Peninsula were similar to the total percent in Prince William Sound (36-37%), but the majority in the former two areas were very lightly oiled (Table 1). Small patches of mousse, sheen and tar balls were observed in June and July, but the majority of the oil either sank, evaporated or had washed up on beaches by the end of May. Tides continued to move oil short distances, thereby coating new and previously cleaned shorelines throughout summer 1989. Winter storms dispersed the majority of surface oil that had not been scoured by cleanup crews. By June 1990, approximately 3% (390 km) of the shoreline in the spill area was considered oiled. Any remaining liquid oil was subsurface.

Figure 3. Terminology used in reporting the reproductive patterns of nesting Bald Eagles (*Haliaeetus leucocephalus*) information gathered during surveys is in unshaded blocks, which allowed calculations of statistics (shaded blocks). The values presented are hypothetical.

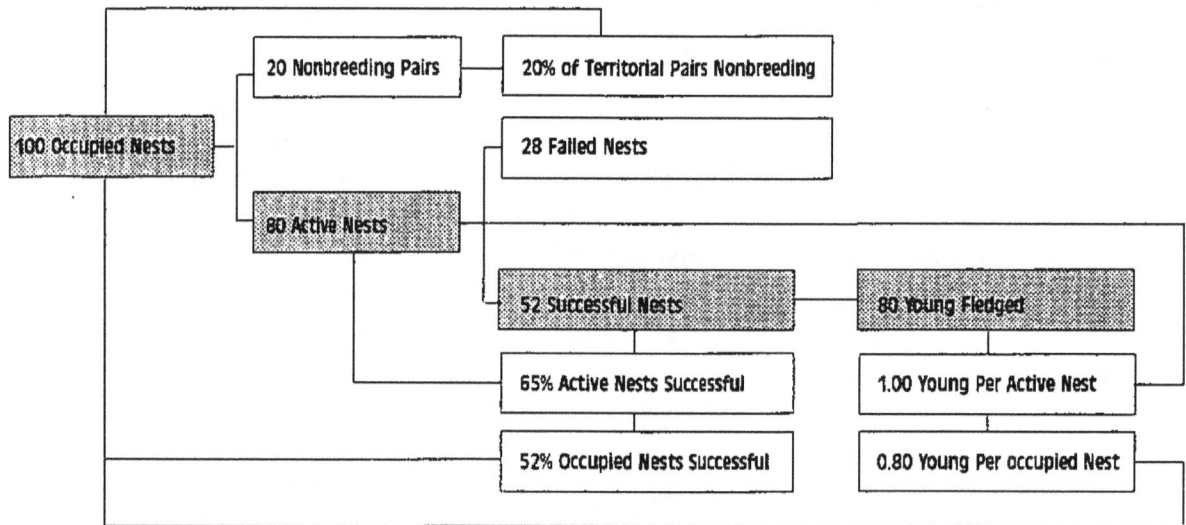

Logistical constraints incurred immediately after the oil spill in 1989 precluded an accurate measure of reproductive success for eagles in most areas. The majority of occupancy surveys were conducted 1-2 months after the spill and oil-related mortalities and nest failures probably had occurred. Estimating the pre-spill breeding population was also hindered by the lack of information collected on pairs that were not actively nesting (nonbreeders and early failures). Young per occupied nest could only be calculated for Prince William Sound and Kodiak (Table 4) in 1989. Reproductive estimates for the remainder of the regions were based on actively nesting or successful pairs. Survey timing and techniques were improved in 1990.

The average for the eight comparison areas was 0.96 young per active nest and 54% nest success (Table 5). There was wide variation in both productivity (0.461.40 young per occupied nest) and active nest success (37-92%). In general, reproductive success among regions was similar in 1989 and 1990 with one exception (Table 4) and similar to that of historical studies (Table 5). The only area obviously affected by the spill was western Prince William Sound in 1989. Only 30% of the occupied nests were successful and only 0.39 young per active nest were produced in 1989. All regions except Katmai produced more than 0.8 young per active nest. In 1990, nest success and production rebounded in Prince William Sound to a level that appeared to be normal. Katmai produced 0.6 young per occupied nest and had less than 50% occupied nest success, but we could not attribute the low productivity and nest success to the effects of oil.

Table 4. Nesting success and productivity of Bald Eagles in southcentral Alaska, 1989 and 1990, after the *Exxon Valdez* oil spill. Numbers in parentheses represent subsets of nests that minimized bias and were used for comparisons between years within a subregion; ND = not determined.

Region [a]	Occupied nets found on both surveys	Young per occupied nest [b]	Percent of occupied nests successful [b]	Young per active nest [b]	Percent of active nests successful [b]	Total occupied nests found [c]	Total young produced [c]
WPWS [e]							
1989	165	0.36	30	0.39	32	165	60
1990	165	1.04	64	1.19	72	165	172
EPWS							
1989	24	0.54	38	0.76	53	·24	13
1990	348	0.74	53	0.89	64	372	276
Kenai [e]							
1989 [f]	0	ND	ND	ND	ND	45 (29)	52 (36)
1990	45	0.92	51	1.00	58	63 (34)	58 (28)
Kodiak [g]							
1989	333	1.20	72	ND	ND	333	399
1990	412	1.05	64	1.07	66	412	431
Katmai							
1989 [h]	0	ND	ND	ND	ND	47	54
1990	45	0.56	47	0.60	50	50	28
APBNWR [i]							
1989	62	ND	ND	1.00	55	69	62
1990	76	0.91	56	1.11	59	76	77

[a] WPWS = Western Prince William Sound, EPWS = Eastern Prince William Sound, Kenai = Kenai Peninsula, Kodiak = Kodiak Archipelago, Katmai = Katmai National Park and Preserve, APBNWR = Alaska Peninsula–Becharof National Wildlife Refuge.
[b] Calculations based only on nests found on occupancy and productivity survey.
[c] Based on all nests found on the productivity survey (nests not found on occupancy survey included).
[d] Subset(s) includes only nests found on both occupancy and productivity surveys in both 1989 and 1990.
[e] Subset(s) includes only nests found on both the 1989 and 1990 productivity surveys.
[f] Kenai Fjords National Park, Seward, Alaska unpublished data.
[g] Kodiak National Wildlife Refuge and adjacent islands; Zwiefelhofer (unpublished).
[h] Yurick (unpublished).
[i] Dewhurst (unpublished). Subset(s) includes nests within the area surveyed in both 1989 and 1990.

Table 5. Nesting success and productivity of actively nesting Bald Eagles in ecosystems not affected by organochloride chemicals. The abbreviation USFWS is U.S. Fish and Wildlife Service.

Area	Years of Study	Active nests	Young per active nest	Percent of active nests successful	Source
Kodiak National Wildlife Refuge	25	24–413	1.00 (0.52–1.20)	65 (44–92)	Zwiefelhofer unpublished
Amchitka Island	1	71	0.86	61	Sherrod et al. (1976)
Chatham Strait [a]	10	15–47	0.91 (0.46–1.23)	60 (37–82)	USFWS unpublished
Kariuk Lake [b]	3	8–14	1.00 (0.6(]1.40)		Hensel and Troyer (1964)
Kenai National Wildlife Refuge [b]	2	22–23	1.20 (1.00–1.44))	75 (72–78)	Bangs et al. (1982)
Tanana River [b] and [d]	3	13–15	1.07 (0.8–1.40)	64 (54–80)	Ritchie (1982)
Copper River Basin [b]	2	37–151	0.64 (0.59–0.84)	42 (40–51)	USFWS unpublished
Copper River Delta [a]	1	59	1.00	64	USFWS unpublished

[a] Marine ecosystem.
[b] Freshwater ecosystem.
[c] Occupancy surveys conducted after hatching, probably overestimated productivity and success.
[d] Productivity surveys conducted after some young fledged on year with lowest productivity.

Discussion

The extent of oiling given in Table 1 differs from that of other studies (Piatt et al. 1990; Bowman et al. 1993; Zwiefelhofer, unpublished). Early reports issued by ADEC and the USFWS estimate 1,300-1,500 km of oiled shoreline in the spill path. We used recent updates by ADEC (Lane, unpublished data) and the U.S. Coast Guard (1993) that estimated 2,400-2,500 km of oiled shoreline. We assumed that the recent updates were the most accurate, but could not explain the differences between the reports.

Our Bald Eagle productivity estimates vary from results presented by others who participated in local Bald Eagle nesting studies after the spill (M. Amaral, USFWS, unpublished data; D. A. Dewhurst, USFWS, unpublished data; M. M. Yurick, National Park Service, unpublished data; Zwiefelhofer, unpublished data). We attribute these differences to interpretation of data. We deleted data that did not meet the criteria outlined in the Methods.

Our comparative sample of historical studies only sampled the actively nesting portion of the population, which probably resulted in an overestimated actual productivity of the breeding population because all pairs occupying territories were not considered. Hensel and Troyer (1964) suggested that 1,418 territorial pairs occupied their study area on Kodiak Island, but only 8-14 actively nested (Table 5). Assuming 18 pairs in the breeding population, the average productivity was 0.59 (range, 0.28-0.78) young per occupied nest. On Amchitka Island, the actual productivity may have been closer to 0.7 young per occupied nest because Sherrod et al. (1976) estimated that 19% of the breeding population never laid eggs. In Chatham Straight (USFWS, Juneau, Alaska, unpublished data), the number of active nests in the study area decreased from 35 in 1985 to 15 in 1987 and then increased to 47 in 1989. In 1987, productivity was reported at 0.8 young per active nest. Assuming there were 47 occupied territories in 1987, productivity was actually 0.25 young per occupied nest. Wide annual variations in the number of active nests in a study area have been documented in other parts of SE Alaska (Hodges 1982, Hansen and Hodges 1985). We do not know if the fluctuations in number of active nests were a result of survey error, birds using alternate sites or territorial pairs not breeding; however, we believe the actual variation in productivity and nest success for occupied nests is greater than we report for active nests in Table 5.

The wide variations and lack of understanding of the breeding population make determining "normal" difficult. Recovery plans for Bald Eagles in the lower 48 specify 1.00 young per occupied nest and 65% occupied nest success for delisting (USFWS 1986). Anthony et al. (1994) suggested 1.00 young per occupied nest is a conservative goal. Populations in the other 48 continental states have been recovering from organochlorine poisoning and their productivity rates are probably not comparable to those of Alaskan populations. Bowman et al. (1995) estimated that 0.86 young per occupied nest would lead to a population growth rate of 2% in Prince William Sound and that approximately 0.7 young per occupied nest would result in a stable population. Buehler et al. (1991) calculated that 0.74 young per occupied nest would result in a stable population in Chesapeake Bay. Both studies agreed with the findings of Grier (1980), who demonstrated that survival was more important than reproduction in Bald Eagle population dynamics. Short-term drops in the reproductive rate may be normal for populations that are near saturation and probably have little effect on the population as a whole. Thus, we believe that the variation in nest success and productivity in Table 5 is normal for the region.

The *Exxon Valdez* leaking oil into Prince William Sound, Alaska. Photo USFWS.

Western Prince William Sound

In 1989, reproductive surveys focused on oiled areas in western Prince William Sound. Productivity (young per occupied or active nest) and nest success (Table 4) were lower than in any historical studies (Table 5) and comparable to those of populations affected by organochlorine pesticides (Sprunt et al. 1973; Stalmaster 1987). The area surveyed also received the heaviest oiling of any region (Table 1). The poor reproductive success can be directly attributed to the spill. Platt et al. (1990) found eagles scavenging on oiled carcasses in 1989. Bowman et al. (1993) found a higher failure rate and decreased production at nests exposed to oil compared to non-oiled nests in Prince William Sound in 1989. Nests with no oil, any oil and heavy oil failed at rates of 65% (71 of 110), 76% (60 of 79) and 88% (36 of 41), respectively (Bowman et al. 1993). The high failure rates for nests on non-oiled beaches indicates either brief exposure may have been enough to cause nest failure or the oiling data were inaccurate (see oiling results above). Brief exposure to oil did cause significant embryo mortality in other avian species (Hartung 1965; Albers 1980), especially if exposure occurred early in incubation (Szaro 1977; Albers 1978).

We believe the majority of documented nest failures were the result of embryo mortality and the toxic effects of oil were persistent throughout the egg laying period. We compared nests first seen occupied in April (n = 127) to those first seen occupied in late May (N = 64). Nesting chronology data collected in Prince William Sound indicate egg laying starts in mid-April and continues through the end of May, with roughly 50% of the nests initiated after 1 May (USFWS, Juneau, Alaska, unpublished data). Productivity (0.34 versus 0.37 young per occupied nest) and nest success (27 versus 32%) was only slightly lower for the April subset. If the toxic effects of oil were short lived, we believe nests initiated later in the season would have had a higher success rate.

Human activity dramatically increased in western Prince William Sound in 1989 because of cleanup activity. Although disturbance early in the nesting season may cause nest failures (Steenhof and Kochert 1982), we do not believe it was a major factor in the poor nest success in 1989. We looked at the timing of nest failures by comparing a sample of nests that were documented as active between 18 April and 5 May (Table 2) and had failed by 1 June. In western Prince William Sound in 1989, 37% (10 of 27) of failures had occurred by 1 June. In eastern Prince William Sound in 1990 (where there was no cleanup activity), 33% (8 of 24) of nests initiated by 5 May had failed by 1 June. The mean difference between the April and May surveys was 30 (range, 15-43) days. Therefore, we believe the majority of birds continued to incubate dead embryos for the entire 34 to 35 day term. Albers (1980) documented that mallards (*Anas platyrhynchos*) also continue incubation for the full period, despite oil-related embryo mortality. In 1989 and 1990, we tried to collect eggs from failed nests and found that scavengers quickly consume eggs from abandoned nests. If failures in 1989 were attributable to disturbance, we believe clutches would have been destroyed and the percent failures observed in May would have been much higher.

Clean up of the oil from the *Exxon Valdez* damaged beaches and intertidal communities were destroyed while much of the sub-surface oil remained to be slowly released into the marine food chain. Photo USFWS.

Once the eggs hatched, survival was apparently high. Of 65 young seen in June, 57 (88%) survived to fledging. All 15 chicks (approximately 8 weeks old) that were radio-tagged in western Prince William Sound in 1989 survived to fledging (USFWS, Juneau, Alaska, unpublished data). Postfledging survival of radiotagged chicks was also considered high (Bowman et al. 1995). Hatching weight (Szaro et al. 1980) and short-term survival (Albers 1980) were normal for chicks that survived oiling during incubation. Pattee and Franson (1982) and Flemming et al. (1982) found normal survival for young of other avian species that had ingested oil.

Oil was still present in 1990 but was mostly subsurface. We did not observe any significant sheens during nesting surveys and do not believe there was any impact on eagle nesting because productivity and nest success in western Prince William Sound (Table 4) were above average in 1990 compared with those of historical studies (Table 5).

Eastern Prince William Sound

We cannot attribute the relatively low productivity observed in eastern Prince William Sound in 1989 to the spill. Prevailing winds and currents pushed the oil and probably most oiled carcasses away from this area. Territorial eagles that were radio-tagged in Prince William Sound from 1989 to 1990 rarely moved more than 2 km during the nesting season and no eagles (n = 30) from eastern Prince William Sound were relocated in the spill area during the breeding season (USFWS, Juneau, Alaska, unpublished data). Thus, eagles from eastern Prince William Sound probably never contacted oil. The low productivity was either attributable to the small sample size or to natural fluctuations in productivity.

In 1990, productivity was approximately 30% lower than in western Prince William Sound (Table 4) and was lower than average for other studies in the region (Table 5). Because productivity was so high in nearby oiled western Prince William Sound, the only probable explanation is natural variation.

Kenai Peninsula

In 1989, we could not calculate nest success or a productivity estimate because initial surveys did not commence until mid June and much of the original data were lost or erased from field maps; however, it appears that productivity was normal if we compare results to the 1990 data. The 1990 productivity (0.92 young per occupied nest) and nest success (58%) were near the average for all areas and years shown in Table 4. Only 6 fewer young (52 versus 58) were found in 1989. Assuming there were 63 (1990 survey) occupied nests in 1989, 0.83 young were produced per occupied nest in 1989; however, initial surveys were conducted sporadically by boat and only one aerial survey was flown. We believe some successful nests were overlooked and total young produced was underestimated because of the lack of an aerial occupancy survey and the inexperience of observers on the productivity survey. If we compare productivity based only on nests observed in both years (the data shown in parentheses), productivity was 51% (1.24 versus 0.82 young per occupied nest) higher in 1989 (Table 4).

Kodiak Archipelago

There was no obvious reduction in Bald Eagle productivity in Kodiak, despite sightings of oiled eagles (Zwiefelhofer, unpublished data). Zwiefelhofer (unpublished data) compared success of nests within oiled plots to historical data and found no significant difference. Estimates of reproductive success in the Kodiak area in 1989 and 1990 were higher than those for any other subregion and were above the historical average for the Kodiak National Wildlife Refuge (Table 5).

Nests of food stressed Black-legged Kittiwakes may be more susceptible to Bald Eagle predation. This Bald Eagle is seen eating Black-legged Kittiwake eggs at a colony in Passage Canal, Prince William Sound, Alaska. Photo by David Irons.

Katmai National Park and Preserve

In 1989, 47 occupied nests were seen between June and August and at least 54 young fledged (Table 4). This is a minimum estimate because field notes indicate the surveyors had a difficult time seeing nests from the water. We do not know the exact dates or locations of many observations because the original data were lost; however, if we assume there were 50 (1990 data) occupied nests, more than 1.00 young were produced per occupied nest in 1989. We believe total young produced were underestimated for the same reasons outlined for Kenai.

The relatively poor nest success and productivity (Table 4) in 1990 is difficult to explain. In surrounding regions (Kodiak, Kenai and APBNWR) and heavily oiled areas in western Prince William Sound reproductive estimates were above average for all survey areas and years. The most likely explanation for these findings is natural fluctuation.

Alaska Peninsula-Becharof National Wildlife Refuge

Productivity and nest success appeared to be normal in both 1989 and 1990 (Table 4) even though one oiled egg was collected in the area surveyed (Dewhurst, unpublished data). Six abandoned or failed nests were examined and no sign of oiling was discovered; two of the nests had been destroyed by brown bears (*Ursus arctos*). Nest success and total young produced were considered minimum estimates. Older young occasionally hide in grass surrounding the nest, giving observers the false impression that the nest had failed. The increase in occupied nests found in 1990 may have been caused by increased surveyor experience and consistency (Dewhurst, unpublished data).

Productivity Compared to Oiling
The apparent lack of reproductive failure outside of western Prince William Sound is difficult to interpret. The total shoreline oiled in Kodiak and along the Alaska Peninsula was similar to that in Prince William Sound. Although roughly five times (15% versus 3%) more shoreline in western Prince William Sound was moderately to heavily oiled in 1989; even nests along lightly oiled and non-oiled beaches had higher than expected failures (Bowman et al. 1993). Laboratory studies (Albers 1978, Albers and Szaro 1978, Coon et al. 1979, Szaro 1979, Szaro et al. 1980) have found that relatively small amounts of oil (5-20 µL) significantly increased embryo mortality. Hehnke (1973) found that eagles switch from a mostly fish to a bird diet on the Alaska Peninsula during a natural die-off of murres. Given the massive die-off (100,000-300,000) of seabirds and drift of carcasses (150 km) (Piatt et al. 1990), it seems likely that eagles would have contacted oil throughout the spill area. The majority (88%) of oiled carcasses were retrieved outside of Prince William Sound.

Prince William Sound
One possible explanation for the apparently normal reproduction outside Prince William Sound is that the oil encountered by eagles was less toxic. Szaro et al. (1980) found Prudhoe Bay crude oil became increasingly less toxic after weathering 2-4 weeks in tap water. The review by Wolfe et al. (1994) suggests a fairly short time-frame for the degradation of *Exxon Valdez* oil after the spill. The oil that washed up in Prince William Sound had been in the water less than 1 week (Figure 1). The oil received some mixing with the tides, but oil and carcasses at the tide line were probably only exposed to water for a fraction of the day. Szaro et al. (1980) found that toxicity of crude oil is not greatly affected by exposure to sunlight and reported that oil at the tide line from a spill in Nova Scotia was largely unaltered after 5 years, in sharp contrast to the findings of Wolfe et al. (1994). Oil on Kenai shorelines had been at sea for 1-2 weeks (Figure 1). The Kenai is typified by steep rocky bluffs with few, small intertidal areas exposed to ocean swells. Oiled carrion was probably not as available to eagles and shorelines received much heavier weathering than in Prince William Sound. Overall, the Kenai also received 50% less oiling (18% versus 36% total shoreline oiled) than other areas (Table 1). At the peak of nesting in early May (USFWS, Juneau, Alaska, unpublished data), the oil was lower in toxicity and more dispersed (Wolfe et al. 1994, 1996).

The oil turned to mousse before it reached Kodiak and the Alaska Peninsula 5-8 weeks after the spill (Figure 1). Szaro et al. (1980) found that, although less toxic, weathered oil still reduced hatching success even a small amount was applied to eggs. Szaro et al. (1980) weathered the oil in small steel containers and observed reduced toxicity, apparently because of evaporation of volatile compounds and the dissolving of water-soluble compounds. In turning to mousse, the oil from Prince William Sound was not only diluted but was also exposed to more air and water per unit surface area. The added time and increased mixing greatly reduced the oil's toxicity (Wolfe et al. 1994).

Analysis of Survey Methodology

Surveys must be timed correctly to obtain an unbiased estimate of reproductive success (Postupalsky 1974; Steenhof and Kochert 1982; Fraser et al. 1983). In Prince William Sound and the Copper River Delta, egg laying starts in the second week of April and 90-95% of nests have been initiated by the third week in May (USFWS, Juneau, Alaska, unpublished data). Nests start failing in the third week of May and approximately 35% of the failures have occurred by 1 June. The timing of nesting events in the other regions appears to be similar to that in Prince William Sound (Hehnke 1973; Zwiefelhofer, unpublished data), although some evidence collected by Dewhurst (unpublished data) suggests nesting may be slightly earlier on the Alaska Peninsula. In Prince William Sound, the majority of active nests were first observed in April. Occupancy surveys in Kodiak and the Alaska Peninsula did not conclude until after 1 June (Table 2). Therefore, nest success and productivity were probably overestimated in Kodiak and the Alaska Peninsula because of early failures being missed on the surveys. This bias may have been accentuated by the spill. Eagles nesting early in the season would have encountered oil on the open water, increasing the possibility of individual mortality and egg oiling. Failures of the early nesting eagles may not have been detected by surveys in late May or early June. By the end of May, the oil had passed through the area and few bird mortalities occurred after that time (Piatt et al. 1990). Thus, we suspect that active nests observed later in the 1989 breeding season had higher success.

Determining the size of the prespill breeding population is difficult because pairs without eggs are not easily recognized as failures (Whitfield et al. 1974, Fraser et al. 1983) and nests abandoned because of adult mortality were impossible to recognize. Failure to lay eggs accounted for 23% of all failures in Oregon (Anthony et al. 1994). In Alaska, where eagle populations may be near saturation, even higher rates of nonbreeding may occur (Hansen and Hodges 1985). The annual fluctuations in active nests seen in historical studies (Table 5, Hodges 1982) support the hypothesis that a significant number of Alaska eagles may not attempt to breed. We did not include an analysis based on occupied nests because few observers recorded these data and the abundance of eagles and nest sites makes the identification of individual occupied territories impossible. Ingestion of oil may inhibit egg laying (Hartung 1965), so a significant number of adults may never have attempted to lay eggs in 1989. Thus, we may have grossly underestimated reproductive failures attributable to the spill.

Kodiak serves as an example of the potential biases. The number of occupied nests increased 24% (333 to 412) from 1989 to 1990. Some increase was probably caused by increased surveyor experience, but there were obviously more active nests in 1990 (Zwiefelhofer, unpublished data). The breeding population on Kodiak is growing (Zwiefelhofer, unpublished data), but a 24% annual increase is not probable. We can also assume that there were more than 412 pairs in 1990 because of the difficulty in recognizing nonbreeding pairs (Whitfield et al. 1974; Fraser et al. 1983; Bowman et al.

1993). Thus, the actual productivity in 1989 was probably much lower than we report because of early failures and nonbreeding pairs being missed on the 1989 surveys. It is impossible to estimate the magnitude of the biases because the actual breeding population was not known in any region.

Population Implications

Bowman et al. (1995), Buehler et al. (1991) and Grier (1980) demonstrated that survival is more important than reproduction in population dynamics. One year of poor reproduction has little impact on the population as a whole. Bowman et al. (1993) predicted that the population in Prince William Sound would return to its prespill size in 4 years, despite oil-related mortality and poor reproductive success in 1989. Large-scale reproductive failure was not evident in any other region. Zwiefelhofer (unpublished data) reported that the nesting population in the Kodiak National Wildlife Refuge (approximately 50% was within the spill area) increased 47% from 1987 to 1992. Although we do not know survival rates of eagles outside of Prince William Sound, it is unlikely that the spill affected the populations as a whole, based on information from Prince William Sound and Kodiak National Wildlife Refuge.

Conclusions

Western Prince William Sound was the only region within the spill zone where a large-scale reproductive failure was evident. The poor reproduction was attributed to the oil spill. Reproduction rebounded in western Prince William Sound in 1990. All other regions appeared to have normal reproduction in both 1989 and 1990; however, because of the lack of prespill data, the wide range in nest success and productivity data from historical studies and survey biases, only large-scale failures would have been evident. It is unlikely that there was any long-term effect on eagle populations in the region as a whole.

Acknowledgements

This study required the cooperation of many individuals from many agencies and private organizations. We thank the following people for participating in Bald Eagle surveys, or providing data or other essential information pertinent to specific regions in the oil spill area and for providing assistance in many other ways: C. M. Adkins, M. Amaral, M. Bill, F. Bird, D. A. Boyce, B. A. Boyle, D. Dewhurst, K. Faber, J. B. Gray, J. I. Hodges, A. Hoover-Miller, J. Hughes, M. J. Jacobson, T. W. Jennings, R. King, K. Kozie, R. Mesta, M. Portner, T. V. Schumacher, M. Tetreau, S. L. Wilbor, D. Williamson, G. Wheeler, H. White, R. E. Yates, M. Yurick and D. Zwiefelhofer. We thank J. D. Fraser and K. L. Oakley for helpful reviews of drafts of this article. This study was funded by the *Exxon Valdez* Oil Spill Trustee Council. This paper is published with the permission of the American Fisheries Society.

Literature Cited

Albers, P. H. 1978. The effects of petroleum on different stages of incubation in bird eggs. Bull. Environ. Contam. and Toxicol. 19:624-30.

Albers, P. H. 1980. Transfer of crude oil from contaminated water to birds eggs. Environ. Res. 22:307-314.

Albers P. H. and R. C. Szaro. 1978. Effects of no. 2 fuel oil on Common Eider eggs. Marine Pollut. Bull. 9:138-139.

Anthony, R. G., R. W. Frenzel, F. B. Isaacs and M. G. Garrett. 1994. Probable causes of nesting failures in Oregon's Bald Eagle population. Wild. Soc. Bull. 22:576-582.

Bangs, E. E., T. N. Bailey and V. D. Berns. 1982. Ecology of nesting Bald Eagles on the Kenai National Wildlife Refuge, Alaska. Pages 47-54. In: W. N. Ladd and P F. Schempf, eds. Proc. of a symposium and workshop on raptor management and biology in Alaska and Western Canada, 17-20 February 1981, Anchorage, Alas. U.S. Dept. Inter., Fish Wildl. Serv., Anchorage, Alas. 335pp.

Bowman, T. D., P. F. Schempf and J. A. Bernatowicz. 1993. Effects of the *Exxon Valdez* oil spill on Bald Eagles. Final report, Natural Resources Damage Assessment, Bird Study 4, U.S. Fish and Wildlife Service, Juneau, Alaska.

Bowman, T. D., P. F. Schempf and J. A. Bernatowicz. 1995. Bald Eagle survival and population dynamics in Alaska after the *Exxon Valdez* oil spill. J. Wildl. Manage. 59:317-324.

Buehler, D. A., J. D. Fraser, J. K. D. Seegar, G. D. Terres and M. A. Byrd. 1991. Survival rates and population dynamics of Bald Eagles on Chesapeake Bay. J. Wildl. Manage. 55:608-613.

Coon, N. C., P. H. Albers and R. C. Szaro. 1979. No. 2 fuel oil decreases embryonic survival of Great Black-backed Gulls. Bull. of Environ. Contam. Toxicol. 21:152-156.

Flemming, W. J., L. Sileo and J. C. Franson. 1982. Toxicity of Prudhoe Bay crude oil to Sandhill Cranes. J. Wildl. Manage. 46:474-478.

Fraser, J. D., L. D. Frenzel, J. E. Mathisen, F. Martin and M. E. Shough. 1983. Scheduling Bald Eagle reproductive surveys. Wildl. Soc. Bull. 11:13-16.

Garrett, M. G., J. W. Watson and R. G. Anthony. 1993. Bald Eagle home range and habitat use in the Columbia River estuary. J. Wildl. Manage. 57:19-26.

Grier, J. W. 1980. Modeling approaches to Bald Eagle population dynamics. Wildl. Soc. Bull. 8:316

Hansen, A. J. and J. I. Hodges. 1985. High rates of nonbreeding adult Bald Eagles in Southeastern Alaska. J. Wild. Manage. 49:454-458.

Hartung, R. 1965. Some effects of oiling on the reproduction of ducks. J. Wildl. Manage. 29: 872-814.

Hehnke, M. F. 1973. Nesting ecology and feeding behavior of Bald Eagles on the Alaska Peninsula. M.S. thesis. Humboldt State University, Arcata, California.

Hensel, R. J. and W. A. Troyer. 1964. Nesting studies of the Bald Eagle in Alaska. Condor 66:282-286.

Hodges, J. I., Jr. 1982. Bald Eagle nesting studies in Seymour Canal, Southeast Alaska. Condor 84:125-127.

Hodges, J. I., Jr., J. G. King and R. Davies. 1984. Bald Eagle breeding population survey of coastal British Columbia. J. Wildl. Manage. 48:99398.

Hodges, J. I., Jr. and F. C. Robards. 1982. Observations of 3,850 Bald Eagle nests in Southeast Alaska. Pages 37-54. In: W. N. Ladd and P F. Schempf, eds. Proc. of a symposium and workshop on raptor management and biology in Alaska and Western Canada, 17-20 February 1981, Anchorage, Alas. U.S. Dept. Inter., Fish Wildl. Serv., Anchorage, Alas. 335pp.

King, K. A. and C. A. Lefever. 1979. Effects of oil transferred from incubating gulls to their eggs. Marine Pollut. Bull. 10:319-321.

Leighton, F. A. 1986. Clinical, gross and histological findings in Herring Gulls and Atlantic Puffins that ingested Prudhoe Bay crude oil. Veterinary Pathology 23:254-263.

Pattee. O. H. and J. C. Franson. 1982. Short-term effects of oil ingestion on American Kestrels (*Falco sparverius*). J. Wildl. Dis. 18:235-241.

Piatt, J. F., C. J. Lensink, W. Butler, M. Kendziorek and D. R. Nysewander. 1990. Immediate impact of the *Exxon Valdez* oil spill on marine birds. Auk 107:387397

Postupalsky, S. 1974. Raptor reproductive success: some problems with methods, criteria and terminology. Pages 21-31. In: F. N. Hamerstrom Jr., B. E. Harrell and R. R. Olendorff, eds. Management of raptors, proceedings of the conference on raptor conservation techniques. Raptor Research Report 2, Raptor Research Foundation, Vermillion, South Dakota.

Ritchie, R. J. 1982. Investigations of Bald Eagles, Tanana River, Alaska, 1977-80. Pages 55-67. In: W. N. Ladd and P. F. Schempf, eds. Raptor management and biology in Alaska and western Canada. U.S. Fish and Wildlife Service (FWS-AKPROC-82), Anchorage, Alaska.

Sherrod, S. K., C. M. White and F. S. L. Williamson. 1976. Biology of the Bald Eagle on Amchitka Island, Alaska. Living Bird 15:143-182.

Sprunt, A. I., IV, W. B. Robertson, Jr., S. Postupalsky, R. J. Hensel, C. E. Knoder and F. J. Ligas. 1973. Comparative productivity of six Bald Eagle populations. Trans. North Am. Wild. Nat. Res. Conf. 38:96-105.

Stalmaster, M. V. 1987. The Bald Eagle. Universe Books, New York.

Steenhof, K. 1987. Assessing raptor reproductive success and productivity. Pages 157-170. In: B. A. Giron Pendleton, B. A. Millsap, K. W. Cline and D. M. Bird, eds. Raptor management techniques manual. National Wildlife Federation, Washington. D.C.

Steenhof, K. and M. N. Kochert. 1982. An evaluation of methods used to estimate raptor nesting success. J. Wild. Manage. 46:885-893.

Szaro, R. C. 1977. Effects of petroleum on birds. Trans. North Am. Wildl. and Nat. Resourc. Conf. 42:374-381.

Szaro, R. C. 1979. Bunker C fuel oil reduces mallard egg hatchability. Bull. Environ. Contam. Toxicol. 22:731-732.

Szaro, R. C., P. H. Albers and N. C. Coon. 1978. Petroleum: effects on mallard egg hatchability. J. Wildl. Manage. 42:404- 406.

Szaro, R. C., N. C. Coon and W. Stout. 1980. Weathered petroleum: effects on mallard hatchability. J. Wildl. Manage. 44:709-713.

Todd, C. S., L. S. Young, R. B. Owen, Jr. and F. J. Gramlich. 1982. Food habits of Bald Eagles in Maine. J. Wildl. Manage. 46:636-645.

U.S. Coast Guard. 1993. T/V *Exxon Valdez* oil spill federal on scene coordinator's report. Vol. 1. U.S. Coast Guard, Department of Transportation, Washington. D.C.

USFWS (U.S. Fish and Wildlife Service). 1986. Recovery plan for the Pacific Bald Eagle. U.S. Fish and Wildlife Service, Portland, Oregon.

Whitfield, D. W. A., J. M. Gerrard, W. J. Maher and D. W. Davis. 1974. Bald Eagle nesting habitat, density and reproduction in central Saskatchewan and Manitoba. Can. Field-Nat. 88:399-407.

Wolfe, D. A., M. J. Hameedi, J. A. Galt, G. Watabayashi, J. Short, C. O'Clair, S. Rice, J. Michel, J. R. Payne, J. Braddock, S. Hanna and V. Salel. 1994. The fate of the oil spilled from the *Exxon Valdez*. Environ. Scie. and Technol. 28:561A-568A.

Wolfe, D. A., M. M. Krahn, E. Casillas, S. Sol, T. A. Thompson, J. Lunz and K. J. Scott. 1996. Toxicity of intertidal and subtidal sediments contaminated by the *Exxon Valdez* oil spill. Am. Fisheries Soc. Symp. 18:121-139.

History and Status of Bald Eagle Nesting and Productivity on the Kodiak Island Archipelago, Alaska

Dennis C. Zwiefelhofer

U.S. Fish and Wildlife Service, Kodiak, AK

The Kodiak Island Archipelago consists of 16 major islands plus numerous small islands and islets located in the western Gulf of Alaska. The archipelago contains approximately 5000 square miles of land area and has an estimated 2500 miles of coastline. The Kodiak National Wildlife Refuge (KNWR) encompasses approximately 58% of the Archipelago's land area on southwest Kodiak and northwest Afognak islands (Figure 1). Development and commercial utilization of Kodiak's coastal habitats have accelerated over the past decade. Through a variety of Congressional land actions (Native Claims Allotment Act of 1906, Soldier's Additional Homestead Act, Alaska Native Claims Settlement Act and Alaska National Interest Land Claims Act) plus greater demands for commercial and recreational opportunities, critical habitat for Bald Eagles is being placed under ever increasing cumulative impacts.

The purpose of this paper is to summarize past Bald Eagle nesting surveys and nesting status on the Kodiak Island Archipelago. Although comprehensive nesting survey for the entire archipelago has not been accomplished, a total of 1402 Bald Eagle nest sites have been identified and plotted. Incidental Bald Eagle nesting information was first collected by KNWR personnel at Karluk Lake in 1952. Chrest (1964) conducted Bald Eagle nesting ecology research on Karluk Lake during the years 1961 to 1963. Bald Eagles nesting within the KNWR were first comprehensively surveyed in 1963 (Hensel and Troyer 1964). Complete survey coverage of refuge lands also occurred during the years 1964-67, 1972, 1975, 1982 and 1987. During the years complete survey coverage did not occur, nesting and productivity surveys were conducted on selected bays and insular habitats of the KNWR No surveys were conducted in 1979, 1981, 1983 and 1984. In 1969, a west side sample area was surveyed for nesting but not for production. Additional Bald Eagle nesting data were collected on the northern (non-refuge) portions of the archipelago as part of the T/V *Exxon Valdez* oil spill assessment studies during 1989 and 1990.

The author stands alongside a Bald Eagle nest tree (below). This nest, used since 1963, is located in Olga Narrows. Photo by Dennis Zwiefelhofer.

Food habits of Kodiak Bald Eagles generally reflect the variety and abundance of food resources available (Grubb and Hensel 1978). Bald Eagles are quick to respond to annual and local food abundances. Dietary shifts from year to year reported by other Alaskan Bald Eagle researchers supports this behavior (Murie 1940, Krog 1953, Hehnke 1973, Sherrod et al. 1976). Grubb and Hensel (1978) found fish comprised 64% of the prey items identified in Kodiak Bald Eagle nests. Salmon (*Oncorhynchus* spp.) made up approximately 50% of the fish species identified. Ungulate carrion has been found to be important to wintering Bald Eagle populations (Imler and Kalmbach 1955, Cole 1972, Servheen 1975, Houston 1978, Stalmaster and Newman 1978, Steenhof 1978, Swenson et al. 1986). Because of the length of time in which surveys have been conducted, the Kodiak Bald Eagle population is likely the best documented nesting population of Bald Eagles in the state of Alaska.

Methods
Bald Eagle nest locations and productivity data were interpreted from historic survey maps. Historic survey map locations were not always clear and some interpolation of the survey locations was done to obtain the final plotted nest sites. Plotting accuracy was estimated to be plus or minus .5 km. Plotted nest sites were consecutively numbered as they were accumulated on the master digitizing maps (1:63,360 USGS topographic maps). Map data were collected using fixed-winged aircraft surveys in the spring to record nesting attempts and late summer to document productivity. Although follow-up late summer sampling of approximately 50% of the early survey's total active or occupied nests was recommended, this guideline was not rigidly followed through the years (Hensel and Troyer 1964). During the 1989 and 1990 surveys, a rotary-winged aircraft was utilized on the northern portions of the archipelago for both the nesting and productivity surveys. Historically, production survey sample sizes ranged from 12% to 99% of the total active nests located during the early nesting survey.

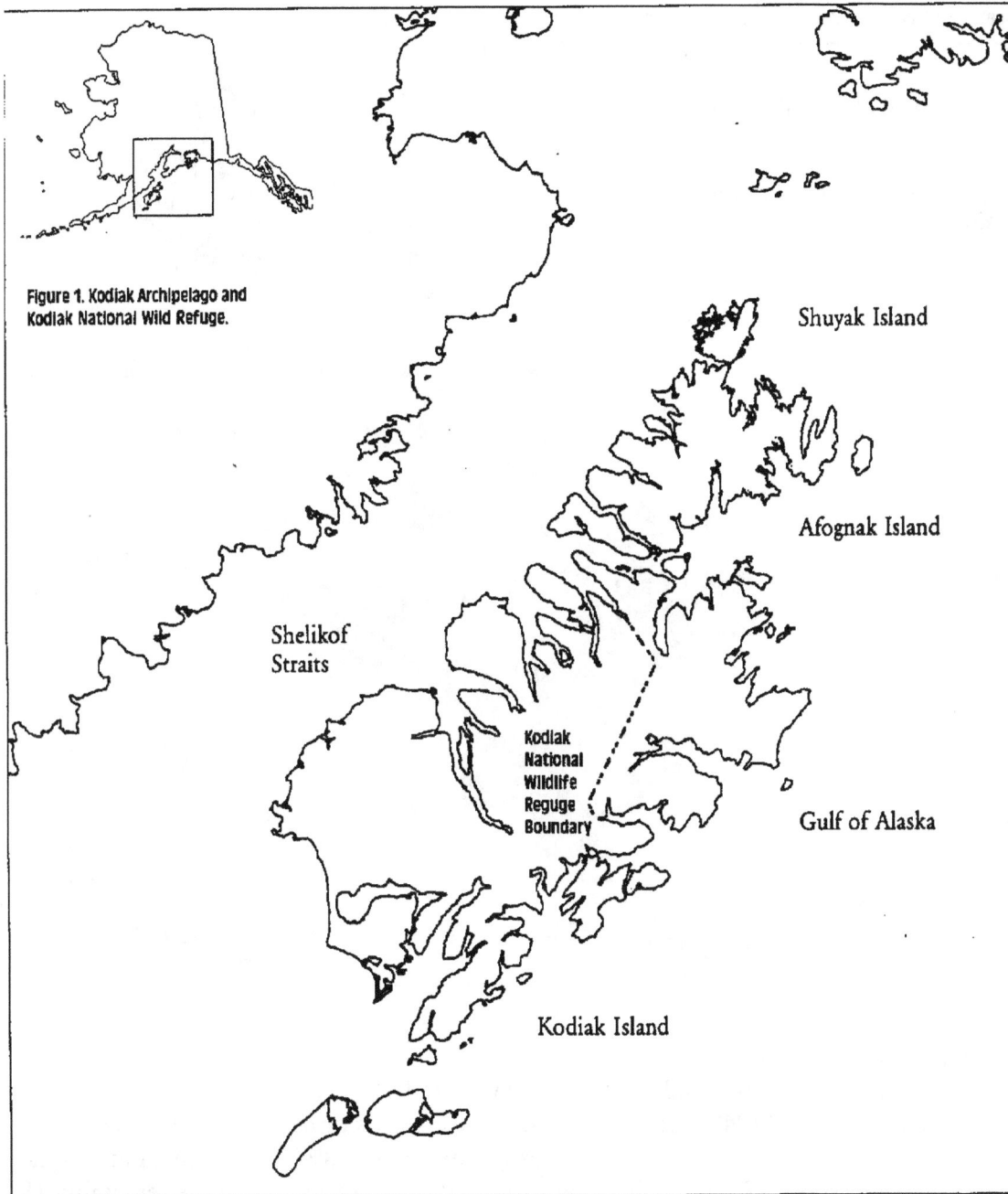

Figure 1. Kodiak Archipelago and Kodiak National Wild Refuge.

Portions of the presented data have been previously reported (Chrest 1964, Hensel and Troyer 1964, Troyer and Hensel 1965, Sprunt et al. 1973). Survey data collected after 1970 appears in KNWR annual narrative reports, but has not otherwise been published. Since 1986, survey plots consisting of five degree longitude-latitude blocks (Figure 2) have been utilized to stratify and randomly sample Bald Eagle nesting habitat when survey coverage of the entire refuge was not possible. The survey plots were used for comparison of data between years. The subset of comparison plots from 1963 to 1990 is primarily coastal data. It was assumed survey coverage within plots remained constant between survey years; therefore, any change seen was considered actual.

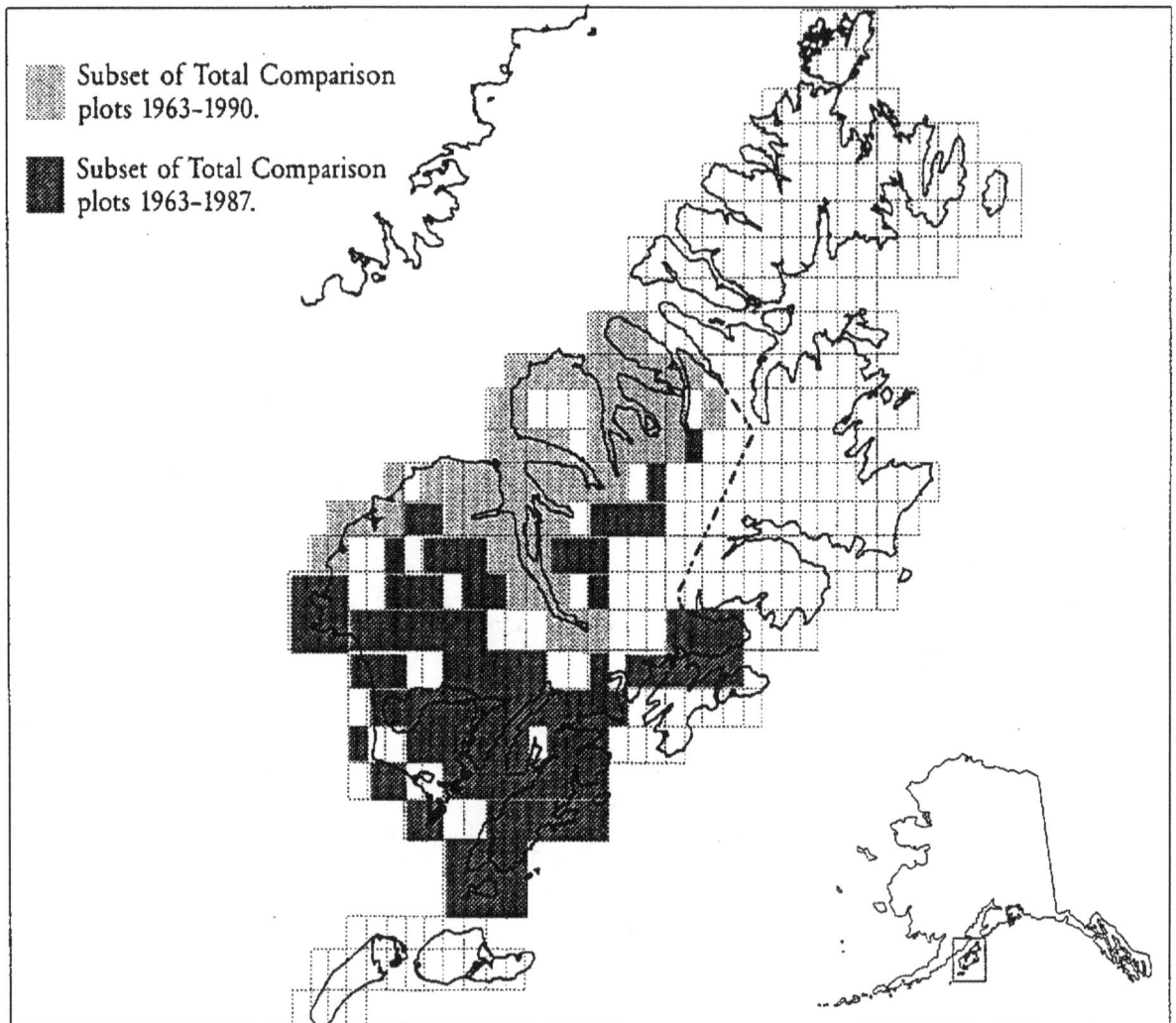

Subset of Total Comparison plots 1963–1990.

Subset of Total Comparison plots 1963–1987.

Results and Discussion

From 1963 to 1990, 1,402 Bald Eagle nest sites were located (Table 1); 1,059 (76%) were found in trees and 343 (24%) occurred on sea stacks, cliffs or as ground nests. Tree species used by nesting Bald Eagles were as follows: 619 (58%) were located in cotton-wood (*Populus* spp.), 422 (40%) in Sitka spruce (*Picea sitchensis*) and the remaining 18 (2%) of the tree nests were found in black birch (*Betula* spp.) or willow (*Salix* spp.) trees. Alder (*Alnus* spp.) trees often occurred in conjunction with cliff habitat and were included with the cliff nests. During years of total refuge survey coverage, mean active nests comprised 60% of the total Bald Eagle nests located (range 49-67%).

Average nesting success was 65% for the years in which productivity was recorded (range 44%-77%). Means of 1.1 young produced per active nest and 1.6 young per successful nest were calculated from the historic data. Occupied nests as defined by Postupalsky (1974) were included with the active nest category.

Figure 3. Bald Eagle nests on the Kodiak National Wildlife Reserve, 1963–1987.

Number of Nests

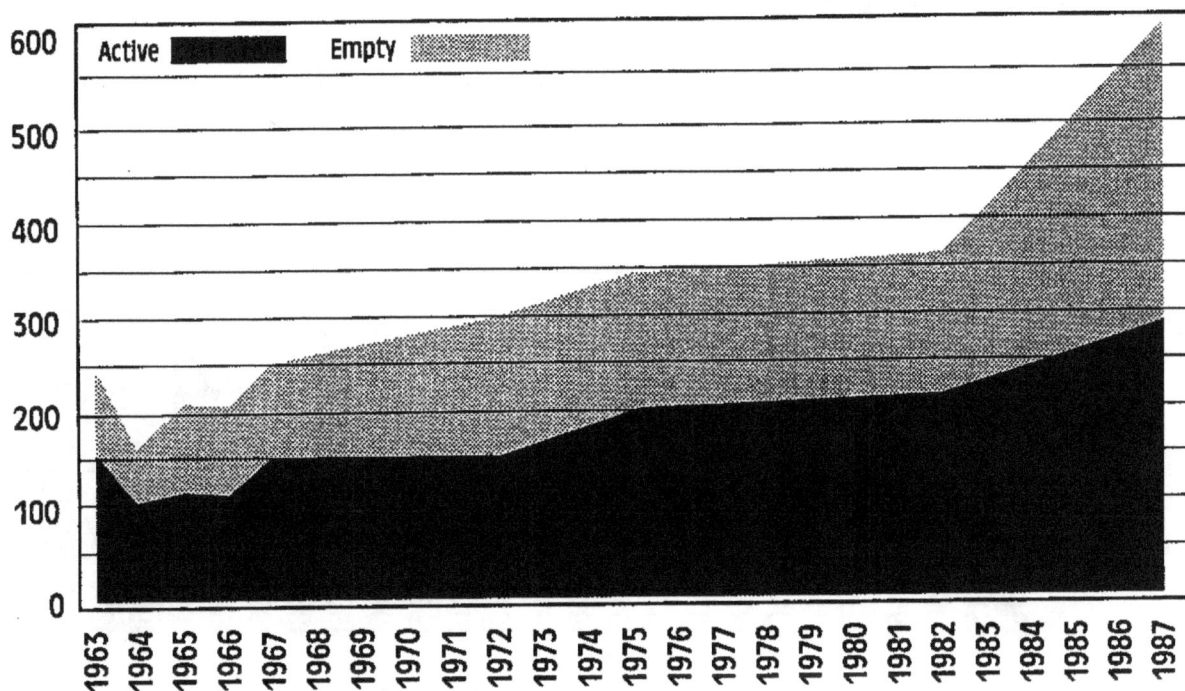

Active ▮ Empty ▨

600
500
400
300
200
100
0

1963 1964 1965 1966 1967 1968 1969 1970 1971 1972 1973 1974 1975 1976 1977 1978 1979 1980 1981 1982 1983 1984 1985 1986 1987

Table 1. Summary of Bald Eagle nest data.

Survey Year	Empty Nests	Active–not rechecked	Active w/ 0 young	Active w/ one young	Active w/ two young	Active w/ three young	Young/Nesting attempt	Total young
1990[a]	380	5	149	108	160	6	1.1	446
1989[b]	308	3	94	94	134	13	1.2	401
1988	119	4	35	57	52	4	1.2	173
1987[a]	318	94	81	66	63	0	.9	192
1986	92	8	39	47	21	1	.9	92
1985	25	1	17	23	18	1	1.1	62
1982[a]	155	197	2	9	14	1	1.5	40
1980	75	11	20	15	10	0	.8	35
1978	67	9	29	19	4	0	.5	27
1977	106	17	10	13	20	0	1.2	53
1976	79	17	10	24	7	1	1.0	41
1975[a]	136	151	18	23	14	0	.9	51
1974	85	48	14	15	17	0	1.1	49
1973	117	54	21	13	8	0	.7	29
1972[a]	135	135	8	8	8	0	1.0	24
1971	9	4	14	13	7	0	.8	27
1970	31	40	6	14	8	0	1.1	30
1968	68	57	11	8	14	2	1.2	42
1967[a]	91	109	17	11	26	0	1.2	63
1966[a]	85	81	15	10	14	0	1.0	38
1965[a]	91	86	16	12	7	0	.7	26
1964[a]	55	48	23	8	13	1	.8	37
1963[a]	95	72	27	20	26	3	1.1	81

[a] Complete KNWR survey coverage.
[b] Includes Afognak, Shuyak, Whale, Respberry, Ban, Amook, Uganik, and Spruce Islands plus the north and west sides of Kodiak Island.

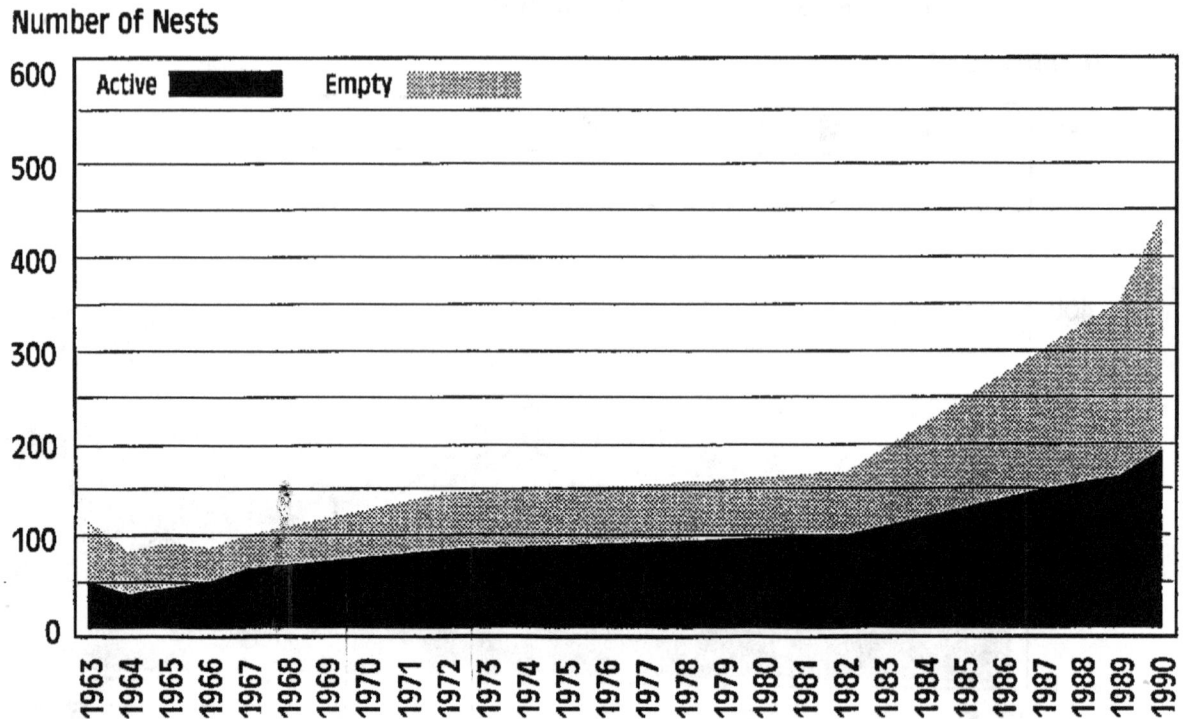

Figure 4. Bald Eagle nests in 61 survey plots on west side of Kodiak National Wildlife Reserve; 1963–1990.

The number of Bald Eagles nesting on the Kodiak Archipelago has increased since 1972 (Figures 3 and 4). Factors contributing to this notable increase have not been identified. The availability of a reliable food source is the habitat parameter most likely to influence Bald Eagle nesting (Swenson et al. 1986, MacDonald and Austin-Smith 1989). Food availability is also one of the most dynamic parameters and, therefore, one of the factors that must be considered when any change in a population is noted. Fish normally constitute a large part of the food resources utilized by Bald Eagles. The availability of salmon would likely influence Kodiak Bald Eagle nesting. Although Kodiak salmon (*Oncorhynchus* spp.) harvest levels have exhibited considerable variance since 1963, an overall increase in total harvest has occurred from 1976 to the present, indicating an increase in the abundance of salmon in the near shore waters of the archipelago (Figure 5). This increased availability of salmon probably has been a factor in the observed nesting increase. Kodiak Island ground fish populations, particularly whiting (*Theragra chalcogrammus*), Pacific cod (*Gadus macrocephalus*) and Pacific tom cod (*Microgadus proximus*) have exhibited a tremendous increase in biomass from the mid-1970's to the late 1980's. Their availability for nesting Bald Eagles, however, is thought to be minimal and therefore not likely a factor in the observed Bald Eagle nesting increase. Kodiak's Pacific herring (*Clupea pallasii*) stocks have also exhibited a biomass increase, but only since 1984 (Prokopowich, pers. comm.).

In 1987, 127 of the total 163 survey plots with Bald Eagle nesting activity contained an average of 7.4 miles (11.9 km) of coastline with a mean of 3.8 nests (range 1-20) per plot. This equates to approximately one Bald Eagle nest for every 2 miles (3.2 km) of Kodiak shoreline.

Kodiak's introduced population of Sitka black-tailed deer has displayed the same surge in numbers during the period Bald Eagle nesting increased. Carrion available from winter-killed deer has also increased. The wind-swept coastal cape habitats on Kodiak generally tend to concentrate wintering deer because of the reduced snow cover. Bald Eagle nest initiation in this habitat type has been observed as early as the end of March or beginning of April. Wintering black-tailed deer are also most likely to be succumbing to the rigors of winter during this period. The availability of deer carrion probably has improved survival rates of all Bald Eagle cohorts and overall body conditions of breeding pairs entering the nesting season. The relative decline in black-tailed deer numbers during the past two years may have an influence on the Bald Eagle population in the future.

The influence of Kodiak weather conditions on Bald Eagle nesting has not been tested. Cold, wet spring weather conditions have been shown to negatively impact other northern Bald Eagle nesting populations (Gerrard and Whitfield 1979, Swenson et al. 1986).

Figure 5. Kodiak area salmon harvest from 1963–1989.

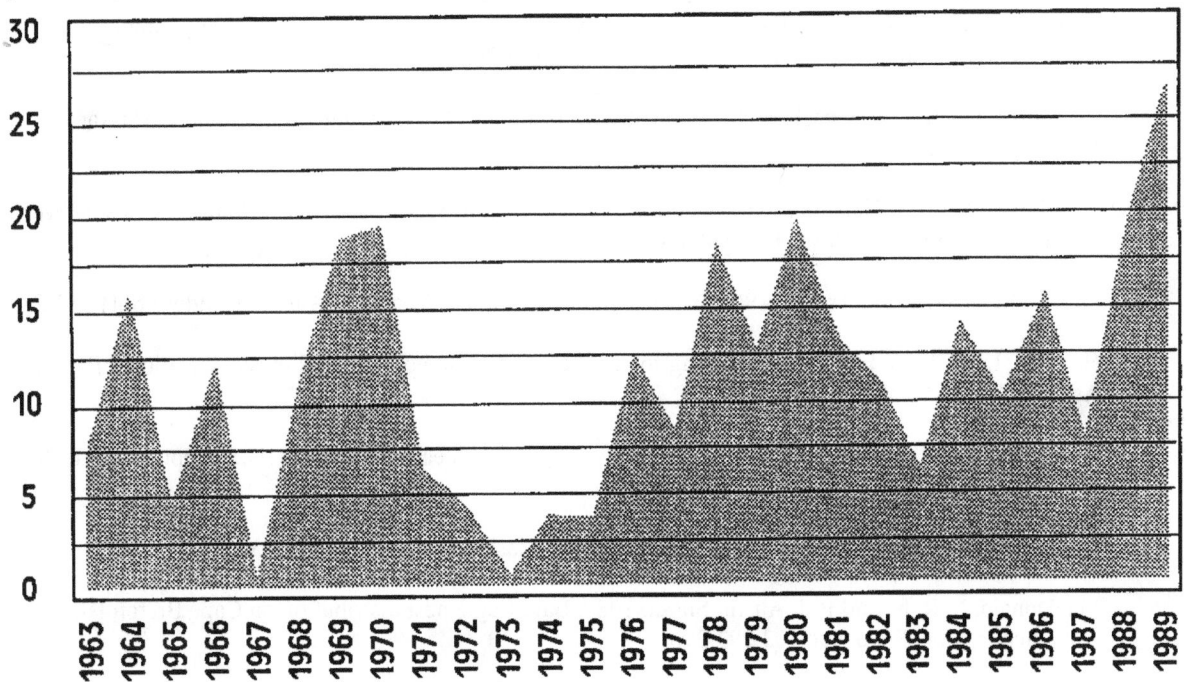

Conclusions and Recommendations

With the removal of Bald Eagle bounties in the late 1950's and the banning of hydrocarbon pesticides in the 1960's, Kodiak's Bald Eagle population have been regulated by natural occurring factors. Although nesting efforts have been on the increase since 1972, overall nesting success and productivity on the archipelago appears to be remaining relatively static. In the future, if complete survey coverage of the KNWR or archipelago is not possible, an effort to use statistically valid sampling will be made. As more of the Kodiak coastline is subjected to a wider variety of user impacts, the undisturbed nesting habitats available to Bald Eagles are being reduced. If the high quality coastal habitats continue to be usurped by man, the nesting Bald Eagles will be pushed into marginal areas that cannot support current population levels.

The factors responsible for the increase of Kodiak Bald Eagle nesting observed since 1972 can only be speculated without further research. Kodiak's Bald Eagle population may be slowly recovering from previous persecution and pesticide use (Patuxent Wildlife Research Center chemical analysis reports) or may have increased beyond historic population densities because of a positive short term environmental change. The elements amenable for the current increase will need to be identified if future cumulative impacts are to be monitored.

Literature Cited

Chrest, H. R. 1964. Nesting of the Bald Eagle on the Karluk Lake drainage Kodiak Island, Alaska. M.S. Thesis. Colorado State University, Fort Collins, CO. 72pp.

Cole, G. F. 1972. Grizzly bear-elk relationships in Yellowstone Park. J. Wildl. Manage. 36:556-561.

Gerrard, J. M. and D. W. A. Whitfield. 1979. An analysis of the "crash" in eagle productivity in Saskatchewan in 1975. Pages 42-48. In: T. N. Ingram, ed. Proc. Bald Eagle conf. on wintering eagles. Eagle Valley Environ., Apple River, Ill., Tech. Rep. BED-79.

Grubb, T. G. and R. J. Hensel. 1978. Food habits of nesting Bald Eagles on Kodiak Island, Alaska. Murrelet 59:70-72.

Hehnke, M. F. 1973. Nesting ecology and feeding behavior of Bald Eagles on the Alaska Peninsula. M.S. Thesis. Humboldt State Univ., Humboldt, Calif. 56pp.

Hensel, R. J. and W. A. Troyer. 1964. Nesting studies of the Bald Eagle in Alaska. Condor 66(4):282-286.

Houston, D. B. 1978. Elk as winter-spring food for carnivores in northern Yellowstone National Park. J. Applied. Ecol. 15:653661.

Imler, R. H. and E. R. Kalmbach. 1955. The Bald Eagle and its economic status. U.S. Dept. Inter., Fish Wildl. Serv. Circular 30. 51 pp.

Krog, J. 1953. Notes on the birds of Amchitka Island, Alaska. Condor 55(6):299-304.

MacDonald, P. R. N. and P. J. Austin-Smith. 1989. Bald Eagle nest distribution on Cape Breton Island, Nova Scotia. Can. Field Nat. 103:293-296.

Murie, O. J. 1940. Food habits of the northern Bald Eagle in the Aleutian Islands, Alaska. Condor 42(4):198-202.

Postupalsky, S. 1974. Raptor reproductive success; some problems with methods, criteria and terminology. Pages 21-31. In: F.N. Hamerstrom Jr., B.E. Harrell and R.R. Olendorff, eds. Management of raptors, proceedings of the conference on raptor conservation techniques. Raptor Research Report 2, Raptor Research Foundation, Vermillio, South Dakota.

Servheen, C. W. 1975. Ecology of the wintering Bald Eagles on the Skagit River, Washington. M.S. Thesis, Univ. Washington, Seattle. 96pp.

Sherrod, S. K., C. M. White and F. S. L. Williamson. 1976. Biology of the Bald Eagle on Amchitka Island, Alaska. Living Bird 15:143-182.

Sprunt, A., IV., W. B. Robertson, Jr., S. Postupalsky, R. J. Hensel, C. E. Knoder and F. J. Ligas. 1973. Comparative productivity of six Bald Eagle populations. Trans. North Am. Wildl. and Nat. Resour. Conf., Washington, D.C. 38:96-106.

Stalmaster, M. V. and J. R. Newman. 1978. Behavioral responses of wintering Bald Eagles to human activity. J. Wildl. Manage. 42(3):506-513.

Steenhof, K. 1978. Management of wintering Bald Eagles. U.S. Fish Wildl. Serv. Biol. Serv. Program FWS/OBS-78/79. 59pp.

Swenson, J. E., K. L. Alt and R. L. Eng. 1986. Ecology of Bald Eagles in the Greater Yellowstone Ecosystem. Wildl. Monogr. 95:146.

Troyer, W. A. and R. J. Hensel. 1965. Nesting and productivity of Bald Eagles on the Kodiak National Wildlife Refuge, Alaska. Auk 82(4):636-638.

Distribution, Abundance and Status of Bald Eagles in Interior Alaska

Robert J. Ritchie and Robert E. Ambrose

Alaska Biological Research Inc., Fairbanks AK and U.S. Fish and Wildlife Service, Fairbanks, AK

Abstract

Information on numbers, distribution and status of Bald Eagles is summarized for six regions of interior Alaska: Upper Yukon, Lower Yukon, Tanana, Kuskokwim, Copper and Susitna rivers. Three hundred and forty-five nesting territories were identified using information from local researchers, a raptor nest atlas and unpublished raptor surveys reports. Nearly 85% of these records were from the Copper, Susitna and Tanana drainages. Extrapolating from known nests and approximate survey coverage per drainage, we estimate that 525 to 725 pairs of Bald Eagles nest in interior Alaska. Information is provided to suggest that substantial increases in the population have occurred since the first half of this century, especially since 1970 and that numbers in some areas have continued to increase. Reasons for this increase may be expanding or rebounding populations on the perimeter of the breeding range, improving health of the population and/or improving environmental conditions e.g., a warming trend. Interestingly, banding and migration data suggest that the interior's population north of the Alaska Range may be influenced by characteristics different from those in the Copper and Susitna drainages. Life history information for interior Bald Eagles is also provided.

Introduction

The Bald Eagle (*Haliaeetus leucocephalus* alascanus) is a dominant resident of Alaska's coastal avifauna from Southeast Alaska north and west through the Bristol Bay region. Regular surveys have provided a basis from which the status of Alaska's Bald Eagle can be determined and support population estimates exceeding 30,000 (Schempf 1989). Alaska's interior population of Bald Eagles however, is relatively small in comparison with the coastal population (Ritchie and Ambrose 1996). With the exception of a few large rivers, Bald Eagles in the interior are dispersed in summer and forced by winter ice and a lack of prey to leave their breeding range for 5-6 months of each year. In this paper we will discuss the distribution and abundance of Bald Eagles in interior Alaska and suggest what physical and biological factors might influence their distribution and abundance. We also will attempt to assess its status, although large areas still require surveys. Our primary sources of information for this paper were results from unpublished raptor surveys, an atlas of raptor nest sites developed for the USFWS in 1981 and personal communications with a number of researchers familiar with each region. Because so many types of surveys, occurring over a wide range of dates, by different observers, form the basis for our discussion, the accuracy of our estimates varies among subregions.

Bald Eagle adult and eaglet in a cottonwood nest. Photo by Phil Schempf, USFWS.

Study Area

The interior study area is described broadly as an area influenced by the continental climatic zone and containing a mix of broad-leaf and conifer vegetation communities, often called the boreal forest. Nearly the entire Yukon and Kuskokwim river drainages are included. We have followed Kessel and Gibson's (1978) boundaries of a Central Region (750,000 km²), which includes the drainages of the upper Copper and Susitna rivers. For the purposes of our discussion the region has been divided into six major areas (Figure 1; drainage areas were calculated from Lamke 1979):

1) UPPER YUKON: Yukon River (Alaska-Canada border to approximately Rampart; Porcupine and its tributaries; Charley, Kandik, Nation, Forty-Mile rivers, Birch and Beaver Creeks; includes the Porcupine Plateau and the Yukon Flats (180,000 km²).

2) TANANA: Tanana River including the Chisana, Nabesna, Delta, Kantishna and other tributaries; Minto Flats and the Tetlin Lake area (118,000 km²).

3) LOWER YUKON: Yukon River west of Rampart to approximately Holy Cross; Koyukuk; includes extensive wetlands associated with the Nowitna and Innoko rivers (190,000 km²).

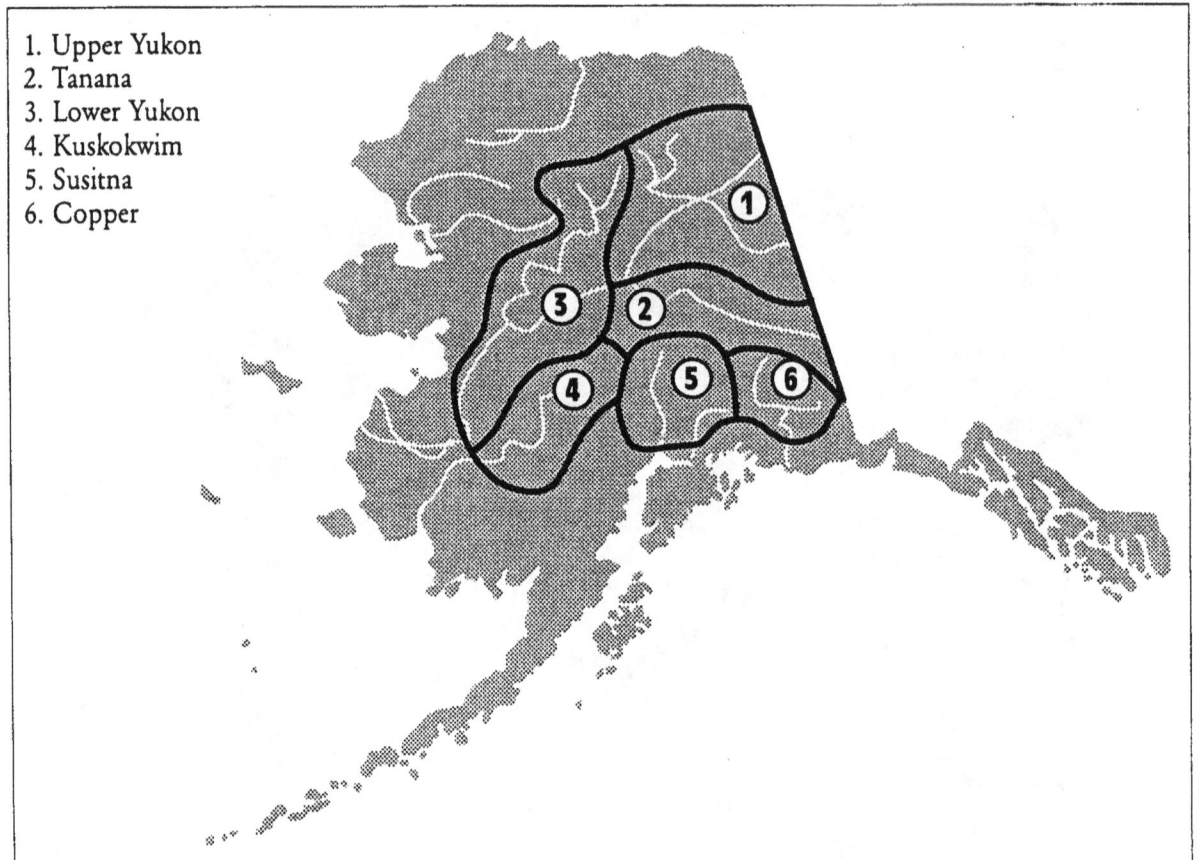

Figure 1. Drainage study areas, Interior Alaska.

4) KUSKOKWIM: Kuskokwim drainage downriver to Aniak; including Holitna River, Hoholitna River and major tributaries of the Kuskokwim River (95,000 km²).

5) SUSITNA RIVER Susitna and its tributaries Skwentna, Talkeetna; Matanuska (60,000 km²).

6) UPPER COPPER Copper from its headwaters to Chitina; including Chitina, Gakona, Gulkana and wetlands in the Nelchina Basin (50,000 km²)

Results and Discussion
Natural History Background
Bald Eagles in interior Alaska are primarily summer residents, arriving as early as late March and departing by freeze-up in mid to late October. Results of three years of migration studies in the upper Tanana River Basin showed peak arrival to occur in late April and peak departure to occur after mid September (Cooper et al. 1991). Regular mid-winter (December-February) observations of Bald Eagles have been recorded on the Tanana River near Delta Junction (Ritchie and Ambrose 1987) and are associated with wintering waterfowl, late salmon runs and extensive open water. Open water in other tributaries of the Tanana may also provide possibilities for over-wintering eagles.

Nest attendance and reconstruction begins in late April. The onset of incubation probably peaks by the second week of May, although hatching in the first week of June near Delta Junction suggests that over-wintering birds or early arrivals may nest earlier (Ritchie 1982). On the Tanana River, more than 70% of breeding pairs produce young and mean productivity was 1.6 (±.4) young per successful pair between 1978 and 1990 (Ritchie 1982, Ambrose unpubl. records). Stalmaster (1987) reported similar rates for boreal populations in Canada. Most young have fledged by late August.

Nests are usually in a dominant tree in a stand close to shorelines. Balsam poplar (*Populus balsamifera*) appears to be the preferred tree for nests along the braided, interior rivers (69%, n=48, Tanana River, Ritchie 1982) and the Susitna River (Parker 1988), but white spruce (*Picea glauca*) are used regularly, especially at off-river sites, or at higher elevation where balsam poplar are less common. Most nests on the Tanana River were within 100 m of a shoreline (Ritchie 1982). Gerrard et al. (1975) suggested that variation in use of trees reflected a preference based on trees available. In addition to trees, Bald Eagles nest on cliffs or on the ground. At least two ground nests have been identified in interior Alaska (upper Susitna, Kessel et al. 1982; Delta, Wilbor 1989). Ground nesting Bald Eagles are common on the coast (Hehnke 1973), but not in the boreal forest.

Food habits information is limited to opportunistic collections at a few nests (Ritchie 1982, Mindell 1983) and observations of hunting eagles. Birds, especially waterfowl, are important in the summer diet of interior Bald Eagles (43% of prey items in nests along the Tanana River, Ritchie 1982). This may be particularly true in spring when most water bodies are still frozen. Fish may also be vulnerable at this critical time if they move through ice-free rapids opening before peak breakup (K. Alt, pers. comm.). Salmon appear to be more important resources in late summer and fall. Barber et al. (1985) suggested that areas of rapids were important to Bald Eagles arriving in spring in a Saskatchewan study area.

Approximately 100 Bald Eagles have been banded along the interior drainages of the upper Yukon, Tanana and Copper rivers since 1984 and we are aware of four relevant recoveries. Two of these records were winter recoveries in the interior regions of North America: a Yukon River eagle was recovered in southcentral British Columbia; and a Tanana River eagle was recovered in northcentral Washington. A third bird, banded in late fall in Glacier National Park, Montana, was recovered the following summer near McGrath (unpubl. banding records, Bird Banding Lab, Patuxent, MD). These recoveries suggest Bald Eagles from interior Alaska winter in continental regions of North America. However, some exchange between coastal and interior areas occurs and this is supported by a record of a long range movement of a subadult Bald Eagle banded in Saskatchewan and recovered near Juneau (Gerrard et al. 1978). Observations along the Copper River near Chitina also suggest movements of Bald Eagles from interior Alaska (Nelchina Basin) to the coast (Cooper et al., 1991).

Regional Abundance and Distribution
Approximately 345 breeding territories or nesting pairs were identified (breeding territory is defined as a nest or series of nests in close proximity to one another, with some recent

[within 10 years] history of use by a pair). The distribution and relative abundance of Bald Eagles in each subregion varies (Table 1). Nearly 85% of known nesting pairs occurred in the Susitna, Copper and Tanana drainages. These three areas also have had regular Bald Eagle surveys.

UPPER YUKON: Raptor surveys on the upper Yukon and tributaries suggest that Bald Eagles are uncommon and dispersed. Most nest records are from drainages south of the Porcupine River including the Black and Charley rivers (M. Britten, pers. comm., Ritchie 1984). Occasional nests have been located in drainages on the south side of the Brooks Range (East Fork Chandalar, Roseneau 1974) and Kandik, Nation, Birch and Forty-Mile rivers (T. Swem, pers. comm., Kuropat 1986). The Yukon Flats, a major wetland, has not been surveyed, but nests have been recorded there during waterfowl surveys (J. Hodges, USFWS, pers. comm.). We can account for approximately 35 nesting pairs in the area and estimate 75-100 pairs in the upper Yukon drainage.

TANANA: Bald Eagle surveys have occurred regularly in the Tanana River basin (Roseneau and Bente 1979, Ritchie 1982, R. Ambrose, unpubl. Notes, T. Doyle, USFWS, pers. comm., Cooper et al. 1991). Bald Eagles are a common breeding bird and we can account for a minimum of 70 pairs along the upper Tanana and Chisana rivers and extensive wetlands near Tetlin Lake. In addition, occasional nests have been identified along the Tanana River below Fairbanks and along its tributaries including the Chatanika, Nabesna, Delta and Nenana rivers. We estimate that 75-100 pairs of Bald Eagles summer along the Tanana River.

LOWER YUKON: With the exception of Peregrine Falcon surveys along the Yukon River and on the upper Koyukuk, no intensive raptor surveys have been undertaken in this area. Bald Eagles are rare breeders along the lower Yukon (Springer et al. 1979, Mindell and Craighead 1981), but approximately 20 nests have been located along the Innoko, Koyukuk and Nowitna rivers (T. Osborne, ADFG, pers. comm., P. Feiger and M. Bertram, USFWS, pers. comm.). We estimate that 50-75 pairs inhabit this region.

KUSKOKWIM: Raptor surveys have occurred on the main Kuskokwim River and some of its tributaries west of McGrath (Ritchie and Ambrose 1976, Mindell 1983). In addition, resource agency personnel have gathered information on a number of nests throughout the area (P. Shepherd, pers. comm., J. Whitman, ADFG, pers. comm.). Approximately 15 pairs have nested on the Holitna and Hoholitna rivers (ADFG, unpubl. maps 1976). With the exception of these rivers, however, Bald Eagles apparently are not common in the Kuskokwim drainage. Only three nests have been located between McGrath and Aniak and Mindell (1983) rarely reported Bald Eagles along 18 rivers in this area and immediately to the west. White and Boyce (1978) also surveyed rivers to the west and rarely located nests. Most tributaries have not been surveyed intensively, but almost all major tributaries have records of scattered nests (J. Whitman, ADFG, pers. comm.). We can account for a minimum of 32 nests in the region and estimate 50-75 pairs in the Kuskokwim drainage.

Table 1. Known and estimated numbers of Bald Eagles in each of six subregions, Interior Alaska.

Region	Percent Surveyed (1)	Known Pairs	Estimated Pairs (2)	Sources
Upper Yukon	<50	35	75-100	Ambrose, unpubl., Ritchie 1984, Kuropat 1986
Tanana	~75	70	75-100	Roseneau 1974, Haugh and Halperin 1976, Roseneau and Bente 1979, T. Swem and P. Knuckles, pers. comm., Ritchie 1982, T. Doyle, pers. comm.
Lower Yukon	<25	20	50-75	Springer et al. 1979, Mindell and Craighead 1981, Amaral 1982
Kuskokwim	<50	30	75-100	Mindell 1983, T. Osborne, P. Feiger, M. Bertram, pers. comm., P. Shepherd, pers. comm.
Susitna	~75	80	125-175	Kessel et al. 1982, Parker 1988, J. Whitman, pers. comm., R. King pers. comm.
Copper	~75	110	125-175	White 1974, White and Cade 1975, Haugh and Halperin 1976, Cooper et al. 1991
Totals		345	525-725	Wilbor 1989, B. Stiedl, pers. comm.

(1) Estimate of area with some history of surveys.
(2) Estimates were derived from total known pairs and approximate area covered; the range (often higher) reflects discussion with observers in each area.

SUSITNA: The Susitna Hydroelectric Project and proposed timber sales promulgated Bald Eagle investigations in this watershed (White 1974, White and Cade 1975, Kessel et al. 1982, Parker 1988). Bald Eagles are common and nests have been found along the Susitna, Talkeetna, Yentna, Skwentna, Chulitna, Beluga and Kahiltna rivers. Nests appear to be uniformly distributed and Parker (1988) estimated 125 pairs for the basin and noted survey totals of 69-76 nests in 1980 and 1988. Additional nests occur on the upper Susitna River (Kessel et al. 1982) and probably occur on other drainages and wetlands in the region. We estimate that 150-200 pairs inhabit the basin.

COPPER A number of raptor surveys have occurred in the Copper River basin (Haugh and Halperin 1976, Amaral 1988, Wilbor 1989, Cooper et al. 1991, B. Stiedl, unpubl. notes). Bald Eagles are common breeders in all major drainages as well as in the extensive wetlands in the Nelchina Basin. A minimum of 110 nesting pairs have been located with concentrations on the Gulkana, mid Copper and upper Gakona rivers. Many of our records are old and drainages including the Slana and Chistochina have not been surveyed. We estimate that 125-175 pairs occupy the upper Copper River.

Although survey coverage explains some of these regional differences, biological and physical factors may influence distribution. The areas where Bald Eagles are most common are closest to dense tidewater populations. Those regions closest to tidewater are also influenced to some degree by maritime weather conditions. Bald Eagle distribution in regions north of the Alaska Range, may be limited by more severe climatological characteristics. Interestingly, Bald Eagles are most dense south of a 30 April iso-breakup line. Leighton et al. (1979) showed that April mean temperature and breeding area density were correlated for a population in Saskatchewan.

Areas with the most dense populations of Bald Eagles in interior Alaska also may have more diverse and seasonally vulnerable prey bases than the majority of wetlands in the interior. For instance, Bald Eagles are fairly common on the Black River in the Porcupine drainage and the Holitna River in the Kuskokwim River basin. Both have late spawning runs of sheefish and chum salmon and early openings in ice cover in spring due to similar favorable hydrologic characteristics (K. Alt, ADFG, pers. comm.).

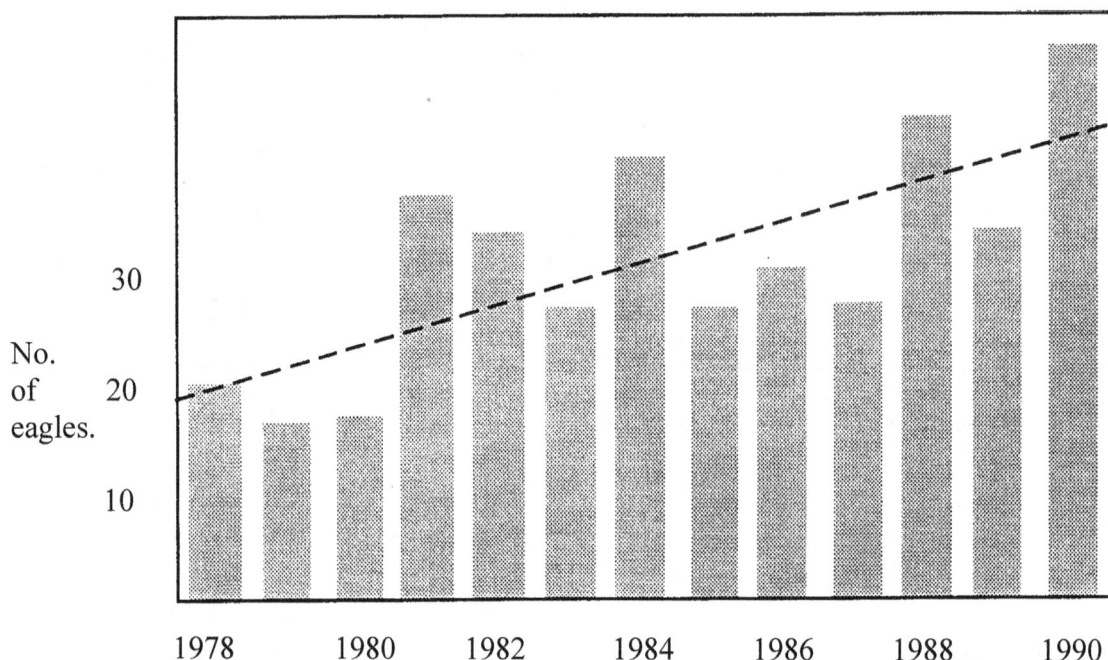

Figure 2. Number of Bald Eagle pairs on the middle Tanana River Alaska. The dashed line represents the apparent increase in Bald Eagle pairs. (Tanacross to Delta River), 1978-1990.

Status

Although Bald Eagles are regular breeders in the interior, little historical information is available for specific Bald Eagle nest sites in the interior, suggesting that they were either overlooked or were much less common than now. Gabrielson and Lincoln (1959) stated that although Bald Eagles are not found along many interior rivers (although common on some) "definite nesting records are lacking, [but it] probably breeds in the interior". This impression was generated from the lack of accounts by early naturalists. For example, the rush of naturalists who traveled through Alaska from the turn of the century through the 1930's noted the Bald Eagle as uncommon or did not list it (Yukon, Dall and Bannister 1869, Kuskokwim, Hinckley 1900, Dice 1920a, 1920b, Yukon, Osgood and Bishop 1900, Blackwelder 1919, Chitina; Tanana, Koyukuk, Murie unpublished notes, Univ. of Alaska

Archives). The nests of other tree-nesting raptors like the Osprey and Red-tailed Hawk, however, often were recorded (Dice 1920b, Murie, unpubl. notes, University of Alaska Archives), suggesting that Bald Eagles may not have been as common a breeder as they are today until sometime after this era. As a matter of fact, Bald Eagles do not fit prominently into ornithological literature for the interior until the 1970's when their special status was an impetus for conducting nesting surveys for proposed industrial developments. Is this apparent change in status related to specific physical or biological phenomena, or is it simply an artifact of sampling effort? We think both factors are involved.

First of all, persecution of the Bald Eagle in Alaska is well documented and influenced their abundance in coastal Alaska. The Bounty Acts of 1917 and 1949 accounted for a minimum of 128,273 eagle mortalities reported between 1917 and 1952 (Robards and King 2008). Hansen and Hodges (1985) suggested that the population in Southeast Alaska was substantially reduced during the bounty period and may have rebounded since that time.

Although most bounties were paid in the southeast and southwest (Robards and King 2008), the bounty's influence on nesting Bald Eagles may have extended into the interior. Recent increases of Bald Eagles in the interior may be associated with this rebound. However, since banding records and migration data suggest that interior birds may not interchange regularly with coastal populations, other mortality factors associated with non-coastal populations in Canada and the 48 states may have played an important part in the noticeable lack of Bald Eagles during the exploration era of Alaska. Persecution did not begin with the bounty system and interior Bald Eagles probably were affected by other human-influenced mortality. For instance, Osgood and Bishop (1900) described trying to collect a female at a nest and although she was too high in the tree "for our No. 4 shot" a passerby shot the male with a rifle! At least in the 1930's through 1970's, sheep ranchers made systematic efforts to exterminate eagles from western states in which interior Bald Eagles may regularly winter (Stalmaster 1987). In addition, the wide use of pesticides influenced many breeding populations in the coterminous United States (Stalmaster 1987) and may have influenced the health of Bald Eagles in interior Alaska. In addition to this apparent change in numbers between approximately 1930 and 1970, Bald Eagles on the Tanana have shown an increasing trend in the past 12 years (Figure 2). Numbers of pairs on the mid-Tanana have increased from 6 to 15 pairs between 1978 and 1990. Although improved survey coverage in some areas may account for some increase, survey effort on the mid-Tanana River has been consistent. Additional studies may provide data to suggest whether these increases are due to the improving health of this population, immigration into this area from rebounding or expanding populations elsewhere, or improving environmental conditions. In regard to the latter, Swenson (1983) makes a case for expansion of breeding range in Canada due to the warming trend especially pronounced in the past forty years.

Summary and Conclusions
In conclusion, nest records suggest that Bald Eagles are most common in the upper Tanana, Copper and Susitna drainages, less common in the Kuskokwim and upper Yukon

drainages and uncommon in the lower Yukon drainage. Bald Eagles may be affected by a number of physical and biological limitations in each of these drainages including the proximity to expanding or recovering populations. Furthermore, the local populations north of the Alaska Range appear somewhat distinct from those in maritime influenced regions south of the Alaska Range.

Since less than 25% of wetlands in interior Alaska have been surveyed intensively for raptors and the density of nesting eagles in areas surveyed varies substantially; it is difficult to generate an estimate for the entire area. Numbers of pairs or nests apparently increased since the middle of this century; information for the Tanana River suggests the population has continued to increase since 1970. With this as background, we would conservatively estimate that 550 Bald Eagle pairs nest in interior drainages. If 70% of these pairs are successful in raising young and raise approximately 1.5 young/successful pair, the total fall population may exceed 1,500 Bald Eagles, excluding non-territorial adults and immatures.

In order to refine our picture of this population and more adequately describe whether or not we have separate subpopulations (maritime influenced versus true interior), we recommend that surveys continue on the Tanana, Susitna and Copper rivers and be expanded to a number of other representative drainages in each area.

Acknowledgements

We would like to acknowledge the many researchers who provided us with information, including T. Swem, P. Feiger, M. Bertram, J. Hodges and T. Doyle of the U.S. Fish and Wildlife Service; T. Osborne, J. Wright and J. Whitman, Alaska Dept. of Fish and Game (ADFG); B. Stiedl, Oregon State University; and P. Shepherd and K. Alt, retired ADFG; P. Knuckles, National Park Service; and L. Rundquist, USDC.

Literature Cited

Amaral, M. J. 1982. Peregrine Falcon survey of the lower Tanana River, Fairbanks to Nenana, Alaska, 1982. Unpubl. Rep., U.S. Fish Wildl. Serv., Anchorage, Alas. 6 pp.

Amaral, M. J. 1988. A survey for nesting birds of prey along the Copper River, Alaska, 1987-1988. Unpubl. Rep., U.S. Fish Wildl. Serv., Anchorage, Alas. 16 pp.

Barber, S., H. A. Stelfox and G. Brewster. 1985. Bald Eagle ecology in relation to potential hydro-electric development on the Churchill River, Saskatchewan. Pages 104-113. In: J. M. Gerrard and T M. Ingram (eds). The Bald Eagle in Canada. Proc. Bald Eagle Days, Winnipeg, Can. 272 pp.

Blackwelder, E. 1919. Notes on the summer birds of the upper Yukon region, Alaska. Auk 36:57-64.

Cooper, B. A., R. J. Ritchie, B. Anderson and L.C. Byrne. 1991. Alaska over-the-horizon backscatter radar system: a synthesis of the avian research program, 1987-1990. Alaska Biological Research Inc. for Arctic Environ. Inform. and Data center. University of Alaska, Fairbanks.

Dall, W. H. and H. M. Bannister. 1869. List of the birds of Alaska, with biographical notes. Trans. Chicago Acad. Sci. 1, part 2:267-210.

Dice, L. R. 1920a. Notes on some birds of interior Alaska. Condor 22:176-185.

Dice, L. R. 1920b. The land vertebrate associations of Interior Alaska. Univ. Mich. Misc. Zool. Occ. Papers, No. 85.

Gabrielson, I. N. and F. C. Lincoln. 1959. Birds of Alaska. The Stackpole Co., Harrisburg, Pa. 922 pp.

Gerrard, J. M. 1985. The status of Bald Eagles in Saskatchewan. Pages 58-61. In: J. M. Gerrard and T M. Ingram, eds. The Bald Eagle in Canada. Proc. Bald Eagle Days, Winnipeg, Canada. 272 pp.

Gerrard, J. M., P. Gerrard, W. J. Maker and D. W. A. Whitfeld. 1975. Factors influencing nest site selection of Bald Eagles in northern Saskatchewan and Manitoba. Blue Jay 33:169-176.

Gerrard, J. M., D. W. A. Whitfield, P. Gerrard, P. N. Gerrard and W. J. Maker. 1978. Migratory movements and plumage of subadult Saskatchewan Bald Eagles. Can. Field-Nat. 92:375-382.

Hansen, A. J. and J. I. Hodges. 1985. High rates of nonbreeding adult Bald Eagles in Southeastern Alaska. J. Wildl. Manage. 49(2):454-458.

Haugh, J. R. and K. C. Halperin. 1976. Evaluation of raptor populations: Portage Glacier area, Denali Highway area, Yukon River pipeline crossing area and Yukon River and Porcupine River tributaries. Unpubl. rep., Bur. Land Manage., Anchorage, Alas. 58pp.

Hehnke, M. F. 1973. Nesting ecology and feeding behavior of Bald Eagles on the Alaska Peninsula. M.S. thesis. Arcata State Univ., Humboldt, Calif. 56pp.

Hinckley, F. C. 1900. Notes on the animal and vegetable life of the region of the Susitna and Kuskokwim rivers. Pages 76-85. In: J. E. Spurr ed. A reconnaissance in Southeastern Alaska in 1889. U.S. Geol. Surv. Ann. Rep. 20, part VII, 1889-1899:31-264.

Kessel, B. and D. Gibson. 1978. Status and distribution of Alaska birds. Studies in Avian Biol. 1:1-110.

Kessel, B., S. O. MacDonald, D. D. Gibson, B. A. Cooper and B. A. Anderson. 1982. Susitna hydro project environmental studies phase I. Annual report on birds and non-game mammals. Univ. Alaska Mus. Unpubl. Rep., Alaska Power Authority.

Kuropat, P. 1986. Beaver Creek raptor survey 1986. Unpubl. rep., Bur. Land Manage., Fairbanks, Alas.

Lamke, R. D. 1979. Flood characteristics of Alaskan streams. U.S. Geol. Surv., WRI 78-129. 61 pp.

Leighton, F. A., J. M. Gerrard, P. Gerrard, D. W. A. Whitefield and W. G. Maker. 1979. An aerial census of Bald Eagles in Saskatchewan. J. Wildl. Manage. 43:61-69.

Mindell, D. P. 1983. Nesting raptors in southwestern Alaska; status, distribution and aspects of biology. Bur. Land Manage., Alaska Tech. Rep. 8. 59pp.

Mindell, D. P. and F. L. Craighead. 1981. Peregrine Falcon status and prey and observations of other raptors on the middle and lower Yukon River, Alaska, 1981. Unpubl. rep., U.S. Fish Wildl. Serv., Anchorage, Alas. 34pp.

Osgood, W. H. and L. B. Bishop. 1900. Results of a biological reconnaissance of the Yukon River region. North Am. Fauna No. 19.

Parker, J. 1988. Susitna Valley Bald Eagle survey. Unpubl. rep., U.S. Fish Wildl. Serv., Anchorage, Alas. 8pp.

Ritchie, R. J. 1982. Investigations of Bald Eagles, Tanana River, Alaska, 1977-80. pp 55-67. In: W. N. Ladd and P F. Schempf, eds. Proc. of a symposium and workshop on raptor management and biology in

Alaska and Western Canada, 17-20 February 1981, Anchorage, Alas. U.S. Dept. Inter., Fish Wildl. Serv., Anchorage, Alas. 335pp.

Ritchie, R. J. 1984. Results of raptor surveys along the Porcupine River and Salmon Fork of the Black River, Alaska, 1984. Unpubl. rep., U.S. Fish Wildl. Serv., Anchorage, Alas. 17pp.

Ritchie, R. J. and R. E. Ambrose. 1976. An investigation of Peregrine Falcon activity and habitat for cliff-nesting raptors in the Kuskokwim River, McGrath to Aniak. Unpubl. rep. prep. for USFS, USFWS, BLM and ADFG. 32pp.

Ritchie, R. J. and R. E. Ambrose. 1987. Winter records of Bald Eagles, *Haliaeetus leucocephalus*, in Interior Alaska. Can. Field Nat. 101:86-87.

Ritchie, R. J. and R. E. Ambrose. 1996. Distribution and population Status of Bald Eagles (*Haliaeetus leucocephalus*) in Interior Alaska. Arctic 49:120-128.

Robards, F. C. and J. G. King. 2008. Nesting and productivity of Bald Eagles in Southeast Alaska-1966. In: Wright, B. A. and P. F. Schempf, eds. Bald Eagles in Alaska.

Roseneau, D. G. 1974. A continuation of studies of raptorial bird nesting sites along proposed pipeline routes in Alaska. Unpubl. rep., Can. Arctic. Gas Study Ltd., Calgary, Alberta. 69pp.

Roseneau, D. and P. Bente. 1979. A raptor survey of the proposed Northwest Alaska Pipeline Company Gas Pipeline route: the U.S.-Canada Border to Prudhoe Bay, Alaska. Unpubl. rep., LGL Ecol. Res. Assoc. Inc., Fairbanks, Alas. 82pp.

Schempf, P. F. 1989. Raptors in Alaska. Pages 144-154. In: B. G. Pendleton, ed. Proc. West. Raptor Manage. Symp. and Workshop. Natl. Wildl. Fed. Sci. and Tech. Series No. 12.

Sherrod, S. K., C. M. White and F. S. L. Williamson. 1976. Biology of the Bald Eagle on Amchitka Island, Alaska. Living Bird 15:143-182.

Springer, A. M., D. G. Roseneau and P. J. Bente. 1979. Numbers and status of Peregrine Falcons on the Colville River, Middle Yukon River and lower Yukon River, Alaska, 1979. Unpubl. rep., LGL Ecol. Res. Assoc., Inc., Fairbanks, Alas. 69pp.

Stalmaster, M. V. 1987. The Bald Eagle. Universe Books. New York. 227pp.

Swenson, J. E. 1983. Is the northern interior Bald Eagle population in North America increasing? Pages 23-34. In: D. M. Bird, N. R. Seymour and J. M. Gerrard, eds. Biology and management of Bald Eagles and ospreys. MacDonald Raptor Research Center. McGill Univ., Raptor Res. Found., Inc. 325pp.

White, C. M. 1974. Survey of the Peregrine Falcon and other raptors in the proposed Susitna River Reservoir impoundment areas. Unpubl. rep. U.S. Fish Wildl. Serv., Anchorage, Alas. 4pp.

White, C. M. and S. Boyce. 1978. A profile of various rivers and their raptor populations in western Alaska, 1977. BLM/AK Tech. Rep. 1:1-77.

White, C. M. and T. J. Cade. 1975. Raptors studies along the proposed Susitna powerline corridors, oil pipelines and in the Yukon and Colville river regions of Alaska. Unpubl. Rep., prep. for USFWS, BLM, NPS, AINA and Amer. Mus. of Nat. History. 28 pp.

Wilbor, S. 1989. An aerial survey for nesting Bald Eagles along the Copper River, upper Delta River, Tangle Lakes, Paxson Lake, the Gulkana River drainage and Gulkana Basin lakes, Alaska, 24-27 May 1989. Unpubl. rep, U.S. Fish Wildl. Serv., Fairbanks, Alas. 5pp.

Bald Eagle photo by Bruce Wright.

Nesting and Wintering Bald Eagle Population Parameters on and Adjacent to the Kenai National Wildlife Refuge, Alaska, 1979-1990.

Theodore N. Bailey, Edward E. Bangs, William W. Larned, Andre J. Loranger, Mary F. Portner, Thomas V. Schumacher and Elizabeth A. Jozwiak

U.S. Fish and Wildlife Service, Kenai, AK

We aerially surveyed nesting Bald Eagles (*Haliaeetus leucocephalus*) on and adjacent to the Kenai National Wildlife Refuge, Alaska each year over 12 years (1979-1990) to document nesting success and productivity. The number of known nesting territories surveyed each year increased from 33 in 1979 to 77 in 1990. We believe most of this apparent increase occurred because of our effort to identify eagle nests during other refuge wildlife surveys and from increased reports from the public. During the study period, the average minimum number of eaglets produced per known nesting pair varied from 0.6 to 1.4 per year. The year of lowest productivity (1990) was associated with the most severe previous winter recorded on the Kenai Peninsula.

Since 1983-84, we also surveyed Bald Eagles by boat and aircraft each winter along two segments of the upper Kenai River. Numbers of observed eagles in winters usually peaked in January or February with a high of 601 recorded in February 1986. The proportion of observed juvenile eagles in the winter population declined from 38% to 12% in the wintering area in the 1980's. The upper Kenai River may be one of the more important wintering areas for Bald Eagles in southcentral Alaska because of its unique ecological attributes. The Kenai River corridor is being rapidly developed and its fisheries are being subjected to increased use. Resource management along the Kenai River is controversial and some issues remain unresolved.

Introduction

The effects of increased human populations on wildlife resources on the Kenai Peninsula in southcentral Alaska, have been significant (Bangs et al. 1982b). Human populations began increasing on the peninsula in the late 1800's and early 1900's. Although some historical population information is available on populations of wildlife such as moose (*Alces alces*), caribou (*Rangifer tarandus*) and wolves (*Canis lupis*) after that time, little information was available for Bald Eagles. The need for information about eagles became apparent in the 1970's and 1980's when development accelerated and human use of fish and wildlife resources on the peninsula increased. As a result, the U.S. Fish and Wildlife Service, at the Kenai National Wildlife Refuge, initiated two series of annual investigations. One study, beginning in 1979, surveyed Bald Eagle nesting and reproductive characteristics (Bangs et al. 1982b). A second, beginning in the winter of 1983-84 studied characteristics of Bald Eagle winter populations along the Kenai River. This report summarizes and discusses the results of those annual investigations.

Study Area

Personnel of the Kenai National Wildlife Refuge monitored nesting and wintering Bald Eagle populations primarily on, but also adjacent to, the 7,972 km² Refuge. The Refuge is located on the northwestern portion of the Kenai Peninsula and encompasses about 30% of its area (Fig. 1). Although Bald Eagles occur along the eastern and southern coastal areas of the peninsula, our investigations did not include this coastal habitat. The Kenai National Wildlife Refuge, like the Kenai Peninsula, is comprised of many wildlife habitats. It includes a permanent ice field and glaciers at the highest elevations, alpine tundra, lowland boreal forest and wetlands and a marine estuary at sea level (Bailey 1984). Of special significance to Bald Eagles are the Refuge's aquatic habitats and fisheries. Over 1,200 freshwater lakes over 2 ha in size and more than 2,100 km of streams provide spawning and feeding habitat for rainbow trout and four species of salmon (*Oncorhynchus* spp.) Dolly Varden (*Salvelinus malma*) and longnose suckers (*Catostomus catostomus*) (Bangs et al. 1982a). Snowshoe hares (*Lepus americana*), several species of waterfowl and carcasses of winter-killed, wolf-killed and vehicle-killed moose are also winter foods of eagles.

Wintering eagles are abundant along the Kenai River on and adjacent to the Refuge because two large lakes in the river system, Kenai Lake and Skilak Lake, release warmer water throughout the winter (Burger et al. 1985). This warmer water often keeps 16 to 24 km sections of river below these lakes ice-free during winters. It also provides a spawning environment for a unique, late-run of coho salmon (*Oncorhynchus kisutch*), an important winter food for Bald Eagles. No other coho salmon run in Alaska is known to arrive and spawn so late. Peak entry of late-run coho into the Kenai River occurs in mid-September and extends through at least mid-December; peak aerial counts of spawning coho were observed in January and February and coho were known to spawn from October through March (Booth 1990).

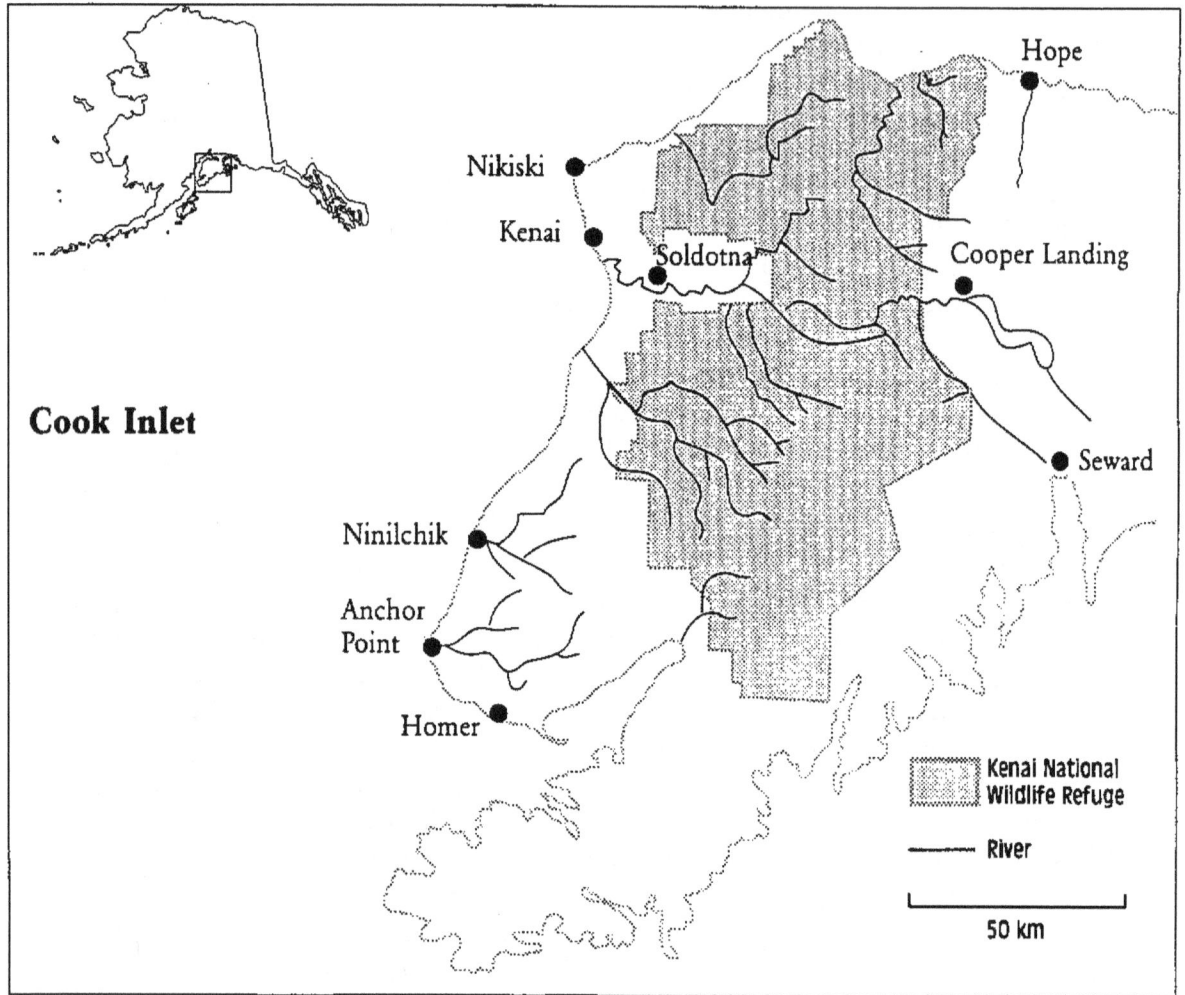

Methods

Bald Eagle Nesting and Productivity Investigations

We conducted low-level, aerial surveys of known, reported and suspected Bald Eagle nesting territories each year using either Piper PA-18 Supercub or Cessna C-206 fixed-wing aircraft. Knowledge of the locations of Bald Eagle nesting territories prior to 1979 was obtained from various refuge staff who had worked on other wildlife surveys during the previous 25 years. After 1979, we kept records of new or reported eagle nests and included them in future surveys. Initially we used a modified quadrat sampling technique (Grier 1977) in 1979 to estimate a population of 40 breeding pairs of eagles on the Refuge north of the Kenai River, but we abandoned this technique as an annual survey method because of its high cost and time requirement. Instead, we flew from one known Bald Eagle nesting territory to another in the spring, usually mid-May and checked each nest to assess nesting attempts. In late summer, usually mid to late July, we flew again to assess nesting success. We attempted to define distinct nesting territories, count the number of nests per territory and characterize the territory by its nearest major aquatic feature. When the previous year's nest was not used, a careful aerial search of the surrounding area was conducted to locate any new nests that might have been constructed.

Winter Bald Eagle Population Investigations

We conducted boat surveys from November through March each winter along two sections of the Kenai River where Bald Eagles concentrated. The first section was 19.8 km in length and extended from the outlet of Kenai Lake (river kilometer (rkm) 131.2) to Jim's Landing (rkm 111.4) (Fig. 2). The second, a 16.8 km section of river, extended from the outlet of Skilak Lake (rkm 50.0) to Bing's Landing (rkm 39.5). If ice conditions prevented use of boats for these surveys, we flew over the same sections of the river using PA-18 or C-206 fixed-wing aircraft to observe eagles. Only one survey per river section was made each winter month, usually in mid-month, using either inflatable rafts or a canoe to float the river. We plotted locations of wintering eagles on maps, distinguished between adults and juveniles and attempted to reduce multiple counts of eagles flying downstream ahead of us by subtracting the number of eagles flying ahead from downstream counts. Juveniles were distinguished by their head color and plumage.

Eagles estimated to be 4 1/2 year-old by head color were classified as adults. Eagles, especially juveniles, were difficult to observe from aircraft and we attempted to develop a correction factor for numbers of eagles missed during aerial surveys. When aerial and boat surveys were conducted simultaneously on January 15, 1986, aerial surveys missed 65% of the eagles observed on the boat survey below Kenai Lakes and 14% of those observed below Skilak Lake. This disparity was likely a result of differences in terrain and perch trees between the two areas. The survey area below Kenai Lake passed through steep mountains, making aerial surveys difficult and eagles there often perched on spruce (*Picea* spp.) trees. The survey area below Skilak Lake was in open lowlands and many perched eagles there were more visible in leafless cottonwood (*Populus* spp.) trees. When combined monthly averages from boat and aerial surveys were compared, aerial surveys missed an average of 57% of the eagles observed on boat surveys. Aerial survey data therefore underestimate the actual number of eagles along the Kenai River in winter.

Results and Discussion
Bald Eagle Nesting Population and Productivity
Nests per territory

The majority (74%) of currently-used and some formerly-used territories included only a single known nest (Table 1). The remaining territories included 2 to 5 nests and the average for all territories was 1.4 nests. Without individually identifiable eagles, we may have overestimated the number of actual territories. For example, we failed to observe any nesting attempts at the Stormy Lake and Swanson River Oilfield nesting territories early in the study, but we later discovered active nests within 3 km of the inactive nests. The active nests were perhaps being used by the same individuals that had been observed at the original nests. We suspect the original nests may have been abandoned because of their proximity to busy roads and intensive human use. In another instance, a frequently-used nest northeast of Beaver Lake was abandoned in 1986, but another nest was discovered in use the same year 4 km from the abandoned nest. Only the newly discovered nest was used by eagles thereafter. Because we suspected that the new nest was in the same territory and used by the same individuals, we continued to count the Beaver Lake area as only one territory. We also recorded instances of nests falling from trees and new nests being built, usually within 3 km of the original nest.

Table 1. Distribution of Bald Eagle nests within nesting territories on and adjacent to the Kenai National Wildlife Refuge, Alaska, 1979-1990.

Description	No. of nests/territory					Total
	1	2	3	4	5	
No. of Territories	60	15	3	2	1	81
Percent of Total	74	19	3	2	1	100

Figure 2. Upper Kenai River showing overwintering Bald Eagle census routes from the outlet of Kenai Lake to Jim's Landing (19.8 km) and the outlet of Skilak Lake to Bing's Landing (16.8 km).

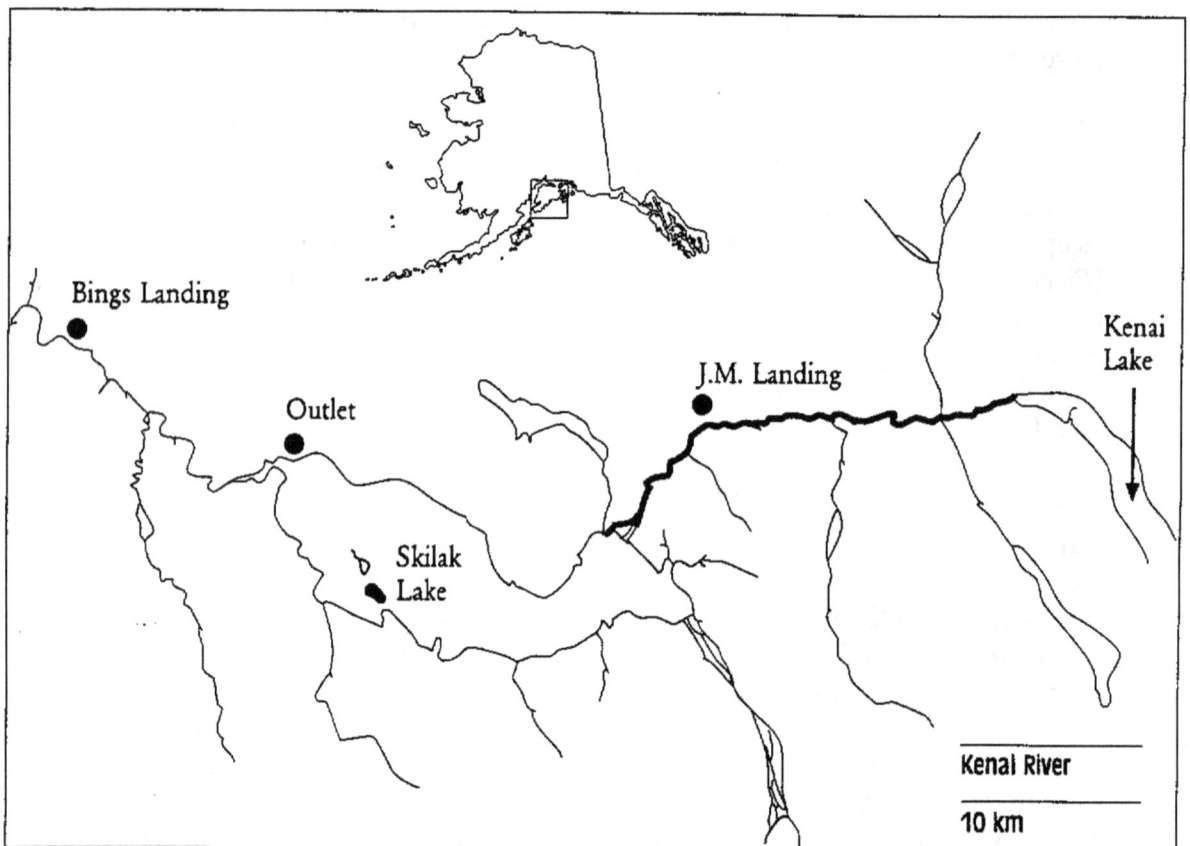

Nesting territory habitat

Forty-eight percent of the identified nesting territories located during the 12 years of our study were in or near riparian habitat associated with a stream or river (Table 2). The next greatest number of territories (38%) were located near lakes. Assignment of some Bald

Eagle nesting territories to a particular nearby aquatic habitat was confusing because their nests were about equidistant to the nearest lake, stream and coastal shoreline. Most nesting territories (50%) were in the watershed of the Kenai River. Fewer were located in the Swanson River drainage and coastal shoreline areas (Table 3). Most territories in the Kenai River watershed were along the river's main channel (22), within the drainage of the Moose River tributary (13), or within the drainage of the Killey River tributary (Table 4). Because of frequent flights over the refuge for other wildlife surveys and an aerial survey of random blocks on the refuge for eagle nests in 1979, we believe the above data reflects actual nest distribution and not survey intensity.

Table 2. Distribution of Bald Eagle nesting territories in relation to nearest major aquatic habitat on and adjacent to the Kenai National Wildlife Refuge, Alaska, 1979-1990.

| | Nearest major aquatic habitat | | | |
	Stream	Lake	Coast	Other
No. of territories	45	35	10	3
Percent of total	48	38	11	3

Nesting Territories, Land Ownership and Refuge Management Zones
Although 61% of the 93 Bald Eagle nesting territories were located within the Kenai National Wildlife Refuge, a substantial percentage (39%) occurred on non-protected lands outside the refuge boundary where there is minimal control over development and human activity. Most off-refuge eagle nesting territories (39%) occurred along the main channel of the Kenai River or its tributaries. Within the refuge, about half of the eagle nesting territories were located within designated wilderness areas which comprise about 68% of the refuge. The other half were located in other refuge management zones.

Nesting Population Trend
We compared numbers of active nesting territories monitored during any one of the first three years of our studies (1979, 1980, 1981) to those monitored in 1990. We assumed at least three years of monitoring were essential to locate most nesting territories used by eagles during the early part of the study. This method of comparison showed a 42% increase in numbers of active nesting territories during the 9 to 12 year period. Most of the observed increase in nesting territories occurred outside the refuge boundaries. However, because of our survey methods, we could not conclusively demonstrate an actual increase in active nesting territories. It is possible that some of the nesting territories monitored in 1990 may also have been used between 1979 and 1981, but were not counted. We also suspect higher counts may have come from our increased aware nests of eagle nests during other aerial wildlife surveys and greater numbers of nest sightings reported by the public.

Table 3. Distribution of Bald Eagle nesting territories within watersheds on and adjacent to the Kenai National Wildlife Refuge, Alaska, 1979-1990.

Watershed

	Kenai River	Swanson River	Fox/Sheep Rivers	Chickaloon River	Kasilof River	Other	Coast Streams	Other
No. of territories	47	11	7	6	3	6	10	3
Percent of total	50	12	7	6	3	6	11	3

Table 4. Distribution of Bald Eagle nesting territories in the Kenai River watershed on and adjacent to the Kenai National Wildlife Refuge, Alaska, 1979-1990.

	Mainstem	Moose River	Killey River	Beaver River	Russian Creek	Funny River	Other
No. of territories	22	13	4	3	1	1	3
Percent of total	47	28	8	6	2	2	6

Table 5. Bald Eagle nesting territories surveyed, nesting success and productivity on and adjacent to the Kenai National Wildlife Refuge, Alaska, 1979-1990.

	Number surveyed	Nests still present	Occupied by eagles	Active	Successful	Failed	Unknown	Total eaglets observe
1979	33	33	24	24	15	8	1	23
1980	33	32	20	20	18	2	0	32
1981	41	39	31	31	21	10	0	34
1982	39	34	27	27	19	7	1	35
1983	42	42	33	33	20	11	2	31
1984	48	47	37	37	24	11	2	37
1985	47	45	32	31	24	4	3	38
1986	60	58	44	43	30	12	1	49
1987	63	54	37	34	26	7	1	43
1988	66	59	39	36	23	11	2	32
1989	68	61	38	37	25	12	0	43
1990	77	73	52	48	18	29	1	29

Nesting Success and Productivity

Nesting attempts, successes and failures and numbers of eaglets produced during the 12 years of the study indicated considerable annual variation in Bald Eagle productivity between 1979 and 1990 (Tables 5, 6 and 7). When current and preceding winter and coho salmon indices data were related to nesting success and eaglets produced (Table 8), no single strong correlation was evident. This suggested these environmental factors either acted in consort with each other, or other factors were involved in influencing eagle productivity. The highest two correlations with nesting success were the number of

Table 6. Bald Eagle brood sizes, observed eaglets and eaglet productivity, Kenai National Wildlife Refuge and adjacent lands, Alaska, 1979-1990.

Year	Nests with observed brood			Total Eaglets	Eaglets/territory	
	1	2	3		Successful	Active
1979	10	2	3	23	1.5	1.0
1980	5	12	1	32	1.8	1.6
1981	9	11	1	34	1.6	1.1
1982	7	8	4	35	1.8	1.3
1983	10	9	1	31	1.5	1.0
1984	10	12	1	37	1.5	1.1
1985	12	10	2	38	1.8	1.4
1986	14	13	3	49	1.6	1.2
1987	10	15	1	43	1.6	1.3
1988	14	9	0	32	1.4	0.9
1989	8	16	1	43	1.7	1.2
1990	7	11	0	29	1.6	0.6

preceding winter days below 0°F (r = 0.62) and the preceding year's commercial catch of coho salmon on the east side of Cook Inlet (r = 0.59). The number of eaglets produced per active territory were most strongly correlated with the preceding year's commercial catch of coho salmon (r = 0.61). The lowest productivity during the 12-year period was documented in 1990 when 60% of the nests failed to produce eaglets. The preceding winter was one of the most severe (coldest average minimum monthly winter temperatures and number of days below 0°F) recorded on the Kenai Peninsula. Much of the upper Kenai River froze from January through March and local snowshoe hare populations, a potential alternate winter food for eagles, were at extremely low levels. We are uncertain if the *Exxon Valdez* oil spill had any effect on Bald Eagle productivity in our study area in 1990. Movement data from a radio telemetry study of wintering eagles indicated that several eagles that wintered along the Kenai River also used marine coastal areas along the Kenai Peninsula, Cook Inlet and Prince William Sound (unpublished data).

Wintering Bald Eagle Population
Distribution along the Kenai River
Aerial surveys in winter along the entire length of the Kenai River from its mouth at Cook Inlet to the outlet of Kenai Lake revealed that the majority of wintering Bald Eagles used only the upper sections of the river above the Moose River confluence. Most wintering eagles were observed along the river from Skilak Lake outlet to 22 km below Skilak Lake (58%), or from the outlet of Kenai Lake to 27 km below Kenai Lake (32%), because these were the sections of the river that normally remained ice-free during

winters. Few eagles wintered below the Moose River, primarily because this section of the river froze during most winters and few carcasses of coho salmon were available as winter food. To avoid dangerous rapids, our float survey areas along the river included only 73% of the river section between Kenai and Skilak Lakes and 76% of the river section from Skilak Lake to the Moose River confluence.

Table 7. Percentage of winter Bald Eagle observations along the entire Kenai River during combined winter aerial surveys, 1983-84 to 1985-86.

Winter	Percent of observations	Kenai River mouth to Moose River (rkm 0-rkm 58)	SAMPLE SIZE Moose River to outlet of Skilak Lake (rkm 58-rkm 80)	Skilak lake outlet to Kenai Lake outlet (rkm 104-rkm 131)
1983-84	5	58	37	505
1984-85	10	60	30	765
1985-86	16	56	28	1085
Average	10	58	32	-

We consistently observed about twice as many eagles in the survey area below Skilak Lake (67%) compared to the survey area below Kenai Lake (33%) (Table 9). Numbers of observed eagles gradually increased in November and December, peaked in January or February and then rapidly declined in March. Peak eagle numbers usually were observed in January in the survey area below Skilak Lake and in February in the survey area below Kenai Lake. The highest monthly number of eagles observed occurred in February of 1986 when 601 total eagles were counted in both survey areas. Numbers of eagles appeared to decline in the following winters to a low during the 1988-89 winter. However, because of extremely cold temperatures, numbers of eagles actually present during 1988-89 and 1989-90 winters may have been slightly underestimated. Ice cover prevented floating the river and lower sightability aerial surveys had to be conducted instead. Even after sightability corrections were made using the combined average correction factor, combined numbers of eagles observed each winter month declined from 1300 during 1985-86 to 696 during 1988-89, a decrease of 46%. We suspect this decline was caused by several cold winters which froze much of the Kenai River and limited the numbers of salmon carcasses available to eagles (Table 8), resulting in higher winter mortality of eagles from starvation. Among the tested variables, the average number of overwintering eagles per survey was most closely related ($r^2 = 0.71$) to the numbers of sport-fishery-caught coho salmon in the Kenai River (Table 8).

Age Composition of the Wintering Bald Eagle Population
The percentage of eagles in juvenile plumage observed during winter surveys was greatest during the winter of 1984-85 (38%). It then gradually declined to 12% during the 1989-90 winter (Table 10). This decline in the percentage of juveniles and the decrease in total numbers of eagles observed, indicated a declining winter population of Bald Eagles between 1985-86 and at least 1988-89. The severity of the actual decline may not have been as pronounced as the observed decline because of the sightability biases associated with aerial surveys that had to be relied upon during the preceding two winters. However,

the decline in numbers and the scarcity of juveniles during the 1989-90 winter, based on boat survey data only, strongly suggested a declining wintering eagle population along the river. We also received reports of dead eagles along the river during the 1988-89 and 1989-90 winters. Some carcasses were retrieved and necropsies revealed that many of the dead eagles died of starvation.

Table 8. Nesting Bald Eagle productivity, observed numbers of overwintering Bald Eagles, winter temperatures and cold periods and late-run Kenai River coho salmon abundance Indices on the Kenai Peninsula, 1979-1990.

Year	Nesting Bald Eagles		Overwintering Bald Eagles (1)			Winter temperatures (2)		Coho salmon harvest(3)	
	Percent nesting success	Eaglets per active nest	Total eagles	Number of surveys	Average per survey	Average monthly temp.	Days Below 0 F	East side Cook Inlet set nets	Kenai R. Sport
1979	62	1.0	-	-		10.8		29,727	3,510
1980	90	1.6	-	-		12.9		40,281	9,545
1981	68	1.1	-	-		17.5		36,031	6,664
1982	70	1.3	-		-	9.3	-	108,383	13,351
1983	61	1.0	395	5	79	19.0	23	37,666	7,549
1984	65	1.1	1273	10	127	16.7	20	36,530	32,029
1985	75	1.4	1300	10	130	11.9	35	69,735	22,146
1986	68	1.2	1151	9	128	13.6	36	77,922	17,551
1987	70	1.3	763	9	85	18.6	15	74,977	8,735
1988	59	0.9	259	4	65	15.3	22	55,419	11,495
1989	66	1.2	377	6	63	6.4	50	81,744	16,195
1990	35	0.6	-	-	-	7.8	49		

(1) Winter = Begins in November 1 of the calendar year and ends March 31 the following year; combined surveys = total of all monthly winter surveys; surveys = number of monthly surveys.
(2) Temperatures in ° F. (Data source: Data collected at Kenai Federal Aviation Administration Airport, Climatological Data, Alaska. National Oceanic and Atmospheric Administration, National Climatic Data Center, Asheville, North Carolina).
(3) Coho salmon indices of abundance: East side Cook Inlet set nets intercept coho salmon primarily spawning in the Kenai River; Kenai River sport harvest are coho salmon caught in the Kenai River by sport fisherman. (Data source: Alaska Department of Fish and Game from Booth 1990).

Distribution Of Wintering Eagles and Land Ownership

In the first three years of winter surveys we classified wintering eagle observations according to their presence within or outside the boundaries of the Kenai National Wildlife Refuge in the survey area below Skilak Lake, the area that supported most of the wintering eagles. The majority (60%, range = 54%-67%) of wintering eagles observed during this period were outside the boundaries of the Kenai National Wildlife Refuge on private, borough and state-owned lands (Figure 3). This distribution of wintering eagles was closely associated with the distribution of spawning late-run coho salmon (Booth 1990) and the availability of their carcasses to eagles in the shallow water at the base of pools and in riffles.

Each winter Bald Eagles on the Homer Spit are fed fish scraps, discards from a cannery. Photo by Allan Ridder.

Conclusions

The nesting Bald Eagle population on and adjacent to the Kenai National Wildlife Refuge appears to have been at least stable and may have increased since first monitored in 1979. Because a significant percentage (39%) of known Bald Eagle nesting territories in the area occur outside the boundaries of the Refuge where they are exposed to development and increasing levels of human activity, there is a potential for loss of eagle nesting territories in this region of the Kenai Peninsula in the future. This is especially a concern along the Kenai River, where many eagle nesting territories presently occur outside the refuge boundary and where controversy still exists about future use of and development along, the river (Anonymous 1986). Although the river corridor was protected in 1984 as the Kenai River Special Management Area under the management responsibility of the Alaska Division of Parks and Outdoor Recreation, agreement has not yet been reached on zoning recommendations to protect natural resources in the area.

Table 9. Numbers of Bald Eagles observed during boat and aerial winter surveys on the Upper Kenai River, Alaska, 1983-84 to 1989-90.

| Winter | | Upper Kenai River | | | | | | | | | |
| | | Kenai Lake to Jim's Landing | | | | | Skilak Lake to Bing's Landing | | | | | |
		Nov	Dec	Jan	Feb	Mar	Nov	Dec	Jan	Feb	Mar	Mean
1983-84	Boat	161	-	26	-		36		207	-	110	79
	Aircraft	-	27		47	34		68	-	35	12	12
1984-85	Boat	13	58	102	129	84	65	210	318	157	137	127
	Aircraft	12	14	59	32	36	35	102	N/A	89	78	46
1985-86	Boat	19	33	81	219	123	29	63	213	382	138	130
	Aircraft	20	34	49	80	39	25	89	187	133	123	78
1986-87*	Boat	73	120	139	59		120	193	228	135	84	128
1987-88*	Boat	34	68	78	100	33	55		169	176	50	85
1988-89	Boat	34	36	-	-		65	124	-	-	-	65
	Aircraft	-	-	14	11	28		24	37	72	31	
1989-90	Boat	30	29	73	-	65	57	123				63
	Aircraft	-	-	-	21			103	19	121	66	
Average	Boat	24	49	80	147	173	61	142	227	212	104	
	Aircraft	16	25	41	38	34	30	86	105	63	81	

*No aerial survey conducted.

Continued health of the nesting Bald Eagle population will depend primarily on the availability and use of undisturbed nesting habitat and the abundance and availability of fish as food. Human sport and commercial harvest of salmon could affect a major source of food for eagles because salmon carcass availability and escapement are the most influential on the quantity of consumable biomass available to overwintering eagles (Stalmaster 1983). Of particular significance to eagles is maintaining an abundance of late-run coho salmon in the Kenai River. The late-run coho in the Kenai River may provide the most important natural food for wintering eagles on the western Kenai Peninsula and perhaps elsewhere. The abrupt decline in eagle productivity documented in 1990, if properly interpreted, also suggests that natural events such as extremely cold winters can reduce the availability of the eagles' winter food supply in the Kenai River. Extremely cold temperatures on the Kenai Peninsula may also increase the energy requirements of eagles beyond that available from their food supply.

Table 10. Adult and juvenile Bald Eagle observed during winter boat or aerial surveys on the Upper Kenai River, Alaska, 1983-84 to 1989-90. Data are from boat surveys unless ice conditions required aerial surveys.

Winter		Upper Kenai River Kenai Lake to Jim's Landing						Skilak Lake to Bing's Landing					
		Nov	Dec	Jan	Feb	Mar		Nov	Dec	Jan	Feb	Mar	% juv.
1983-84	Adults	13	20	18	28	9	22	44	142	24	76	396	
	Juveniles	3	7	8	19	3	14	24	65	11	34	188	32
1984-85	Adults	9	40	70	75	50	34	118	198	103	91	788	
	Juveniles	4	17	32	54	34	31	86	120	54	46	478	38
1985-86	Adults	16	25	51	107	78	17	41	131	264	87	817	
	Juveniles	3	8	30	112	44	11	22	76	115	50	471	37
1986-87	Adults	-	53	78	89	36	74	147	176	96	61	810	
	Juveniles	-	20	42	46	19	41	42	46	34	20	310	27
1987-88	Adults	18	46	62	84	27	32		140	146	40	595	
	Juveniles	16	22	15	15	5	23		29	27	8	160	21
1988-89	Adults	24	30	12	10	27	30	110	20	36	67	366	
	Juveniles	10	1	2	1	1	35	14	4	1	5	74	17
1989-90	Adults	24	27	59	21	60	46	111	92	17	108	565	
	Juveniles	6	2	14	0	5	11	12	11	2	13	76	12

The declining trend in the wintering eagle population along the Kenai River and the declining proportion of juvenile eagles in this population during the 1980's are difficult to interpret. Since movement data from our radio telemetry studies (Kenai N.W. R.) suggests Bald Eagles from areas throughout southcentral Alaska come to the Kenai River to overwinter, eagles may have to use other wintering areas when the upper Kenai River freezes. However, starving eagles found along the Kenai River suggests other options for winter feeding areas may be limited. Simultaneous investigations of wintering eagle populations throughout southcentral Alaska could help clarify observed population trends on the Kenai Peninsula.

Figure 3. Approximate distribution and average densities of overwintering Bald Eagles along the Kenai River from the outlet of Skilak Lake to Bing's Landing, 1983–86.

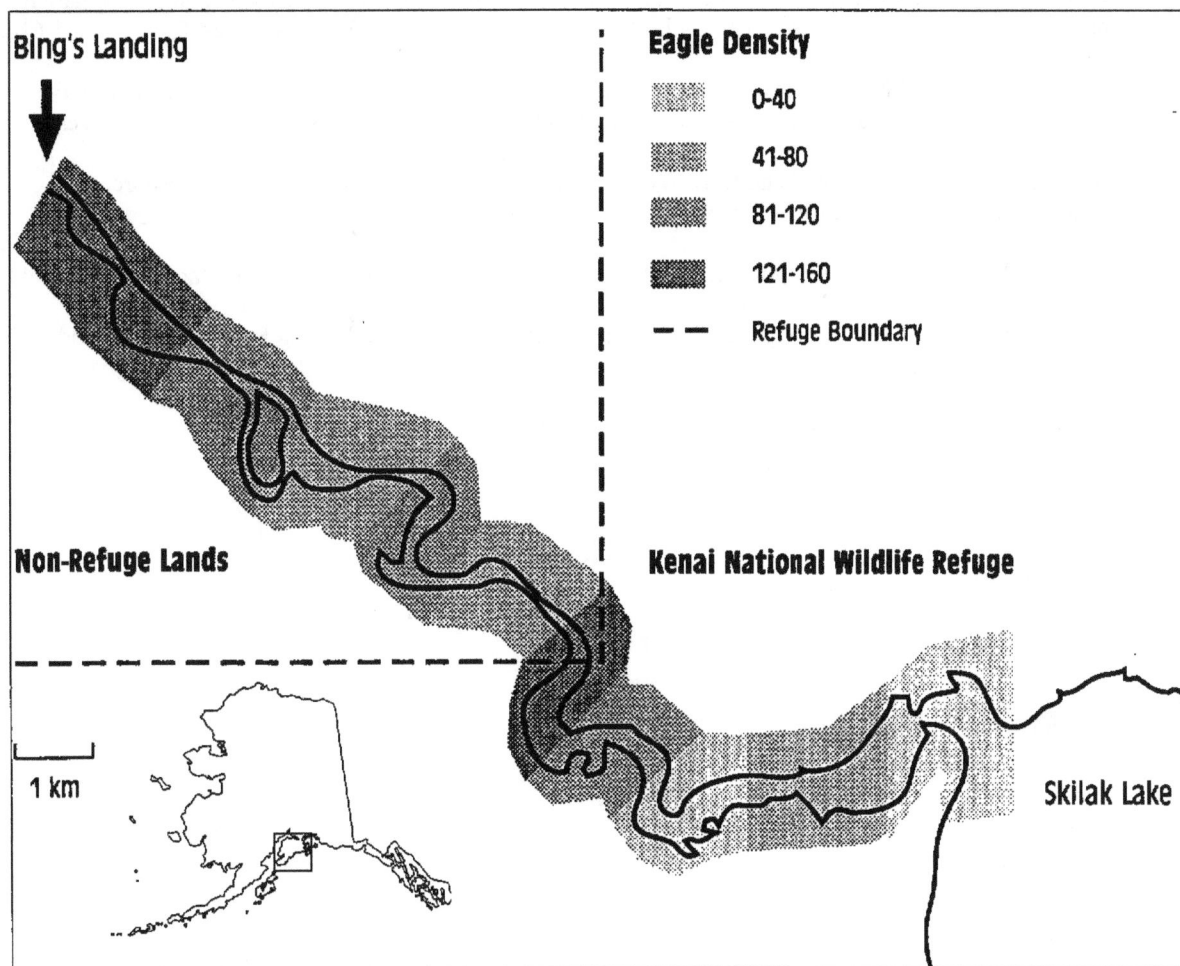

Acknowledgements

We thank refuge managers J. E. Frates, R. D. Delaney and D. W. Doshier for their support of these Bald Eagle investigations; refuge pilots V. D. Berns, R. A. Richey, R. D. Delaney and R. K. Johnston for flying aerial surveys; and S. Crampton, M. Kesterson, E. Kord, R. McAvinchey, C. Paez, E. Sharpe, W. Staples and L. Tutterow for helping census wintering eagles.

Literature Cited

Anonymous. 1986. Kenai River comprehensive management plan. Alaska Dept. Nat. Res. and Kenai Peninsula Borough, Anchorage, Alas. 384pp.

Bailey, T. N. 1984. Technical supplement: Terrestrial habitats and wildlife species. Kenai National Wildlife Refuge comprehensive conservation plan, environmental impact statement and wilderness review. Kenai Natl. Wildl. Refuge, Soldotna, Alas. 72 pp.

Bangs, E. E., T. N. Bailey and V. D. Berns. 1982a. Ecology of nesting Bald Eagles on the Kenai National Wildlife Refuge, Alaska. Pages 47-54. In: W. N. Ladd and P. F. Schempf, eds. A Symposium and Workshop on Raptor Management and Biology in Alaska and Western Canada. U.S. Fish Wildl. Serv.,

Anchorage, Alas. 335pp.

Bangs, E. E., T. H. Spraker, T. N. Bailey and V. D. Berns. 1982b. Effects of increased human populations on wildlife resources of the Kenai Peninsula, Alaska. Trans. North Am. Wildl. Nat. Res. Conf. 47:605-616.

Booth, J. A. 1990. Run timing and spawning distribution of coho salmon (*Oncorhynchus kisutch*) in the Kenai River, Alaska and their relation to harvest strategies. M. S. Thesis. Montana State Univ., Bozeman.

Burger, C. V., D. B. Wangaard and R. L. Wilmot. 1985. Kenai River salmon in a unique resource in southcentral Alaska. U.S. Fish Wildl. Ser, Fish Wildl. Leaflet 3. 14 pp.

Grier, J. W. 1977. Quadrat sampling of a nesting population of Bald Eagles. J. Wildl. Manage. 41:438-443.

Stalmaster, M. V. 1983. An energetics simulation model for managing wintering Bald Eagles. J. Wildl. Manage. 47:349-359.

History and Status of Bald Eagle Population and Productivity Studies on the Alaska Peninsula, Alaska

Donna A. Dewhurst

U.S. Fish and Wildlife Service, King Salmon, AK

Bald Eagles are abundant along the waters of the Pacific Ocean throughout Alaska (Murie 1959); however, baseline information on the relative abundance, distribution and production is lacking for much of the Alaska Peninsula (Sowls 1982). Some specific parts of the Alaska Peninsula have detailed records of eagle nesting and local population counts, such as for inland portions of Katmai National Park and Preserve and for the Pacific Coast of the Alaska Peninsula/Becharof National Wildlife Refuge. The major portion of the Peninsula has only scattered records of general surveys and incidental sightings.

The objectives of this report are: 1) to provide an overview of the complicated history of Bald Eagle surveys recorded on the Alaska Peninsula, 2) to compare survey methods and study areas and 3) to summarize survey results.

Study Area

The Alaska Peninsula extends 725 km (450 mi) from Kamishak Bay south to Isanotski Strait. The Peninsula splits Bristol Bay and the Bering Sea on the northwest side from the Pacific Ocean on the southeast side. The volcanic Aleutian Mountain Range lies along the east side forming a Pacific Coast that is rocky and deeply incised with many fjords. West of the Aleutian Range, the land slopes gradually to the Bering Sea, forming relatively flat terrain with numerous lakes and large, meandering rivers.

Most of the land on the Peninsula is under federal and state management. Federal management units (Figure 1) include: Katmai National Park and Preserve, Alaska Peninsula/Becharof National Wildlife Refuges, Aniakchak National Monument and Preserve, Izembek National Wildlife Refuge, Alaska Peninsula Unit of Alaska Maritime National Wildlife Refuge, the McNeil River Game Sanctuary, Izembek Game Refuge and the Egegik, Pilot Point, Cinder River, Port Heiden and Port Moller Critical Habitat Areas are the state management units on the Peninsula (Figure 1). The western portion of the Peninsula is mostly owned by Native villages, regional corporations and the state of Alaska.

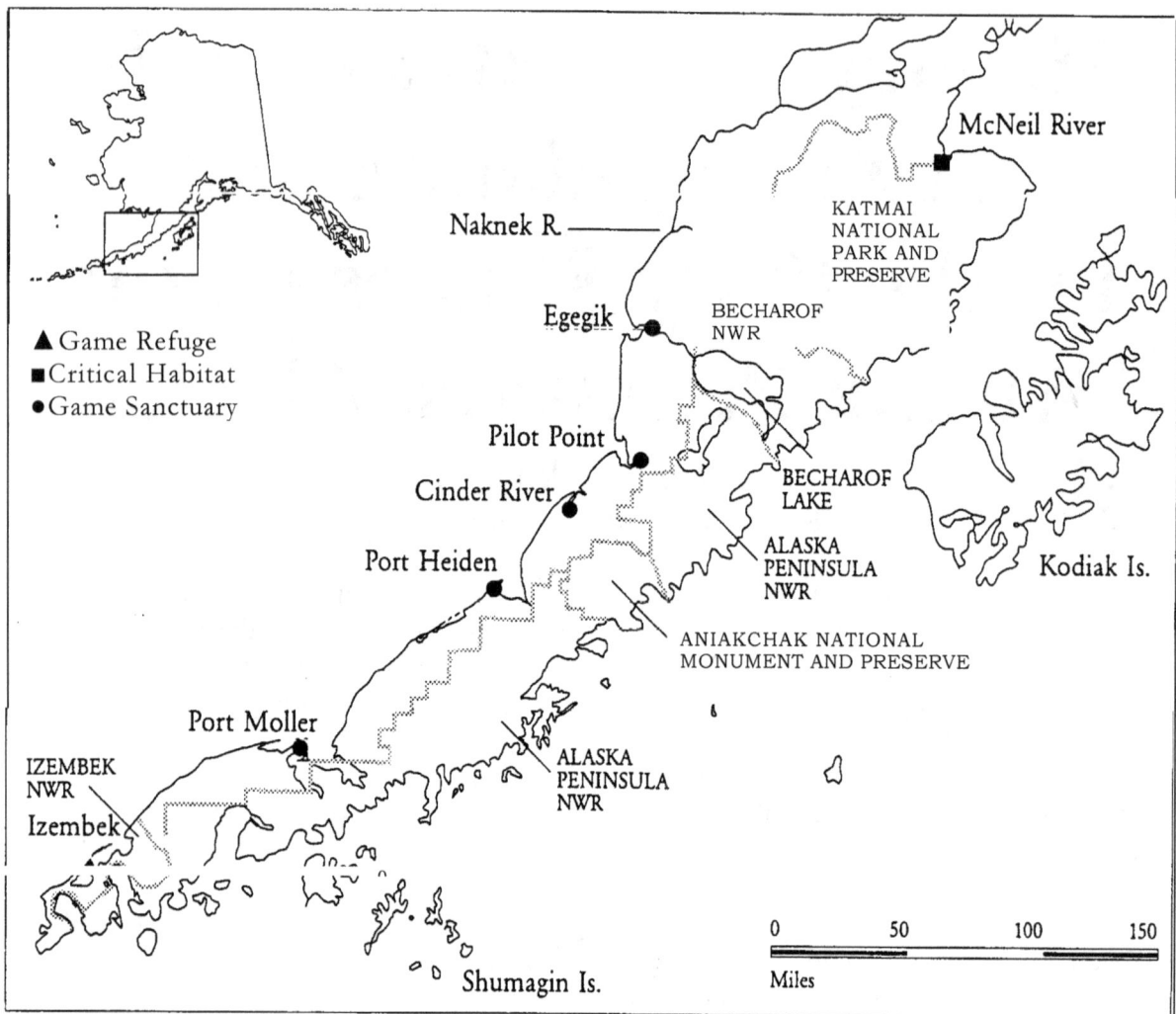

Figure 1. locations of federal land management units, Alaska state game refuges, critical habitat areas and game sanctuaries on the Alaska Peninsula, Alaska.

Methods

Methods used in the earliest Bald Eagle surveys on the Alaska Peninsula were not recorded (Murie 1959), but surveys were likely made by boat or on foot. Records consisted of data from visits to easily accessible nests to record locations and general natural history. The first recorded methodical eagle surveys occurred in the 1970's and can be divided into nesting/productivity surveys and population surveys (Table 1).

Nesting and Productivity Surveys

Hehnke (1973) conducted the first recorded Bald Eagle nesting study on the Alaska Peninsula and incorporated his findings into a Masters thesis. Hehnke's study involved individual nest visits and examined the feeding ecology of nesting eagles.

Troyer (1975-1979) initiated the use of fixed-wing aircraft for Bald Eagle nesting surveys on the Peninsula. Troyer (1975-1979) concentrated his work on Katmai National Park (Katmai), but also surveyed the Pacific Coast of Becharof Refuge. Aerial (fixed-wing) nesting surveys of Katmai were continued by Jope (1983-1987) and Sowls (1988), but these later surveys concentrated on the inland lakes portion of the Park.

Along the Peninsula's Pacific Coast, Bailey (1978) initiated a six-year period of Bald Eagle nesting surveys using inflatable boats. These inflatables were used to circumnavigate the islands of the Alaska Peninsula Unit of Alaska Maritime Refuge and also gain foot access to nests. Islands, from Sanak north to Kamishak Bay, were systematically surveyed for both eagles and colonial seabirds (Table 1).

Aerial surveys (fixed-wing) of the Pacific and Bering Sea coasts of the Peninsula were conducted in the 1980's incidental to spring and fall surveys for Emperor Geese (King 1980-1990, Berns 1984, Mumma 1985). Nest locations were recorded for general areas (bays, rivers). Numbers of adult and juvenile eagles observed were also noted.

In 1989, the 11-million gallon *Exxon Valdez* oil spill occurred in Prince William Sound, Alaska, eventually spreading to the Pacific Coast of the Alaska Peninsula. More precise Bald Eagle nesting and productivity data was needed to assess the impacts along the Peninsula. Helicopter nesting surveys was started in 1989 on the Pacific Coast of the Becharof Refuge and Ugashik Unit of the Alaska Peninsula Refuge (Dewhurst 1989, Table 1). The nearshore islands of Alaska Maritime Refuge were included in the survey effort. Eagle nesting surveys conducted by the National Park Service in 1989 included surveys of the Katmai coast using helicopters and motor vessels (Yurick 1989) and the Aniakchak coast using inflatable boats and a motor vessel (Payer 1989). In 1990, the helicopter surveys were expanded to cover the entire monitored portion of the Alaska Peninsula coastline, from Kamishak Bay south to Stepovak Bay (Dewhurst 1990, Portner 1991). Both active and inactive nests were mapped and revisited at least once to determine productivity. Nest site habitat selection studies were based on habitat types described for the Aleutian Islands by Sherrod et al. (1977), with the addition of a "trees" category and data stratification using mainland versus island.

Aniakchak National Monument and Preserve
Population surveys
The first attempt to survey the Alaska Peninsula's Bald Eagle population comprehensively enough to achieve a population estimate was made by Hodges (1983), using fixed-wing aircraft. A stratified random plot quadrat sample method was developed with plots established for the Peninsula. The nearshore islands of Alaska Maritime were included in the surveys. The population survey was repeated by Payne (1987), but did not include all the nearshore islands and only covered Cape Kubugakli south to Stepovak Bay. Nests and their contents were also recorded as part of these surveys. Helicopter surveys conducted in 1989 and 1990 provided further data on the number and distribution of adult and juvenile Bald Eagles along the Pacific side of the peninsula (Dewhurst 1989, 1990).

Table 1. Summary of all Bald Eagle nesting and population surveys conducted on the Alaska Peninsula, Alaska, 1911-1990.

Source	Location*	Methods	Notes
Wetmore (1911)**	Morzhovol Bay	Unknown	General observations
Hehnke (1973)	Unknown	Unknown	Nesting study and feeding ecology
Troyer(1975-1979)	KNPP-Inland and Pacific Coast	Fixed-wing	Nest mapping and productivity
Bailey (1978)	AMNWR-Shumagins	Inflatable boat	General census and nest mapping
Troyer(1980)	KNPP-Naknek River	Fixed-wing	Nest mapping and productivity
Bailey and Faust (1980)	AMNWR-Sandman Reefs	Inflatable boat	General census and nest mapping
King (1980-1990)	Pacific and Bristol Bay Coasts - all areas including INWR	Fixed-wing	General census Incidental to Goose surveys
Bailey and Faust (1981)		Inflatable boat	General census and nest mapping
Sowls (1982)	AMNWR-Mitrofania to Sutwik Islands	Motor vessel	General census and nest mapping
Bailey (1983)	KNPP, AP/BNWR, ANMP, AMNWR	Inflatable boat	General census and nest mapping
Hodges (1983)	AMNWR-Sanak and Pavlof Islands	Fixed-wing	Stratified random plots population surveys
Jope (1983-1987)	KNPP, AP/BNWR, ANMP, AMNWR	Fixed-wing	Nest mapping
Nishimoto (1984)	KNPP Inland Lakes	Inflatable boat	General census and nest mapping
Berns (1984)	AMNWR-Chlachl Islands	Fixed-wing	Census incidental to Emperor Goose survey
Mumma (1985)	AP/BNWR-Pacific	Fixed-wing	Census incidental to Emperor Goose survey
Payne (1987)	AP/BNWR-Pacific	Fixed-wing	Stratified random plots population surveys
Sowl (1988)	AP/BNWR-Pacific	Fixed-wing	Nest mapping
Dewhurst (1989)	KNPP-Inland Lakes	Helicopter	Nest mapping and productivity
Payer (1989)	AP/BNWR, AMNWR, ANMP-Pacific	Motor vessel	Nest mapping and productivity
Yurick (1989)	ANMP-Pacific	Inflatables	Nest mapping and productivity
McManus and Thrailkill (1989)	KNPP-Pacific	Motor vessels, heli.	Nest mapping
	KNPP-American Creek	Inflatable boat	Nest mapping and productivity
Dewhurst (1990)	AP/BNWR, AMNWR, ANMP-Pacific	Helicopter	Nest mapping and productivity
Portner (1991)	KNPP-Pacific	Helicopter	
*Location abbreviations:	KNPP-Katmai National Park and Preserve AP/BNWR-Alaska Peninsula/Becharof National Wildlife Refuge ANMP-Aniakchak National Monument and Preserve AMNWR-Alaska Maritime National Wildlife Refuge, AK Peninsula Unit INWR-Izembek National Wildlife Refuge		

**See Murie (1959) for reference

Results and Discussion

Nesting Surveys

Due to the variability in survey methods and areas used for nesting studies on the Alaska Peninsula, results will be compared only in similar study areas.

On Katmai National Park, early nesting survey efforts were concentrated on the inland lakes (Naknek, Brooks, Nonvianuk, Coville and Grosvenor). Survey results summarized by Jope (1987, Table 2), indicated a relatively stable nesting population in Katmai's interior. Troyer (1980) also surveyed the Naknek River drainage from 1976-1979, documenting a yearly average of 17.8 nests producing 26.3 eaglets. The Pacific coast of Katmai National Park and Preserve was surveyed by Troyer during the same time period (1974-1977) yielding an average of 27.3 nests. Troyer compared the nesting habitat selection of coastal versus interior nesters (Table 3), finding a habitat shift from hardwoods to rocky cliffs, reflecting the relative lack of trees along the coast.

Nesting eagles along Katmai's Pacific coast received more intensive scrutiny during 1989-1990 (Yurick 1989) due to the oil spill damage assessment studies. Nesting habitat selection along the coast paralleled Troyer's (1975-1979) studies, with 11% of the 1989 nests in trees (hardwoods and evergreens combined) and 17% tree-nests in 1990 (Table

4) (Yurick 1989, Portner 1991). Nesting data on use of rocky habitats (sea stacks, ridges, hillsides) on the Katmai coast was not recorded (Sherrod et al. 1977). General incorporation in habitat comparisons (Table 4) was possible for Portner (1991) data, but not for Yurick (1989) data.

Table 2. Results of aerial surveys of nesting Bald Eagles, Katmai National Park and Preserve (Jope 1987).

| Water Body | 1975-81 average | 1983 | | 1984 | | 1985 | | 1986 | | 1987 | | |
	Pairs on nests	Pairs on nests	Roosting eagles	Pairs on nests	Roosting eagles	Pairs on nests	Roosting eagles	Pairs on nests	Roosting eagles	Pairs on nests	Pairs not on nests	Roosting eagles
Brooks Lake	2.3	3	3	3	5	1	4	3	2	0	0	4
Naknek Lake	3.3	5	9	1	18	1	23	1	8	4	0	19
Savonoski / Grosvenor River	2.7	2	8	1	3	1	6	3	3	1	0	0
Coville Lake	0.7	1	0	-	-	4	1	4	4	0	0	5
Grosvenor Lake	3.4	1	8	-	-	1	9	0	4	0	0	4
American Creek	1.3	1	1	-	-	0	5	1	6	2	0	4
Nonvianuk Lake	0.6	6	3	-	-	2	8	2	3	2	1	1
Kulik Lake	0.1	0	1	-	-	0	3	0	1	0	0	0
Kukaklek Lake	-	-	-	-	-	-	-	-	-	0	0	0
Alagnak Nonvianuk River	-	-	-	-	-	-	-	-	-	0	0	0
TOTAL	14.3	19	33	-	-	10	59	14	31	13*	2	41*

* Notes that these totals include the 4 nesting pairs and 4 roosting eagles observed on the Alagnak/Nonvianuk River, which was not surveyed in previous years.

Sowls (1982) conducted the earliest documented nesting survey of the Alaska Peninsula/Becharof Refuges' Pacific Coast in 1973 using the motor vessel Aleutian Tern, but recorded only 15 nests from Cape Kubugakli to Cape Kunmik. Bailey's (1978) extensive surveys via inflatable boat during the 1970's and early 1980's yielded maps of specific eagle nesting sites and the first counts in the islands (Table 5), providing a baseline for all future coastal nesting surveys. Troyer's (1975-1979) survey efforts on Katmai extended down the Becharof Refuge coast averaging seven nests from Cape Kubugakli to the Kekurnoi Islets. These data corresponded to nine nests observed during the 1989 helicopter survey (Dewhurst 1989). Payne's (1987) surveys, using fixed-wing aircraft, provided the first comprehensive mapping of nests along the coast south to Stepovak Bay (excluding islands). A total of 101 nests were recorded; however, specific nest site data are not available.

Table 3. Bald Eagle nesting habitat use on Katmai National Park, 1974-1977 (Troyer 1975-1979).

| Habitat Types | Habitat Use by Area | |
	Coastal Nests	Interior Nests
Rocky Cliffs	111(82%)	3(3%)
Hardwood Trees	15(11%)	28(30%)
Evergreen Trees	10(7%)	61(67%)
Total	136	92

The helicopter eagle nesting surveys conducted during 1990 along the Alaska Peninsula/Becharof Refuges' coast duplicated Payne's 1987 survey. Use of helicopters in

1990 resulted in recording 139 nests (Dewhurst 1990) in the same study area examined by Payne (1987). Extending portions of this survey on Aniakchak Monument and the islands of Alaska Maritime Refuge resulted in observations of 106 additional nest sites. In another comparison of survey methods on Aniakchak Monument, 13 nests were documented during 1989 boat surveys (Payer 1989) which corresponded to 17 nests found in 1990 using helicopters (Table 4, Dewhurst 1990).

Table 3. Bald Eagle nesting habitat use on Katmai National Park, 1974 - 1977 (Troyer 1975-1979).

Habitat Types	Habitat Use by Area	
	Coastal Nests	Interior Nests
Rocky Cliffs	111 (82%)	3 (3%)
Hardwood Trees	15 (11%)	28 (30%)
Evergreen Trees	10 (7%)	61 (67%)
Total	136	92

Figure 2. Distribution of 1990 Bald Eagle nests among available habitat types along the Pacific Coast of the Alaska Peninsula, Alaska, including nearshore islands (N=245 nests).

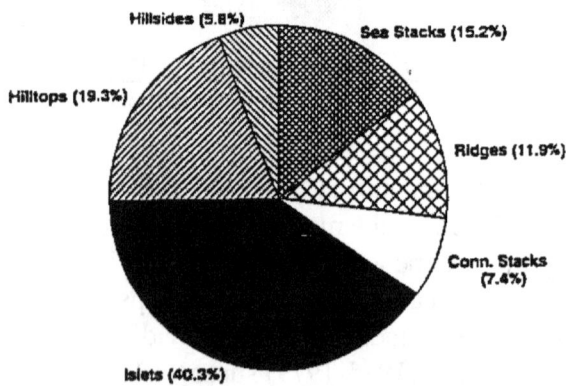

Figure 3. Bald Eagle nest habitat selection on nearshore islands of the Alaska Peninsula, Alaska, May–July 1990 (N=100).

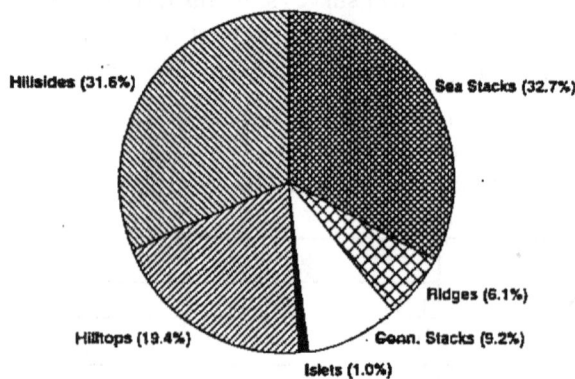

Note that these totals include the 4 nesting pairs and 4 roosting eagles observed on the Alagnak/Nonvianuk River, which was not surveyed in previous years. Bailey's (1978) extensive surveys via inflatable boat during the 1970's and early 1980's yielded maps of specific eagle nesting sites and the first counts in the islands (Table 5), providing a baseline for all future coastal nesting surveys. Troyer's (1975-1979) survey efforts on Katmai extended down the Becharof Refuge coast averaging seven nests from Cape Kubugakli to the Kekurnoi Islets. These data corresponded to nine nests observed during the 1989 helicopter survey (Dewhurst 1989). Payne's (1987) surveys, using fixed-wing aircraft, provided the first comprehensive mapping of nests along the coast south to Stepovak Bay (excluding islands).

Table 4. Bald Eagle nesting habitat preferences in the 1990 study area of Kamishak Bay to American Bay, subdivided into the respective management units (Dewhurst 1990, Portner 1991).

Habitat types[a]	Number of active nests						
	Katmai Park	Becharof Refuge	Ugashik Unit[b]	Chignik Unit[b]	Maritime Refuge	Aniakchak Monument	Total
I) Sea stacks	13	8	10	14	0	5	50
II) Coastal ridges	4	1	0	26	0	2	33
III) Connected stacks	1	0	1	14	0	3	19
IV) Islets/Islands	8	-	-	-	-	-	8
–I Sea stacks	-	0	0	0	32	0	32
–II Ridges	-	0	1	0	5	0	6
–III Conn. stacks	-	0	0	0	9	0	9
–IV Smaller islets	-	0	0	0	1	0	1
–Va Hilltops	-	0	0	3	17	0	20
–Vb Hillsides	-	0	2	5	25	0	32
Va) Hilltops	2	3	12	27	0	5	44
Vb) Hillsides	9	2	0	10	0	2	24
X) Trees	8	0	0	0	0	0	8
Total	45	14	26	99	89	17	290

[a] Habitat types:
I–Sea Stacks (pinnacles sticking out of sea)
II–Ridges (small peninsulas still connected to the mainland)
III–Connected sea stacks (stack joined to the mainland by a lower saddle)
IV–Islet/Island (land width greater than height) combined with other habitat types
Va–Hilltops (top of any portion of mainland)
Vb–Hillsides (sides of hill or cliffs on the mainland)
X–Trees (includes hardwoods and conifers)
[b] Units are part of the Alaska Peninsula National Wildlife Refuge

Table 5. Summary of Bald Eagles counts using inflatable boats conducted along the Pacific Coast of the Alaska Peninsula (Bailey 1978, 1980, 1981, 1983, 1984 and Nishimoto 1984).

Location	Year(s) surveyed	Eagles sighted	Nests sighted
Kamishak Bay-Jute Bay	1981	123[a]	26
Jute Bay-Amber Bay	1980	141	29
Sutwik, Mitrofania Islands	1979	70	12
Shumagin Islands	1973-1986	150	43
Sandman Reefs	1973-1978	47	7
Pavlof, Chiachi, Sanak Islands	1983-1988	91	15

[a] Totals are from published surveys and observations on various islands from fox eradication work, seabird surveys and other missions. Data from some areas like the Shumagins represent notes from visiting different islands over a period of years, but the overall area was not completely surveyed in any single year. Less attention was given to islands without seabird colonies and these ares were likely under-represented in the totals (Bailey, pers. comm., Homer, Alas., 2/91).

Table 6. A comparison of 1989 and 1990 Bald Eagle nest occupancy and productivity along the Pacific Coast of the Alaska Peninsula, Alaska (Yurick 1989, Dewhurst 1990, Portner 1991).

Kamishak Bay to Cape Kubugakli	1989	1990
Total nests surveyed[a]	60	70
Occupied and/or active nests	60	48
Successful nests	49	20
Nesting success rate[b]	82%	42%
Fledglings	47[c]	28
Fledglings per occupied/active nest	–	0.62
Fledglings per successful nest	1.20	1.27

Cape Kubugakli to Cape Kunmik[d]		
Total nests surveyed	72[a]	106[e]
Occupied and/or active nests	72	78
Successful nests	40	41
Nesting success rate[b]	55%	53%
Fledglings	62	70
Fledglings per occupied/active nest	0.86	0.90
Fledglings per successful nest	1.55	1.71

[a] Includes "empty" nests. Note empty nests were not recorded during the 1989 surveys.
[b] Nests discovered during the later surveys were not included in this calculation for either 1989 or 1990.
[c] Data is based on only the 39 nests monitored for productivity in 1989.
[d] Data from Cape Providence and Aiugnak columns was only collected in 1990 and was not included in calculations.
[e] During 1990 surveys, empty nests were those occupied in 1989 but not in 1990. Other abandoned nests (without fresh nesting material) were not documented due to problems with distinguishing Bald Eagle nests from those built by Gyrfalcons, Rough-legged Hawks and Common Ravens.

Examining 1990 data from Cape Kubugakli to American Bay, habitat types used for 245 nests indicated a strong preference toward islands/islets (Figure 2). Upon further stratification of habitat types, preferences among the island nesters tended toward sea stacks and hillsides (Figure 3). The total lack of usable trees along this portion of the Alaska Peninsula parallels that of the Aleutian Islands, as does resultant nest site selection (Sherrod et al. 1977, Payer 1989, Dewhurst 1989, 1990).

Table 7. Estimates of Bald Eagle population size and densities, Cape Kubugakli to Chichagof Bay (excluding islands), Pacific Coast of the Alaska Peninsula/Becharof National Wildlife Refuges, Alaska, based on stratified random sample aerial surveys conducted by Payne (1983), 8-13 June 1983.

Stratum[a]	N	n	N(N-n)	s^2y	y	Yn = Nyn
Low	22	13	198	3.39	1.77	39
Medium	22	13	198	7.64	4.84	107
High	11	6	55	17.60	6.00	66
Totals	55	32	451	28.63	12.61	212

Adult population estimate = 212 ± 40.2 (95% CI)

Immature Bald Eagle population estimate

Stratum[a]	N	n	N(N-n)	s^2y	y	Yn = Nyn
Low	22	13	198	0.00	0.00	0
Medium	22	13	198	1.40	0.69	15
High	11	6	55	0.17	0.17	2
Totals	55	32	451	1.57	0.86	17

Immature population estimate = 17 + 9.4 (95% CI)
[a] Symbol definitions:
   N = Total plots available for sampling
   n = Number of plots sampled
   s^2y = Variance between sample plots
   y = mean eagles per sampled plot
   Yn = Estimated population of eagles in stratum

Productivity Surveys

Nest surveys conducted as part of the oil spill damage assessment provided means for a two-year comparison of productivity along the Alaska Peninsula (Table 6). Nest productivity of refuge nests (Cape Kubugakli to Cape Kunmik) in 1990 closely paralleled that of 1989 with 0.90 fledglings per occupied and/or active nest (Table 6). Nest productivity as measured by number of fledglings per successful nest was higher for refuge nests than for those in Katmai Park (Kamishak Bay to Cape Kubugakli), but did not vary significantly between survey years for both areas (Table 6). Nest productivity on the Alaska Peninsula was also very comparable with other Bald Eagle populations surveyed during the oil spill assessment except for Prince William Sound. Over the same study period (1989-1990), nest productivity on Kodiak Island was 1.63-1.66 (fledglings per successful nest), on the Upper Copper River was 1.61-1.72 and in Southeast Alaska was 1.39-1.52 (Schempf et al. 1990).

Bald Eagle clutch sizes were first successfully documented on the Alaska Peninsula in 1990 on the nests surveyed by helicopter from Cape Kubugakli to American Bay. In 37 cases, incubating adults did not permit observation of nest contents. Of the 154 nests where nest contents were observed, clutch size frequencies were: 0 eggs: 22, 1 egg: 24, 2 eggs: 73 and 3 eggs: 35, producing a mean clutch size of 1.78 eggs (Dewhurst 1990).

By conducting replicate surveys of refuge nests during incubating, hatching and fledging, it was possible to examine individual breeding pair productivity. Using 1990 data (Dewhurst 1990) and tallying only nests with known contents, 192 eggs yielded 85 downy eaglets and 70 fledglings. Pair productivity was 0.36 or one fledgling per every three eggs laid. Hatching success was surprisingly low (85 hatchlings per 192 eggs - 44%); while brood rearing success was relatively high (70 fledglings per 85 hatchlings = 82%). Brood rearing success was very comparable to 1989 survey (Dewhurst 1989) results of 57 fledglings per 68 hatchlings = 84%.

The causes of nest failure were generally unknown, but during 1990 surveys (Dewhurst

1990), brown bears (*Ursus arctos*) destroyed five nests, surprisingly all on islands: Wide Bay-2, Aiugnak Columns-2 and Chiginagak Bay-1. In these documented cases, a bear was observed on the respective islands and nests were physically destroyed. All surveyed nest sites were within range of brown bears, with access limited only by severe topography (narrow sea stacks, remote ledges).

Young Bald Eagles await their next meal. Photo by Scott Gende.

Population Surveys

Based on stratified random plot surveys conducted using fixed-wing aircraft, Hodges (1983) estimated the population of Bald Eagles along the Pacific Coast of the Alaska Peninsula to be 1442 adults and 418 immatures, using 95% confidence intervals. Hodges (1983) speculated that they observed about 90% of the adult eagles present on the shorelines of the plots. The nearshore islands of Alaska Maritime Refuge contained the best eagle habitat with the highest densities being present on the Shumigan, Semidi and Sanak islands. Eagle densities averaged 7.0 eagles/plot as compared to 8.5 eagles/plot on the Kodiak Archipelago.

Payne (1987), using the same methods as Hodges (1983), conducted a replicate survey, but covered only the mainland portion of the Peninsula between Cape Kubugakli and

Chichagof Bay (Table 7). Eagle densities averaged 12.6 adults/plot and 0.9 immatures/plot, which was considerably higher than recorded by Hodges (1983).

Conclusions and Recommendations

Methodology for Bald Eagle nesting and population surveys on the Alaska Peninsula has evolved from boats to fixed-wing aircraft to helicopters, improving survey accuracy and precision, but not cost effectiveness. Helicopters appeared to be the only way to accurately map nests along the Peninsula's Pacific coast due to the complexity of terrain. Funding was available for additional surveys due to the 1989 *Exxon Valdez* oil spill. Nests observed during these comprehensive surveys along the Pacific Coast during 1989 and 1990 were digitized into an ARC/INFO computer database. A similar survey effort should be made for the Pavlof Unit of the Alaska Peninsula Refuge and the Shumigan, Pavlof and Sanak islands to complete the picture. All coastal Bald Eagle nesting surveys should be conducted by helicopter to maintain survey accuracy and safety. Once mapped, nests should be monitored at least every three years, perhaps on an area rotation system due to the vast distances involved. For population size monitoring, use of the stratified random plot survey method via fixed-wing aircraft should be initiated on a five-year basis to census the Peninsula's interior.

Acknowledgements

I would like to thank the following people for their co-operation in providing historical data and reviewing this manuscript: Chris Dau, Izembek National Wildlife Refuge; Ed Bailey, Alaska Maritime National Wildlife Refuge; Mary Portner, Regional Oil Spill Office; Steve Hurd and Ron Squibb, Katmai National Park and Preserve.

Literature Cited

Bailey, E. P. 1978. Breeding seabird distribution and abundance in the Shumigan Islands, Alaska. Murrelet 59:82-91.

Bailey, E. P. and N. H. Faust. 1980. Summer distribution and abundance of marine birds and mammals in the Sandman Reefs, Alaska. Murrelet 61:6-19.

Bailey, E. P. and N. H. Faust. 1981. Summer distribution and abundance of marine birds and mammals between Mitrofania and Sutwik Islands south of the Alaska Peninsula. Murrelet 62:34-42.

Bailey, E. P. 1983. Reconnaissance of the Pavlof and Sanak Islands, Alaska, May 1983. Unpubl. rep., U.S. Fish Wildl. Serv., Homer, Alas. 25pp.

Berns, V. 1984. Fall Emperor Goose surveys-Alaska Peninsula/Becharof National Wildlife Refuge. Unpubl. rep., U.S. Fish Wildl. Serv., King Salmon, Alas. 3pp.

Dewhurst, D. A. 1989. Bald Eagle nesting and reproductive success along the Pacific Coast of the Alaska Peninsula/Becharof National Wildlife refuge, Cape Kubugakli to Cape Kunmik, 10 May-25 July 1989. Unpubl. rep., U.S. Fish Wildl. Serv., King Salmon, Alas. 15pp.

Dewhurst, D. A. 1990. Bald Eagle nesting and reproductive success along the Alaska Peninsula, Cape Kubugakli to American Bay, 9 May-28 July 1990. Unpubl. rep., U.S. Fish Wildl. Serv., King Salmon, Alas. 43pp.

Hehnke, M. F. 1973. Nesting ecology and feeding behavior of Bald Eagles on the Alaska Peninsula. M.S.

Thesis, Calif. State Univ., Humboldt. 56pp.

Hodges, J. 1983. Alaska Peninsula Bald Eagle survey, 1983. Unpubl. rep., U.S. Fish Wildl. Serv., Juneau, Alas. 18pp.

Jope, K. L. 1983-1987. Nesting Bald Eagle survey, Katmai National Park and Preserve. Unpubl. annual admin. rep., Natl. Park Serv., King Salmon, Alas.

King, R. 1980-1990. Spring and fall population surveys on Emperor Geese in southwestern Alaska. Unpubl. annual admin. reps., U.S. Fish Wild. Serv., Fairbanks, Alas.

McManus, B. and R. A. Thrailkill. 1989. Eagle nest location maps, Katmai National Park and Preserve, American Creek. Unpubl. admin. rep., Natl. Park Serv., King Salmon, Alas. 7pp.

Mumma, D. 1985. 1985 spring Emperor Goose surveys, Alaska Peninsula/Becharof National Wildlife Refuge. Unpubl. rep., U.S. Fish Wildl. Serv., King Salmon, Alas. 38pp.

Murie, O. J. 1959. Fauna of the Aleutian Islands and the Alaska Peninsula. North Am. Fauna No. 61. 406pp.

Nishimoto, M. 1984. Survey of selected islands along the Alaska Peninsula during the spring of 1984. Unpubl. rep., U.S. Fish Wildl. Serv., Homer, Alas. 28pp.

Payer, D. C. 1989. 1989 biological resources survey and oil spill impact assessment: Aniakchak National Preserve. Unpubl. rep., Natl. Park Serv., King Salmon, Alas. 48pp.

Payne, J. 1987. Initial Bald Eagle inventory along the Alaska Peninsula. Unpubl. rep., U.S. Fish Wildl. Serv., King Salmon, Alas. 4pp.

Portner, M. 1991. Bald Eagle nest survey 1990 - Katmai Coast. Unpubl. rep., U.S. Fish Wild. Serv., Anchorage, Alas. 15pp.

Schempf, P. F., T. Bowman, J. Bernatowicz and T. Schumacher, 1990. Assessing the effects of the *Exxon Valdez* oil spill on Bald Eagles. Unpubl. rep., U.S. Fish Wildl. Serv., Juneau, Alas. 48pp.

Sherrod, S. K., C. M. White and F. S. L. Williamson. 1977. Biology of the Bald Eagle on Amchitka Island, Alaska. Living Bird 15:143-182.

Sowls, K. 1988. Bald Eagle survey - Katmai National Park and Preserve. Unpubl. admin. rep., Natl. Park Serv., King Salmon, Alas. 7pp.

Sowls, L. W. 1982. A reconnaissance of the breeding distribution of colonial nesting seabirds on the south coast of the Alaska Peninsula, May 30- June 19, 1973. Unpubl. rep., U.S. Fish Wildl. Serv., Anchorage, Alas. 46pp.

Troyer, W. 1975-1979. Bald Eagle nesting and productivity surveys of Katmai National Monument. Unpubl. annual admin. reps., Natl. Park Serv., Anchorage, Alas.

Troyer, W. 1980. Bald Eagle production - Naknek Drainage. Unpubl. admin. memo., Natl. Park Serv., Anchorage, Alas. 1p.

Yurick, M. M. 1989. 1989 raptor nest inventory and productivity survey, Katmai National Park and Preserve. Unpubl. rep., Natl. Park Serv., King Salmon, Alas. 14pp.

Distribution and Status of Bald Eagles in the Aleutian Islands

G. Vernon Byrd and Jeffrey C. Williams

U.S. Fish and Wildlife Service, Homer, AK

The Bald Eagle reaches the western edge of its breeding range in the Rat Island group of the Aleutian Islands (Am. Ornith. Union 1983). In the treeless Aleutians, the species nests on the ground, often on small islets and sea stacks near larger islands.

Bald Eagles are top level predators in the Aleutian food web, which is dominated by marine elements. The Aleutian region is geographically isolated, has a sparse human population and has been a National Wildlife Refuge since 1913. Nevertheless, the ecosystem has been strongly influenced by human activities. The major perturbations include: introduction of Arctic and red fox by trappers prior to 1930, occupation by military personnel during World War II, nuclear testing, current military operations and commercial fishing activities.

Relatively little is known about the ecology of Bald Eagles in the Aleutian Islands, but several site-specific studies have provided insight into their breeding biology (Sherrod et

al. 1976, White et al. 1977) and food habits (Murie 1940, Sherrod et al. 1975). In addition, Bald Eagle nests were delineated on most islands during seabird surveys throughout the Aleutians from the mid-1970s to the mid-1980s (Early et al. 1981, Nysewander et al. 1982 and unpubl. files of Alaska Maritime National Wildlife Refuge).

Red fox photographed near Nikolski, Aleutian Islands. Photo by Bruce Wright.

Here we summarize available published and unpublished information on distribution, abundance, habitat use, reproductive performance and food habits of Bald Eagles in the

236

Aleutian Islands. The available information provides a reasonably complete description of the status of the species, but data are inadequate to reflect more than short-term trends. To remedy this shortcoming, a strategy for monitoring Bald Eagle populations at selected sites is suggested.

Distribution and Abundance

Although the Bald Eagle currently nests only as far west as Buldir Island in the western Rat Island group of the Aleutians, the species formerly nested at least as far west as the Soviet Commander Islands (Figure 1). According to Stejneger (1885), the breeding population of eagles was declining in the Commander Islands in the early 1880s and by the 1930s Bald Eagles occurred there only as occasional stragglers (Johansen 1961).

The former status of Bald Eagles in the westernmost group of the Aleutians, the Near Islands, is unclear. Turner (1886) reported that they did not breed there and he saw only a single bird during the 11 months he lived at Attu. In the 1930s, Murie (1959) saw only 2 eagles, both at Agattu, during extensive field observations in the Near Islands and the local Aleuts told him that they seldom saw eagles. In apparent contrast Murie (1959) concluded, probably erroneously, that there was a substantial westward movement of Bald Eagles from the Rat Islands to the Near Islands in fall based upon 6 band recoveries supposedly from Attu. It now seems likely that the Attu natives, who trapped foxes in the Rat Islands, took the eagles for bounty there but reported the bands from Attu after they returned home (Murie et al. 1937, R. D. Jones, Jr. pers. comm., C. M. White pers. comm.).

Estes and Palmisano (1974) speculated that Bald Eagles may have been more common in the Near Islands prior to Russian occupation because the decimation of the sea otter by Russian fur hunters drastically changed the trophic structure of the nearshore ecosystem. They suggested that when otters were removed, sea urchins overgrazed kelp beds and thus adversely affected the entire food web that was based upon benthic macrophytes, including eagles. A similar pattern may have occurred in the Commander Islands.

Figure 1. Location map of Aleutian Islands.

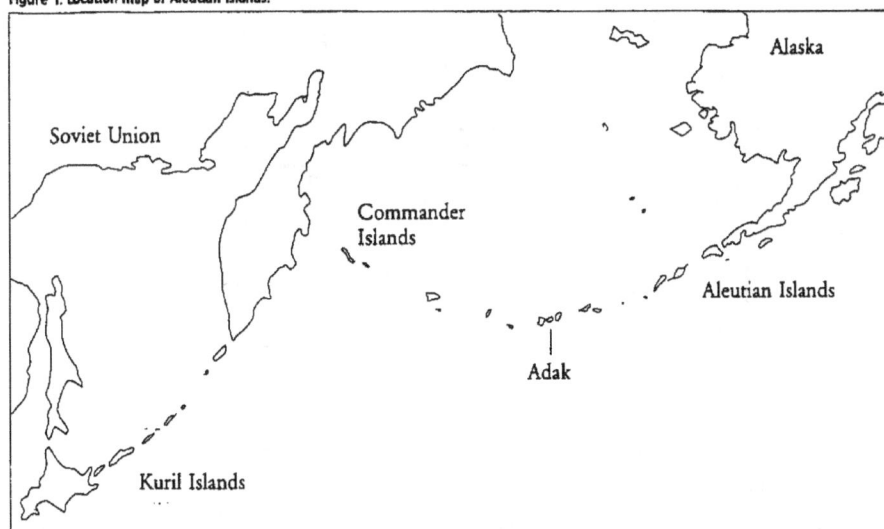

Figure 2. Map depicting the estimated number of Bald Eagle nests or territories by island group in the Aleutian Islands, Alaska. A ">" symbol preceeding the estimate indicates an incomplete survey of at least one island in the group.

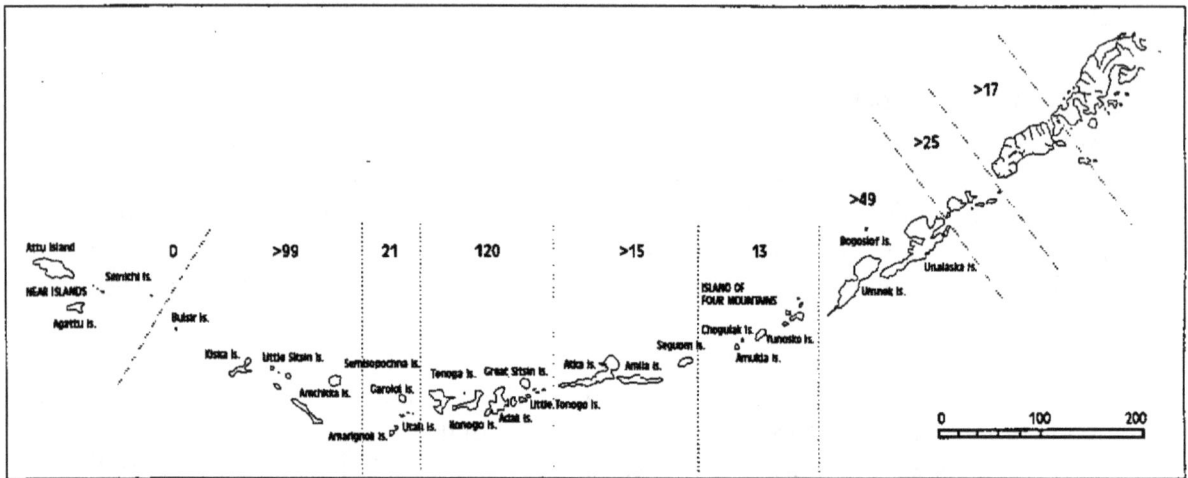

In any case, Bald Eagles currently nest only as far west as Buldir Island (Figure 2, Byrd and Day 1986), but they commonly nest east of there (Turner 1886, Murie 1959, Early 1982). We do not yet have accurate surveys of eagle nests for every island in the Aleutians, but most islands have been surveyed at least once since 1976. We were able to account for 331 nesting territories (Table 1) and estimate that approximately 70 more nests may occur in areas not completely surveyed such as Atka, Amlia, Umnak, Unalaska and Unimak. Therefore, we place the minimum number of nesting eagle pairs in the Aleutians at approximately 400.

Table 1. Bald Eagle breeding population estimates by island group in the Aleutian Islands, Alaska.

Island Group	Total Breeding Pairs	Density mean	s.d.	n
Near Islands	0	-	-	-
Rat Islands	>99	7.6	2.9	7
Delarof Islands	21	6.8	4.9	6
West Andreanof Islands	120	11.9	6.7	11
East Andreanof Islands	>15	-	-	-
Islands of Four Mountains	13	19.8	13.7	5
Fox Islands West Fox Islands	>49	-	-	
Krenitzin Islands	>25	13.8	27.2	5
Unimak and Adak	>17	-	-	-
Total	>331			

The largest populations occur in the Rat Islands, especially at Amchitka and in the western Andreanofs, particularly at Adak (Figure 2). Early (1982) estimated that the Aleutians contained approximately 600 nesting pairs of Bald Eagles, but his extrapolation was based only upon available data for densities in the area from Adak westward. We now believe that application of these densities to areas farther east is inappropriate.

There is no basis for judging whether Bald Eagle nesting populations have changed over the long term from the Rat Islands eastward. However, several complete nesting surveys at Kiska, Amchitka and Adak suggest there is at least short-term stability throughout the region (Table 2).

Bald Eagles perched on stored cod pots in Unalaska. Photo by Bruce Wright.

Estimated nesting densities in different groups of the Aleutian Islands vary from about 1 pair per 7 km of coastline to 1 pair per 20 km (Table 1). Densities apparently are higher in the Rat and Delarof Island groups than farther east, but incomplete data for several areas makes critical evaluation of this pattern difficult.

Table 2. Reproductive parameters of Bald Eagles In the Aleutian Islands, Alaska.

Year (a)	Location	Clutch size		Hatch success (b)		Fledge Success (c)	
		Mean	No. of nests	Mean	No. of nests	Mean	No. of nests
1936-37	Overall Aleutians	1.79	34	-			
1969	Amchitka	1.91	46	1.54	57	1.51	53
1970	Amchitka	-	-	1.78	56		
1971	Amchitka			1.73	68	-	-
1972	Amchitka			1.53	71	1.42	72
1974	Amchitka	-	-	1.72	64	-	-
1980	Amchitka	1.78	18	1.58	44	1.48	44
1981	Adak	2.37	27	1.83	35	1.69	12
1982	Adak	-				1.52	<34
1983	Adak	2.07	15				
	Mean	1.96		1.68		1.52	
	Std. Dev.	0.23		0.11		0.10	

(a) 1936-37 (Murie 1959), 1969-1974 (Sherrod et al. 1976), 1980 (Heglund and Reiswig 1980), 1981 (Reiswig 1981b), 1983 (Kline 1983).
(b) Young chicks/nest where ≥1 chicks hatched

(c) Fledglings/nest where >1 chick fledged.

There is considerable variation in estimated nesting densities between individual islands, even within the same group. Amchitka Island has a particularly high density of nesting eagles compared to other large islands for which intensive surveys are available. Amchitka has approximately 1 pair per 3 km in contrast to Adak, which has 1 pair per 8 km, Kanaga and Kiska with 1 pair per 7 km and Tanaga with 1 pair per 17 km.

Nesting density in the Aleutians is probably a function of available nest sites and food. Amchitka has a particularly high number of sea stacks for use as nest sites and the broad intertidal bench surrounding the island (an unusual feature in the Aleutians) provides a diverse nearshore foraging area year-round. Further, the removal of introduced foxes on selected islands has allowed the recovery of several species of native birds including Rock Ptarmigan, Glaucous-winged Gulls and ducks, all prey of eagles.

Age Ratios

Sherrod et al. (1976) reported an age structure of about 66% adult and 34% immature eagles at Amchitka from 1970 to 1972. They speculated the local dump was responsible for the high survivorship of immature eagles. After humans left Amchitka in 1974 and closed the dump, the proportion of immature eagle age classes decreased by over half the following year (Sherrod et al. 1976). At Adak, age ratios of Bald Eagles recorded on Christmas bird counts from 1972 to 1989 indicate a similar trend. In 1975, the local dump was converted from a dump-and-burn operation to a landfill, making garbage less available to eagles. There was a decline in the average annual proportion of immature eagles from 64% before the change to 47% thereafter.

These estimates of the proportion of immature eagles in populations at Amchitka and Adak may be biased due to differing observability of the age classes, but they should still provide an indication of trends.

Inter-Island Movements

Bald Eagles are considered year-round residents in the Aleutian Islands (Murie 1959, White et al. 1971). However, inter-island movements, especially to nearby islands, occur in response to food availability (Sherrod et al. 1976). For example, Bald Eagles concentrate around the military base at Adak during winter because of food scraps available from outside Navy galleys and at the landfill. During winter surveys in 1989 and 1990, no more than 5 eagles were seen on 5 islands just east of Adak, which usually contain at least 17 nesting pairs in summer. We speculate these eagles traveled to Adak to scavenge at the dump and outside Navy galleys.

We are aware of only 2 cases of inter-island band recovery other than that reported by Murie (1959). One involved a nestling banded at Amchitka and seen 3 years later at Adak some 300 km east of Amchitka (Sherrod et al. 1976). The other case involved 2 nestlings banded at Adak, one of which was eventually recovered at Atka, 250 km east of Adak. These few data suggest an eastern movement of some young eagles, but probably most young eagles remain near their natal areas. About 80% of the recoveries of Adak banded nestlings are from Adak.

Nest Sites

The maritime tundra of the Aleutian Islands provides only ground nest sites for Bald Eagles. Sherrod et al. (1976) identified 5 types of Bald Eagle nest substrates at Amchitka; islets, sea stacks, ridges, hillsides and connected sea stacks (Figures 3 and 4). Two of these substrates-islets, which are wider than tall and sea stacks, which are taller than wide-are separated from main islands. About 54% of the eagle nests at Adak were on islets or sea stacks (Reiswig 1981a) whereas 46% were in these habitats on Amchitka (difference not significant, p>0.1).

Figure 3. An idealized section of coastline showing the five nesting substrates of Bald Eagles in the Aleutian Islands, Alaska.

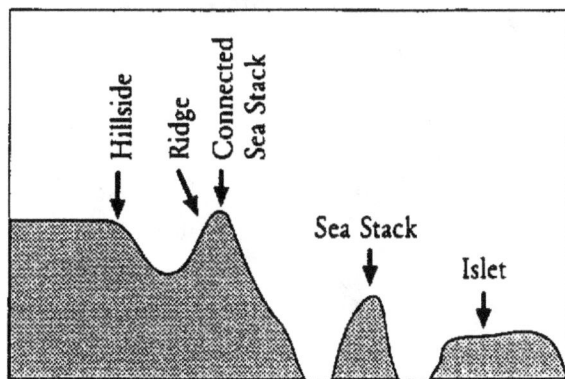

Most nests were located on or near the coast. For example, the mean distance from nests to the sea at Adak was 7 m, excluding 2 nests found more than 50 m inland (Reiswig 1981a). The mean elevation of nests was about 19 m on Adak (Reiswig 1981a) and 13 m on Amchitka (Sherrod et al. 1976).

Bald Eagle nests in the Aleutians are relatively small compared to the large nests found elsewhere in Alaska (Murie 1959, Sherrod et al. 1976). At the extreme, little or no nest material is added to the substrate and the young are reared in a well-trampled bare spot on a pinnacle (Murie 1959). Nests on Amchitka, typical of those found in the Aleutians, varied from 1.2 m to 2.1 m in diameter and the accumulation of nest material rarely exceeded 30 cm in height (Sherrod et al. 1976).

Most nests are found within the Elymus-umbel plant community (Byrd 1984) and nesting material is generally composed of common plants from nearby. Vegetation used in nest construction includes: dried stalks of *Heracleum lanatum* and *Angelica lucida*, kelp (e.g., *Nereocystis*) and *Sphagnum* spp. (Murie 1959, Sherrod et al. 1976).

The choice of nest sites throughout the Aleutians may have been influenced by the presence of introduced Arctic foxes. Sherrod et al. (1976) argue that nests on fox-free islands are more frequently found in accessible locations than are nests on islands with high densities of foxes.

Breeding Schedule and Reproductive Success

In the Aleutians, nest building begins as early as 20 January (Sherrod et al. 1976). Egg laying occurs from late March to May and peaks in mid-April. Hatching occurs from early May to late June. Eaglets usually fledge from early July to late August, with the peak in mid-August (White et al. 1971, Sherrod et al. 1976, Byrd and Day 1986 and unpubl. files of Alaska Maritime National Wildlife Refuge).

Figure 4. In the Aleutian Islands, Bald Eagle nest on offshore seastack or connected pinnacles such as this one at Adak. Photo by Vern Byrd.

Figure 5. This typical Aleutian nest, the trampled bare area on the left half of the pinnacle, illustrates the normal sparsity of nest material. Photo by J. Williams.

Productivity

About 20% of the nests that were considered active (those that had adults present throughout the spring) at Amchitka in 1969 never contained eggs (Sherrod et al. 1976). We have no other estimates of the proportion of attended nests that are inactive.

Six estimates of average clutch size are available for Aleutian sites (Table 2). The mode was 2 eggs in most cases and the overall average was 1.96 for all available data sets. Little variation was noted in hatch success, defined as the mean number of young in successful nests among the 8 estimates available (Table 2). The overall mean was 1.68 young per successful nest. The differences between the means of clutch size and brood size in the 4 cases where both estimates were available in the same year (Table 2) suggest that about 0.3 eggs per nest (range 0.12-0.54) failed to hatch (about 15%).

Approximately 1.5 eaglets fledged in nests where at least one young fledged. There was little inter-year variation (Table 2). About 78% of the pairs at nests with eggs were successful in hatching at least 1 egg in 1969 (Sherrod et al. 1976), the only year for which such data are available.

Food Habits
Prey Delivered to Nests

Available descriptive data on prey delivered to eagle eyries suggests birds are relatively important (Table 3). The most frequently taken species are seabirds including Northern Fulmar, shearwaters, Glaucous-winged Gull, murres and auklets and murrelets (see references in Table 3). At Amchitka, sea otter pups and Norway rats each comprised about half each of the mammalian prey taken by eagles (Sherrod et al. 1975, Heglund and Reiswig 1980). Ground squirrels are taken frequently at Unimak Island in the eastern Aleutians where they are native (Murie 1940). A pair of eagles at Ogliuga apparently favored this prey since they had to travel 8 km to Kavalga Island, the only island in the group where ground squirrels were introduced.

Locally, fish were important prey brought to nests (Table 3). The major species recorded were Atka mackerel, sculpins and greenling (Murie 1940, Krog 1953, Sherrod et al. 1976). The importance of fish as a food item delivered to nests may be far underestimated because fish may be consumed whole so that little evidence remains.

The account presented here for Bald Eagle prey provides a general description, but studies are lacking which quantify preference, or sample prey in such a way that variations among locations, seasons and individual pairs are adequately addressed. It is clear that some individuals are regularly prone to take certain types of prey (Sherrod et al. 1976), but the majority of eagles are opportunistic and use the most available prey (Grubb and Hensel 1978). For example, as a result of over-exploitation by fur hunters there were few sea otters on Amchitka in the 1930s and Murie.(1940) found no sea otter pups in eagle eyries. In later years as the local population of otters increased, sea otter pups were found more frequently in eagle eyries (Krog 1953, Sherrod et al. 1976, Heglund and Reiswig 1980).

Table 3. Summer prey of Bald Eagles in the Aleutian Islands, Alaska based upon examination of remains at eyries.

Year (a)	Location	No. of items	Bird	Food Class Mammal	Fish	Invert.
1936	Aleutians	74	58.9(b)	5.3	18.8	16.1
1937	Aleutians	325	86.0	7.6	6.1	
1953	Amchitka	29	24.0	21.0	55.0	
1969-70	Amchitka	89	57.0	28.0	15.0	
1971-72	Amchitka	480	61.3	23.1	14.0	0.6
1973	Bogoslof	15	93.3	6.7	-	
1974-76	Buldir	83	100.0			
1979	Buldir	26	100			
1980	Amchitka	43	25.6	46.5	27.9	
1990	Ogliuga	9	50.0			

(a) 1936-37 (Murie 1940), 1953 (Krog 1953), 1969-70 (White et al. 1971), 1971-72 (Sherrod et al. 1976), 1973 (Byrd et al. 1980), 1974-76, 1979 (refuge files), 1980 (Heglund and Reiswig 1980), 1990 (G.V. Byrd pers. comm.)

(b) Percent of total prey items

Foods and Feeding Behavior

The relative importance of specific prey to adult and sub-adult Bald Eagles has not been quantified in the Aleutians. Nevertheless, general observations provide a means of describing the response of eagles to normal seasonal variations in prey and to less predictable stochastic events such as beach-cast whales, which suddenly provide large amounts of food.

Most large Aleutian Islands have numerous small streams which contain Dolly Varden and spawning pink salmon. While some pairs feed on Dolly Varden all summer, each August and September eagles congregate along streams to feed on spawning salmon. As the salmon availability declines and winter approaches, eagles must switch to other prey such as gulls, various species of ducks, sea otters and nearshore fish.

Figure 6. Bald Eagles scavenge garbage dumps primarily in the winter after other bird species migrate and salmon have spawned. Photo by Mike Boylan.

Seabirds begin to congregate near breeding islands by May and provide a major source of food in most parts of the Aleutians through early-to-mid August. Beach-cast marine mammals, including sea otters, sea lions and whales attract eagles particularly in winter. Beaked whales and sperm whales are the primary cetaceans eagles regularly scavenge. Refuse dumps and other sources of scrap food concentrate eagles in winter (Figure 5).

These situations have been recorded at Unalaska (K. Griffin pers. comm.), Adak and Amchitka (Sherrod et al. 1976). Sherrod et al. (1976) reported that 85% of the eagles on Amchitka were present at the dump after a severe snow storm in 1970. The dump at Adak may additionally attract eagles from nearby islands in winter. The supplemental winter food provided in landfills probably increases survival, especially of young eagles.

At Adak, eagles have become quite bold and have been known to take downed waterfowl before hunters were able to retrieve them. Eagles will frequently steal fish as fishermen reel them in and have been known to take stringers of fish even while fishermen stood nearby. In winter, eagles will flock to the site of caribou kills before hunters finish field dressing the animals.

Threats and Conservation Issues

Currently the most obvious mortality factor for eagles in the Aleutians is electrocution at Adak. In 1978, when year-round records began, 50 eagles were electrocuted on overhead power lines at the Navy base. The next year, the U.S. Fish and Wildlife Service and the Navy began a program to install perches on poles above high voltage lines. Initially, perches were placed on poles in areas known for high concentrations of eagles. In subsequent years, perches were added on every pole where eagles were found electrocuted and the number of electrocutions declined to levels well below the 1978 level (Figure 6). Approximately 10 to 15 eagles are still electrocuted annually at Adak. Perches will continue to be added to poles and the Navy is gradually replacing overhead lines with underground cables (Soil Conservation Service 1990). Eagles were also electrocuted at Amchitka when overhead power lines were used there in the early 1970s (Sherrod et al. 1976). Currently, overhead power lines are not used at Amchitka or other sites inhabited by people in the Aleutians.

Several eagle nest sites were destroyed at Amchitka during nuclear testing in the late 1960s and early 1970s (Fuller and Kirkwood 1977, White et al. 1977), but apparently the birds used alternative sites because breeding populations have remained relatively stable. Some nests also must have been destroyed during World War II activities such as bombings at Kiska, but there are no data to judge the long term impacts of such activity. Most eagle nesting areas in the Aleutians are not likely to be affected by future development since National Wildlife Refuge regulations and the wilderness status of most islands offer special protection.

Chemical toxicants have been used on several islands in the Aleutians to remove introduced Arctic fox (Bailey and Kaiser 1990). Baits containing poisons were purposely kept small to avoid attracting eagles and there appeared to be no inadvertent take of eagles (Byrd et al. 1988).

Bounty hunting of eagles could have been a major source of mortality in the Aleutians. Murie (1936) reported that after the 1924 to 1925 trapping season on Ogliuga Island in the Delarof Island group, 104 pairs of eagle talons were left in the trapper's cabin there. Bounty collection by Aleuts could have locally affected Bald Eagles (Murie 1959).

Figure 7. Electrocution of eagles is a significant mortality factor at Adak. Installation of perches on heavily used power poles has reduced the number of eagles electrocuted to 10-15 annually. Photo by Vern Byrd.

Introduced foxes may have adversely affected Bald Eagles in the Aleutians. It is possible that foxes keep eagles from nesting in otherwise suitable locations (Sherrod et al. 1976), but more importantly, foxes and introduced rats have eliminated most large ground-nesting birds, thus reducing an important prey resource for eagles. Apparently eagles seldom prey on foxes in the Aleutians (Murie 1959). It will be interesting to determine whether eagle populations increase at Kiska or other islands as the avifauna begins to recover following fox removal.

As indicated above, beach-cast marine mammals provide a winter food source for Bald Eagles which may be important. Northern sea lion and harbor seal populations are declining in the Aleutians (Merrick et al. 1987), thus the reduction in abundance of these sources of food could adversely impact eagles in the future.

Information Needs

Baseline data on nesting populations and reproductive performance are available for Amchitka and Adak, but no monitoring system is in place to detect trends. Island-wide surveys of nest sites need to be conducted about every three years to record changes in nesting density. Furthermore, study areas need to be delineated at these two islands so that samples of nests may be checked during the period of mid-eaglet rearing to estimate the average number of young per nest as an indication of overall reproductive performance.

To complete the Aleutian nest census, islands not yet entirely surveyed should be censused for eagle nests. Other islands should be resurveyed whenever possible.

Literature Cited

American Ornithologists Union. 1983. Check list of North American birds. Sixth ed. Allen Press Laurance, K. A.

Bailey, E. P. and G. W. Kaiser. 1990. Impacts of introduced predators on nesting seabirds in the northeast Pacific. In: K. Vermeer, ed. Proc. of Pacific Seabird Group Symposium on Status, Ecology and Conservation of Marine Birds in the Temperate North Pacific.

Byrd, G. V. 1984. Vascular vegetation of Buldir Island, Aleutian Islands, Alaska compared to another Aleutian island. Arctic 37:37-48.

Byrd, G. V. and R. H. Day. 1986. The avifauna of Buldir Island, Aleutian Islands, Alaska. Arctic 39:109-118.

Byrd, G. V., G. J. Divoky and E. P. Bailey. 1980. Changes in, marine bird and mammal populations on an active volcano in Alaska. Murrelet 61:50-62.

Byrd, G. V., G. T. McClellan and J. P. Fuller. 1988. To determine the efficacy and environmental hazards of Compound 1080 (sodium fluroacetate) as a control agent for Arctic fox (*Alopex lagopus*) on Kiska Island, Aleutian Islands Unit-Alaska Maritime National Wildlife Refuge (AIU-AMNWR)(Field investigations). Unpublished final Progress Report to Env. Prot. Agency.

Early, T. J. 1982. Abundance and distribution of breeding raptors in the Aleutian Islands, Alaska. Pages 99-111. In: Ladd, W. N. and P. F. Schempf, eds. Proceedings of a symposium and workshop on raptor management and biology in Alaska and western Canada. U.S. Fish and Wildlife Service, Anchorage, Alaska. 335pp.

Early, T. J., K. Hall and B. Minn. 1981. Results of a bird and mammal survey in the central Aleutian Islands, summer 1980. U.S. Fish and Wildlife Service Report, Adak, Alaska.

Estes, J. A. and J. F. Palmisano. 1974. Sea otters: their role in structuring nearshore communities. Science

185:1058-1060.

Fuller, R. G. and J. B. Kirkwood. 1977. Ecological consequences of nuclear testing. pp. 627-649. In: M. L. Merritt and R. G. Fuller, eds. The environment of Amchitka Island, Alaska. National Technical Information Service, Springfield, Virginia.

Grubb, T. G. and R. J. Hensel. 1978. Food habits of nesting Bald Eagles on Kodiak Island, Alaska. Murrelet 59:70-72.

Heglund, P. J. and B. Reiswig. 1980. 1980 Raptor survey: The breeding Bald Eagle population of Amchitka Island, Alaska. U.S. Fish and Wildlife Service Report, Adak, Alaska.

Johansen, H. 1961. Birds of the Commander Islands. Auk 78:44-56.

Kline, N. 1983. Adak Bald Eagle study-1983 progress report. U.S. Fish and Wildlife Service Report, Adak, Alaska.

Krog, J. 1953. Notes on the birds of Amchitka Island, Alaska. Condor 55:299-304.

Merrick, R. L., T. R. Loughlin and D. G. Calkins. 1987. Decline in abundance of the northern sea lion, *Eumetopias jubatus*, in Alaska, 1956-86. Fishery Bulletin 85:351-365.

Murie, O. J. 1936. Biological investigations Aleutian Islands and southwestern Alaska-April 23-September 19. 1936. U.S. Fish and Wildlife Service Report, Washington, D.C.

Murie, O. J. 1940. Food habits of the northern Bald Eagle in the Aleutian Islands, Alaska. Condor 42:198-202.

Murie, O. J. 1959. Fauna of the Aleutian Islands and Alaska Peninsula. North American Fauna 61:1-364.

Murie, O. J., V. B. Scheffer, J. H. Steenis and H. D. Gray. 1937. Report on biological investigations in Aleutian Islands, Alaska. U.S. Fish and Wildlife Service Report, Washington, D.C.

Nysewander, D. R., D. J. Forsell, P. A. Baird, D. J. Shields, G. J. Weiler and J. H. Kogan. 1982. Marine bird and mammal survey of the Aleutian Islands, summers of 1980-81. U.S. Fish and Wildlife Service Report, Anchorage, Alaska.

Reiswig, B. 1981a. Progress report: movement and breeding biology of Bald Eagles on Adak Island, 01-01-81 to 11-3181. U.S. Fish and Wildlife Service Report, Adak, Alaska.

Reiswig, B. 1981b. Bald Eagle nest survey, 1981, Amchitka Island. U.S. Fish and Wildlife Service Report, Adak, Alaska.

Reiswig, B. 1981c. Eagle nest survey-Little Tanaga, Umak, Kanu, Takadak, Asuksak and Aziak Islands. Unpublished data, U.S. Fish and Wildlife Service, Adak, Alaska.

Sherrod, S. K., J. A. Estes and C. M. White. 1975. Depredation of sea otter pups by Bald Eagles at Amchitka Island, Alaska. J. of Mammal. 56:701-703.

Sherrod, S. K, C. M. White and F. S. L. Williamson. 1976. Biology of the Bald Eagle on Amchitka Island, Alaska. Living Bird 15:143-182.

Soil Conservation Service (SCS). 1990. Natural resources management plan-naval complex, Adak Island, 1990. Draft Report U.S. Geological of Agric. Soil Conservation Service. Anchorage, Alaska.

Stejneger, L. 1885. Results of Ornithological explorations in the Commander Islands and in Kamtschatka.

Government Printing Office. Washington, D.C. 382pp.

Turner, L. M. 1886. Contributions to the natural history of Alaska. U.S. Army Signal Service, Government Printing Office, Washington D.C. 226pp.

White, C. M., W. B. Emison and F. S. L. Williamson. 1971. Dynamics of raptor populations on Amchitka Island, Alaska. BioScience 21:623-627.

White, C. M., F. S. L. Williamson and W. B. Emison. 1977. Avifaunal investigations. Pages 227-260 in M.L. Merritt and R.G. Fuller, eds. The environment of Amchitka Island, Alaska. National Technical Information Service. Springfield, Virg.

Bald Eagles in Western Alaska

John M. Wright

Alaska Department of Fish and Game, Fairbanks, AK

When Bald Eagles (*Haliaeetus leucocephalus*) are envisioned, most people picture regal white-headed birds in a background of dark green conifers or grey-barked cottonwoods. This is to be expected, for coastal spruce-hemlock and riparian forests are home to the majority of Alaska's Bald Eagles. But Bald Eagles are also found in other parts of Alaska, including the treeless tundra coasts and scattered patches of boreal forest of Bristol Bay and western Alaska.

This report provides information on the distribution and abundance of nesting Bald Eagles on the northern side of the Alaska Peninsula through Bristol Bay and north through coastal western Alaska to the Noatak River drainage (Figure 1). In Kessel and Gibson's (1978) scheme of biogeographic regions, this corresponds to the northern portion of their Southwestern Region and most of their Western Region. The majority of this area lies west of tree line with tundra the dominant habitat.

Methods

A variety of sources have been used in the compilation of information for this report. Because few systematic surveys for Bald Eagles have been reported from the region, most information was in the form of personal communications and unpublished notes. Much of the data was collected by biologists with the U.S. Fish and Wildlife Service (FWS), National Park Service (NPS) and Alaska Department of Fish & Game (ADF&G). Surveys of sufficient detail to develop estimates of eagle density have been conducted in only a few areas in the region. Several potential sources of information were not available when this paper was prepared and, undoubtedly, many knowledgeable sources were never identified.

A minimum estimate of the number of breeding pairs in this region of Alaska may be derived from the information gathered for this report, but several qualifiers must accompany this attempt:

1) the data comes from a variety of sources (e.g., specific raptor surveys, waterfowl surveys, fisheries surveys, birding tours, walrus research, air taxi pilot reports);
2) different observer platforms were used (e.g., fixed-wing and helicopter aerial surveys, boats and river rafts, on foot);
3) in many cases recent information has been combined with 15-20 year-old data when current data was lacking; and
4) for several locales only incomplete coverage (of any data) was available.

Breeding Distribution and Abundance

Nesting Bald Eagles are found in coastal areas from the western tip of the Alaska Peninsula near Izembek Lagoon, north to Goodnews Bay. Inland from the coast, nesting Bald Eagles are found on the Alaska Peninsula throughout Bristol Bay, north to the Yukon and Andreafsky rivers and occasionally as far north as the Unalakleet River. A very preliminary minimum estimate of the number of Bald Eagles for the entire region would be 160-175 nesting pairs.

For the following discussion, the region has been broken down into the following subregions: north side of the Alaska Peninsula, Naknek River drainage, Kvichak River drainage, Nushagak River drainage, Togiak, Yukon/Kuskokwim Delta and North of the Yukon drainage (Figure 2).

North Side of the Alaska Peninsula

On the north side of the Alaska Peninsula, southwest of, but not including the Naknek River drainage, approximately 30 nest sites are known. Nineteen sites were active in the Port Moller/Herendeen Bay/ Nelson Lagoon in a single year, 1976 (Gill et al. 1981). This is the only locale that has been thoroughly surveyed in this subregion. No information was found for the Port Heiden/Black Lake, Cinder River and Egegik/Becharof Lake locales. With Bald Eagles using a variety of nest sites in this subregion, including bluffs, cliffs, pinnacles, sand dunes, shrubs, balsam poplar (*Populus balsamifera*) trees and man-made structures, many locales that on first sight might be considered unsuitable for nesting require a detailed search before they can be considered vacant.

Bald Eagle gliding. Photo by Daniel Zatz. Naknek River Drainage

In the Naknek River drainage, an average of 16 active nests occur annually. Over the past 15 years, more than 30 different nest sites have been located. Recently about two thirds have been found in spruce (*Picea*) trees, with the remainder in balsam poplars; but in the 1970's poplar nest sites outnumbered spruce nests 2.4 to 1 (Katmai Natl. Park unpubl. rep.). One ground nest on a small island in Naknek Lake was reported in the late 1960's (D. Gibson pers. comm.) and occasional cliff nests on islets were reported in the 1970's (W. Troyer, Katmai Natl. Park, unpubl. rep.).

Kvichak River Drainage
Around 35-40 nests are likely active each year in the Kvichak River drainage. About 15 of these are found on the Alagnak River and the lakes it drains. Iliamna Lake and the streams feeding into it have not been systematically surveyed, but at least 10 nesting pairs are probably found there. Eleven active nests were found around Lake Clark and drainages feeding into it in 1990. The majority of nests in Lake Clark National Park are found in balsam poplar trees (J. Fowler, pers. comm.).

Williamson and Peyton (1962) discuss the historical abundance of Bald Eagles in the Iliamna Lake area and suggest their numbers have increased markedly since 1900. At the turn of the century, Osgood saw just one Bald Eagle on this large lake and only five in total while crossing the peninsula (Osgood 1904). By the 1930's and 40's, Bald Eagles were considered common in most natural history reports from the area.

Nushagak River Drainage
A minimum of 25 nesting sites have been reported over the years by a variety of sources. Twelve of these were in the Mulchatna River drainage, with the remainder from the Wood/Tikchik Lakes and the Nushagak River. Nearly all reports are of tree nests, though a ground nest has been observed on an island in Tikchik Lake.

Togiak
Forty-five to fifty nests are likely active in this subregion each year. Inland from the immediate coast, Togiak National Wildlife Refuge (NWR) personnel have accumulated records for 40 nest sites, with approximately 25 active each year (L. Hotchkiss and D. Campbell, Togiak NWR unpubl. rep.). Most nests are found in deciduous trees clustered in groves (90%, mostly balsam poplar), or spruce standing alone on the tundra (10%), though at least one nest has been found atop a rock outcrop on a tundra-covered hill. A recent survey of the coast in the center of the subregion found 11 active nests. These nests were on pinnacles, cliffs and bluffs overlooking the sea (J. Wright, unpubl. data).

Yukon/Kuskokwim Delta
Few nesting Bald Eagles have been reported from this primarily flat, open expanse of wet tundra. About five nests have been seen in the lower Kuskokwim drainage, mostly on tributaries south of the main river. Two nests have been reported on sloughs of the Yukon River in the vicinity of Marshall and 3 or more may be active annually in the Andreafsky drainage. White and Boyce (1978) reported 2 nests on the Anvik River, on the lower river below the mouth of the Yellow River. All reports from this subregion were of tree nests.

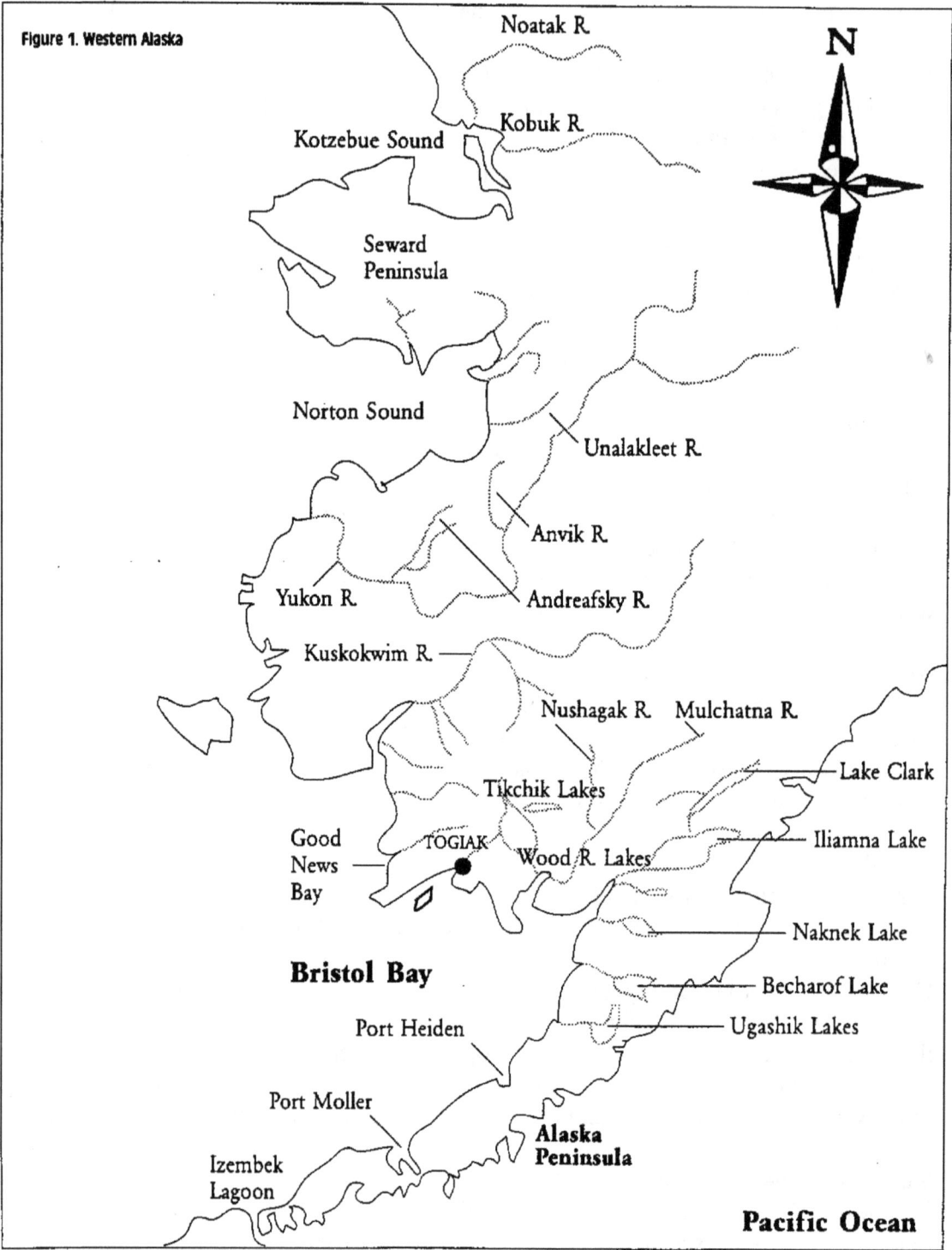

Figure 1. Western Alaska

Noatak R.

Kobuk R.

Kotzebue Sound

Seward
Peninsula

Norton Sound

Unalakleet R.

Anvik R.

Yukon R.

Andreafsky R.

Kuskokwim R.

Nushagak R.   Mulchatna R.

Lake Clark

Tikchik Lakes

Iliamna Lake

Good
News
Bay

TOGIAK

Wood R. Lakes

Naknek Lake

Bristol Bay

Becharof Lake

Port Heiden

Ugashik Lakes

Port Moller

Alaska
Peninsula

Izembek
Lagoon

Pacific Ocean

Figure 2. Subregions of western Alaska.

North of the Yukon Drainage

Yukon/Kuskokwim Delta

Nushagak River Drainage

Kvichak River Drainage

Togiak

Naknek River Drainage

North Side of the Alaska Peninsula

N

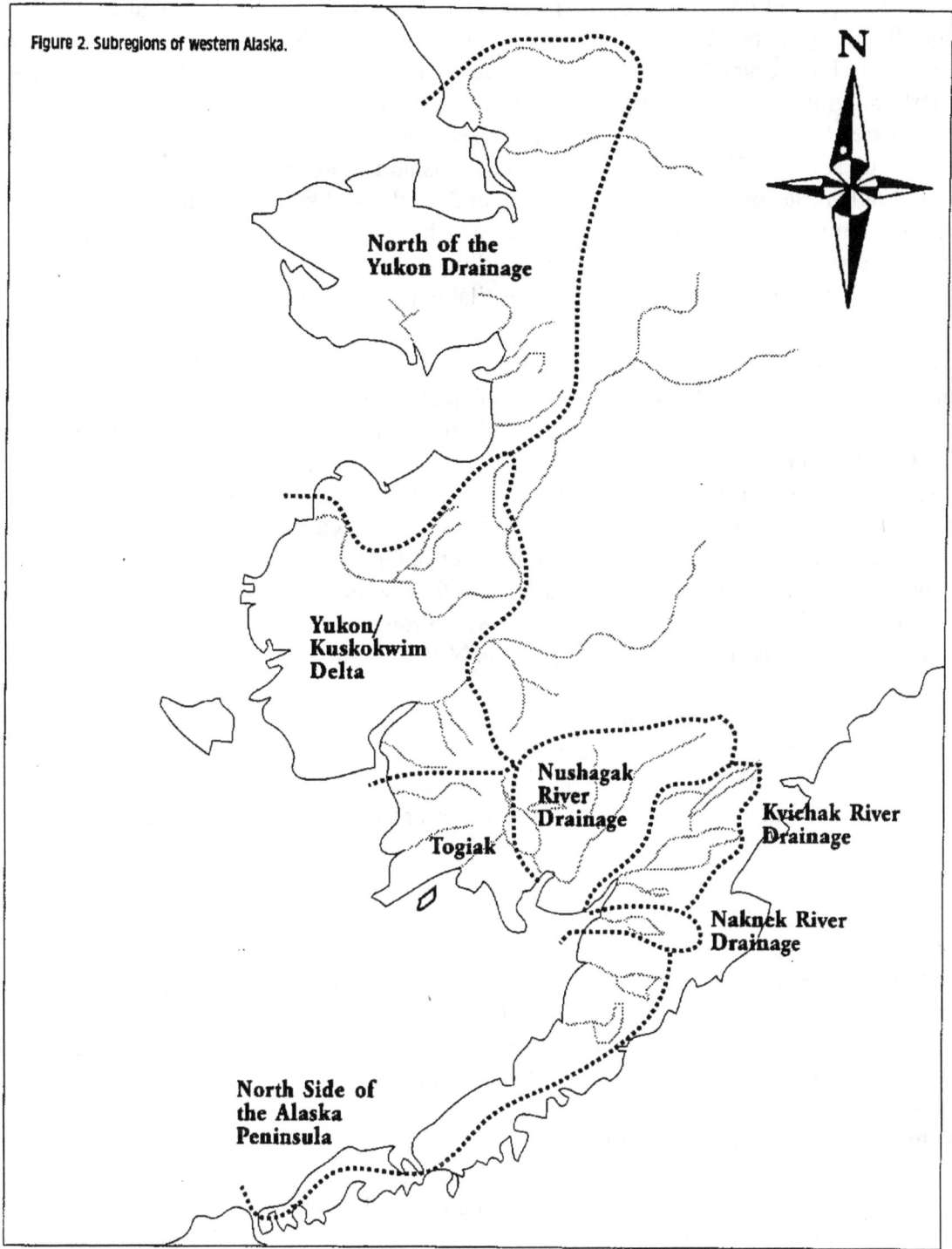

Nesting Density

Four areas have been surveyed with sufficient intensity to determine nesting density. The Port Moller area was surveyed completely by air and boat in 1976 (Gill et al. 1981, R. Gill pers. comm.). Nineteen active nest sites were located along approximately 160 miles of shoreline, roughly 1 nest per 8.5 miles (13.5 km). In Katmai National Park, aerial surveys have been conducted in most years since the mid-1970s. In 1988, 402 miles of lake and river shore were surveyed. Twenty active nests were counted, equaling 1 nest per 20 miles (32 km) (Katmai Natl. Park unpubl. rep.). The NPS also conducted aerial surveys in Lake Clark National Park. Five active nests were found in 1990 around Lake Clark, roughly 1 nest per 25 miles (40 km) of shoreline (J. Fowler, pers. comm.). The fourth area to be intensively surveyed was the coast in the vicinity of Togiak. A helicopter survey of 212 miles of mainland and island shores in 1990 found 11 active Bald Eagle nests, or approximately 1 nest per 20 miles (32 km). Golden Eagles were seen at 4 sites mixed in with the Bald Eagles (J. Wright, unpubl. data). Data are accumulating in other areas, such as Togiak National Wildlife Refuge; density estimates for large blocks of land within the region may be available in the future.

Productivity

Information on the number of young raised to near fledgling age is available from three areas. At Port Moller in 1976, an average of 1.9 young were found in 15 successful nests (R. Gill, unpubl. data). From 1976-79 in Katmai National Park, the average number of young per successful nest ranged from 1.6 to 2.2 (n = 12 to 16 nests). Considering all active nests found earlier in the season, productivity ranged from 1.2 to 1.8 (n = 15 to 22 nests, W. Troyer, Katmai Natl. Park, unpubl. rep.). On the Togiak NWR, the number of young per successful nest ranged from 1.5 to 1.9 between 1986-88 (n = 7 to 20 nests). The number of young per active nest for 1987-89 ranged from 0.95 to 1.15 (n = 11 to 26 nests, L. Hotchkiss and D. Campbell, Togiak NWR, unpubl. rep.).

Broods of three young were surprisingly common in some years at Katmai National Park. In 1976, 6 of 12 successful nests held three young. From 1977-79, the percentage of successful nests with three young ranged from 7-27%. At Port Moller in 1976, 2 of 15 successful nests held three young. No broods larger than two were reported from Togiak NWR.

Fall and Winter Distributions

Late-spawning red salmon (*Oncorhynchus nerka*), fall runs of silver salmon (*0. kisutch*) and fall-staging waterfowl provide locally concentrated food sources at many sites in the region. Although no systematic effort has been made to identify fall congregation sites of Bald Eagles in this region, several have been noted: Port Moller in August, but dispersed by September; and, Savonoski River between Naknek Lake and Lake Grosvenor in October (173 eagles, including 136 subadults, seen in mid October 1975, W Troyer, Katmai Natl. Park, unpubl. Rep.).

A number of Bald Eagles overwinter in the region. In the Port Moller area, four adults and six subadults were seen in January 1977 and up to 20 adults in December were reported by local residents (Gill et al. 1981). On the Naknek River, 4-5 adults and 8-10 sub-adults were commonly seen in winter (D. Russell, pers. comm.). Approximately 20 eagles remain on the Togiak NWR over winter (L. Hotchkiss and D. Campbell, Togiak NWR, unpubl. rep.) and from one to a few adults were regularly seen just off the refuge at the river outlets of the Wood River lake system.

Prey

Information on prey taken by Bald Eagles has been reported from just one nest site in the region. Prey remains were collected at a coastal nest in the Togiak subregion in the early 1970's. Remains of salmon (*Oncorhynchus* spp.), wolf fish (Anarhichadidae), kittiwakes (*Rissa* sp.) and Tufted Puffins (*Fratercula cirrhata*) were identified (M. Dick, unpubl. FWS rep.).

Literature Cited

Bailey, A. M. 1948. Birds of arctic Alaska. Denver Mus. Nat. Hist., Popular Ser. 8:1-317.

Gill, R. E., Jr., M. R. Petersen and P. D. Jorgensen. 1981. Birds of the northcentral Alaska Peninsula, 1976-1980. Arctic 34:286-306.

Kessel, B. and D. D. Gibson. 1978. Status and distribution of Alaska birds. Studies Avian Biol. 1:1-100.

Mindell, D. P. and R. A. Dotson. 1980. Raptor surveys and river profiles in the Kuskokwim, Unalakleet and Yukon River drainages, Alaska, 1979 and 1980. Bur. Land Manage., Anchorage Dist. Off., Anchorage, Alas.

Osgood, W. H. 1904. A biological reconnaissance of the base of the Alaska Peninsula. North Am. Fauna No. 24, 86pp.

White, C. M. and D. A. Boyce, Jr. 1978. A profile of various rivers and their raptor populations in western Alaska, 1977. U.S. Bur Land Manage., Rep. BLM/AK/TR/78/01, Anchorage, Alas.

Williamson, F. S. L. and L. J. Peyton. 1962. Faunal relationships of birds in the Iliamna Lake area, Alaska. Biol. Papers Univ. Alaska 5:1-73.

Personal communications and others who provided information:

Lee Anne Ayres, NPS, Kotzebue; Rachel Brubaker, FWS, Kotzebue; Diane Campbell, FWS, Togiak NWR, Dillingham; Chris Dau, FWS, Izembek NWR, Cold Bay; Jim Dau, ADF&G, Kotzebue; Donna Dewhurst, FWS, King Salmon; Bob Dittrick, Wilderness Birding Adventures, Anchorage (Nushagak); Joe Fowler, NPS, Lake Clark Natl. Park, Port Alsworth; Dan Gibson, Univ. of Alaska Museum, Fairbanks; Robert Gill, FWS, Anchorage (Port Moller); Sue Hills, FWS, Fairbanks (Alaska Peninsula); Mike Hikes, FWS, Togiak NWR, Dillingham; Rod King, FWS, Fairbanks (Alaska Peninsula, Togiak); Lee Hotchkiss, FWS, Anchorage (Togiak); Dan Hourhan, Alaska State Parks, Anchorage (Nushagak); Brian McCaffery, FWS, Yukon Delta NWR, Bethel; Bob Nelson, ADF&G, Nome; Bob Ritchie, Alaska Biological Research, Fairbanks; Scott Robinson, Bur. of Land Management, Fairbanks (Unalakleet, Seward Peninsula); Dick Russell, ADF&G, King Salmon; Mike Spindler, FWS, Galena (Kotzebue Sound); Ron Squibb, NPS, Katmai Natl. Park, King Salmon; Ted Swem, FWS, Anchorage (Togiak); Randall Wilke, FWS, Fairbanks (Alaska Peninsula).

The Status of Bald Eagles in the Yukon Territory, Canada

D. H. Mossop

Yukon Territorial Government (retired), Whitehorse, Yukon, Canada

The Yukon initiated an inventory of its breeding birds of prey in the early 1970's. This work has focused on large falcons and other raptors primarily where input was needed for making land use decisions. The information from these surveys has been entered into a dataset on the Yukon Government IBM mainframe for analysis as required. Over the years, a systematic survey has been conducted as funding has become available. The strategy was to design a standard survey and data format so the overall data base can expand in a meaningful way (Hayes and Kale 1979).

The Bald Eagle has been recorded during these surveys as one of the target species. Priority, however, has focused on other raptors when habitats have been selected for field work; the coverage for breeding Bald Eagles has rarely been as complete. However, the highly visible nature of the species enhances its coverage through incidental sightings. Coverage accuracy in the case of the higher priority large falcons has been estimated at an average 80% in the habitat actually surveyed (Mossop 1988). For Bald Eagles, accuracy is likely about 75%, similar to that suggested for other study areas (Grier et al. 1981).

Methods

Breeding population

Most raptor inventory surveys in the Yukon have been conducted by aircraft, usually by helicopter. Some initial surveys were conducted by boat, but effectiveness of this survey method for identifying breeding Bald Eagles in the large flood plains of many Yukon rivers has not been considered foolproof. Air surveys have been timed to correspond with late incubation or early brood rearing. Perched or incubating adults have been found to be highly visible. Virtually all waterways surveyed by boat have been resurveyed by air over the years.

The term "nest site" has taken the meaning of an area around an occupied nest which is reasonably assumed to be defended. Stick nests within 2 km of attending adults have been assumed to be the same "site".

At each nest site, its accurate location has been mapped at 1:250,000 and assigned its UTM coordinates which act as a permanent identifier. The species, condition and height of the nest tree have been recorded along with the distance from water. The presence of alternate nests in the area has been recorded. The presence of adult(s) and the productivity parameters at the nest have been noted including the estimated age of young. For management purposes, analyses of breeding populations of riparian nesting species like Bald Eagles and Peregrine Falcons have been by major drainage basin. The Yukon inventory has divided the territory into seven basins; various ones have received differing levels of attention (Figure 1).

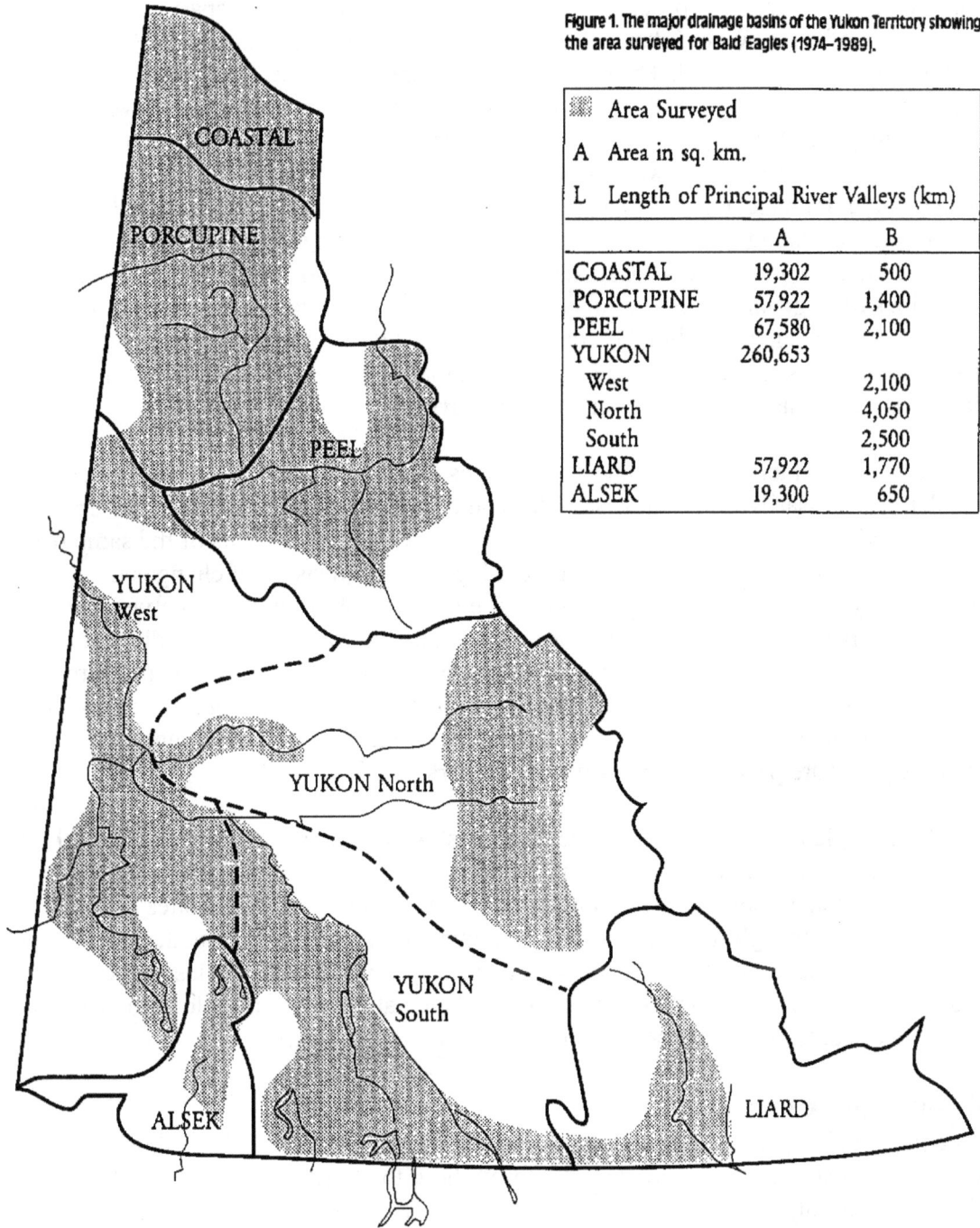

Figure 1. The major drainage basins of the Yukon Territory showing the area surveyed for Bald Eagles (1974–1989).

	Area Surveyed
A	Area in sq. km.
L	Length of Principal River Valleys (km)

	A	B
COASTAL	19,302	500
PORCUPINE	57,922	1,400
PEEL	67,580	2,100
YUKON	260,653	
West		2,100
North		4,050
South		2,500
LIARD	57,922	1,770
ALSEK	19,300	650

The task of extrapolating Bald Eagle population parameters to these entire drainages varies greatly and simply cannot be done with precise confidence in most cases. Nevertheless, an initial look at the known breeding numbers gives a relatively good generalized impression of the status of the Bald Eagle and points out where future work should be prioritized.

All data were coded and stored as a SAS (Statistical Analysis System) data set. Analysis has been by standard SAS procedures allowing the lumping and comparing of parameters in a variety of ways. Where statistical significance is indicated, tests are by Chi squared at the 90% confidence level. The process of judging coverage was approached in two ways: by the linear distance of water courses surveyed and by the area surveyed within each drainage. In the first case, the average linear shoreline distance between nest sites was calculated and numbers were simply then expanded to extrapolate breeding numbers to the whole drainage. Only river valleys, which were considered large enough to be suitable eagle nesting habitat, were measured in each drainage. As a standard, only those rivers recognized in surveys of Canada's hydrometric network were measured. The entire shorelines of large lakes were included. Concurrently, the measured area of coverage for birds of prey in general within the drainage was used as a percent to extrapolate potential breeding numbers. This value is calculated as a matter of course in the reporting of population analysis of raptors throughout the territory.

Quantifying productivity at the known nest sites is difficult because site visits were not regular or necessarily of the same sample. The best indication from the Yukon drainages is a lumped sample of visits over the years of survey. No repeat visits of the same nest within one year were included. This, although giving no measure of changes in productivity over the years, suggests a relative measure of productivity between areas and allows comparison with eagle populations elsewhere. The attendance of adults at nest sites tends to be the weakest statistic in our single visit survey simply because birds not productive in that year may not be in the immediate area when the survey was conducted. The proportion of sites producing young and the average number of young per nest site over the years are probably more useful indicators.

The Bald Eagle is the one raptor in the northwest which lends itself to identification of critical feeding and concentration areas due to its traditional use of salmon spawning streams and sometimes waterfowl staging areas in late summer. These sites become known mostly through fisheries research and incidental observations made by trappers and others on the land. The importance of these staging and feeding sites to the local eagle populations is undoubtedly enormous and a cataloguing of their locations and the numbers of eagles in attendance has accumulated over the years.

Results and Current Status

Breeding Bald Eagles have been recorded in all drainage basins of the Yukon. The species is considered a common breeder throughout the territory. Across the territory nest sites were virtually always located in trees (one rock site out of 162); large spruce trees in riparian sites dominated (58%) while the rest were in deciduous trees (42%). Differences did occur in the density of breeders between drainage basins, however and productivity differences also seem apparent from some parts of the territory.

1) North Slope (Coastal)

Only two breeding pairs have been identified in the drainages flowing into the Beaufort Sea. Coverage has been about 90% of both the major drainages and of the area. Clearly these habitats are well north of the Arctic Circle with few nesting trees and a very short open water season are marginal breeding habitat for Bald Eagles. Golden Eagles, meanwhile, are by far the most common breeding raptor in the region suggesting the differing strategies of the two eagle species create differing opportunity at high latitude.

Productivity of Bald Eagles in North Slope drainages is hard to assess, but indications are of a relatively low breeding effort. Of the two nest sites, only one is known to have produced young in the last 5 years.

2) Porcupine River

This drainage straddles the Arctic Circle, but contains some rich wildlife features including the wetlands of Old Crow Flats and the large salmon runs of the Porcupine River. The Bald Eagle is a fairly common breeder throughout.

Twenty-four different nesting sites are in the data file for the Porcupine drainage. Coverage by area in the drainage has been estimated at 80% and 70% by watercourse. This suggests a breeding population of between 37 and 43 pairs. An average linear watercourse distance between nests averaged 32 km. Productivity at these nest sites was assessed from 36 annual visits to different nests. The visits span the period from 1977 to 1984. Occupancy by adults averaged 53% and 42% produced young. The production averaged two young per successful nest.

A concentration of eagles is associated with spawning salmon in the upper Porcupine drainage, including the Fishing Branch River. It is possible that most of the eagles breeding in the Porcupine Basin may concentrate in that area in late summer.

3) Peel River

This large drainage in the north eastern portion of the territory lies mostly south of the Arctic Circle and contains relatively productive wetlands. It harbors no Pacific salmon runs, but is used extensively by the very productive Mackenzie River delta fish populations.

Twenty-six different Bald Eagle nest sites are known from the basin. Coverage was estimated at 60% by area and 50% by watercourse distance. A breeding population of between 54 and 123 pairs is suggested. Inter-nest distance along waterways averaged 17 km. Productivity measurement is from a sample of 52 annual visits over the period from 1978-1982. In that period, 69% of nest sites were found attended by adults and 50% of nests produced young. An average of 1.5 (± 0.2) young were being raised at successful nests. No eagle concentrations are known to occur in this area.

4) Yukon North

This section of the large Yukon River basin includes the mainstream of the Yukon River and its two largest tributaries, the Stewart and the Pelly rivers. Several salmon runs are included and the valleys of the large rivers have relatively productive wetland habitats. Twenty-three Bald Eagle nest sites are known from the region. Coverage by area was 40% and 30% of the linear waterway distance was surveyed. A breeding population of between 72 and 96 pairs is suggested. Linear distance between pairs averaged 42 km. There were 27 visits over the period from 1978-1982. An average of 81% of the sites were attended by adults and overall 63% produced young. An average of 1.4 young ($\pm$ 0.4) were produced per successful nest.

No staging or concentration sites are known for the drainage although coverage in this mostly remote drainage during late summer has been negligible.

5) Yukon West

This area includes the large tributaries of the Yukon which drain the northern flanks of the St. Elias Mountains. Several salmon runs occur in these drainages and extensive wetlands used by a variety of waterfowl species are in the hinterlands.

Twenty-one nesting sites are known from the area. Coverage was 60% by area, 60% by waterway, translating into a potential population of about 41 pairs. Linear distance between pairs averaged 51 km. At these sites, 25 visits were made over the years 1978-1988. Sixty-eight percent of nest sites were found attended by adults and 44% produced young. The average number of young per successful nest was 1.3 ($\pm$ 0.2).

Two concentrations of eagles are known in the region. One concentration of up to 100 eagles occurs on the Kluane River north of Kluane Lake in association with a salmon spawning area. The other, about 25 birds similarly associated with salmon, occurs on the upper White River near the mouth of the Koidern River.

6) Yukon South

This includes an area dominated by the large headwater lakes of the Yukon River. Several salmon runs occur and the lake systems are relatively productive. The Yukon tends to be dominated by the mountains of the coast ranges limiting Bald Eagle habitat to the valley bottoms.

Fifty-two different nest sites are known from this area. Coverage was 54% by area and 44% by watercourse, suggesting a population between 138 and 158 nest sites. Average linear watercourse distance between sites was 16 km. Visits to individual nest sites over the period 1977-1988 totaled 59. On these visits, 62% of sites were found attended by adults and 44% produced young. On average, successful pairs were raising 1.7 ($\pm$ 0.2) young.

Four small fall concentrations of eagles occur. One concentration of up to 50 eagles is on the Teslin River in association with a chinook salmon spawning area. Another (up to 30 eagles) on the Nisutlin River is associated with staging waterfowl and a chinook salmon run. Small concentrations of eagles (estimated at 20 and 50) are also known from the Big and Little Salmon rivers in association with spawning chinook salmon.

7) Alsek River

This area includes a diverse region of some large lakes and rivers harboring salmon in the southern territory, but also includes a large area of high mountains and glaciers. The eagle habitat is closely linked with the Yukon south segment and perhaps should be considered part of that area.

Nine Bald Eagle nests are known from the area. With an estimated 50% of the area covered and 75% watercourse coverage, the population may be between 15 and 22 pairs. Distance between sites was about 25 km. Productivity from 13 annual visits over the period 1978-1989 showed 69% of sites occupied and 39% producing young. On average, successful pairs were producing 1.6 ($\pm$ 0.4) young.

A small concentration (averaging 5-15 birds) occurs annually in association with salmon runs to the upper Tatshenshini River near the village of Klukshu about 30 km west of Haines Junction on the southern border of Kluane National Park.

Table 1. Estimated number of Bald Eagle nest sites in the Yukon Territory by drainage basin.

Drainage	Known nest sites	Yukon Totals	
		Extrapolated by area	Extrapolated by inter-nest distance
North Slope	2	3	3-4
Porcupine	24	37	42
Peel	26	54	123
Yukon River (north)	23	72	96
(west)	21	41	41
(south)	52	138	158
Alsek	9	22	15
Liard	5	31	63
Total	162	398	552

8) Liard River

This is a relatively large drainage in the south eastern portion of the territory which drains eastward into the Mackenzie system. It has been poorly surveyed and the known Bald Eagle population is not thought to be indicative of total numbers.

Five nest sites are known. With coverage less than 20% by area and 10% by waterway, a population of between 31 and 63 pairs is suggested. Seven visits show an average occupancy of 57% and an average of 39% of nests producing young. No eagle concentration areas are known for the region.

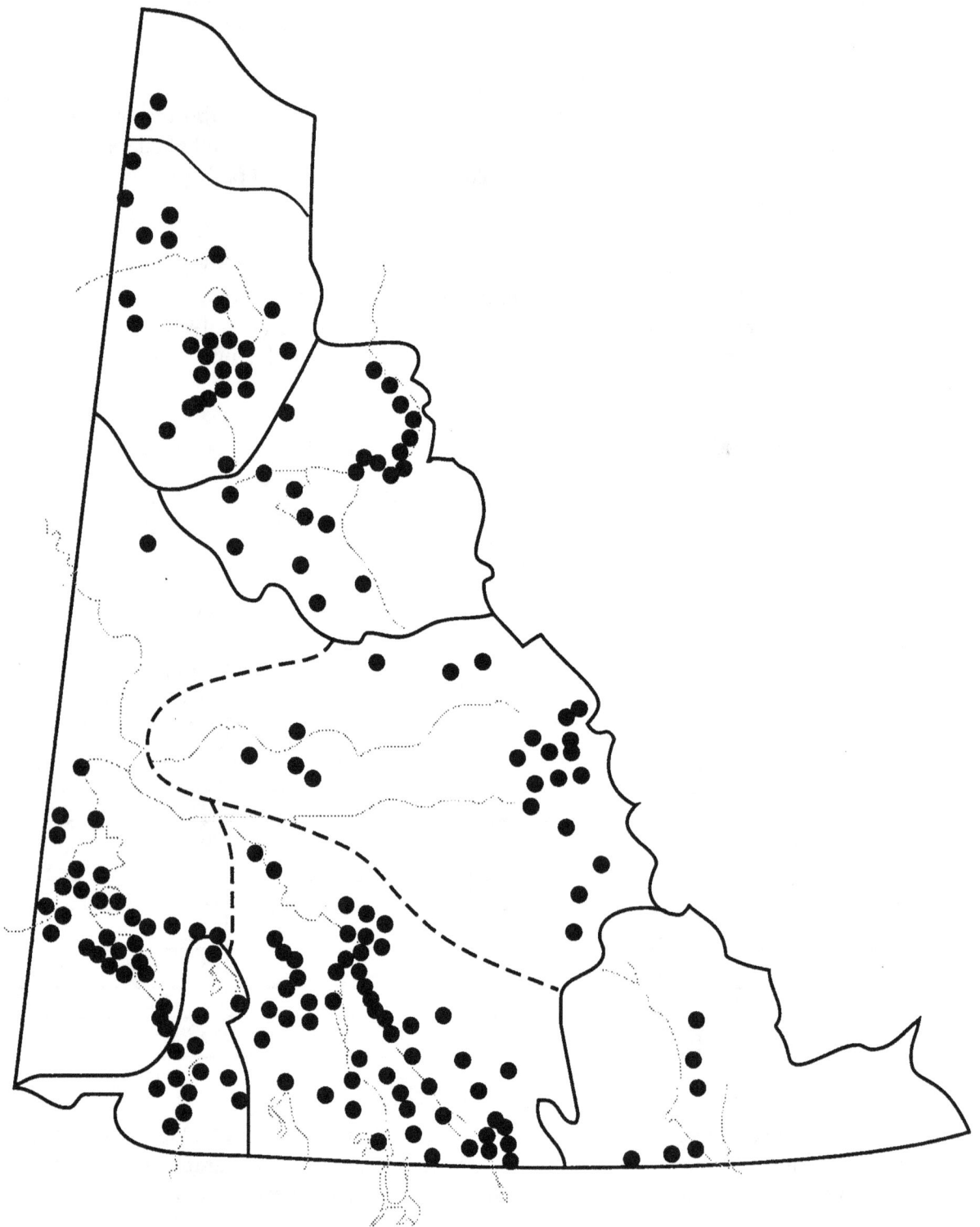

Figure 2. Locations of known nest sites of Bald Eagle from survey 1974-1989.

Discussions and Conclusions

With the possible exception of the North Slope, breeding pairs of Bald Eagles are found throughout Yukon. No evidence exists to suggest any trend in their numbers. Ignoring the possible differences in density between drainages, it is clear that the breeding range of the species must be considered to include the whole territory (Figure 2).

Location of known nest sites
In total, 163 Bald Eagle nest sites are known throughout the Yukon. Depending on the reliability of methods of extrapolation this could translate to a total population of somewhere between 400 and 550 breeding sites (Table 1). Clearly these numbers depend substantially on the estimates of coverage and the overall estimate of accuracy. Because there is no area where Bald Eagle surveys have been a priority, there is no way to check these estimates. They are based on assumed visibility and coverage relative to the other birds of prey being surveyed more completely in the same area. A refinement of these extrapolations will await a specific survey of Bald Eagles in some significant area of the territory.

The breeding densities suggested are low when compared with prime eagle nesting habitat in Saskatchewan and Manitoba (Leighton et al. 1979, Koonz 1983). The Yukon's 482,000 km² may support 500 breeding pairs or one nest site per 960 km². However, it is questionable whether the Yukon with its mountain-valley habitats can be compared to the more homogeneous habitats in Saskatchewan and Manitoba. The linear measure of shoreline has more promise for extrapolating and comparing Yukon's eagle densities and perhaps Bald Eagle populations in general (Whitfield et al. 1974). The Yukon's 16,520 km of principal waterways average one nest site per 30-40 km. This compares to 17-19 km per nest site from the areas mentioned above, suggesting Yukon populations in the medium to low range by comparison.

The differences between Yukon drainage areas are significant in some cases. The North Slope with its 175 km average distance between nest sites is probably best viewed as non-eagle habitat. While the Peel and Yukon south drainages (17 km and 15 km between sites) compare closely with southern eagle populations. The rest of the Yukon averages 39 km between sites. Productivity parameters from the various drainages show no significant differences. On average, 39%-63% of nest sites were producing young annually. No significant difference could be detected in the production of young from the successful nests in the various drainages. Using the lumped sample of all nests visited in all years, productivity averaged 1.6 ± 0.19 (s.d.) young per successful nest site. These values are well within the ranges for reproductive statistics of Bald Eagles throughout North America (Stalmaster 1987).

The total population of Bald Eagles migrating annually out of the Yukon, based on the survey data and all the assumptions noted, is at best a relatively shaky estimate. Nevertheless, it appears that between 800-1,100 adults, approximately 300-480 young of the year and an unknown number of subadults (perhaps 150-250) are in the 1,250-1,900 "fall flight" population. The best overall impression is of a stable, normally productive population at medium to low density, occupying suitable habitat throughout the riparian systems of the territory.

A total population of 315 eagles is estimated at the eight known staging sites. Clearly, not all eagles in the Yukon fall population are accounted for. These high latitude, interior eagles are critically dependant on late summer salmon runs. It is hoped a more complete inventory of these important staging habitats will accumulate over time and a further understanding of eagle migration strategy, particularly in the far north, will emerge.

Literature Cited

Grier, J. W., J. M. Gerrard, G. D. Hamilton and P. A. Gray. 1981. Aerial visibility bias and survey techniques for nesting Bald Eagles in northwestern Ontario. J. Wildl. Manage. 45(1):83-92.

Hayes, R. and W. Kale. 1982. Yukon raptor population data storage and retrieval system. Dept. Renewable Resour., Yukon Territorial Gov., Whitehorse.

Koonz, W. 1985. An update on the status of the Bald Eagle in Manitoba. Pages 55-57. In: J. M. Gerrard and T N. Ingram, eds. The Bald Eagle in Canada. Proc. of Bald Eagle Days, 1983.

Leighton, F. A., J. M. Gerrard, P. Gerrard, D. W. A. Whitfield, W. J. Maher. 1979. An aerial census of Bald Eagles in Saskatchewan. J. Wildl. Manage. 43(1):61-69.

Mossop, D. 1988. Yukon raptor population inventory project, 1987-88. Dept. Renewable Resour. Yukon Territorial Gov., Whitehorse.

Stalmaster, M. V. 1987. The Bald Eagle. Universe Books, New York. 227pp.

Whitfield, D. W. A., J. M. Gerrard, W. J. Maher and D. W. Davis. 1974. Bald Eagle nesting habitat, density and reproduction in central Saskatchewan and Manitoba. Can. Field-Nat. 88:399-407.

Current Management

Shoot the Damned Things! Alaska's War Against the American Bald Eagle

R. N. DeArmond

Historian, Sitka, AK

Bald Eagles have not always enjoyed public favor especially in Alaska.

"The eagle is a nice bird. We like to see it - on twenty-dollar gold pieces. Sentimentally, it is a beautiful thing, but in life it is a destroyer of food and should be killed wherever found."
Douglas Island News, August 6, 1920

"The eagle is a curse to the rest of the animal kingdom and the sooner it is exterminated the better off the game will be."
The Valdez Miner, April 17, 1920

Those paragraphs appear to have reflected the feelings Alaskans had held about the Bald Eagle since at least 1917 and would hold for a considerable time in the future. On April 6, 1917, the United States declared war on Germany. And the following day, April 7, the Alaska Territorial Legislature took the first steps toward declaring war on the American Eagle.

America's war against Germany lasted just short of 19 months. Casualties were 116,708 killed, 304,002 wounded. Alaska's war against the eagles lasted for 36 years, from 1917 until 1953, with a couple of short armistices. Casualties were 120,195 confirmed killed, according to the reports of the Territorial Treasurer. The number of kills for which no bounty was paid, number of wounded and number of missing in action are incalculable. The House and Senate of the Third Alaska Territorial Legislature received slightly different eagle bounty bills on the same day. Their introduction was no doubt triggered in part by the recommendation of a federal official, E. Lester Jones, the deputy U.S. Commissioner of Fisheries. In a report on his 1914 investigations in Alaska, Jones condemned eagles as destructive of salmon and wrote, "British Columbia has a bounty on these destructive birds and I think that it would be the means of saving many salmon and their spawn if the United States government would place a similar bounty on them in Alaska."

For once, most Alaskans agreed with the recommendation of a federal official! The perceptions of many Alaskans regarding eagles coincided with that of Jones and moreover, sheep ranchers in the Aleutians and fox farmers along the coast claimed that eagles preyed on their lambs and pups. The war in Europe may have been a factor, too. Even before the United States entered the fray, people were being urged to conserve energy and food. Each of the eagle bounty bills was titled, "An Act to preserve the food supply of Alaska and placing a bounty on eagles."

The House bill, No. 39, was introduced by Rep. Isaac Sowerby, a Juneau insurance agent who was serving his first term in the legislature. The bill got a "Do Pass" from the Committee on Fisheries, Fish and Game. If there was any debate, it was not reported by either of Juneau's two daily newspapers and the bill sailed through on a 13-2 vote with one member absent.

The two who voted against the bounty bill were Rep. Frank Cannon, a Knik hotel owner and Charles M. Day, who was engaged in the transportation business at Valdez. Their votes may well have resulted from fiscal caution rather than avian sympathy. The bill carried an appropriation of $7,500 and the treasury of the fledgling Territory was far from overflowing. In the upper chamber, Senator James R. Heckman of Ketchikan, a merchant, banker, cannery-man and a resident of Alaska for more than 30 years, saw his eagle bounty bill pass unanimously. Heckman's bill was then withdrawn in favor of the Sowerby bill, which also received unanimous approval. The Sowerby bill then went to Governor John F. A. Strong who signed it into law on April 30.

The law provided for a bounty of 50 cents on each eagle, to be paid by the Territorial Treasurer upon presentation of both feet of the eagle, with a certificate that "no poison or other means that might cause the wanton destruction of other birds and animals" were used.

The legislative action that encouraged the slaughter of the American Eagle was ignored by the press, both in and out of Alaska. With the United States just getting into the war in Europe, the editorials in Alaska newspapers ran heavily to patriotism. "Talk Patriotism or Don't Talk," admonished the Anchorage Times and there were editorials in a number of papers paying tribute to the American flag and extolling its virtues. But the eagle did not even get an obituary.

Before the next session of the Territorial Legislature rolled around in 1919, one Senator had a change of heart on the eagle bounty law. He was Senator Dan Sutherland, who at that time hailed from the village of Ruby on the Yukon River but who had previously been the U.S. Marshal for Southeastern Alaska.

On the 8th day of the session, Senator Sutherland introduced a bill to suspend the bounty law for two years. He explained that he wanted a survey made to determine what damage was actually being done. The bill went to the Fisheries Committee, chaired by Senator Heckman and of which Senator Sutherland was a member. The third member was Senator Thomas C. Price of Anchorage and he voted with the other two on a "Do Pass" recommendation.

When the bill came up for second reading, however, it was recommitted to the Fisheries Committee "to give some people of Juneau an opportunity to be heard." Committee hearings were not reported in those years and the press ignored this one, but whatever was said was enough to change two votes. Senators Price and Heckman recommended that the bill be indefinitely postponed.

Sutherland's bill next went to a Committee of the Whole which gave it the deep six with a 7 to 1 vote for indefinite postponement. And the legislature appropriated $5,000 to pay the bounty on 10,000 more eagles.

Photo: A bounty hunter from Territorial days examines eagle claws collected in Southeast Alaska. This photo was taken in 1936. Courtesy of Alaska State Museum.

During the years Bald Eagles were killed for bounty some bounty hunters were said to kill mainly the non-breeding juvenile birds, leaving the adults to produce birds for next years' bounty hunting. It was during the 1920 political campaign in Alaska that the press, both in and out of Alaska, began to take note of the eagle bounty. Dr. William T. Hornaday, zoologist and author of numerous books on wildlife and nature, wrote in Natural History magazine:

"Eagles are now more than rare all over the country except in Alaska and even there they will not last long if the territorial authorities keep up the present bounty of fifty cents which in their unwisdom they are paying on the head of every eagle killed."

The New York Times quoted from the article in its "Topics of the Times" column on June 26, 1920.

"Dr. Hornaday was already known in Alaska for his advocacy of greater protection of the brown bear and had suggested that Admiralty Island be made a bear preserve. That came under the heading of conservation, a nasty word in Alaska ever since President Teddy Roosevelt locked up the coal fields in 1906."

Commented The Alaska Daily Empire on its editorial page:
"One of the menaces to Alaska is non-resident hobby riders, most notorious among whom is Gifford Pinchot, but not the least of whom is Dr. Hornaday."

Territorial Senator Dan Sutherland was a part of that 1920 campaign, running on the Republican ticket for the office of Delegate in Congress from Alaska. The campaign was a bitter one and Sutherland was viciously attacked by some Alaska newspapers for, among other things, his defense of the eagle. The two quoted items at the beginning of this article were a part of that campaign. But despite the attacks, Sutherland won the office that year and for several subsequent terms. In 1930, while Delegate, he testified before the House Committee on Agriculture on an eagle protection bill. He told the committee:
"In 1919 I introduced a bill to suspend the bounty until a survey might be made to know what damage might be done by the killing of eagles. As a consequence of my attitude - and I was a minority of one - I incurred considerable ridicule throughout the Territory and in my early campaigns for Congress it was a little embarrassing to be known generally as the only friend the eagle had in Alaska."

But Sutherland himself had undergone another conversion. He confessed to members of the committee that in 1919 he had acted out of sentiment and said that he had learned, both through his own observation and through talking with others, how destructive the eagle actually was. He asked the committee members to exempt Alaska from the eagle protection bill it was considering. They acceded to his wish.

That, presumably, left the eagle without a single friend in Alaska.

Certainly the bird had no friend in Anthony J. Dimond of Valdez, a freshman senator in the 1923 legislature. He introduced a bill to increase the bounty from fifty cents to a dollar. It passed both houses unanimously and was signed into law by Governor Scott C. Bone on April 11. Dimond served two four-year terms in the Alaska Senate and spent a dozen years as Delegate in Congress from Alaska before being appointed U.S. District judge at Anchorage. While in Congress he secured the exclusion of Alaska from the provisions of the Eagle Protection Act of 1940.

The increase in the bounty to $1 raised eagle-shooting from a hobby to a business. The 1923 appropriation of $8,000 for bounty payments was not nearly enough and the 1925 legislature came up with $10,000 more to pay for the accumulated backlog of eagle claws. Then it appropriated another $20,000 for the next biennium.

When news of the $1 bounty reached New York, the American Nature Association, according to The New York Times, "as a first move in a campaign for the repeal of the Alaska bounty law, issued an appeal to every school teacher in the United States to file a protest on behalf of his class." Either the teachers failed to respond or the protests were ignored.

The Fraternal Order of Eagles, a national organization, also expressed displeasure, but aside from occasional rumblings of protest from conservation and bird protection organizations, the eagle bounty program sailed easily through the years of the Great Depression. And despite some tight territorial budgets, the legislators managed to find some funds to buy eagles' feet - as much as $15,000 for one biennium, $12,000 for another.

Then came a new governor for Alaska and the federal Act of June 8, 1940, prohibiting the taking or possession of Bald Eagles. Delegate Tony Dimond managed to get Alaska excluded from that Act, but Governor Ernest Gruening took up the cause of the eagle. In his first message to an Alaska legislature, delivered on January 29, 1941, the governor said:

"Since the last meeting of the legislature, eagles on which the Territory has been paying a bounty of one dollar have been protected by federal statute. It is now against the law to kill an eagle anywhere in the United States except Alaska. While Alaska was exempted out of consideration for existing territorial legislation, it would seem reasonable for us to move in the direction of practice now established everywhere else and at least to cease paying a bounty on this national bird."

The Territorial Board of Budget urged the legislature to review the entire bounty system, including the bounties on wolves, coyotes and hair seals, in view of the very tight money situation.

Two days after the governor spoke, Senator O. D. Cochran of Nome introduced Senate Bill No. 1 to repeal the eagle bounty law. The bill was vigorously debated. Senator LeRoy Sullivan, also of Nome, argued that the law should be kept on the books to preserve Alaska's control over a predator, but that no money need be appropriated when funds were limited.

Senator Edward Coffey of Anchorage urged retention of both the law and the appropriation. In his election district were all of Alaska's sheep ranches and many fox farms and Coffey was himself a fisherman. When it appeared that he might lose on a 5-3 vote, he made an unusual request and the Senate, in an unprecedented action, granted it. Coffey asked that Representative William A. Egan of Valdez be given the privilege of the floor to discuss the bill.

Egan, at 26, was the youngest member of the 15th Territorial Legislature, serving his first term and beginning a long political career. Just what he told the Senators on that February day was not reported in the press, but he undoubtedly spoke on behalf of his constituents among the fox farmers and sheep ranchers with a strong defense of the eagle bounty. Whatever he said, it was enough; the bill was defeated.

It was not the last time that Gruening and Egan would line up on opposite sides of an issue. Nor would it be the last time that Egan won the battle. In this instance, however, while he won on the repeal, he failed to get an appropriation for eagle bounties.

In 1943 an eagle bounty repeal was again before the Senate, but this time it was Governor Gruening who was given the privilege of the floor. He told the Senators that if the law was not repealed he believed the President would issue an executive order banning the killing of Bald Eagles in Alaska.

That threat did not scare four of the Senators and again the bill was killed on a tie vote. But some overnight arm twisting brought a reconsideration motion and Senator H. H. McCutcheon changed his vote.

Over in the House, however, Rep. Egan had positioned himself as chairman of the Committee on Fisheries, Fish and Game which would have jurisdiction over the bounty repeal bill. It reached his committee on February 20 and never again saw the light of day. Again, however, there was no appropriation to pay eagle bounties.

Although he made it clear that he had no personal animosity toward the Bald Eagle and was acting only at the behest of many of his constituents, Egan's zeal in the matter won him the nickname "Eagle Bounty Bill."

Soon after the 1943 legislative session ended, Egan joined the Air Force and went off to help fight his country's war. He thus missed the 1945 session of the legislature, which had had its membership increased from 24 to 40. In his absence the 1917 eagle bounty law was repealed on a vote of 14-2 in the Senate and 15-7 in the House.

In the 1946 General Election, Egan was swept back into the House, outpolling the other 13 candidates in his district. Just why he waited until the 40th day of the session to introduce a new eagle bounty bill is not known, but it was a tactical mistake. His bill provided for a $5 bounty on each eagle and carried a $15,000 appropriation, but that was whittled down in second reading to $3 and $9,000. Egan got the bill passed by a 17-7 vote but not until after the deadline for transmitting bills to the Senate. Egan did some pleading and the Senate finally accepted the bill, only to put it to death on a 15-0 vote for indefinite postponement.

That made the future for an eagle bounty look pretty bleak, but Egan was no quitter and he was back with another bill in 1949. The bill sailed through both houses with the bounty set at $2. In the House only Mrs. Essie Dale of Fairbanks voted against it.

In the other chamber, Senator Frank Barr of Fairbanks raised the lone voice in defense of the eagles. "For the privilege of seeing them impressively in flight, I'm willing to throw them a few fish," he declared. And he was joined by Senators Victor C. Rivers and Gunnard Engebreth, both from Anchorage, in voting against the bill.

Governor Gruening wrote an impassioned veto message - but he did not veto the bill. He pointed to the fact that the Continental Congress in 1782 had adopted the Bald Eagle as the national symbol and cited an item from the Denver Post: "The Alaska legislature, hoping to become the 49th state under the wings of the eagle, nevertheless voted Wednesday to place a bounty on eagles."

The governor quoted statements by officials of the U.S. Fish & Wildlife Service which recited threats of Congressional action, strong protests from conservation groups and a wasteful expenditure of territorial funds. "These arguments were presented before the legislature," the governor added, rather plaintively. "Nevertheless, they adopted the measure by votes that came close to unanimity. Therefore out of respect for the overwhelming sentiment among the legislators in favor of its passage, I will allow the bill to become law without my signature."

Some legislature watchers, however, believed that the governor needed Senator Egan's vote on a number of administration bills and would have lost it with a veto. The 1949 appropriation for eagle bounties was $15,000, but it was not enough. The next legislature made a deficiency appropriation of $2,000, plus $15,000 more for the 1951-53 biennium.

But in 1953 the attitude changed completely in what one reporter dubbed "the mutiny on the bounty." The bounty repeal bill was introduced in the Senate and even "Eagle Bill" Egan voted for it. The only dissenting vote came from Senator Percy Ipalook of Barrow. In the House the bill went to second reading without a committee referral, then was advanced and passed 22-0 with two members absent.

Gone, probably forever, were the days when a pair of shriveled eagle claws hanging on the wall behind the cook stove in a Last Frontier cabin was the equivalent of two bucks in the bank.

Law Enforcement and the Bald Eagle Protection Act

Jerry A. Cegelske

U.S. Fish and Wildlife Service, Fairbanks, AK

The Bald Eagle Protection Act provides for the protection of eagles and their nests. How the Act is used or not used is based on the circumstances of the violations involved. Oftentimes the results are not what is expected or desired. This leads to the use of other federal laws to protect eagles.

The Bald Eagle Act, 16 USC 668, which took effect on June 8, 1940, was enacted when Congress recognized that the Bald Eagle was threatened with extinction. The Act states in part "whoever, without being permitted to do so, shall knowingly, or with wanton disregard for the consequences of his act take, possess, sell, purchase, barter, offer to sell, purchase or barter, transport, export or import, at any time or in any manner, any Bald Eagle commonly known as the American Eagle, or any Golden Eagle, alive or dead, or any part, nest or egg thereof of the foregoing eagles, or whoever violates any permit or regulation pursuant to sections 668 to 668d of this title, shall be fined not more than $5,000, or imprisoned not more than one year or both."

Section 668 (a) of the Act authorizes the taking, possession and transportation of specimens for scientific, or exhibition purposes of public museums, scientific societies and zoological parks or for the religious purposes of Indian tribes, or when it is deemed necessary to permit the taking of such eagles for the protection of wildlife or of agricultural or other interests, in a particular locality.

Section 668 b (b) of the Act authorizes the forfeiture of all guns, traps, nets and other equipment, vessels, aircraft and other means of transportation used in the unlawful activities concerning the species.

The Act also provides for civil penalties to be assessed against persons who violate the law. The words "knowingly, or with wanton disregard for the consequences of his act" are not in the civil penalty section, thus requiring a lower burden of proof from the government. It is a monetary penalty only with no imprisonment possible.

As used in the Act, the term "take" includes also pursue, shoot, shoot at, poison, wound, kill, capture, trap, collect, molest or disturb.

Since its enactment, there have been several amendments. Although enacted on June 8, 1940, the law did not take effect in Alaska until it was amended for statehood in 1959.

Golden Eagles came under the protection of the Bald Eagle Protection Act in 1962. This amendment also authorized the take of eagles for the religious purposes of Indian tribes. Another amendment in 1972 authorized the Secretary of the Interior to permit the taking, possession and transportation of Golden Eagles for the purpose of falconry, except that only Golden Eagles which would be taken because of depredations on livestock or wildlife may be taken for purposes of falconry.

Timothy Bowman with a dead immature Bald Eagle found during studies after the *Exxon Valdez* oil spill. Photo by USFWS.

The Eagle Act has usually taken second place to the Endangered Species Act of 1975 in the lower 48 states for prosecution of eagle shooters due to the endangered and threatened status of the eagle in the contiguous U.S. The Endangered Species Act provides for penalties of $20,000 and one year in jail.

The Eagle Act was enhanced with the passage of the Fine Enhancement Act of 1987, 18 USO 5625 which makes a misdemeanor punishable by imprisonment for more than six months and a fine of up to $100,000.

When the sale of eagle feathers is involved in a violation, the Migratory Bird Treaty Act, 16 USC 705, enacted on August 16, 1916, is usually substituted for the Eagle Act. The reason for this is that under penalty section, 16 USC 707, of the Migratory Bird Treaty Act, the sale of migratory bird feathers is a felony calling for a $2000 fine and two years in jail. This brings the potential penalties up to $250,000 for an individual and $500,000 for an organization or corporation, due to the effects of the Fine Enhancement Act of 1987.

Some of the unpermitted takes of eagles in Alaska are as follows:
Electrocutions: Eagle electrocutions occur in a variety of locations in Alaska. This problem is being addressed in new construction planning and consultation.

Oil Spills: The *Exxon Valdez* oil spill resulted in the suspected deaths of large numbers of eagles due to the effects of oil. Additional eagle deaths can be expected around any oil spill which kills other wildlife which eagles feed on.

Prosecution of the take of eagles resulting from the *Exxon Valdez* oil spill were not sought under the Eagle Act due to the requirement that the government prove that the take was done knowingly and with wanton disregard for the consequences of the act. Prosecution was considered under the Migratory Bird Treaty Act.

Trapping: Trapping can and does take a large number of eagles if it is not done properly. There are frequent reports of eagles trapped or of eagles flying around with traps on their legs.

Shooting: Shooting takes a large percentage of eagles both in Alaska and in the lower continental United States. Eagles transplanted from Alaska to other states have suffered mortality due to shootings. Almost every community in Southeastern Alaska has had eagles shot in their area.

Trapping and shooting probably place the heaviest burden on eagle populations in Alaska. In trapping, even if the eagle is released in what appears to be an unharmed condition, the eagle will not have a good chance of survival if tissue damage is extensive or if the temperature has been below freezing, when the lack of blood flow allows the feet to freeze.

The trapping of eagles is illegal without a permit even if it is unintentional. When the price of bobcat hides climbed in the late 70's, large numbers of Golden Eagles were taken by bobcat trappers in the western states.

In April of 1987 a trapper pled guilty to violating the Eagle Act by catching three eagles on the Kenai National Wildlife Refuge. The trapper was fined $500, ordered to pay $204 to the veterinarian to which he took one of the eagles and was ordered to contribute $500 to a fund established for the care of injured eagles. The trapper also forfeited his refuge trapping permit for failure to check his traps every seven days. All three eagles died of exposure.

In 1984, a man came to the Fish and Wildlife Service Law Enforcement office in Ketchikan to tell of finding three eagles in wolf traps several months before. No prosecution was sought because the person released the dead birds from the traps and allowed the carcasses to float away with the tide.

One of the major differences between the incidental trapping of eagles and shooting them is intent. A marten or wolf trapper does not want eagles in his traps although he may be careless in setting them. The eagle shooter obviously has the intent to kill the eagle.
In June of 1988, two twelve year old juveniles shot a nesting eagle off the south end of Douglas Island near Juneau. Due to complications and procedures in prosecuting juveniles, no prosecution was obtained on them. They did forfeit the two rifles used in the violation. Did they learn not to shoot eagles, or did they learn not to talk about shooting eagles in front of those who would report their actions?

Even eagles which are injured and supposedly protected are not safe from people. In August 1988, a one eyed eagle was being maintained at the Fish and Wildlife warehouse in a locked cage behind a locked gate, awaiting shipment to the Alaska Raptor Rehabilitation Center in Sitka, Alaska. After being shown the eagle by a second person who was trespassing, the violator stated he wanted the talons and left. He later returned with bolt cutters, cut both locks and proceeded to hit the eagle and then cut the legs and head off. Blood was splattered three feet up on the sides of the warehouse. The violator spent six months in jail for trespassing and enrolled himself in a drug and substance abuse program as drugs and alcohol made him violent and uncontrolled. Upon pleading guilty to taking the eagle, the subject was sentenced to continued attendance in the drug program, served probation and paid $40 for the two locks.

Valentines day 1983 was the start of one of two investigations into what is probably the shooting of the greatest number of eagles by one person since the Eagle Act took effect in Alaska. The end results do not reflect that fact nor was a trial held which would expose what was happening.

On Valentines day 1983, a family of four were at the shooting range by the dump of a logging camp on Prince of Wales Island, Alaska. As the wife was leaving with the children to walk home, she heard a shot, looked up and saw an eagle fall from a tree. Approximately one minute later, the manager of the camp was observed driving from where the shot was fired with a rifle in the gun rack of the pickup. As a result of the witness moving away and a second witness involved in later actions moving away, the government declined to pay the cost of bringing the witnesses from the mid-west for the trial and instead settled for a civil penalty. The penalty was $1000 and there was no admission expressed or inferred by reason of the compromise. That civil penalty was completed on March 8, 1985 and the killing did not stop during that time although several people knew what was happening and chose not to do anything about it.

In May 1987, information was received that about 20 eagle carcasses were found in the logging camp dump. An investigation revealed that parts of what was believed to be at least 30 eagles were located in the area of the dump. After an extensive investigation and the offering of a substantial reward, two witnesses came forward with statements that they had seen the subject shoot eagles or saw him leave the area where the witness saw an eagle shot. Both of these violations occurred during the time of the first investigation. One of the witnesses stated the subject had frequently told him of shooting "X" number of eagles that day. When added up, the specific numbers that the witness could remember were between 60-70 eagles. The second witness was fishing under a bridge when he heard a vehicle stop on the bridge. The witness heard a shot and saw an eagle fall from a tree. Climbing the bank and onto the road he was able to see and identify the subject leaving the area. In a plea bargain, the 68 year-old violator plead to one count of taking an eagle and paid a fine of $750 and spent 30 days in jail and was on one year of active probation.

This penalty can be compared with another Eagle Act case. In September 1986 a civil penalty of $3812.50 was assessed a man who shot a transplanted Golden Eagle which was sitting on a post in a cow pasture in Georgia. This civil penalty was issued after the subject had completed an affidavit admitting to shooting the eagle, had a jury trial and was found not guilty. The penalty was equal to the cost of the transplant.

In the Cordova area, a man was standing next to his skiff on the shoreline, about 200 yards from a fishing vessel. He observed a rifle barrel come out of a window and looked in the direction it was pointed and saw an eagle. A second man saw an eagle flying, heard a shot and saw the eagle fall. Looking to where the shot came from, he saw a rifle barrel being pulled back into the fishing vessel cabin. The vessel was seized and the subject was interviewed and completed an affidavit admitting to shooting the eagle. The violator pleaded not guilty and at the trial stated that the agents threatened him with the loss of his vessel if he did not admit to shooting the eagle. The first trial ended in a hung jury as did the second trial.

It seems as if we have not learned to value or cherish our natural resources and wildlife in the 300 years since European settlers first appeared on our eastern shores or in the two centuries our nation has existed. Are eagles not to be valued above their status as rifle targets? Tourists visiting Alaska who have not had the opportunity to see eagles in their home states do cherish the sight of eagles.

As the human population grows and demand for resources increases, the loss of nesting habitat and nest trees will increase along with nest disturbances. Logging operations take nest trees but it also opens up areas allowing nest trees to be blown down by winds when buffering trees are removed. On Long Island an eagle nest tree was observed where every tree within approximately 100 yards had been removed. How many October and November storms will it take before it falls?

Road construction is a continued problem with heavy equipment, blasting and construction activity around nesting eagles, scaring them off the nests during critical periods causing the loss of eggs.

Mining activities also cause disturbances of eagle nests and possible nesting failures. At the development of one mining claim, helicopters were arriving and departing within 100 yards of the nesting eagles and resulted in a suspected nest abandonment.

People purchase land from state land sales knowing of eagle nest trees on the property and then ask how to remove or construct around them. Some people purchase land from others and only later when they inspect the land do they find out about the eagle nest tree. During a telephone conversation a Southeast Alaskan developer explained how he could remove an eagle nest tree from his property and make it look like wind damage or an accident in cutting a second tree. His actions would be totally illegal as his intent was the removal of the eagle nest tree and thus the nest.

Construction for national defense can even be a cause of disturbance to nesting eagles. The Back Island submarine testing facility construction is suspect in the disturbance of the nesting eagles there (Canterbury 2008).

The Southeast Alaska area has hundreds of eagle nests. The enforcement of the Eagle Act at so many locations is an impossible task. Some construction sites are monitored; however, such monitoring is usually not adequate. Eagles which are disturbed may continue to nest well after the disturbance. Once the nest is abandoned, the eggs are subject to predation, which destroys evidence.

What can be done to slow this loss of both bird and nest? What is needed is a change in attitude among all people, that their individual actions will influence the "take" of an eagle or nest, whether it is with a rifle, trap, bulldozer, or chainsaw?

Individual action is important, especially by those who know of and have direct knowledge of violations. While not threatened by extinction in Southeast Alaska, eagle populations around human population centers are under pressure from development. Pressure on eagle populations will increase without active involvement by those knowledgeable of violations. The alternative is a decline in the species with increased regulations and restrictions on development and human activities.

Literature Cited

Canterbury, J. 2008. Bald Eagle reaction to construction on Back Island, Alaska. In: Wright, B.A. and P.F. Schempf, eds. Bald Eagles in Alaska.

Cooperative Management of the Bald Eagle in South Coastal Alaska

Fred B. Samson

U.S Forest Service, Missoula, MT

Wildlife is abundant in the south coastal forests of Alaska and the Bald Eagle (*Haliaeetus leucocephalus*) is among the most prominent species. Most forests in south coastal Alaska are managed by the U.S. Department of Agriculture, Forest Service, for multiple use. Timber harvested from the Tongass National Forest in Southeast Alaska supports local economies and contributes to the economies of Pacific Rim nations. Recreation and commercial fishing are important on both the Chugach National Forest in southcentral Alaska and the Tongass and both industries impact regional economies and those of other nations. More than 12,000 adult eagles are thought to reside on the Tongass National Forest and their distribution and abundance is believed to be very similar to what it was in pre-settlement times. Eagle nesting densities in the Tongass, about one nest per 1.25 miles of saltwater shoreline, are the highest reported in North America. Less is known about eagles on the Chugach National Forest, but summer populations may range from 2000 to 3000 adults and winter concentrations total about 2500 eagles (P. Schempf U.S. Fish and Wildl. Serv., pers. comm.).

As mandated in the National Forest Management Act of 1976 and its implementing regulations, the Forest Service has primary responsibility for managing wildlife habitat on National Forest System lands in south coastal Alaska. That includes habitat for Bald Eagles. In addition, the Forest Service is charged to enforce such federal legislation relating to eagles as the Bald and Golden Eagle Protection Act (1972, 16 US 668) and the Migratory Bird Treaty Act (1918, 16 US 703). Some state legislation also protects Bald Eagles on National Forest Service lands. Title 16 of the Alaska State Statutes 16.4-0, Section 16.05.920 provides for the protection of birds and specifically their nests and eggs, against disturbance.

The U.S. Department of the Interior, Fish and Wildlife Service, like the Forest Service, must meet the requirements of the Bald and Golden Eagle Protection Act, the Migratory Bird Treaty Act and similar legislation. Unique among all agencies, the Fish and Wildlife Service has authority to issue permits as exceptions to normal protection provided eagles by the Bald and Golden Eagle Protection Act and the Migratory Bird Treaty Act. Such permits are related to scientific or educational needs and native ceremonial (religious) uses.

Given both shared and unique legal responsibilities for management of the Bald Eagle, the Forest Service and the Fish and Wildlife Service have cooperated for more than three decades in managing Bald Eagles in south coastal Alaska. This paper reviews the progress of cooperative management since the establishment of the initial Memorandum of Understanding in 1968 and describes current activities to improve eagle management under the Interagency Agreement of 1990.

The 1960s

The Forest Service Manual provides direction and responsibilities for resource management including those efforts that involve cooperation among both state and federal agencies. In 1968, the Alaska Region of the Forest Service initiated a review of Forest Service Manual direction for eagle management. The proposed direction was presented to the Fish and Wildlife Service in 1968 by Sig Olson, then Chief, Branch of Wildlife Management (Olson 1968). A subsequent review of Fish and Wildlife Service eagle management in Alaska by Fred Robards, Eagle Management Studies and John Findley, Regional Director, Portland, Oregon, suggested it would be useful to coordinate the efforts of both agencies. The coordination included the following:

• The Forest Service was to provide to the Fish and Wildlife Service information on the location of proposed land management activities.

• The Fish and Wildlife Service was to map Bald Eagle nest locations.

• Liaison with the State of Alaska was acknowledged as important, although interest in the eagle by the state was minimal.

• Both agencies were to seek information on issuance of permits that would allow cutting of eagle nest trees when necessary to protect agricultural interests such as logging.

• Though it was not included in the Memorandum of Agreement, it was acknowledged that need existed to evaluate the Forest Service 330-foot protective radius around each eagle nest.

In September 1968, a Memorandum of Understanding was signed by the Forest Service and the Fish and Wildlife Service (USFS and USFWS 1968). That document required the Forest Service to provide the Fish and Wildlife Service with information on proposed logging activities; the Fish and Wildlife Service was required to map eagle nest locations and to establish adequate beach markers to mark locations of eagle nest trees. The Forest Service was also required to apply to the Fish and Wildlife Service for a permit if it wished to allow felling a tree containing an eagle nest. A revision of this Memorandum of Understanding required the Fish and Wildlife Service to locate and mark nest trees with "Wildlife Tree" signs provided by the Forest Service.

The 1970s

The 1970s witnessed a series of changes in federal agency cooperative eagle management. Under a 1974 Memorandum of Understanding (USFS and USFWS 1974), the Forest Service was to include clauses and specifications in timber sale contracts to protect eagle nests. Joint investigations by both agencies were to precede issuance of any permit to disturb or cut an eagle nest tree. Furthermore, contacts between the two agencies on policy and program direction were to be through the Regional Forester and Area Director. The major change in the 1974 Memorandum of Understanding was a provision to maintain a 330-foot radius buffer around each eagle nest tree and to exclude all logging, road building, or other activity within that zone.

Bald Eagle nest trees on the Tongass National are marked by the U.S. Fish and Wildlife Service. Note that this tree still has remnants of ladder rungs nailed to it so the eaglets could be collected for bounty. Photo by Jack Hodges, USFWS.

The mid-1970s began with a judicial opinion of a request to remove 30 eagle nest trees in the right of way for the proposed Juneau to Haines highway (Stevens 1976). The request from the State of Alaska, Commissioner of Highways, was based on the Forest Service and Fish and Wildlife Service Memorandum of Understanding, which, under certain conditions, permits entering the 330-foot buffer surrounding a nest. Section 2 of the , as amended, 16 US 668 et seq. (1970) does allow the Department of Interior "to permit the taking of such eagles for the protection of wildlife or of agricultural or other interests in any particular locality. "The judicial opinion rendered, however, was that "other interests" did not include road building and the Forest Service and Fish and Wildlife Service Memorandum of Understanding could not be used as partial justification for cutting eagle nest trees.

In 1978, another revised Memorandum of Understanding (USFS and USFWS 1978) provided habitat protection to eagle habitat beyond nest trees, specifically including feeding and perching sites. Perch (and presumable feeding) sites were described as dominant trees, over 24 inches in diameter (or largest available if smaller than 24 inches) at breast height and within 40 yards of the high tide line. Protection for the perch sites was to be provided by a cluster of trees in each 100 yards of beach front. Furthermore, this buffer was to be maintained in event the nest on a nest tree became unusable for any reason.

The 1980s

Version 5 of the Memorandum of Understanding (USFS and USFWS 1984) was signed in 1984. In this version, key provisions of the 1978 memorandum were retained. Specific tree size requirements for perch and feeding sites included a definition for a group (i.e., 3-10) of trees. The memorandum also stated such trees should provide good visibility for birds using them, thus they should have open crowns and/or spike tops. The joint analysis that the 1978 memorandum required in cases where the 330-foot radius was to be entered now required the Fish and Wildlife Service to provide a list of habitat recommendations if a variance to the Memorandum of Understanding was requested by the Forest Service. The Fish and Wildlife Service also would be required to state reason(s) why, a variance to the Memorandum of Understanding was denied. Reasons why a variance was denied, including habitat recommendations, were to be addressed in the project Environmental Assessment or Environmental Impact Statement and considered by the Forest Service Interdisciplinary Team in developing alternatives for land use activities. The Fish and Wildlife Service also agreed to provide current field data to the Forest Service and both agencies agreed that "eagle nests properly distributed along the shoreline must be present in perpetuity."

In 1989, the Forest Service conducted a review of Bald Eagle habitat management (USFS 1989) across the Region. Participants in this review included Fish and Wildlife Service personnel and Forest Service biologists from the Tongass National Forest, the Chugach National Forest and the Regional Office.

Key findings of this review included three observations:

• Population estimates based on Fish and Wildlife aerial plot counts show an increase in Bald Eagle numbers from about 7,000 birds in the early 1970s to more than 12,000 in 1987.

• Relatively few variances to the Memorandum of Understanding are requested and fewer are approved.

• Cooperation between the agencies is good.

In addition, the activity review identified several important needs for eagle management on National Forest lands. They included:

• Development of population and habitat goals.

• An increase in field level interchange of information between the two agencies.

• An increase in the awareness of all eagle management requirements, i.e., perching and feeding sites.

The activity review noted that:

• Some state and federal land holding agencies are not aware of the Forest Service/Fish and Wildlife Service cooperative management program.

• The eagle translocation program-shipping young eagles from the Tongass National Forest to assist other states in building eagle populations-should be continued.

• The current Memorandum of Understanding is directed toward the Tongass National Forest. Emphasis is needed for the Chugach National Forest as well.

• Little or no information exists on inland eagle habitat use.

The review further proposed that the two agencies should:

• Amend the revised Tongass Land Management Plan to include protection of wintering habitat.

• Monitoring of eagle populations is needed.

• Initiate a cooperative study to identify sources of disturbance and assess their significance to Bald Eagles.

• Establish an up-to-date approach to inventory and maintenance of the eagle nest tree data base.

• Revise the Memorandum of Understanding, given that the Forest Service will fund the ongoing eagle nest survey and related activities.

Some, but not all, of the recommendations related to cooperative eagle management noted in the 1989 review of Bald Eagle management in south coastal Alaska are underway or completed. The eagle translocation project is continuing, the draft revised Tongass Land Management Plan provides for the protection of wintering habitats and information on eagle habitat use on the Chugach National Forest is becoming increasingly available.

In May 1990, an Interagency Agreement for cooperation in management of the Bald Eagle in south coastal Alaska was signed by the Forest Service and the Fish and Wildlife Service (USFS and USFWS 1990). An Interagency Agreement, in contrast to a Memorandum of Understanding, allows for the transfer of monies from one agency to another. An example of such a transfer is the recent transfer of monies from the Forest Service to the Fish and Wildlife Service for a study of the effects of disturbance on nesting

Bald Eagles-a need first noted in the late 1960s.
Future projects involving transfer of Forest Service monies to the Fish and Wildlife Service include the development of an automated data base (including a Geographic Information System) compatible to both agencies, use of satellite location systems to map eagle nest sites, personnel training and gaining further crucial information on winter eagle habitat needs. These tasks, identified in the 1989 eagle habitat management review, will be given serious consideration in forthcoming years.

The Future
The Fish and Wildlife Service established a committee of Fish and Wildlife Service biologists (Steglietz 1990) to prepare a synthesis document outlining Bald Eagle management zones for eagle habitat and nests in Alaska (USFWS, undated). Other agencies such as the Forest Service will at some future time have an opportunity to comment on those guidelines.

The Interagency Agreement between the Forest Service and Fish and Wildlife Service, however, provides the only current set of established guidelines for eagle management in Alaska. Through two decades, the Memorandum of Understanding, now an Interagency Agreement, has been revised on seven occasions, an average of every 3.1 years. It is generally felt that the process has set high standards for eagle management throughout Alaska.

Despite the successes in cooperative management, there are opportunities to improve eagle management in Alaska. One example would be to consider applying the concept of ecological management. Management of the Northern Spotted Owl (*Strix occidentalis*) throughout the Pacific Northwest is based on ecological provinces. A province is a large area, often a sizable portion of a state and each province differs in vegetation from bordering provinces. Differences in vegetation among provinces, in turn, leads to differences in prey species, prey distribution and prey abundances. Territory size of spotted owls as well as key life history characteristics is highly dependent on prey availability. Within each province, territory size, mortality and natality rates are monitored, allowing for the estimation of population trends and, over time, viability of the subspecies.

In southeast and southcentral Alaska, little information is available to describe life history characteristics of Bald Eagles or effects of disturbance on eagle nesting success. Such information is needed to more effectively manage eagles. As with many raptors, including the spotted owl, information unique to a province or region is a basic requirement for effective management. The Forest Service is currently funding a study through the Fish and Wildlife Service to determine the effects of disturbance and will continue to provide funding for eagle surveys (Anthony and Bibles, 1997). Information from both an in-depth study and surveys should provide an expanded ecological and scientific basis for developing a Bald Eagle management plan. Such a plan could encompass more than one nest and perhaps an ecological unit such as a watershed, habitat management area, or province-a most useful possibility for future eagle management.

Literature Cited

Anthony, R. G. and B. D. Bibles. 1997 Assessment of the potential effects of human activities on Bald Eagle productivity and behavior on Prince of Wales Island, Alaska. Unpubl. rep. Oregon State Univ. Corvallis, OR. 103pp.

Olson, S. T. 1968. Letter to Chief, Division of Recreation, Lands, Wildlife and Watershed Management, 6 May. On file, U.S. For. Serv. Reg. Office, Juneau, Alas.

Steglietz, W. 1990. Letter to M. Barton, 21 August. On file, U.S. For. Serv. Reg. Office, Juneau, Alas.

Stevens, T. 1976. Letter to B. A. Campbell, 9 July. On file, U.S. For. Serv. Reg. Office, Juneau, Alas.

U.S. Fish and Wildlife Service, undated. Bald Eagle basics. U.S. Fish Wildl. Serv., Alaska Reg., Anchorage, Alas. 20pp.

U.S. Forest Service. 1989. Bald Eagle habitat management activity review, July 1989. On file, U.S. For. Serv. Reg. Office, Juneau, Alas.

U.S. Forest Service and U.S. Fish and Wildlife Service. 1968. Memorandum of Agreement, 21 June. On file, U.S. For. Serv. Reg. Office, Juneau, Alas.

U.S. Forest Service and U.S. Fish and Wildlife Service. 1974. Memorandum of Understanding, 26 April. On file, U.S. For. Serv. Reg. Office, Juneau, Alas.

U.S. Forest Service and U.S. Fish and Wildlife Service. 1978. Memorandum of Understanding. 14 November. On file, U.S. For. Serv. Reg. Office, Juneau, Alas.

U.S. Forest Service and U.S. Fish and Wildlife Service. 1984. Memorandum of Understanding. 23 January. U.S. For. Serv. Reg. Office, Juneau, Alas.

U.S. Forest Service and U.S. Fish and Wildlife Service. 1990. Interagency Agreement. 15 May. On file, U.S. For. Serv. Reg. Office, Juneau, Alas.

Removal of Alaskan Bald Eagles for Translocation to Other States

Michael J. Jacobson

U.S Fish and Wildlife Service, Juneau, AK

Bald Eagles (*Haliaeetus leucocephalus*) were first captured and relocated from Alaska in 1981 when the state of New York requested eagles in an effort to re-establish a viable nesting population (Cain and Hodges 1981). As in most of the contiguous 48 states, New York's Bald Eagle populations had declined drastically and by the mid-1970s was reduced to a single unproductive nesting pair (Nye 1982). Suitable habitat remained and prey sources were present to support a growing population of Bald Eagles. An infusion of young birds was needed to become a viable population in the area.

Alaska was selected as a reliable donor of young because of its abundance of eagles. Each year from 1981-1990 Southeast Alaska provided young Bald Eagles for translocation to one or more of the lower-48 states (Jacobson 1987). Over 300 eagles had been captured and relocated since 1980. The young eagles were removed from wild nests, transported to lower 48 states, reared in hacking towers (artificial nests on human-made towers) until capable of flight, usually at 11 or 12 weeks of age and then released into the wild. New York received the majority of Alaskan eagles, the remainder have gone to Missouri, Indiana, North Carolina and Tennessee.

Study Area

The project was designed to remove Bald Eagle nestlings from the same region each year. A study area was established in Southeast Alaska, west and southwest of Juneau along a portion of Lynn Canal and Chatham Strait (Figure 1). The shoreline habitat was composed of old-growth coastal rainforest dominated by Sitka spruce and western hemlock (Cain and Hodges 1981, Cain et al. 1982).

The study area was divided into a removal (experimental) area and an adjacent control area where no young were removed (Figure 2). The removal area consisted of 211 km (131 miles) of shoreline and the control area totaled 84 km (52 miles) of shoreline. The entire study area was within the Tongass National Forest. The amount of eagle nesting habitat within the study area remained unchanged throughout the 1981-1990 period. In 1987 an additional 30 eaglets were removed from a location outside of the study area which contained similar habitat. This separate location was south of Juneau on the eastern side of Stephens Passage and Frederick Sound (Figure 1).

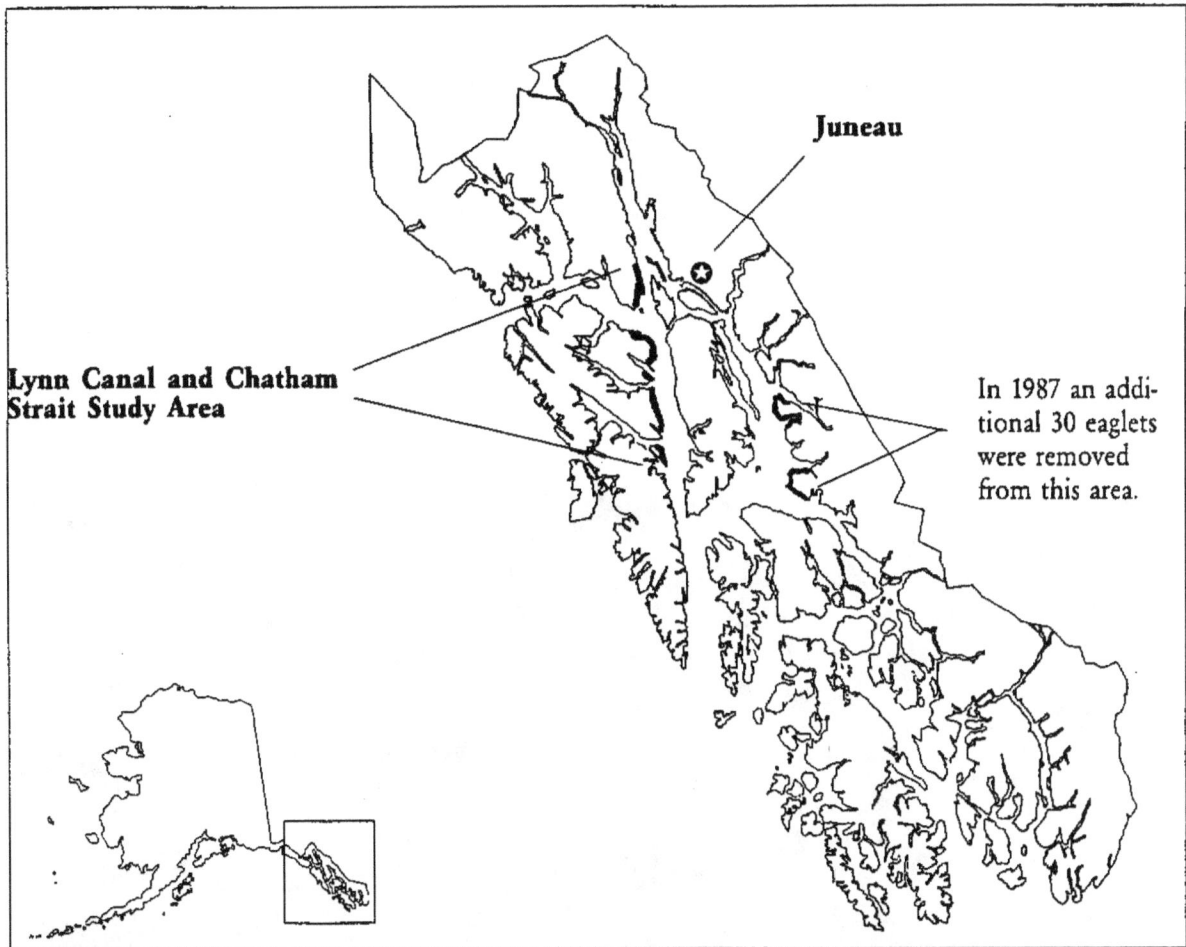

Figure 1. Map of Southeast Alaska showing the study area and additional collection sites for Bald Eagle nestlings.

In the map: Juneau; Lynn Canal and Chatham Strait Study Area; In 1987 an additional 30 eaglets were removed from this area.

Methods

Aerial surveys of the study area were conducted by helicopter in mid-May to find active nests. Follow-up surveys were flown in July to locate successful nests, determine the number of young, estimate the age of young and evaluate if the nest trees could be safely climbed. Active nests were defined as those with eggs or an adult in incubating position. Successful nests were those that contained one or more young at the time of the survey. The nest activity surveys were conducted from May 12 to May 18 and nest success surveys were flown between July 6 and July 18. Adult eagles were counted in July by fixed-wing aircraft.

Two observers participated in each helicopter survey. The pilot also helped with the search for nests and birds. The primary observer (Jacobson) remained the same during all surveys from 1984 through 1990. The survey for active nests in May was conducted during two consecutive days and averaged nine hours of flight time; whereas the July survey was completed in a single day and averaged five hours. Only adult eagles with white head and tail were observed nesting.

Bald Eagle capture area, Couverden Islands and the Chilkat Peninsula. Photo by Mike Jacobsen.

Figure 2. Bald Eagle nestling removal and control locations of the Lynn Canal and Chatham Strait study area.

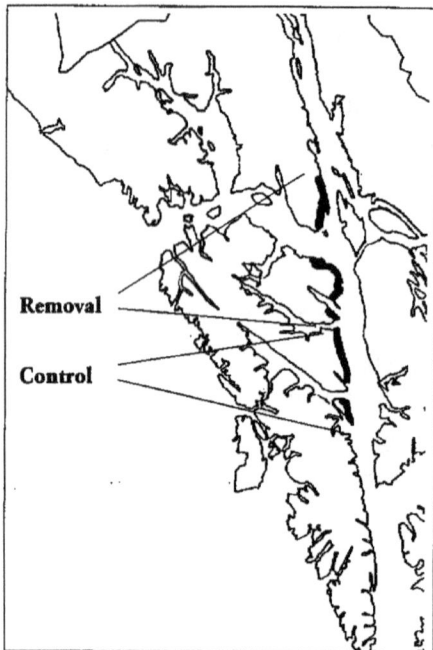

Removal

Control

The usual procedure for capturing eaglets was to shuttle two capture crews of two to three people each to shore by skiff. Nest trees were climbed using climbing spurs, ropes and rappelling equipment. An average of 4 to 6 trees could be climbed daily by two crews depending on the distance between nests, difficulty of climbing and the weather conditions. When a climber reached a nest, an eaglet was placed in a padded nylon bag and carefully lowered to the ground. Young were 6 to 8 weeks of age when removed from nests.

Eaglets were then taken by skiff to a larger vessel and placed in standard air kennels. While on the vessel, young were provided a constant supply of fresh fish and the kennels were cleaned daily. All eaglets were leg-banded and treated with antiectoparasite powder following collection. Upon returning to Juneau, they were immediately flown to lower-48 states via private charter or commercial airline.

Chip Grafe ascends and descends these Bald Eagle nesting trees to remove a young eaglet for relocation to Tennessee. Photos by Mike Jacobson.

Results and Discussion

A total of 279 eaglets (50% of available young) were removed from the original study area during 1981-1990. Table 1 summarizes the results of all surveys through the 10-year period.

Productivity Surveys

In the removal area, the number of active nests in May ranged between 36 and 89 with an average of 64 over all years. Successful nests ranged from 22 to 61 with an average of 38. Sixty-three percent of all active nests were successful in producing one or more young. Successful nests averaged 1.44 young, with a range of 1.16 to 1.69. No nest contained more than two young in the removal area during the entire 1981-1990 period.

The control area, which contained 40% of the shoreline distance of the removal area, had a range of 15 to 47 active nests, with an average of 32. Successful nests varied between 10 and 33, with an average of 19. Sixty-two percent of all active nests successfully produced one or more young in the control area. Young per successful nest averaged 1.40, with a range of 1.20 to 1.69. Three young were seen in a single nest on only one occasion in the control area.

Table 1. Bald Eagle productivity data and census results in Lynn Canal and Chatham Strait, Southeast Alaska, 1981-1990.

		Year										Mean
		1981	1982	1983	1984	1985	1986	1987	1988	1989	1990	
Nests surveyed	Removal	123[a]	131[a]	170	173	185	211	166	182	187	202	173
	Control	80	86	88	94	100	102	82	84	85	90	89
Active nests[b] (Percent)	Removal	--	58[a]	70	36	52	66	53	66	88	89	64
		--	(44)	(41)	(21)	(28)	(31)	(32)	(36)	(47)	(44)	(36)
	Control	--	33	21	27	35	29	15	40	47	43	32
		--	(38)	(24)	(29)	(35)	(28)	(18)	(48)	(55)	(48)	(36)
Successful nests[c] (Percent)	Removal	22[a]	34	31	28	30	37	35	48	61	58	38
		(18)	(26)	(18)	(16)	(16)	(18)	(21)	(26)	(33)	(29)	(22)
	Control	15	27	13	18	13	14	10	29	33	23	19
		(19)	(31)	(15)	(19)	(13)	(14)	(13)	(35)	(39)	(26)	(21)
Percent active nests successful	Removal	--	59	44	78	58	56	66	73	69	65	63
	Control	--	82	62	67	37	48	66	73	70	54	62
Young produced	Removal	26[a]	48	36	40	43	60	50	81	96	83	56
	Control	18	37	20	25	16	20	12	49	50	32	28
Young per active nest	Removal	--	0.83	0.51	1.11	0.83	0.91	0.94	1.23	1.09	0.93	0.93
	Control	--	1.12	0.95	0.93	0.46	0.69	0.80	1.23	1.06	0.74	0.89
Young per successful nest	Removal	1.18	1.41	1.16	1.43	1.43	1.62	1.43	1.69	1.57	1.43	1.44
	Control	1.20	1.37	1.54	1.39	1.23	1.43	1.20	1.69	1.52	1.39	1.40
Young removed		17	21	20	31	33	30	28	46	30	23	28
Adults in April (by boat)	Removal	--	--	354	--	--	--	--	--	--	--	--
	Control	--	--	143	--	--	--	--	--	--	--	
Adults in July (by plane)	Removal	--	276	354[d]	229	244	321	143	179	130	--	217
	Control	--	--	143[d]	85	104	106	70	73	72	--	85

[a] Adjusted for several small islands which were not surveyed in these years.
[b] Active nest - A nest with eggs or an apparent incubating adult on the nest.
[c] Successful nest - A nest at which one or more young were observed at the time of the survey.
[d] Surveys in 1983 conducted by boat.

In both the removal and control areas, the years 1988, 1989 and 1990 showed a surge in the number of active and successful nests. Productivity reached a peak in 1989 with 96 young in the removal area and 50 young in the control, compared to an average of 56 and 28 respectively (Figure 3).

The old-growth spruce/hemlock forest provided an abundance of Bald Eagle nesting habitat and the density of nests was high in the entire study area. The removal area averaged 0.82 nests per km (1.32 nests per mile) of shoreline, while the control area averaged 1.06 nests per km (1.71 nests per mile) of shoreline.

Active and successful nest densities were somewhat higher in the control area. An average of one active nest could be found for every 3.3 km (2.0 mi.) of shoreline in the removal area and every 2.6 km (1.6 mi.) in the control area. An average of one successful nest was found for every 5.5 km (3.4 mi.) in the removal area and 4.4 km (2.7 mi.) in the control.

Population Surveys

Counts of adult Bald Eagles were conducted by fixed-wing aerial survey during seven years (1982, 1984-1989) in the removal area and six years (1984-1989) in the control area. The density of adult Bald Eagles was nearly identical in both the removal and control areas. The average number of adult eagles observed in the removal area was 217, or 1.03 adults per km (1.66/mi.) of shoreline. In the control area, the average number of observed eagles was 85 adults, or 1.01 per km (1.64/mi.) of shoreline.

Hansen and Hodges (1985) reported that many adult Bald Eagles in Southeast Alaska do not breed annually. Based on the seven years of July counts in the removal area, a minimum of 59% of adult Bald Eagles occupied nests and 35% of adults successfully raised young. The six years of census data in the control area showed an average of 75% of adults occupied nests and 45% of adults successfully raised young.

The adult population, as counted by aerial survey in July, was highest in 1986 for both removal and control areas, but was variable throughout the study, no doubt due to such factors as weather and attraction to food sources. On warm sunny days eagles often soar on thermals at high elevations, so they can be missed during a low level aerial survey (Jacobson 1987). This also suggests that a single census on one day in July is not adequate to properly quantify the adult eagle population. The number of adult eagles recorded in July decreased after 1986. The reason for the reduction is not fully known but was common to both the removal and control areas.

Figure 3. Total young produced in the Lynn Canal and Chatham Strait study area.

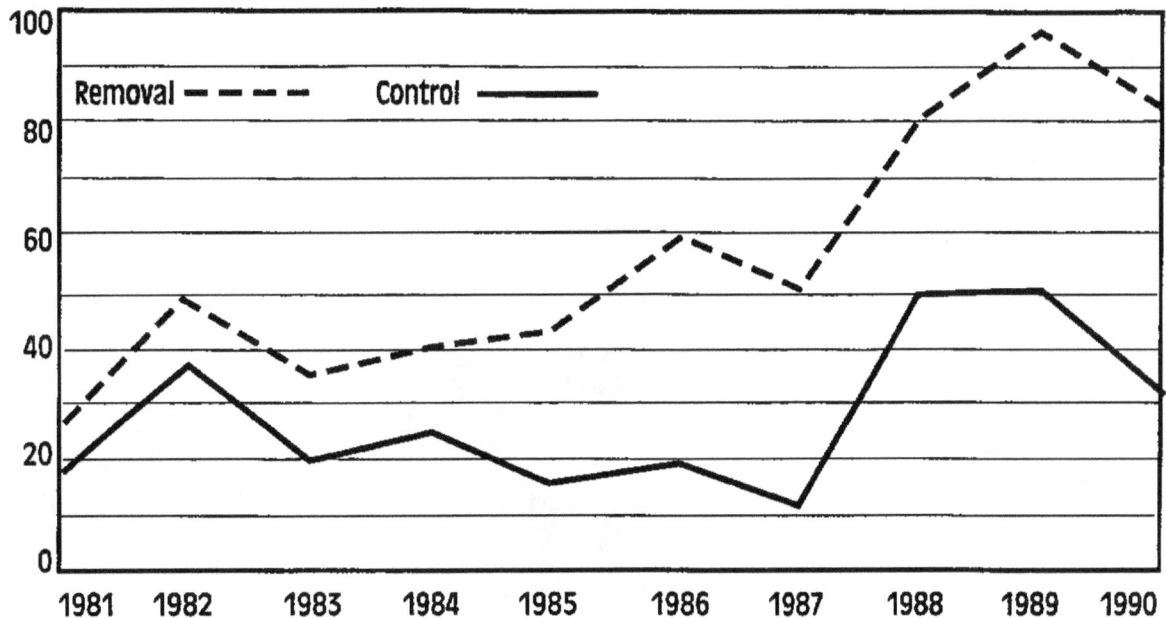

The percentages of active and successful nests and the number of young were highly correlated between the removal and control areas through the 10 year period of the study (Table 1). The proportion of all nests active in both the removal and control areas was identical (36%) and the proportion of all nests that were successful in both the removal and control areas was nearly identical (22% versus 21%).

It was impossible to determine the reaction of specific pairs of adult eagles to the removal of their young. Eagles were not individually marked and it was impossible to identify breeding territories occupied by particular pairs from year to year. Rather than attempt to monitor individual eagles, surveys were conducted to monitor the population and reproductive trends.

Perhaps when young were taken from a pair of adults, that pair may have been more persistent in nesting the following year. Even if they were less likely to nest the following year, there was apparently an abundance of non-breeding adult eagles ready to "fill in" and become breeders, thus concealing any possible effects of removal of young during the prior year(s).

Bald Eagle nestlings are placed in animal shipping containers. Photo by Mike Jacobsen.

Also, the study area is a relatively small part of an extensive coastal shoreline and forested region that supports a large population of Bald Eagles. Over 12,000 adult Bald Eagles are estimated to occur in Southeast Alaska (Jacobson 1989). This large pool of birds could have buffered the effect of removing young from nesting pairs in the study area because there were so many other eagles from the surrounding region to potentially fill any vacancies.

Even though 50% of available young were taken from the removal area during this study, there was no indication of a detrimental affect on the Bald Eagle population. Productivity was not affected by the removal of a major portion of the young during the previous nesting season.

Lower 48 States

The ultimate measure of success for this or any Bald Eagle translocation project is the establishment of a self-sustaining wild population in the region where they are released. New York pioneered the hacking of Bald Eagles on a small scale in 1976, then expanded the effort in 1981 with large numbers of eagles from Alaska. Of the 178 Alaska eagles taken to New York, 175 were successfully reared and released by hacking (P. Nye, pers. comm.). New York's interim goal was the establishment of 10 breeding pairs by 1990.

This goal was achieved in 1989 and enabled New York to end their hacking project that year. The long range goal is 40 breeding pairs by the year 2000. Some of the eagles released in New York have also successfully nested in adjacent states.

Missouri began a Bald Eagle hacking project in 1981 with a small number of birds from Wisconsin (J. Wilson, pers. comm.). At that time Missouri had no nesting Bald Eagles and had not had an active nest since 1960. However, hacked Bald Eagles became established and augmented naturally occurring eagles in Missouri. In 1990 there were 4 successful nests that produced a total of 8 young. The first of 30 Alaska eagles were translocated to Missouri in 1986.

A total of 29 Bald Eagles were reintroduced into North Carolina from 1983 to 1988. Of these, nine young were received from Alaska (in 1987), but only one survived after being released. Most of the Alaskan eagles died from avian malaria (T. Henson pers. comm.). When its reintroduction program began in 1983, North Carolina had no known nesting Bald Eagles. The last documented nesting pair failed to produce young in 1971. Even though eagles from Alaska did not fare well in North Carolina, some of the eagles reintroduced from other areas have survived. As of 1990, a total of 31 young had been produced from wild nests in North Carolina (7 young from 3 nests in 1990) and the number of breeding pairs continued to rise.

Bald Eagle nestlings are placed in bags and slowly lowered to the ground. Photo by Mike Jacobsen.

Indiana began reintroducing Bald Eagles in 1985, with the goal of establishing at least 5 breeding pairs in the state by the year 2000 (Castrale 1990). The final year of planned releases took place in 1989. A total of 73 eagles were released (36 from Alaska). In 1989

Indiana had its first nesting pair of eagles in over 90 years.

Tennessee also reintroduced Bald Eagles and received 64 young eagles from Alaska during 1986-1990. Prior to 1983, a successful nestling pair of Bald Eagles had not been sighted in Tennessee since 1961. In 1990, 8 nests successfully produced 17 young. The goal was to have about 25 successful nests by the year 2000. Kentucky also benefited from Tennessee's hacking program as some of the eagles moved into Kentucky to nest (R. Hatcher, pers. comm.).

The Bald Eagle is making a strong comeback in much of the contiguous United States and its numbers will likely continue to increase, due in part to translocation projects. Reintroduced young have survived and established themselves. They are reaching maturity and breeding successfully. The translocation of Alaskan Bald Eagles proved to be a successful method to reestablish viable breeding populations in other parts of the country.

Editor's Note: The translocation of Bald Eagles; from Alaska ended in 1993. California was added to the group of states that received Alaskan eagles. From 1981 to 1993 a total of 394 Bald Eagle young were removed from nests in Alaska for translocation to lower 48 states (the study area at Lynn Canal and Chatham Strait provided 357 of the total). Bald Eagle numbers have greatly increased across the contiguous United States. In 1995 the Bald Eagle was reclassified under the Endangered Species Act from endangered to threatened in the lower 48 states. Hopefully, it will never again be necessary to translocate Bald Eagles from Alaska.

Literature Cited

Cain, S. L. and J. I. Hodges. 1981. Involvement of the U.S. Fish and Wildlife Service in the New York state Bald Eagle reintroduction project. Unpubl. rep., U.S. Fish Wildl. Serv., Juneau, Alas. 8pp.

Cain, S. L., J. I. Hodges and P. Nye. 1982. The capture of Alaska Bald Eagles for translocation to New York and related productivity studies 1982. Unpubl. rep., U.S. Fish Wildl. Serv., Juneau, Alas. 6pp.

Castrale, J. S. 1990. Bald Eagle restoration efforts in Indiana, 1989-1990. Indiana Dept. Nat. Resourc., Div. Fish Wildl., Mitchell. 6pp.

Hansen, A. J. and J. I. Hodges. 1985. High rates of non-breeding adult Bald Eagles in Southeastern Alaska. J. Wildl. Manage. 49(2):454-458.

Jacobson, M. J. 1989. A survey of the adult Bald Eagle population in Southeast Alaska. Unpubl. rep., U.S. Fish Wildl. Serv., Juneau, Alas. 6pp.

Nye, P. E. Status, research and management of Bald Eagle nesting territories in New York. Federal Aid to Endangered Species New York Project E-1-6. Performance Rep. 11-2.

Personal Communication

Hatcher, R. 1991. Tennessee Wildl. Resourc. Agency, Henson, T. 1991. North Carolina Wildl. Resourc. Comm., Nye, P. 1990. New York State Dept. Environ. Conserv., Wilson, J. 1991. Missouri Dept. Conserv., Jefferson City.

A Review of the Natural History of a Reestablished Population of Breeding Bald Eagles in New York

Peter E. Nye

New York State Department of Environmental Conservation, Delmar, NY

Despite the bounty resulting in the removal of more than 100,000 Bald Eagles from the Alaskan population during the first half of the twentieth century, Bald Eagles can be considered secure and even at saturation levels in Alaska. This is undoubtedly due to the maintenance of undisturbed, suitable habitat and an abundant food supply. Similarly, much of Canada boasts abundant Bald Eagle populations.

Within the entire contiguous United States, however, the Bald Eagle is classified as either endangered or threatened. Human pressures, particularly expressed as habitat loss, disturbance, killing and more recently, persistent chemical poisoning, have been responsible for the steady and dramatic decline of our national symbol in the lower 48 states. Bald Eagle populations hit their nadir here in the early 1970s, at the same time that the reproductive contaminant DDT was banned nationally (1972) and the ground breaking Endangered Species Act was passed (1973). Breeding populations were reduced by as much as 80% from historic norms in many areas, while in others, such as within New York, the species was completely extirpated.

By the mid-1970s, attention began to focus on the restoration of Bald Eagles and other raptorial species hard hit by DDT, into remaining vacant but suitable habitats. Efforts to bolster and actually restore dwindling or extirpated populations of breeding Bald Eagles in the United States began in Maine in 1974 with the transplant of two eggs from wild nests in Minnesota in exchange for two eggs in nests in Maine.

Three restoration techniques have been employed in the recent Bald Eagle recovery effort including egg transplants, fostering and hacking. Bald Eagle hacking, pioneered in New York State in 1976, has been the most widespread and successful technique. Following years of trial and refinement, hacking has become a popular and relatively straightforward method of releasing nestling age Bald Eagles into a given environment in hopes of reestablishing nesting pairs in the area.

The objective in hacking is to act as surrogate, yet inconspicuous, parents during the in-cage pre-fledging period and to conduct the hack in such a manner that the birds fledge with the highest degree of "natural" fears, instincts and abilities possible. We want hacked eaglets to have as good a chance, or better, at growth, development and independence as wild nestlings. Years of learning have revealed that techniques used in the hacking process, more than any other variable, can and do influence the quality of the hack. Bear in mind that "quality" can be measured in a variety of ways, including time to fledging and dispersal and ultimately in survival (and/or mortality).

This hacking tower, located in New York, allows a commanding view by the eaglet(s) and security from predators. The adjacent scaffolding houses the feeding platform and blind. Photo by Peter Nye.

Selection of hacking sites is of extreme importance and should include the following considerations:

1) a clean, abundant fish food supply, usually a source very accessible to inexperienced eagles,

2) an area of limited or no human use or disturbance,

3) an area with documented historic eagle use and

4) an area suitable for nesting, should hacked eagles survive and decide to nest.

The hacking process involves the acquisition of young eagles, preferably six to eight weeks of age and their placement into artificial nests on man-made towers in suitable habitat, somewhat simulating natural nesting conditions. Eaglets are housed in 2.4 m square cages, usually two birds per cage. Hacking towers are constructed in a variety of ways with several important considerations including:

1) sufficient space for confined eagles to exercise and develop normally,

2) availability of a choice between protection from and exposure to the elements,

3) easy flight access both to and from the tower, including several potential perching locations,

4) sufficient isolation of the tower from any human activity to encourage use of the structure by fledged eagles and

5) placement of the tower in a suitable habitat location (site selection) and orienting birds properly to the chosen location (view).

Once in residence, young eagles require a continuous (preferably fresh) supply of food and minimal human contact until fledging time. Fresh water is also desirable, yet not essential, for caged eaglets. Since fledging generally occurs between 11-13 weeks of age, hacked eagles are confined within their tower cage for approximately 4-6 weeks. Close attention must be kept on potentially overly aggressive interactions with nest mates during this time and to ensure that all birds are feeding regularly. Detailed observations are greatly aided by use of remote video surveillance systems. These systems allow continuous daylight observation of caged eaglets without human contact or disturbance.

Prior to fledging, each eaglet is given a patagial (wing) marker and tail-mounted radio transmitter. Upon complete development of the flight feathers, cage doors are opened and eagles are allowed to fledge. An extensive network of perches outside of each cage ensures plenty of opportunity for young eagles to hop around and test their wings prior to fledging. Some individuals exhibit an immediate fledging response, while others may take up to a week before attempting their first flight. Special precautions are taken to ensure the release, usually conducted during early morning darkness, is as quiet and un-stressful as possible for the eagles.

Some eagles upon fledging leave the hacking area almost immediately, never returning, while others show a marked dependence on the hack tower in excess of seven weeks after fledging. The duration of stay, or weaning from the hacking towers, is believed to be linked to the fitness and survival of these eagles. After the release, fresh food continues to be provided on the hack tower and the lack of human contact becomes even more important for those eagles remaining in the immediate area. Aided by the use of short-term radio transmitters, post-fledging observations are made to ensure the welfare of each hacked eagle during the critical first few weeks of its independence. Additional remote feeding areas are also established as birds range from the hacking tower.

Historically, many parts of New York, especially the Adirondacks and the Great Lakes shorelines, provided suitable Bald Eagle nesting habitat. Large wetlands, such as those surrounding Oneida Lake, were favored locations. At least 75 locations have been confirmed to have had nesting Bald Eagles since 1800. The size of the New York breeding population at any one time is unknown, although it would seem reasonable that at least between 50-100 pairs occurred here during the most suitable times. By about 1960, only a dozen pairs were estimated to still exist and by 1974, only a single, non-productive pair remained in the entire state at a location in Livingston County in western New York. Although barren, this last pair proved to be suitable foster parents and successfully accepted and fledged eight foster eagles over a five-year period. Due to the lack of sufficient nesting birds to act as foster parents, however, hacking, or the hand-rearing to independence of nestling eagles in the absence of parent birds, was the primary option available for the attempted reestablishment of the species in New York.

Bald Eagle hacking began in 1976 in New York under the guidance of Tom Cade and was modeled after similar techniques just developed for Peregrine Falcons. Since that time, 15 additional states and the province of Ontario have initiated eagle hacking projects of varying sizes at approximately 30 locations, mostly within the eastern Unites States. By 1990, over 1,000 eagles had been released by these hacking projects. The vast majority (over 80%) of eagles for hacking have been collected directly from wild nests, with Alaska, by far, supplying the greatest number of birds. The remainder have come mostly from wild eggs collected in Florida and hatched in captivity at the Sutton Avian Research Center in Oklahoma. A small percent of the birds has come from totally captive sources such as Patuxent and selected zoos. The overall successful fledging rate for hacked eagles is extremely high, exceeding 95% for all projects and all years.

Between 1976 and 1980, 23 eagles were hacked at a single New York location in an experimental effort to determine if hacking was feasible for Bald Eagles. All results, including the successful establishment of a nesting pair of hacked eagles in 1980, indicated that the technique worked. Eaglets for these experimental years were obtained from captive sources at Patuxent and from wild nests in the Great Lakes. Based on these results, a plan was prepared to launch a large-scale management effort to hack 175 additional eaglets at additional sites in New York. Alaska was chosen as the donor state for these eagles, due to their abundance. The eagles simply could not be supplied from the lower 48 states.

Between 1981 and 1988, 175 additional nestling eagles were reared and released by hacking at four sites within New York. As noted, all of these birds were collected from wild nests in Alaska. A study area in Southeast Alaska, consisting of a control and a removal zone, was established for the eight-year collection program. Techniques and effects of collection have been discussed elsewhere in these proceedings by Jacobson. Once collected, eaglets were returned to New York State as quickly as possible, usually by private jet.

Eaglets aboard the M/V Surfbird in crates for shipment to New York. Photo by Jack Hodges, USFWS.

Following release, movements of hacked eaglets were carefully monitored and recorded. Similar to movement studies of wild fledglings, no clear preference as to direction or distance was observed. Movements of the eaglets can be generally characterized as random wandering for at least the first few years of their life.

Overall known mortality of New York hacked eagles is 16% (32 of 198 birds), undoubtedly a minimum. The majority of all known deaths (79%) occurred within three months of fledging, corresponding to the time of early independence when all young raptors are known to be most vulnerable. The primary cause of death of New York hacked eagles has been shooting, accounting for 50% of all mortalities.

Emaciation/starvation or young eagles simply not learning to make it on their own, was the next leading cause of death, but only accounting for 25% of the cases. This is not surprising and indeed was expected, since fledgling Bald Eagles typically spend from 3-12 weeks within the nesting territory honing their flight and prey-capturing abilities while watching their parents. Other causes of mortality in order of magnitude included disease, suffocation, electrocution and vehicle collision. On the brighter side, survival at least appears to be equaling mortality.

Sexual maturity in Bald Eagles generally occurs at five years of age, although can occur at four years, particularly in unstressed (e.g., un-crowded) conditions. Of 150 potentially sexually mature New York hacked eagles (5 years of age through 1990), 16% (24) are definitely known to have survived to adulthood. Again, this number must be considered a minimum, since there are undoubtedly birds we are not aware of or that may have lost their wing tags and, therefore, are not countable. This represents a minimum survival to sexual maturity for approximately one of every six hacked eagles. Such data is extremely useful to others interested in establishing nesting Bald Eagles by hacking and in particular, it tells how many eagles may need to be released in any given location. Adult survival seems to be skewed slightly to females (13 females versus 8 males, 3 sex unknown), for unknown reasons. During the hacking process, male eaglets are typically the most annoyed and stressed. Males are also known to fledge sooner and leave the hack site earlier than do females, which may decrease their survival chances.

The first New York hacked eagles began breeding in 1980, at age four, 146 km (91 mi) from their release site. By 1990, 14 breeding pairs of Bald Eagles were confirmed within New York, all a direct result of hacking projects. In addition, New York hacked eagles are currently nesting in at least two other locations outside of the state, in Pennsylvania and in New Hampshire. Nearly 90% of all nesting New York hacked birds made their first nesting attempt at either four or five years of age. Fifty percent of all first time breeding attempts were successful. Of 55 total breeding attempts by New York hacked eagles since 1980, 65% have been successful, resulting in the fledging of 51 young, or 0.93 young per nesting attempt. These figures are comparable to other wild eagle populations under study. The national recovery goal for the Bald Eagle is 1.00 young per breeding attempt. As our New York nesting birds gain in breeding experience (and provided they receive sufficient protection from human disturbance) we fully expect to exceed this level. For example for 1990, 12 breeding pairs of eagles produced 15 young for a value of 1.25 young per nesting attempt.

Known turnover of our adult breeders currently stands at only 5% over a 13 year period, much less than in other raptorial species such as Peregrine Falcons. Wing tags have allowed this close, long-term monitoring of our New York hacked eagles. They have also provided us with significant insight into initial nest territory establishment by these hacked birds.

Seventeen New York hacked eagles (12 females, 5 males) have been positively identified as to release origin and subsequent nesting site. Although no favored direction could be detected of nest sites from release sites, a sexual bias based upon distance is clearly expressed. Males exhibited a definite tendency to establish nesting territories closer to their release site than did females. Males moved an average of only 58 km (36 mi, range

0-146 km, 0-91 mi) while females moved an average nearly 3 times greater, of 161 km (100 mi, range 14-386 km, 9-240 mi). The important lesson here is, if you want nesting eagles close to your release site, favor males. No hacked eagle has been found to be nesting further than 386 km (240 mi) from its release site.

The breeding chronology of recently reestablished New York nesting eagles has been found to be within the date-range consistent with our region, as opposed to dates expected from the locale of origin of these birds. In other words, transplanted Alaskan eagles adopt to the breeding chronology of their "new" surroundings. Recent egg dates have ranged from 8 March to 23 April. Hatchlings have been observed between 16 April and 30 May. Fledged young have been confirmed from 15 July to as late as 31 August. Current New York nesting eagles are showing a clear preference for dominant, live, white pine trees. Forty seven percent of all nest trees selected have been white pines (7 of 15 trees) while other tree species have been chosen on only single occasions. Other species used include red oak, red maple, silver maple, red pine, hemlock and an elm snag. Height to the nests have ranged from 7.6 m (25') to 33.5 m (110'), with an average height of 22.4 m (73').

Two current New York nesting situations bear special mention, both involving three adults. At one location, in an apparent display of polygamy, one male has been taking care of two females at separate nests spaced approximately .5 km (1/3 mile) from each other. For two consecutive years, the male has shared incubation duties with both females at both nests and provided food to young at both nests in 1989 when two young successfully fledged from each nest. One of these two nests has failed in 1990, due to an apparent infertile egg. The other nest hatched and fledged a single young. The second situation involves polyandry at a single nest site. Here, two males and a single female have been nesting, apparently quite harmoniously for four consecutive years. The trio have successfully fledged five young during this time and are still together. The reasons for these unusual behaviors is unknown, although the lack of a sufficient reservoir of breeding adults in the overall population may be a plausible explanation.

Although production of young is important within the context of an expanding Bald Eagle population, it is actually the survival of young and adult birds that is the critical determinant in population direction. Using a stochastic model for population growth developed by Grier, population parameters for hacked Bald Eagles in the eastern United States were input and three random situations covering a 20-year period were run to determine the direction of this nascent population. Two primary sets of survival conditions were applied to determine their affect on population growth. The first assumed a 60% first-year mortality and 15% per year thereafter. The second assumed a 50% first-year mortality and only 10% thereafter.

Under condition 1, with a higher mortality, the population shows early growth while young eagles are still being hacked, but then levels off and begins to actually decline following the cessation of releases. Under condition 2, with more favorable survival conditions, the overall population continues to grow even once hacking has ceased. Survival data accumulated for New York eagles thus far, indicates that we are squarely within the survival range depicted under the growth scenario of condition 2.

The New York breeding Bald Eagle population is currently expanding at an annual rate of between 25-75% per year. Should this rate of growth continue, we will easily reach and surpass our recovery goal of 40-50 nesting pairs by the mid-1990's.

Despite some initial concern and hesitation by both biologists and the public, Alaskan Bald Eagles are indeed "making it" in New York and making it successfully. They have adapted to local conditions and now form the basis of a strong and expanding regional population. The citizens of the state of Alaska should take great pride in providing the opportunity for the squanderers to the south, to reestablish our national symbol. Hopefully, we will all learn a valuable lesson from these experiences of the past and make it unnecessary for future generations to take these costly and Herculean steps.

Editor Note: New York's Bald Eagle breeding population has continued to increase steadily. By 1998 there were 40 nesting pairs of Bald Eagles in the state.

Jack Hodges inspects a Bald Eagle nest in Sitkoh Bay. Photo courtsey of USFWS.

Human Disturbance and Bald Eagles

James D. Fraser and Robert G. Anthony

Virginia Polytechnic Institute and State University, Blacksburg, VA; Oregon State University, Corvallis, OR

The decline of Bald Eagle populations in the lower 48 states has been attributed largely to habitat destruction, shooting and the effects of DDT and other contaminants (e.g., Belding 1890, Harlow 1918, Broley 1958, Howell 1962, Sprunt et al. 1973, Wiemeyer et al. 1984). However, as early as 1960, some workers suggested that human disturbance may also be detrimental to the species (e.g., Cunningham 1960). In this paper, we examine the effects of human disturbance on Bald Eagle populations and focus on anthropogenic sources of disturbance. We define human disturbance as any human presence or activity that causes an eagle to alter its physiological state or behavior (e.g. Fraser 1985).

Behavioral Responses to Human Presence
Disturbance in foraging areas
The 1970s and 1980s saw the beginnings of experimental efforts to determine the distance at which various human activities produce behavioral responses by eagles. Most studies were conducted in feeding areas and involved intentional approaches to eagles to determine the distance at which birds flushed. Most flush distance obtained in this way was less than 500 m.

Distance within and among studies varied somewhat, apparently for a variety of reasons. Stalmaster and Newman (1978) reported that flush distances of adults were greater than those of immature and subadult birds. That result, however, could not be repeated by other workers who conducted similar studies in different regions (Russell 1980, Knight and Knight 1984, Wallin and Byrd 1984, Smith 1988, Buehler et al. 1991).

Several workers reported that flush distances were greater in areas that had little human use than in areas used more frequently by people; they cited this as possible evidence that eagles in the high human use areas became habituated to the presence of people (Stalmaster and Newman 1978, Russell 1980). Similarly, Buehler et al. (1991) reported greater flush distances in winter on the Chesapeake Bay than in summer, when human use of the bay was greatest. In contrast, flush distances in a North Carolina reservoir increased from spring to late summer (Smith 1988).

As Knight and Knight (1984) pointed out, there may be differences among areas or over time and unrelated to habituation, that result in changes of a population's flush distance. In Washington, for example, eagle flush distance appeared to be negatively related to food availability (Knight and Knight 1984). In Smith's North Carolina study, limited radiotelemetry data indicated that some individuals stayed in the study population only briefly. Thus changes in flushing response could have reflected the changing composition of the study population.

Perhaps the most important variable affecting flush distance is the visibility of the intruder. In most studies, the disturbance stimulus was clearly within sight of the subject eagles. However, in studies on the Nooksack and Skagit rivers in Washington (Stalmaster and Newman 1978), flush distances caused by people approaching eagles in open river and riverbank habitats were greater than those caused by people approaching through dense vegetation. This was probably because the eagles did not detect people in the vegetation until they were quite close. These results support the idea of providing vegetative buffers near eagle areas to prevent eagles from seeing people.

Flush distances provide a measure of the extent to which eagles will tolerate people, but there is also an "agitation distance" (McGarigal et al. 1991) which is greater than the flush distance and within which humans elicit behavioral and physiological responses from eagles even though the birds do not flush. McGarigal et al. (1991) estimated the agitation distance for eagles foraging on the Columbia River estuary by determining the usual foraging areas of breeding eagles, placing an occupied boat within those areas and then noting the distances from the boat where use declined. Almost all eagles in that study avoided perches within 300-400 m of the boat and some eagles avoided perches within 800 m.

The work by McGarigal et al. (1991) also showed that disturbance to eagles depends on the type of human activity involved, the distance to the activity, the time of day and the eagle location and activity. One must also consider the encounter rates of the various human activities under consideration. In the Columbia River estuary, for example, encounter rates were highest for trains, followed by aircraft and boats; eagles rarely encountered automobiles or pedestrians because of the large wetlands between the roads and the eagle use areas. Eagles were most frequently disturbed by automobiles and next most frequently by pedestrians, aircraft and boats; trains did not disturb eagles.

One might interpret these results as evidence for habituation, but this is not necessarily correct. Although disturbance rates were low for boats (6.4%), the number of encounters with boats was much higher, so that boats caused 80% of all flush responses by eagles. Only a few flush responses were caused by pedestrians, automobiles or aircraft because of the low encounter rates. All eagles flushed when boats approached within 100 m. No differences in flush rates or distances were attributed to nesting stage, cloud cover, eagle appetite, age, breeding status, or residence. However, eagle perch height, eagle activity and time of day influenced flush rate and distance. Eagles that were perched on or near the ground flushed in response to approaching humans more often than eagles perched in trees (Table 1).

Eagles flushed in response to human activities more often before 0800 than after 1000, but the time of day did not have a significant effect on flush distance. Although flush distances have varied from study to study, trials conducted under similar conditions resulted in comparable flush distances (Table 2). This suggests that there may be a general tolerance threshold for foraging eagles.

Table 1. Mean flush distances for factors with significant effects on Bald Eagle flush rates and distance for human activities on the Columbia River estuary, 1985-86 (from McGarigal et al. 1991).

Factor and level	Flush distance		KW or MWa	
	n	Mean	SE	P
Eagle perch height				
1 m	17	251	24	10.34
1-10 m	17	146	21	(0.006)
10m	16	180	24	
Eagle activity Foraging or feeding	33	167	15	175
Resting or other	17	242	26	(0.030)
Time of Day 0600 hrs	11	153	31	5.17
0600-0800 hrs	18	224	21	(0.160)
0800-1000 hrs	10	189	32	
1000 hrs	11	185	35	

KW = Kruskall-Wallis analysis of variance for factors with >2 levels; MW = Mann-Whitney U-Statistic for factors with 2 levels.

Disturbance at nests
In contrast to studies of foraging eagles, less work has been done to examine the distances at which humans elicit behavioral responses from nesting eagles. In Minnesota, a single person slowly approaching a nest in open view resulted in flush distances averaging 476 m (Fraser et al. 1985). Flush distance increased with the number of previous disturbances at a nest, decreased as the season progressed and was greater in mid-day than in the morning or the evening.

The strong positive correlation between flush distance and the number of previous disturbances suggests that, rather than becoming habituated to disturbances at the nest, eagles became sensitized. In this study, the same observer approached the nest from the same direction at each subsequent disturbance. Thus, it is possible that the eagles began to recognize a behavior pattern that would result in a very close approach to the nest, which might account for the increasing flush distance.

Disturbance at roosts
Most information about disturbance at roosts is anecdotal. However, Smith (1988) fired rifle and shotgun blasts at 200 m increments while approaching a roost in North Carolina after eagles had settled in for the evening. Eagles flushed when shots were fired at 600 m and 400 m, but not when shots were fired at 800 m and 1000 m. Eagle use of this roost on the nights of the shooting was lower than on other nights, but rebounded to pre-experiment levels on the nights after the shooting.

Population Responses to Human Activities

Information about behavioral responses to human activities is important because it provides managers with an empirical framework they can use to design buffer zones around important habitats. Ultimately, however, disturbance is only a problem for eagles if it changes their population parameters. In this section we examine the evidence that human activities change natality, mortality and dispersion in eagle populations.

Table 2. Bald Eagle flush distances (M) in response to various human activities.

Activity at Foraging Areas	Average distance	Range	Source
Pedestrian (River, Riverbank)	131	15->300	Stalmaster and Newman 1978
Boat	393	112-540	Wallin and Byrd 1984
Canoe	178		Knight and Knight 1984
Boat	137	0-395	Smith 1988
Pedestrian	270	191-246	Smith 1988
Boat	215	40-475	Buehler et al. 1991
Boat	197	50-468	McGarlgal et al. 1991
at Nests Pedestrian	497	57-991	Fraser et al. 1985

Effects on Natality Rates

Early studies of the effects of human disturbance on Bald Eagles focused on the impact of disturbance on natality rates, in part because of the many nest failures observed in the 1960s and 1970s and in part because nesting parameters are far easier to measure than survival or dispersion parameters.

Grubb (1976) found that, for nests within 0.25 miles of human developments, successful nests were significantly farther from the development (mean distance = 130 yards) than nests that did not produce young. Similarly, Anthony and Isaacs (1989) reported that mean productivity was lower at sites altered by logging or other human activities than it was in pristine, unaltered sites. They also found that productivity was negatively correlated with proximity to clear cuts, main logging roads and non-recreational activities. In contrast, McEwan and Hirth (1979), Mathisen (1985) and Fraser et al. (1985) failed to find evidence that human activities in their study sites were depressing reproduction. Similarly, Grier (1969) found no difference in the productivity of nests where young had been banded when compared to nests that had been censused only from a distance. The differing results in these studies may be attributable to differing levels of disturbance in the various study areas, or to methodological variation.

Effects on Eagle Distribution

Nest sites: A number of observations of eagles abandoning nests after local disturbances have been reported (Broley 1947, Murphy 1965, Thelander 1973, Anthony and Isaacs 1989). Movement away from developments may have been partly responsible for Grubb's finding that productive nests were farther from disturbances than unproductive nests since 30 of 52 unproductive nests were not active. In Minnesota, new nests adjacent to developed shoreline were farther from the water than nests on undeveloped shoreline and nests were farther from houses than would be expected if shoreline sections were chosen randomly (Fraser et al. 1985). Similarly, in Maryland, nests were significantly farther from structures and paved roads than were random points (Andrew and Mosher 1982). In Oregon, Anthony and Isaacs (1989) found that recently used nests within a breeding territory were farther from logging roads, recreational facilities and improved roads than old nests, suggesting a shift in nesting away from human activities.

This Bald Eagle nesting tree is within 30 m of two homes. Two years after this nest was built the eagles switched to a more remote nesting tree 400 m away and 100 m from the nearest home. Photo by Bruce Wright.

Foraging areas: The effect of recreational boating and shoreline use was examined at Jordan Lake, North Carolina by Smith (1988). Eagle densities were greatest along the segments of shoreline that received the lowest use by people. That fact alone could have been accounted for by differential habitat selection by people and eagles. For that reason, Smith compared eagle densities and human densities on weekdays with densities found on weekends. Jordan Lake is a favorite recreational area for many people from the Raleigh-Durham area and human use was much greater on weekends than during the weekdays. Eagle numbers, counted by shoreline surveys, were significantly lower during weekends than during weekdays. Smith estimated that the threshold density of boats which caused changes in eagle density was 0.5 boats/km².

In a similar analysis, Buehler et al. (1991) showed that eagles were less likely to be found on Chesapeake Bay shoreline segments with pedestrian traffic or adjacent boat traffic than on segments without such traffic. Moreover, they found that eagles were less likely to use developed shoreline (i.e. shoreline with buildings) than undeveloped shoreline. Any level of development on a 250 m long shoreline strip was sufficient to reduce the probability of eagle use, but development at or above a density of one building per hectare resulted in a probability of eagle use approaching zero. Thus, they assumed that Chesapeake Bay shoreline developed to that extent no longer serves as eagle habitat.

Effects on Survival

We are unaware of evidence that disturbance has negatively affected Bald Eagle survival. This is not surprising given the number of confounding variables that would affect such an analysis and the difficulty of even estimating survival rates. However, based on energetics modeling, Stalmaster (1983) predicted that disturbance could increase total energy needs of eagles and could also interfere with food acquisition. In a food stressed population, this could lead to reduced survival rates. Such effects would be more likely to occur in Canada and Alaska than in the 48 conterminous states because eagle populations in the former areas are more likely to be at or near the carrying capacity of the environment than other populations. Populations in the lower 48 states were depressed to well below carrying capacity by DDT and shooting and are still recovering from those effects.

Summary and Conclusions

The normal activities of eagles can be disrupted by human activities. The distance at which any given activity disrupts normal behavior varies with the nature of the activity, the individual eagle involved, the visibility of the activity from the eagle's point of view and a variety of other environmental factors. Nevertheless, a conservative rule of thumb is that when humans walk or boat within 400-500 m of eagles in the lower 48 states, many eagles will be disturbed. Our casual observations suggest that Alaska eagles may be more tolerant of humans than are birds in the rest of the United States, but this remains to be tested.

In some cases, human disturbance may cause nesting failure. Moreover, eagles that are subjected to disturbance during the breeding season may seek new, more remote nest sites. Non-breeding eagles avoid pedestrians, boaters and human dwellings such that excessive human presence on the shoreline can depress the carrying capacity of habitat that is otherwise quite suitable.

While some have suggested that eagles may habituate to human disturbance, there is no hard evidence that this is happening in the areas which are currently experiencing the greatest human densities. Thus it appears that the long-term well-being of eagles depends upon maintenance of more or less remote shorelines where human-eagle interactions are minimized.

*Editor's Note: During 1985-1992, D. G. Roseneau. and P. J. Bente designed and tested methods for building. artificial Bald Eagle (*Haliaeetus leucocephalus*) tree nests and directly and indirectly relocated nesting pairs (Roseneau 1990; Roseneau and Bente 1987, 1989, 1993; Roseneau et al. 1986, 1987). The work was conducted for the Alaska Energy Authority as part of a multiyear study to develop management techniques for mitigating potential impacts of hydroelectric projects built in areas supporting Bald Eagle nesting populations. The above photograph shows a natural appearing, weather resistant nest designed to provide drainage and withstand high winds and heavy snow loads. By the conclusion of the 1992 breeding season, Bald Eagles had used nine (60%) of 15 nests installed in spruce (*Picea* sitchensis *and *Picea* glauca) *and balsam poplar (*Populus* balsamifera) *trees in the Tanana and Susitna river drainages and upper Kachemak Bay and a nest mounted on top of an experimental tripod erected in the Susitna River Valley. Also, during the study, one pair of eagles was successfully relocated from their natural nesting territory to an artificial territory about 488m away by moving their eight-week-old young to an artificial nest and temporarily blocking their natural nest with a steel*

cone (the first direct relocation of breeding Bald Eagles) and another pair was indirectly moved to a new location in their nesting territory by coning their nests.

Literature Cited

Andrew, J. M. and J. A. Mosher. 1982. Bald Eagle nest site selection and nesting habitat in Maryland. J. Wildl. Manage. 46:383-390.

Anthony, R. and F. Isaacs. 1989. Characteristics of Bald Eagle nest sites in Oregon. J. Wildl. Manage. 53(1):148-159.

Belding, L. 1890. Land birds of the Pacific district. California of Sciences Occasional Papers II. Sacramento, Calif.

Broley, C. L. 1947. Migration and nesting of Florida Bald Eagles. Wilson Bull. 59:3-20.

Broley, C. L. 1958. The plight of the American Bald Eagle. Audubon 60(4):162-163, 171.

Buehler, D. A., T. J. Mersmann, J. D. Fraser and J. K. D. Seegar. 1991. Effects of human activity and shoreline development on Bald Eagle distribution and abundance on the northern Chesapeake Bay. J. Wildl. Manage. 55(2): 282-289.

Cunningham, R. L. 1960. The status of the Bald Eagle in Florida. Audubon 62(1): 24-26, 41, 43.

Fraser, J. D. 1985. The impact of human activities on Bald Eagle populations-a review. Pages 68-84. In: J. M. Gerrard and T. N. Ingram, eds. The Bald Eagle in Canada. White Horse Plains Publishers, Headingly, Manitoba.

Fraser, J. D., L. D. Frenzel and J. E. Mathisen. 1985. The impact of human activities on breeding Bald Eagles in north-central Minnesota. J. Wildl. Manage. 49:585-592.

Grier, J. W. 1969. Bald Eagle behavior and productivity responses to climbing to nests J. Wildl. Manage. 41:438-443.

Grubb, T. G. 1976. A survey and analysis of Bald Eagle nesting in western Washington. M.S. Thesis, Univ. of Washington, Seattle. 87pp.

Harlow, R. C. 1918. Notes on the breeding birds of Pennsylvania and New Jersey. Auk 35:18-29.

Howell, J. C. 1962. The 1961 status of some Bald Eagle nest sites in east-central Florida. Auk 79:716-718.

Knight, R. L. and S. K. Knight. 1984. Responses of wintering Bald Eagles to boating activity. J. Wildl. Manage. 48:999-1004.

Mathisen, J. E. 1985. Effects of human disturbance on nesting Bald Eagles. J. Wildl. Manage. 32:1-6.

McEwan, L. C. and D. H. Hirth. 1979. Southern Bald Eagle productivity and nest site selection. J. Wildl. Manage. 43:585594.

McGarigal, K., R. C. Anthony and F. B. Isaacs. 1991. Interactions of humans and Bald Eagles on the Columbia River estuary. Wildl. Monogr. 115:1-47.

Murphy, J. R. 1965. Nest site selection by the Bald Eagle in Yellowstone National Park. Proc. Utah Acad. Sci. 42:261-264.

Roseneau, D. G. 1990. Bradley Lake hydroelectric project Bald Eagle program 1989: Summary of 1989 monitoring activities. Interim report by LGL Alaska Research Association, Inc. for the Alaska Energy Authority, Anchorage, Alas. 4 pp.

Roseneau, D. G. and P. J. Bente. 1987. Bradley Lake hydroelectric project Bald Eagle program 1987: Surveys of nesting populations, experiments with artificial nests and methods for indirectly relocating nesting pairs. Annual report by LGL Alaska Research Association, Inc. for Stone and Webster Engineering Corp., Englewood, CO and for the Alaska Energy Authority, Anchorage, Alas. 32 pp. plus figures.

Roseneau, D. G. and P. J. Bente. 1989. Bradley Lake hydroelectric project Bald Eagle program 1988: Surveys of nesting populations, experiments with artificial nests and methods for indirectly relocating nesting pairs. Annual report by LGL Alaska Research Association, Inc. for the Alaska Energy Authority, Anchorage, Alas. 31 pp. plus figures.

Roseneau, D. G. and P. J. Bente. 1993. Bradley Lake hydroelectric project Bald Eagle program 1986-1991: Bald Eagle nest surveys and experiments with artificial nests and translocation of nesting pairs in Kachemak Bay, Alas. Final report by BioSystems Alaska for the Alaska Energy Authority, Anchorage, AK. 180 pp. plus folding maps.

Roseneau, D. G., P. J. Bente and J. D. Woolington. 1986. Artificial nests and nest structures built for Bald Eagles (*Haliaeetus leucocephalus*) in the Tanana and Susitna river drainages, August-September 1985. Interim report by LGL Alaska Research Association, Inc. for Harza-Ebasco Susitna Joint Venture and for the Alaska Energy Authority, Anchorage, Alas. 28 pp.

Roseneau, D. G., P. J. Bente and J. D. Woolington. 1987. Bradley Lake hydroelectric project Bald Eagle program 1986: Prefabrication and installation of artificial nests and nesting structures, direct relocation of nesting pairs and coning natural nests. Annual report by LGL Alaska Research Association, Inc. for Stone and Webster Engineering Corp., Englewood, CO and for the Alaska Energy Authority, Anchorage, Alas. 40 pp. plus figures and maps.

Russell, D. 1980. Occurrence and human disturbance sensitivity of wintering Bald Eagles on the Sauk and Suiattle rivers, Washington. Pages 165-174. In: R.L. Knight, G. T. Allen, M. V. Stalmaster and C. W. Servheen, eds. Proc. Washington Bald Eagle Symposium. The Nat. Conserv., Seattle, Wash.

Smith, T. J. 1988. The effect of human activities on the distribution and abundance of the Jordan Lake-Falls Lake Bald Eagles. M. S. Thesis, Virginia Polytechnic Inst. and State Univ., Blacksburg, VA.

Sprunt, A., W. B. Robertson, Jr., S. Postulpalsky, R. J. Hensel, C. E. Knoder and F. J. Ligas. 1973. Comparative productivity of six Bald Eagle populations. Trans. N. Amer. Wildl. Conf. 38:96-106.

Stalmaster, M. V. 1983. An energetics simulation model for managing wintering Bald Eagles. J. Wildl. Manage. 47:349-359.

Stalmaster, M. V. and J. R. Newman. 1978. Behavioral responses of wintering Bald Eagles to human activity. Journal of Wildlife Management 42:506-513.

Thelander, C. G. 1973. Bald Eagle production in California, 1972-1973. State of California Department of Fish and Game. Wildlife Branch Administrative Report No. 73-5. 17pp.

Wallin, D. O. and M. A. Byrd. 1984. Caledon Park Bald Eagle study. Unpublished report, Department of Biology, College of William and Mary, Williamsburg, VA. 53pp.

Wiemeyer, S. N., T. G. Lamont, C,. M. Bunck, C. R. Sindelar, F. J. Gramlich, J. D. Fraser and M. A. Byrd. 1984. Organochlorine pesticide, PCB and mercury residues in Bald Eagle eggs, 1969-1979 and their relationships to shell thinning and reproduction. Archives of Environmental Contamination and Toxicology 13:529-549.

Bald Eagle Reaction to Construction on Back Island, Alaska

Jackie Canterbury
U.S. Forest Service, Ketchikan, AK

Introduction

In March of 1986, the U.S. Navy announced its selection of Back Island in Behm Canal, Southeast Alaska, as the preferred site for a proposed submarine acoustic measurement facility, or SEAFAC. Back Island, the site of the facility, constitutes 120 acres of island habitat. It is located within the Tongass National Forest, about 13 air miles north-northwest of the city of Ketchikan, Alaska. The island lies along the southern shore of western Behm Canal, between Betton Island to the southwest and Grant Island to the northeast (Figure 1). The interior of Back Island is forested mostly with western hemlock (*Tsuga heterophylla*) and western red cedar (*Thuja plicata*). Old-growth Sitka spruce (*Picea sitchensis*) dominate portions of the shoreline, providing suitable sites for eagle nesting and perching. *Vaccinium* spp. and salal (*Gaultheria shallon*) dominate the shrub layer.

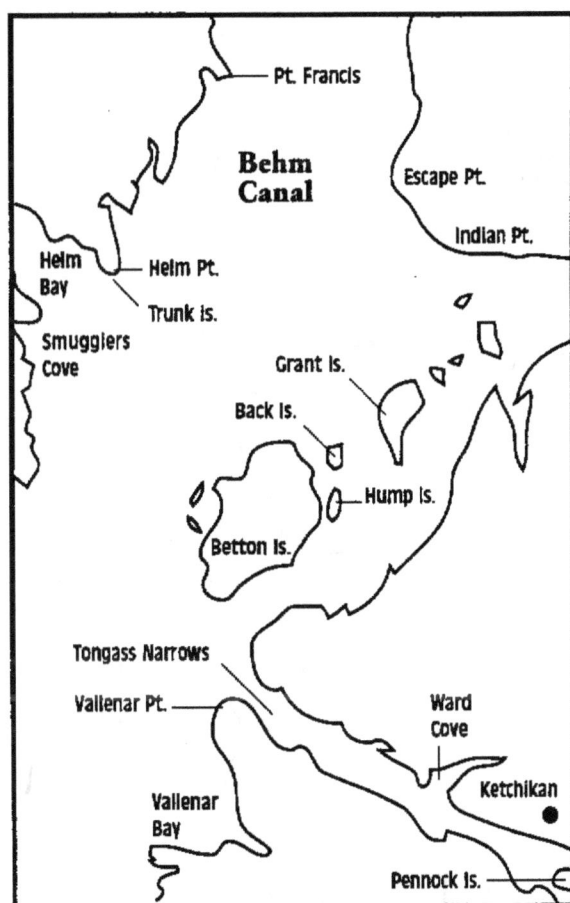

Figure 1. Back Island in Western Behm Canal.

Plans for the SEAFAC facility consist of an underwater measurement site, located in the center of western Behm Canal; a static site, located to the northwest of Back Island; and supporting shore facilities on Back Island. The shore facilities consist of the operations area on the northwest side of the island and the dock area on the west side. The dock is a 268-foot long, 16-foot wide pile supported pier (Figure 2). The shore facility required the clearing of approximately 15 acres, which included the approach to the dock, access road to the operations area, operations area and clearing for security fences. Clearing of the 15 acres began in November, 1989.

During the planning stages of this project, it was recognized that construction and operation of the acoustic measurement facilities could potentially affect Bald Eagle activity on Back Island. In Alaska, the Bald Eagle is protected under the Bald Eagle Protection Act (16 USC 668-668d). The act makes it illegal to take, possess, disturb or molest eagles, eagle parts, eggs or nests. The Bald Eagle and its habitat have been given additional protection through a Memorandum of Understanding between the Forest Service (FS) and the Fish and Wildlife Service (FWS). In 1985, the FWS (Alaska Region, U.S. Department of the Interior) and FS (Alaska Region, U.S. Department of Agriculture) drafted an interagency agreement outlining the responsibility of each agency to protect and manage Bald Eagles and their habitat within National Forests in Alaska (Samson 1998). This Memorandum of Understanding specifically addresses disturbance associated with blasting within one-half mile of eagles or active nests. Construction of the road, dock and facility would all occur within a one-half mile radius of nest #67. Thus, a "Back Island Bald Eagle Monitoring Plan" was developed in 1989 between the FS and FWS.

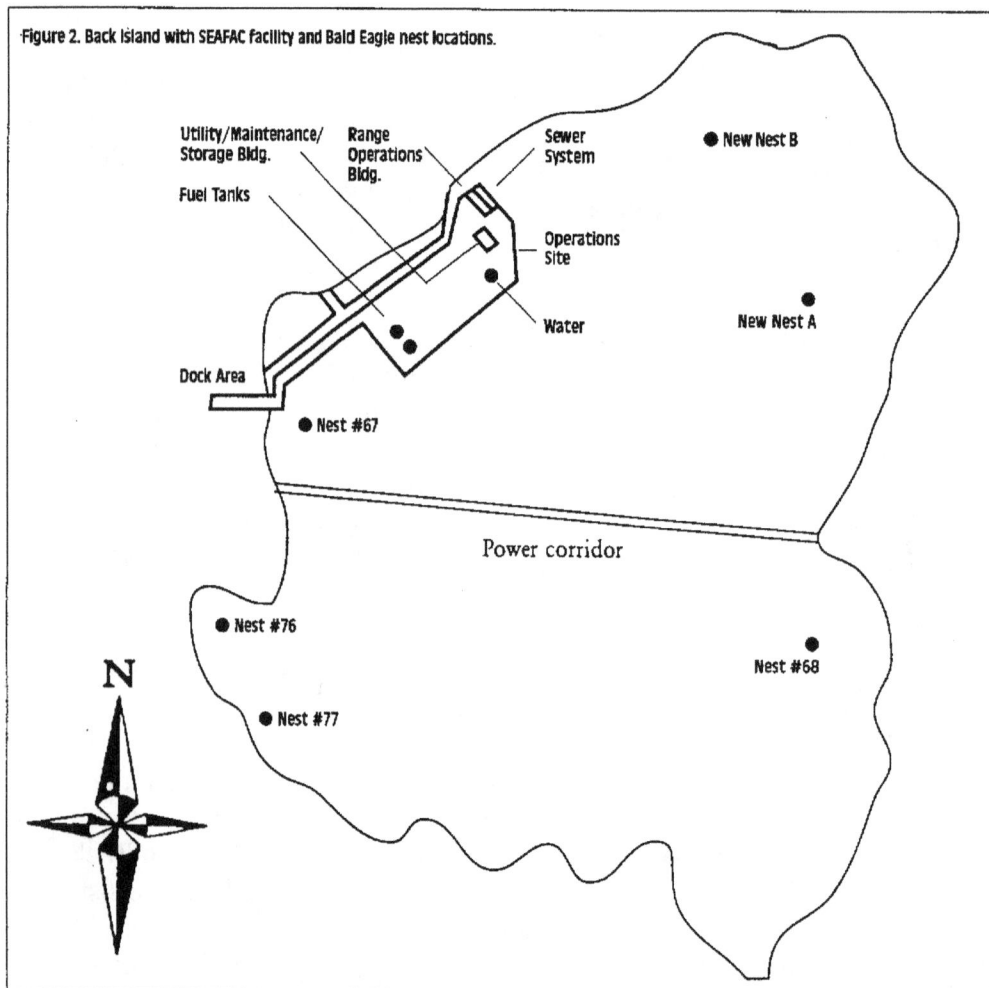

Figure 2. Back Island with SEAFAC facility and Bald Eagle nest locations.

Methods

The Monitoring Plan was developed to address the behavioral responses of resident breeding Bald Eagles to the activities associated with construction of the facility and was to be implemented during construction of the road, dock and facility. Field observation data were to be collected regarding the responses of eagles to various construction activities. The observer was to be responsible for determining the reproductive period of a nest, monitoring coastline for possible changes in nesting location, identifying a nest's occupancy status, interpreting eagle behavior in conjunction with construction activities, recording eagle behaviors during the monitoring periods and determining if the reproductive success of a nest were in jeopardy. Background information in the plan states that human activity near nest sites may result in reproductive failure by Bald Eagles (Stalmaster et al. 1985). Stalmaster has also suggested that human disturbance can disrupt breeding by reducing the occupancy, activity, success and/or productivity of nests or by causing total desertion of the nesting territory (Stalmaster 1987). In birds of prey, the impacts of disturbance have been documented, including nesting failures (Boeker and Ray 1971) and lowered nesting success (Wiley 1975, White and Thurow 1985).

The agreement called for monitoring of eagle nest #67 and all active nests on the west side of the island. Nest #67 was emphasized because it is 200 feet from the facility and it had been active since 1986. Observations, in lesser detail, were to be recorded on all other nests located on other portions of the island: #68, #76, #77 (a remnant nest) and two new nests found in 1990, numbered A and B.

Aerial surveys of Back Island have been conducted from 1986-90. Those surveys gathered information on nest location, activity and productivity. The proposed development of SEAFAC was the impetus for the surveys. Historical nesting data of Back Island is given in Table 1. Data were not available for 1987.

Table 1. Historical Bald Eagle nesting by year on Back Island collected by aerial survey.

Nest Number	1986	1988	1989	1990
67	A	A, N	A, N	1
68			A	*
76		T	A	I
New nest A				A, I
New nest B				I

A = Active (bird or egg on the nest).
N = Nestling(s) (nestlings seen or heard).
I = Inactive (no birds or eggs on nest).
T = Territorial activity (adults perched near nest).
* = No data (no data available).

Monitoring of nesting territory establishment, nest reconstruction, nest activity (adults sitting in the nest or evidence of eggs), nesting and fledgling(s) stages of development began February 21, 1990 and extended to August 31, 1990. Prior to collecting observation data, a general reconnaissance of the island was completed to determine locations of the Bald Eagle pairs. Behavioral information was collected and activities such as perching, foraging, vocalizing and flying were noted for each eagle forming a territorial pair. Nest #67 and #76 were observed at the same time because of location. New Nest A and new Nest B were observed together, also because of location. Observation time for #68 was less because of distance from the SEAFAC facility. A nesting territory was defined as a confined locality where nests are found, usually in successive years and where no more than one pair has ever bred at one time (Steenhof 1987). The observations were designed to begin prior to nest establishment so the field observer could become familiar with the locations of Bald Eagle nests, Bald Eagle behavior and locations for observations. Field observations were collected an average of two days per week, three to six hours per day. In winter, hours were often shortened due to weather and amount of daylight.

Observations of eagle behaviors for example perching, foraging, vocalizing and behavior associated with disturbance, were primarily made from a 17-foot Boston Whaler boat, though some observations were made from helicopter or on the ground. Ground observations were generally conducted only when necessary to verify boat observations of activity of nearby nests and adjacent nests on Betton Island. The Betton Island nests, used as a control, were not randomly selected but were chosen on the basis of logistics.

Two aerial surveys were flown during 1990 for Back Island and Betton Island. The purpose of the surveys was to determine Bald Eagle nest occupancy/success and verify nest locations. The objective of the first survey, flown May 24, was to count the number of pairs associated with nesting territories and the number of pairs with eggs. The goal of the second survey, flown July 17, was to count the number of successful pairs and the number of fledgling-age young.

A sound level meter was used to monitor noise levels on the ground associated with construction activities near new Nest B. The sound meter was used once.

Results

Construction of the road, dock and facility began in the fall of 1989. Eagle observations began in February, which coincided with the dock construction phase. During that time noise levels were high due to pile driving activities associated with the dock construction. Three Bald Eagle nests were known to occur at the onset of the monitoring project and two additional nests were identified during the monitoring process (Figure 2). Eagle nest tree #67, located on the western shore of Back Island, is about 200 ft from the road construction. Nest #76 is located approximately 800 ft from the facility on the SW point of the island. Nest #77 is located 45 ft south of nest #76, was identified as a remnant and was not observed on a regular basis. Because alternate nests are often within a few yards of each other #77 may be an alternate for nest #76. Eagle nest tree #68 is located on the eastern shore of Back Island about 1600 ft away from the site and about 500 ft from the power corridor.

The nesting success of the resident Bald Eagles on Back Island and adjacent Betton

Island are shown in Table 2. All three Betton Island nests exhibited all stages of reproduction through nestling success. In contrast, no nests on Back Island advanced to the nestling stage. An association exists between ranking of disturbance and degree of nesting advancement. Ranking of disturbance was determined by field observation of construction activities within each territory. Each nest was ranked from most disturbed (1) to least disturbed (6). Nest #67 which was closest to the facility and experienced the most disturbance, ranked number one.

Table 2. 1990 Bald Eagle nesting advancement on Back island and adjacent Betton Island.

Island	Nest	Pair In territory From-To (month)	Work on nest Yes/No	Adult in nest From-To (month)	Eggs Yes/No	Nestling Yes/No	Rank of Disturbance* 1 = most; 6 = least
Becton	66	02-08	Yes	04-05	Yes	Yes	6
Betton	65	02-08	Yes	04-05	Yes	Yes	6
Betton	64	02-08	Yes	04-05	Yes	Yes	6
Back	Nest A	02-08	Yes	08	Yes	No	5
Back	68	02-08	Yes	05	No	No	4
Back	Nest B	02-08	Yes	No	No	No	3
Back	76	02-08	No	No	No	No	2
Back	67	02&07	No	No	No	No	1

* Ranking of disturbance was determined by field observation of construction activities within each nesting territory.

Nest #67, with a ranking of 1, did not advance beyond territorial pairing. Nest #67 was never occupied in 1990. This is one of the oldest nests on the island and was active in 1986, 1988 (with nestlings) and 1989 (with nestlings) (Table 1). In 1987, no data were available. The nest is visible from the water and 200 ft from the road to SEAFAC. Because this road serves as an access road, high levels of activity have occurred since November, 1989, when clearing of the land and road building to the waste area began.

Blasting and drilling began December 6 1989 and continued periodically through February. Building of the access road began December 9, 1989. Although this area has been historically active, little eagle use was observed during the monitoring period. Of approximately 50 hr observation time of this nest, eagles were observed perched near the nest for only 3.5 hr and foraging near the nest for 3 hr. While there was intermittent territorial use, there was no nest reconstruction and no use was seen at the nest tree.

Nest #76 was not occupied in 1990, although there was an adult pair in the territory. The nest is visible from the water and on a prominent point in the SW section of the island. The dock area of SEAFAC is approximately 1,000 ft from the nest. High noise levels were associated with the construction of the dock which began March 12, 1990. The first piles were driven in March and drilling was completed May 2, 1990. Constant activity was observed in the area in the form of approaching boat traffic, heavy construction and human activity. Boat traffic consisted of one jet boat, several smaller transport boats and barges off-loading equipment. One adult pair were observed in the territory since the beginning of observations. Of approximately 50 hr of monitoring time of this nest, an eagle pair was observed 43 hr perched in the territory. There was no nesting activity observed in 1990, although the nest was active in 1989 (Table 1).

New Nest B was identified in May 1990 in the operations section of SEAFAC. It is visible from the water, approximately 200 ft from the beach. The nest is 199 ft from the operations site waste area. Because the nest was not identified earlier, a 330-foot buffer was not provided, making it more vulnerable to disturbance. Construction activities began in the waste area November 14, 1989, with rudimentary road building after the trees were cut. After identification of the nest in May, the operation of equipment the last 200 ft of the waste area was restricted. Construction activities were monitored in June and noise levels 199 ft from the nest were measured at 75 decibels. Of the 50 monitoring hours of the nest, an eagle pair was observed 31 hours perched in the territory. No eagles nested in this territory, although nest reconstruction was observed in May 1990. This nest may be an alternate for nest #67. Or it may be what is referred to as a frustration nest, partial or entire nests constructed after breeding failure. This may have been constructed after the abandonment of #67. The area may also be the nesting territory of a Bald Eagle pair.

Nest abandonment leads to certain death of eaglets. Photo by Steve Cain.

An adult eagle was briefly observed in the nest in May, however, the nest did not produce young. Of the approximately 20 hr observation time of this nest, a pair of eagles were observed 16 hr perched in the territory. The nest was active in 1989 (Table 1). The nest is not visible from the water, is 800 ft from SEAFAC and 500 ft from the power corridor (Figure 2). Disturbance to this eagle pair was observed July 30, 1990. Heavy equipment was operating in the power corridor near the beach. As the area was approached by boat, the eagles were observed with heads thrown back, giving the scream call. The birds then flew around the operating heavy equipment. Two eagles from the territory of new Nest A joined them and all four eagles flew together, calling.

New Nest A was identified in May 1990 in the NE section of Back Island. It is visible from the water, approximately 150 ft from the beach. The distance from the end of the access road to this nest is 600 ft. There had been a Bald Eagle pair in the territory since observations began. Of 50 hr of monitoring this nest, a Bald Eagle pair was observed perched in this territory 46.5 hr. In April, a subadult Bald Eagle performed the circling display for approximately fifteen minutes. A territorial chase ensued, the adult Bald Eagle extending talons to harass the subadult. This was observed on three occasions in spring 1990. On the basis of these observations and the large size of new Nest A, it appears that this territory has been historically active. During the aerial survey flown May 24, one egg was seen in new Nest A, thus the nest was thought to be active. However, observations from boat before and after the survey were not consistent; the female was not seen incubating the egg, but was perched with the male 90% of time observed. On July 26, nest reconstruction was observed. Then, on August 24 the female was observed for two hr on the nest in incubating posture.

Three nests on Betton Island, located about one mile west of the western shoreline of Back Island, were used for the control group. Betton Island received approximately 30 hr of monitoring time. Due to close proximity to Back Island, nest #66 was also observed while observing nest #67 and #76 on Back Island. No construction activity occurred on the island and the habitat is comparable. Though it is in close proximity to Back Island, noise levels were insignificant and human activity, other than research observations, was absent. All nests observed on Betton Island were active and produced young: #66 produced two fledglings, #65 and #64 each produced one. No unoccupied nests were identified in the observed portion of Betton Island.

Discussion

As evidenced by the historical breeding data (Table 1) and the 1990 nesting abandonment (Table 2), nesting was adversely affected by disturbance. On the basis of approximately 150 observation hours at Back Island from February 21 to August 24, 1990, it appears that nesting success was influenced by human activities. Human activity near nest sites has been suggested to result in reproductive failure by Bald Eagles (Stalmaster 1987). Of importance at Back Island was the eagle's breeding chronology and the timing of construction activities. Increased levels of disturbance were taking place during the most critical times of Bald Eagle nesting, egg laying and incubation. Noise levels were higher than ever experienced. Human activity, insignificant in past years, was increasing. This may have been reason for the early abandonment of nest #67 and development of the frustration nest. Eagles vary widely in their response to human activity. Some pairs of eagles will tolerate activity near the nest, others are not as permissive, as evidenced by the 1990 nesting success rate of Back Island. Raptors in frequent contact with human activities tend to be less sensitive to additional disturbances than raptors nesting in remote areas (Newton 1979). Similarly, whether or not there will be detrimental effect may depend on several factors, including the stage of nesting cycle and the duration of the disturbance (Gerrard and Bartolotti 1988).

Gerrard and Bartolotti (1988) state, "Studies of the effects of human activities near eagle nests have yielded variable results, although most suggest that people have a negative effect on nesting success. It is easy to be misled or get false impressions of the influence that humans have on the productivity of nesting eagles because of examples of a few tame individuals. Some eagles are fairly tame, but others are extremely upset by the presence of humans even hundreds of yards away from their nest. Much of the variability in behavior may perhaps be attributed to learning. Experience with a specific kind of disturbance generally has one of two effects on the eagle's subsequent behavior toward that disturbance. The bird may habituate to it, that is, show no adverse reaction, for it has learned that there is nothing to fear. Alternatively, eagles may become so sensitized that they react with ever-increasing intensity." This was observed in July near nest #68.

A correlation can be made between the absence of the production of young and a change in the level of disturbance on Back Island. There were five nests on Back Island in 1990. The nest closest to the facility, #67, receiving the highest ranking of disturbance, advanced the least in 1990. No eagles on Back Island produced young in 1990, yet there is a record of strong historical use (Table 1). Of the three nests observed on Betton Island, where disturbance was low to nonexistent, nesting advancement extended to the nestling stage in all nests (Table 2).

Conclusion and Recommendations
Much of the landscape in Southeast Alaska has not experienced activity at the levels of the Back Island project. Although Back Island is within the Clover Pass Scenic Area, past activity has been limited to recreational boat traffic and an occasional picnic on the island. Hunting pressure has not been significant (Bob Wood, ADFG biologist, pers. comm.).

Evidence suggests a strong negative relationship between the amount of disturbance as a ranking and the nesting advancement of Bald Eagles on Back Island. Construction activity produced increased noise and levels of human activity. Future long-term management recommendations, though, will require the collection of additional data.

The recommendation is to continue the monitoring program to determine what happens to the birds when construction disturbances decrease and the facility begins operation, which will be in 1991. Nesting raptors may or may not reuse the same nesting territory the year following the disturbance.

The monitoring program format should be similar to that which existed this year for consistency, though with increased intensity. All nests on the island should be given equal weight as disturbance has occurred in some form near all five nests and will likely continue, but at various levels. Field observations would be made two times per week from March 1 through August 31, 1991. I recommend routine use of a noise meter, perhaps placing one at each nest site. Time lapse cameras could be used to monitor nests and could be placed with the noise meter at each nest site or at selected sites. This could be a cooperative study with the USFWS who have the equipment. A project such as this would require additional funding, but could produce significant research and management implications.

The general SEAFAC operations plan should concentrate on minimizing SEAFAC disturbance to the nests during the critical stages of egg laying and incubation, establishing a 330-foot buffer for all active nests. It is known that falcons nesting in remote areas may be more sensitive to human activities (Newton 1979) and more restrictive management involving disturbance to the birds may be necessary. Operating guidelines might include the use of a propeller boat instead of a jet boat and general land noise kept to a minimum at recommended times.

Acknowledgements

Without the financial assistance of the United States Navy, this project would not have been possible. I especially thank Jane Noll West for her support and guidance throughout this project. I would like to acknowledge Cole Crocker-Bedford, Rick Hauver and Jack Gustafson who provided valuable comments on earlier versions of the paper. Additionally, I would like to acknowledge Dave Perkins for his field assistance at the beginning of the project and Paul Crowl for his technical maintenance advice.

Editors' Note: Back Island was resurveyed by the U.S. Fish and Wildlife Service during June 1998. None of the original nests observed during this study were found. Two new nests were found on the south shore at Back Island; both were inactive.

Literature Cited

Boeker, E. L and T. D. Ray. 1971. Golden Eagle population studies in the Southwest. Condor 73:463-467.

Gerrard, J. M. and G. R. Bortolotti. 1988. The Bald Eagle: haunts and habits of a wilderness monarch. Smithsonian Inst. Press, Washington, D.C. 178pp.

Newton, I. 1979. Population ecology of raptors. Poyser Ltd., Hertfordshire, England. 399pp.

Samson, F. B. 1998. Cooperative management of the Bald Eagle in south coastal Alaska. In: Wright, B.A. and P.F. Schempf, eds. Bald Eagles in Alaska.

Stalmaster, M. V., R. L., Knight, B. L. Holder and R. J. Anderson. 1985. Bald Eagles. Pages 269-290. In: E. R. Brown, tech. ed. Management of wildlife and fish narratives. U.S. Dept. Agric., For. Serv., R6-F&WL 192-1985, Portland, Oreg. 332pp.

Stalmaster, M. V. 1987. The Bald Eagle. Universe Books, New York, N.Y. 227pp.

Steenhof, K. 1987. Assessing raptor reproductive success and productivity. Pages 157-170. In: B. A. Giron Pendleton, B. A. Millsap, K. W. Cline and D. M. Birds, eds. Raptor management techniques manual. Sci.

Tech. Ser. 10. Natl. Wildl. Fed., Washington, D.C. 420pp.

White, C. M. and T. L. Thurow. 1985. Reproduction of Ferruginous Hawks exposed to controlled disturbance. Condor 87:14-22.

Wiley, J. W. 1975. The nesting and reproductive success of Red-tailed Hawks and Red-shouldered Hawks in Orange County, California, 1973. Condor 77:133-139.

Nesting Bald Eagles in Urban Areas of Southeast Alaska

Nathan P. Johnson

Alaska Department of Transportation and Public Facilities, Juneau, AK

In Southeast Alaska (Figure 1), Bald Eagles (*Haliaeetus leucocephalus*) which have chosen nest sites in or near urban areas are often acclimated to high levels of human activity. The Alaska Department of Transportation and Public Facilities (ADOT&PF) has found that for these "urban eagles," current U.S. Fish and Wildlife Service (FWS) guidelines on blasting and general highway construction to prevent disturbance of nesting Bald Eagles under the Bald Eagle Protection Act can be too restrictive.

The FWS basic stipulations to protect nesting Bald Eagles state that to permit eagles to initiate nesting activities there should be no heavy construction work within 100 m of a nest from March 1 to May 15 and this period should continue to August 31 if the nest is occupied (Hodges 1982b). If the nest is not occupied by May 15, construction activities within 100 m can proceed. For blasting, the timing restrictions remain the same, but the buffer zone is 800 m.

Some recent ADOT&PF projects involved blasting and heavy equipment work near eagle nests within the FWS buffer zones and time frame. The pairs of eagles using these nests successfully raised young during the affected nesting seasons. In addition to this field information, ADOT&PF undertook this study to evaluate the existing literature on disturbance of nesting eagles and methods of monitoring disturbance. Based on the findings of the study, the department recommends the Federal Highway Administration (FHWA) develop a Memorandum of Agreement (MOA) with the FWS to: a) on a case by case basis, mitigate and/or monitor potential impacts from construction on eagle nest trees to prevent disturbance and b) undertake research to better define disturbance. Increases in location and design costs due to mitigation and/or monitoring on a case by case basis will more than offset the minimization of both construction delays and elevated costs due to the presence of active eagle nests adjacent highway construction projects.

Figure 1. Alaska relative to the Lower 48.

Background and History of Disturbance Studies

The federal Bald Eagle Protection Act of 1940 prohibits the taking of Bald Eagles (including nests or eggs) at any time or in any manner without a permit. As defined in the act, taking includes "molest or disturb." However, nowhere in the act (or implementing regulations) are these two terms defined. To date, case law offers the only definition of what may constitute "molest or disturb."

The eastern region of the U.S. Forest Service (USFS) implemented a policy of establishing buffer zones around individual Bald Eagle nest trees in 1963 (Mathisen 1968). It is unclear whether the FWS concept of buffer zones evolved from this policy or was established independently.

Early Studies

Early investigations of potential impacts of human activities on nesting Bald Eagles have been documented in the literature (Lincer et al. 1978, U.S. Army Corps of Engineers 1979). Quantification of impacts in these studies has been general, focusing on the human activities involved, then attempting to measure nest abandonment or lowered productivity as an indication of disturbance. Nests were usually grouped into disturbed and undisturbed categories.

One of the first studies to evaluate human disturbance as a potential cause of nesting failure among Bald Eagles was carried out in the Chippewa National Forest in Minnesota (Mathisen 1968). Results indicated specific types of human activities did not significantly disturb nesting eagles. A major component of the disturbances were human recreational activities which took place from mid June throughout the rest of the summer. These activities occurred after nests were established and the young hatched, the two most critical time periods from a disturbance standpoint. Nest occupancy and fledging of young were used as measures of nesting success.

Two other researchers (Jueneman and Frenzel 1972) on the Chippewa National Forest classified four different levels of disturbance within a mile of nests. Analysis of the data showed a negative relationship between both apparent nesting activity and measured production as compared to degree of disturbance. The ratio of activity to productivity was better with lesser disturbance.

A study on the Kenai National Wildlife Refuge in Alaska (Bangs et al. 1987) separated eagle nests into disturbed and undisturbed categories. Human disturbance was not quantified and apparently no statistical analyses were made of the productivity data, but the study indicated human disturbance can decrease productivity.

Another study in the Chippewa National Forest (Fraser et al. 1985) found no evidence that under management policies at that time, natural or induced human activities had any major impact on Bald Eagle reproductive success. The authors concluded that, "birds at unsuccessful nests, as a group, were not exposed to higher levels of human activities than birds at successful nests." The investigators went so far as to suggest "experiments in which a substantial number of eagles are disrupted to the point of nest failure by a variety of human activities will have to be carried out in a number of different areas in order to address this question (of the affects of human disturbance on nesting eagles) adequately. The relatively stable population of eagles in Alaska and Canada could be used in such studies."

The use of the word "disrupt" i.e., to break apart, rupture, to throw into disorder or to cause to break down, implies that levels of disturbance which do not cause nest abandonment are acceptable. This approach is extreme and unnecessary. The investigator's straight line approach toward a nest with pausing at 20 m intervals in plain view, until the attending adult(s) flushed, is unnatural human behavior and is directly threatening to nesting birds. It appears the technique was designed for statistical analysis rather than duplicating normal human-induced disturbance factors. The principle investigator of the FWS Eagle Management Studies Program in Southeast Alaska (M. Jacobson, unpubl. data) agrees that any direct threats by man can significantly impact breeding behavior and success.

More recent work in western Oregon (Anthony and Isaacs 1989) characterized 201 Bald Eagle nest sites in three different forest types over four nesting seasons. Mean productivity was "lower at sites altered by logging or other human disturbance," particularly clear cuts, main logging roads and non-recreational human activities. In given nesting territories, most newer, more recently used nests were farther from human activities than associated older nests in these same territories.

The researchers measured many variables to characterize individual nest trees, the forest stand surrounding each nest tree and human activity. Many of the human activity categories were actually measurements of habitat alteration over time rather than direct impacts of day to day human activities on nesting birds. Clearcut logging and associated roadways plus non-logging roads and highways, public facilities and private homes were some of the major human activities measured.

Other studies (Murphy 1965, Retfalvi 1965, Weekes 1974) have also demonstrated lowered productivity and site desertion associated with human disturbance at Bald Eagle nest sites.

Activity Budget Approach

The current approach to quantifying impacts of disturbance to raptors is typified by the use of the activity/energy budget on peregrines in the Sagavanirktok River drainage in Alaska (Ritchie 1987). The technique consists of determining the energy budgets of undisturbed nesting birds and then statistically comparing them with the energy budgets of those same birds (or other nesting pairs) under disturbed conditions. The activity/energy budget is the amount or percent of time (energy) expended by an animal in performing various behavioral activities as determined through field monitoring.

In this study, behavioral and environmental data were recorded on both activity and disturbance forms for each half hour of observation at each nest site. Observations focused on the attending adult at the nest or in the adjacent cliff area. During experimental disturbances, intensive observations were made on the focal bird. Each recorded disturbance was described by several characteristics: 1) behavior of the birds prior to disturbance, 2) type of disturbance (other species, helicopter, light truck), 3) degree of reaction of the birds (none, mild, moderate, severe), 4) duration of disturbance (time within restricted zone), 5) duration of reaction of the birds, 6) direction (in relation to falcons), 7) distance (closest linear distance to falcons for all disturbances and altitude for avian predators and aircraft), 8) noise level (none, low, medium, high) and 9) visual stimulus (none, unlikely, probably, positive).

Experimental disturbances included construction and maintenance equipment, airplanes, river boats, snow machines and people on foot. The type and timing of experimental disturbances were varied to simulate both normal and unusual disturbance activities. The author tested the "hypothesis that time spent in each activity category did not differ among the two disturbed and the undisturbed activity budgets .." He then used a battery of nonparametric analyses of variance to determine levels of significance. He concluded that the disturbances studied "did not cause significant changes in the time spent in important behaviors (e.g. incubation) and did not cause measurable impacts on occupancy or productivity."

While no significant differences in activity budgets with regard to specific human activities indicates no disturbance, significant differences may begin to define disturbance from a biological standpoint, i.e., reduction in current and future productivity. For example, operation of heavy equipment adjacent to a nest in the early morning hours may significantly reduce parental feeding behavior of newly hatched young to the point of lowering productivity.

The basic activity budget approach is also applicable to Bald Eagles (Cain 1985). This pioneering study on quantifying the nesting activity (time) budgets of Bald Eagles in Southeast Alaska concluded "Detailed accounts of nesting time budgets are needed to develop criteria for Bald Eagle management in areas where the potential for human disturbance is of concern." Remote, time-lapse movie cameras were used to "document the amount of time adults spent at incubating, brooding and feeding at the nest, with specific emphasis on: the division of these activities between the male and female, temporal changes in time budgets and the effects of several environmental parameters on nesting time budgets."

Time-lapse photography provided instantaneous, single frame exposures every 90 seconds. The films were developed and then analyzed with a time-lapse analyzing projector. Activity data were punched directly into a computer for analysis. Results indicated significant differences in both individual and pair activity budgets with regard to human disturbance, incubation, brooding, prey deliveries, feedings and effects of weather on nesting activities. With respect to disturbance, the author concluded that reactions were variable, "but that most eagles were extremely sensitive to intrusion during incubation and for the first one or two weeks after hatching."

Video equipment has also been used to monitor nesting Bald Eagles in California and Arizona (Garcelon et al. 1988). These continuous "real time" observations lend themselves to a variety of analyses unlike time-lapse photography which records data at preset intervals.

Habitat Disturbance

Observations and data collected during most of the disturbance studies discussed above attempted to measure only the direct impacts of human activities on the nesting eagles themselves. The more important long-term problem of the loss of Bald Eagle nesting habitat due to human activity (disturbance) must always be kept in mind (Corr 1974, Hodges 1982b, Fraser et al. 1985, Anthony and Isaacs 1989). Existing nest trees will eventually be lost from one cause or another such as decay, blow-down or human activities and, therefore, over the long-term, alternative sites must be available to maintain viable eagle populations.

In a study of the relationships of Bald Eagle nesting to forestry practices near Petersburg, Alaska, from 1967 through 1969 (Corr 1974), nest sites located in the fringe of timber left along the beach as a result of logging were found to be highly susceptible to windthrow. In one winter, 1968-1969, 20% of the known nests were lost to storm damage. Buffer zones of 660 ft. and reduction of beach strip logging to ensure potential nest sites were recommended.

In an attempt to minimize impacts on eagle nests and nesting on federal lands in Southeast Alaska, the U.S. Forest Service and the FWS entered into a Memorandum of

Understanding (MOU) in 1968. It requires the FS to "establish and maintain a minimum five-chain radius habitat management buffer zone around each Bald Eagle nest tree and exclude all land use activity within the zone." It also provides a mechanism for possible variances to these buffer zones. However, the FS and the FWS jointly agree that to "maintain the Bald Eagle nesting population at natural levels of abundance, a sufficient number of trees, suitable for supporting eagle nests and properly distributed along the shoreline, must be present in perpetuity." Neither "natural levels" nor "sufficient numbers" are defined.

In 1979 and 1980, Bald Eagle nests in Southeast Alaska were surveyed before and after logging to assess the adequacy of the 100 m buffer zone to protect nests and nesting habitat (Hodges 1982b). Few of the clear cuts in the study were adjacent to the 100 m buffer zones. However, had clear cuts been adjacent to all buffer zones, "loss (due to windthrow) would have averaged 17% of the buffer zone after just a five-year period." If the clear cuts had "surrounded the 100 m buffer zone, potential would exist for much greater losses to blow-down." The author concluded, "the loss of nesting habitat from blow-downs adjacent to clear cut areas will probably cause the most serious long-term problems for eagles under the existing management policy." Similar problems have been documented in the coterminous states (Anthony and Isaacs 1989).

The potential loss of future nesting habitat becomes heightened in urban areas where land ownership shifts from unreserved public lands (those left in their natural state) to public use and private lands. The Bald Eagle Protection Act can be implemented to protect nesting eagles and existing nest trees but cannot exclude construction of highways, homes, businesses and other urban amenities in areas which may some day provide future eagle tree nest sites. Thus, the availability of potential nest trees may be dependent on reservation of parcels of unreserved public lands and fortuitous retention of suitable sites on private lands.

Legal Definition of Disturbance
Even though evidence clearly demonstrates eagles can be disturbed to the point of deserting their nests and/ or young, legal action to halt such activities seems to require proof of negligence or show of intent to do harm. The Bald Eagle Protection Act itself states, "Whoever .. shall knowingly, or with wanton disregard for the consequences of his act take..." A case in point (Schempf 1982) involved an eagle nest on private property in the Juneau area which was being developed. The owner was observed clearing and burning brush near the nest site in March. He was informed of the presence of the nest, given a copy of the Bald Eagle Protection Act and advised not to disturb the birds from March through July. He indicated he would not disturb the area. The eagles selected the site and nested. In late April, the owner, disregarding his earlier statement, began clearing and burning again. Drifting smoke disturbed the adult eagles. The owner was warned again. The adults abandoned the nest in late June. Subsequent field investigation revealed a dead eaglet at the base of the nest tree. The owner and an employee were each fined $200 for what Schempf called an "open and shut case of willful disturbance that ultimately caused the death of the eaglet."

While existing case law may define disturbance from a legal standpoint, there is a difference between the point of successful criminal prosecution and a more conservative point of acceptable management impacts due to disturbance (Schempf, unpubl, data). From both legal and biological standpoints, there is a need for a functional, biological definition of disturbance. An emerging approach to defining disturbance is maintaining long-term productivity Assuming adequate food resources, the number of available nest sites and the number of young raised per nest site each year are the key factors of the long-term productivity equation. Of course, productivity data must be balanced against mortality and survival rates.

Questions which must be addressed in fine tuning this definition are: Should it include an assessment of current and potential levels of Bald Eagle productivity? Should it include measurement of lowered productivity during the time of disturbance? How would this be measured? Would it require abandonment of nest, eggs or young? Would successful nesting in successive years counterbalance specific levels of disturbance due to human activities, particularly during years of high eagle populations?

Development of a functional definition of disturbance is also in the best interest of state and federal highway agencies. It should lead to more cost effective and expeditious development of public works projects.

Raptor Biology and Behavior, Effects on Potential Nesting Disturbance

For most raptors, the main habitat requirements for nest selection and successful rearing of young are: 1) adequate food supplies prior to and throughout the breeding season, 2) a satisfactory nest site with associated perching areas and 3) visibility of adjacent territory/ feeding grounds (Snow 1973, Lincer et al. 1978, Hayes and Mossop 1982, Stalmaster et al. 1985, Sidle et al. 1986). The more completely these three conditions are met, the less raptors are disturbed by human activities.

Work with Peregrine Falcons (*Falco peregrinus* anatum) in the Yukon Territory indicates that "physiological condition of breeding females may be the key factor in regulating annual breeding success (Hayes and Mossop 1982)." Breeding success was considered to be strongly and inversely tied to the energy requirements expended during spring migration by breeding females and could affect the psychological as well as physiological conditioning of the birds. Does this type of preconditioning also affect the breeding success of Bald Eagles? Evaluating the physiological condition of nesting eagles may be a base ingredient in any monitoring program and should include quantitative and qualitative measures of available food sources within individual nesting territories.

An interesting situation with respect to preconditioning in nesting Bald Eagles seems to occur annually in the Chilkat Valley near Haines, Alaska (Jacobson, unpubl. data). Observations during late spring nesting surveys conducted by the FWS in the mid- to upper Chilkat Valley show average, though often variable, densities of active nests. However, their observations during production surveys flown later in the summer indicate very low nesting success. The middle Chilkat Valley, with its abundant winter food source of spawning salmon, is an important over-wintering area for Bald Eagles, particularly young birds. A certain percentage of young and maturing birds may orient to the area, making their first nesting attempts there. During the spring and early summer, the large spawning runs of salmon are not present, however. The low nest success rates may be due to inexperience, or the reciprocal impacts of high nesting density versus an inadequate food supply. These nesting pairs may be severely stressed, making them very susceptible to even low levels of human disturbance. In this situation, any loss of productivity due to human disturbance of a marginal breeding population may be insignificant. Also, early termination of what may normally be an unsuccessful nest might possibly free up food resources for another marginal pair to raise their young to fledging.

Human activity may also increase the local food supply and thus concentrate eagles (Musselman 1949). Bald Eagles frequently used a garbage dump on Amchitka Island, Alaska (Sherrod et al. 1976). A high percentage of use was by sub-adult eagles, however, adults did use the dump as a supplemental food source. During the winter and early spring months, the dump may have been an important supplemental food source for young birds and potential nesting pairs.

An experimental winter feeding program for eagles was carried out in Maine from 1981 through 1985 (McCollough 1986). During this period, 98,000 kg of carrion were dispensed at feeding stations in four major eagle wintering areas. First- and second-year birds became heavily dependent on the artificial food source, with older birds less dependent. Analysis of banded birds showed productivity of local populations near feeding sites was enhanced.

The relative health of any population under study must be considered along with preconditioning when attempting to determine the effects of human activities on nesting Bald Eagles. The estimated Bald Eagle population of Southeast Alaska was approximately 7,000 adults for both 1967 and 1977 (King et al. 1972, Hodges et al. 1979). In the FWS's Seymour Canal Study Area in Southeast Alaska, productivity exhibited a broad scale decline in 1979, 1980 and 1981, dropping by almost 50% for unknown reasons (Hodges 1982a). The most recent aerial census of Bald Eagles in Southeast Alaska indicated a total adult population of close to 12,000 birds (Jacobson, unpubl. data).

The Bald Eagle population may be peaking in Southeast Alaska (Jacobson, unpubl. data). The rate of population increase is slowing and reproductive rates are dropping off. With large population fluctuations over an extensive area in Southeast Alaska, there remains a provocative question which should be addressed in any definition of "disturbance" from a biological standpoint. What is the real biological impact of one year of reduced or missing production from one to a few nests either on a local population or the larger regional population? Long-term cumulative impacts of individual projects must also be considered.

Another important variable which must be considered is the individuality of the birds. For Peregrine Falcons, variations "in response to a disturbance exists between individuals, ..

in one individual over time, .. and in one individual's reaction to different types of disturbance." Also, " a complex array of factors may influence a peregrine's response to disturbance and perhaps more important, the reaction of the falcon in any particular instance is highly unpredictable." Factors which might affect a given bird's response to disturbance are "nature of the disturbance, type and severity, frequency and duration, distance from nest site, height of nest above river, presence of intervening topographical features, time relative to reproductive phenology" and "sex, age and breeding status of the individual(s)." (Amaral 1982) This same difficulty of predicting the effects of a given type of disturbance applies to individual Bald Eagles because of their variable responses to human activity (Stalmaster et al. 1985).

The variability of reactions of individual Bald Eagles to the climbing and placing of cameras in eagle nest trees or adjacent trees was documented in a study of Bald Eagle nesting activities on Admiralty Island, Alaska (Cain 1985). One female returned to the nest while the camera was still being mounted in a tree less than 30 m from the nest. At another nest, the female returned within a few minutes of the researcher's descent from the camera tree. At a third site, the male was the first to return, but not until nearly 2 1/2 hours following camera installation.

The individuality of raptors also influences the degree to which particular birds or pairs of birds can become habituated to human activities (Fraser et al. 1985, White and Thurow 1985). Habituation is the non-reaction of an animal to non-threatening, usually repetitive events, although there is often a behavior threshold beyond which the involved disturbance is unacceptable. At that point, avoidance behavior sets in and nest abandonment may occur. This threshold, for raptors in general (Ritchie 1987), is "influenced by season, age, sex, previous breeding experience, health of birds, weather and/or prey availability."

Analysis of data gathered on the Chippewa National Forest (Fraser et al. 1985), suggests "eagles avoid human settlements when building new nests." Settlements consisted of clusters of houses occupied throughout the year. The availability of nest trees in the area was not the limiting factor (Mathisen, unpubl. data). However, based on recent observations (1986-1988), some newer territories have been established closer to the housing areas. This is probably a result of habituation and/or the population approaching saturation density. Current nesting data indicate a slowing of the population growth rate coupled with a reduction in productivity.

The fact that Bald Eagles nest and successfully raise young in urban areas demonstrates that the required nesting habitat is present and any needed physiological preconditioning dependent on availability of foods has been met. Man-caused disturbance factors are usually greater in urban than wilderness or rural areas, so it follows that these breeding pairs of eagles are tolerant of, or have become habituated to, some degree of human disturbance. Several current researchers (Ambrose, Cain, Lincer, Mathisen and Ritchie, unpubl. data) agree.

From 1981 through 1987, 215 nestling Bald Eagles have been captured by the FWS in

Southeast Alaska for translocation to the contiguous 48 states (Jacobson 1987). The bulk of these birds, 180, came from the Chatham Strait study area which mainly includes the eastern coastline of both the lower Chilkat Peninsula and Chichagof Island. These 180 eaglets constitute a 59% removal of the 303 young available on the entire study area over the seven-year period. A control area is located near the removal area. Study data show "an increasing trend in production of (total young) for the experimental area and a decreasing trend for the control area." The high productivity rate could be due to the removal of the nestlings which "may have actually created a positive reproductive response in the experimental area." In addition, the number of young raised per occupied nest was identical for both the experimental and control areas. Therefore, the author concludes, "no detrimental effect on productivity has been detected from removal of young during the seven-year study period."

Recent work by the FWS Eagle Management Program indicates nest densities along the Juneau road system, particularly the Auke Bay area, are higher than in many non-roaded portions of Southeast Alaska. Also, productivity appears to be comparable to, or in some cases exceed, other surveyed areas.

The FWS has collected several year's of nesting success data for both the Juneau urban area and their remote Seymour Canal study area on Admiralty Island. These data should be analyzed to determine the degree to which overall impacts of urbanization have affected long-term eagle nesting success and productivity.

The argument can be made that the Mendenhall River estuary, biologically rich Auke Bay marine waters and associated uplands are prime eagle nesting habitat and that eagle nesting densities and productivity were substantially higher prior to urbanization. This may be so. Unfortunately, no historical productivity data are available to substantiate this hypothesis. On the other hand, the data indicate that as long as nest sites are available, the eagles will occupy them and successfully produce young at rates similar to nests in non-urbanized areas. This would tend to indicate the limiting factor is the number of available nest sites (or territoriality) rather than food supplies or disturbance by human activities in the area. The FWS Southeast Alaska Eagle Management specialist feels there is no one limiting factor (Jacobson, unpubl. data). He suggests food supplies may be the key. If food is plentiful and trees are available for nesting, then the eagles will use the trees to nest.

Urban Eagles in Southeast Alaska -The Need for Case by Case Assessment

As demonstrated in the four cases discussed below, the Bald Eagle's tolerance of, or acclimation to, human disturbance in urban areas, at least in Southeast Alaska, can be quite high (Figure 2).

Stabler Point: This nest is located along biologically rich Auke Bay, near Juneau, Alaska. Prior to highway construction in the area, the nest tree was approximately 50 m from the top edge of a 20 m rock cliff. Following highway construction, the nest was less than 15 m from the edge of the cliff. Historically, the nest has been regularly productive.

Eagles successfully raised two young in the nest during the 1981 and 1982 nesting seasons when removal of the rock face through the use of explosives and general highway construction activities occurred.

Figure 2. Southeast Alaska

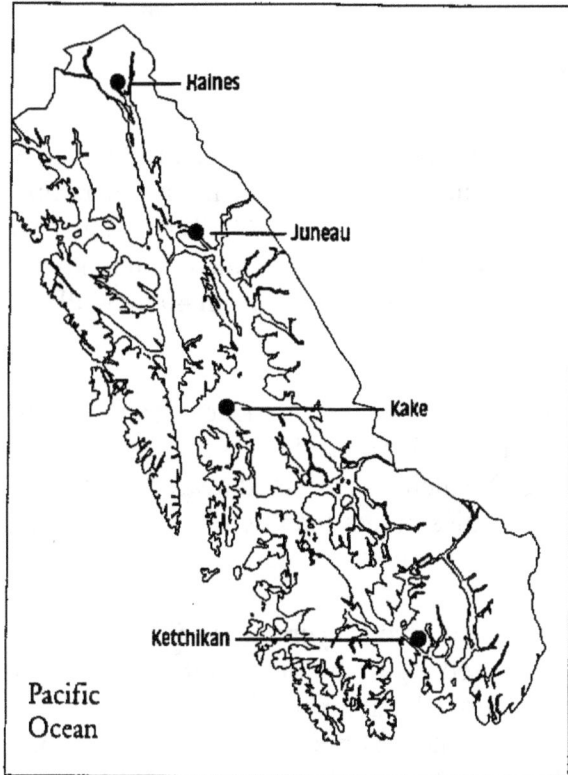

Recommendations in the ADOT&PF construction contract required blasting within 800 m and general construction activities within 100 m be suspended during the March 1 to April 30 nest selection period. If the eagles selected the nest, the restrictions would continue through August 31. If they did not select the nest by April 30, construction could resume.

In 1981, the contractor did not finish drilling and blasting by March 1 and asked for a three week extension. The FWS required blasting and construction to be monitored to prevent substantial disturbance of the nesting eagles. Fourteen rock blasts were monitored from March 3 through March 13, 1981. During these shots, eagles attending the nest flew nine times (64%) and did not fly five times (36%). Other reactions such as raising wings and staring in the direction of the blasts indicated some level of disturbance.

Construction noise levels measured at the base of the nest tree ranged from 40 to 50 dBA. Light planes flying nearby registered 55-65 dBA. Background noise levels ranged from 40-50 dBA. Aircraft overflights ranged from the mid-50 to 70 dBA range with peaks at 75 and 80 dBA.

At least seven shots occurred the next year from March 2 through March 17. Reactions of the nesting eagles were not monitored, nor were any noise measurements taken.

North Tongass: This project consisted of reconstructing the North Tongass Highway from the Ketchikan city limits to the Ward Cove bridge. One large area of rock blasting occurred in the Ward Cove Cannery area. Two eagle nests are located near the rock removal area, one at about 230 m distance and the other at about 500 m. Over the past several years, one or the other nest has been occupied, however, during the 1988 blasting period, both nests were occupied (Jacobson, unpubl. data). At least one young was fledged at each site.

In March 1988, ambient noise levels, mainly due to aircraft traffic, were measured twice at the nest nearest the blast area. Noise levels from 18 aircraft were measured during one hour on the first day and from eight aircraft during one hour on the second day. Noise levels generated by these aircraft generally ranged from the mid-50 to mid-60 dBA range. Two helicopter flyovers registered 65-67 and 75-76 dBA. The loudest noise levels were produced by two DeHavilland Beaver aircraft, 78 dBA and 94 dBA. General highway traffic noise averaged in the 40-50 dBA range with highs in the 50-60 dBA range. Two rock blasts were monitored at a point 60 m closer to the blast from the nest site. One registered 54 dBA and the other less than 50 dBA.

At the nest farther from the blast area, ambient noise levels were monitored for only one one-hour period and no blasts were monitored. Again, aircraft were the main generators of noise, with 10 overflights. Half of the aircraft registered in the 50-60 dBA range. Two helicopters measured 63-66 dBA, two Beavers registered 60-67 dBA and one unknown aircraft registered 70-72 dBA. General highway traffic noise ranged from 40 to 50 dBA. This site was noticeably quieter.

Both nests are well within the 800 m buffer zone for blasting recommended by the FWS. Blasting and removal of the first lift of rock occurred prior to eagle nest selection. Succeeding blasts were below the edge of the cliff which was oriented away from the eagle nests. The blasts were small, generated velocities of less than two feet per second at 30 m distance and occurred on a regular basis, usually 10:00 a.m. daily.

Fred Meyers: This nest is located to the north behind Fred Meyers. It is 15-20 m from the Old Glacier Highway in Juneau and has been used regularly for a number of years. In 1988, firewood logging occurred throughout the nest selection period. Some trees within 10 m were felled. General noise levels at the base of the nest tree were monitored in mid June during a one-hour period from 3:00 to 4:00 p.m. General highway noise from the Egan Expressway (approximately 400 m distant) ranged from mid-50's to low-60's dBA. Peak vehicle noises and light planes at the Juneau International Airport averaged 68 dBA. Nineteen sight-seeing helicopter overflights averaged 78 dBA. The helicopter flights most likely started in mid-May with the beginning of the tour boat season. This would have followed nest selection and probably hatching. Also in mid June, a bulldozer was used to grade the vacant lot across the Glacier Highway at about 75-100 m from the nest. FWS personnel on a helicopter survey, July 27, 1988, found two young in the nest. On August 31, 1988 one fledged young was seen perched near the nest.

Kake: This nest is located adjacent Keku Road about 1.5 km south of Kake and just north of the Alaska Marine Ferry Terminal. No noise or other disturbance data are available for this nest which has been regularly active over the last several years. The nest tree is located approximately 30 meters from the centerline of Keku Road, 30 m from the communities' diesel-fueled power generating and transformer station, 40 m from an active fuel tank farm, 10 m from fuel supply lines, 60 m from a service station, 70 m from a heavy equipment maintenance station, 75 m from a new port facility, 45 m from an operating cannery and 170-330 m from an intermittently used rock quarry. All of these facilities are in plain view of the eagle nest. Also, heavy equipment from road graders to logging trucks frequently traverse the road.

The conclusions of the following study probably apply to all raptors, including Bald Eagles and the mandates of the Bald Eagle Protection Act. The work deals with a study of the protection of Peregrine Falcons from disturbance under the Endangered Species Act of 1973 (Amaral 1982) based on a review of the literature and the results of a questionnaire the FWS sent out to biologists who have worked closely with the peregrine and other raptors in Alaska.

Citing several cases documenting the variability of reactions among individual peregrines to human disturbance, Amaral concludes, "it is extremely difficult to draw upon observations of individual birds or pairs to make inferences about the sensitivity or behavior of an entire population or species." This same variability of peregrines to a particular response "poses something of a dilemma to (any) attempt to develop protection measures."

The author acknowledges that the current recommended restrictions on human activities near peregrine aeries "are not inviolable." They are intended to aid responsible agencies as to whether proposed activities may affect the peregrine. When a proposed action might violate any of the restrictions, the initiator of the action "must enter into consultation with (the FWS) to examine in detail the proposed activity and its effect on" the peregrine. This type of "biological assessment" is required under Section 7 of the Endangered Species Act.

Two pertinent responses quoted from the review of the questionnaire are:
1. "All respondents affirmed that the distance at which restrictions should apply should depend on the nature of the activity, time during the breeding season and local topography. The desirability of a case-by-case review was expressed."

2. "All respondents agreed that human activities should be restricted near nest sites. Approximately 50% of (the) biologists who answered the question qualified their answers, stating that the nature of the intrusion, distance from eyrie and presence of intervening topography should be considered and that human activity need not be restricted in all cases."

Researchers in Minnesota (Fraser et al. 1985) concluded, "Not only are individual eagles likely to differ in their response to disturbance, but the same eagles may respond differently at different times..." Because this tolerance to human disturbance can vary among populations, they strongly recommended that "buffer zones be based on data from each managed population and, to the extent possible, from observations of specific pairs of eagles." This supports the concept for creating management plans for individual pairs of nesting eagles (Mathisen et al. 1977). Several other researchers agreed that guidelines need to be developed on a case-by-case basis (Ambrose, Grubb, Schempf and Ritchie, unpubl. data).

The general application of the FWS guidelines (800 m for blasting and 100 m for general construction during nest selection and nesting) in urban areas certainly may not always be appropriate. Case by case analysis in FHWA project development procedures should expedite needed public works projects and save money, yet adequately maintain nesting viability of Bald Eagles in urban areas. However, case by case analyses will have to be based on field research, particularly activity (time) budget studies tailored to specific Bald Eagle nesting situations.

A researcher is about to collect data on these two urban eaglets. Photo by Scott Gende.

Proposed Research
Proposed research consists of two approaches:

1. Analyze existing nest location and productivity data for the Juneau road system collected by the FWS over the last 3-4 years.

2. Design and implement an activity (time) budget study similar to Bald Eagle work on Admiralty Island (Cain 1985). Personnel from ADOT&PF and the staff of the Raptor Management Studies program of the FWS in Juneau should participate in the design and review of both projects. This cooperation is encouraged by the Federal Fish and Wildlife

Coordination Act. However, the actual design, field work where required, analysis and report writing should be undertaken by a third party acceptable to both agencies.

Analysis of the existing nest and productivity data is needed to determine the general impacts of human disturbance (including construction and existence of highways) on nesting Bald Eagles. While these data were collected adjacent to the Juneau road system, they are probably representative of other urban areas in Southeast Alaska. Results of this work will most likely influence the design of the more complex activity (time) budget study.

Analysis of the existing FWS file data would parallel recent work on Oregon Bald Eagles (Anthony and Isaacs 1989). While this study concentrated on "non-urban" eagles, the factors measured and analytical techniques used should be applicable to the Juneau roadside data. Particular measures of disturbance for the proposed analysis of the Juneau data include existence of a highway between the nest tree and beach, distance to road, distance to nearest structure, distance to commercial development, plus some level of disturbance and/or habitat quality. Nest characteristics and annual productivity factors to be tested include tree species, depth of forested area adjacent nests, nest condition, tree height, height of nest, distance to waterfront, elevation, number of years occupied, number of years productive and number of young produced. Statistical analysis will be based mainly on multiple regression of the productivity and nest site factors versus the potential disturbance factors.

Following completion of this general study, the next logical step in gaining a better understanding of the potential impacts of human-induced disturbance on eagles in the urban environment would be to repeat work similar to the energy (time) budget study of nesting eagles on Admiralty Island (Cain 1985). Quantifiable disturbance factors must be added. The first task would be to measure the existing disturbance factors and activity (time) budgets of eagles which successfully nest in an urban situation adjacent to a proposed highway project corridor. Activity (time) budgets should then be quantified during construction of the project. Comparison of these two activity budgets would indicate the significance of the construction impacts on the nesting birds. Results from this type of work would be biologically credible and a great help in determining what types of disturbance, at what levels, may impact Bald Eagle nesting success. It would also help mold a working biological definition of disturbance and set the criteria for evaluation of individual nest sites on a case by case basis.

Recommended Approach
The following procedure for assessment of potential disturbance of nesting Bald Eagles on a case by case basis and incorporation of needed stipulations in design and construction projects is recommended.

1. In consultation with the FWS, assess known eagle nests during the reconnaissance and location phase which lasts one to two years. Measure ambient conditions, particularly human disturbance in relation to the nesting sequence. Evaluate potential disturbance of nesting eagles by proposed construction techniques, including affects on wind firmness of

nesting trees. Consider use of habituation to acclimate the birds to minimize impacts of construction. Include required/recommended procedures in the project environmental document.

2. Incorporate required/recommended procedures into the design phase of the project. Initiate habituation, if necessary, at this time. Identify potential construction disturbances which may significantly alter nesting behavior, thereby halting construction.

3. Clearly list, in the project bid documents, any limitations on construction procedures or timing (as determined in 1 and 2 above). Clearly state conditions under which field monitoring may be required. List any known conditions under which work will or can be modified, curtailed, or rescheduled.

4. During construction, perform field monitoring (using a trained observer) to assure contractor compliance with stipulations as spelled out in contract bid documents. Where necessary, monitor eagles to track those situations which might require project alteration or shutdown.

5. Summarize field data and notes in a project construction monitoring report. The report should assess the project construction guidelines to minimize disturbance as stipulated in the bid documents and how they were implemented during construction. This report should include recommended changes or improvements for future projects. A copy should be sent to the FWS for their review and comment.

6. Monitor nest use and productivity in succeeding years to confirm the level of construction impacts. Without banding, nest site tenacity is an unknown. However, assuming nest sites are the limiting factor in urban areas, continued use of the site following construction may indicate no appreciable impacts from construction activities.

Conclusions

Protecting nesting Bald Eagles near highway construction projects is not always a simple matter of merely applying the buffer zones and timing constraints as recommended by the FWS. The 100 m buffer zone for general construction, 800 m buffer zone for blasting and the timing restriction of March through August for active nests are often too restrictive. This is particularly true for eagles nesting in urban areas. In Southeast Alaska, the March through August closure is three-fourths of the average construction season. Unnecessary restrictions on construction timing or techniques can significantly increase project costs. An array of variables including food supplies, satisfactory nest sites and innate and learned behavior of individual birds can greatly affect nest site tenacity of any given pair of Bald Eagles. The greater the nest site tenacity, the less potential disturbance due to construction activities. To address this variability, each nesting pair must be addressed on a case by case basis. As demonstrated in the case studies presented in this paper, construction can often proceed within the FWS recommended buffer zones and timing restriction.

A systematic methodology to assess nesting eagles on a case by case basis should be developed in consultation with the FWS. This approach to maintaining long-term productivity of eagle nests adjacent urban construction projects should show good faith intent to abide by the mandates of the Bald Eagle Protection Act. Addressing the potential construction impacts on nesting Bald Eagles and prescribing mitigation measures in the project NEPA document, plus implementing the agreed to stipulations to prevent disturbance during construction should also avoid legal action.

Incorporation of realistic, enforceable stipulations in project environmental and construction bid documents in a timely manner is necessary. It would allow the maximum flexibility necessary to schedule highway projects to minimize design and construction costs.

Acknowledgements

I would like to thank Skip Ambrose, Mike Jacobson and Phil Schempf of the U.S. Fish and Wildlife Service; Bob Ritchie of Alaska Biological Research; Art Dunn, Mike McKinnon and Van Sundberg of the Alaska Department of Transportation and Public Facilities; and Irv Lloyd of the Federal Highway Administration for their ideas and helpful criticism. Without Vanda Randolph's patience and proficient typing, preparation of this report would have been a headache. Funding for this project was made available through the Federal Highway Administration.

Literature Cited

Amaral, M. 1982, Recommended restrictions for protection of Peregrine Falcons in Alaska. Pages 217-233. In: W. N. Ladd and P F. Schempf, eds. Raptor management and biology in Alaska and western Canada. U.S. Fish Wildl. Serv., FWS/AK,'PROC-82. Anchorage, Alas. 335pp.

Anthony, R. G. and F. B. Isaacs. 1989. Characteristics of Bald Eagle nest sites in Oregon. J. Wildl. Manage. 53(1):148-159.

Bangs, E. E., T. N. Bailey and V. D. Berns. 1987. Ecology of nesting Bald Eagles on the Kenai National Wildlife Refuge, Alaska. Pages 47-54. In: W. N. Ladd and P. F. Schempf, eds. Raptor management and biology in Alaska and western Canada. U.S. Fish Wildl. Serv., FWS/AK/PROC-82. Anchorage, Alas. 335pp.

Cain, S. L. 1985. Nesting activity time budgets of Bald Eagles in Southeast Alaska. M. S. Thesis, Univ. Montana, Missoula. 47pp.

Corr, P. O. 1974. Bald Eagle (*Haliaeetus leucocephalus* alascanus) nesting related to forestry in southeastern Alaska. M. S. Thesis, Univ. Alaska, Fairbanks, 144pp.

Fraser, J. D., L. D. Frenzel and J. E. Mathisen. 1985. The impact of human activities on breeding Bald Eagles in north-central Minnesota. J. Wildl. Manage. 49(3):585-592.

Garcelon, D. K., T. G. Grubb and S. Porter. 1988. Video surveillance systems for monitoring nesting raptors. Paper presented at the 1988 Annual Meeting, Raptor Res. Found., Inc., Minneapolis, Minn.

Hayes, R. and D. H. Mossop. 1982. The recovery of an interior Peregrine Falcon population in the northern Yukon Territory. Pages 234-243. In: W. N. Ladd and P. F. Schempf, eds. Raptor management and biology in Alaska and western Canada. U.S. Fish and Wildl. Serv., FWS/AK/PROC-82. Anchorage, Alas. 335pp.

Hodges, J. I. 1982a. Bald eagle nesting studies in Seymour Canal, Southeast Alaska. Condor 84:125-127.

Hodges, J. I. 1982b. Evaluation of the 100 meter protective zone for Bald Eagle nests in Southeast Alaska. Unpubl. rep., U.S. Fish Wildl. Serv., Juneau, Alas. 11 pp.

Hodges, J. I., J. G. King and F. C. Robards. 1979. Resurgence of the Bald Eagle breeding population of southeast Alaska. J. Wildl. Manage. 43: 219-221.

Jacobson, M. J. 1987. The capture of Alaskan Bald Eagles for translocation to other states and related productivity studies-1987 Unpubl. rep., U.S. Fish Wildl. Serv., Juneau, Alas. l2pp.

Jueneman, B. G. and L. D. Frenzel. 1972. Habitat evaluations of selected Bald Eagle nest sites in the Chippewa National Forest. Trans. 34th Am. Midwest Fish Wildl. Conf., Des Moines, Ia. 4pp.

King, J. G., F. C. Robards and C. J. Lensink. 1972. Census of the Bald Eagle breeding population in Southeast Alaska. J. Wildl. Manage. 36(4):1292-1295.

Lincer, J. L., W. Clark and M. N. France, Jr. 1978. Working bibliography of the Bald Eagle. Raptor Information Center. Nat'l. Wildl. Fed., Washington, D.C.

Mathisen, J. E. 1968. Effects of human disturbance on nesting Bald Eagles. J. Wildl. Manage. 32(1):1-6.

Mathisen, J. E., D. E. Sorenson, L. D. Frenzel and T. C. Dunstan. 1977. Management strategy for Bald Eagles. Trans. North Am. Wildl. and Nat. Res. Conf. 42:86-92.

McCollough, M. A. 1986. The post-fledging ecology and population dynamics of Bald Eagles in Maine. Ph.D. Thesis, Univ. Maine, Orono. 132pp.

Murphy, J. R. 1965. Nest site selection of the Bald Eagle in Yellowstone National Park. Proc. Utah Acad. Sci., Arts and Letters 42:261-264.

Musselman, T. E. 1949. Concentrations of Bald Eagles on the Mississippi River at Hamilton, IL. Auk 66:83.

Retfalvi, L. I. 1965. Breeding behavior and feeding habits of the Bald Eagle (*Haliaeetus leucocephalus*) on San Juan Island, Washington. M.S. Thesis, Univ. B.C., Vancouver.

Ritchie, R. J. 1987. Response of adult Peregrine Falcons to experimental and other disturbances along the Trans-Alaska Pipeline System, Sagavanirktok River, Alaska, 1985, 1986. Unpub. rep., Alas. Biol. Res., Inc., Fairbanks, Alas. 92pp.

Schempf, P. F. 1982. U.S. Fish and Wildlife Service involvement with raptors in Alaska. Pages 12-18. In: W. N. Ladd and P. F. Schempf, eds. Raptor management and biology in Alaska and western Canada. U.S. Fish and Wildl. Serv., FWS/AK/PROC-82. Anchorage, Alas. 335pp.

Sherrod, S. K., C. M. White and F. S. L. Williamson. 1976. Biology of the Bald Eagle on Amchitka Island, Alaska. Living Bird 15:143-182.

Sidle, W. B., L. H. Suring and J. L. Hodges, Jr. 1986. The Bald Eagle in Southeast Alaska. Wildl. Fish. Habitat Manage. Notes, No. 11, U.S. Dept. Agric., For. Serv., Alas. Reg., Juneau, Alas. 29pp.

Snow, C. 1973. Habitat management series for endangered species. Report No. 5: Southern and northern Bald Eagle. Bur. Land Manage. 58pp.

Stalmaster M. V., R. L. Knight, B. L. Holder and R. J. Anderson. 1985. Bald Eagles. Pages 269-290 In: E. R. Brown (Tech. ed.) Management of wildlife and fish habitat in forests of Western Oregon and Washington. Part I - Ch. Narratives, U.S. Dept. Agric., For. Serv., Pub. No. R6-F&WL 192-1985. Portland,

Oreg. 332pp.

U.S. Army Corps of Engineers. 1979. The northern Bald Eagle (*Haliaeetus leucocephalus* alascanus). A literature survey. U.S. Army Corps of Engineers, Seattle, Wash. 86 pp.

Weekes, F. M. 1974. A survey of Bald Eagle nesting attempts in southern Ontario, 1969-73. Can. Field-Nat. 88:415-419.

White, C. M. and T. L. Thurow. 1985. Reproduction of Ferruginous Hawks exposed to controlled disturbance. Condor 87:14-12.

Unpublished Data
Ambrose, R. E. USFWS, Cain, S. L. National Park Service, Grubb, T. G. U.S. Forest Service Exp. Station, Jacobson, M. J. USFWS, Lincer, J. L. Eco-Analysts, Inc., Mathisen, J. E. Chippewa National Forest, Ritchie, R. J. AK. Biol. Research, Inc. and Schempf, P. F. USFWS.

Habitat Structure of Bald Eagle Nest Sites and Management Zones near Juneau, Alaska

M. Hildegard Reiser and James P. Ward, Jr.

Rocky Mountain Experiment Station, Flagstaff, AZ

Knowing how much space and what kinds of forest habitat Bald Eagles need is crucial to making effective decisions about resource management. This study, conducted near Juneau, Alaska, examines specific characteristics of Bald Eagle nest trees, forest structure around the nest tree and forest structure within both the current management zone and a larger area beyond the management zone.

As urban and wild lands come into increasingly closer contact and as demands on wildlife and other natural resources increase, effective and sound ecological management of these resources becomes more critical. This is particularly true in Southeast Alaska where timber harvesting and coastal development continue to threaten Bald Eagle (*Haliaeetus leucocephalus*) populations. No longer can we simply rely upon the vast acreage of Alaska to ensure minimal impacts on North America's largest population of Bald Eagles (King et al. 1972, Hodges et al. 1979). Current minimal standards and guidelines may protect against direct human disturbances to nesting Bald Eagles, but these measures may be insufficient to maintain a healthy landscape, which is necessary for ensuring the existence of future populations (Connor 1979, Sidle et al. 1990). Thus, sound management solutions are currently needed for maintaining eagle populations in Southeast Alaska.

Quantitative descriptions of habitat used by Bald Eagles are a prerequisite to establishing effective management strategies. Although general habitat descriptions are reported for active Bald Eagle nests in Southeast Alaska (Hodges and Robards 1982, Sidle et al. 1990), quantitative descriptions of habitat around nest sites used by Bald Eagles are not available.

The purpose of this study is to provide an additional understanding of area requirements and characteristics of the habitat used by Bald Eagles for nesting and perching in the vicinity of Juneau, Alaska. In this paper we:
1) quantify and compare characteristics of specific trees eagles used for nesting and perching and

2) quantify and compare characteristics of habitat found,

    a) immediately around nest trees,

    b) within a 100 m radius management zone around nests (currently proposed by the USDA Forest Service for protecting eagle nest sites) and

    c) outside the management zone but within a 0.5 km area potentially used by eagles during the breeding period.

Study Area

We studied Bald Eagle habitat use around North Douglas Island, Mendenhall Peninsula and various small islands located in Auke Bay and Fritz Cove in Southeast Alaska (Figure 1). Western hemlock (*Tsuga heterophylla*) and Sitka spruce (*Picea sitchensis*) dominated the overstory in this coastal temperate rainforest. The understory trees, particularly along coastal shorelines, consisted of Sitka alder (*Alnus crispa* sinuata), willow thickets (*Salix* spp.) and occasionally black cottonwood (*Populus balsamifera* trichocarpa).

Human activity was evident on the study area. Public road use, air transport and residential development occurred on the mainland and on north Douglas Island. The islands were less developed, although we observed trail use along the shorelines. Boating, primarily for fishing, was a frequent activity within coastal waterways of the study area.

Most of the habitat used by the eagles was on lands currently administered by the Tongass National Forest or recently transferred to state or city jurisdiction. Some nest (8 of 23) and perch (14 of 33) sites that we examined were located on privately owned lands.

Figure 1. General location of the Auke Bay/Fritz Cove study area near Juneau, Alaska.

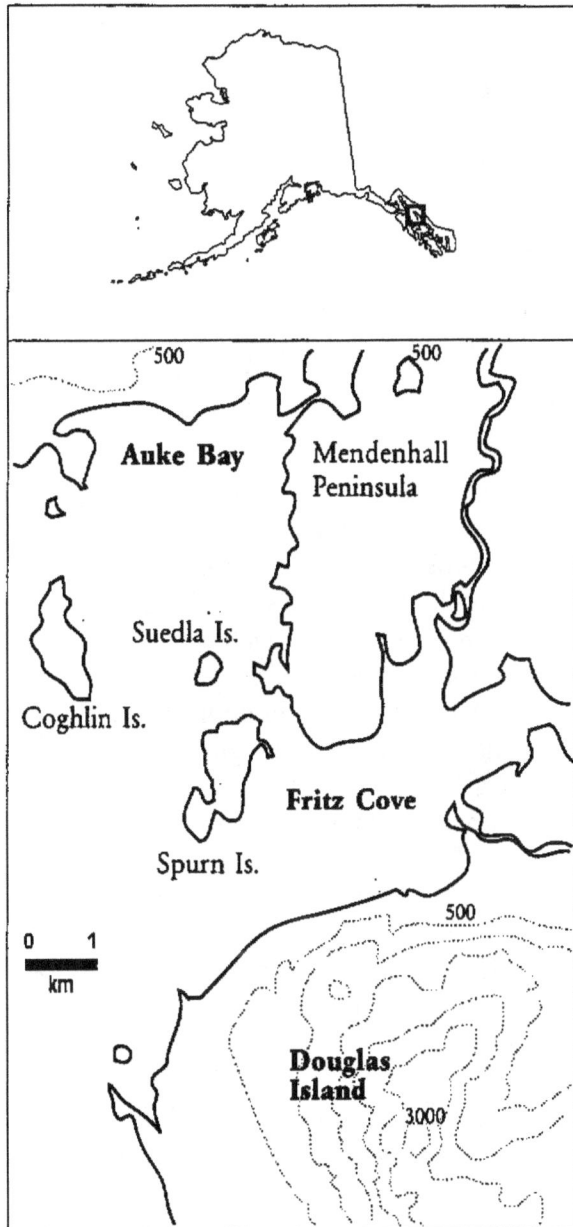

Methods

We characterized areas used by Bald Eagles for nesting by sampling and quantifying habitat within a series of systematic plots (0.05 ha). These plots were placed at and around trees used by eagles (Figure 2). In addition to sampling used habitat, we sampled randomly selected trees and plots in order to quantify any features that eagles may have selected within their domain.

Microhabitat and macrohabitat were sampled at 23 Bald Eagle nests randomly selected from a set of 66 nests previously located by the U.S. Fish and Wildlife Service during 1971 to 1989. We also sampled the microhabitat at 33 perch sites, randomly selected from 190 observations gathered during this study and 17 trees not used for nesting, but similar in diameter to nest trees and found within 15 m of known nests. Because sampling effort was constrained by available resources, we were not able to examine all of the nests and perches known to us. Though we allocated effort for sampling 23 non-nest trees, we could not find trees that met our "non-nest" criteria at six sites.

The purpose of microhabitat sampling was to characterize nest, perch and non-nest trees used by Bald Eagles. We report here on six variables describing tree structure and composition including: 1) tree species, 2) tree crown category, 3) tree height, 4) tree diameter, 5) elevation at the tree's base and 6) overhead canopy closure at the tree (Figure 2A).

Figure 2A-2C. Configuration of plots used to sample habitat characteristics near Bald Eagle nests.

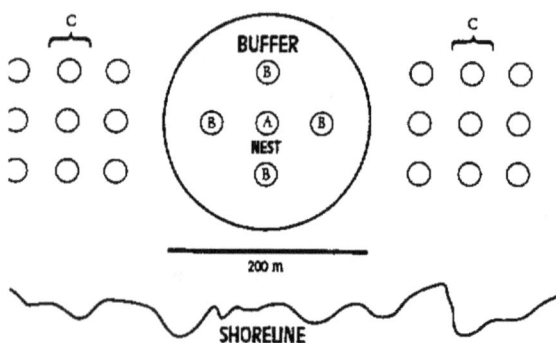

Tree species and a tree crown category (normal slender, broken top live, unbroken top dead, deformed top, or double top; Hodges and Robards 1982) were recorded for each nest, perch and non-nest tree. Tree height (in m) was measured using a clinometer. Tree diameter at breast height (DBH, in cm) was measured with a steel tape. The elevation (in m) of the tree base above sea level was measured using an altimeter or taken from a topographic map. Overhead canopy closure (in %) was estimated as an average of 4 ocular tube readings taken from each of 4 stations (16 total readings). Stations were located at the base of each tree along 2 perpendicular axes radiating through the center of the nest tree with the first axis established parallel to the main shore closest to the tree.

We sampled macrohabitat in order to describe forest stand characteristics within and outside of a 100 m management zone proposed by the Forest Service. Macrohabitat sampling was conducted at 5 plots within the circular management zone (Figure 2B), including 1 plot centered at a Bald Eagle nest tree (Figure 2A) (after B. Noon et al., pers. comm.) and within 4 plots randomly selected from a grid of possible plots situated outside of the management zone but within a 0.5 km area considered to represent habitat used by nesting eagles (Hodges and Robards 1982, Figure 2C). This configuration formed a 200 m x 500 m sampling area which was oriented along the shoreline.

Within each plot, we tallied: 1) the number of trees by species, 2) estimated live tree density and basal area for 3 diameter classes (1 to 30 cm, > 31 to 45 cm and > 46 cm) using the point-quarter method (Brower and Zar 1984) and 3) estimated overhead canopy closure (in %) using an average of 4 ocular tube readings taken from stations placed 12.5 m from the plot center along the plot axes. Plot axes were defined in the same manner as described above.

Micro- and macrohabitat features were quantified using standard descriptive statistics. Univariate statistical methods were used to quantify differences in habitat features among sampling regimes (i.e., among tree types or among nest sites and management zones). Statistical tests were considered significant at the 5% level.

Results and Discussion
Tree Characteristics
Selection of nest tree species varies over the geographic range of the Bald Eagle. Bald Eagles in the Juneau vicinity appeared to select western hemlock ($x^2 = 4.14$, df =1, p = 0.042; Figure 3). Eagles used western hemlock significantly more for nesting than for perching ($x^2 = 9.07$, df = 1, p = 0.003; Figure 3). Hodges and Robards (1982) found only 20% (n = 776) of eagle nests in western hemlock in Southeast Alaska; however, relative density of tree species was not available from their study for evaluating tree availability. In coastal areas of the Pacific Northwest, Douglas fir (*Pseudotsuga menziesii*) and Sitka spruce were predominantly used for nesting (Anthony et al. 1982, Stalmaster et al. 1985). Low use of Sitka spruce may be a reflection of past logging practices. Many of the large Sitka spruce had been logged from the islands located in our study area by the early 1900's (Rakestraw 1981).

With the exception of crown top conditions, structural characteristics of Bald Eagle nest trees were similar to previously reported descriptions (Anthony et al. 1982, Stalmaster et al. 1985, Wood et al. 1989). Crown conditions of nest trees were significantly different from perch tree crowns ($x^2 = 14.80$, df= 6, p = 0.022), but not significantly different from non-nest tree crowns ($x^2 = 9.16$, df = 5, p = 0.10) in our study area (Figure 4). Most nests were located in trees with normal, bushy crowns (40%, n = 9; Figure 4). Bushy crowns may protect the nestlings from the rain and solar radiation. Both perch and non-nest tree crowns were predominantly normal, slender crowned (Figure 4). Crown conditions of eagle nest trees near Juneau differ from those in other geographic areas. The low proportion of trees with broken or dead tops (17%) was dissimilar to the nest tree crown conditions found by Hodges and Robards (1982, 38%) in Alaska, or Grubb (1976, 48%) in Washington.

Nest trees tended to be a dominant or co-dominant tree in the surrounding stand. Nest tree heights (=30.0 m) were significantly taller than perch trees ($x^2 = 24.9$ m; t = 2.49, df = 54, p = 0.016), while nest trees were found at significantly higher elevations ($x^2 = 11.6$ m) relative to perch trees ($x^2 = 4.1$ m; t = 3.47, df = 49, p = 0.001; Figures 5 and 6). Bald

Eagle nest trees had greater, but not significantly different, diameters than non-nest and perch trees (Figure 7). Overhead canopy cover at non-nest, nest and perch trees was similar (Figures 8 and 9).

Figure 3. Tree species used by Bald Eagles on randomly selected sites near Juneau, Alaska. SISP=Sitka spruce, WEHE=western hemlock, and BLCO=black cottonwood. Sample sizes are in parentheses.

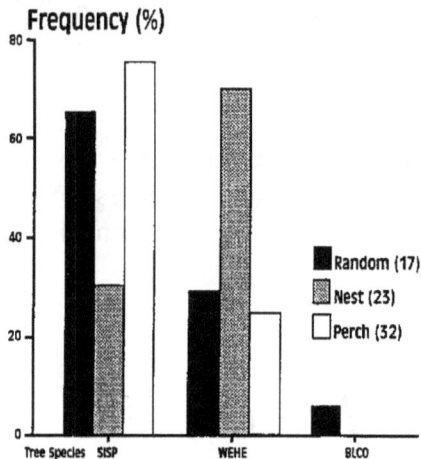

Figure 4. Crown condition of trees used by Bald Eagles near Juneau, Alaska. Sample sizes are in parentheses.

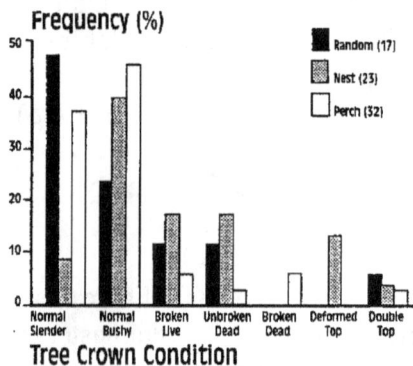

Plot Characteristics

The number of western hemlock per plot was significantly different at the nest, inside and outside of the management zone (Kruskal-Wallace H =12.24, n = 23, 56, 72 plots, respectively, p = 0.002; Table 1). Fewer western hemlock were found near nest trees, an increasing number were counted within the management zone and even more were found outside the management zone. Sitka spruce exhibited the opposite trend, but this trend was not statistically significant. The density of all trees around eagle nests in the Juneau vicinity (498 trees/ha; Table 2) was greater than densities recorded in other geographic areas (e.g., 109 to 166 trees/ha throughout the Pacific Northwest; Anthony, et al. 1982). The coastal areas around the Juneau area were heavily logged since European settlement in 1880 (Rakestraw 1981). Thus, in this dense secondary growth forest, the eagles may be selecting the least dense stands to nest within, or eagles may be selecting large residual trees in patches of forest where the growth of smaller trees is limited (by shading and nutrient competition). Whether or not the eagles are exhibiting a real preference for sparser stands is not clear.

Basal areas of pole sized trees, saw timber sized trees and trees of similar size (DBH) to nest trees, were lower immediately around Bald Eagle nests than in stands within and outside the 100 m management zone (Table 3). However, this difference was not statistically significant. Basal area for all tree sizes (79.6 m²/ha) was slightly greater than those recorded from other areas in the Pacific Northwest 57.9 m²/ha to 70.9 m²/ha (Anthony et al. 1982). Overhead canopy closure was similar at Bald Eagle nests, inside and outside of the management zone (Figure 8).

Table 1. Number of trees (± s.e.) at and around Bald Eagle nests near Juneau, Alaska, summer 1989. Sample size signifies number of plots used to estimate the mean.

Tree species	Nest (n=23)	Number of trees In buffer (n=56)	Outside buffer (n=72)
Sitka spruce	5.9 (1.32)	5.2 (0.60)	4.8 (0.43)
Western hemlock	10.0 (1.89)	13.2 (1.13)	15.4 (0.98)*

*Indicates a significant difference among the 3 plot types for the 2 tree species.

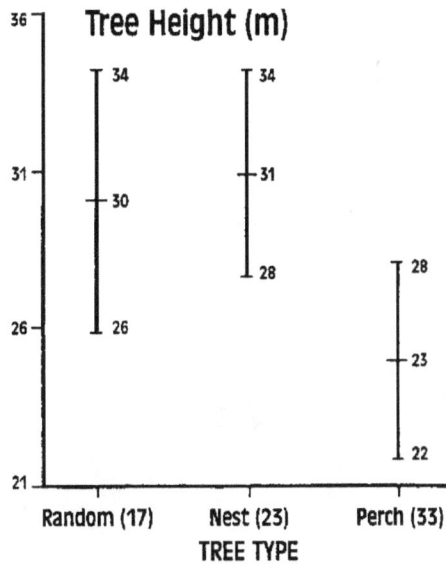

Figure 5. Heights of non–nest (random), nest, and perch trees (m) (mean ± 95% C.I.) used by Bald Eagles near Juneau, Alaska. Nest trees were significantly taller than perch trees (p=0.016, t=2.49, df=54). Sample sizes are in parentheses.

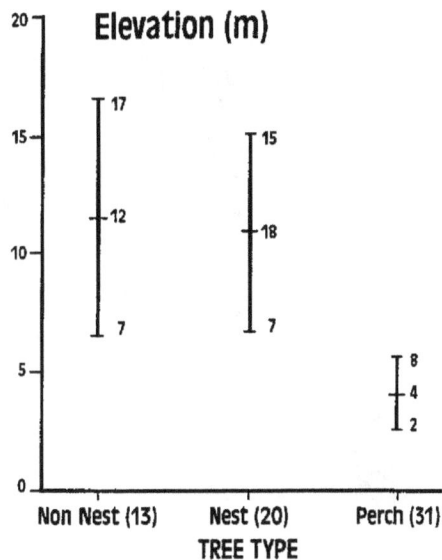

Figure 6. Elevation above sea level (m) (mean + 95% C.I.) of non–nest (random), nest, and perch trees used by Bald Eagles near Juneau, Alaska. Sample sizes given in parentheses.

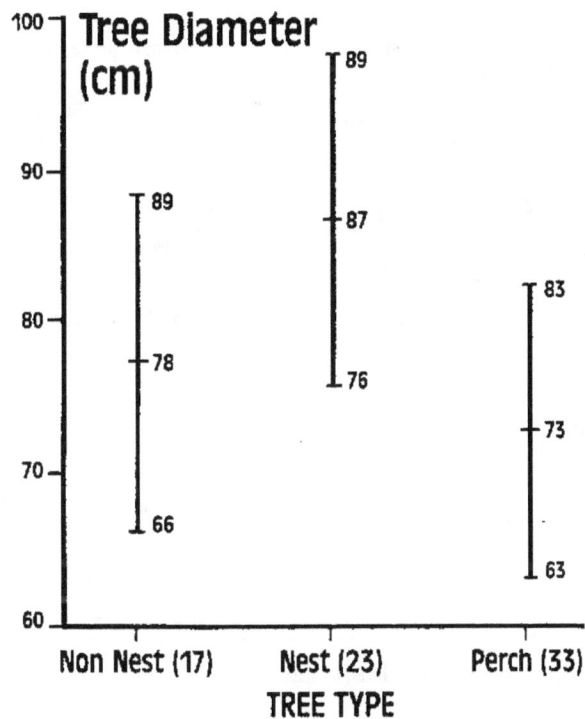

Figure 7. Tree diameter (cm) (mean + C.I.) of non–nest (random), nest, and perch trees used by Bald Eagles near Juneau, Alaska. Sample sizes given in parentheses.

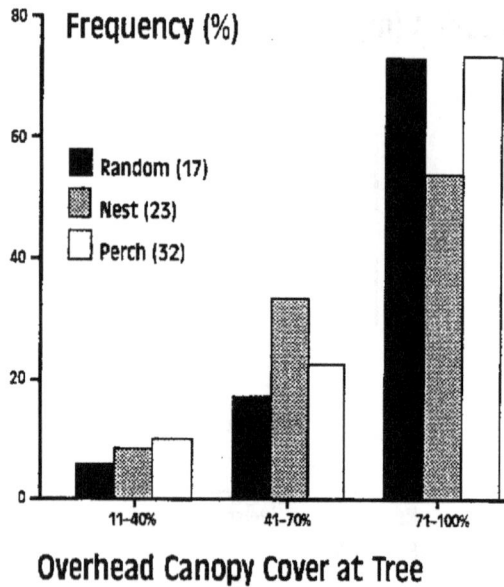

Figure 8. Overhead canopy cover at non-nest (random), nest, and perch trees near Juneau, Alaska. Sample sizes given in parentheses.

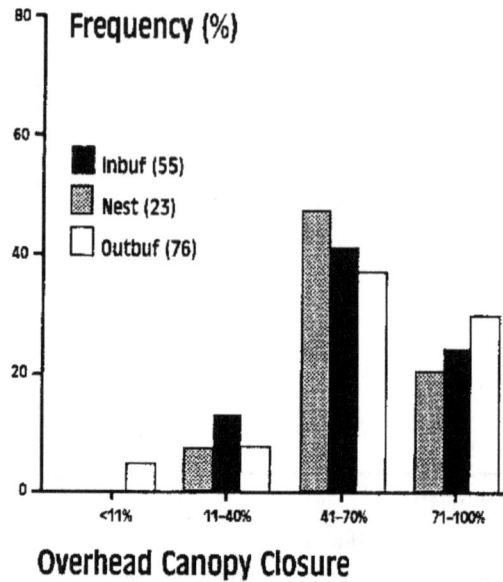

Figure 9. Overhead canopy cover at nest plots (nest), and plots within the 100 m radius management zone (inbuf), and outside of the 100 m management zone (outbuf), but within the 0.5 km x 0.2 km potential use area near Juneau, Alaska. Sample sizes given in parentheses.

Table 2. Tree density (± s.e.) at and around Bald Eagle nests in the vicinity of Juneau, Alaska, summer 1989. Standard errors are given in parenthises.

Tree size		Mean density (trees/ha)		
		Nest (n=23)	In buffer (n=56)	Outside buffer (n=72)
All sizes		326.0 (± 33.0)	497.6 (± 36.5)	468.7 (± 34.9)
Pole	(10–30.5 cm)	453.8 (± 94.7)	814.0 (± 112.7)	734.8* (± 93.3)
Saw timber	(> 30.5 cm)	294.3 (± 37.0)	396.2 (± 35.9)	398.9 (± 41.7)
Nest[1]	(> 46 cm)	292.2 (± 63.8)	374.1 (± 44.6)	346.8 (± 51.0)

* Indicates that the density of trees was significantly lower at the nest compared to the vicinity around the nest. (p = 0.035, F = 5.53, df = 2).
[1] Trees of similar diameter as trees used for nesting by Bald Eagles in the vicinity of Juneau, Alaska.

Table 3. Tree basal area (± s.e.) at and around Bald Eagle nests in the vicinity of Juneau, Alaska, summer 1989.

Tree size	Mean basal area (m²/ha)		
	Nest (n=23)	In buffer (n=56)	Outside buffer (n=72)
All sizes	47.9 (± 11.7)	79.6 (± 13.3)	67.0 (± 10.5)
Pole (10–30.5 cm)	13.6 (± 4.5)	23.6 (± 5.1)	19.8 (± 4.2)
Saw timber (> 30.5 cm)	73.6 (± 18.5)	103.0 (± 27.0)	104.1 (± 17.9)
Nest[1] (> 46 cm)	106.4 (± 38.1)	153.4 (± 31.7)	124.2 (± 27.0)

[1] Trees of similar diameter as trees used for nesting by Bald Eagles in the vicinity of Juneau, Alaska.

Management Implications

A regional landscape approach to raptor management has been used for Bald Eagles in the Pacific Northwest (Stalmaster, et al. 1985) and for accipiters in the eastern U.S. (Falk 1990). This concept is being considered for management of populations of the Northern Spotted Owl (*Strix occidentalis caurina*) in the Pacific Northwest (Thomas et al. 1990) and for Northern Goshawk (*Accipiter gentilis*) populations in southwestern U.S. (R.

Reynolds, pers. comm.).

In this approach, the goal is to create management zones that are large enough to maintain the benefits from fully functioning ecological units that are under consideration. For example, in Southeast Alaska, Bald Eagles are concentrated and probably dependent, on forested zones along the coast and fresh water tributaries with salmon runs. Thus, enough landscape should be provided to ensure the habitat needs for an adequate number of Bald Eagles to maintain the population through time.

Within a landscape, structural diversity operates at different scales depending on a species perception of its environment (Hunter 1987). In this study, we examined 4 "human-designated" scales of Bald Eagle habitat use: 1) specific characteristics of nest trees, 2) forest structure immediately around the nest tree, 3) forest structure within a currently utilized management zone and 4) forest structure around a larger use area beyond this zone suggested in the literature.

At the smallest scale of habitat use, Juneau area Bald Eagles seem to be choosing characteristic trees, an emergent or co-dominant tree within a stand, with a large diameter. This pattern has been observed elsewhere (Anthony et al. 1982, Stalmaster et al. 1985, Wood et al. 1989).

Bald Eagle adult and eaglet in Sitka spruce tree nest. Photo by Phil Schempf, USFWS.

At the second scale of habitat use, a spatial pattern emerged. The forest immediately around the nest was sparser than the surrounding forest. This may allow for easier observation of approaching intruders and provide easier access to the nest structure. The forest structure appears relatively uniform away from the nest tree. It is a multi-layered and dense forest. The denser forest stands around a nest site could provide screening from more distant disturbances and neighbors and provide some measure of protection from the wind. Trees situated in open conditions are subject to windthrow (P. Schempf, pers. comm.).

We did not notice any significant differences in forest structure between the third and fourth scale of habitat use, the two management zones. However, use of habitat by eagles at the fourth scale would include a greater number of perches, likely increasing the chance of foraging success.

We found that nests averaged 0.65 km apart along the shorelines in the Juneau vicinity. In a concurrent study (Reiser and Ward, in prep), radio-marked Bald Eagles utilized an area approximately 0.55 km wide by 1.25 km length of shoreline. This area is twice as large as the expanded management zone (the fourth scale of habitat use) that we examined. Thus, the scale of the landscape used to manage Bald Eagles in the Juneau vicinity and possibly Southeast Alaska should be expanded to ensure the habitat needs of this species.

Other components to consider in a habitat management strategy for the Bald Eagle include the distribution of perch trees and the distance of perch sites to the nest trees (Reiser and Ward, in prep). Moreover, the availability of prey may influence perch site selection, requiring additional adjustments in the size and placement of management zones. Finally, the reproductive history of each eagle nest site should be evaluated in relation to habitat structure and prey availability to provide information for linking habitat and population management.

Acknowledgements

We wish to thank P. Schempf, M. Jacobson and B. Conant, U.S. Fish and Wildlife Service and A. Doyle, U.S. Geological. of Agriculture, Forest Service, for their valuable input and support of this project. We also gratefully acknowledge the logistical support and general assistance provided by C. Johnson, S. Gilbertson and B. Grochow, the City of Juneau Land and Parks and Recreation Offices. This work would not have been possible without the labor and devotion of C. Blair, intern and the many School for Field Studies (SFS) students, who collected data as part of a Bald Eagle Ecology course during the summer 1989. Financial support of this project was provided by the SFS, Beverly, Massachusetts.

Literature Cited

Anthony, R. G., R. L. Knight, G. T. Allen, B. R. McClelland and J. I. Hodges. 1982. Habitat use by nesting and roosting Bald Eagles in the Pacific Northwest. Trans. North Am. Wildl. Nat. Resourc. Conf. 47:332-342.

Brower, J. E. and J. H. Zar. 1984. Field and laboratory methods for general ecology (2nd ed.). Wm. C. Brown Publ., Dubuque, Ia. 226pp.

Connor, R. N. 1979. Minimum standards and forest wildlife management. Wildl. Soc. Bull. 7:293-296.

Falk, J. A. 1990. Landscape level raptor habitat associations in northwest Connecticut. M.S. Thesis, Virginia Polytech. Inst. State Univ., Blacksburg. 116pp.

Grubb, T. G. 1976. A survey and analysis of Bald Eagle nesting in western Washington. M.S. Thesis, Univ. Washington, Seattle. 87pp.

Hodges, J. I. and F. C. Robards. 1982. Observations of 3,850 Bald Eagle nests in Southeast Alaska. Pages 37-46. In: W. N. Ladd and P F. Schempf, eds. Proc. of a symposium and workshop on raptor management and biology in Alaska and Western Canada, 17-20 February 1981, Anchorage, Alas. U.S. Dept. Inter., Fish Wildl. Serv., Anchorage, Alas. 335pp.

Hodges, J. I., J. G. King and F. C. Robards. 1979. Resurvey of the Bald Eagle breeding population in Southeast Alaska. J. Wildl. Manage. 43:219-224.

Hunter, M. L., Jr. 1987. Managing forests for spatial heterogeneity to maintain biological diversity. Trans. North Am. Wildl. Nat. Resour. Conf. 52:60-69.

King, J. G., F. C. Robards and C. J. Lensink. 1972. Census of the Bald Eagle breeding population in Southeast Alaska. J. Wildl. Manage. 36:1292-1295.

Rakestraw, L. W. 1981. History of the United States Forest Service in Alaska. U.S. Geological. Agric., For. Serv., Alaska Hist. Comm. 221pp.

Sidle, W. B., L. H. Suring and J. I. Hodges, Jr. 1990. The Bald Eagle in Southeast Alaska. U.S. Dept. Agric., For. Serv., Wildl. Fish. Habitat Manage. Notes. R10-MB-114. 29pp.

Stalmaster, M. V., R. L. Knight, B. L. Holder and R. J. Anderson. 1985. Chapter 13. Pages 269-290. In: E. R. Brown, ed. Management of wildlife and fish habitats in forests of western Oregon and Washington. U.S. Geological. Agric., For. Ser., Pac. Northwest Reg.

Thomas, J. W., E. D. Forsman, J. B. Lint, E. C. Meslow, B. R. Noon and J. Vemer. 1990. A conservation strategy for the Northern Spotted Owl. Interagency Sci. Comm. to Address the Conserv. of the Northern Spotted Owl. Portland, Oreg. 458pp.

Wood, P. B., T. C. Edwards, Jr. and M. W. Collopy. 1989. Characteristics of Bald Eagle nesting habitat in Florida. J. Wildl. Manage. 53:441-449.

Appendix 1.

Non-nest (random), nest and perch tree variables
Tree species
Crown condition (Categories are normal slender, broken top & alive, unbroken top & dead, deformed top & alive, doubled top & alive)
Nest height (in m)
Elevation above water (in m) from the base of the tree
Diameter at breast height (DBH) (in cm)
Overhead canopy cover
Nest, inside buffer, outside buffer forest stand variables
Number of trees by species Density (trees/ha) of trees Basal area (m ^{2}/ha) of trees
Overhead canopy closure (in %)

The Alaska Chilkat Bald Eagle Preserve: How It All Began

Raymond R. Menaker

Newsman, Haines, AK

Let me introduce you to the Alaska Chilkat Bald Eagle Preserve-a place that is unique-because what you find there you won't find anywhere else; because it's the only preserve in the state of Alaska; because people set it up before it was too late; because Bald Eagles and people are able to look at each other there without fear; because preservationists and industry people created it together; because the preserve is inclusive rather than exclusive; and because it is habitat for a wide variety of birds: waterfowl, songbirds, raptors; wildlife: moose, bear, wolves, coyotes; fish: salmon, trout, eulachon; humans: skiers, airboaters, snow machiners, hunters, trappers, fisherfolk, hikers, berry pickers, photographers, sightseers and researchers.

The Tlingit people knew about the preserve area long ago. They watched the eagles gather and disperse. They knew the connection between salmon and eagles. They knew that when the birds ate well, people could too. Early non-Native settlers knew about the eagles also. The soldiers at Fort William H. Seward, or "Chilkoot Barracks," knew about the eagles-in the days of the federal bounty on eagles, soldiers supplemented their government pay with bounty funds. Lots of folks knew about the fall and early winter gathering of countless Bald Eagles on the shores of the Chilkat River near the Chilkat Indian village of Klukwan. The National Audubon Society learned of the eagle concentration in 1970, when a Haines resident wrote to the society to suggest that Audubon should look into the need to preserve the habitat that was the basis for the gathering.

Two years later, the area's legislative representative, Morgan Reed of Skagway, proposed a bill to set aside an area in the Chilkat Valley as a protected habitat for the eagles that gather there each fall. He asked for local views about his proposal-and he got them. In one of the biggest meetings held in Haines to that point, a large number of people objected strongly to a fish and game habitat area, citing interference with local economic development and access to private lands. They also claimed that eagles were already protected by federal and existing state statutes. Reed agreed to withdraw the bill. Nonetheless, in June of 1972 a bill creating a 4,800-acre critical habitat area on the Chilkat River became law without the governor's signature.

By the late 1970s the Haines area was depressed economically. Two sawmills had closed. Special legislation had been passed to permit long-term state timber sales. A long-term sale of local timber that would permit one mill to open was being held up by litigation. And onto the scene came the National Audubon Society with a proposal for a four-year study of the Chilkat Bald Eagles.

Bald Eagles gather along the Chilkat River, in the Alaska Chilkat Bald Eagle Preserve. Photo by Scott Gende.

In May of 1980, while the U.S. Congress was trying to resolve the Alaska lands issue, there appeared in the Senate bill a section that declared the annual gathering of the eagles "a unique national resource." That section called for a three-year study of the eagles and it authorized land swaps permitting the U.S. to acquire private or state lands in the area of the eagle study. Elected officials and community organizations fought to remove any reference to the Chilkat eagles from the legislation. Groups favoring and groups opposing sent lobbyists to Washington and the Alaska state government also entered the fray. Governor Jay Hammond wrote then-Senator Gary Hart, who sponsored the eagle section in the bill: "At present, there are no plans for development in areas currently thought to be of great importance to the eagles. To alleviate concern about the future possibility of such actions prior to completion of the studies I am declaring a moratorium on all major development activities within the essential Bald Eagle habitat."

This is to include any planning for road and bridge construction. Customary and traditional uses important to the welfare of local residents and which in past years have not adversely impacted the eagles will continue to be permitted in these areas. Such uses will include, but are not necessarily limited to, hunting, fishing, trapping, subsistence, prospecting, general recreation and both motorized and non-motorized access.

The state agreed to fund studies during the moratorium.

A Haines-Klukwan Cooperative Resource Study Committee made up of local citizens and state agency people worked to coordinate studies of the area. By late 1981, when the Alaska Legislature was considering a proposal to create a state forest system, the Resource Study Committee recommended setting aside an area for eagle protection in the proposed Haines area state forest. Apparently the community had tired of the bitter wrangling that the several years of depressed economy had generated. Apparently people were tired of the claims and counter-claims that eagles, preservationists, the federal government and conservationists from the Lower 48 were responsible for both the local economic woes and the moratorium on development in about 53,000 acres while the resource studies were underway.

In late January 1982, however, a day-long Saturday meeting in Haines got nowhere. State agency representatives, local timber interests, local conservationists and local government officials were unable to agree on what was needed. But then, as so often happens in Alaska, the weather and the transportation system stepped in. The State folks bundled themselves up to return to Juneau. Snow began to fall. The nearby mountains disappeared. And the airlines shut down. The state ferry system, the only other means for public travel south, was not scheduled until the next day. Someone suggested an evening get-together to rehash the eagle/forest problem. And, lo and behold! a set of essential needs for eagle habitat, for reasonable access, for in-holder rights, for transportation, for subsistence and traditional use, for timber and mineral industry use were discussed, debated and-wonder of wonders-agreed upon informally.

From that Saturday it was all downhill. Oh, there were plenty of small uphill stretches, but by late February there was agreement among a very diverse set of interests on a very carefully worded legislative bill. Actually, it was a bill that no one really liked in total, but it was a bill that everyone could live with.

Imagine, if you will, a community in which for several years folks would shout each other down at public meetings, where the letters to the editor columns in the local newspaper were full of vituperative name-calling, where industry advocates were often seen as out to cut every tree, where eagle and fish habitat advocates were often seen as trying to lock up the whole Chilkat Valley. Think of what it meant for eight widely different groups to agree upon legislation that set up a Haines State Forest Resource Management Area that let the timber industry know where it could operate on a long-term basis, that guaranteed habitat for eagles and the fish they depend upon and that allowed the customary and traditional uses of the areas involved to continue as they'd been going on for generations.

Those eight signatories to the Alaska Chilkat Bald Eagle Preserve and Haines State Forest Resource Management Area legislation were: Schnabel Lumber Company, the major local timber industry representative, the Haines chapter of the Alaska Miners Association, the National Audubon Society, the U.S. Fish and Wildlife Service, Lynn Canal Conservation, the major local conservation organization, Southeast Alaska Conservation Council, the mayor of the City of Haines and the mayor of the Haines Borough.

The signatories agreed that no changes would be permitted in the wording of the bill unless all eight approved and they urged the governor to sign it. In a letter sending the proposed legislation to then Governor Hammond the signatories wrote: "We are convinced that this `Alaskan Solution' has the potential for adequately protecting local, state, national and international resource values and other interests in the Chilkat and Chilkoot valleys and could well serve as a model for resolving similar conflicts elsewhere in the State. Furthermore, successful implementation of this legislation once passed should demonstrate to all Alaskans and to the Nation as a whole that protection and management of resource values and other interests can in fact be successfully accomplished."

Note that there was not general support for the proposed legislation from the Native community. The people of the Chilkat village of Klukwan questioned whether the state had the right to create a state preserve on land to which they had a claim that was at that moment being litigated. Numerous Native allotment applications were still stalled in bureaucratic red tape and the applicants wondered what would happen to their allotments that were within either the Bald Eagle Preserve or the state forest. The proposed bill carefully excluded private land from the preserve and the forest and specifically treated Native allotments-both approved and pending-as not in the preserve and forest.

The bill also created a 12-person Alaska Chilkat Bald Eagle Preserve Advisory Council with representation from the State Division of Parks, the State Division of Forestry, the State Department of Fish and Game, the U.S. Fish and Wildlife Service, the mayors of the City of Haines and of the Haines Borough, the President of the Council of the Chilkat Indian Village of Klukwan, the President of the Chilkoot Indian Association, the President of Klukwan, Inc. (the for-profit Native corporation created by the Alaska Native Claims Settlement Act), the local business community, the Upper Lynn Canal Fish and Game Advisory Committee and a conservation organization.

On June 15, 1982 Alaska's Governor, Jay Hammond, signed the bill into law, establishing the Alaska Chilkat Bald Eagle Preserve and the Haines State Forest Resource Management Area.

For eight years the preserve advisory council has been fighting for funding for the preserve. It convinced the legislature in 1990 to provide some operating funds. The council also has been working to be sure everyone understands that although the preserve is part of the state parks system, it is not a park. Part of the uniqueness of the preserve is that even though it is set up for eagles and their habitat and fish and their habitat-not for people-its location alongside a major highway makes it a tremendous drawing card for visitors. Because the preserve is part of the parks system, the instinct is to treat it like a park; but everyone connected with writing the enabling legislation wanted to be sure that the activities that had been customary and traditional and at the level and means prior to preserve statutes-were continued. Special regulations that differ somewhat from standard park regulations were created by the advisory council.

In closing, I'd like to point out that what started out as an attempt to protect eagles and fish and their habitat has become a world-class tourist attraction. It has been interesting and rewarding to see that many people who had steam coming out of their ears at the thought of setting aside an inch of ground for eagles-what was often phrased as "locking up the valley"-are now proudly proclaiming Haines as the "Eagle Capital of the World" and recognizing the eagle preserve as an important addition to the economy of the region. Proponents and opponents of the eagle preserve smile at each other now, talk with each other now and listen to each other now. It may not be easy, but resource conflicts can be resolved. Perhaps that's the most important thing about the Alaska Chilkat Bald Eagle Preserve.

Bald Eagle Banding in Alaska

Kimberly Titus and Mark R. Fuller

Alaska Department of Fish and Game, Juneau AK; Raptor Research and Technical
Assistance Center, Boise, ID

Bird banding is important for research and management of wildlife. Modern bird banding originated in Denmark in 1890 (USDI Fish and Wildlife Service 1986) and subsequently, banding activities spread across Europe and the United States. Since 1920, the banding of migratory birds in the United States and Canada has been under the joint direction of the U.S. Fish and Wildlife Service (USFWS; formerly the Bureau of Biological Survey) and the Canadian Wildlife Service. The USFWS Bird Banding Laboratory (BBL) manages banding data on about 1.1 million birds and receives about 50,000 encounters annually (D. Bystrak, pers. comm.).

Bird banding is most effective when used for specific management goals or research objectives. Often bird banding contributes to descriptions of movements, migration patterns, philopatry and longevity. Banding is also an important method for estimating survival and harvest rates (e.g. Anderson 1975, Nichols and Hines 1987) and banding and colormarking of breeding pairs provide data about demography and mating behavior (e.g., Woolfenden and Fitzpatrick 1984). Studies such as these have specific banding protocols as part of their design. In addition much banding has been done to achieve other objectives that require handling birds (e.g., studies of nestling development or molt, wildlife rehabilitation) or in conjunction with education or recreation. Information from these banding efforts is seldom analyzed (J. Tautin, pers. comm.). Bald Eagle banding often occurs in this context, where the actual banding and results from banding usually have been incidental to the overall study objectives. Nevertheless, examination of long-term patterns associated with the encounters from banded Bald Eagles has provided some important natural history information (Gerrard and Bortolotti 1988). We review information that was obtained from banding Bald Eagles in Alaska and relate it to topics such as movements and longevity.

Methods

Three terms are commonly used in reference to bird banding data. An encounter is a report about a previously banded bird. Encounters include recaptures of banded birds, recoveries and sightings. A recovery is a banded bird found dead and reported to the BBL. Thus, a recovery relates only to a dead bird and is a terminal record. Sighting is the process of reading and reporting a band number on a live bird without actually capturing the bird. Sightings include the reading of a band, usually with a telescope and observations of color-marked birds. Colored leg bands or patagial markers, often labeled with large numbers and letters, provide a unique identification for individual birds or cohorts.

We obtained Bald Eagle data from the BBL banding and encounter files. Information about continent-wide Bald Eagle bandings and encounters was available from a listing for 1955 through 1985. We used this as a basis for comparison to some of the Alaska information. Alaska banding and encounters were obtained for 1956-1990. BBL banding summary files contain the following information: bird species (using American Ornithologists Union codes, e.g., 352.0 for Bald Eagle), date, sex (for Bald Eagles the sex is usually unknown), location (in 10 minute latitude/longitude blocks), permit number (agency or individual who did the banding) and status codes (e.g., normal wild bird, rehabilitation bird, color banded, radio transmitter attached). The recovery/encounter file may also contain information on how, when and where the encounter was obtained.

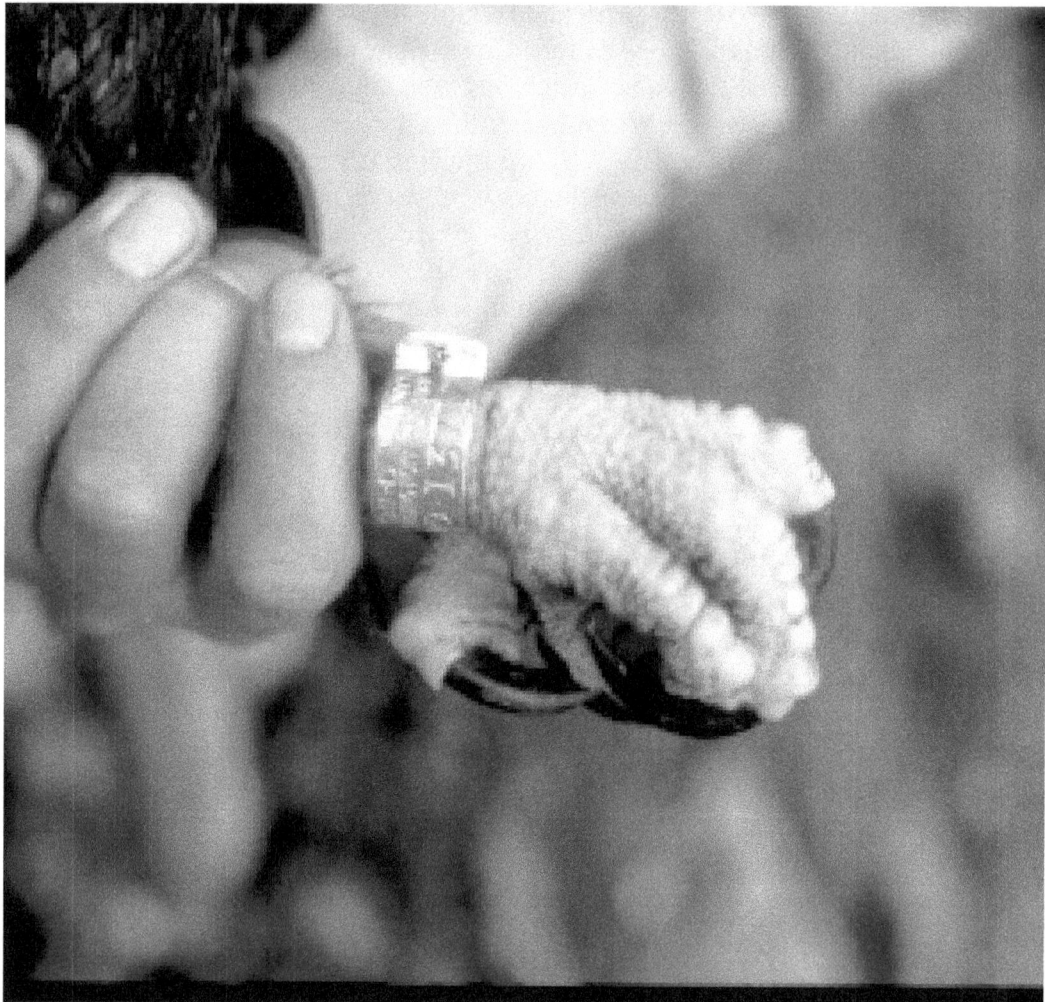

U.S. Fish and Wildlife Service band on the leg of an adult Bald Eagle. Photo by Mike Jacobson.

Results and Discussion
Bald Eagles Banded
In Alaska 1,185 Bald Eagles were banded and 73% of these occurred since 1980 (Figure 1). Throughout North America, 12,441 Bald Eagle banding records were processed from

1955 through August of 1985. During this period the largest numbers were banded in Wisconsin (2,254), Michigan (1,105), Ontario (911), Minnesota (734), Alaska (720), Nova Scotia (512) and Saskatchewan (495). Nestlings banded in Michigan, Minnesota and Wisconsin accounted for 33% of the total number of banded Bald Eagles in North America.

The status codes assigned to each banded bird indicated that many Bald Eagles were not handled solely for banding. Activities that alter the "normal wild bird" status included attaching a radio transmitter, obtaining a blood sample, holding and transporting a bird prior to release, using a color marking technique and rehabilitation. These activities can limit the uses of banding data because some analyses require that only normal wild banded birds can be included (Brownie et al. 1985). This restriction is based on the assumption that some activities alter the probability of a future encounter.

Only 39% of the Bald Eagles banded in Alaska were banded as "normal wild" birds, while continent-wide 61.5% of all Bald Eagles were banded as normal wild birds. Forty-eight percent of Alaskan Bald Eagles were banded in the month of July because banding of nestlings generally occurs during this period. The proportion of nestlings banded was 59% of all Alaskan eagles banded and continent-wide, 86% of all Bald Eagles were banded as nestlings. There has been more emphasis on the capture and hence banding of free-flying Bald Eagles in Alaska than elsewhere (Robards 1967, Cain and Hodges 1989). The number of Bald Eagles banded as adults (the ATY-after third year category) in Alaska was 25%, while continent-wide adults made up only 4%.

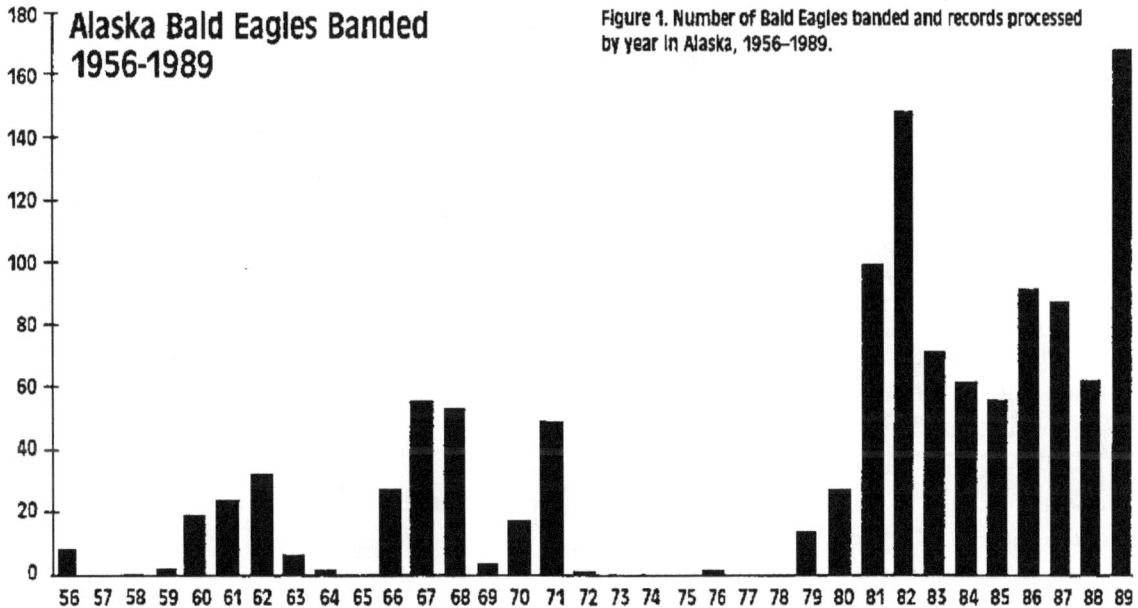

Figure 1. Number of Bald Eagles banded and records processed by year in Alaska, 1956–1989.

Several USFWS studies accounted for 83% of the Alaska Bald Eagle banding. The objectives of these studies often do not rely on banding Bald Eagles as the main marking method. For example, T. N. Bailey captured, banded and radio-marked 22 Bald Eagles wintering along the upper Kenai River to document movements. Staff of the Alaska Maritime National Wildlife Refuge color-marked and banded about 197 Bald Eagles on

Adak Island to learn about their association with a garbage dump and about inter- and intra-island movements. Hansen et al. (1984) captured, radio-tagged and banded 31 Bald Eagles in the Chilkat Valley to understand the movements of these eagles in the Chilkat Valley and throughout Southeast Alaska. D. Zwiefelhofer of Kodiak National Wildlife Refuge banded 239 Bald Eagles (20% of the Alaska bandings). USFWS staff from the Juneau Office of Migratory Bird Management and Raptor Management Studies have banded 544 (64% of Alaska Bald Eagle bandings), mostly when they were handled for primary purposes other than banding. Data from encounters of birds banded in this manner usually provide supplemental data for the objectives and sometimes anecdotal information about the cause of death, longevity or movements.

Bald Eagle Encounters and Movements

Few Bald Eagle encounters occur in Alaska compared with continent-wide encounters. Across North America, 12.5% of 12,441 Bald Eagles banded were encountered, but only 3.5% of 1,185 Bald Eagles banded in Alaska have been processed by the BBL. Encounters by the public (vs. special efforts of biologists) likely are closely related to human densities in areas where eagles occur. We expect a low encounter rate in Alaska owing to the low human density and the poor chance of the public encountering a banded bird in a remote location.

Most sightings of color-marked Bald Eagles are not reported to the BBL, yet biologists can benefit from specific color-marking and banding of Bald Eagles. For example, McCollough (1986, 1989) designed a mark-resight study that provided information on postfledging survival rates, molting sequence and aging of Bald Eagles in Maine, with his resight data then becoming part of the continent-wide data base. Sightings provided data on many released birds, for example, Bald Eagles that were translocated from one area to another and where young, captive-bred birds are released (Sherrod et al. 1989, Nye 1998, Wood et al. 1990). Sightings also provide very useful information from programs in which wild birds are banded to study movements and use of local resources such as food or roost sites (Helander 1985, McCollough 1986). In Alaska, sightings could provide many data at concentrations of birds feeding on salmon runs and along shorelines where nests are common.

Information about the circumstance of encounters is available for some banded birds. Encounter information from Alaska includes:
29 "found dead"
1 skeleton with band
2 shot
2 caught due to injury
1 caught in a trap (not a bird trap)
1 caught due to a car
3 caught due to striking wires/towers
1 caught and released by bander and
1 only the band number was available.
The "found dead" category includes a variety of causes, but often information is insufficient for an explanation for a cause of death.

An Alaskan encounter is a longevity record for the Bald Eagle (Cain 1986, Klimkiewicz and Futcher 1989). The individual eagle was banded on the Chilkat River in November 1965 when it was judged to be at least 3 years old. Subsequently, the bird was captured and released on the north end of Admiralty Island in 1984 and Cain (1986) estimated it to be at least 21 years, 11 months of age.

Of the 41 encounters of Bald Eagles banded in Alaska, 36 were in Alaska. A nestling banded in Saskatchewan and recovered dead south of Juneau four years later was the only Bald Eagle banded outside Alaska and encountered in the state. Five Bald Eagles banded in Alaska were recovered to the south (Table 1). Three of these were banded and radio-tagged in association with the Chilkat River studies (Hansen et al. 1984, Hodges et al. 1987) and were later recovered in southern coastal areas. Two Bald Eagles banded in interior Alaska were recovered to the south: R. Ambrose banded a nestling on the Tanana River that was recovered in northwest Washington and T. Swem banded a nestling on the Kandik River that was recovered in south-central British Columbia. Banding (Figure 2) and telemetry studies (Hodges et al. 1987) indicate movements of Bald Eagles between Alaska and British Columbia (Campbell et al. 1990). Additional study could confirm the idea that interior Alaska Bald Eagles use different migration routes and wintering areas than coastal Bald Eagles (Ritchie and Ambrose, 2008).

Table 1. Dates and locations of five Bald Eagles banded in Alaska and encountered outside the state at a later date.

Age	Date banded	Date encountered	Lat–long banded[1]	Lat–long encountered[1]	Location encountered
HY[2]	10/20/81	1/25/82	59°20'–135°50'	46°20'–123°50'	Washington state
HY	10/20/81	10/17/82	59°20'–135°50'	49°10'–125°50'	British Columbia
ATY[3]	10/21/81	1/12/82	59°20'–135°50'	50°30'–127°30'	British Columbia
L[4]	6/24/84	3/6/85	64°10'–146°40'	48°50'–122°20'	Washington state
L	7/25/84	9/2/88	65°30'–141°20'	51°30'–122°20'	British Columbia

[1] The latitude and longitude, to the nearest 10' of the original banding and subsequent encounter.
[2] HY = A bird capable of sustained flight and known to have been hatched during the calendar year in which it was banded.
[3] ATY = A bird now in at least its fourth calendar year of life.
[4] L = Local; a young bird incapable of sustained flight; a nestling.

There were 12 encounters (two recently provided by J. Williams) from the 197 Bald Eagles banded on Adak Island: 11 encounters were on Adak Island and one was on Atka Island, about 140 km to the east. These encounters indicate that Bald Eagles from the Aleutian Islands do not migrate, but occasionally make inter-island movements to local food sources (Sherrod et al. 1977).

Some bandings and encounters of Bald Eagles banded in Prince William Sound after the *Exxon Valdez* oil spill in 1989 are included in the Alaska banding data. However, these data are incomplete and none of the encounters are of normal wild birds.

Conclusions
Historically, banding provided the only regular information about the movements and survival of Bald Eagles (Broley 1947). Today, especially in Alaska where enormous efforts usually are required to capture and handle these birds, banding supplements color- or radio-marking. Consequently, Bald Eagle banding usually provides supplemental and

anecdotal information of the kind we summarized. Currently, many options for designing and analyzing data obtained from banding and color marking animals are available.

Nichols (1992) presents a general review of the models and types of information commonly acquired from marked animals (e.g., population size and survival estimates) and Lebreton et al. (1992) give detailed explanations of new "capture-mark-recapture" procedures. Also, Bald Eagle data are used in an example of another new procedure to estimate population size (Arnason et al. 1991). Use of these methods can increase the information available from future bandings of Bald Eagles.

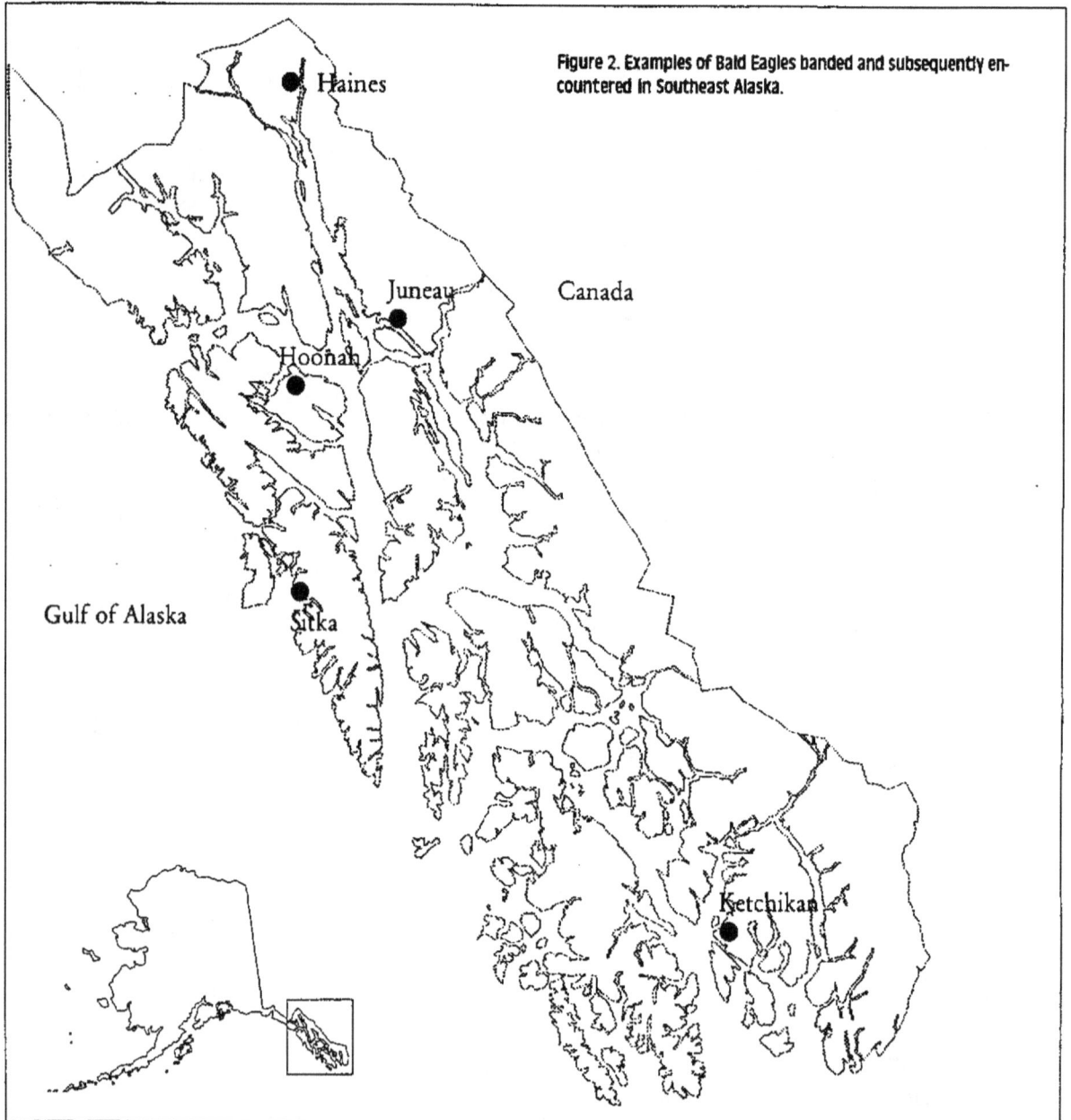

Figure 2. Examples of Bald Eagles banded and subsequently encountered in Southeast Alaska.

Acknowledgements

Many persons participated in banding projects and we appreciate their efforts. Important contributions were made by D. Zwiefelhofer (Kodiak National Wildlife Refuge), T. N. Bailey (Kenai National Wildlife Refuge), J. Hughes (Alaska Department of Fish and Game), R. Ambrose (USFWS-Fairbanks), J. Williams and staff from the Aleutian Islands Unit-Alaska Maritime National Wildlife Refuge and J. King, B. Conant, J. Hodges, P. Schempf and M. Jacobson (USFWS Migratory Bird Management, Juneau. J. E. Hines (USFWS-Patuxent Wildlife Research Center) and E. L. Boeker (National Audubon Society) provided the continent-wide Bald Eagle banding summaries in 1986 and J. Bladen (USFWS, Office of Migratory Bird Management) provided the Alaskan Bald Eagle summary files in a timely and convenient format. We thank D. Evans, S. Houston, M. Kralovec and J. Tautin for comments about our draft manuscript.

Editors' Note: A second eagle from those banded on the Chilkat River has been encountered and established a new Bald Eagle longevity record of 28 years, 0 months of age (Schempf, P. R, 1997 Bald eagle longevity record from Southeastern Alaska, J Field Ornithol. 68(1): 150-151.)

Literature Cited

Anderson, D. R. 1975. Population ecology of the Mallard: V. Temporal and geographic estimates of survival, recovery and harvest rates. U.S. Fish Wildl. Serv. Resour. Publ. 125. 110pp.

Anonymous. 1984. North American bird banding-Volume 1. Can. Wilds. Serv., Ottawa, Ontario, Canada. Various pages.

Arnason, A. N., C. J. Schwarz and J. M. Gerrard. 1991. Estimating closed population size and number of marked animals from sighting data. J. Wildl. Manage. 55:716-730.

Broley, C. L. 1947. Migration and nesting of Florida Bald Eagles. Wilson Bull. 59:3-20.

Brownie, C., D. R. Anderson, K. P. Burnham and D. S. Robson. 1985. Statistical inference from band recovery data: a handbook. Second ed. U.S. Fish Wildl. Serv. Resour. Publ. 156. 305pp.

Cain, S. L. 1986. A new longevity record for the Bald Eagle. J. Field Ornithol. 57:173.

Cain, S. L. and J. I. Hodges. 1989. A floating-fish snare for capturing Bald Eagles. J. Raptor Res. 23:10-13.

Campbell, R. W., N. K. Dawe, I. McTaggart-Cowan, J. M. Cooper, G. W. Kaiser and M. C. E. McNall. 1990. Birds of British Columbia. Vol. II. Nonpasserines. Royal British Columbia Museum. Mitchell Press, Vancouver, B.C. 636pp.

Gerrard, J. M. and G. R. Bortolotti. 1988. The Bald Eagle-haunts and habitat of a wilderness monarch. Western Producer Prairie Books, Saskatoon, Sask. 177pp.

Hansen, A. J., E. L. Boeker, J. I. Hodges and D. R. Cline. 1984. Bald Eagles of the Chilkat Valley, Alaska: ecology, behavior and management. Final rep., Chilkat River Coop. Bald Eagle study., Natl. Audubon Soc., Anchorage, Alas. 27pp.

Helander, B. 1985. Colour-ringing of White-tailed Sea Eagles in northern Europe. Pages 401-407 In: I. Newton and R. D. Chancellor, eds. Conservation studies on raptors. Int. Counc. Bird Prot. Tech. Publ. No. 5.

Hodges, J. I., E. L. Boeker and A. J. Hansen. 1987. Movements of radio-tagged Bald Eagles, *Haliaeetus leucocephalus*, in and from southeastern Alaska. Can. Field-Nat. 101:136-140.

Klimkiewicz, M. K. and A. G. Futcher. 1989. Longevity records of North American birds, supplement 1. J. Field Ornithol. 60:469-494.

Lebreton, J. D., K. P. Bumham, J. Clobert and D. R. Anderson. 1992. Modeling survival and testing biological hypotheses using marked animals: a unified approach with case studies. Ecol. Monogr. 62:67-118.

McCollough, M. A. 1986. The post-fledging ecology and population dynamics of Bald Eagles in Maine. Ph.D. diss., Univ. Maine.

McCollough, M. A. 1989. Molting sequence and aging of Bald Eagles. Wilson Bull. 101:1-10.

Nichols, J. D. 1992. Capture-recapture models. Using marked animals to study population dynamics. BioSci. 42:94-102.

Nichols, J. D. and J. E. Hines. 1987. Population ecology of the Mallard: VIII. Winter distribution patterns and survival rates of winter-banded Mallards. U.S. Fish Wildl. Serv. Resour. Publ. 162. 154pp.

Nye, P. E. 1998. A review of the natural history of a reestablished population of breeding Bald Eagles in New York. In: Wright, B. A. and P. F. Schempf, eds. Bald Eagles in Alaska.

Ritchie, R. J. and R. E. Ambrose. 2008. Distribution, abundance and status of Bald Eagles in Interior Alaska. In: Wright, B.A. and P. F. Schempf, eds. Bald Eagles in Alaska.

Robards, F. C. 1967. Capture, handling and banding of Bald Eagles. Unpubl. rep., U.S. Geological. Inter., Bur. Sport Rsh. Wildl., Juneau, Alas. 25pp.

Sherrod, S. K., C. M. White and F. S. L. Williamson. 1977. Biology of the Bald Eagle on Amchitka Island, Alaska. Living Bird 15:143-182.

Sherrod, S. K., M. A. Jenkins, G. McKee, D. H. Wolfe, Jr. and S. Tatom. 1989. Restoring nesting Bald Eagle *Haliaeetus leucocephalus* populations to the southeastern United States. Pages 353-358. In: B. U. Meyburg and R. D. Chancellor, eds. Raptors in the modern world. Proc. III World Conf. Birds of Prey and Owls. Berlin.

USDI Fish and Wildlife Service. 1986. Bird banding-the hows and whys. Conserv. Note 5. 7pp.

Wood, P. B., D. A. Buehler and M. A. Byrd. 1990. Bald Eagle. Pages 13-21. In: Proc. southeast raptor manage. symp. and workshop. Natl. Wildl. Fed., Washington, D.C.

Woolfenden, G. E. and J. W. Fitzpatrick. 1984. The Florida Scrub Jay: demography of a cooperative-breeding bird. Mongr. in Pop. Biol. No. 20. Princeton Univ. Press. Princeton, N.J. 406pp.

Survey Techniques for Bald Eagles in Alaska

John I. Hodges

U.S. Fish and Wildlife Service, Juneau, AK

Introduction

Interest in obtaining information about Bald Eagle (*Haliaeetus leucocephalus*) populations in Alaska probably began with Imler (1941). His food habits studies commenced 24 years after the territorial government established a bounty system to reimburse citizens for dead eagles. After serving as a factor in eagle mortality for 35 years, the bounty was removed in 1953, again altering the population dynamics of the Bald Eagle. Later, additional pressures confronted the eagle population in the form of logging operations, fishing practices, fluctuations in prey base and removal of chicks for translocation to the eastern United States.

Surveys have been used to estimate eagle population parameters and to monitor changes. The first region-wide population survey was conducted by King et al. (1972) in Southeast Alaska using an airplane. Intensive boat searches for Bald Eagle nests began in 1969 (Hodges 1984). Since then survey techniques have evolved and expanded to all parts of Alaska.

Adult Bald Eagles and their nests are easily observed compared to most other bird species. Even though the visibility rate may be as low as 50% on a given survey, there is still good justification for the survey if repeatability and consistency are practiced. Observer bias, or differential abilities by observers, is a pestering factor in many surveys, but it can be addressed with diligent training or bias estimation.

Population Surveys

Population surveys are used to determine the number of individual birds associated with a given area. The techniques presented here assume that the eagles are located within viewing distance of some body of water.

Fixed wing: High wing airplanes are preferred because observers are usually looking down on perched eagles. Coastlines, river corridors or lake shores are flown at an altitude of approximately 30 m above the substrate (tree tops or ground) with a viewing angle of 45 degrees downward. One or two observers are located on the right side of the plane. The pilot should be used to scan for soaring eagles and observe perched eagles whenever safety permits.

The flight path should be flown in a way that maximizes observability and minimizes air sickness. Right turns around a sharp point of land requires an increase in aircraft altitude to avoid a steep turn that would cause the lowered wing to obstruct the observers' view. Wide coves are flown with left turns and may require decreased altitude to avoid obstructing the observers' view with the landing gear, a particular concern with float planes. If the cove is too tight to allow a comfortable left turn over the water, then the flight path should cross the far shoreline and commence a right turn just landward of the shore to keep the observer looking down at the coastal habitat (See Figure la). A string of islands can often be surveyed with a figure 8 pattern that takes less time and reduces the G forces on the plane and its occupants (See Figure 1b). During left turns the island habitat will be on the pilot's side and the observers will look across out the left windows. Survey airspeed should remain at least 50% above stall speed at all times.

Figure 1. Suggested flight path for a narrow cove or a string of islands.

a. Narrow Cove

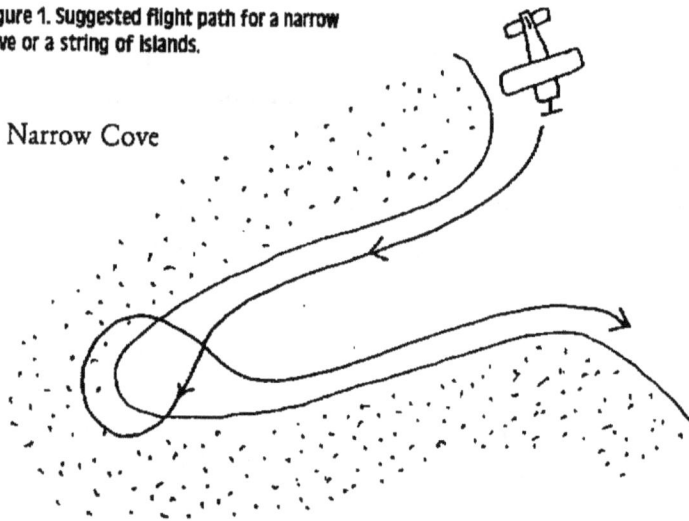

b. String of Islands

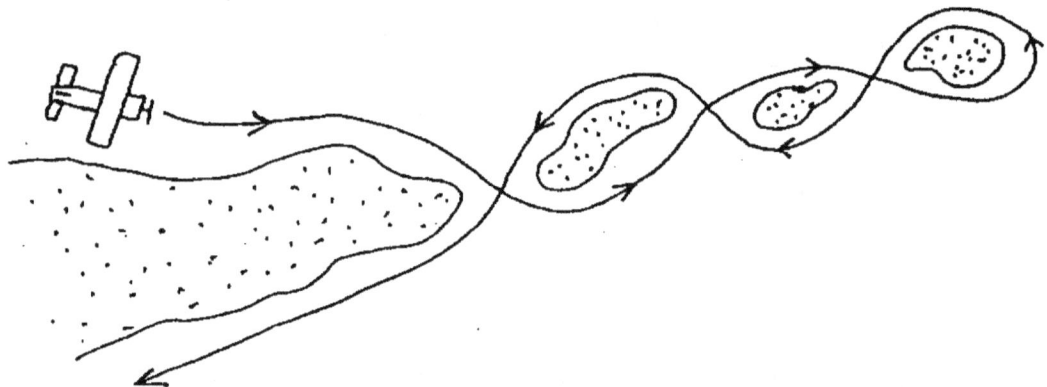

Observations can be plotted onto maps or recorded into an onboard computer. Linking the computer to the Global Positioning System (GPS) navigation radio in the airplane works well except for those cases when the eagle or nest is not immediately adjacent to the airplane. Manual mapping will usually be more accurate than GPS mapping when landmarks are abundant but less accurate when landmarks are scarce.

Helicopter: Generally the same survey procedures apply when conducting a population survey by helicopter. Slower safe airspeeds are possible, which result in more gentle turns and more observation time per unit of habitat.

Boat: Population surveys by boat are conducted at slow speeds under 10 km/h. Distance from shore is a compromise between maintaining proximity to the coastal habitat and a setback distance that allows a perspective of the trees behind the shoreline face. Binoculars can be used to scan with increased acuity. An intense boat survey will provide a much better survey for immature eagles in dense foliage than an aerial survey. Eagles that flush in the direction of travel should be monitored to avoid double counting.

Timing: Ideally, population surveys should occur at a time when eagles are not clumped in distribution. Traditionally surveys have been conducted in the spring during incubation, providing auxiliary information about nesting attempts. This time of year has drawbacks. In coastal areas with coniferous forests, incubating adults will be less visible to observers in an aircraft than perched eagles and they may be totally hidden from the view of a boat. Herring and eulachon runs also occur in spring causing large concentrations of eagles. Perhaps a better time for population surveys in coastal areas would be late June before the salmon runs commence. Interior rivers must be surveyed before the trees have leafed out, which necessitates surveys during incubation.

Age ratios: Perched eagles are generally not used to estimate the ratio of immature eagles to adults eagles because immature eagles are more difficult to see. Assuming that adults and immatures have the same probability of flushing or flying, we can use the age ratio observed for flying eagles to represent the age ratio of eagles in the study area. This also assumes that adult and immature eagles in flight have an equal probability of being recorded.

Sources of error: Weather conditions can have a significant effect on the distribution of eagles and consequently on the population survey. During clear weather eagles are more likely to soar, particularly if the weather has been wet during the preceding days. The eagles want to dry their wings and see where the latest food source may be. This behavior will decrease the number of eagles seen along the shoreline or river survey.

Observer differences in ability, experience and interest also will affect the results of the survey. These effects can be major sources of variability and ways of dealing with them are discussed under Observer Bias at the end of this paper.

Nest Surveys
Nest location data is often required to assist in resource development planning and to avoid violations of the Bald Eagle Protection Act. For this reason nest surveys usually fall under the category of censuses.

Fixed wing: Fixed wing surveys for Bald Eagle nest structures are very effective in cottonwood or balsam poplar habitat during the period when leaves are not present. Fixed wing nest surveys are not recommended for locating nests in conifer trees especially in the heavy coastal forests.

Helicopter: Helicopters may be used to locate nests in heavy coastal forests but it is likely that numerous passes over the habitat will be required to locate a high percentage of the nests. Nest surveys should be flown in a manner similar to population surveys but at a slower airspeed and often at a lower elevation.

Boat: Boat surveys for nests are usually superior to other survey modes because of the very slow speeds and the careful scrutiny which can be given to the forest. Exceptions include areas where nests are removed from shore and impossible to view from the water. The ground based observer has time to carefully plot the location of each nest on a detailed map.

This turbine powered beaver, N-754, was designed for conducting aerial surveys. Photo courtesy of USFWS.

Timing: Nest surveys must be done before leaf-out in cottonwood and balsam poplar habitat. Aerial surveys of nests in coniferous forests are best done during incubation because adults on the nest platform facilitate the detection of active nests. During the early part of the nesting season boat surveys can benefit from the excited behavior of adults near their productive nest.

Sources of error: Non-detection of nests is caused by inadequate coverage of the study area or the concealed nature of some nests. Observer training is critical to a good survey.

Productivity Surveys
Productivity surveys provide a measure of effort on the part of nesting pairs to produce offspring. They may occur at any time between nest initiation in spring and fledging in late summer.

Fixed wing: Productivity surveys by fixed wing aircraft are generally unsuccessful. Fully feathered young can be observed in openly exposed nests, but this excludes most nests in cottonwood trees or under the canopy of large coastal trees. Fixed wing surveys of feathered young are possible to a limited extent in Interior coniferous forests and in treeless areas such as the Aleutian Islands and the Alaska Peninsula. Incubating adults can be observed before leaf-out in cottonwood stands or to a limited degree in conifer stands.

Helicopter: Helicopter is the preferred means of conducting productivity surveys (Hodges 1984). Eggs may be counted if the adult flushes from the nest, although purposely flushing the adult is not recommended because eagles taking sudden flight can damage the eggs. Young of all ages can be seen if foliage does not block the observer's view of the nest. Nestlings under three weeks of age may be difficult to count if they are huddled close together. Helicopter surveys should not be used to count young after they have reached the age of 8 weeks because the young may prematurely fledge from the nest if frightened by the helicopter.

Caution and vigilance on the part of the helicopter pilot are necessary for safely hovering in the vicinity of an active eagle nest. Some eagles can be expected to attack the helicopter. Evasive action requires moving away from the eagle rapidly and if possible directing the downwash of the helicopter towards the eagle.

Boat: Boats are usually not useful for conducting productivity surveys. However, they can be used in a rudimentary fashion to locate nests that are actively defended by adults. This behavior is usually an indication of the presence of young or eggs. If the young are more than 7 weeks old they can often be observed from a boat.

Nest climbs: Trees may be climbed to count the young before they reach the age of 8 weeks. After this age the young may prematurely fledge at the sight of the climber gaining access to the nest. Nests with eggs should not be climbed because of the high likelihood of causing nest desertion by the adult (Cain 1985).

Surveys of Concentration Areas
When food becomes available in large quantities, Bald Eagles concentrate in large numbers. These concentrations can have as many as 3000 eagles in a 4 km section of river feeding on spawning salmon, or 200 eagles in a 2 km section of shoreline feeding

on spawning herring or 100 eagles in 100 m of beach feeding on a humpback whale carcass.

Survey technique is a matter of placing the observer in a position or series of positions in which he/she can count all eagles present. Ground access and the use of a spotting scope are preferred. Fixed wing aircraft have been used in areas inaccessible for ground access. Helicopters are not recommended because of the higher disturbance level that flushes a large percentage of the eagles.

Documentation of communal roosts in Alaska is limited to a few areas where wintering eagles concentrate on a food source that is close to a stand of heavy coniferous timber. More work in this area is needed.

Age ratios: Good age ratio information for large numbers of adult and immature eagles is easily obtained at feeding concentrations. Further breakdown of the immature segment of the population is possible if the observer can get close enough to the birds. The plumage, beak color and eye color are all used to split the immatures into age classes (Wheeler and Clark 1995). How well these classes correspond to year classes is not known. Bald Eagles mature at differing rates possibly due to food availability and/or social interactions with other eagles.

Design
The goals of a good survey should be to achieve accuracy and repeatability. A complete census accomplishes this best but is not often possible. Random plots have been successfully used in coastal Alaska and British Columbia (King et al. 1972 and Hodges et al. 1984). Random segments of shoreline have also been used (Robards and King 2008).

In northern areas square grids do not work well as the basis for a plot design. At the corners of a large study area the plots become highly skewed relative to the cardinal directions. Also, the square grid pattern is difficult to repeat by another researcher at a later date without the use of the original design maps. An alternative system has been used to survey Bald Eagles from Unimak Island in Alaska to Vancouver, British Columbia which eliminates these two problems. The north and south boundaries of all plots are parallel to the lines of latitude and the east and west boundaries are parallel to the lines of longitude. Each plot is nearly square in shape, the north boundary being slightly narrower than the south boundary. The plots are all the same height and the same width at the center. Another researcher can exactly duplicate the plots by simply knowing the plot number and the two formulas shown in Figure 2.

Straight line transects can be used to sample habitats that tend to be uniformly distributed throughout the study area. For example, in the instance of a broad river plain with intricate patterns of small lakes, a fixed transect width is chosen, such as 200 or 400 m. The long transects are subdivided into segments of fixed length. Sightings are preferably recorded by exact location but alternatively by segment.

Compute Center point (I, J) as:

$$LAT_j = LAT_o + h \cdot J$$
$$LON_i = LON_o + I \, (h/cos(LAT_j))$$

where,

(I, J)	= Column I and Row J
LAT$_o$	= Latutude for Row 0
LON$_o$	= Longirude for Column 0
h	= Height of each plot in degrees

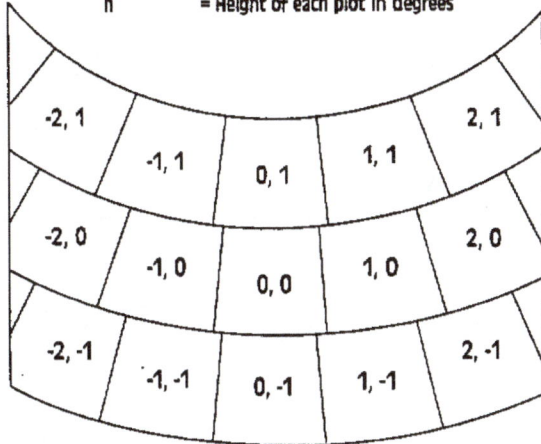

Observer Bias

Observer differences can have potentially serious effects on the accuracy of surveys. Observer training is highly desirable even if an attempt is made to adjust survey results to account for observer bias. For example, estimating the number of missed nests is of no value if the nest locations are needed for planning habitat protection.

Three methods will be discussed to measure the amount of observer bias in the aerial survey setting. The first method is comparison of a complete ground count with an aerial count. This is the preferred method. Ground counts in Alaska are usually conducted from a boat. Boat observers must be well trained and dedicated and must see all of the eagles. Ideally the air and ground counts would be conducted at exactly the same time, but realistically the boat surveys require much more time and the assumption that the same number of eagles are present for both surveys becomes increasingly suspect.

The second method for measuring observer bias uses a form of the Peterson Index to determine the number of eagles missed by two observers in one aircraft or boat (Magnusson et al. 1978). This method will not estimate eagles that were impossible for either observer in the craft to see. The assumptions are (1) that sightings by both observers occur independently; and (2) that the probability of spotting each object is the same for all objects, but can vary between observers.

The first assumption is met by having the front seat observer record the rear seat observations as well as his own. If the front seat observer sees an eagle he waits to record it until it has passed the wing tip. If the rear seat observer sees an eagle, he communicates the sighting just as the eagle passes the wing tip. The front observer records an eagle as having been seen by both of them if he saw the eagle and he also heard the rear observer call out the eagle. The front observer records an eagle as having been seen by him alone if he sees the eagle and fails to hear the rear observer call it out as it passes the wing tip. The front observer records an eagle as having been seen by the rear observer alone if he hears an eagle called out but has not seen it. The formula for the estimated number of eagles that both observers missed (M) is where:

F = Number seen by front seat observer only.

R = Number seen by rear seat observer only.

B = Number seen by both observers.

Figure 3. Correction factors (CF) to use in the Petersen index method of estimating observer bias for six possible probability of detection curves. The estimated number of animals missed by both observers is multiplied by CF.

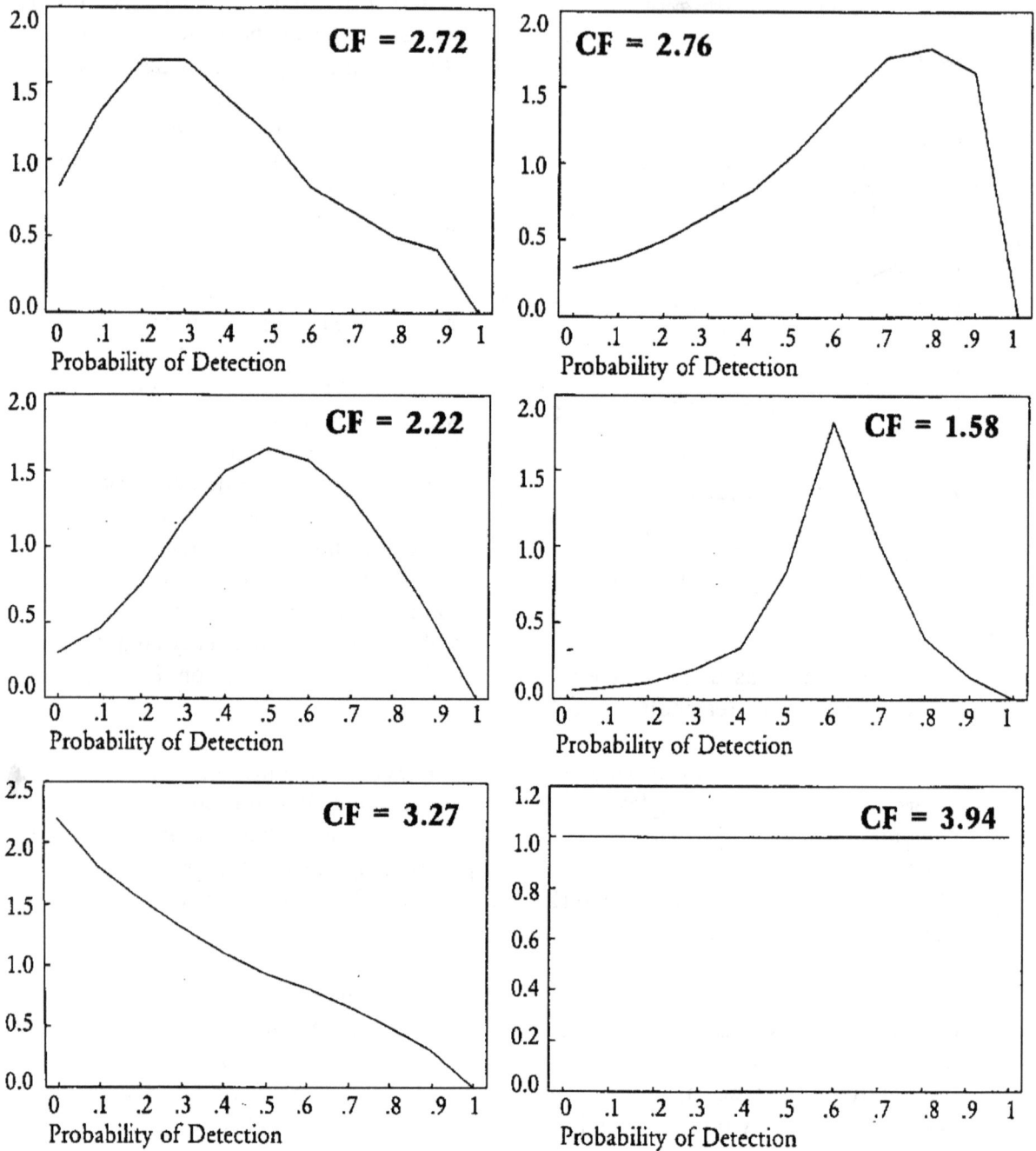

The second assumption of equal detection probability for each animal is unlikely to hold true in wildlife surveys. Magnusson et al. (1978) concluded that this assumption was not critical for their alligator nest surveys but in general the error in estimating M increases as the probability distribution of detectability deviates from a single point. Species that are difficult to detect have a larger segment of the population in the missed by both category (M) and thus the accuracy in estimating M becomes more critical.

Six hypothetical detection probability distributions (Figure 3) were chosen to determine the inaccuracy in estimating M. It was assumed that the probability distribution was identical for both observers. The correction factor (CF) needed to make the estimate of M unbiased in each case was significant. Bald Eagles, for example, might have a distribution which is weighted toward birds which are likely to be observed and would require using CF = 2.76 in the equation for M.

In the absence of good information on the true detection probability distribution of the population being surveyed one should use a correction factor of CF = 2.5 when estimating M. This strategy would certainly be superior to ignoring the correction factor as suggested by Magnusson et al. (1978).

Another approach for handling deviations from the second assumption of equal probability of detection for all animals is to stratify the observations based on an estimate of each animal's detectability. For example, eagles could be classed into three strata by the observers, (A) obvious or easy to see, (B) not obvious but not difficult to see, (C) difficult to see. The analysis would occur separately by stratum. This will help improve the estimate of M for all strata combined if a significant proportion of the population is not difficult to see.

The third method of estimating observer bias involves the use of radiotagged eagles. First, the radioed eagle is visually located while one of the observers remains blindfolded. Then the blindfold is removed and a normal flight path is flown to determine if the observer having no prior knowledge of the radioed eagle's location is able to locate the eagle. An important advantage of this technique is that it includes eagles that have zero probability of being seen from the survey aircraft in normal survey mode.

Literature Cited

Cain, S. L. 1985. Nesting activity budgets of Bald Eagles in Southeast Alaska. M.S. Thesis. Univ. of Montana, Missoula. 47pp.

Hodges, J. I. 1984. Bald Eagle nesting studies in Seymour Canal, Southeast Alaska. Condor 84:125-127.

Hodges, J. I., J. G. King and R. Davies. 1984. Bald Eagle breeding population survey of coastal British Columbia. J. Wildl. Manage. 48:993-998.

Imler, R. H. 1941. Alaskan Bald Eagle studies. USDI Report. Denver, Colo. 17pp.

King, J. G., F. C. Robards and C. J. Lensink. 1972. Census of the Bald Eagle breeding population in Southeast Alaska. J. Wildl. Manage. 36: 1292-1295.

Magnusson, W. E., G. J. Caughley and G. C. Grigg. 1978. A double survey estimate of population size from incomplete counts. J. Wildl. Manage. 42:174-176.

Robards, F. C. and J. G. King. 2008. Nesting and productivity of Bald Eagles in Southeast Alaska-1966. In: Wright, B. A. and P. F. Schempf, eds. Bald Eagles In Alaska.

Wheeler, B. K. and W. S. Clark. 1995. A photographic guide to North American raptors. Academic Press, Inc., San Diego, Calif. 198pp.

Graphic Depiction of Bald Eagle Habitat Use Patterns

Richard E. Yates, B. Riley McClelland and Carl H. Key

National Park Service, Glacier National Park, MT

Specific temporal and spatial use patterns are valuable in determining sensitive times and areas of Bald Eagle (*Haliaeetus leucocephalus*) use, allowing appropriate management or mitigation actions to be developed. The method accommodates study of one to several Bald Eagles, long- or short-term data sets, radio transmitter or visual locations, varying degrees of precision and various sampling schemes.

Introduction

Managers of Bald Eagle habitat must be aware of the relative importance of specific forage and roost sites at breeding and wintering areas in order to augment habitat protection and enhancement efforts. Identification of key habitat areas is of particular importance in breeding areas where Bald Eagle productivity is low. Depicting daily or seasonal shifts in Bald Eagle use of available habitat aids in identification of areas with conflicting human activity. Based on detailed information, management of human activities, perch and roost trees and screening vegetation can reduce disturbances at critical times. Home range programs such as "McPaal" (Stuwe and Blowhowiak 1986) and the Use-Zone concept (Mont. Bald Eagle Working Group 1986) include general areas of Bald Eagle use, but do not incorporate temporal shifts or the weighted importance of specific foraging and perching areas. In this paper we discuss a method of identifying key use areas on a daily or seasonal basis.

Study Area

Glacier National Park (GNP) is located along the Continental Divide in northwestern Montana. Within the 1 million acre park, six Bald Eagle breeding areas occur within forested mountain valleys, at lakes ranging in size from 360 ha. to 2,761 ha. More than 1.8 million people visit GNP each year. Our study focused on Lake McDonald, the largest lake in the park, located on the west slope of the Continental Divide. All six perennial streams that flow into Lake McDonald have some type of human activity and facilities associated with their inlets. The Going-to-the-Sun Highway, which bisects the park, parallels the lake's eastern shore.

Productivity for GNP's six pairs of breeding Bald Eagles averaged 0.63 young per occupied nest from 1982 through 1990. This low productivity contrasts with a reported recent increase in productivity for the rest of Montana's breeding Bald Eagle population (Flath and Hazelwood 1986). Montana had 94 occupied Bald Eagle territories in 1990; 71

were successful (76%) and 1.37 young fledged per occupied nest (D. Flath pers. comm.). The Lake McDonald breeding area had low productivity (0.44 young per occupancy from 1982 through 1990) and a high level of human activity, making it a management priority for Bald Eagle enhancement.

Methods

Between March 1986 and August 1987, we logged 3,172 hrs observing Bald Eagle habitat use at the Lake McDonald breeding area. Precise determination of Bald Eagle movements and home range requires the use of radio transmitters (Griffin 1978, Frenzel 1984). The adult male was captured at Lake McDonald on 15 March 1986 using a floating fish (Cain and Hodges 1989).

Orange, vinyl wing-markers coded with black characters (A-01) were attached around the patagium of each wing (Young 1983) and a U.S. Fish and Wildlife Service band was placed on the right leg. A Telonics Inc. (Mesa, Ariz.) backpack transmitter with an activity tip-switch (weight 56 g, guaranteed battery life 14 months) was attached by fitting a Teflon harness around the eagle's body (a method previously used by D. Garcelon pers. comm.).

Transmitter locations were used mainly as aids in obtaining visual locations of the eagle. Observations of the male were made with binoculars and variable-power telescopes at distances of 0.5 km to 5 km to avoid influencing eagle activity. Blocks of observation hours were varied daily so that all daylight hours were sampled at least once each week. More emphasis was placed on morning and evening periods, when eagles were most active.

Individual perch locations and durations were plotted daily on USGS 7.5 min topographic maps. A modified-minimum-area-polygon method (Harvey and Barbour 1965) was used to map the nesting home range by connecting outer perching and soaring locations within the study area. Other information recorded at the time of location included: weather, perch time at each location, behavior of individual eagles, identification of food items and observation time.

Perch-Site Frequency Calculation

Mapped perch sites were digitized with UTM coordinates to the nearest 10 m using the "Digit" program (developed by coauthor C.H.K) and a Numonics tablet digitizer. All UTM locations were then imported into a database file containing date, time, duration and activity information for each specific location of the eagle. Locations were segregated by specific seasonal observation periods using a database search and exported to ASCII files. Within each ASCII file, perch durations were aggregated within 25 m of a representative perch site. Minutes of eagle presence at each aggregate point were divided by the total observation time to yield a standardized index of eagle use per unit of observation time for each seasonal observation period. These values were used to scale circle sizes around each aggregate point on the seasonal study area maps. Perch sites were mapped using circles whose radii were proportional to the relative amount of time spent at each location (Figure 1). Times less than 10 min were assigned the same scaling value for the smallest circle size. Study area drainages and lakes were plotted on maps to provide location information. These previously digitized data were obtained from GNP's Geographic Information System (Wherry et al. 1985). The aggregate site points and their corresponding scaled circles were plotted using the "Plot" program (developed by coauthor C.H.K). Maps of roost-site use were generated in a similar manner, using number of roost nights at a specific location divided by the total number of roost nights documented. This quotient was used to scale circle sizes which were plotted on a location map of Lake McDonald.

Lake McDonald, Glacier National Park, Montana. View is up-lake toward the Bald Eagle nesting territory and the snow-capped peaks of the Continental Divide. The home range of the single nesting pair encompasses the entire lake and surrounding area. Photo by B.R McClelland.

A map of the Primary Use Zone, the area in which at least 75% of the eagle's use occurred (Mont. Bald Eagle Working Group 1986), was prepared using an 18-month compilation of the male's perch sites in the Lake McDonald area (Figure 1). It indicated the year-around composite of male eagle habitat use and not seasonal patterns.

Primary Applications

We prepared perch-site location maps covering eight selected seasonal periods and a single map of the male's roost sites at Lake McDonald during the 18 month study period (Yates 1989). Nest failures in 1986 and 1987 occurred in April. The nesting periods for both years began with courtship (mid-March) and continued until the nest was abandoned (late-May). Other seasonal periods were determined by identifying major shifts in habitat use by the male.

We compared the male's habitat use during the spring of 1986 and the spring of 1987 (Figure 2). The decrease in the amount of use near the Upper McDonald Creek inlet may indicate a change in the prey base, an increase in disturbance at that inlet, or a behavioral change within the nesting pair due to mate replacement in April 1987. Comparison of the male's habitat use during the spring and summer of 1987 (Figure 3) shows a marked decrease in time spent at Lake McDonald. Causes for this dramatic shift in habitat use probably resulted from changes in prey availability and increased disturbance due to the influx of thousands of summer park visitors.

Roost-site use at Lake McDonald (Figure 4) revealed at least three areas where the male spent most nights. The roost near the Upper McDonald Creek inlet is used mostly in autumn, when kokanee salmon (*Oncorhynchus nerka*) spawn along the adjacent shoreline. The roost near the nest is mainly used during the nesting season and the roost along the northwest shore of the lake is used during spring, summer and autumn.

Other Applications

The use of radio transmitters may be used to depict locations of one bird over time or of several birds (using different maps for each bird) during the same time period. Habitat use by a fledgling and an adult, the members of a breeding pair or by several wintering eagles may be easily contrasted.

Documentation of specific perch- or roost-site use by many different birds also can be depicted by recording the amount of time a site is used and plotting circles for each site on a single map. Large or small data sets from adequate sampling schemes can be used to plot habitat use because the method generates relative amounts of use. Documentation of habitat use can yield important information without using expensive telemetry equipment. However, if the precision of representing an actual perch-site or foraging location is decreased (e.g. a point may be digitized to the nearest 100 or 1000 m), telemetry data without visual observations could be used (Crenshaw 1985). Satellite-telemetry data also can be used if the corresponding location error is considered. Sampling schemes will vary according to specific questions being addressed. The method can be refined to provide perch information for specific times of the day by plotting perch locations and durations only for specified hours.

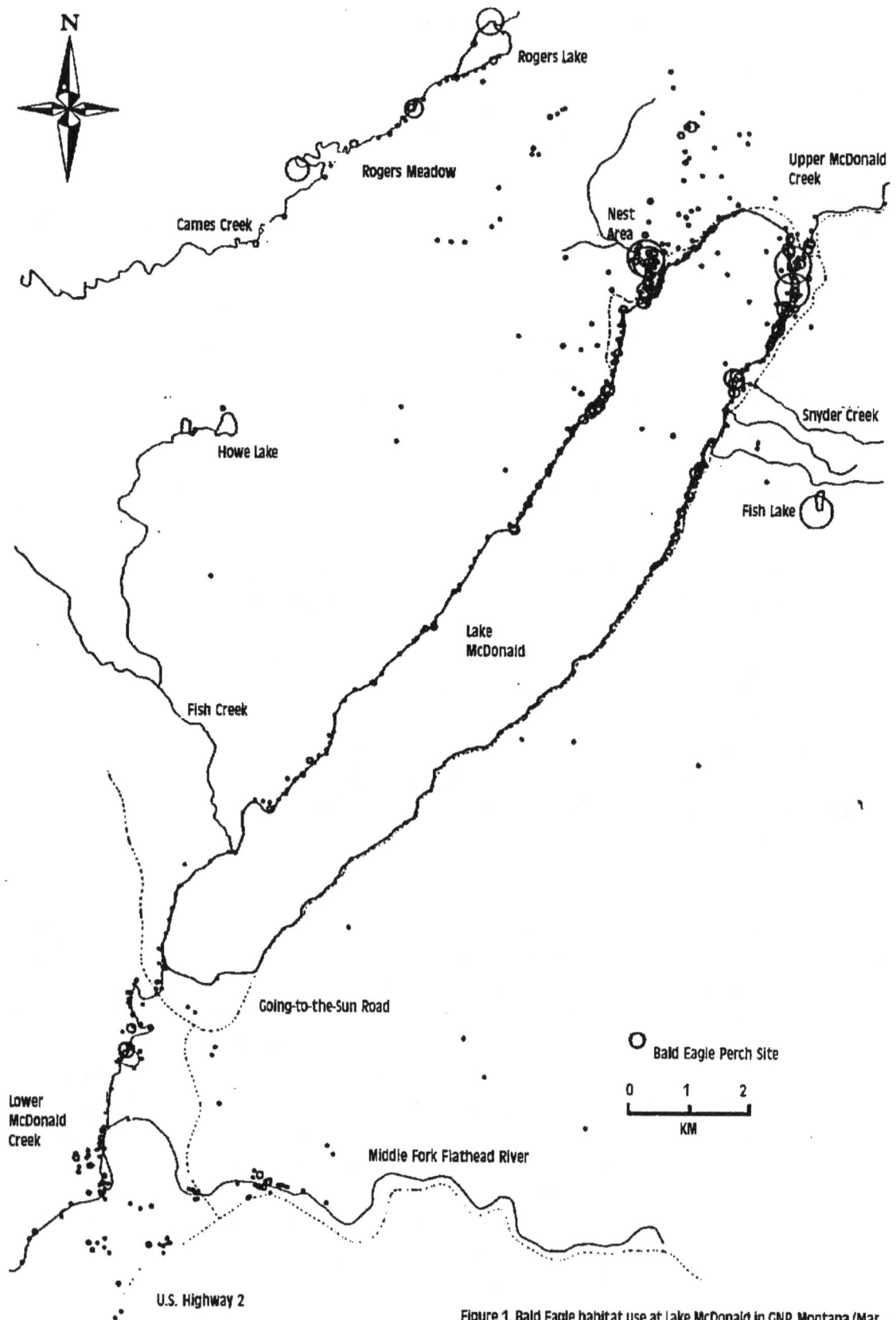

Figure 1. Bald Eagle habitat use at Lake McDonald in GNP, Montana (Mar 1986–Aug 1987). Circles depict the relative time spent at corresponding perch locations by an adult male.

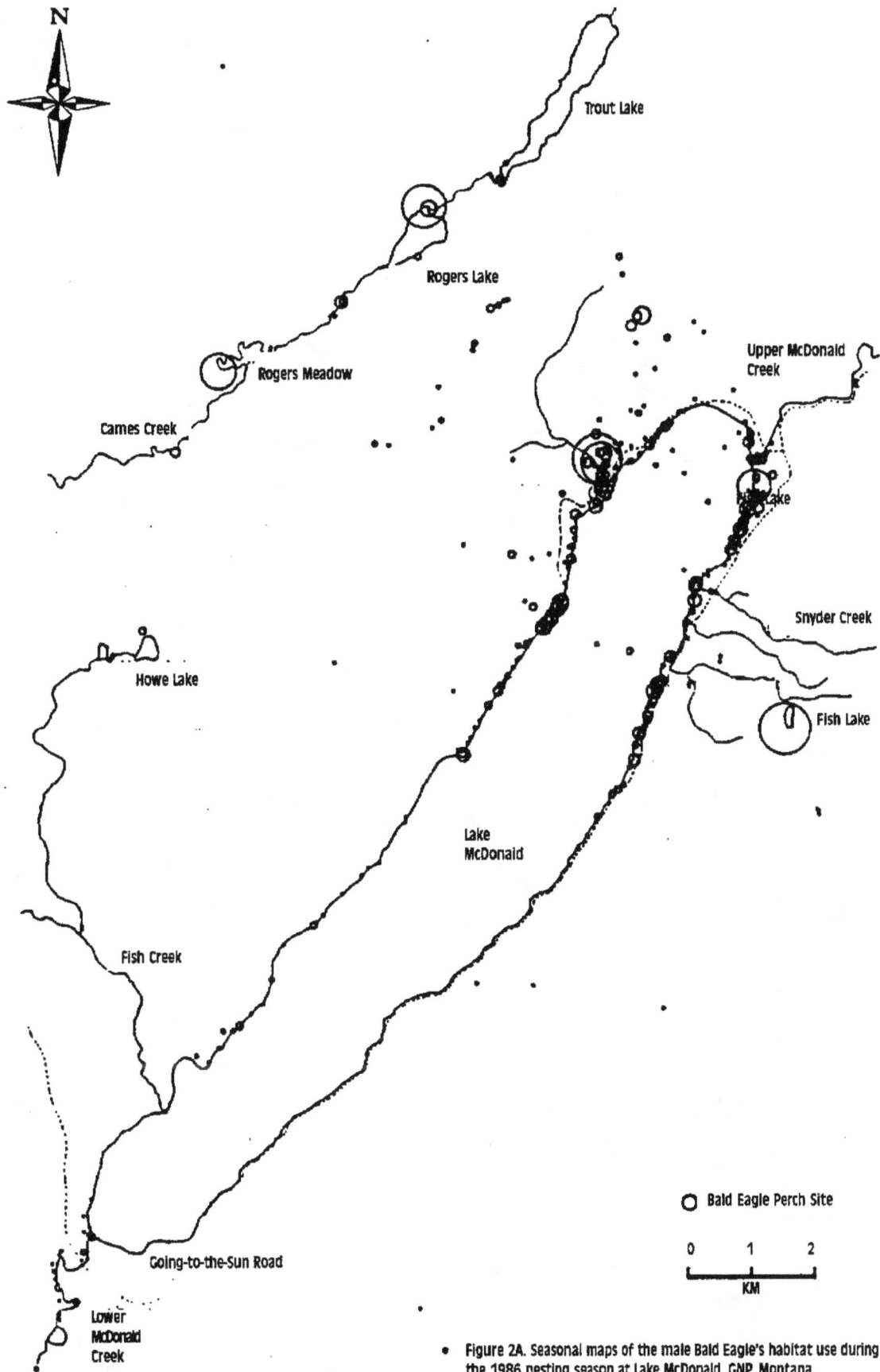

Figure 2A. Seasonal maps of the male Bald Eagle's habitat use during the 1986 nesting season at Lake McDonald, GNP, Montana.

Trout Lake

Rogers Lake

Rogers Meadow

Cames Creek

Upper McDonald Creek

Snyder Creek

Howe Lake

Fish Lake

Lake McDonald

Fish Creek

Going-to-the-Sun Road

Lower McDonald Creek

○ Bald Eagle Perch Site

0   1   2
KM

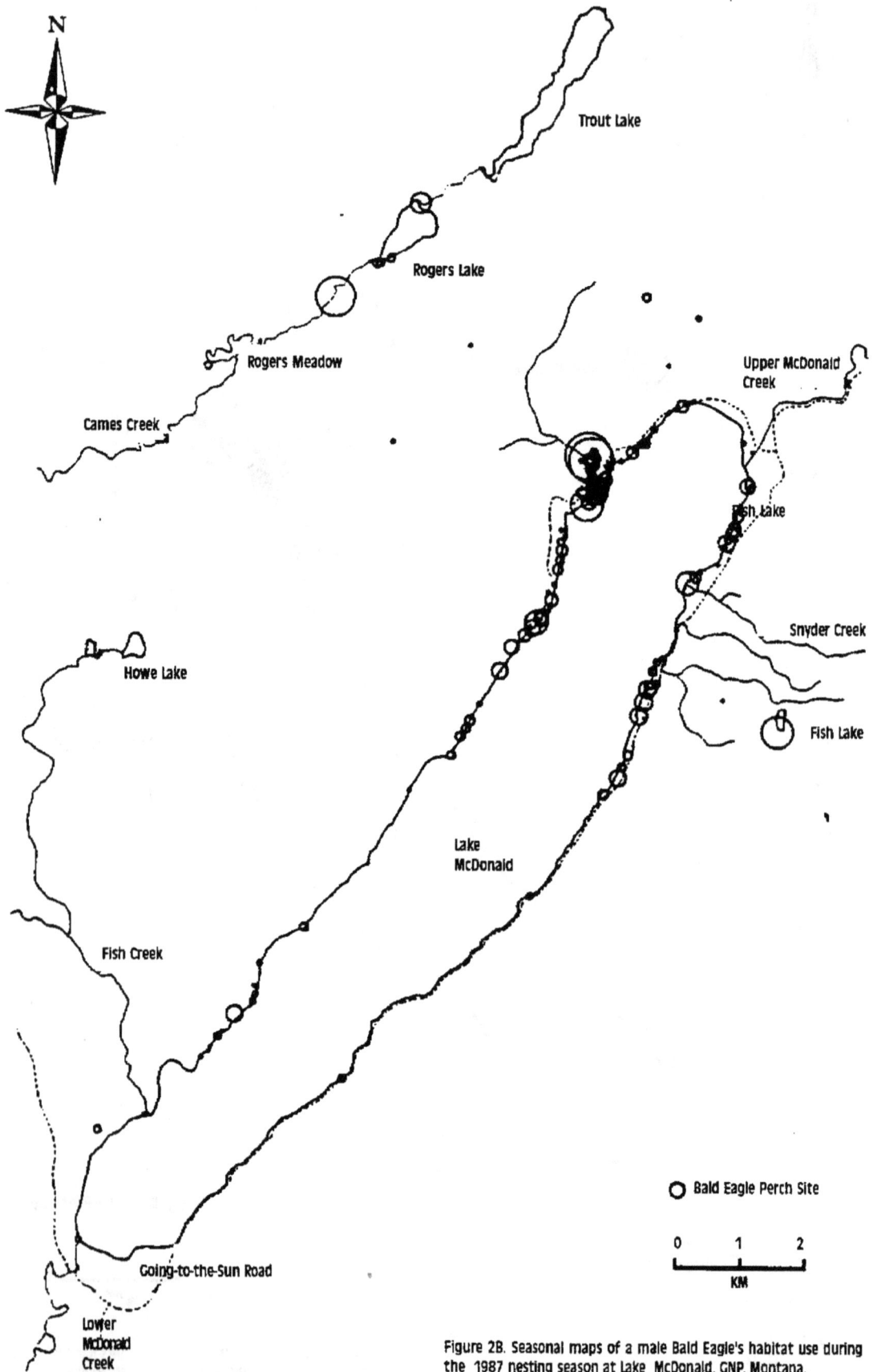

Figure 2B. Seasonal maps of a male Bald Eagle's habitat use during the 1987 nesting season at Lake McDonald, GNP, Montana.

Trout Lake

Rogers Lake

Rogers Meadow

Upper McDonald Creek

Cames Creek

Fish Lake

Snyder Creek

Howe Lake

Fish Lake

Lake McDonald

Fish Creek

○ Bald Eagle Perch Site

0   1   2

KM

Going-to-the-Sun Road

Lower McDonald Creek

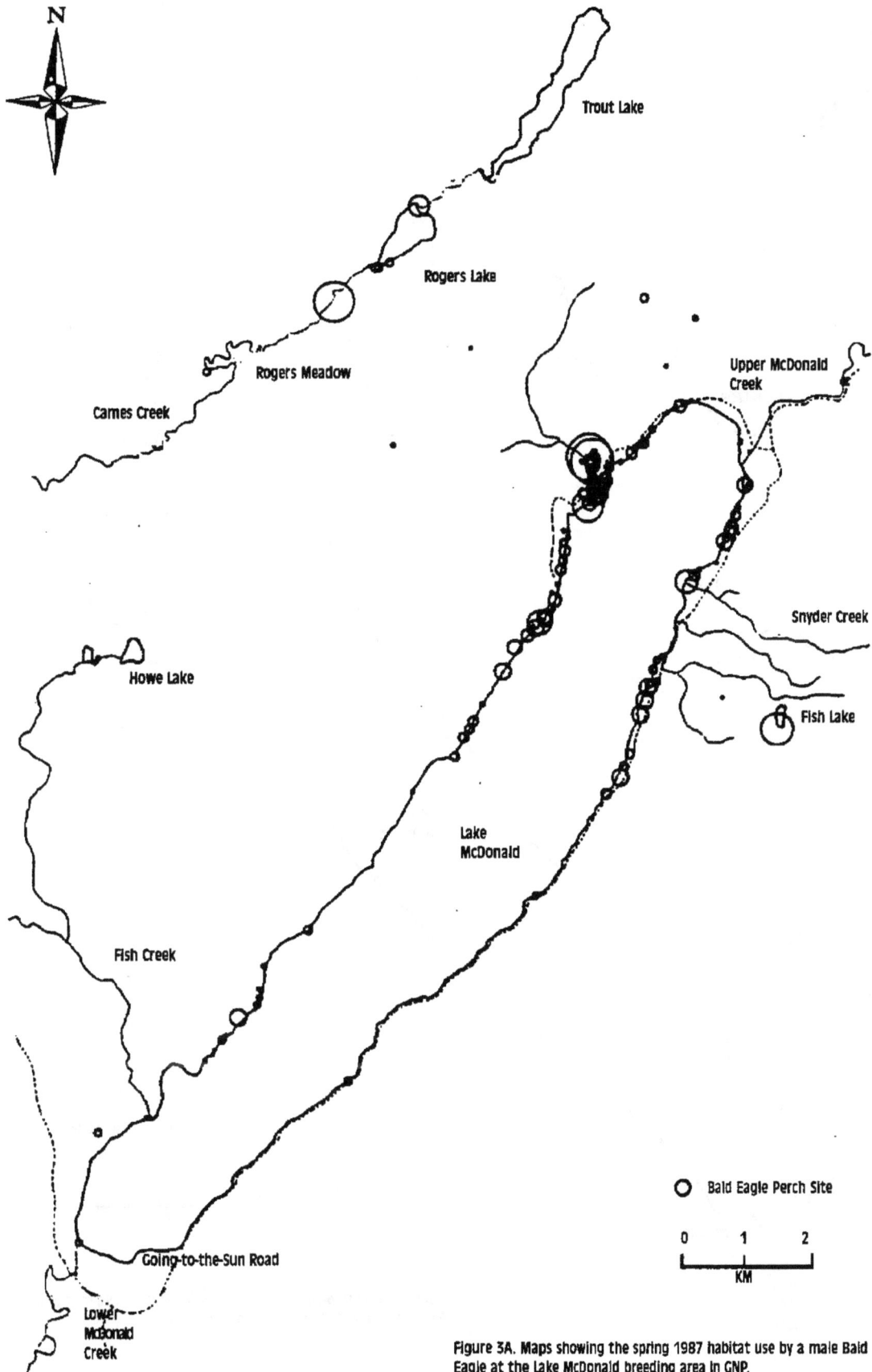

Figure 3A. Maps showing the spring 1987 habitat use by a male Bald Eagle at the Lake McDonald breeding area in GNP.

Trout Lake

Rogers Lake

Rogers Meadow

Carnes Creek

Upper McDonald Creek

Snyder Creek

Howe Lake

Fish Lake

Lake McDonald

Fish Creek

○ Bald Eagle Perch Site

0   1   2

KM

Going-to-the-Sun Road

Lower McDonald Creek

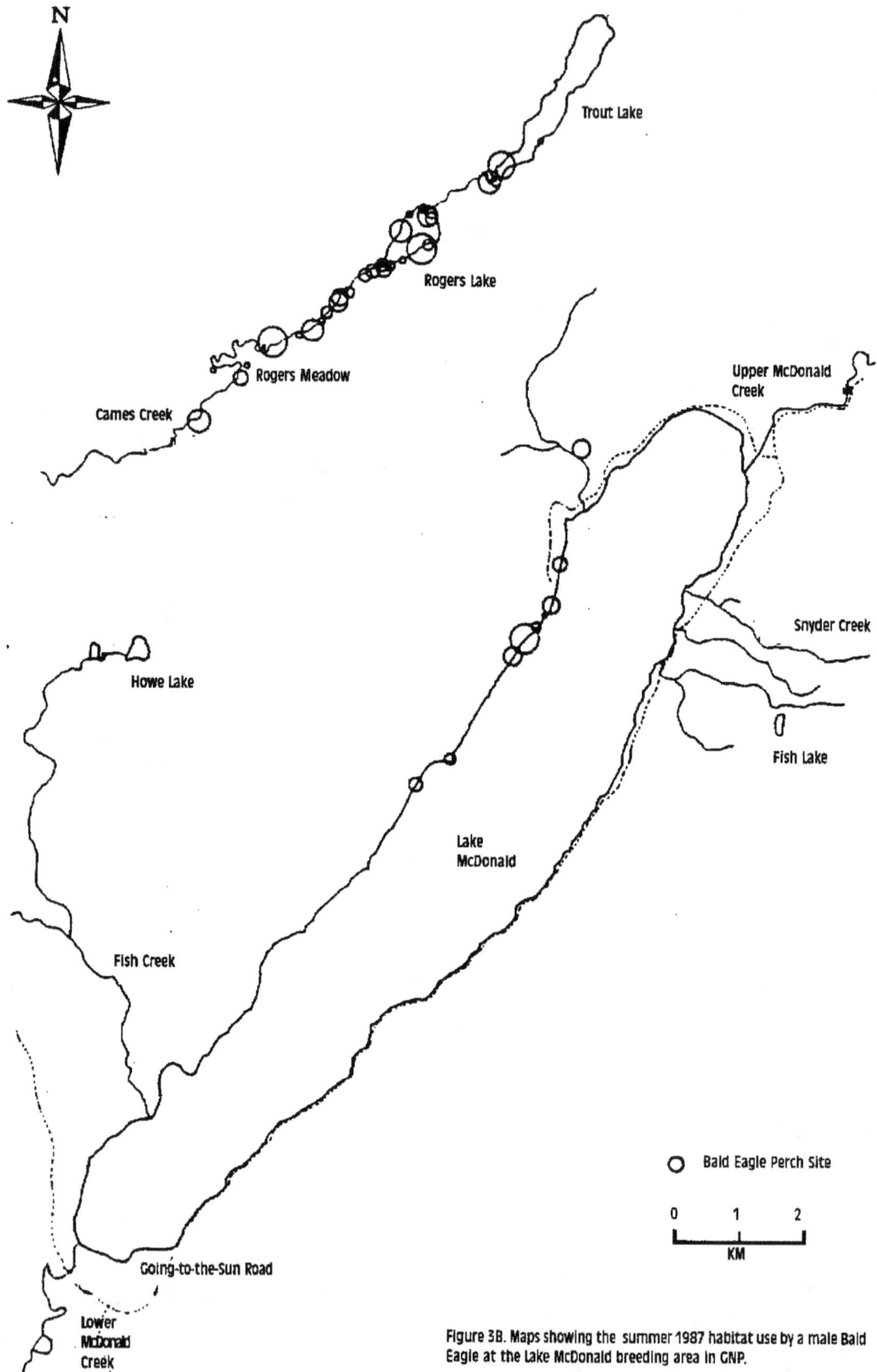

N

Trout Lake

Rogers Lake

Rogers Meadow

Cames Creek

Upper McDonald Creek

Snyder Creek

Howe Lake

Fish Lake

Fish Creek

Lake McDonald

○ Bald Eagle Perch Site

0   1   2
KM

Going-to-the-Sun Road

Lower McDonald Creek

Figure 3B. Maps showing the summer 1987 habitat use by a male Bald Eagle at the Lake McDonald breeding area in GNP.

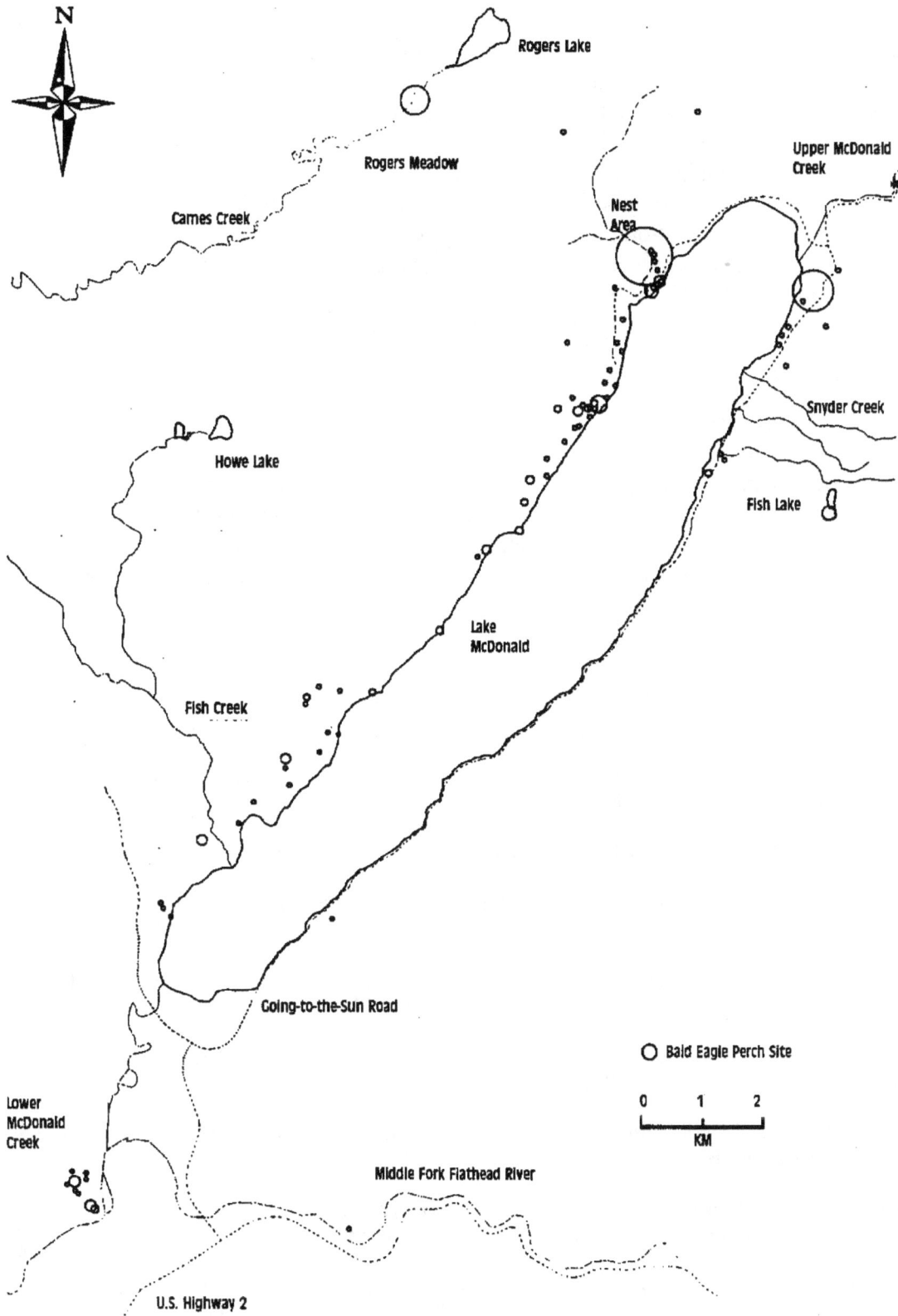

Figure 4. Male Bald Eagle's roost-site use at Lake McDonald in GNP (March 1986–August 1987).

Management Implications

Depicting Bald Eagle use areas by this method not only delineates important forage, perch and roost sites, but also identifies significant times of the year, season or day. Managers can use this information to identify hours and areas of eagle/human conflict. Shifts in use of key areas may indicate changes in the prey base, disturbance factors or success of implemented management recommendations. An example of seasonal shifts in habitat use was made by comparing the locations and sizes of circles for two maps (Figure 3). If a change in foraging habits were the result of human disturbance, managers would need to know the effect of any positive actions (such as area closures or boating restrictions) taken to reduce those disturbances. Depiction of Bald Eagle habitat use patterns before and after management actions is important in determining their success or failure.

Acknowledgements

Partial funding for this project was provided by the U.S. National Park Service and by a U.S. Dept. of Agriculture McIntire-Stennis Grant obtained through the Montana Conservation and Forest Experiment Station, University of Montana. We thank R. Bennetts, E. Caton, R. Ljung, P. McClelland and M. McFadzen for their dedicated assistance in the field. Dr. H. Zuuring reviewed an earlier draft and provided helpful comments.

Literature Cited

Cain, S. L. and J. I. Hodges. 1989. A floating-fish snare for capturing Bald Eagles. J. Raptor Res. 23(1):10-13.

Crenshaw, J. G. 1985. Characteristics of Bald Eagle communal roosts in Glacier National Park, Montana. M.S. Thesis, Univ. Montana, Missoula. 85pp.

Flath, D. and R. Hazelwood. 1966. Up, up and away-Montana's soaring eagles. Montana Outdoors 17(3).

Frenzel, R. W. 1984. Environmental contaminants and ecology of Bald Eagles in southcentral Oregon. Ph.D. Thesis, Oreg. State Univ., Corvallis. 143pp.

Griffin, C. R. 1978. The ecology of Bald Eagles wintering at Swan Lake National Wildlife Refuge, with emphasis on eagle-waterfowl relationships. Ph.D. Thesis, Univ. Missouri, St. Louis. 185pp.

Harvey, M. J. and R. W. Barbour. 1965. Home range of *Microtus ochrogasteras* determined by a modified minimum area method. J. Mammal. 40(3):398-492.

Montana Bald Eagle Working Group. 1986. Montana Bald Eagle management plan. U.S. Dept. Inter., Bureau Land Manage., Billings, Mont. 61pp.

Stuwe, M. and C. E. Blowhowiak. 1986. Micro computer program for the analysis of animal locations. Conserv. and Res. Cent., Natl. Zool. Park, Smithsonian Inst., Washington, D.C. 18pp.

Wherry, D. B., J. A. Hart, C. H. Key and S. A. Bain. 1985. An operational interagency GIS: the Glacier National Park/Flathead National Forest project. Pages 58-67. In: Proceedings for PECORA 10 Remote Sensing in Forest and Resource Management, Ft. Collins, Colo.

Yates, R. E. 1989. Bald Eagle nesting ecology and habitat use: Lake McDonald, Glacier National Park, Montana. M.S. Thesis, Univ. Montana, Missoula. 102pp.

Young, L. S. 1983. Movements of Bald Eagles associated with autumn concentrations in Glacier National Park. M.S. Thesis, Univ. of Montana, Missoula. 102pp.

Behavioral Studies in the Alaska Rain Forest

Johanna Fagen and Robert Fagen
University of Alaska Southeast, Juneau, AK

The mist-bound lives of Alaska's rainforest animals exert special fascination. The coastal forests are remote from population centers, the animals themselves are difficult to observe, the country in which they live is vast and rugged and the area as a whole is relatively little-known and little-publicized. Because of these factors, viable populations of species like the Bald Eagle and entire forest landscapes persist on Alaska's coasts. However, their survival is not assured. Individual humans, interacting with individual forest animals, will ultimately decide the future of these species. Long-term study of animal behavior in this natural setting is essential to define requirements for survival, to monitor and inventory individuals and communities and to assess the effects of human activity and management policy. To cover such wide-ranging topics adequately, the discussion will need to address issues of many different kinds.

General Overview

The two sections that will follow are entitled "Biological Context" and "Observing and Recording." The common basis of these discussions is the observation that although every ecological setting offers unique biological relationships for study along with varying practical difficulties, scientists have developed standard techniques for observing behavior that work well in a variety of settings. These humane techniques are equally useful for studying eagles in a Southeastern Alaska rainforest, baboons in an African grassland and human children in a laboratory preschool. When using these techniques, it is essential to recognize the special qualities and the natural and cultural history of each specific setting for behavior - unique and distinct, as in the three cases cited above. This context inevitably contributes to the interpretation of field observations and even to the perception of ongoing behavior. The overall scientific context for these and all such studies is the realization that individual animals have distinct, unique personalities which affect behavior, ecology and evolution. Similarly, individual forest trees may well be distinct in ecologically significant ways. New information on Alaskan rainforest plant individuality could shed light on forest animal behavior and deserves systematic study from an ecological perspective. Full understanding of individual distinctiveness in animals and its diverse implications for population, landscape and evolutionary dynamics is essential for management of wildlife and fish resources. An adequate appreciation of these relationships in the specific context of each particular wildlife viewing opportunity is equally essential if an interpretive, educational or wildlife tourism program is to achieve its goals of quality experience for the participants. Information on unique individuals and their behavior is an essential element of scientifically-based monitoring and resource inventory, as well as economic and ecological modeling. This information contributes to management of wildlife-human interactions, resource management with important population-level consequences, better public information about wildlife re-sources and wildlife-oriented education and interpretation. Often, these information needs flow from explicit management mandates and administrative direction, as based in enabling legislation. To meet these needs, it is essential to conduct long-term behavioral research on known individual animals at specific field sites whose characteristics are known to favor research of this sort.

The following section, entitled "Biological Context," expands the first of the three points made above under "General Overview:" Each setting for behavioral studies has special qualities that must inform any study from its outset. In particular, the Southeastern Alaska rainforest is a biome with special qualities that affect literally everything a behavioral researcher sees and does in the field. These special qualities include the proximity of glacier ice and the history of recent glaciation. These factors have created and today continue actively to shape a special environment, termed the periglacial environment. This setting has produced unique relationships between animals and landscapes and these relationships, in turn, both mold and reflect unique characteristics of both animals and landscapes. In the periglacial environment of Southeastern Alaska, land and water interpenetrate. The conventional distinction between "terrestrial" and "marine" science needs to be set aside, as it does not apply here and becomes counterproductive or even misleading whenever attempts are made to retain it in practice. In Southeastern Alaska, landscapes are seascapes and vice versa. Every particle of land and every drop of water in Southeastern Alaska, like the country itself, integrates sea and land in an emergent whole, a fact that is fundamental to the ecology of the entire coastal rainforest biome. This recognition acknowledges ecological reality and the impact of geological history, both of which deserve consideration by human activities and organizations concerned with the forest and its animals.

In our section on "Biological Context," we also enumerate and discuss the special characteristics of animals that, make their home in the periglacial environment of the coastal rainforest biome where land and ocean interpenetrate. These characteristics include large body size, long lifespan, low reproductive potential, large brains, ecological dependence on entire landscapes rather than on specific habitat types, playfulness both as young and as adults, a potential for long-distance dispersal over both land and water and strong individual personalities. This pattern is common to all of the forest's major animal groups, both mammals and birds. Because strong individual differences persist and because low reproductive potential and delayed maturity together mean that population-level changes are slow, rare events can have profound consequences for individuals, populations and landscapes. These characteristics of Alaskan rainforest animals further justify the critical need for long-term studies of known individuals of key animal species in varied areas of the forest.

In this paper, the term "ethologist" is used to indicate a student of the behavior of animals under natural conditions. The science of ethology, comprising much of current-day research on animal behavior, includes both field and laboratory studies. A college course in animal behavior or comparative psychology will cover most of the field of ethology as currently defined.

It is not the purpose of this paper to address the important safety considerations for behavioral research in the Alaska rainforest. Safety considerations are exclusively and entirely the responsibility of the legally-specified parties, which may include the researcher and/or the entity that administers the actual work. This chapter is solely intended to address scientific issues relating to behavioral studies in the Alaska rainforest. Appropriate training on safety and health procedures must be obtained from certified professionals by any individual wishing to do such behavioral research before going into the field.

Bald Eagles and other birds take advantage of spawning sand lance. Photo by Bob Armstrong.

Biological Context
Southeastern Alaska is a geologically-young periglacial landscape. The history of its

animals involves repeated glaciations, a changing climate and the mass extinctions of Alaska's Pleistocene. Relationships between animals and their physical and biotic environment that have developed in Southeastern Alaska over the past 10,000 years are the joint outcome of long-term cycles and rare events involving individuals or individual ecological sites. Knowledge of history and long-term study of individual behavior are essential to understand these outcomes and their current-day consequences.

Rare events, such as periods of food scarcity and abundance, glacial recession and the emergence of new land, favor large-brained, intelligent, large bodied, behaviorally plastic predators, scavengers and generalists with highly-developed dispersal abilities (Geist 1978). Southeastern Alaska has some of the largest concentrations of Bald Eagles, brown bears, orcas (killer whales), Steller sea lions and river otters. Many of these species and additional species in this biome such as the Common Raven, are among the consummate generalists of the animal kingdom.

As a broad generalization, the feature that most sharply differentiates them from other animal species is the use of entire landscapes to survive. This generalization holds especially well for brown bears, but the same principle applies, in varying degrees, to many other Southeastern Alaska animal species.

The vertebrate species most commonly encountered in ecology and animal behavior textbooks (Anolis lizards, rhesus macaques, coniferous forest warblers, Red-winged Blackbirds, voles, sticklebacks, juncos, etc.) display a kind of ecology that is much more familiar, relatively well-studied by scientists and fairly typical of most animal species. They depend on just a few particular features of a large area, but can get along without the rest as long as that one particular feature is present in sufficient quantity. Some of these species, like juncos and sticklebacks, may be prominent in periglacial environments, may exhibit one or more features marking them as ecological generalists and/or may be good dispersers, but do not depend on entire landscapes for survival. (In Southeastern Alaska, where land and sea fuse together, "earthscape" is perhaps a better term than landscape or seascape. Scientists working in the rainforest are burdened with inadequate terminology based in western European and urban North American lifestyles.) After a few months in the field in Southeastern Alaska, patterns of individualistic, landscape-oriented resource use become apparent to even the untrained observer. To cite three casual examples from our own experience, a Sitka black-tailed deer swam from island to island and ate kelp, a brown bear dug for clams and two brown bear cubs handled and mouthed a small flatfish (flounder or sole). Foraging and diet of these species and their individual members is diverse in Southeastern Alaska because of the interpenetration of marine and terrestrial elements in each actual habitat.

The life cycle of any salmon species found in Southeastern Alaska illustrates the interdependence of saltwater and terrestrial organisms. A good year for salmon is generally a good year for seals, bears, eagles, ravens and gulls. The salmon caught by a bear or an eagle may also feed Mew and Bonaparte's gulls, Northwestern Crows and ravens, as well as fertilizing the sedges in an estuary, a 400-year old Sitka spruce in the forest and a buttercup in the alpine.

When a salmon run fails, poor nutrition, poor reproductive success or migration may change the composition of a deme or population of animals. Loss or displacement of key individuals may affect social behavior, cultural transmission or habitat use within a population. The failure of the pink salmon run in 1988 in upper Seymour Canal was a unique event superimposed on a canon of long-term environmental cycles. Indeed, rare events may determine a population or species' history more than "the daily rhythms of birth, feeding, sex and death" (Gould 1989). A valid picture of the life of any species and particularly species of the sort we are discussing here, can only emerge after known individuals of the species are studied across major natural cycles and over several generations.

Observing and Recording Behavior

After many hours of watching an individual, a trained observer will begin to notice distinct behavioral acts emerging from many behavioral states. It is at this point that you realize an animal is not just shaking its head, but it is shaking its head at another animal and sending a subtle message. It may seem a contradiction then to state that an observer should be careful not to prejudice his or her observations by recording what he or she "thinks" is happening. In order to record what the ethologist sees objectively it is necessary first to see the behavior as distinct movements. A purely verbal description of movement may be inadequate.

Seeing behavior and thinking in movements are essential research skills for studies in any habitat. To acquire these skills involves real discipline and long hours of training by a qualified teacher. Concentration and focus, freedom from preconceptions about behavior, the learned ability to perceive both small details of movement and large patterns of movement and above all patience are essential (Darling 1937). Most people can learn to do all of these things well, but it takes time. Training in non-biological areas, such as dance, clinical psychology or classroom observation, often involves these same skills.

Thinking in terms of body movements and movement patterns helps scientists observe behavior more clearly and accurately. Movement research has contributed formal systems of notation, new modes of analysis and new concepts of movement to the study of behavior (Golani 1976, Pellis 1981 and Fagen 1990). Although the early pioneers of movement research (e.g., Eshkol and Wachmann 1958, Laban 1960) recognized the broad implications of their findings, dancers and students of behavior are only now coming to recognize that their fields have much in common. Today, students of behavior increasingly include some form of movement analysis in their professional training.

To study a species, you must first get to know an individual. This truism seems incontestable. However, in the past, scientists were unaware of the importance of individual effects at the population level. As ecologists, ethologists or resource managers, they were trained to study a population of animals and make generalizations about the species. Individuals whose behavior was deviant from the group were not thought to deserve much scrutiny. However, in large-brained, intelligent mammals, the importance of the individual in cultural transmission and innovation is beginning to be recognized. Jane Goodall had observed more than a decade of peaceful living within chimpanzee troops at Gombe Stream before witnessing the first cannibalistic attack (Goodall 1986). Over the next four years only one infant was raised. The innovation of cannibalism of infants by two cooperating individuals at Gombe Stream (Goodall 1986) is a prime example of individual behavior affecting the demography and reproductive success of the population.

If you are fortunate to be able to study a species whose members are large, visible and all with individually distinct pelage or feathers, identification of individuals will be easy. However, getting to know individuals is usually not that simple and it is often necessary to depend on a combination of identifying factors. Answers to the following questions will help identify many individuals: Is the animal male or female, young or old, exceptionally large, small, fat, thin? Does it have offspring and how many? Does it have any scars, spots, stripes? Does it spend most of its time in one area? Is it seen with another animal? How does it interact with other known individuals? Does it have a strange gait, or any man-made marks such as tags, radio collars or streamers?

Once an individual is identified it must be named. It is often easiest to name it for its distinguishing characteristic. However, names such as Scarface or Mom may imply behavior or personality. Lehner (1979) examines some of the biases names create.

Avoiding bias is important in another area of ethology, that of sampling. Methods for obtaining valid samples of behavior are various (Lehner 1979) and include a method called focal-animal sampling that is particularly useful for studying known individuals (Altmann 1974). In focal-animal sampling, each individual in a group is observed for the same length of time in random order. This method benefits the animals as well as the observer, because no animal is observed for such a long period of time that it becomes uncomfortable at being watched.

This consideration of focal-animal sampling raises the point that the welfare of animals is important for all research. Increasing numbers of researchers are putting the animals first by choosing study questions and observational techniques that are compatible with the animals' long-term and short-term well-being. There is no shortage of crucially-important problems of this sort, both in field and in laboratory settings.

Literature Cited

Altmann, J. 1974. Observational study of behavior: sampling methods. Behaviour 49:227-267

Darling, F. F. 1937. A herd of red deer. Oxford Univ. Press, London.

Eshkol, N. and A. Wachmann. 1958. Movement notation. Weidenfeld and Nicolson, London.

Fagen, R. 1990. Playing with danger and dancing with strangers. Anthrozoos 4:4-6.

Geist, V. 1978. Life strategies, human evolution, environmental design: toward a biological theory of health. Springer-Verlag, N.Y.

Golani, I. 1976. Homeostatic motor processes in mammalian interactions: a choreography of display. Pages 69-134. In: P. P. G. Bateson and P. H. Klopfer, eds. Perspectives in ethology, vol. 2. Plenum, N.Y.

Goodall, J. 1986. The chimpanzees of Gombe. Belknap Press, Harvard Univ. Press, Cambridge, Mass.

Gould, S. J. 1989. The horn of Triton. Nat. Hist. 12:18-27.

Laban, R. 1960. The mastery of movement. 2nd ed. Macdonald and Evans, London.

Lehner, P. 1979. Handbook of ethological methods. Garland STPM, N.Y.

Pellis, S. 1981. A description of social play by the Australian Magpie *Gymnorhina tibicien* based on Eshkol-Wachman notation. Bird Behaviour 3:61-79.

Photographing Bald Eagles

Robert H. Armstrong

Alaska Department of Fish and Game (retired) and University of Alaska Southeast, Juneau, AK

One only needs to spend time at the Alaska Chilkat Bald Eagle Preserve to realize the attraction that Bald Eagles have for photographers. Professional photographers cluster at every turnout and points in between. They come from all over the United States and from other countries. They make their living with photography in a variety of ways, but all agree that eagle photographs are among their best sellers (Armstrong 1986). Many tours are scheduled to this preserve and seeing an individual among them without a camera would indeed be a rare sight. Even people traveling to points further north stop to photograph these majestic birds perched along the highway.

Photography also is used to gather scientific information about Bald Eagles. Time-lapse cameras have been used at eagle nests to determine such behavior as incubation and brooding time by sex and number of prey deliveries (see Cain 2008). Photography also has been used successfully to study behavior in other raptors (Enderson et al. 1972, Wille 1979).

Whatever the purpose, getting close enough to photograph eagles is difficult and in doing so photographers can often stress and even harm eagles. Regulations, guidelines and written ethics exist to help protect Bald Eagles in Alaska from overzealous photographers. Also, the use of certain techniques and equipment can help photographers obtain good photographs without undue stress to the eagles. I will discuss all of these subjects in this paper.

Regulations, Guidelines, Ethics

"Wildlife photographers generally consider their activities to be non-consumptive, that is they do not harvest wildlife like hunters, trappers and fishermen. But photographers can take a toll of their subjects, causing increased stress and even death. Therefore, it is important to keep in mind that the welfare of the wildlife is more important than the photograph."

This statement from Photographing Wildlife in Alaska by Wright and Arnason (1980) certainly seems to be true for Bald Eagles. Just approaching eagles usually causes them to flee long before they are within camera range. Once feeding eagles are disturbed they usually completely evacuate the area (Hansen et al. 1984) and do not return to feed until several hours later (Stalmaster and Newman 1978). Attempting to photograph eagles at their nest site may cause the birds to abandon the nest (Armstrong 1987). Even biologists working carefully around nesting eagles have caused abandonment and death of the young (Cain 2008).

Regulations restricting photographic activities around eagles are few. Probably the only established law that directly affects photographers throughout Alaska is the Bald Eagle Protection Act (BEPA; 16 U.S.C. 668688d). The most pertinent part of this act prohibits molestation or disturbance of eagles at their nests. Because of this possibility a permit from the United States Fish and Wildlife Service is required to build a photographer's blind near an eagle nest. Also Alaska state law (11 AAC 21.120) requires authorization to build a wildlife observation blind on the Alaska Chilkat Bald Eagle Preserve.

Certain guidelines exist for the Alaska Chilkat Bald Eagle Preserve that would affect photographers. In summary these guidelines are: (1) stay off the flats, (2) view eagles only from the area between highway and river, (3) do not disturb the fish in any way and (4) stop and park only in designated turnouts.

Ethics for photographing eagles are difficult to establish. All photographers develop their own ethics as their experience increases. What is ethical for one photographer may be unacceptable to another. It seems nearly impossible to approach eagles without causing them some stress, but perhaps it is the degree of stress that we should be most concerned about. Members of the Alaska Society of Outdoor and Nature Photographers pledge that "No action will be taken that will adversely impact my subject or natural setting" (Walker 1986). Although this statement is open to differing interpretations, I cannot think of a better one.

Equipment

The best source of information I found on photography is John Shaw's book The Nature Photographers Complete Guide to Professional Field Techniques (1984). Shaw's suggestions for lenses, tripods and cameras are in my opinion, ideal for photographing eagles.

For photographing Bald Eagles in flight I like to use a 300 mm, internal focusing, f4.5 telephoto lens. This size is light and easy to hold by hand. The internal focusing feature (IF) changes the optical elements within the lens rather than the length of the lens as standard lenses do. This means that IF lenses have rapid and smooth focusing, a real plus when working with fast-moving eagles. A motor drive is also a real asset when working with eagles in flight.

For perched and feeding eagles, a longer telephoto lens may be needed. Most professional photographers at the Alaska Chilkat Bald Eagle Preserve use the very expensive and fast (f2.8-5.6) 400 to 600 mm telephoto lenses (Armstrong 1986). The faster lenses let in more light so they focus more easily. They also allow you to use faster shutter speeds that help stop both eagle and camera movements.

According to Shaw (1984) you should use the shortest focal length you can because the longer the focal length the more vibration is magnified. Because of vibration when using telephoto lenses a good steady tripod is a must. The brands I see most often used are the heavier models of Bogen and Gitzo. Some eagle photographers use additional support such as a monopod. The use of a cable release, self timer, or mirror lock-up all help to reduce camera movements or vibration and help yield a sharper image.

I use my 300 mm lens with a 1.4x extender for perched and feeding eagles. The extender make my lens a 420 mm f/6.4. This may not be the very best setup, but it is a compact, affordable package that yields marketable results. Shaw recommends against using any teleconverters larger than 1.4x because the loss of light, shutter speed and photo sharpness may be unacceptable.

A telephoto lens was necessary to take this picture without disturbing the eagle. Photo by Bob Armstrong.

There is some specialized equipment that might help to obtain outstanding photographs of Bald Eagles. Some devices allow you to trigger your camera from a distance or allow the bird to trigger the camera for you. This would allow you to put a camouflaged camera close to where an eagle perches or feeds and use a shorter focal length lens to get a different perspective not possible with a long telephoto lens. Combining motor drive with infrared triggering and radio controlled devices, you can trigger the cameras from up to about 60 m away (with infrared) to between 300 m and 700 m away (with radio control). I have used the infrared devices with considerable success on many different species of birds, but I have not yet tried them with eagles. They should work wherever an eagle regularly comes to a specific spot to feed or perch. Most popular camera brands sell these devices, but they usually work only on cameras of the same brand.

One device, the Dale Beam, could be used at a known feeding or perching spot. The Dale Beam is a photo tripper that contains an infrared transmitter and receiver. It sends out a pulsed beam of infrared light which is bounced off a small reflector and back to the built-in sensor. An eagle breaking the beam, by flying or stepping through it, would trigger the camera. I have successfully used the Dale Beam for birds and found it to be very well built and able to withstand considerable abuse.

Some photographic devices might have an application to Bald Eagle research. The Dale Beam, for example, can be used with 9 to 24 volt DC power and would last many days without attendance. Data backs available for 35 mm cameras can be programmed to fire the camera at any interval you select. Their usefulness would be greatest if used in conjunction with a bulk film magazine. Some researchers have successfully used remote time-lapse camera units (Enderson et al. 1972, Wille 1979, Cain 1998).

Temple (1972) describes the construction of timelapse motion picture cameras. These units usually consist of a movie camera, an intervalometer, a photocell and a battery pack. Cain (1998) used the intervalometer to take single-frame exposures every 90 seconds and the photocell turned the system off at night to save batteries and film. The camera was housed in a 50 caliber ammunition box lined with polyurethane foam to muffle sound and prevent condensation.

Techniques

The greatest challenge in photographing eagles is getting close enough. Even when using long telephoto lenses, such as 400 mm, you need to be closer than 20 m for a frame-filling photo. In one study of eagle behavior in which the birds were approached by an observer, the mean distance at which eagles flushed was 196 m for adults and 99 m for juveniles and flushing distance generally ranged between 25 and 300 m (Stalmaster and Newman 1978). These distances are much greater than the range at which one could obtain good photographs. So how do we get close to eagles?

One method is to find an area where eagles are accustomed to human activity. The best place I know of is the Alaska Chilkat Bald Eagle Preserve during the months of November and December (Warden 1985). Eagles perch and feed in the area between Mile 18 and Mile 24 of the Haines Highway often within 15 m to 30 m of the viewing areas (Hirschmann 1988). If spawned-out salmon are available along the spring-fed channels close to the road and if most other channels farther out are frozen, one can almost be assured of good photographic opportunities. Along roadways eagles are usually accustomed to automobiles and cars can be used as a blind. On many occasions I have slowly driven up to an area where eagles were feeding and been able to obtain good photos without leaving my automobile or disturbing the birds. Window mounts, such as the one made by Bushnell, help steady the camera. Any movement within the automobile can cause camera shake, so working alone is usually best.

This Eagle's fish catching technique is captured using a motor drive, large telephoto lens and high speed Film. Photos by Bob Armstrong.

For many years eagles have been fed fish scraps in Homer, Alaska. Photographers are allowed in the area but only if they stay in their car (Walker 1988). The reasoning for this is obvious because the minute one steps out of a car all the eagles flush and often do not return that day. I have also found this to be true wherever I have used a car as a blind. According to Lee Rue III (1984) there is no better way to photograph eagles than by baiting the birds with carrion. He recommends using road-killed wildlife. Skunks should be transferred outside the car, however!

In Alaska I have found fish parts and carcasses to be ideal bait for luring Bald Eagles close enough for photography. When food is plentiful, however, such as during the time when salmon spawn, baiting usually does not work. It is illegal to use the whole carcass of some sport caught fish as bait for eagles. According to the Alaska Department of Fish and Game (1990), "Except for whitefish and suckers, the intentional waste or destruction of any species of sport-caught fish for which bag limits, seasons or other regulatory methods and means are provided, is prohibited, except that the head, tail, fins and viscera of legally taken sport fish may be used for bait or other purposes." Under special circumstances you may be able to obtain a scientific or educational collecting permit from the Alaska Department of Fish and Game that would allow the use of sport fish. Also, I believe there is no regulation against collecting and using dead spawned-out salmon as bait for eagles or using any fish, such as staghorn sculpins, not considered a game fish.

Approaching Bald Eagles by boat may allow you to get close enough for photography. In many areas of Alaska, boats, like cars, are a familiar sight to Bald Eagles and the birds often accept their presence. For example, Bald Eagles feeding on spawning herring may ignore a kayaker paddling nearby. I have often closely approached eagles perched in a tree near shore with my bright yellow skiff. Sometimes presenting a floating fish beneath a perched eagle elicits an almost immediate spectacular dive and snatch of the fish from the water surface. To make fish float, simply inject their body cavity with air from a football pump and needle. Using styrofoam to float fish and working below an eagle's nest should be avoided. Accidental ingestion of styrofoam may harm eagles and photography near a nest site may cause the adults to abandon the nest.

Photographing eagles in flight requires certain techniques for success. It is nearly impossible to react quickly enough for single frame photos of flying eagles. I usually set my motor drive in the continuous mode and fire it in bursts of 3 to 6 as I am following the eagle in flight. Prefocusing on a floating fish can also help you obtain "in-focus" photos of flying eagles.

You can hand hold the camera most successfully if you use a shutter speed equal to or larger than the length of your lens. For example, sharp photos can be taken with a hand-held 300 mm lens at 1/500 sec but are less likely at 1/125 sec. However, with practice and luck spectacular photos of flying eagles with sharp head and blurred wings can be taken at the slower shutter speeds (Oberle 1988). I obtain the highest percentage of in-focus, sharp photos of flying eagles by using Ektachrome 400 at f/11 and 1/1000 sec on a sunny day. However, since Kodachrome is more marketable I usually settle for 1 to 3 sharp photos of flying eagles for every 36 exposure roll.

Editors' note: In recent years we have seen Bob and other professional photographers using digital cameras.

Literature Cited

Alaska Department of Fish and Game. 1990. Alaska sport fishing regulations summary. 4pp.

Armstrong, B. 1986. Chilkat eagles and photographers. Alaska Outdoor Photographer Newsletter. Alas. Soc. Outdoor and Nat. Photographers. Dec. p. 3-4.

Armstrong, B. 1987. Photographing birds at nests. Alaska Outdoor Photographer, Newsletter Alas. Soc. Outdoor and Nat. Photographers. March p. 2-3.

Cain, S. L. 1998. Time budgets and behavior of nesting Bald Eagles. In: Wright, B.A. and P.F. Schempf, eds. Bald Eagles in Alaska.

Enderson, J. H., S. A. Temple and L. G. Swartz. 1972. Time-lapse photographic records of nesting Peregrine Falcons. Living Bird 11:113-128.

Hansen, A. J., E. L. Boeker, J. I. Hodges and D. R. Cline. 1984. Bald Eagles of the Chilkat Valley, Alaska: ecology, behavior and management. Final rep., Chilkat River Coop. Bald Eagle Study, Natl. Audubon Soc. and U.S. Fish Wildl. Serv, Anchorage, Alas. 27pp.

Hirschmann, F. 1988. The eagles have landed. Alaska Soc. Outdoor and Nat. Photographers Newsletter. December. p. 7.

Oberle, F. 1988. The flight of eagles. Audubon January p 72-77.

Rue, L. L. III. 1984. How I photograph wildlife and nature. World Almanac Publ., New York, N.Y. 287 pp.

Shaw, J. 1984. The nature photographers complete guide to professional field techniques. Am. Photographic Book Publ., New York. 144pp.

Stalmaster, M. V. and J. R. Newman. 1978. Behavioral responses of wintering Bald Eagles to human activity. J. Wildl. Manage. 42:506-513.

Temple, S. A. 1972. A portable time-lapse camera for recording wildlife activity. J. Wildl. Manage. 36(4): 944-947.

Walker, T. 1986. On ethics. Alaska Soc. Outdoor and Nat. Photographers Newsletter. 2(3):2.

Walker, T. 1988. Eagle report. Alaska Soc. Outdoor and Nat. Photographers Newsletter. 4(2):6.

Warden, J. 1985. Tips on photographing at the eagle preserve. Alaska Soc. Outdoor and Nat. Photographers Newsletter. 1(9):3.

Wille, F. 1979. Den gronlandske havorns *Haliaeetus albicilla* groenlandicus Brehm. fodevald-metode of forelobige resultater. (Choice of food of the Greenland White-tailed Eagle-method and preliminary results.) Dansk orinithologisk Forenings Tidsskrift. 73:165-70.

Wright, J. and P. Arneson. 1980. Photographing wildlife in Alaska. Nongame Wildlife Prog., Div. Game, Alaska Department of Fish and Game, 333 Raspberry Road, Anchorage, Alas. 99503.

Raptor Rehabilitation

Noele Weemes

Juneau Raptor Center and Auke Bay Laboratory, NOAA, Juneau, Alaska

Raptor rehabilitation is the rescue, medical treatment and release of orphaned or injured birds of prey. A raptor rehabilitator must possess a good working knowledge of the natural history and physiology of many types of birds, because most raptor centers provide care and rehabilitate non-raptor species too.

In Alaska, there are currently three raptor centers; the Juneau Raptor Center (JRC), Juneau, Alaska, the Alaska Raptor Rehabilitation Center (ARRC), Sitka, Alaska and Birds Treatment and Learning Center (Bird TLC), Anchorage, Alaska. These centers share the same goals and work closely with one another by providing and sharing knowledge and new information. Sometimes, a bird may be transported between facilities. For example, the Juneau Raptor Center, which is an all volunteer organization, transports birds that require constant care and much physical therapy to the ARRC or Birds TLC who have full-time staffs, avian specialist veterinarians and large flight cages.

People from all over Alaska rescue and ship injured Bald Eagles via airplane or boat. In many instances, an eagle is injured locally and volunteers rescue the bird. Volunteers from Juneau have gone swimming in the Mendenhall River, climbed trees, jumped head first into garbage dumpsters and hiked many miles - just to highlight a few of the exciting adventures. When an eagle arrives at the center, it is given an identification number and is taken into the clinic for an evaluation. It usually requires two to three people to perform a medical examination on the injured bird. Raptors use their talons and beak for defense, so leather gloves and jacket should be worn to protect oneself from serious injuries. Most raptors remain fairly calm when their head is covered and a leather falconry hood or a blanket can be used to cover the head while performing the examination. Some things done during the examination include an observation for vigilance, inspection of flight and tail feathers, as well as inspection of wings and feet for broken bones, palpation of crop for food and breastbone for fitness, examination of skin elasticity for hydration level and pupillary dilation in the case of a concussion. Many Bald Eagle patients that are treated at the centers are dehydrated and some what emaciated. Injured birds usually have difficulty in obtaining an adequate amount of food and use most of their energy maneuvering on foot trying to locate prey. Patients that are malnourished and/or dehydrated are tubed with fluids into their crop for several days before given solid food such as fish. In Juneau, after initial examination at the center, eagles are taken to one of the local animal hospitals for full-body X-rays and blood evaluation. Veterinarians prescribe medicine, which usually consists of antibiotics to treat an infection from a wound or illness.

Rehabilitation may require days for some patients, but for others it may take months. Some birds lose muscle strength and must go through physical therapy and regain physical fitness in a large flight cage. After rehabilitation and final reevaluation, many birds are released back into their natural habitat where they may once again live in freedom. However, some birds' injuries are so severe that they can not survive in the wild; these birds are considered nonreleasable and are usually placed in breeding or educational facilities throughout the United States. Alaskan nonreleasable Bald Eagles have been placed in facilities such as: the Toledo Zoo in Ohio, Thompson Park Zoo in New York, Orange County Zoo in California and Dollywood in Tennessee.

Bald Eagle recovering in open mew at Juneau Raptor Center. Photo by Juneau Raptor Center.

Raptor centers in the United States are permitted by U.S. Fish and Wildlife and can house injured raptors on a rehabilitation permit or an educational permit. Educational permits are given to raptors who have been determined nonreleasable and will be used for public display. Raptors on a rehabilitation permit must not be kept on display for public viewing because it is important that birds do not get habituated to humans.

Education is a very important component of all raptor centers. Since rehabilitation alone cannot solve the many problems that wildlife populations encounter, wildlife educators must increase public awareness. Many Bald Eagle injuries are human-related. Every year Alaskan rehabilitators treat victims of gun shot, lead poisoning, leg hold traps and entanglement in fishing line. It is an important responsibility of raptor centers to educate the public about conservation. Many nonreleasable birds participate and travel to educational programs all over the country. We hope by giving people the opportunity to see a magnificent bird of prey up close that they will want to help protect it and the environment in which it lives.

The event of releasing recovered Bald Eagles back into the wild often draws a crowd and the media. Photo by Juneau Raptor Center.

This recovered juvenile Bald Eagle is being released in the foothills of Anchorage after being rehabilitated by TLC volunteers. Photo by David Predeger.

Research is also a component of raptor centers. The Alaska Raptor Rehabilitation Center collects blood which is used in a genetic study at the University of Minnesota. Eagles that are released back into the wild are required to be banded with U.S. Fish and Wildlife bands in the case that these bird are ever recovered. In 1993 an injured Bald Eagle was rescued by hikers in Haines and sent to the Juneau Raptor Center for medical treatment. This eagle had been banded in the winter of 1965 by a biologist who banded 39 Bald Eagles on the Chilkat River in Haines, Alaska. Records kept by the biologist did not indicate the age estimate at time of banding. Since eagles mature at age five and estimating age after maturity is close to impossible, if the bird had been banded as <1 year of age, it would have been 28 years of age at time of recovery which is the longevity record for the Bald Eagle (Schempf, 1996).

Volunteers are an important component of raptor rehabilitation centers. Many volunteers provide daily husbandry for the birds housed at the center. Enclosures must be kept clean and sanitary to help prevent the spread of disease. Perches are scrubbed and disinfected, gravel substrate is raked and feathers are picked up.

Fish, rats, rabbits and quail are the main diets prepared for raptors which are supplemented with a multivitamin called Vita-hawk. Food not consumed within a day is thrown away and water bowls are given fresh water. A food intake log is kept for all birds which helps the operations manager monitor the diets and health of birds at the center.

I am a volunteer at the Juneau Raptor Center because I enjoy rehabilitating injured birds and watching as they fly back to freedom. When I was young, my mother would bring home orphaned baby birds and I would help my mother care for them. When they had fledged, we would release them in a safe area. Childhood exposure to my mother's compassion for animals has given me a lifelong ambition to care for creatures in distress.

Rehabilitation can be very demanding. Some of my days seem quite long because I must work my bird care schedule around my full-time job. It is not uncommon for me to tube feed an eagle, rebandage another one's foot and clean both of their kennels before going to work in the morning.

Some of my evenings and weekends are spent picking up new patients and caring for the educational birds at the center. Sounds like a large amount of work, but I am assisted by other volunteers who enjoy handling and caring for the birds - just like I do!

Rehabilitation can be rewarding and heartbreaking. In the month before writing this, there have been two bird patients that have been very memorable. The first was a Bald Eagle that was reported to be on the ground and unable to fly. As I approached the bird, I noticed its foot stained with blood. After the bird was captured by several volunteers, we realized that the foot had suffered from a compound fracture and had been almost completely amputated. The foot could not be surgically repaired. The eagle showed no sign of pain, but it was evident that this bird would no longer have a good quality of life and was euthanized.

The second patient was a Boreal Owl that had collided with something, most likely a car. The owl was suffering from a concussion and was given an injection of steroids to decrease the swelling on its brain. I had to tube feed the owl at first, but after a couple of days he began to eat the mice that I placed in his kennel. Shortly afterwards, the owl was ready for release. As I opened my hand for the release, the owl flew into the branches high up in a nearby tree. A couple of minutes later he vanished into the forest.

Table 1. Raptors treated by Alaska raptor centers, 1984-1996.					
Center	Released	Placed	Died	Unknown	Total
ARRC	113	89	255	0	457
TLC	78	27	62	45	212
JRC	37	27	49	0	113
total	228	143	366	45	782
% of total	29.2%	18.3%	46.8%	5.7%	100%

During 1984-1996, the raptor centers in Alaska have treated approximately 782 eagles (Table 1). Injuries have been a result of natural causes, as well as human-related causes. Almost one-third of all eagles treated were successfully released back into the wild. Nearly one-fifth have been placed into educational and captive breeding programs throughout the country. As I researched this topic, I was given medical records and reports from the three centers. I was amazed to see the number of gunshot and trap victims. That is one reason why raptor centers must educate people about raptors and their importance in nature. Ecologically we may not be making a difference, but we can increase public awareness.

If you are interested in becoming a raptor center volunteer or member in Alaska, please contact:
Bird TLC, 1142 H Street, Anchorage, AK 99501, (907) 274-1186

Alaska Raptor Rehabilitation Center P.O. 2984, Sitka, AK 99835, (907)747-8662

Juneau Raptor Center, P.O. Box 34713, Juneau, AK 99803

Basic handling of eagles for rescue and shipment to raptor center
An eagle appears to be suffering from an injury
1. If there is a local raptor center in the area call them. One can reach the Juneau Raptor Center by calling the state troopers, police department, or local veterinarians.

2. It is important that you also look around the area where you find the bird for clues to what happened to it. For example, are there nearby power lines?

3. Try to work in a team if possible.

4. It's best that your hands and arms are protected from its talons and beak. Now is the time to put on leather gloves and a thick jacket if you have them.

5. Approach eagle with blanket or some large fabric (coats have many times been used).

6. Drape blanket over eagle making sure the head is covered.

7. Holding wings in with elbows, scoop eagle into chest.

8. Have someone assist in the location of legs and talons.

9. Once they locate a foot, grab on to it so that you are holding one in each hand.

10. Eagles can be shipped to the centers in a pet kennel or large box. Most local airlines have kennels available. Alaska Airlines and charter services will fly birds to the facilities.

Literature Cited

Schempf, P. F. 1996. Bald Eagle longevity record from Southeastern Alaska. J. Field Ornithol. 68(1):150-151.

Bald Eagles in a Changing Land

Bald Eagle Research Needs and Opportunities in Southeast Alaska

James G. King

U.S. Fish and Wildlife Service (retired), Juneau, AK

The Bald Eagle, symbol of our nation, has had serious difficulties coping with the increase of human activity throughout its range. If the Bald Eagle is to survive, wild and free and abundant, as human populations double and, double again we must learn a great deal more about the needs and capabilities of this magnificent bird. There is no better place to focus this research than in Southeast Alaska, where Bald Eagles remain more abundant than anywhere else in the nation and where human activity is still outweighed by large expanses of untouched wilderness.

Scott Gende prepares to measure the growth of this nestling Bald Eagle. Note the new flight feathers. Photo USFWS.

Bald Eagle research is needed in two main areas: basic biological requirements and relationship with humanity. Research opportunities in Southeast Alaska can be further subdivided under three habitat types: wilderness settings, areas of resource exploitation by humans and urban settings. Combining the two subject areas of research with the three habitat types gives us six divisions that cover major research needs:

Biology/Wilderness Sites: Bald Eagles evolved in a wilderness setting and that is where they are best adapted. We need to know a great deal more about their life history when they are undisturbed by humans. Subjects that need more investigation include: feeding habits under optimum and adverse conditions, selection and defense of nesting territories through the life span, comparison of nest sites (ground, cottonwood, hemlock, spruce), pair fidelity, daily movements, seasonal migration, rearing young, young learning to forage on their own, longevity, mortality factors, competitors, disease and parasites.

Biology/Resource Exploitation Sites: As Alaskans develop natural resources we must identify and accommodate eagle needs that are affected by development. Areas of research should include: fluctuations and changes in fish stocks on which eagles depend, what happens after removal of large trees suitable for nesting, disturbances caused by road traffic, tourist activity and boats and rafts; attraction of eagles to dumps and other sites where they may pick up poisons.

Biology/Urban Sites: In the early 1900s, when fish canning and fur farming were primary industries in Southeast Alaska, the Bald Eagle was considered a nuisance, a competitor and a threat to these enterprises. Eagles were destroyed wherever practical and exterminated in the vicinity of towns. In the second half of the century, with legal protection and a more enlightened public attitude, eagle numbers are rebuilding.

Territorial pressures within the eagle population are forcing more birds to seek feeding sources and nesting sites within urban settings. Eagles that elect an urban life are subject to a number of problems not faced by their rural relatives. Trees large enough for nesting may be scarce and farther from the water, food sources may occupy places also used by people, power lines and other structures may pose a threat, dumps may mix poisons with food sources, moving vehicles are a danger and all sorts of disturbances can occur. Research could lead to reducing dangers and providing necessities so that eagles can thrive in the urban setting.

Relations With People/Wilderness Sites: Interaction between eagles and people in a wilderness setting is minimal. Research is needed as per above. Research is also needed to ensure that visitors, photographers, perhaps researchers themselves and other people do not interfere with the natural conditions important to eagles. Managers of the national parks, national forests and national monuments must have a better understanding of the interaction between eagles and people if they are to fulfill their environmental and legal mandate to protect the portion of this wilderness wildlife population under their jurisdiction in perpetuity.

Relations With People/Resource Development Sites: The greatest need for research perhaps exists in this category, where resources are being exploited, but where there is plenty of room for eagles and they have prospered in the past. The Chilkat Valley above

Haines may be the best place in the world to do such research. The fishing, timber, mining, transportation and tourism industries, as well as development of private land, all impact a high density of nesting eagles and the greatest fall feeding concentration of Bald Eagles in the world. All these human activities are increasing and are often interdependent. How much timber and fish can be removed, how much more highway and river traffic can be accommodated and how much development of private land can occur are vital questions that must be addressed if the eagles are to prosper in the area? Detailed observations of how eagles are coping and review of development plans are imperative now.

Removal of old-growth timber along beaches throughout Southeast Alaska and the existing programs to protect eagle nest trees are two areas that need scientific review. Are the small protected areas around nest trees attracting people or other creatures to the detriment of eagles? Do the large trees so protected eventually blow down? Will removal of a portion of the beach fringe where no nest is present now ultimately limit nesting and the eagle population to a level below what the food source has sustained in the past? Can nest structures be provided in areas where nest size trees have been eliminated? Is protection comparable and adequate on federal, state, borough and private lands?

Relations With People/Urban Sites: In the past wildlife was unceremoniously destroyed in cities. Today we are a little more tolerant and we have enacted laws for protection of wildlife. As a result, we are finding that some species can do well in an urban setting. In Southeast Alaska, Bald Eagle populations are still increasing after having been reduced earlier in the century and they are reinvading the towns from which they were exterminated. It turns out that a good many residents and tourists are excited about having eagles as part of the urban scene.

Urban eagles have some problems their country cousins avoid and they cause some problems for people. If Bald Eagles continue to increase in the Lower 48 states, eventually there will be urban populations in much larger cities and problems may become more serious. The relatively small cities of Southeast Alaska, particularly Juneau, would be a very good place to research the management of Bald Eagles in an urban setting.

Some aspects needing investigation in this regard are: identification and modification of structures such as power lines, where eagles have accidents and cause public expense, methods of moving eagles that try to nest in places where they are a nuisance, methods of attracting eagles to nesting sites where they might be an asset, artificial nesting structures that could be built where nesting trees have been removed, urban food resources for eagles, including the possibility of establishing fish sources, investigation into how much space eagles need and how they interact with other urban wildlife and domestic animal life.

The rehabilitation and accommodation of eagles that become sick or injured is another area that enjoys popular support and requires research. Maintenance of eagles that cannot be returned to the wild and their use for display, education or research is an almost untouched field.

Urban governments should have management plans for eagles that can be incorporated into comprehensive plans and enforced by ordinances. Perhaps new federal legislation could be designed to encourage such planning. The whole arena of the legal standing of eagles needs review and adjustment in accord with current public values.

Conclusion

Bald Eagle research is needed to collect the information necessary to properly manage and protect the species. It offers exciting opportunities and challenges. Southeast Alaska is the best place to do it. The American public will enthusiastically support it and it will lead to perpetual abundance of our national symbol-living free but in close association with our people.

The Bald Eagle Bibliography

Annette Nelson-Wright

University of Alaska Southeast

When it is sighted, our Nations emblem, the Bald Eagle, often causes people to stop and gaze in awe upon its majestic presence. While almost everyone could identify an eagle, few could easily access abundant data on *Haliaeetus leucocephalus*, the Bald Eagle. It was only recently that a comprehensive bibliography was compiled by John Maniscalco for the Bald Eagle Research Institute in cooperation with National Wildlife Federation and the U.S. Fish and Wildlife Service. The National Wildlife Federation published the Bald Eagle bibliography in 1979, then gave the University of Alaska Southeast permission to update and maintain it. The bibliography is now housed in the William A. Egan library at the University of Alaska Southeast Juneau campus. Available via computer disk or hard copy, the bibliography will serve as an invaluable reference to those researching eagles.

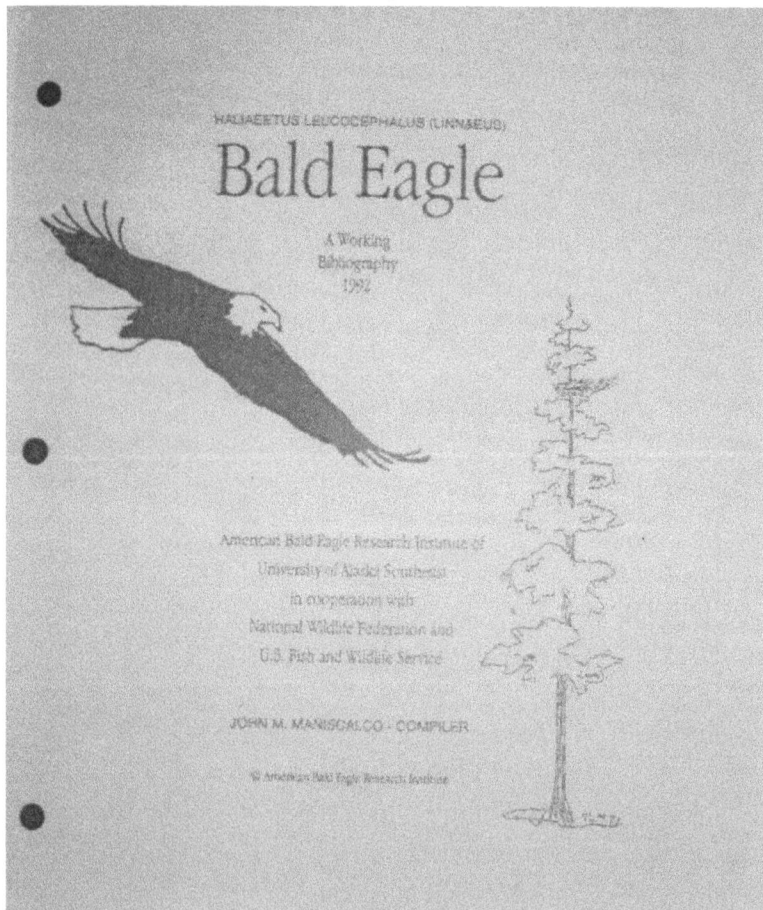

Information on eagles which existed in the popular literature, newsletters, scientific journals, technical and status reports had been assembled by the National Wildlife Federation but was outdated (ca. 1976). The work of John Maniscalco in 1992 updated and organized the data and put it into a workable format, one that could be easily utilized by the novice or the master and made eagle information readily available to all.

With a bibliography compiled, plans exist to update it as it is feasible. In our rapidly advancing world, both ecologically and technologically the availability of this data becomes increasingly important. Those aware of the history of eagles may help ensure healthy populations for generations to come.

Bald Eagles and the Tourist Industry in Alaska

Judy Shuler

Travel Planner, Juneau, AK

Tourism is a complex industry that encompasses a broad spectrum of large and small businesses. In Alaska, tourism is a family home with a few spare bedrooms used for bed and breakfast guests and it is an international cruise line with ships carrying thousands of passengers north every summer. It is a wilderness guide service with a handful of employees leading small groups of adventurers and it's a commercial bus line with hundreds of employees transporting thousands of people.

Tourism ranks third among Alaska's industries in gross dollar volume, following oil production and commercial fishing. It is Alaska's largest private sector employer, creating the equivalent of more than 10,000 year-around jobs to serve more than one million visitors a year from all over the world.

Whether they come by cruise ship or state ferry, in motor homes or by airliner, most Alaskan visitors come for essentially the same reasons. They come to experience the wilderness mystique that surrounds Alaska. They come for a spiritual bonding with nature, in whatever terms they choose to define that experience. And they come to see wildlife.

How visitors feel about their Alaskan experience may be colored by the weather, the mood of the traveler or the way the traveler is treated by the bus driver or the hotel clerk. It will include expectations versus reality. Did they catch the fish they thought they would? Were bears actually fishing along the salmon stream, as they had expected? Did a humpback whale breach right next to the boat, as they had hoped?

Much, too, will depend on the travelers' own interest in their surroundings, their capacity for observation and their attention span. Some may be like the tourist I met at the Auke Bay ferry terminal near Juneau. It was a pleasant summer day, midway between brilliant sun and gray rain. Eagles were manning their usual tree-top look-out posts across the road from the terminal. Several travelers watched in awe, but this man was not impressed. On his entire north-bound cruise, he said, he had seen nothing but mountains, trees and snow. His assessment of Alaska: "This is the most boring place I've ever been." Fortunately, this man is not typical of Alaskan visitors.

The fastest-growing segment of the travel industry is that portion called "soft adventure." That includes outdoor experiences sometimes described as having "active days and comfortable nights." People who travel this way might cheerfully hike all day in chilling rain, but come evening, they want a hot shower and a soft bed. Guides for these outdoor activities are avid naturalists, accomplished birders, professional outdoor photographers. Soft adventure travelers expect in-depth information from knowledgeable guides.

In these kinds of travel experiences, where encountering nature is the primary goal, Bald Eagles and other wildlife become the focus.

The fall gathering of Bald Eagles in the Chilkat Valley, with its unique opportunities for photographing Bald Eagles and observing their behavior, is a prime example of soft adventure.

It is difficult to estimate how many visitors come especially to see Bald Eagles in the Alaska Chilkat Bald Eagle Preserve and impossible to guess what part eagles play in attracting visitors to other parts of coastal Alaska. But even part-time counts of visitors to the Chilkat Valley number in the hundreds every year and the Haines Visitor Bureau reports it received.

Virtually every major professional wildlife photographer in the country has stopped along the banks of the Chilkat during the eagle concentration. And through their lenses, the Chilkat phenomenon has been viewed by thousands of people through calendars, magazines and books.

My first journey to the Valley of the Eagles came on a field trip with the Juneau Audubon Society perhaps 10 years ago. Although we were all local residents of Southeast Alaska, it was for most of us the first visit to the annual gathering of eagles. We spotted our first eagle in the semi-darkness of an early November morning, perhaps halfway to the heart of the great concentration. We leaped from the bus in great excitement. Hands fumbled as we raced to set up tripods and attach telephoto lenses. Our guide graciously concealed what must have been great amusement and assured us there would be more eagles ahead. There were many hundreds.

I would like every Alaska visitor to share some of the excitement we felt in seeing the Bald Eagles and I think tour guides would find great satisfaction in leading their guests in that sense of discovery.

In a survey I took at the 1990 Alaska Visitor Association convention, all the tour operators who filled out the questionnaire reported seeing eagles daily on their tours. Half said visitors were very excited upon seeing a Bald Eagle and half said visitor response ranged between very excited and interested.

Respondents were also asked if they would like more information about Bald Eagles to share with visitors. All but one said "yes."

This leads into what I believe is an important role for the tourism industry. Its member businesses and associations, large and small alike, can speak out on behalf of protection of habitat for the Bald Eagle and other wildlife.

Representatives of Alaska's other resource-based industries-timber, commercial fishing, mining, petroleum-have become strong advocates for policies that favor and strengthen their use of resources. Their activism will only accelerate in the days ahead.

What if members of the tourism industry, currently Alaska's third largest industry in gross dollar revenues, realized they have a vested interest in protecting the natural resources that are crucial to the product they market? Enhancing tourism may depend on better docks, more camper parks, more hotels. But all these amenities will be incidental if Alaska loses its ability to provide the wildlife and scenic values that attract visitors in the first place.

We need to educate the travel industry about their need to become advocates for the environment. People within tourism have a tremendous opportunity to share with visitors the need to care for the natural environment, both here and in their home communities around the world.

Is the Bald Eagle important in Alaska tourism? Absolutely. But tourism can be important to the eagle, too. It is up to us to nurture that synergism.

Tourism and timber harvest both impact wildlife, but clear cuts are much more obvious, as seen in Hobart Bay, Southeast, Alaska. Photo by Phil Schempf, USFWS.

The Haines Story

David E. Olerud

Educator and Merchant, Haines, AK

Haines is a small town geographically located between the Chilkat and Chilkoot river systems in the northern part of Lynn Canal in Southeast Alaska. To the north by way of the Haines Highway are our Canadian neighbors and to the south by water or air is Juneau and the remainder of Southeast Alaska.

This northern part of Southeast Alaska is blessed with resources commonly associated with geographic youth. Its ruggedness, beauty and purity are enjoyed and loved by those who live there and never forgotten by those who visit and return to their homes elsewhere.

The people who live in Haines, whether they were born there or were transplanted, have such characteristics as independence, pride, resourcefulness, productivity and possibly a healthy streak of stubbornness. These are the same qualities one would find in most healthy communities, but Haines residents possibly have these characteristics a trifle more than most folks.

When I was given the privilege of living in this part of the world, everything was very simple and yet, in its own way, very complex. Customs and traditions were very strong-so strong they could control the behavior of new arrivals. I will never forget the respect for the land that meant so much to all. There was no waste of the moose or goat people hunted. There was no waste in harvesting the sea or the plants from the land and those activities provided a large percentage of the food people consumed. These natural resources were and still are very important assets to people of the Haines area.

I will never forget the pure and simple way that people helped one another, often as simply as in the 1960s, when the postmistress kept the post office open on Christmas Eve to distribute Christmas gifts that had come in the latest mail. In those days the problems of the outside world seemed far away and we handled ours with one poorly-trained policeman. Life was indeed simple. But there was a strong desire to have community improvements such as a new high school. The old high school gym was so small that when spectators in the balcony got excited, the basketball backboards would sway, adding another variable to the skills needed to play the game.

The economy at that time was limited. Commercial fishing was dominant, with Haines Packing Company providing the greatest cash flow on a part-time basis. State and federal government, the Haines gas pipeline, highway work and many new school teaching jobs provided local employment. Tourism and logging were in their infancies, with minerals having already declined from the heyday of gold rush days.

At that time the eagle was not considered a valuable natural resource. In fact, some people picked up extra cash by shooting eagles for the bounty offered by the Alaska Territorial government from 1917 to 1953. Yes, life was simple and organized, but the complexity of our country and its future demands were coming closer.

As the years progressed, economic development and the use of local resources to create a higher standard of living became a goal for many Haines people. The timber industry grew and as mobility developed within the Lower 48 states, the Haines tourism industry flourished. Meanwhile, the fishing industry in Haines declined when Ward Cove Packing purchased Haines Packing and consolidated its operations at Excursion Inlet, 75 miles south of town. Even when the Haines pipeline was closed down in 1970, the overall economy was growing and with it the public infrastructure, demanding a stronger tax base. Things were getting more complex.

In the river valleys near Haines, a combination of geographic phenomena attracts great seasonal concentrations of eagles (Boeker 2008, Menaker 2008). This unique occurrence, which the people of Haines took as a normal part of their life, became of strong interest to people throughout the United States in the early 1970s. Left by themselves, the people of Haines would have lived with and appreciated the eagles for many generations to come. But pressures from outside the valley demanded that resources should be thought about, listed and set aside, covered by strong words to guarantee their existence. This mentality was new to the people of Haines, but it was understandable to the minds of outsiders, for whom the Bald Eagle represented an endangered species. For Haines people these events meant the simple handshake signifying understanding and commitment was replaced by a lack of trust.

All the social reactions a sociologist could predict occurred in response to these outside pressures. Fears and frustrations, anger and resentments became commonplace. Ultimately, however, on June 20, 1982, the 48,000 acre Alaska Chilkat Bald Eagle Preserve was established, enlarging the original critical habitat area.

Even before establishment of the preserve, the people of Haines had begun to understand the correlation of the eagle with future environmental health. In 1977, meetings had taken place to discuss what could be done to further the positive relationship between humans and the eagle. In the early 1980s, with the help of Hans Fluehler of Montreal and Douglas DeVries from Vermont, the American Bald Eagle Foundation became a federally approved, tax exempt reality, dedicated to understanding the complexity of the Chilkat River Valley and making that understanding available to the rest of the world.

As people began to understand the importance of the eagle as a resource, they began to contribute time, money and effort to create an eagle information center in Haines. The city donated land; and volunteers from Haines and as far away as Indiana and Alabama cleared the land, hauled fill, laid a foundation, raised walls, put on a roof, put up siding and hung doors and windows. More than $300,000 was contributed; the eagle information center was opened in spring 1991. Educational displays and video presentations change and grow year after year.

The center will make it easier for people to understand the eagle and its relationship to environmental health. People who visit the center can take new understanding home and in turn make our planet a better place on which to live. It will be a gift from Alaska, a state that has not yet been damaged by population density.

When the Alaska Chilkat Bald Eagle Preserve was created in Haines, federal and state monies were to have been appropriated for ongoing research on the eagle. Unfortunately, the money never materialized. In a way, the preserve has become a 48,000-page book full of valuable information whose pages have never been turned.

A Bald Eagle waits for a chance to feed on salmon along the Chilkat River. Photo by Scott Gende.

But the private sector and common citizens are strongly attracted to our Nation's symbol. The Bald Eagle is a litmus test of our time. Our responsibility to future generations is to leave the Nation's symbol healthy and strong.

Editor's Note: In 1996, Mr. Olerud and others of the American Bald Eagle Foundation, University of Alaska Southeast and other private and public sectors have redesigned and re-designated the original research institute as the Jay Hammond Bald Eagle Research Institute or the Bald Eagle Research Institute. The Institute's principle objects are to promote research and education programs designed to enhance the survival and propagation of the Bald Eagle.

Literature Cited

Boeker, E. L. 2008. Eagles on the Chilkat: Winter ecology. In: Wright, B.A. and P.F. Schempf, eds. Bald Eagles in Alaska.

Menaker, R. R. 2008. The Alaska Chilkat Bald Eagle Preserve: How it all began. In: Wright, B.A. and P.F. Schempf, eds. Bald Eagles in Alaska.

American Bald Eagles At Home in the World

Hans C. Fluehler

Businessman, Montreal, Quebec, Canada

To any naturalist in the world certain place names carry overtones of excitement and longing. One of these is Alaska, name of a state famous for untouched wilderness, wildlife and relative remoteness from the usual haunts of mankind.

Unfortunately for nature and for wildlife, this beautiful balance is being put to the test more and more. Alaska's much cherished clean environment is losing its lustre. The *Exxon Valdez* oil spill brought us all to a brutal awakening. The world followed in dismay the pollution of shorelines and the struggle for survival by entrapped waterfowl, seals, otters, eagles and other species. Our wildlife, our environment, became victims of the failure of a whole industrialized nation. All the finesse of modern world technology could not help.

A juvenile Bald Eagle. Photo by Mike Jacobson.

Fortunately, wise people in Alaska and other parts of the world have been observing the steady degeneration of nature, the brutal and careless grab of land, the destruction of wildlife and the pollution of air and water. Although not always popular, they have slowed down the deadly tidal wave by legislating wilderness parks, resource management areas, eagle preserves and bird sanctuaries. We should all be grateful for their foresight. Luckily, a broad, new stream of conservation consciousness has started to run through states and provinces. At no other time is this miraculous change of mind more evident than during election campaigns. Environment and nature are definitely in!

Even more fortunate, there are signs of action. In the United States demonstrated its bipartisan commitment for waterfowl and wetlands with the long overdue passage of the North American Wetlands Conservation Act. By working in cooperation with the Canadian Wildlife Service and provincial conservation agencies, as well as with Ducks Unlimited, they are setting an encouraging example of collaboration involving two countries and a model conservation organization.

This new vigor promoting a safer environment has also reached the corporate world. More and more initiatives are becoming the trademark of industrial leaders. "The Greening of Corporate Canada" or "MacDonald's environmentally friendly packaging" are now part of headlines in financial magazines. People are even talking about global warming now.

As Patrick Carson, vice-president of environmental affairs for Loblaw International Inc. of Toronto said recently, "Businesses have to realize they can no longer divorce their balance sheets from nature's bottom line."

Many North American companies have already recognized this and are finding financial rewards by responding to consumer demands for environmentally friendly products and production methods. One of the challenges for business leaders and politicians in the 1990s is to hammer out a set of international principles that will enable businesses to progress technologically and economically and to benefit shareholders and the population at large without harming the fragile environment.

What has all this to do with the American Bald Eagle?
Eagles have long had a dominant place in religious and political symbolism of humankind and they have an even longer history as a symbol of earthly power. For thousands of years the eagle underlined the mightiness of emperors, kings, warriors and statesmen. The history of North America is living proof of the eagle's powers and grace. Few symbols have had a bigger impact on men of different origins, cultures and colours.

The American Bald Eagle Foundation, in close cooperation with the Bald Eagle (Jay Hammond) Research Institute, the University of Alaska Southeast and the Government of Alaska should work to help the Bald Eagle flourish once again in all the Lower 48 states and Canada. Thus, we cannot only help an endangered species to survive, but we can also help the inhabitants of this continent to better air, a safer environment and happier coexistence. As members of the American Bald Eagle (Jay Hammond) Research Institute we have the obligation to help the many millions living in the present civilization realize how essential nature is for our culture and our survival.

Resurrection of the Bald Eagle on this continent is the goal of our involvement. With the help of wildlife specialists, industrial leaders, politicians and governments we shall be able to show the world an example of wildlife management gone right. While history is important and nostalgia is nice, the time is now, to make our strongest stand for the Bald Eagle.

Photo by Bob Armstrong.

Index

C

www.ingramcontent.com/pod-product-compliance
Lightning Source LLC
Chambersburg PA
CBHW080603270326
41928CB00016B/2907